On Global Justice

On Global Justice

Mathias Risse

PRINCETON UNIVERSITY PRESS

PRINCETON AND OXFORD

Copyright © 2012 by Princeton University Press
Published by Princeton University Press, 41 William Street, Princeton, New Jersey 08540
In the United Kingdom: Princeton University Press, 6 Oxford Street, Woodstock,
Oxfordshire OX20 1TW

press.princeton.edu

Jacket Photograph: *Earth* by Yuri Arcurs. Courtesy of Dreamstime.

Library of Congress Cataloging-in-Publication Data

Risse, Mathias, 1970–
    On global justice / Mathias Risse.
        pages cm
    Includes bibliographical references and index.
    ISBN-13: 978-0-691-14269-2 (cloth : alk. paper)
    ISBN-10: 0-691-14269-6 (cloth : alk. paper) 1. Internationalism. 2. Distributive
justice. 3. Human rights. I. Title.
    JZ1308.R57 2012
    340′.115—dc23   2011053393

British Library Cataloging-in-Publication Data is available

This book has been composed in Sabon and Univers

Printed on acid-free paper. ∞

Printed in the United States of America

10 9 8 7 6 5 4 3 2 1

Für meine Eltern, Josef und Maria Risse,
In grosser Achtung und mit viel Liebe

And for my wife, Kozue Sato Risse,
Who has done the most beautiful thing for me

Contents

Preface

IN JAMES JOYCE'S SHORT STORY "The Boarding House," we learn about one character that "she dealt with moral problems as a cleaver deals with meat" (*Dubliners*, 1992, 58). That person presumably cut through all complexities of a moral question by formulating a clear and strong position that simply ignored all voices of doubt. The contemporary debate about global distributive justice is not amenable to this kind of approach. In an increasingly politically and economically interconnected world, it is hard to ascertain what justice requires. It is difficult to spell out how principles of justice apply, to begin with, and hard to assess what they entail for pressing political questions ranging from immigration to trade and climate change.

The two traditional ways of thinking about justice at the global level either limit the applicability of justice to states or else extend it to all human beings. The view I defend rejects both these approaches and instead recognizes different considerations or conditions based on which individuals are in the scope of different principles of justice. To my mind, finding a philosophically convincing alternative to those approaches is the most demanding and important challenge contemporary political philosophy faces (one that in turn reflects the significance of the political issues that are at stake). It is in light of my confidence in the importance of this kind of work—but indeed only when taking that perspective—that I feel like the "good author" in Nietzsche's *Human, All Too Human,* "who really cares about his subject" and therefore "wishes that someone would come and destroy him by representing the same subject more clearly and by answering every last question contained in it" (1996, 57).

My own view, and thus my attempt at meeting the aforementioned challenge, acknowledges the existence of multiple *grounds of justice*. This book seeks to present a foundational theory that makes it plausible that there could be multiple grounds of justice and to defend a specific view of the grounds that I call *internationalism* or *pluralist internationalism*. Internationalism grants particular normative relevance to the state but qualifies this relevance by embedding the state into other grounds that are associated with their own principles of justice and that thus impose additional obligations on those who share membership in a state. Other than shared membership in a state, it is humanity's common ownership of the earth that receives the most sustained treatment. And it is probably in the conceptualization of common ownership as a ground of justice that my view seems strangest.

To demonstrate its philosophical fruitfulness, I develop my view for a broad range of topics, including immigration, fairness in trade, and obligations resulting from climate change, but also human rights, obligations to future generations, and others. I am not concerned with familiar questions about the state's constitution and internal structure beyond what is required to show that shared membership in a state is a ground of justice to which particular principles of justice apply. I inquire about the state only in a global perspective. This book is about global justice as a philosophical problem, and about political problems on which principles of justice bear at the global level. Nonetheless, my view does regard the state as special within a theory of global justice, and this distinguishes my approach from more cosmopolitan approaches.

I have incurred many debts in the course of thinking about and writing this work. The book sums up most of the work I have done since coming to Harvard in 2002. I am grateful for the environment at the Harvard Kennedy School, where foundational philosophical inquiry is possible and where not only is one surrounded by social scientists, whose expertise is often helpful for matters of global justice, but the primary interest is in solving the world's political and economic problems, including problems raised by globalization. Such problem solving inevitably leads to questions about what kind of world we should have. Enter political philosophy. Philosophy and real life intersect. Philosophy need not always be useful to be worthwhile, nor will it always contribute as much as those who seek its guidance might hope. Philosophical inquiry rarely leads to concrete policy advice unless much of what most people currently believe and much of how our institutions work is taken as constraining what such advice could look like. Nonetheless, we do need visions for the future of the world. If such visions try to dispense with political philosophy, they forfeit conceptual tools that are plainly needed to develop and defend them. At the same time, political theory that proceeds with too little connection to the problems that preoccupy those who want to change the world often is complacent and boring, as is philosophical inquiry that mostly investigates its own nature and thinks of political discourse only as one source of input for metaethical analysis.

Some of the early work on this book was done while I was on leave in 2003–4 at Harvard's Center for Ethics and the Professions. My various projects in the field of global justice came together as a book while I was at Princeton's Center for Human Values in 2006–7—a happy place that had already helped me with the completion of my dissertation on matters of collective rationality a decade earlier. Conversations with Charles Beitz especially during that year, but also earlier and later, have been much appreciated, as is the general example he sets for all of us working in this area. In 2008, Harvard's Weatherhead Center for International Affairs funded a small conference on my manuscript. I am grateful to the center and the participants for the feedback that this event generated. The Weatherhead Center also provided funding for a semester of leave in 2008. Over the years I have presented this material at dozens of talks and conferences, mostly in the United States and Europe, but also in Israel and Japan. I am indebted to many who commented on my ideas during these discussions.

For research assistance I am indebted to Craig Nishimoto. My faculty assistant, Derya Honça, has been working on this book as long as I have. I am indebted to her not only for much library research but also for many editorial suggestions. Micha Glaeser and Gabriel Wollner read a substantial part of the manuscript. Both saved me from many errors and improved the argument in countless ways. Arthur Applbaum has read all the chapters in some version or other, often several times, and his comments unfailingly improved their substance. His support and input over the years have been invaluable. The penultimate version of the book benefited enormously from Allison Dawe's keen editorial eye and deep philosophical acumen. She embodies the Platonic idea of a philosophical editor. Her suggestions prompted major rearrangements of the material in this book, as well as changes in the arguments of every chapter. She, too, saved me from numerous errors. My debts to Applbaum, Dawe, Glaeser, and Wollner are greatest.

Though they have not been directly involved with this book, I must also thank my advisers at Princeton University, Richard Jeffrey (deceased 2002) and Paul Benacerraf, as well as the supervisor of my thesis in mathematics, Robert Aumann of the Hebrew University of Jerusalem, for doing their best to teach me how to approach complex questions. Long ago, Wolfgang Spohn, Rüdiger Bittner, and Klaus Reisinger at the University of Bielefeld showed me through their teaching and feedback on my writings what sort of thing philosophical work was supposed to be. Later, at Yale, where I held my first teaching position, Shelly Kagan and Robert Adams had that same impact on me (mutatis mutandis). Being Gopal Sreenivasan's teaching assistant at Princeton in 1996 showed me that political philosophy was what I needed to do. Michael Blake and Malgorzata Kurjanska have co-authored articles and Robert Hockett has done research with me from which they have graciously allowed me to use material in this book. Blake was a colleague at Harvard for several years. Since his departure he has remained a valued friend and fellow traveler. Leif Wenar, too, has been a friend and respected fellow traveler for many years. Leif Wenar and Charles Beitz reviewed this book for Princeton University Press. Their comments led to substantial revisions of every chapter. I am deeply grateful for their intellectual engagement and patience with this book.

Other colleagues, friends, or students who have read parts of the book or shared thoughts with me on some of the themes I discuss include Eric Beerbohm, George Borjas, Dan Brock, Simon Caney, Ian Carter, Eric Cavallero, Howard Chang, Tom Christiano, Bill Clark, Norman Daniels, Angus Deaton, David Estlund, Nir Eyal, Archon Fung, Axel Gosseries, Elizabeth Harman, Nicole Hassoun, Ricardo Hausmann, Wilfried Hinsch, Robert Hockett, Bill Hogan, Nadeem Hussain, Aaron James, Sandy Jencks, Frances Kamm, Michael Kessler, Rahul Kumar, Robert Lawrence, Jenny Mansbridge, Andrew March, Daniel Markovits, Jamie Mayerfeld, Joseph Mazor, David Miller, Joseph Millum, John O'Neill, Japa Pallikkathayil, George Pavlakos, Thomas Pogge, Jonathan Quong, Christopher Robichaud, Dani Rodrik, Andrea Sangiovanni, Debra Satz, Tim Scanlon, Alexander Schwab, Matthew Noah Smith, Markus Stepanians, John Tasioulas, Moshik Temkin, Dennis Thompson, Dan Wikler, Andrew Williams, and Ken Winston. I am deeply grateful to them, as well as to all those colleagues who have reviewed different parts of this material over the years. Needless to say, all remaining errors are entirely my own.

The interaction with all the people mentioned, as well as the engagement with the questions that this book addresses and an awareness of the tremendous significance of these questions, has made the writing of this book a truly humbling experience. One thing I hope the collective efforts of those who have helped me taught me is that philosophical problems rarely are the sort of thing one can approach "as a cleaver deals with meat." Another Joyce character provides better inspiration, stating that "above all things else, we must avoid anything like being or becoming out of patience" (*Finnegans Wake*, 1976, 108).

I would also like to thank the wonderful staff at Princeton University Press for making sure this material would actually appear as a book. Ian Malcolm had checked in with me over a number of years to see if I was writing a book, and was perhaps surprised when the answer eventually switched from "no" to "yes." I am very grateful to him for his encouragement and for creating a home for this book at Princeton. After his departure Rob Tempio took over and made sure that what Ian had begun would come to fruition. Marjorie Pannell did a wonderful job as a copyeditor, as did David Luljak in putting together the index and Karen Fortgang in overseeing the production process. I very much appreciate their terrific work.

To others I owe a debt of a more personal nature that is even greater in magnitude and that I will not record in detail. If you do not know who you are, I have failed already. But I hope you do.

Cambridge, April 21, 2011

Acknowledgments

I am grateful for permissions to use this material:

Chapter 2 draws on "What to Say about the State," *Social Theory and Practice* 32, no. 4 (2006): 671–98, and contains a section drawing on Michael Blake and Mathias Risse, "Two Models of Equality and Responsibility," *Canadian Journal of Philosophy* 38, no. 2 (2008): 165–201.

Chapter 3 also draws on "What to Say about the State."

Chapter 6 contains a section drawing on "Does Left-Libertarianism Have Coherent Foundations?," *Politics, Philosophy, and Economics* 3, no. 3 (2004): 337–65.

Chapter 7 draws on "Common Ownership of the Earth as a Non-Parochial Standpoint: A Contingent Derivation of Human Rights," *European Journal of Philosophy* 17, no. 2 (2009): 277–304. Chapter 7 also contains a section drawing on "The Right to Relocation: Disappearing Island Nations and Common Ownership of the Earth," *Ethics and International Affairs* 23, no. 3 (2009): 281–300.

Chapter 8 draws on Michael Blake and Mathias Risse, "Immigration and Original Ownership of the Earth," *Notre Dame Journal of Law, Ethics, and Public Policy* 23, no. 1 (2009): 133–67; Michael Blake and Mathias Risse, "Migration, Territoriality, and Culture," in *New Waves in Applied Ethics,* ed. Jesper Ryberg, Thomas Petersen, and Clark Wolf (Aldershot: Ashgate, 2007), 153–82; and "On the Morality of Immigration," *Ethics and International Affairs* 22, no. 1 (2008): 25–33.

Chapter 13 draws on "A Right to Work? A Right to Leisure? Labor Rights as Human Rights," *Journal of Law and Ethics of Human Rights* 3, no. 1 (2009): 1–41.

Chapter 14 draws on "Fairness in Trade I: Obligations from Trading and the Pauper Labor Argument," *Politics, Philosophy, and Economics* 6, no. 3 (2007): 355–77; and Malgorzata Kurjanska and Mathias Risse, "Fairness in Trade II: Export Subsidies and the Fair Trade Movement," *Politics, Philosophy, and Economics* 7, no. 1 (2008): 29–56.

Chapter 15 draws on "Do We Owe the Poor Assistance or Rectification?," *Ethics and International Affairs* 19, no. 1 (2005): 9–18; "How Does the Global Order Harm the Poor?" *Philosophy and Public Affairs* 33, no. 4 (2005): 349–76; and "What We Owe to the Global Poor," *Journal of Ethics* 9, nos. 1–2 (2005): 81–117.

CHAPTER 1

The Grounds of Justice

1. When Thomas Hobbes devoted *De Cive* to exploring the rights of the state and the duties of its subjects, he set the stage for the next three and a half centuries of political philosophy. Focusing on the confrontation between individual and state meant focusing on a person's relationship not to particular rulers but to an enduring institution that made exclusive claims to the exercise of certain powers within a domain. Almost two centuries after Hobbes, Hegel took it for granted that political theory was merely an effort to comprehend the state as an inherently rational entity. And 150 years later, the American philosopher Robert Nozick could write that the "fundamental question of political philosophy is whether there should be any state at all" (1974, 4).[1]

Two central philosophical questions arise about the state: whether its existence can be justified to its citizens to begin with, and what is a just distribution of goods within it. As far as the first question is concerned, philosophers from Hobbes onward have focused on rebutting the philosophical anarchist, who rejects the concentrated power of the state as illegitimate. For both sides of the debate, however, the presumption has been that those to whom state power had to be justified were those living within its frontiers. The question of justice, too, has been much on the agenda since Hobbes, but it gained centrality in the last fifty years, in part because of the rejuvenating effect of John Rawls's 1971 *A Theory of Justice*. Again, the focus was domestic, at least initially.

However, real-world changes, grouped together under the label "globalization," have in recent decades forced philosophers to broaden their focus. In a world in which goods and people cross borders routinely, philosophers have had to consider whether the existence of state power can be justified not just to people living within a given state but also to people excluded from it (e.g., by border controls). At a time when states share the world stage with a network of treaties and global institutions, philosophers have had to consider not just whether the state can be justified to those living under it but whether the whole global order of multiple states and global institutions can be justified to those living under it. And in a world in which the most salient inequalities are not within states but among them, philosophers have had to broaden their focus for justice, too, asking not only what counts as a just distribution within the state but also what counts as a just distribution globally.

My focus in this book is on the last of these new problems, although what I have to say will be relevant to the other two new problems as well. I consider the question of what it is for a distribution to be just globally and offer a new reply: a new systematic theory of global justice, one that develops a view I call *pluralist internationalism*. Up to now, philosophers have tended to respond to the problem of global justice in one of two ways. One way is to say that the old focus on justice within the state was, in fact, correct. The only distributions that can be just or unjust, strictly speaking, are within the state. The other response is to say, by contrast, that the old focus on justice within the state was completely wrong. The only relevant population for justice is global. Leading theories of justice within the state, such as Rawls's, should simply be applied straightforwardly to all of humanity. This usually yields the result that global distributions are radically unjust.

This book defends a view between those two, one that improves on both. I agree with the second view that we *can* talk about global justice, that global distributions are just or unjust. But I agree with the first view that nonetheless, the state has a special place in accounts of justice. Domestic justice—justice within the state—and global justice have different standards, and the former are more egalitarian. Theories of domestic justice like Rawls's cannot simply be transferred to the global scene. That means that the global distribution of various goods is not as radically unjust as it would be if domestic justice did apply straightforwardly. Nonetheless, global distributions turn out to be unjust in various important ways.

I defend my view by developing a pluralist approach to what I call the *grounds* of justice. These, roughly, are the reasons why claims of justice apply to a certain population. Some grounds apply only among those who share a state, while others apply universally or almost so. Some—membership in a state, common humanity—have been explored before, though I hope to show that they should be understood in new ways. But other grounds—common ownership of the earth, membership in the global order, subjection to the global trading system—have not been explored in this context before, and I hope to show they have a substantial contribution to make. From a plurality of grounds of justice we get a plurality of principles of justice—again, some of which apply only within the state and some of which apply globally or almost so. We also get a host of real-world applications, to matters as diverse as illegal immigration, climate change, the global regulation of trade, and the provision of essential drugs. The British philosopher Bernard Williams once said of contemporary moral philosophy that it had "found an original way of being boring, which is by not discussing moral issues at all" (Williams 1993, xvii). Political philosophy too is susceptible to such a problem, but I hope the wide range of concrete applications in this book will prevent it from sharing this fate.

Inquiries into global justice differ from those into international justice by not limiting inquiry to what states should do. They question the system of states itself, and assess alternative arrangements. We must broaden our view about what is involved in justifying states, and we must adopt a broader perspective on the scope of justice. In the rest of this book, I investigate these grounds one by one, exploring the principles they generate. At the end, I consider the implications of the resulting list of principles for institutions. I return to the state, and also consider—as an example of what can be said about a global institution—the World Trade Organization (WTO). This allows me to return as well to the two other new problems described above that globalization has raised for political philosophy, the problem of justifying the state to outsiders and the problem of justifying the global order to all. In the remainder of this chapter, though, I will set the stage for the rest of the book by making what I have said so far more precise.

2. Let me start by saying a bit more about globalization. *Globalization* denotes processes that erode the political and economic importance of national boundaries and increasingly affect life chances through the system of rules that constitutes the global order. Globalization is actually not new. It traces back to developments that began in the fifteenth century through the spread of European control, continuing with the formation of new states through independence or decolonization. In 1795, Kant could write that the "community of the nations of the earth has now gone so far that a violation of right on one place of the earth is felt in all" (*Perpetual Peace,* 1970b, 330). Political philosophers of the seventeenth and eighteenth centuries, such as Hugo Grotius, Christian Wolff, Samuel Pufendorf, John Locke, Emmerich Vattel, or Immanuel Kant, explored questions about *that* stage of globalization. They developed the doctrine of sovereignty, explored under what conditions one could acquire non-European territories, and debated what kind of ownership there could be of the seas.

The "major fact about the 19th century is the creation of a single global economy," writes the historian Eric Hobsbawm, "an increasingly dense web of economic transactions, communications and movements of goods, money and people" (1989, 62). The creation of this economy reflected the spread of European control. By the end of the nineteenth century, political philosophers such as Alexis de Tocqueville and John Stuart Mill were busy justifying why non-Europeans should endure political dependence. A period of devising rules for the spread of empire gave way to a period of justifying its persistence. After World War II, "global governance" came into its own, and talk about a "global (political and economic) order" and an "increasingly interconnected world" has become commonplace and appropriate.

While this global order has no government, it comprises treaty- and convention-based norms regulating territorial sovereignty, security and trade, some property rights, human rights, and the environment. Politically, the UN Charter codifies the most significant rules governing this system. Economically, the Bretton Woods institutions—the International Monetary Fund, the World Bank, and later the General Agreement on Tariffs and Trade and the WTO—form a network intended to prevent war and foster worldwide betterment. Jointly with more powerful states, these institutions shape the economic order. At *this* stage of globalization philosophers must worry about the normative issues that such governance raises.

These developments in the world have prompted changes in the concerns of political philosophers, in particular, a new interest in global distributive justice. So let me turn to saying something in general about how I understand distributive justice. In what follows, "justice" means "distributive justice" unless otherwise specified. (It is a controversial matter what other kinds of justice there are.) Distributive justice determines what counts as an acceptable distribution of holdings. Principles of distributive justice are propositions in the first instance about the distribution of some good in some population. They take this form: "The distribution of good G in population P is just only if...." These principles entail further propositions about duties (for agents and institutions) and claims (of individuals). The principle says "only if"—the right-hand side states a necessary condition of the distribution on the left-hand side being just, not a sufficient condition. This leaves space open for there being multiple principles of justice: there could be more than one principle even for the same good and the same population.

A theory of distributive justice explains why certain individuals have particularly stringent claims to certain relative or absolute shares, quantities, or amounts of something. The relevant population for a principle of justice usually consists of individuals living at a given time, but it need not. To use some examples that will be relevant later in the book, it can be a population of states or one of different generations. Two especially important populations in what follows are the population of all humanity, the whole population living on earth (at present, those two groups happen to be identical), and the population within a particular state. I sometimes talk about the "scope of, or associated with, a principle" to mean the relevant population for that principle.

Whatever it is whose distribution is at stake is the *distribuendum, metric,* or *currency* of justice. The relevant goods for a principle of justice are potentially heterogeneous and range from quite concrete things (material goods) to quite abstract things (primary goods, legal rights) and even (potentially) subjective states (satisfaction, happiness). It can be controversial whether something is an appropriate candidate to be a good whose distribution is a matter of justice, but facing that controversy is part of the job of someone defending a specific principle of justice. Principles of justice need not specify an exactly equal distribution. Few that have been seriously defended do. But they can be more or less egalitarian. A paradigmatic example of an egalitarian principle is Rawls's "difference principle," which says (roughly) that the distribution of goods within a population is just only if any differences in holdings benefit the worst-off.

Principles of justice have *grounds*. The grounds are those considerations or conditions based on which individuals are in the scope of principles. We may think of this in two (roughly equivalent) ways. First, these are the features of the population (exclusively held) that make it the case that the principle of justice holds. Second, these are a set of premises that entail the principle of justice. These premises can be partly normative. Grounds can support more than one principle, but these will have the same population. Grounds are features of populations, and a vague ground may correspond to a vague population. Different grounds can support principles that apply to the same population. The same principle could be supported by different grounds. Principles of justice trivially entail stringent claims. Every member of the relevant population has a stringent claim to whatever its share of the relevant good would be if the distribution was just. Principles, distribuenda, grounds, and scopes must form a coherent theory. I will say that they are respectively *associated* with each other.[2]

Principles of justice also trivially entail "obligations, or duties, of justice" for somebody. ("Obligation" and "duty" I use interchangeably.) For each principle there is some individual or institution or other agent that has an obligation to do what it can, within limits, to bring about that sort of just distribution—that is, to bring it about that the relevant stringent claims are satisfied. Exactly which agents have this obligation for which principles, though, is a matter to be settled in particular theories of justice. It is a controversial matter whether the obligations that follow from principles of distributive justice are the only "obligations of justice" there are (just as it is controversial what other kinds of justice there are). It is commonly agreed, though, that obligations of justice are not the only sorts of *moral* obligation, and that among moral obligations, obligations of justice are especially stringent.

Alan Ryan (1993) reminds us that in Shakespeare's *Merchant of Venice,* Shylock makes his demand for a pound of his delinquent debtor's flesh in terms of justice, and until the clever Portia finds a device for voiding the contract, the presumption is that it must be granted. Demands of justice are the hardest to overrule or suspend. Kant goes too far insisting there is no point for human beings to continue to live on earth unless justice prevails. Still, justice plays its central role in human affairs because it enables persons to present claims of such stringency.[3] "We can't leave it to insurance companies to deliver justice," J. M. Coetzee has the protagonist of his novel *Disgrace* say (2000, 137). This is amusing precisely because of the stringency of justice. We speak about justice in the family, at the workplace, or in competitions. There is justice as a personal virtue, a constitution of character or disposition to help ensure others have, or are, what they should have or be. Domestic distributive justice is also often called *social justice*.

Those are the central concepts of justice. Here are some other concepts that in due course will play a role in this book. There is a demand of reasonable conduct on person P to perform action A if and only if it would be unreasonable for P not to do A, and if and only if P can reasonably be expected to do A. If P has a duty of justice to do A, then there is a demand of reasonable conduct that P do A, but not vice versa. Demands of reasonable conduct can be less stringent than duties of justice. I will mostly be interested in cases in which there are demands of reasonable conduct without corresponding obligations of justice. In such cases I talk of "mere" demands of reasonable conduct. Moreover, a person has a moral right to X if and only if someone else has a moral obligation to let that person have X. We can distinguish moral rights from positive rights (e.g., legal rights, conventional rights, etc.). It is a matter of empirical research what legal rights someone in a given country has, say. It is a matter of philosophical inquiry what moral rights someone has. Positive rights can enter theories of justice as goods to be distributed; moral rights can enter as part of the grounds of a principle of justice.[4]

3. Reflection on global justice has become mandatory not only because of globalization. Our understanding of domestic justice itself requires such reflection. Samuel Fleischacker (2004) argues that the modern conception of social justice incorporates several premises.[5] First, each individual has a good that deserves respect: individuals are due rights and protections to that end. Justice is not (merely) a matter of realizing, say, a divine order.[6] Second, some share of material goods is among the rights and protections everyone deserves. Third, what each person deserves is rationally and secularly justifiable. ("Where mystery begins, justice ends," Edmund Burke once wrote [1982, sec. 53].) Fourth, the distribution of these goods is practical: it is neither a fool's project nor self-undermining, like attempts to enforce friendship. Fifth, it is for the state (and conceivably other political entities) to achieve justice.

This conception captures commitments about how fates are tied and about the specials claims and duties generated thereby that are strikingly unusual by historical standards. Instead of each individual having a good worthy of respect, as is often taken for granted now, only people of a certain race or status may demand respect for their good, whereas the good of others can allegedly be realized only through a relationship of inferiority. Instead of individuals being due certain rights, and instead of there being rational and secular justifications, as is now often assumed, justice may require of persons to occupy positions based on divine or natural law, or as otherwise determined by an ideology not subject to scrutiny. Governments may be accountable only to God, as the Psalmist's David recognized responsibility only to God for sending his beloved's husband to die (Psalm 51:4: "Against thee, thee only, have I sinned"). Instead of material goods being among the distribuenda, only honors may be. Instead of there being efforts to achieve a certain distribution, that distribution may be considered an unalterable fact. Or there may be reasons not to do anything about it, such as divine grace, or a perception that intervention creates moral failings (say, because it conflicts with other values, e.g., liberty) or is practically undoable. Finally, instead of the state's being charged with maintaining a just distribution, the task may be left, say, to churches.

But if each individual has a good deserving of respect, we must ask whether corresponding duties expire at borders. If material goods are among the rights and protections everyone deserves, we must ask whether this depends on where people live. If rights require rational justification, we must ask whether such justification is available only for principles that hold within the state. Plausibly, entities other than states too ought to strive for justice. In his *Enquiry Concerning Human Understanding,* Hume has Epicurus ask those who believe in a provident God, "Are there marks of a distributive justice in the world?" (1975, 141). Suitable secularized and modernized versions of this question must now indeed be raised about the world, not merely about a state. Assuming that Fleischacker's analysis of our modern conception of social justice is correct, as I think it is, we can see how this conception points beyond itself: it naturally leads to an inquiry into global justice.

4. Distributive Justice is the genus of which relationism and nonrelationism are species. Relationists and nonrelationists disagree about the grounds of justice. "Relationists" think principles of justice hold only among persons who stand in some essentially practice-mediated relation. "Nonrelationists" think all principles of justice apply among all human beings regardless of what relations they share. A reference to practices keeps nonrelationism from collapsing into relationism. The relation of "being within 100,000 kilometers of each other" is not essentially practice-mediated, nor is, more relevantly, that of "being a fellow human." I talk about "essentially" practice-mediated relations since there may be practices associated especially with this latter relation that are dispensable to understanding its content.[7]

Relationists may hold a range of views about the nature of the relevant relations, and they may think there is only one relational ground or several. Relationists are motivated by concerns about "relevance," the moral relevance of practices in which certain individuals stand. Such practices may include not only those that individuals chose to adopt but also some in which they have never chosen to participate. Globalists think there is only one relevant relation, and that relation holds among all human beings in virtue of there being a global order. (To remember its relationist meaning, readers should connote this term with global order rather than with globe.) Statists, too, think there is only one relevant relation, and think that relation holds (only) among individuals who share membership in a state.

Globalists may well concede there used to be a relevant difference between state and global order but assert there no longer is. Whatever relations are supposed to be so important among the people sharing a state that they ground principles of justice now exist among the whole population of the earth (or perhaps most of it, those living isolated from the modern world excepted). Since the relevant relation-sharing community has now expanded, principles of justice apply only globally (or almost globally). All relationists owe an account of why relations should be all-important for the applicability of justice. Globalists owe an account of what it is (exclusively) about involvement with the global order that generates demands of justice. Similarly, statists owe an account of what it is (exclusively) about shared membership in states that does so.

Statists and globalists disagree about ground and scope but agree that there is only one ground, and that it is relational. Relationists may also agree about the scope and agree that there is only one ground while disagreeing about that ground. In chapter 3 we encounter *coercion-based* and *cooperation-based* statists. Both think the people who respectively stand in the justice relationship are those who share a state. They disagree about whether it is in virtue of cooperative or coercive practices that justice applies. What is distinctive of a ground is the account of the conditions and considerations that are norm-generating. Those who think cooperative practices are crucial to shared membership in a state have a different view of the grounds than those who think coercive practices are. It should be noted that globalism is a view about *grounds*, not about the scope that is consistent with a nonrelationist ground. Talk about "non-relationist globalism" is oxymoronic.

Nonrelationists deny that the truth about justice depends on relations. They think principles of justice depend on features that are shared by all members of the global population, independent of whatever relations they happen to be in. Rather than focusing on relevance, nonrelationists seek to avoid the "arbitrariness" of restricting justice to regulating practices. Globalization may have drawn our attention to the fact that justice applies globally, but in fact it always did. The versions of nonrelationism seriously defended in the literature take the scope of justice to be global, including all of (and only) humanity. But nonrelationists could in theory determine the scope differently. One could limit justice to a subset of humanity by insisting on the normative importance of sex or race. Or one could insist that justice must have all sentient beings in its scope, at least higher animals and conceivably rational Martians.[8]

Nonrelationists (of the mainstream sort) owe us an account of what it is that members of the global population have in common—if not some relations—that make it the case that principles of justice apply to the global population. "Common humanity" is an obvious possible answer, but there could be others. Commonly, nonrelationism is defended as a view committed to one ground, but there could be several. For nonrelationists for whom common humanity is the only ground, justice is a property of the distribution of advantage, broadly understood. While for relationists, individuals stand in the justice relationship if they have special claims within particular practices, for this kind of nonrelationist that relationship is distinguished by the absence of special claims.

One term I have little use for is "cosmopolitanism." According to a well-known definition, cosmopolitanism consists of three positions:

> First, individualism: the ultimate unit of concern are human beings, or persons.... Second, universality: the status of ultimate unit of concern attaches to every living human being equally—not merely to some sub-set, such as men, aristocrats, Aryans, whites, or Muslims. Third, generality: this special status has global force. (Pogge 1994, 89)

None of the views I discuss in this chapter denies moral equality among persons; each has capacities to make sense of individualism, universality, and generality. What is crucial is how rich a notion of moral equality one should endorse and how it relates to political and distributional equality. It is in this regard that those views disagree with each other and with my own view, which I introduce in section 5. One response is to use different notions of cosmopolitanism, perhaps distinguishing weaker from stronger versions. Another is to stop using that term in debates about distributive justice. This second response strikes me as the right one. While the term is suitable to describe a love of humanity or the evanescence or fluidity of culture, it has outlived its usefulness for matters of distributive justice. We have learned the basic cosmopolitan lesson: moral equality is an essential part of any credible theory of global justice. We live on a "cosmopolitan plateau." But we should conduct the philosophical debate about global justice in the terms discussed in this chapter.[9]

5. Qua relationists, statists and globalists oppose nonrelationism. At the same time, globalists and nonrelationists oppose statism in a significant way. The state is "normatively peculiar" (from a standpoint of justice) if and only if there are some principles of justice that apply only within states. Statists endorse the normative peculiarity of states; globalists and nonrelationists reject it. Disagreements among statism, globalism, and nonrelationism notwithstanding, they all assume a single justice relationship. (Or, that is, statism, globalism, and the common versions of nonrelationism do.) Alternatively, one may deny that all principles of justice have the same scope and the same ground. That is what *internationalism* does, the view I defend in this book.

Internationalism shares with statism a commitment to the normative peculiarity of the state. Internationalism also holds that nothing as egalitarian or demanding as Rawls's account of justice (see below) applies outside of states, though it does apply inside the state. At the same time, internationalism accommodates multiple grounds, some of which are relational and some not. Therefore, I also talk about "pluralist internationalism." Internationalism agrees with globalism that the global order generates its own principles of justice and with nonrelationism that not all grounds are relational and that common humanity is a ground. But the principles thus generated are much weaker than those that apply within states. Using the term "internationalism" for my view is apt because it recognizes the applicability of principles of distributive justice *outside* and *among* ("inter") states. Internationalism's inherent pluralism transcends the distinction between relationism and nonrelationism, formulating a view "between" the two common views that principles of justice either apply only within states (as statists think) or else apply to all human beings (as globalists and nonrelationists think).[10]

My defense of pluralist internationalism in this book accepts a twofold challenge: first, to show why statism, globalism, and nonrelationism are insufficient and why a view combining relational and nonrelational grounds is promising; and second, to illustrate the fruitfulness of my view by assessing constructively what principles are associated with different grounds. Altogether I explore five grounds. I recognize individuals as human beings, members of states, co-owners of the earth, as subject to the global order, and as subject to a global trading system. For common humanity, the distribuendum is the range of things to which a certain set of natural rights entitles us; for shared membership in a state, it is Rawlsian primary goods; for common ownership of the earth, it is the resources and spaces of the earth; for membership in the global order, it is again the range of things to which a set of rights generates entitlements; and for subjection to the global trading system, it is gains from trade.

For concreteness, I assume that the principles of domestic justice are something like Rawls's principles. For our purpose it suffices to establish that especially demanding, egalitarian principles hold domestically. But I do explore how domestic justice must integrate principles associated with other grounds. For each ground we must demonstrate "distributive relevance": we must show that principles of the form "The distribution of good G in population P is just only if ..." hold within certain populations. The burden of proof is on those who wish to introduce additional grounds. Nonetheless, I do not claim that I have identified all grounds: membership in the European Union is a contender, or more generally, different forms of membership in transnational entities. Certain grounds stand out because human affairs render them salient before the background of political realities and philosophical sensitivities. "Social justice" demarcates the relevance of membership. "Global justice" demarcates the salience of not one but several grounds: those mentioned and possibly others for which one must argue.[11]

One might worry that my approach brings under the purview of "distributive justice" much that may fit under justice, but not *distributive* justice. Indeed, internationalists do not say, for instance, that "'humanity' ought to come before justice in the determination of social and political priorities" (Campbell 1974, 4). Common humanity does not stand in contrast to justice but is one ground. Thereby my view acknowledges an important truth in nonrelationism. The issues that I claim fall under distributive justice are tied. The connection is that all grounds bear on the distribution of *something* that is both significant for individuals and salient at the political level, and that all claims based on different grounds place stringent demands on states and other agents. It is possible to think of humanitarian duties as opposed to justice for a narrowly conceived notion of justice. However, there is pressure to think of these duties as stringent, which renders this contrast uncompelling. Internationalism contrasts humanitarian with *other* duties of justice. There does remain some awkwardness in thinking of all the issues in this book in terms of distributive justice. Nonetheless, on balance, there is good reason to do so.

Another worry is that, at its core, distributive justice concerns material goods and opportunities: extending the term to include all the distribuenda that I just mentioned my account recognizes for different principles makes justice too amorphous. However, it is impossible to theorize about justice while embracing that intuition. Reflection creates pressure to take a more abstract standpoint to obtain a coherent and plausible approach. Recent theories of justice use abstract distribuenda, to make plausible that any two individuals ought to have an equal share of them, including opportunities, well-being, social bases of self-respect, or expectations for life trajectories. Some distribuenda are not the sort of thing one can *distribute*. One can affect their distribution only indirectly.

Reflection on statism, globalism, nonrelationism, internationalism, and perhaps other positions that one might want to formulate about the grounds of justice becomes especially urgent once we confront a broader spectrum of alternatives to states than those that lack coercive institutions and therefore are at issue with anarchists. That spectrum includes societies with coercive institutions other than states or governments. Of interest are not primarily political organizations that predate states, such as city-states, city leagues, empires, or feudal structures. Instead, of interest are a world state, a world with federative structures stronger than the UN, one with a more comprehensive system of collective security, one where jurisdictions are disaggregated, or one where border control is collectively administered or abandoned entirely. Reflection on such structures matters greatly in an interconnected world where enormous differences in life prospects persist.[12]

6. John Rawls is an interlocutor throughout, second only to Hugo Grotius, whose work I discuss in chapter 5. I introduce parts of Rawls's theory throughout (especially in chapters 2 and 3) as needed. Let me say a bit about his approach, and about how mine differs from his. At the core of Rawls's theory is a proposal for two principles of domestic justice (e.g., Rawls 2001, 42):

1. Each person has the same indefeasible claim to a fully adequate scheme of equal basic liberties, which scheme is compatible with the same scheme of liberties for all.
2. Social and economic inequalities are to be arranged so that they are both (a) attached to offices and positions open to all under conditions of fair equality of opportunity and (b) to the greatest benefit of the least advantaged.

The second part of the second principle is the *difference principle*. Priority is given to the first principle, and within the second to the first clause.

Conflicts between the principles are decided in favor of the first. Conflicts between the two parts of the second principle are resolved in favor of the first part. The distribuenda presupposed by these principles are what Rawls calls the social primary goods: basic rights and liberties, freedom of movement and free choice of occupation against a background of diverse opportunities, powers and prerogatives of offices and positions of authority and responsibility, income and wealth, and the social bases of self-respect (Rawls 2001, 58–59).

The rights captured by the first principle are political and civil rights: freedom of thought and liberty of conscience; political liberties (e.g., rights to vote and to participate in politics) and freedom of association, as well as rights and liberties specified by the integrity (physical and psychological) of persons; and finally, rights and liberties covered by the rule of law (ibid., 44). The second principle adds demanding conditions regarding socioeconomic inequalities. Fair equality of opportunity requires measures much beyond removing discrimination in the provision of access to offices and positions. What is required instead are arrangements that enable people to be healthy and well educated enough to be genuinely competitive, regardless of what segment of society they belong to. The difference principle then regulates the distribution of the remaining social primary goods. It asks us to compare feasible institutional arrangements that distribute these goods and to identify the respectively least advantaged. We should choose that arrangement that makes its least advantaged better off than the respectively least advantaged are under any other arrangement. Rawls assumes this condition will work out favorably for everybody in society, so that remaining differences in primary goods do indeed benefit everybody.

These principles do not regulate all aspects of people's lives. They regulate the *basic structure* of society and apply only to people who share such a structure. The basic structure is the way in which the major social institutions fit together into one system and how they assign fundamental rights and duties and shape the division of advantages from cooperation. Institutions that constitute this structure include the political constitution, the different forms of property, the legal system of trials and other legal procedures, the organization of the economy (norms enabling the production, exchange, and consumption of goods), and also the nature of the family (Rawls 1999c, 6–7; 2001, secs. 4, 15, 16).

Among those who share a basic structure, then, the principles of justice respond to the question of how to distribute social primary goods. Rawls uses a social contract argument to approach this question. The traditional form of this argument envisages a state of nature in which individuals live together before there is political authority. The answer to the question of what contract they would agree to is supposed to determine the scope and limits of justified state power. Since few such contracts have been made, and since it will be no longer binding on the living even where one was made in the past, one may think about a hypothetical contract instead. But Rawls does not employ an argument of either form. His "aim is to present a conception of justice which generalizes and carries to a higher level of abstraction the familiar theory of the social contract found, say, in Locke, Rousseau, and Kant" (1999c, 10).

This generalization involves an expository device Rawls calls the "original position." In the original position, people are behind a "veil of ignorance," so that

> no one knows his place in society, his class position or social status, nor does any one know his fortune in the distribution of natural assets and abilities, his intelligence, strength, and the like. I shall even assume that the parties do not know their conception of the good or their special psychological propensities. The principles of justice are chosen behind a veil of ignorance. This ensures that no one is advantaged or disadvantaged in the choice of principles by the outcome of natural chance or the contingency of social circumstances. Since all are similarly situated and no one is able to design principles to favor his particular condition, the principles of justice are the result of a fair agreement or bargain. (1999c, 11)

The original position models the idea of equality among participants. This device captures reasonable limitations on arguments they can make in support of principles of justice. Individuals can enter the original position any time by accepting these constraints. Based on reasoning that we explore in more detail in chapter 2, Rawls concludes that, given these reasonable limitations, participants would choose his principles.

Rawls is a relationist, and specifically a statist. He famously calls justice "the first virtue of institutions, as truth is of systems of thought," and talks about "justice in social cooperation" (1999c, 3).[13] "Distributive justice," says his expositor Samuel Freeman (2007a) by way of highlighting Rawls's relationism, "poses the general problem of fairly designing the system of basic legal institutions and social norms that make production, exchange, distribution, and consumption possible among free and equal persons" (305–6). Many aspects of advantage and its distribution are natural facts. But "what is just and unjust," says Rawls (1999c, 87), are not these facts but instead "the way that institutions deal with these facts."

Rawls's relationism also bears on his choice of distribuendum. Let me briefly explain this point, both as a way of expounding Rawls's approach and to illustrate the reach of the distinction between relationism and non-relationism. Rawls's *Theory* itself provides little argument for primary goods over other currencies.[14] To show how primary goods, or something like them, become inevitable as currency, I introduce a *publicity constraint* that excludes subjective distribuenda.[15] Since citizens encounter conflicts of interest, they need a currency they can regulate with reasonable effectiveness and can verify with some certainty and without information depending on declarations of or intrusions upon persons. Since free and equal citizens take themselves to be judges of the extent to which their pursuit of the good succeeds, public deliberation *ought* not to assess subjective welfare. Since one cannot expect others to take one's word for the relevant data, dissenters either must intrude upon a citizen's mental life or decide her satisfaction for her. Neither is acceptable.[16]

There are objective distribuenda other than primary goods, including Ronald Dworkin's "resources" or Amartya Sen's "capabilities." But for citizens to support policies in a suitably informed way, the basic structure must be regulated in terms of a currency they can use in deliberations. Currencies that are too abstract or complex fail that test, so we need a guidance constraint on the choice of distribuenda. These two constraints are plausible within Rawls's theory because his principles regulate practices, membership in a state. These constraints lead toward primary goods. It is hard to see how to support primary goods over competitors if these criteria are unavailable. Nonrelationists may grant that such criteria matter practically. But they object to their bearing on the determination of what principles of justice are, and to distribuenda that lack plausibility without these criteria. Rawls's relationism is critical for his choice of primary goods as distribuenda.[17]

7. Let me explain how pluralist internationalism relates to Rawls's view. Rawls's main subject is domestic justice. His later *The Law of Peoples* (Rawls 1999b) adds an approach to international justice by way of sketching the foreign policy of a society that applies his principles (or something like them). Relationists like Rawls can recognize duties to those with whom one does not share the relevant relation, such as membership in a given state. But those duties could not be duties to realize the principle that arises from *that* ground (in the example, principles applying within that state). They could be duties of some kind *other* than duties of justice; or they could be duties of some kind of *justice* other than distributive justice.

Thomas Nagel (2005) adopts the former approach. A statist like Rawls, Nagel insists that principles of justice hold only within states. In *The Law of Peoples,* Rawls adopts the latter approach. Rawls implicitly acknowledges a distinction between duties of *distributive* justice held within states and duties of justice that may hold otherwise. The duty of assistance to "burdened societies" that Rawls recognizes is not one of *distributive* justice (1999b, 106, 113–20). Duties of distributive justice concern shares in a system of economic production and exchange, which Rawls thinks presupposes a basic structure.[18]

Rawls never asks how to justify states to outsiders. Nor does he explore what distinguishes states from other structures. *A Theory of Justice* took for granted that political philosophy had mostly solved the problem of justifying the state to the anarchist. What was left to do was primarily to develop an account of justice. But the state has since become problematic in ways in which it never was for Rawls. It is to that state of affairs that my book reacts. Unlike Rawls's, my concern is not primarily with domestic principles of justice but with arguments that set the stage for their selection and with considerations about the place of the state in a politically and economically interconnected world that constrain their formulation. I inquire about the state in global perspective.

For concreteness, I assume that something like Rawls's principles holds domestically (primary goods being the distribuendum). I accept "something like Rawls's principles" because perhaps we should permit less inequality than Rawls allows (Barry 2005), or more (Nagel 1997). One may take the first stance, for example, if one thinks inequality (of some sort) is problematic as such. One may take the latter stance, for instance, if one thinks it matters more than Rawls allows how inequalities have arisen. Rawls regarded his principles as one form of a credible liberal egalitarianism, other forms of which may allow for more inequality. However, a complete formulation of principles that apply to the state must be longer, and must correspond to a broader range of duties at the global level, than Rawls allows. The main challenge for my pluralist internationalism is to make good on that claim.

Rawls's approach to justice is motivated by his philosophical method. He begins with domestic justice and works "outward" from there to the Law of Peoples, and "inward" to local associational justice (2001, 11). Domestic justice is presupposed by the other subjects. As Freeman (2007a) says:

> The principles that appropriately regulate social and political relations depend upon the kinds of institutions or practices to be regulated, and these principles are to be "constructed" on the basis of ideas that are central to the functioning of those institutions or practices and people's awareness of them. (270)

This approach has been called "political constructivism." Freeman plausibly sees it as integral to Rawls's rejection of global principles of distributive justice. The convictions and intuitions that must be in reflective equilibrium (to use a term I spell out in chapter 2) to obtain a theory of justice concern the practices and institutions within which we lead our lives. These convictions are less developed outside the domestic setting.[19]

Indeed, we must take as given a global political order whose principal subdivisions consist of units roughly like the current state, but be open to the possibility that the best justification for doing so requires (possibly considerable) modifications in the norms of the system as we find them. We cannot pretend to be able to invent a global order from scratch (a thought that chapters 15 and 16 develop in detail). After starting with the state, we can ask what is normatively peculiar about it, and whether there ought to be states, as well as bring into focus the state's duties to those outside it. But we do not therefore need to agree with Rawls that there are principles of distributive justice that apply domestically and must be articulated first, and that then there may well be other principles of justice (not distributive justice) that apply globally. Contrary to Rawls—and this is the major difference between his approach and mine—I argue that states are subject to principles of distributive justice also on account of the other considerations reflected in the grounds-of-justice approach, and that there are several grounds of justice, of which some are relational and some are nonrelational.

What is perhaps most distinctive about my approach is the significance I give to humanity's collective ownership of the earth, inspired by the work of the seventeenth-century Dutch jurist and philosopher Hugo Grotius. Inquiring about ownership of the earth offers insights into immigration, obligations to future generations, obligations arising from climate change, and even human rights. In this respect my approach differs from Rawls's, but also from just about all other major contemporary theories of global distributive justice.[20]

8. In a nutshell, I formulate a view of global justice "between" two standard views, that principles of justice either apply only within states or else apply to all human beings. There are different principles with different relevant populations (scopes) and grounds of different types. The chapters in part 1 primarily discuss the state, and thus shared membership in a state as a ground of justice, but that discussion also includes an account of common humanity as a ground (chapters 2–4). Then part 2 explores humanity's collective ownership of the earth (chapters 5–10). In part 3 I turn to international structures, the global order and the international trade regime (chapters 11–14). Finally, I explore two remaining questions that arise from my view, both pertaining to institutions. First, I assess whether there ought to be a system of multiple states to begin with, and second, I explore how the state's various obligations to bring about a just world mesh together, and start doing the same for global institutions (part 4, chapters 15–18).

Throughout, I successively develop a theory of human rights, to the extent required to explain how such a theory fits into a theory of global justice. I fall short of offering a complete list of human rights. Chapter 4 introduces a conception of human rights as rights that persons have in virtue of the distinctively human life. Chapter 7 begins work toward another conception that understands such rights as membership rights in the global order. Collective ownership of the earth is one source of such rights. Chapter 11 continues the work on this conception and integrates the distinctively human life as another source of rights. The conception from chapter 4 will therefore be fully integrated into the conception of human rights as membership rights in the global order, the conception I propose in this book. Chapters 12 and 13 explore how my conception makes sense of certain human rights.

Let me summarize chapter by chapter. In part 1, chapter 2 characterizes shared membership in a state as a ground and explores how this characterization bears on the selection of domestic principles of justice. Chapter 3 elaborates on differences between and among my pluralist view, statism, and globalism by looking at contemporary debates involving statism and globalism. Together, chapters 2 and 3 establish the state's normative peculiarity, and they also show that the principles of justice that hold in a state are especially demanding (broadly egalitarian) principles of justice. Chapter 4 explores what justice requires in virtue of common humanity and defends my pluralist view against a prominent version of nonrelationism. To that end, I develop a conception of human rights that individuals hold in virtue of being human. The grounds in part 1 are shared membership in a state and common humanity.

Part 2 explores collective ownership of the earth. Since this approach is now uncommon, chapter 5 explores how one of its protagonists, Hugo Grotius, put it to work. An even more important interlocutor than Rawls, Grotius is also a source of inspiration for my discussions of duties from climate change, in chapter 10, and of a human right to pharmaceuticals, in chapter 12. Chapter 6 systematically develops the idea that humanity collectively owns the earth, selecting a conception I call Common Ownership.[21] Chapter 7 begins work on my conception of human rights as membership rights in the global order. Common Ownership is one source from which to derive such rights. Chapter 8 applies the ownership approach to immigration, arguing that states can reasonably be expected to allow immigration to the extent that they are underusing their share of three-dimensional space. Chapter 9 explores how Common Ownership illuminates duties toward future generations, and chapter 10 assesses the implications of Common Ownership for duties resulting from climate change.

Part 3 turns to international structures, discussing two remaining grounds, shared membership in the global order and shared subjection to the global trading system. Thinking of membership in the global order as a ground of justice acknowledges that the earth is covered by a system of states and that there are international organizations that aim to be of global reach. World trade is highly structured and subject to numerous conventions. Involvement with the trading system too constitutes a ground. The trading system is part of that order. States too are parts of it. Nevertheless, particular principles of justice apply to them, and the same is true for the global trading system.

Chapter 11 continues to develop the account of human rights as membership rights in the global order. Part 3 includes two studies of how to apply this conception to questions of the sort, "Is there a human right to X?" (Chapter 7 also offers one such study, concerning the question of whether there is a human right to relocation for inhabitants of disappearing island nations.) Chapter 12 explores whether there is a human right to essential pharmaceuticals. Chapter 13 assesses whether labor rights are human rights. Exploring the fifth ground, chapter 14 discusses how justice applies to trading. Chapter 18, in part 4, completes the discussion of trade by assessing the WTO.

Parts 1–3 explore the different grounds. Taking internationalism as established, Part 4 addresses two remaining questions, both pertaining to institutions. My approach makes the normative peculiarity of states central, as well as the existence of a system of multiple states. But states exist only contingently. If it were morally desirable for the state system to cease to exist, then my theory of global justice could not offer us an ultimate ideal of justice. That ideal would be offered by a vision of the political arrangement that should replace the system of states. So we must explore whether it is true that morally there ought to be no system of states but instead there ought to be either no states or else a global state. Answering that question is also relevant to answering the two questions concerning justification posed earlier in chapter 1. If there ought to be no state system, then it cannot be justified to people subject to it.

Chapter 15 considers several arguments that find fault with the way we live now, the system of states. We explore four strategies one may deploy (a) to identify faults of the state system and (b) to use the identified moral failings to reach the conclusion that there ought to be no system of states, and thus no global order. Chapter 16 offers a sweeping objection to any attempt to argue toward the conclusion that the state system ought to cease to exist. There remains a nagging doubt about whether there ought to be states at all; nevertheless, morally and not merely pragmatically speaking, we ought not abandon states now, nor ought we aspire to do so eventually.

Chapters 17 and 18 explore a question that we also encounter at several points throughout the book: what obligations do various institutions have to bring about a just world? In chapter 17 I focus on the state, drawing together the threads of my discussion and asking how the various obligations on the state to bring about a just world mesh together. In chapter 18 I begin the task of doing the same for global institutions by focusing on one, the WTO. In addition to questions of justice, we also encounter questions of accountability.

Let me add two caveats. First, the grounds-of-justice approach offers a comprehensive view of obligations of distributive justice. This involves a fair amount of categorization. This categorization will often be somewhat artificial, and in many cases the material of this book could have been organized differently. Obligations of justice at the global level are often overdetermined and can be captured in various ways. Second, by virtue of its pluralism, internationalism triggers the question of how to think about situations where principles derived from different grounds conflict. The structure of this book obscures the significance of this question since I more or less look at one ground at a time. Only in chapter 17 do we directly face the question of how to combine principles associated with different grounds. There I make a proposal for how to rank-order the different principles stating obligations of justice as they apply to the state. That list is an expansion of Rawls's principles. The rank-ordering will be controversial and will not be readily accessible to conclusive argumentation that would rule out alternative orderings. That, however, is in the nature of a genuinely pluralist theory.

Shared Citizenship and Common Humanity

CHAPTER 2

"Un Pouvoir Ordinaire"

Shared Membership in a State as a Ground of Justice

1. In a little-known 1677 essay, Leibniz has two diplomats wonder about the status of princes of the Holy Roman Empire of the German Nation. These princes had obtained a great deal of independence in the Treaty of Westphalia in 1648, but they were also beholden to the empire. Were these princes, at least those with sizable territories, "sovereign" or not?[1] To shed light on the empire's confusing realities, Leibniz distinguishes "Majesté" from "Soveraineté," the former being the "supreme right to command, or the supreme jurisdiction" (le droit supreme de commander, ou la supreme jurisdiction) and the latter a ruler's "legitimate and regular power to force one's subjects to obey, while [that ruler] could not himself be so constrained other than through war" (un pouvoir legitime et ordinaire de contraindre les subjects à obëir, sans qu'on puisse estre constraint soy même si ce n'est par une guerre) (Leibniz 1864, 352). Princes are sovereign in virtue of their day-to-day power to rule, a power Leibniz calls "ordinaire." Although the emperor's authority is higher, and although he may also be sovereign in some territories, where he is not he must go to war to enforce his authority.

This chapter seeks to establish shared membership in a state as a ground of justice. I first identify what it is about shared membership that makes it the case that some principles of justice apply only in states.[2] Then I make it clear why demanding, broadly egalitarian principles of justice apply to those who respectively find themselves in the scope of that ground. To be "broadly egalitarian," a principle must be concerned with the relative socioeconomic status of the individuals in its scope and forbid some inequalities in that status.[3] Our topic is philosophically both intriguing and difficult. It is intriguing because on the face of it, it must be surprising that some principles of justice would apply only within one institution. It is difficult because it is hard to identify a feature of life in a state that is genuinely unique to states (especially because of institutions that have proliferated globally that share some features) and can be the foundation for a successful argument to the relevant principles.

This chapter goes straight to my solution for this problem, but chapter 3, which is tightly connected to this one, also explores various proposals that fail. This chapter does not yet address the possibility that the same principles also apply on grounds other than shared membership in states. Chapter 3 does so. Since I understand the normative peculiarity of states such that there are principles of justice that apply *only* within states, we can fully establish this peculiarity only in chapter 3. Nonetheless, this chapter contributes much of the argument to make that case, and thereby contributes to the development of internationalism.[4]

Leibniz had part of the solution to our problem. The contrast between the coercive powers he observed in the princes and the emperor has a parallel in the contrast between the powers of states and global institutions such as the UN. One component of what is peculiar about shared membership in states turns out to be what Leibniz said was distinctive about princes, "the legitimate and regular power to force their subjects to obey," or the immediate day-to-day power to enforce rules, without having to go to war. States not only have coercive power but, as I will say, they coerce "immediately." But if Leibniz had one part of the solution, Rawls had the other. Also unique to states is a special sort of cooperation, what Rawls called "reciprocity." These two ideas can be combined to identify the ground we are looking for: the feature of life in states that explains why especially demanding principles of justice apply within states. An elaboration of the richness of an account of membership in states is essential for my claim that such principles apply to those who respectively share membership in a state.

To fix ideas (and to set aside the complex history of this concept; see Skinner [1989] and Geuss [2001]), I adopt Kavka's (1986) notion of the state:

> To be a State, an organization must be *preponderant* in power, in a given geographic region, in the sense that it can physically overpower internal competitors and generally discourage aggression by outsiders. This means it can successfully enforce its rules and judgments against any public internal opposition if it chooses to do so, except possibly in the special case of its being replaced in accordance with established and recognized internal procedures, for example, elections. And it provides sufficient actual enforcement against internal and external transgressors that its citizens are seldom forced to resort to anticipatory action . . . to protect themselves. . . . And a State is simply an organized society with a territory and government. (158)

These criteria apply in degrees. Many countries in Africa, Central and South America, Western and Southern Asia, and Eastern Europe have low state capabilities. Some states fulfill Kavka's criteria to so small a degree that we may call them "quasi-states" (Jackson 1990). Nonetheless, when talking about the current state system, I talk about entities as characterized by Kavka, and assume there are many of them.[5]

2. To characterize shared membership in a state as a ground, let us begin with the manner in which states are coercive. Coercion is characterized by two features. First, it creates conditions under which person P has no reasonable alternative but to do A. Second, coercion involves a threat: P has no reasonable alternative but to do A because otherwise the coercive agent seriously worsens P's circumstances. I refer to the condition under which the first feature is present as "Nonvoluntariness" and to the condition under which the second is present as "Threat." Enforcement agents such as the police are coercive, but not all coercion is wrongful. All I claim about coercion is that it involves these conditions. On any natural understanding of what a threat is it involves a lack of voluntariness, but not each time something is done involuntarily is a threat present. Since Nonvoluntariness itself also is a plausible condition on the applicability of principles of justice, some of our investigations (especially in chapter 3) involve that condition as such.

One might wonder whether coercion itself characterizes the ground of shared membership. Chapter 3 discusses this approach, but the brief response is that some kind of coerciveness is also present in global institutions. So if arguments from coercion to principles of justice succeed, proponents might have inadvertently supported globalism rather than the normative peculiarity of the state. The question becomes whether there is a way of adding detail to the account of coercion above so that it is unique to states, or at least not shared by global institutions. This is where we can take the hint from Leibniz.

While coercion generally involves Nonvoluntariness and Threat, the state's coerciveness assumes a more specific character. (So the kind of state coerciveness I am about to introduce entails Nonvoluntariness and Threat, but not vice versa.) What is characteristic of the state is the *unmediated* nature of the interaction of individuals with their government. Exploring the manner in which states coerce, Michael Blake (2001) and Thomas Nagel (2005), for instance, stress the unmediated nature of this interaction, the *immediacy* of the interaction between individuals and state. Blake thinks only states coerce immediately. Similarly, Nagel admits that "the newer forms of international governance share with the old a markedly indirect relation to individual citizens and that this is morally significant" (139). But while neither of them elaborates on it, it behooves us to explore this theme to understand the normative peculiarity of the state.

The relevant notion of immediacy has nothing to do with spatial proximity. Instead, the immediacy of the interaction between individuals and state is characterized on two dimensions, a legal one and a political one. (I often simply talk about legal or political immediacy.) The legal aspect consists in the directness and pervasiveness of law enforcement. State enforcement agencies have direct, unmediated access to bodies and assets. Since many facets of the dealings of citizens among each other (including all property dealings, ranging from the purchase of a cup of coffee to ownership of firms and conditions on inheritance and bequest) are regulated, enforcement is pervasive for most individuals subject to it. The political aspect consists in the significance of the environment that the state provides for the realization of basic moral rights, a significance that captures the profundity of this relationship. Below I elaborate on the notion of reciprocity in Rawls. Rawls did not explore state coerciveness in detail, but my account of legal and political immediacy can be embedded in his sort of *ideal* theory.[6]

To elaborate, let us consider first the *legal* dimension. Like Leibnizian princes, states ideally possess the ability of unmediated law enforcement. Bureaucracies, courts, and police may seize, incarcerate, fine, or otherwise penalize individuals. Enforcement agencies may have nested or overlapping jurisdictions, for instance in federal systems. Sometimes states do without many or even any enforcement agencies to which all citizens are subject. (The early nineteenth-century United States is an example.) Still, even if law enforcement is decentralized, this is based on prior decisions (or historical processes) that states may in principle alter. While law enforcement may assume many forms, living in a state means living in an environment where enforcement agencies (at least potentially) have such access pervasively, and where it is up to internal processes to regulate what form such access takes and to what constraints it is subject.[7]

We can reformulate Max Weber's (1921) view that states possess a territorial monopoly of the legitimate use of force by saying that a state is a system of rules that guides interactions among individuals in a territory, accompanied by enforcement mechanisms that can reach individuals directly. The relationship between citizens and the state is such that there is no organization "in between," in the sense that that organization's legitimate prerogative is to offer protection against the state's enforcement agents, parallel to how state agencies are charged with protecting citizens from other individuals and other states. The legal framework may include agencies whose purpose is to protect individuals from other agencies (public defenders, appellate courts, etc.) or may allow citizens to delegate this task to other individuals (e.g., lawyers). But none of this undermines the contrast I am after.

Not all citizens are within reach of the state at all times, nor are all their assets. And not all individuals subject to a state's authority are citizens: some are temporary workers, illegal immigrants, or tourists.[8] Still, the nature of state power, by way of contrast with other entities, can be characterized in terms of directness and pervasiveness. The relationship between citizens and Leibnizian princes is like that, whereas the interaction between citizens and the Leibnizian majesty is not. Some laws may not effectively be under a state's control. However, even such laws require the enforcement mechanisms of the state. This statement by Cover (1986), about state coercion—"A judge articulates her understanding of a text, and as a result, somebody loses his freedom, his property, his children, even his life" (1601)—may be contrasted with Ruggie's (2005) claim that "international officials or entities may be endowed with normative authority that comes from legitimacy, persuasion, expertise, or simple utility; but they lack the basis and means to compel" (330). International organizations exercise power, and this fact matters in chapter 3. But they do so mediated through states.

One might object that while international organizations do not exert power in an immediate way, the Mafia might. To this, two counterarguments might be raised. First, although this account of the legal aspect of immediacy might apply to the Mafia to some extent, my account of its political aspect does not. Second, to the extent that there are similarities, they reveal what is problematic about the manner in which organized crime exercises power. Augustine famously asked what, absent justice, would be the difference between states and robber bands ("Remota itaque iustitia quid sunt regna nisi magna latrocinia?," *De Civitate Dei Contra Paganos libri XXII*, bk. iv). A nonstandard way of understanding the force of this question is that *to the extent that* robber bands are like states, *they too* are under pressure to abide by principles of justice.

As far as the *political* dimension is concerned, states provide the environment in which basic rights are, or fail to be, realized. For me to have freedom of speech, as it is commonly understood, is for me to be able to speak my mind to those around me; it does not depend on governments elsewhere refusing to publish my views, even if such refusals mean I cannot reach the audience I am most eager to reach. For me to have freedom of conscience, as it is commonly understood, is for me to be able to practice my religion where I live, not for my religion to be accepted elsewhere, nor does it mean for me to be able to travel anywhere my religion may require me to go. If the Saudis were unexpectedly to prevent pilgrimages, this would not undermine freedom of conscience of Muslims in Michigan. For me to enjoy freedom of association, as it is commonly understood, is for me to be able to associate with like-minded persons in an area where we are subject to the same jurisdiction; it does not depend on my ability to meet people far away, even if I have no other like-minded people in the same jurisdiction. International organizations can monitor violations or set incentives for states to respect rights. But whether individuals can exercise rights is a function of their immediate environment.[9]

One might worry that these claims are true only to the extent that what rights "mean" is a matter of how, presumably, most people would understand them. But a better way of proceeding is to explore what rights *properly understood* entail. Such an analysis would involve an exploration of the interests that explain the importance of the rights. That exploration would find, for instance, that some of the interests that explain the importance of freedom of religion do transcend boundaries. (Here we may think of the Muslim pilgrimage.) But we must be careful not to lose touch with the world in which we live. It is possible to construct scenarios where the exercise of basic rights depends only to a small extent on one's immediate environment. An example is a religion that requires ongoing travel to remote locations and requires nothing that involves one's immediate environment. However, a world in which such cases are common is quite different from ours. The kind and quantity of available counterexamples to my claim about basic rights are unlikely to undermine the special importance of the immediate environment for the realization of those basic rights in our world.

Individuals in failed or abusive states may have claims on other states (to asylum, say). Other states may have duties or prerogatives (to intervene on their behalf, say) that they would not have if these persons did not live in failed or abusive states. In war, too, special conditions obtain in which individuals have rights against other states, for instance as prisoners of war. Nevertheless, in states that instantiate the criteria we took from Kavka (1986), and so in well-functioning states, it is the state in which individuals live that guarantees their basic rights. (On the question of whether there ought to be states at all, see chapter 16.) That the environment in which rights must be guaranteed is the state, rather than a smaller or larger unit, is a corollary of my discussion of legal immediacy.

 While the legal dimension of immediacy captures the directness and pervasiveness of the relationship between state and citizens, the political dimension captures its profundity. One might object that, say, individuals living in Manhattan can realize their basic rights to a larger extent than people living in bad parts of the Bronx. It is municipalities, even boroughs, rather than countries that provide the environment on which the realization of rights depends. However, the fact that law enforcement in the United States is organized in a manner that makes the realization of rights vary across municipalities could *in principle* be changed through a political process.

3. Legal and political immediacy, then, characterize what is peculiar about state coerciveness, and so illuminate the form that Threat and Nonvoluntariness assume within states. But the two kinds of immediacy do not exhaustively describe shared membership in a state as a ground of justice.

What supports the thesis of the normative peculiarity of the state is not merely its coerciveness but also the fact that the state is a particular kind of cooperative endeavor. Membership in a state is also characterized by *reciprocity*, the joint participation in maintenance and reproduction of the state.

The notion of reciprocity figures prominently in Rawls's theory of justice. I integrate my account of immediacy with Rawls's account of reciprocity to obtain what I call an enlarged Rawlsian account of membership. Section 4 further elaborates on the richness of this account by exploring an account of responsibility that is closely tied to it. Rawls's notion captures successful participation in the society he envisages (the kind of participation that, in ideal theory, most people engage in most of the time). Rawls works with the "fundamental idea of society as a fair system of cooperation" (1993, 14; 2001, 5). What is crucial is reasonable acceptability to free and equal citizens of principles that govern constitutional essentials.[10] This does not mean coerciveness fails to enter. For Rawls explains the nature of the political, in contrast to the personal, the associational, or the familial, as a relationship within the basic structure, which, as he presumes methodologically, we enter by birth and exit by death (1993, 41, 137, 222; 2001, 40, 93, 182). Also, "cooperation is distinct from merely socially coordinated activity. . . . Cooperation is guided by publicly recognized rules and procedures that those cooperating accept and regard as properly regulating their conduct" (1993, 16). The regulation *of* a fair system of cooperation is regulation *by* coercive power.

My account of immediacy can be embedded in Rawlsian ideal theory. In our world, and within the range of "realistic utopias" (see chapter 16), the kind of society for which Rawls offers his theory of reciprocity will plausibly also be characterized by legal and political immediacy. To see why one should regard legal and political immediacy as part of ideal theory, one should not think of the possibilities of abuse available to states with a pervasive law enforcement apparatus any more than one should think of the possibilities of abuse available to a fair system of cooperation because it may be effective. One should think of the ideal of equal citizenship that is inseparable from immediacy. Immediacy makes sure no power in between state and citizens undermines equal citizenship. Feudal structures offer examples of such intermediate powers. Much of what I say about immediacy is implicit or explicit in Rawls. So I assume that my account of immediacy is part of this enlarged Rawlsian account.

One might think that in ideal theory, no coerciveness should be present. But one must still distinguish between ideal theory and the requirements of morality that apply only to "the saint and the hero" (Rawls 1999c, 419). Conflicts of interest remain, and occasionally people will fail to comply. For this reason it is hard to subtract coerciveness from ideal theory altogether (though its exercise would presumably be diminished). Immediacy is in any event part of the ideal of equal citizenship.

Those engaged in social cooperation are equal and free citizens. The basic structure is the way in which the major social institutions fit together, how they assign fundamental rights and duties and shape the allocation of advantages arising through cooperation. Two points matter. First, interaction among equal and free citizens requires their ability to conclude agreements. We need a structure that guarantees that those agreements are made freely and under fair conditions. Second, the basic structure is the environment in which abilities and talents flourish. We cannot know what we would have become otherwise. The importance of the basic structure has affinities to legal and political immediacy. One may talk about "social immediacy" to capture the ways in which the basic structure guarantees the space in which individuals can flourish. "Reciprocity" is the term Rawls uses for the relation between citizens who do their part in this cooperative system. As Rawls (1993) explains,

> the idea of reciprocity lies between the idea of impartiality, which is altruistic (being moved by the general good), and the idea of mutual advantage understood as everyone's being advantaged with respect to each person's present or expected future situation as things are. (16–17; see also Rawls 2001, 49 n.)

Reciprocity plays two roles for Rawls. First, it characterizes a relation that obtains in a state (as Threat, Nonvoluntariness, and immediacy do), namely, that of the interaction of free and equal citizens in maintaining a basic structure. In virtue of what such a structure *is*, this relation captures a dense form of cooperation. Reciprocity partly determines the conditions under which certain principles of justice apply. Second, reciprocity captures a situation in which individuals already do their part as prescribed by justice. What I need now is reciprocity of the (logically prior) former sort.

How Andrea Sangiovanni (2007) characterizes the modern state speaks to this point:

> When well-functioning, these basic state capacities [the basic extractive, regulative, and distributive capacities central to any modern state], backed by a system of courts, administration, and military, free us from the need to protect ourselves continuously from physical attack, guarantee access to a legally regulated market, and establish and stabilize a system of property rights and entitlements. Consider further that state capacity in each of these areas is not manna from heaven. It requires a financial and sociological basis to function effectively, indeed even to exist. . . . Citizens and residents, in all but the most

extreme cases, provide the financial and sociological support required to sustain the state. It is they who constitute and maintain the state through taxation, through participation, in various forms of political activity, and through simple compliance, which includes the full range of our everyday, legally regulated activity. Without their contributions to the de facto authority of the state—contributions paid in the coin of compliance, trust, resources, and participation—we would lack the individual capabilities to function as citizens, producers, and biological beings. (20–21)

Sangiovanni offers this as an account of the reciprocity among citizens of a state. We can think of this account as a somewhat more concrete version of Rawls's idea of reciprocity.

4. Rawls's notion of reciprocity and my account of immediacy merge into an overall account of shared membership in a state as a ground of justice, the enlarged Rawlsian account of membership in a state. Let us explore another aspect of Rawls's theory to illustrate the richness of this account.[11] I recall here that it is in virtue of ideas about shared membership that primary goods are acceptable as currency of justice. Shared membership is essential also to the way in which ideas of responsibility factor into domestic distributive justice. Rawls articulates an idea of a social division of responsibility that has puzzled many. However, that idea can be spelled out in a plausible way within the enlarged Rawlsian account of membership. That it is also tied to such a view of responsibility highlights the philosophical richness of that account.

An extended discussion of responsibility is notoriously absent from Rawls's *Theory of Justice,* and is never prominent on his agenda. But Rawls does offer the following account in several subsequent essays (emphasis added):

> This conception [of justice] includes what we may call a *social division of responsibility*: society, the citizens as a collective body, accepts the responsibility for maintaining the equal basic liberties and fair equality of opportunity, and for providing a fair share of the other primary goods for everyone within this framework, while citizens (as individuals) and associations accept the responsibility for revising and adjusting their ends and aspirations in view of the all-purpose means they can expect, given their present and foreseeable situation.[12]

One might think what "currency" to choose for justice is conceptually prior to and independent of how individuals and society divide responsibility. Why, then, would Rawls claim that his view of responsibility is *implicit* in the choice of social primary goods?

A fair system of social cooperation can exist over time only if, first, the possession of certain goods is regulated such that the fairness of the interaction and the participants' freedom and equality persist over time, which leads to primary goods as a metric of justice. Second, such a system persists only if citizens *as a collective body* assume responsibility for organizing the basic structure so as to support such a system of cooperation. Otherwise, the aggregative effect of individual decisions (on markets, say) may over time undermine the status of some as free and equal citizens. Third, cooperation remains fair, and individuals remain free and equal, only if they do not unreasonably burden each other with the costs of their decisions. Variations in preferences and tastes

> are seen as our own responsibility. . . . That we can take responsibility for our ends is part of what free citizens may expect of one another. Taking responsibility for our tastes and preferences, whether or not they have arisen from our actual choices, is a special case of that responsibility. As citizens with realized moral powers, this is something we must learn to deal with. (Rawls 1993, 185)

Let us consider now T. M. Scanlon's (1998) distinction between *responsibility as attributability* and *substantive responsibility*. "To say that a person is responsible, in this sense, for a given action," he says, explaining the former, "is only to say that it is appropriate to take it as a basis of moral appraisal of that person." In contrast, judgments of substantive responsibility "express substantive claims about what people are required (or . . . not required) to do for each other" (248). Substantive responsibility does not simply follow from facts of attribution. Applying Scanlon's distinction to the passage I just quoted from Rawls, we see that individuals must take substantive responsibility for tastes and preferences *regardless* of whether those are attributable to them. They must do so against the background of a basic structure whose social positions are regulated by Rawls's principles. Attributability does not bear on substantive responsibility.

We can now see that Rawls's division of responsibility is *implicit* in the choice of social primary goods in the sense that both the former and the latter are essential to the conception of society as a fair system of cooperation among free and equal citizens. What accounts for the choice of primary goods is what accounts for the endorsement of a social division of responsibility, namely, the concern to maintain a system of fair cooperation, which depends on both. The question of the "currency" of justice does *not* arise prior to the question of who is responsible for what. Both questions are answered simultaneously. Rawls's discussion proceeds in terms of a fair system of cooperation among free and equal citizens. "Reciprocity" denotes successful participation in such a system. The enlarged

Rawlsian account of membership, in turn, includes this idea of reciprocity. So Rawls's idea of a social division of responsibility (and the argument for its appropriateness) can be recast within that account of membership.

For G. A. Cohen (1989), "the primary egalitarian impulse is to extinguish the influence on distribution of both exploitation and brute luck," where "[a] person is *exploited* when unfair advantage is taken of him, and he suffers from (bad) *brute luck* when his bad luck is not the result of a gamble or risk which he could have avoided" (908). In Rawls's conception of responsibility, concerns about exploitation and brute luck enter derivatively of the idea of maintaining a fair system of cooperation, rather than by capturing a "primary egalitarian impulse." Justice is not (at least not primarily) about redressing inequalities imposed by nature or misfortune but about providing resources to realize moral powers. A notion of responsibility is added accordingly.

Rawls's notion of responsibility does not gain respectability by being useful for an account of the free will problem. It is not reducible to notions of responsibility current in that context, such as responsibility drawing on causal involvement or voluntary choice. This notion cannot play such roles, in much the same way that conceptions are unsuitable to ensure that burdens are distributed in a manner that guarantees the continuation of fair cooperation among free and equal citizens. The fact that primary goods are chosen as distribuenda because they are what free and equal citizens need entails that moral responsibility should not influence an individual's guaranteed share and thus her substantive responsibility. This notion of responsibility is thoroughly political, fitting only for the relationship of shared citizenship. Its importance and peculiarity add depth to my enlarged Rawlsian account of shared membership.

5. Before I connect the enlarged Rawlsian account to principles of justice that are limited to those who share a state, let me contrast my approach to the normative peculiarity of states with a very different approach to that subject, *nationalism*. I have accounted for shared membership in terms of dense relationships of coerciveness and cooperativeness. Appeals to nationality or shared nationhood have played no role. If instead one tries to account for the state's normative peculiarity in terms of nationality, there will be a naturalness to the existence of states that also gives a prima facie response to the question of why there ought to be states to begin with. As opposed to that, I must discuss separately the question of whether there ought to be states at all (chapter 16).

Nevertheless, there are good reasons not to account for the normative significance of shared membership through shared nationality. I cannot do justice to the substantive reasons that have been offered in support of a nationality-based approach to this topic. Still, I should explain why I do not account for that significance by appeal to shared nationhood, and what relevance shared nationhood may nevertheless have in the view I develop. Isaiah Berlin has suggested that nationalism

> entails the notion that one of the most compelling reasons, perhaps the most compelling, for holding a particular belief, pursuing a particular policy, serving a particular end, living a particular life, is that these ends, beliefs, policies, lives are *ours*. This is tantamount to saying that these rules or doctrines or principles should be followed not because they lead to virtue or happiness of justice or liberty . . . or are good and right in themselves . . . rather they are to be followed because these values are those of *my* group—for the nationalists, of *my* nation. (1981, 342–43)

We must distinguish *civic* from *ethnic* nationalism, depending on how one develops the attitude Berlin expresses.[13] Both allow us to formulate the thesis of the state's normative peculiarity. The civic conception is often connected to Ernest Renan's (1996) *Qu'est-ce qu'une Nation?*, a work first delivered as a lecture in 1882. A nation is a voluntary association of individuals, "a daily plebiscite." There are special obligations among fellow citizens because they have actually accepted them. This may not involve an oath or something similarly explicit, but civic nationalism emphasizes the manner in which individual *wills* maintain a closely knit community. The ethnic conception is associated with Herder's *Outline of a Philosophy of the History of Man* (1800). This view ties the stance that one ought to follow rules or principles "because these values are those of *my* group" to objective features of social life, such as language and tradition. These supposedly shared features are taken to generate duties.

In both versions, shared national identity establishes the normative peculiarity of the state. No appeal to the state's coerciveness or cooperative nature is then required to argue for its normative peculiarity. Appeals to the importance of nationhood of either sort lead to nationalism as the principle "which holds that the national and the political unit should be congruent" (Gellner 1983, 1). David Miller (1995) argues that shared nationality is a powerful source of identity, although he denies that it generates any clear specification of duties toward compatriots (which must emerge from public discourse). Without bonds of nationalism, Miller suggests, bonds of citizenship are very thin, psychologically *and* normatively. I submit that the view developed in this chapter rebuts Miller's stance as far as the normative dimension is concerned.[14]

In addition, there are well-known problems with both versions of nationalism. Shared nationality does not generally possess the voluntary nature on which civic nationalism focuses. Since it is therefore based on a misguided understanding of the nature of shared nationality, it cannot give us an account of how shared nationality would generate obligations. Ethnic nationalism is problematic because its central considerations do not generally apply to all relevant people. In any event, it does not provide us with an intelligible way of generating obligations in the first place. Therefore it is a considerable advantage of my internationalism that it does not enlist nationhood to explain what is special about membership in a state.

Nonetheless, nations frequently are cohesive groups in which individuals care about each other more than about others (being "teammates in life"; Wellman 2003, 270). Thus, often "my nation is an appropriate object of partial attitudes because it, more than other similarly sized groups, has allowed me to act with others to produce significant human goods" (Hurka 1997, 155). The nation's welfare often improves through political autonomy. As David Miller stresses, bonds of citizenship are easier to maintain with support from bonds of nationalism. I accept these points as reasons why people do or do not wish to live together. As John Stuart Mill puts it in *Considerations on Representative Government*, "Where the sentiment of nationality exists in any force, there is a prima facie case for uniting all the members of the nationality under the same government, and a government to themselves apart" (1991, 310). Appeals to nationality are relevant for drawing boundaries. They are irrelevant when we ask what duties hold among those who share a state, and why they do.

6. The enlarged Rawlsian account characterizes shared membership as a ground of justice. Immediacy and reciprocity are jointly sufficient to that end. Next I sketch how this account is connected to principles of justice. We must make sure that the relations unique to states are essential to the argument, so that one cannot readily reconstruct it with some substitute relation to support the result that the same principles apply globally. I "sketch" this connection in the sense that I seek to show how an account of shared membership enters into the argument for the selection of principles. Once the role of the enlarged Rawlsian account transpires, questions remain about the *precise formulation* of the principles, and about the arguments needed to support them. Such questions are not my concern, and addressing them involves a vast literature that explores whether Rawls's arguments for his proposal succeed.

What needs to become clear, however, is how this enlarged Rawlsian account leads to broadly egalitarian principles. For concreteness I will assume, then, that Rawls's principles are the correct principles domestically. Since I endorse these principles, I cast my discussion of how to connect shared membership in a state to principles of justice in the Rawlsian framework. Nonetheless, these principles must also be combined with principles associated with grounds other than shared membership in a state. The list of principles that generate duties for a government is an extension of the list that Rawls provides, with small changes in those principles that originate in the need to produce a combined list of all such principles. After all, those who share membership in the state also find themselves in the scope of principles of justice *with others*, for instance, in the scope of principles that concern humanity's collective ownership of the earth. Chapter 17 presents such an extended list.

Rawls's principles are the following (e.g., Rawls 2001, 42):

1. Each person has the same indefeasible claim to a fully adequate scheme of equal basic liberties, which scheme is compatible with the same scheme of liberties for all.
2. Social and economic inequalities are to be arranged so that they are both (a) attached to offices and positions open to all under conditions of fair equality of opportunity and (b) to the greatest benefit of the least advantaged.

Rawls actually begins with a more general conception of justice:

All social values—liberty and opportunity, income and wealth, and the social bases of self-respect, are to be distributed equally unless an unequal distribution of any or all of these values is to everyone's advantage. (1999c, 54)

The general conception (which is broadly egalitarian) allows for inequalities with regard to all social primary goods. The prioritizing within the principles becomes reasonable only once circumstances allow for effective realization of the liberties in the first principle (1999c, sec. 26). As long as concerns about survival dominate, people can permissibly prioritize survival over basic liberties.

Membership in states amounts to an intensely cooperative endeavor that is coercively regulated. However, the sought-after principles do not regulate all interaction. The question that principles of justice are supposed to answer is, how should the *basic structure* be regulated? In light of the enlarged Rawlsian account of membership, the question that principles of justice are supposed to answer is equivalent to this one: how should the basic structure be regulated, given that shared membership is characterized by immediacy and reciprocity? The distribuenda, for Rawls, are social primary goods. These goods are provided by the basic structure. We can therefore again reformulate the question that principles of justice are supposed to answer: how should the distribution of social primary goods be regulated, given that shared membership in a state is characterized by immediacy and reciprocity?

As we noted in chapter 1, Rawls uses a social contract argument to answer this question, one that involves the "original position" as an expository device. Behind the veil of ignorance, Rawls argues, individuals would adopt a *maximin* approach: they would seek to maximize their share in social primary goods in the worst-off position. Individuals would compare different ways of regulating the distribution of goods, inquire of each proposal which group would fare the worst, and choose the one that left the respectively worst-off better off than any alternative. According to Rawls, that reasoning leads to his (broadly egalitarian) principles. The first principle guarantees that the integrity of each person is protected, the first part of the second principle ensures that society makes substantive efforts to create equal opportunities for all, and the second part of the second principle makes sure the kinds of advancement in society that natural and social advantages permit benefit everybody, including the least well-off.

I have yet to explain how the enlarged Rawlsian account of membership enters into his argument. To do so, we should note that Rawls does not think a decision behind the veil is final. The principles thus chosen must "match our considered convictions of justice or extend them in an acceptable way" (1999c, 17). Otherwise,

> we have a choice. We can either modify the account of the initial situation or we can revise our existing judgments, for even the judgments we take provisionally as fixed points are liable to revision. By going back and forth, sometimes altering the conditions of the contractual circumstances, at other withdrawing our judgments and conforming them to principles, I assume that eventually we shall find a description of the initial situation that both expresses reasonable conditions and yields principles which match our considered judgments duly pruned and adjusted. (1999c, 18)

Once we have reached such a point, intuitions and principles are in reflective equilibrium. So we obtain principles of justice through a multistage process of revising both moral intuitions and the setup of the original position. Ultimately we obtain an account of the original position that delivers principles that fit the considered convictions of those who live in the society regulated by the principles. The original position—and thus the idea that principles of justice are principles chosen under certain circumstances—is indeed only an expository device; it systematizes ideas and constructs arguments in support of principles that must hold up in a court of considered intuitions.

Rawls's own intuitions are driven by the moral arbitrariness of natural assets and social status. "We are led to the difference principle," he says,

> if we wish to set up the social system so that no one gains or loses from his arbitrary place in the distribution of natural assets or his initial position in society without giving or receiving compensating advantages in return. (1999c, 87)

But what could Rawls say to opponents who decline to set up the social system that way? It matters now that we seek to identify principles for those who share membership *in a state*. Such members are free and equal persons. But it is a big step from this view of personhood to the kind of process that leads to the selection of Rawls's principles.

Membership in a state is participation in its maintenance and reproduction, an intensely cooperative, reciprocal endeavor that is coercively regulated as captured by the two aspects of immediacy. The profundity and pervasiveness of coercion impose burdens on those who are subject to the state. They also characterize the significance that membership has for them. Primary goods are provided through everybody's cooperation. These are ways of articulating how persons are in relevant ways *equally* and *significantly* invested in and subject to a state, and *in that sense*, as participants in this endeavor, are fundamentally alike. It is this fundamental alikeness whose content is described by immediacy and reciprocity that creates a default status for an equal distribution of social primary goods, placing a heavy burden of proof on those who prefer an unequal distribution.

This point matters, first of all, when we describe the original position. Again, in the original position "no one knows his place in society, his class position or social status, nor does any one know his fortune in the distribution of natural assets and abilities, his intelligence, strength, and the like." These features are judged to have no bearing on the selection of principles of justice. They are so judged by way of comparison with the manner in which all members of a state are fundamentally alike. Nobody has special entitlements, based on features that are undeserved assets of genetic makeup or social standing, to a social product that all members have collectively provided under conditions of reciprocity and immediacy. That some are strong or smart does not per se create entitlements since strength and smartness contribute only marginally to the cooperatively intertwined activities of all.

Rawls's guiding intuition that natural assets and social status are morally arbitrary and should not create entitlements to distributive shares is valid precisely because members of a state are fundamentally alike in the ways I described. Members do not equally contribute to the creation of public goods. Nonetheless, they are equal in their contributions and participation in very significant ways. Of course, *all* human beings are fundamentally alike in the sense that they partake of a distinctively human life (chapter 4). What matters here is alikeness *of a particular content*, namely, as described by immediacy and reciprocity. For this reason the argument I am developing cannot be reconstructed with some substitute relation that is present globally, to argue that the same principles hold globally.

Second, the fundamental alikeness of members in a state matters when we judge whether the principles devised in the original position are bearable for them. The "strains of commitment" (Rawls 1999c, 153f) must be borne by members who are expected to contribute to the provision of a social product under conditions of immediacy and reciprocity. If principles are found to be straining too far the members' ability to commit to their realization, the process of reflective equilibrium formation continues. This process ends only once we identify principles that are acceptable both ex ante, in the original position, and ex post, once individuals live in society and bear the consequences of their choices. In both scenarios, again, the fundamental alikeness of members as far as reciprocity and immediacy are concerned creates a default position for an equal distribution of social primary goods. Shared membership puts considerable pressure on the acceptability of inequalities in social and material status, as well as on the acceptability of inequalities in the value of civil and political liberties ("pressure" of the sort I illustrated by way of looking at the kind of claims one can make based on strength or intelligence). Individuals who do not jointly participate in such a relation are not alike in ways that create such pressure.

Here I note two points. First, the enlarged Rawlsian account of membership does not just imply that the distribution of primary goods must be *justifiable* to members. This account enters by way of constructing constraints on admissible arguments for the selection of principles of justice, and by thereby creating a presumption of equality in the distribution of primary goods. These constraints ensure that broadly egalitarian principles emerge from the process that generate reflective equilibrium. Nonetheless—and this is the second point—immediacy and reciprocity, and hence my account of shared membership as a ground of justice, do not bear on the content of the principles beyond what I have stated. Their precise content would be determined as part of this reflective equilibrium process. Once the original position is set up, arguments competing with Rawls's proposal could be developed. Any proposal that wins that debate must be acceptable ex post as well, until reflective equilibrium is reached.

Rawls thinks deviations from equality are acceptable if they are to everybody's advantage. Space remains for disagreement about acceptable deviations from equality. There is controversy about how to integrate *natural* primary goods, such as health, intelligence, attractiveness, and so forth, to the extent that those bear on shares in social primary goods. Nothing I have said addresses whether individuals should receive compensation for disadvantages in natural primary goods, or whether instead there is less of an obligation to attend to social disadvantage the more the disadvantage arises from natural differences. Similarly, nothing I have said bears on how, or whether, general sociological insights (hence the kind of insight available in the original position) about effects of inequality on human beings should affect the selection of principles of justice. Perhaps we should permit less inequality than Rawls allows (as Barry [2005] argues), or more (as Nagel [1997] argues). But in what follows, I assume that something like Rawls's principles hold, where the "something like" captures the lacuna I am now leaving.

Let me conclude. This chapter has shown that there are principles of justice that apply within states. Strictly speaking, this refutes globalism and nonrelationism since both hold that all such principles apply globally. I have not yet established the normative peculiarity of the state since that notion entails that there are principles that apply *only* in states. We can do so only in chapter 3. (My argument leaves open the strange possibility that the same principles apply both globally and within the state, in virtue of different grounds.) Nonetheless, this chapter has provided a significant part of my argument for the normative peculiarity of states, and thereby contributes to the development of internationalism. What principles of justice apply globally remains open.

CHAPTER 3

Internationalism versus Statism and Globalism

Contemporary Debates

PART I. EXPLORING STATISM

1. Chapter 2 characterizes shared membership in a state as a ground of justice and shows how that ground generates demanding principles. The argument there is meant to support internationalism. Internationalism transcends the distinction between relationism and nonrelationism by recognizing both relational and nonrelational grounds. Therefore, I must defend it against three views identified in chapter 1: statism, the view that all principles of justice apply within states, owing to a single ground, a relation among people that is present only within the state; globalism, the view that all such principles apply globally, owing to a single ground, a relation between people that is present among everyone living under the global order; and nonrelationism, the view that all such principles apply globally, owing to a single, nonrelational ground.

Other views are possible, but I do not explore them. Since each of those competitors endorses the view that there is a single ground, they must be rebutted by the constructive exercise of developing a pluralistic view of the grounds of justice. This book as a whole does so. Nonetheless, my view receives additional support through an engagement with prominent versions of the competitors. This chapter explores contemporary debates about statism and globalism. Chapter 4 addresses a version of nonrelationism. Such scrutiny increases the plausibility of my view as a contender for a theory of global justice, and sharpens our understanding of its contributions to contemporary debates.

Part I of this chapter addresses a debate among statists. Statists need a necessary condition for justice to apply. They must tell us what it is about states that renders such principles applicable, and does so only in states. The quest for such a condition ends inconclusively. This result leads to a pluralist view of the grounds of justice, and enables me to state internationalism more precisely than before. The result "leads" to such a view in a heuristic sense. To use a distinction from the philosophy of science, the debate among versions of statism turns out to be a context of discovery for internationalism as a contender for a plausible theory of global justice. This book as a whole provides the context of justification. Part II engages with the most prominent version of globalism, the view defended by Beitz (1999). Beitz thinks that Rawls's principles hold globally. To engage with Beitz we first look at the merits of relationism, and then make use of the enlarged Rawlsian account of membership from chapter 2 to argue that Rawls's principles do not apply to the global order. This discussion also completes my case for the normative peculiarity of states.

2. According to *coercion-based statism*, what distinguishes membership in a state is its coerciveness; according to *reciprocity-based statism,* it is its intense form of cooperation. Let us explore what we can say on behalf of these views.[1] Michael Blake (2001) accounts for the state's normative peculiarity, and offers a characterization of membership in states as a ground of justice, in terms of the presence of coercive structures. It is because of the Autonomy Principle ("all human beings have the moral entitlement to live as autonomous agents, and therefore have entitlements to those circumstances and conditions under which this is possible"; Blake 2001, 267) that such justification is necessary. The notion of autonomy captures a vision of persons controlling their destiny to some extent. An autonomous life is possible only for somebody who has the mental capacities to pursue projects, enjoys an adequate range of valuable options, and is free from coercion and manipulation (what Joseph Raz [1986, 369–78] calls the "conditions of autonomy").

What makes the relationship between state and citizens special is the need to justify coercion *to them*, but not to others not subject to such coercion. Forms of coercion, according to Blake, can be justified by hypothetical consent. In particular, property law must be so justified. Persons who share a property regime have claims on each other as far as their relative economic standing is concerned. Most property law is domestic. Blake seems to propose a *necessary* condition for justice to apply. Blake himself may not be a statist. His account could be developed into a pluralist view. Nonetheless, his approach offers one way of developing *coercion-based statism*.

As opposed to Blake, Andrea Sangiovanni (2007) argues that coerciveness is no such necessary condition. Sangiovanni constructs the following scenario:

> Imagine an internally just state. Suppose all local means of law enforcement— police, army, and any potential replacements—are temporarily disarmed and disabled by a terrorist attack. Suppose further that this condition continues for several years. Crime rates increase, compliance with the laws decreases, but society does not dissolve into a war of all against all. Citizens generally feel a sense of solidarity in the wake of the attack, and a desire to maintain public

order and decency despite the private advantages they could gain through non-compliance; this sense of solidarity is common knowledge and provides reassurance that people will (generally) continue to comply with the law. The state continues to provide the services it always has; the legislature meets regularly; laws are debated and passed; contracts and wills drawn up; property transferred in accordance with law, disputes settled through legal arbitration, etc.

Sangiovanni argues that the legal system still requires the same justification as before because membership remains *nonvoluntary*. Nonvoluntariness is still present, but not Threat. People have no viable alternative to membership because of the costs of starting a life elsewhere. A group of objectors (who think the broadly egalitarian principles of justice that held before no longer apply) could be rebutted by a reference to that point. Since Threat is not central to the normative peculiarity of the state, coercion cannot be either. Instead, says Sangiovanni, it is Reciprocity that is central for the normative peculiarity of the state. Sangiovanni's view too is consistent with a pluralist approach. But it also provides us with a way of developing *reciprocity-based statism*.

Let us recall that Sangiovanni describes the modern state this way:

> When well-functioning, these basic state capacities [the basic extractive, regulative, and distributive capacities central to any modern state], backed by a system of courts, administration, and military, free us from the need to protect ourselves continuously from physical attack, guarantee access to a legally regulated market, and establish and stabilize a system of property rights and entitlements. Consider further that state capacity in each of these areas is not manna from heaven. It requires a financial and sociological basis to function effectively, indeed even to exist.... Citizens and residents, in all but the most extreme cases, provide the financial and sociological support required to sustain the state. It is they who constitute and maintain the state through taxation, through participation, in various forms of political activity, and through simple compliance, which includes the full range of our everyday, legally regulated activity. Without their contributions to the de facto authority of the state—contributions paid in the coin of compliance, trust, resources, and participation—we would lack the individual capabilities to function as citizens, producers, and biological beings. (20–21)

While this makes for a clumsier statement than what I said in chapter 2 to introduce Threat and Nonvoluntariness, I use the term "Reciprocity" from now on to capture these conditions of individuals jointly participating in the maintenance of a state.

Let me add to this discussion of problems with the coercion-based statism inspired by Blake. If it is *because of the Autonomy Principle* that coercion requires justification, anything requires justification that affects whether people have a reasonable range of options. One way of affecting whether people live under such conditions is by coercing them, but others include *removing* options and setting incentives that determine whether people can rise above poverty. The International Monetary Fund (IMF) may need to decide on a loan for a country. (Let us assume the IMF is not to blame for that country's problems.) No coercion is involved since there is no threat, but the IMF affects whether people there can lead autonomous lives. In light of the Autonomy Principle, the IMF must justify its action just as well as if it had used threats. Differences between coercion and incentive setting notwithstanding, one cannot argue for the normative peculiarity of the state by saying *both* (a) that states coerce while the global order merely sets incentives *and* (b) that the reason why (only) states require special justification is the Autonomy Principle.

Thomas Nagel (2005) offers another way of developing coercion-based statism (and in fact is such a statist), arguing that

> it is this complex fact—that we are both putative joint authors of the coercively imposed system, and subject to its norms, i.e., expected to accept their authority even when the collective decision diverges from our personal preferences—that creates the special presumption against arbitrary inequalities in our treatment by the system.... This request for justification has moral weight even if we have in practice no choice but to live under the existing regime. The reason is that its requirements claim our active cooperation, and this cannot be legitimately done without justification—otherwise it is pure coercion. (128–29)

While Nagel and Blake agree that what requires justification is the state's coercive apparatus, Nagel finds the source of this need in the fact that we are both authors and subjects of coercion. States join international organizations in response to (innocuous) incentives, whereas coercion involves threats. For Nagel it is the presence of threats per se (rather than the violation of any principle through them) that records a crucial difference between states and such organizations.

Nagel's view too is open to the concern that states and international structures share relevant features. Suppose the IMF will lend funds to a country threatened by economic chaos only if it reforms. Or suppose a country changes its trade policies to comply with WTO agreements. "Why not say," inquire Cohen and Sabel (2006),

> that citizens in member states are expected to take account of WTO decisions, which have binding legal force: that they ought not to oppose a new trade regulation that is made pursuant to a WTO finding? (168)

Increasing interconnectedness renders it ever less plausible that the global order does not coerce. Another example is the following. Members of the European Parliament are elected by direct vote. While the impact of the parliament on the EU is much smaller than the impact of national parliaments on domestic politics, the joint presence of this parliament and the European Commission entails that the EU exerts coercion that has EU citizens as both authors and subjects. Nagel rightly argues that a difference between citizenship in a state and membership in international organizations is that one does not generally assume the former voluntarily but does so assume the latter. Nonetheless, both involve coercion (including threats) in cases of noncompliance. Moreover, once citizenship or membership has been assumed, resigning may not be a reasonable option. Since what matters is the presence of threats per se, differences between citizenship in states and membership in international organizations are insufficient to draw a salient contrast in terms of coercion between citizenship and such membership.

Statists are ill-advised to base their case on as controversial an issue as precisely what counts as a reasonable alternative or a threat rather than an incentive, and how much of a moral difference there is between scenarios that involve an absence of reasonable alternatives as well as a threat and scenarios where "legitimacy, persuasion, expertise, or simple utility" (Ruggie 2005, 330; see also chapter 2, section 2, of this book) create reasons for states to act in certain ways. Statism should not assume that a morally significant difference between states and other entities is that only the former coerce.[2]

3. The proper response to these problems is not to replace coercion-based statism with reciprocity-based statism. We should instead rethink statism altogether. To that end I argue first that, while Threat is not a necessary condition for justice to apply, neither Nonvoluntariness *nor reciprocity* is such a condition either. I do so by discussing other scenarios in the manner of Sangiovanni's example. All of this will be a discussion internal to statism, and the presumption throughout is that statists seek to justify the applicability of broadly egalitarian principles of justice within states. The first scenario creates an objection to the necessity of Nonvoluntariness:

> Imagine an internally just state. Suppose that, for whatever reason, perhaps just to indulge in a gigantic philosophical experiment, many individuals elsewhere in the world wish to create a situation that renders membership in that state voluntary. They have the patience and ability to do so. To lure people away from that state, those experimenters create a social environment continuous with what the targeted emigrants are accustomed to—*except* that principles

of justice will not fully apply. No matter how many people relocate, the improvements of their situation cannot be seen as outcomes of just redistributive principles that are in place elsewhere (perhaps only because they would receive more than justly they ought to). Emigrants would have their moves paid for and would get generous start-up funds to allow them a social status above what they used to have.

Yes, it is hard to imagine such a scenario, but not much harder than to imagine a post-attack state where law enforcement lapses while everything else continues as before. This scenario eliminates Nonvoluntariness from a just state.[3] Suppose some people dispute that broadly egalitarian principles continue to apply. Exit has never been so easy. Since Threat persists for those who stay, these objectors must continue their participation in the state. They complain that Threat persists unjustly, and advocate resistance. But it seems that, if broadly egalitarian principles were acceptable before, Threat and Reciprocity, jointly with the fact that exit may not lead to a scenario in which such principles would hold, still suffice for demanding such principles. Statists should conclude that Nonvoluntariness is not necessary to render principles of justice applicable.[4]

The next scenario is more important for the dispute we presently consider:

> Imagine an internally just state. Suppose in response to biological warfare, most individuals become lethargic and considerably less interested in cooperating with each other even where that is to their advantage. Suppose those with blood type O negative (of whom there are few) are less affected. Law enforcement continues to exist, at a minimal level. Other states are not affected, and offer no reasonable exit options. Gradually, economic, political, legal, and social ties loosen. Trust and solidarity diminish because most people do not care enough about themselves and each other. The state more and more ceases to provide many of the services it used to provide; the legislature almost never meets; property is rarely transferred, but disputes hardly arise because most people do not care.

Alternatively, one could formulate a scenario in terms of excessive aggressiveness. The point is to envisage cooperation sinking below the level where Reciprocity applies. The level of cooperation will then have decreased to a point where it is so minimal that nobody is making a sufficient sacrifice for the maintenance and reproduction of the state to have a claim against others. Again, these thought experiments are fanciful, but if they are more so than the earlier ones, it is a matter of degree. Suppose a group of objectors of blood type O negative insist that principles of justice no longer apply. They insist that what little enforcement is left of such principles is unjust. Most people will be too lethargic to resist, but theorists should rebuke these objectors. As there are no reasonable exit options, and as remaining enforcement may still seriously worsen lives, individuals have the same claims of justice as before. Statists should conclude that Reciprocity is not necessary for the applicability of broadly egalitarian principles.

So none of the contenders we have considered is *necessary* for the statist's case. I have conducted this inquiry without using the notion of immediacy from chapter 2 since this debate has so far been conducted without it. Nonetheless, since immediacy is the form that Threat and Nonvoluntariness assume in states, the examples involving Threat and Nonvoluntariness also exclude immediacy as a necessary condition for the applicability of broadly egalitarian principles. The upshot of our inquiry is not as counterintuitive as it might seem. The outlandish nature of our thought experiments shows that Threat, Nonvoluntariness, and Reciprocity (and, if we may now add the result of our discussion in chapter 2, immediacy) occur together. Worlds in which only two of them hold are far from ours in logical space. If one defends statism, it is important to identify a necessary condition for principles of justice to apply. However, we encounter candidates for such a condition in discourses where we take them to be *jointly sufficient* for demands of justice to arise, which makes it hard to isolate one as *necessary*.

To illustrate, we may consider resistance to libertarianism. One could resist libertarianism by appealing to intuitions that draw on any of these factors. "We are all involved," one may say, "in creating the social product within which each of us operates. It makes little sense to think of what each should get for her participation merely in terms of her marginal contribution, which is what drives wages in capitalist economies. We must all cooperate to maintain such a system, also as customers or consumers, and comply with rules. No account of entitlements can undermine this point." Or one may say, "Nothing gives individuals property rights that can be bequeathed and inherited at will and thereby resonate through the ages. Since such rights are conventional but coercively maintained, they ought to be arranged so that each person can make a living."

Finally, we can make a similar point with reference to the fact that property regimes apply to individuals without alternatives to staying within the state. "I have no other place to go, within reasonable limits. The reason for this is that human beings have developed living arrangements of a certain sort. That gives me a claim to have this society arranged such that I can make a decent living." These intuitions must be embedded in a theoretical framework, and must be refined if our target is to end up with conditions that generate principles that do not also apply globally. The point now is merely that there is no *single* factor such that libertarians could say, "If I can persuade you on *that* point, I win." Repudiating any one of these conditions cannot undermine the antilibertarian stance as long as the others remain available.

We can trace the interconnectedness of these conditions also by noting that Threat, Nonvoluntariness, and Reciprocity all appear in Rawls, which is nicely documented by the fact that defenders of competing views on the normative peculiarity of states find support in Rawls. Nagel (2005) points out that arbitrary inequality is problematic for Rawls only within given societies: "What is objectionable," he says, "is that we should be fellow participants in a collective enterprise of coercively imposed legal and political institutions that generates such arbitrary inequalities" (128). Blake (2001) too is eager to establish the compatibility of his view with Rawls (285–89), enlisting passages where Rawls emphasizes the exercise of coercive power. Sangiovanni (2007) quotes from Rawls in support of his reciprocity-based view (75–77). Moreover, Beitz (1999) elaborates on the significance of reciprocity by way of arguing that the proper context in which to find the relevant sort of reciprocity is the global order as such (130–31). Beitz thereby also contributes to an understanding of Rawls that makes reciprocity central to Rawls's account of shared membership.

So both Threat and Reciprocity appear in Rawls. Rawls also notoriously assumes that we are born into a society and do not leave it, thus stipulating Nonvoluntariness.[5] He assumes that society is a certain way, and Threat, Nonvoluntariness, and Reciprocity all provide intuitive input that informs his view of society. The question of precisely what constitutes the grounds of justice has only recently gained attention. In pretheoretical thinking, these factors appear together, which makes it hard to isolate one as *necessary* for justice to apply. This is the point that the thought experiments make.

4. Let us draw some conclusions. I use the term *nongraded*, or *monist*, *internationalism* for the view that principles of justice either do or do not apply, that they do apply within states, and thus among people who share membership in a state, and only then. Nongraded or monist internationalism is identical to statism. Introducing this terminology allows us to connect statism to other views that endorse the normative peculiarity of the state. Coercion-based and reciprocity-based statism are versions of monist or nongraded internationalism. Since their view presupposes a single justice relationship, finding a necessary condition for the applicability of justice is essential for statists. Such a condition, first, must apply only to states, and second, must be of sufficient significance to support the claim that justice applies only if that condition holds. However, neither coercion-based nor reciprocity-based statism is plausible.

Perhaps statists could argue that a necessary condition is that any two of our three conditions hold. The desired condition would be a disjunction over three conjunctions.[6] A necessary condition for the applicability of justice is that there be *some* thickness to the relevant interaction, its precise nature being irrelevant. But this move is problematic. Let us consider combining any two of the scenarios that excluded Threat, Nonvoluntariness, and Reciprocity individually as necessary conditions—for example, the post-attack state in combination with the easy-exit situation. Law is not enforced *and* it is easy to leave, but Reciprocity still applies. Does justice apply? We are now losing our grip on these situations; it is hard to see what to think. Statists are ill-advised to pursue this argument.

Reciprocity, Threat, and Nonvoluntariness all are fixations of conditions that occur in different versions, weaker or stronger. Reciprocity is a strong form of cooperation, whereas immediacy captures the form that Threat and Nonvoluntariness assume in states. Threat and Reciprocity capture forms of what Julius (2003) calls "framing," ways of getting others to further one's interest. In conjunction with this observation, the difficulties in formulating monist internationalism suggest that it misconstrues the challenge in determining the logical relationship between conditions that potentially generate principles of justice and those principles themselves. (On the word "suggest," see below.) Monist internationalism understands that challenge as a quest for identifying a (conceivably complex) necessary condition for the applicability of uniquely defined principles of justice. But if indeed the conditions characterizing shared membership in a state as a ground are jointly sufficient to generate principles of justice (as chapter 2 argued), we can sensibly inquire about a set of weakened versions of the conditions that apply to states and explore whether they *too* generate principles of justice, which would be *different* principles nonetheless.

Graded internationalism holds that different principles apply depending on the associational (social, legal, political, economical) arrangements. Different arrangements are characterized by a set of considerations that renders the respective principles applicable, all of which are principles of justice. Some considerations, or a disjunction over combinations of them, are necessary to render the *respective* principles applicable, but there may be others that are not indispensable but that, if present, also provide reasons for why these principles apply. Jointly these considerations suffice to render the principles applicable. Chapter 2 began the work to establish graded internationalism, and thus the inquiry to which our discussion in part I of this chapter leads. Shared membership in states is characterized by reciprocity and immediacy. Weakened versions of these conditions apply elsewhere. The principles that respectively apply would all be equally stringent in virtue of being principles *of justice*. Nonetheless, some principles may be more demanding than others if they affect more aspects of the lives of those in their scope, or if they impose duties that are more difficult to satisfy. (Both points would then also be reflected in the respective distribuenda.)

What is crucial is that graded internationalism abandons the idea that theorizing justice delivers a unique ground in favor of the idea that there are different principles of justice with different grounds and relevant populations (scopes). Again, it is the observation that none of the conditions we have explored is necessary for the applicability of justice but that they jointly suffice to characterize the state's normative peculiarity, in conjunction with the fact that Reciprocity, Threat, and Nonvoluntariness are fixations of conditions that occur in different versions, that leads us to ask of a set of weakened versions of those conditions that apply to the state whether they *too* generate demands *of justice*, presumably different from those that apply within states. Graded internationalism recognizes different grounds, all of them relational, but endorses the state's normative peculiarity. Let me illustrate how *weaker* versions of principles that apply within states may apply in other associative structures by looking at the WTO. The WTO is an organization in which most countries are members or observers. The WTO treaty is a "single undertaking": members must accept the whole package. Through the treaty on Trade-Related Aspects of Intellectual Property Rights, the WTO regulates at least one domain of property.

The WTO is characterized by weakened versions of conditions that apply to states. First, members do not join because of a threat, but, arguably, categorically staying away is not a reasonable option. Chapter 2 characterized the state's coerciveness as profound and pervasive. Although it falls short of that standard, the WTO dispute settlement system too is coercive because it can impose sanctions. A second, similar point applies to reciprocity. Although the WTO deals with trade in a broad sense, this falls far short of reciprocity in states. Third, as Blake has emphasized, the state regulates most property. Since I have characterized the state's normative peculiarity in terms of sufficient conditions, we can add more conditions to the relevant set. While the WTO does not generally regulate property, it does regulate intellectual property rights, and indirectly regulates some prices (e.g., through antidumping or countervailing duties). For the global trading system, it is hard to argue for the extensive transfers embodied by domestic taxes. Still, asserting that these conditions do not generate *any* demands of justice, while conditions in states generate broadly egalitarian principles, is implausible. Chapter 18 discusses the WTO at length. I have used it here merely for the sake of illustration.

Chapter 1 began with an account of justice according to which envisaged disagreement is about determining a *uniquely fixed* ground and scope.

Principles of justice are a uniquely fixed list (*"the* principles of justice"*) that applies among those who stand in that unique "justice relation" (Julius 2006). But according to the graded view, principles of justice are *different principles* associated with *different grounds*, and depend on what norm-generating conditions apply respectively. Principles of justice regulate how these considerations respectively bear on distributions. The term "principles of justice" operates like a logical variable rather than a name.

Of course, nonmonists too need to look for necessary conditions for the applicability of respectively different principles. But problems with that endeavor matter less than for statists. Less weight rests with the determination of necessary conditions. We no longer attempt to determine a condition such that people could not stand in *the* (uniquely fixed) justice relationship unless they satisfied that condition. Central for nonmonists is the constructive task of spelling out different grounds and principles associated with them, as well as explaining why other (possibly stronger) principles are not associated with them. This task is *constructive* because it involves an investigation of various grounds, and thus delineates the agenda that this book pursues and that differs from focusing on the determination of necessary conditions for the applicability of uniquely defined principles. We can answer the question of why principles that apply within states do not apply, say, in the WTO or the global order by investigating those entities and by arguing that within them, one can press only certain demands. So, indeed, and sensibly, graded internationalism construes the challenge in determining the logical relationship between conditions that potentially generate principles of justice and those principles themselves rather differently from monist internationalism.

If graded internationalism now seems clearly more plausible than its monist (statist) cousin, one might wonder if anybody actually is a *monist* internationalist. Nagel (2005), for one, holds such a view. In the history of reflection on the state, statism has been the default position, either in virtue of theoretical commitments or, more commonly, in virtue of the comparative neglect of systematic theorizing about duties outside states. The commitments involved in nonmonism are substantial: it abandons the idea that there is only one combination of grounds-cum-scope-cum-principles that neatly describes a unique justice relationship. It is one thing to have doubts about monism, or even to grant special treatment in terms of justice to those outside the immediate context in contrast to the rest of the world (as the Greeks did by distinguishing among fellow citizens, Hellenes, and Barbarians, as the Talmud did by recognizing Samaritans and others that observe Noah's commandments as a closer category of association than other peoples, or as John Stuart Mill did by distinguishing between civilized and barbarian peoples); it is another to have a well-developed alternative.

Now that we have introduced a nonmonist view, we should take seriously the idea that some grounds could be relational and others not. One view about how principles of justice apply is that they apply only within states. Competing views hold that the ground of justice consists in common humanity or a shared involvement in a global economic system (so that, either way, all human beings stand in the justice relationship with each other). A sensible response to the ensuing debate is to explore whether there is an intermediate view that abandons the view that principles of justice are entirely state-focused without forfeiting the state's normative peculiarity. While graded internationalism moves in this direction, it captures a narrow view of the conditions under which justice applies. Perhaps there is no deep conflict between relationism and nonrelationism. Integrating relationist grounds into a theory of global justice pays homage to the idea that individuals find themselves in, or join, associations and that membership in some of them generates duties. Integrating nonrelationist grounds means taking seriously the idea that some duties of justice do not depend on associations. Another revision leads to *pluralist internationalism*, or plainly *internationalism*, as I have called it so far.

Statism's inability to find a straightforward necessary condition for the applicability of justice, in conjunction with the fact that Reciprocity, Threat, and Nonvoluntariness all are fixations of conditions that occur in different versions, indeed merely *suggests* that we should abandon monism. The second transition, from graded to pluralist internationalism, is motivated by the fact that the nonrelationist's insistence that there should also be nonrelationist grounds, given that now we recognize a multiplicity of grounds, looks much more plausible than her insistence that there should only be nonrelationst grounds. Once we do recognize such a multiplicity, there is indeed no longer a plausible ex ante reason to limit a nonmonist view to relationist grounds. Internationalism succeeds if (and, what matters presently, *only* if) we can show that the proposed grounds are indeed grounds of justice. Our discussion of versions of statism provides a helpful context of discovery for this view. The actual defense—the context of justification—is a separate matter. This book as a whole explores what principles are associated with different grounds, and so gives content to and defends my view.[7]

In light of the preceding discussion, I can state my proposed pluralist internationalism more precisely than in chapter 1. Pluralist internationalism holds the following:

1. There are different grounds of justice, some relational and some not.
2. A range of considerations (including coerciveness and reciprocity) applies within the state as a set of jointly sufficient conditions to render particular

principles of justice applicable. (I assume these principles are Rawls's principles but have not offered a full argument for that view.)

3. Weakened versions of these conditions hold within other political arrangements and generate principles of justice.

4. There are grounds characterized by considerations that we cannot understand as weakened versions of conditions that hold within states (especially common humanity and collective ownership of the earth).

I have characterized shared membership in a state as a ground of justice in terms of *jointly sufficient* conditions. One possibility I leave open is that immediacy and Reciprocity are respectively by themselves sufficient to generate broadly egalitarian principles. This ground would then itself be pluralistic.

PART II. EXPLORING GLOBALISM

5. The most prominent version of *globalism* appears in the work of Charles Beitz. Beitz (1999) distinguishes a strong from a weak thesis about distributive duties. The weak thesis is that the global order is subject to *some* principles of justice. The strong thesis (which he defends) is that Rawls's principles apply globally. Beitz argues not only that there are no relevant differences between the domestic and global setting but also that the global order includes the kind of structures that render Rawls's principles applicable. Internationalism incorporates Beitz's weak thesis while rejecting its strong cousin.

Against Beitz, I argue that the normative richness of shared membership reveals differences between states and other entities that make it plausible that Rawls's principles apply domestically but not globally. Strictly speaking, chapter 2 refuted globalism as well as nonrelationism, since both views deny that any principles apply specifically in states. I have argued that there are principles that hold within states, although it is still open whether the same, or equally strong, principles also hold globally. Suppose there is an argument from some relation that is present globally to equally strong principles of justice. (One would need to think about how the presence of these principles is consistent with what we have established for the state, but let us set this aside.) That argument would *not* establish globalism as such but a view one may call "maximally egalitarian pluralism," which captures much of the appeal of globalism. To rebut globalism in spirit, we must rebut maximally egalitarian pluralism, too. If we can rebut Beitz, we will have done so, and thereby also have completed the case for the state's normative peculiarity.

Beitz's strategy is mostly negative: he finds it implausible to limit Rawls's principles to states, which is to deny that the sort of argument presented in chapter 2 can succeed. At this stage I presume it can, and indeed, the argument in chapter 2 is at the core of my response to Beitz. A rebuttal of Beitz's view leaves supporters of maximally egalitarian pluralism with the possibility of offering a positive argument. But since Beitz's view is important to the contemporary debate, it behooves us to engage with it explicitly. That discussion also makes clear why that positive case is hard to make.

The conflict between globalists and defenders of maximally egalitarian pluralism, on the one side, and those who endorse the normative peculiarity of the state on the other concerns the nature and relative importance of certain *relations*. It is therefore useful to begin by exploring in more detail than we did in chapter 1 why relationism could be a sensible view at all. (Arguments to that effect also support the inclusion of relationist grounds in a pluralist view once we take nonrelationism seriously.) Below I use this investigation to formulate an objection to Beitz. Defenses of relationism may draw on at least two strategies. To begin with, it is hard to demonstrate the applicability of duties in the first place, especially duties of justice. Arguing that somebody *ought* to do something is to make a strong claim. Without relations in which individuals stand, we cannot grasp how duties surpass a basic level. The second strategy is that human beings have reason to value certain relations, which bears on the applicability of justice. Let me elaborate.

Let us begin with the first strategy. I do not deny that there are *natural* rights and duties of justice (see chapter 4). But arguments in their support depend on natural attributes of persons and facts about the nonhuman world, and must be acceptable to all reasonable people. Claims of justice cannot succeed *merely* because of the significance of something for the claimant. We need reasons why others ought to provide what is significant. Nonrelationists can most readily meet that challenge if we restrict it to rights and duties pertaining to elementary human concerns, such as satisfying basic needs. Duties pertaining to *relative* rather than *absolute* economic status in particular are (at the very least) easier to establish, and more demanding, if we can resort to relations to make that case.

To illustrate, let us consider T. M. Scanlon's (2003d) influential discussion of objections to inequality, and hence to differences in relative economic status. Scanlon identifies five reasons to pursue greater equality: (1) to relieve suffering or severe deprivation, (2) to prevent stigmatizing status differences, (3) to avoid unacceptable forms of power or domination, (4) to preserve the equality of starting places required by procedural fairness, and (5) because procedural fairness sometimes supports a case for equality of outcomes. As Scanlon explains, (2) and (5) are the clearest expressions of egalitarianism. Reason (4) is consistent with considerable inequalities, and so is only weakly egalitarian. Reasons (1) and (3) are not egalitarian at all. Scanlon argues that Rawls uses (2)–(5), and perhaps (1) as well, to argue for his difference principle. That principle is supported by both egalitarian and nonegalitarian reasons.

Crucially, even the force of (3) and (4) depends on the relations that individuals share. For instance, to explain what counts as unacceptable forms of power, we should explore how the relevant individuals respectively contribute to the maintenance of a political and economic system, and hence also what the political and economic ties among them are to begin with. Some exercises of power are unacceptable regardless of what relations individuals stand in. But the more ties there are among individuals, the more possibilities there are for them to contribute to the maintenance of relations, which generates rationales to resist certain exercises of power. Similarly, to assess how much reason there is to preserve the equality of starting places on behalf of procedural fairness it is essential to assess what kinds (and range) of procedures individuals are jointly subject to. Thus, if we seek to argue for obligations pertaining to relative standing without making use of relations, there is little we can say. We can derive more demanding obligations if we make use of relations.

The second strategy in defense of relationism appears in Samuel Scheffler's (2001a) account of the link between special relations and responsibilities. Relations create responsibilities because having reason to value relations noninstrumentally just *is* to have reasons to see oneself under, and to actually have, special obligations. To attach noninstrumental value to a relationship with somebody means

> to be disposed, in contexts which vary depending on the nature of the relationship, to see that person's needs, interests, and desires as, in themselves, providing me with presumptively decisive reasons for action, reasons that I would not have had in the absence of the relationship. (Scheffler 2001a, 100)

For reasons to be presumptively decisive means they could in principle be outweighed although they present themselves as reasons on which an agent must act. Skepticism about such responsibilities succeeds only if we have no reasons at all to value our relations noninstrumentally.[8] The case is clear for family ties and friendships but less clear for political relations. Beitz (1999) does not use such reasoning to support his globalism. To do so one would have to show that membership in, or subjection to, the global order is a relation we ought to value. Beitz wonders instead about the relevance of such arguments *even* for shared membership in states (212). Simone Weil makes a stronger point: "The State is a cold concern, which cannot inspire love, but itself kills, suppresses everything that might be loved; so one is forced to love it because there is nothing else. That is the moral torment to which all of us today are exposed" (1971, 114).

We can appreciate skepticism about this defense of relationism by noting how this strategy is used elsewhere. An example is Bernard Williams's (1981) discussion of attachments:

> The point is that somewhere one reaches the necessity that such things as deep attachments to other persons will express themselves in the world in ways which cannot at the same time embody the impartial view, and that they also run the risk of offending against it. They will run that risk if they exist at all; yet unless such things exist, there will not be enough substance or conviction to a man's life to compel his allegiance to life itself. Life has to have substance if anything is to make sense, including adherence to the impartial system. (18)

And Susan Wolf (1992) has this to say:

> Morality sets limits on what one can do in the context of a friendship or love relationship, but, for the most, part, these relationships advance moral goals rather than threaten them. For in addition to being an immeasurable and profound source of human happiness—a moral goal if ever there was one—such relationships provide by far the most natural and effective setting for the development of moral sentiments and virtues. Sympathy for a friend teaches and encourages one to have sympathy also for a stranger. (247–48)

Should we *really* endorse similar statements about shared membership in a state, let alone in the global order? As far as the state is concerned, I think the answer is affirmative after all. Hardly anybody has emphasized the value of shared citizenship more than Rousseau. According to his *Social Contract* (1968, first published in 1762), what matters most about persons is that they are, and can exercise the offices of, citizens. However, Rousseau demands of citizens intense participation, especially in shared deliberation.[9] Such participation is less suitable for territorial states than for the city-states about which Rousseau wrote primarily. Nonetheless, people do have reason to value shared citizenship.

Citizenship has less day-to-day relevance for many than family and friendships. But what matters is not whether relations are ordinarily valued but whether they are *valuable*. Being respected as a citizen means *not* being subject to all sorts of harmful political arrangements. It is easy to forget the value of citizenship, given that struggles for emancipation have succeeded in many places, such as emancipation of the working class, women, or oppressed ethnic groups. It is easy to forget the value of citizenship if police abuse, manipulated trials, or silencing of the press is exceptional. For much of history this has not been the case anywhere, it continues not to be so in many places most of the time, and it continues not to be so just about everywhere some of the time.

One might say that reminders of such evils show only that citizenship should be valued *instrumentally*. But citizenship is a status, and in valuing a status, instrumental and noninstrumental aspects are closely intertwined. According to Mason (1997), for instance, citizenship has *intrinsic* value because qua citizen,

> a person is a member of a collective body in which they enjoy equal status with its other members and are thereby provided with recognition. This collective body exercises significant control over its members' conditions of existence (a degree of control which none of its members individually possesses). It offers them the opportunity to contribute to the cultural environment in which its laws and policies are determined, and opportunities to participate directly and indirectly in the formation of these laws and policies. (442)

Citizenship offers such opportunities and is thus intrinsically valuable. But where such opportunities exist, individuals are also protected from abuse in many ways, which renders citizenship also instrumentally valuable. Valuing citizenship is continuous with the statements from Williams and Wolf.

6. We are now ready to engage Beitz (1999). Capturing globalist resistance to supporters of the normative peculiarity of the state, Beitz argues that global interdependence

> involves a pattern of transactions that produce substantial benefits and costs; their increased volume and significance have led to the development of a global regulative structure.... Taken together, these institutions and practices can be considered as the constitutional structure of the world economy: their activities have important distributional implications. (148–49)

Beitz argues that if Rawls's case for his principles succeeds, their content should not change by enlarging the scope of the original position.[10] He takes for granted that Rawls thinks of the grounds of justice (largely) in terms of a cooperative scheme, and argues that the global order is relevantly like what Rawls claims about states. So the principles that Rawls restricts to states (including the difference principle) apply globally. Beitz does not distinguish sharply between cooperative and coercive approaches. He recognizes that nonvoluntariness is present in the global order. So the argument against Beitz cannot be that he misidentifies the grounds of justice by excluding coerciveness.[11]

Beitz considers two objections to the view that Rawls's principles apply globally (1999, 154–61). The first insists that interdependence is necessary but insufficient for the applicability of justice. The global order lacks effective decision-making mechanisms, as well as any real sense of community, and these, the objector says, are also necessary for a political entity to be subject to standards of justice. Beitz responds that these differences fail to show that principles of justice do not *apply* globally. Instead, they show that it is harder to *implement* them. According to the second objection, features of cooperation within states override the requirements of global principles *even if* justice applies globally. Rich countries may deserve their advantages because of differences in organization or technology. Beitz responds that this would mean to base entitlements on arbitrary factors like those that, as Rawls insisted, ought not affect one's share of goods. He rejects this move much as Rawls rejects principles drawing on undeserved social or genetic characteristics. But this objection is relevant only if we grant that (uniquely conceived) principles apply globally because of the existence of a global basic structure. Since I deny this, I ignore the second objection.

To reply to Beitz's response to the first objection, we must identify differences between membership in a state and membership in the global order that bear on the applicability of justice. These need to be differences to which globalists cannot plausibly respond that they matter to the *implementation* of justice rather than to its *applicability*. I have elaborated on the richness of shared membership in a state in chapter 2 to capture such differences.[12] The aspects of immediacy are normatively relevant because they provide reasons why individuals can make claims on shares of collectively produced benefits. Profundity and pervasiveness of coerciveness impose burdens on those who are subject to states. They also characterize the significance that shared membership in a state has for them. Primary goods are provided through intensely cooperative behavior. I also elaborated on the idea of responsibility that applies within a society characterized by those conditions. All these are ways of articulating how individuals are (in relevant ways) equally and significantly invested in and subject to a state (and in that sense, qua participants in a particular social endeavor, are fundamentally alike), which creates redistributive pressure without parallel in other contexts.

Shared membership puts pressure on the acceptability of inequalities in social and material status at the domestic level, as well as on the acceptability of inequalities in the value of civil and political liberties. Individuals who do not jointly participate in such a relation are not alike in ways that create such pressure. Domestic interdependence does not merely differ from but is considerably (and sufficiently much, to make a difference for justice) *stronger* than what we find globally. The differences—characterized by reciprocity and immediacy—are not differences in the difficulties involved in *implementing* justice. They are differences pertaining to what *reasons* people have to make claims on each other. These differences repudiate a core move in Beitz's globalism, to insist that no plausible distinction sets domestic structures apart. Especially the difference principle is very demanding, asking of individuals to comply with socioeconomic arrangements that put differences among them into the service of all. The conditions characterizing the state's coerciveness and cooperativeness are sufficiently demanding and comprehensive to explain why the difference principle applies. Relations characterized by much weaker or less comprehensive conditions are not.[13]

In section 5 I noted the strategies supporting relationism. These strategies are that, first, arguing that somebody *ought* to do something is to make a strong claim (i.e., without relations in which individuals stand, we cannot grasp how duties surpass a basic level), and second, that human beings have reason to value certain relations, which bears on the applicability of justice. We can now construct the following argument using these strategies. First, we enlist these strategies to support relationism. Second, we turn to the enlarged Rawlsian account of shared membership to show that, via those strategies, this particular relation generates especially demanding duties of justice. If the two strategies in support of relations work *at all* (as indeed they do), they support *stronger* obligations among those who share membership in a state than among those who merely share the global order.

So the strategies that support *the very family* of views to which globalism belongs (relationism) support the view that, as far as justice is concerned, there are relevant differences between the domestic and the global context. It should be noted that although I offer this argument against globalism, a version of it also works as an argument against statism: if we think we need relations to get stronger principles of justice than we can get with no relations, then it will be plausible to think that thinner relations yield weaker principles. This in turn leads us from both globalism and statism toward pluralism.

7. But could globalists not insist that, differences between the domestic and the global level notwithstanding, global interdependence *suffices* to render (unique) principles of justice applicable? The global order as a whole *nevertheless* is where justice applies, and we should account for differences between the domestic and the global level in some way *other than* by taking them to imply that there is a difference as far as the applicability of (uniquely determined principles of) justice is concerned.

But this is a difficult road to take. Once we see how the extended Rawlsian account of shared membership bears on the selection of principles of justice, and once we realize that the global order does not share the conditions that are central to that account, we must ask, *how else* could these differences matter? Perhaps the threshold of conditions that must be present for justice to apply is lower than what is formulated by the enlarged Rawlsian account. Global interconnectedness will do. The differences between the domestic and the global level would then offer substantive elaboration of the fact that people who share a state stand in the justice relationship. But individuals who merely share the global order *already* stand in that relationship. Only a constructive account of principles of justice that apply in the global order as such provides a conclusive answer to this move. Part 3 of this book offers such an account, one that supports the reasoning of this chapter. If so, what I have called maximally egalitarian pluralism is implausible.

Defenders may proceed in two ways. First, they may grant that there are important differences between shared membership in a state and in the global order, and that these differences matter for justice, but insist that I neglect important considerations that imply that, all things considered, we cannot drive a wedge between principles of justice as they apply globally and domestically. The second response, too, grants these differences but insists that we should transform the global order into an entity characterized by the same forms of coerciveness and cooperativeness as, in ideal theory, the state is. The state of affairs at the global level is deficient in implementing an ideal that applies to it. In a sense this second response would actually abandon globalism.

Pressing the first reply, Cavallero (2010) argues that there is an international property regime (private law and investment treaties) that constitutes a significant portion of property entitlements worldwide. This regime entails the regular use of coercion against the nationals of one society by the enforcement agencies of other societies and international bodies without providing viable exit options. Therefore, says Cavallero, differences between the domestic and global scenario cannot bear on the applicability of justice. Sometimes, he says, foreign powers threaten vital interests by means of puppet governments. There is then no relevant difference between a domestic scenario, where enforcement is immediate, and the global order, where it is not. Leibniz's emperor, we recall from chapter 2, does not have to fight if he can manipulate the princes.

However, legal and political immediacy do not merely capture certain practices in some states. They are also part of ideal theory because of their significance for equal citizenship. If states possess properties of immediacy, no power in between state and citizens undermines equal citizenship. But the aforementioned sort of intervention is not part of ideal theory. It is the kind of problem a global order ought to limit. While there are similarities between enforcement at the domestic and global level, only in the former case are these activities part of ideal theory. Moreover, since immediacy is part of ideal theory, my account of shared membership in states helps explain why intervention is problematic. *To the extent* that states correspond to the extended Rawlsian ideal of membership, efforts by some governments to transform others into puppets are *especially* offensive. For then others use for their purposes a relation characterized both by its significance for and its enormous impact on its participants.

These responses lead to the second way in which globalists may proceed. Why not say that, especially in light of the presence of such interferences at the international level, we ought to transform the global order into a setting characterized by the same form of coerciveness and cooperativeness as, in ideal theory, the domestic scenario is? This response entails advocacy for a *world state* of sorts, the subjection of all of humanity to a common political authority.

That is also how Rawls sees the situation (1999b, 36, 48). Yet he denies that we should aim for a world state. Following Kant, he thinks world government "would either be a global despotism or else would rule over a fragile empire torn by frequent civil strife as various regions and peoples tried to gain their political freedom and autonomy" (36). Also, according to Rawls's political constructivism (see chapter 1), considered convictions of justice arise within the practices and institutions we live with. They are attuned to the structure and demands of those institutions. It is hard to support a world state within Rawls's methodology. But even globalists and nonrelationists do not generally do so, partly because of considerations of feasibility, partly because of its potentially undesirable features (likely oppressiveness, excessive homogeneity, inefficiency, soullessness). Chapter 16 revisits this subject. We will see there that we should indeed not aim to create a world state.[14]

8. Let me conclude. This chapter contributes to the development of internationalism by exploring contemporary debates about statism and globalism. Part I of this chapter has explored the debate about necessary conditions for the applicability of principles of justice that statists must engage in. The quest for such a condition has so far ended inconclusively. This result leads to my pluralist view of the grounds of justice, in a heuristic sense. My view must be defended separately, and this book as a whole does so. Still, this assessment of a debate among statists (monist internationalists) generates good reasons to take internationalism seriously. I could also offer a more precise account of my view than chapter 1 provided.

Part II of this chapter has engaged with the most prominent version of globalism. I have argued that Rawls's principles do not apply globally. The enlarged Rawlsian account of membership from chapter 2 reveals important differences between the global order and states. Features of membership in states lead to the difference principle, but those of membership in the global order do not. In light of that discussion, maximally egalitarian pluralism is implausible. That discussion also completes my case for the normative peculiarity of the state, at least in all plausibility. The logical possibility remains that some other ground delivers the same principles as shared membership in a state, but this no longer seems a plausible prospect. If readers disagree, the subsequent discussions of other grounds will address their position. Much of the remainder of this book develops internationalism by exploring additional grounds: common humanity, humanity's collective ownership of the earth, membership in the global order, and shared subjection to the global trading system. The global interconnectedness central to Beitz's case I put to a different use, making it an integral component of a conception of human rights as membership rights in the global order that I start developing in chapter 7.

CHAPTER 4

What Follows from Our Common Humanity?

The Institutional Stance, Human Rights, and Nonrelationism

PART I. THE INSTITUTIONAL STANCE

1. In 2000, the UN General Assembly committed governments to eradicating extreme poverty by adopting the Millennium Development Goals.[1] Two years later, the High-Level Panel on Financing for Development insisted that no country could expect to meet these goals

> unless it focuses on building effective domestic institutions and adopting sound policies including: Governance that is based on participation and the rule of law, with a strong focus on combating corruption; disciplined macroeconomic policies; a public expenditure profile that gives priority to investment in human capital, especially basic education and health, the rural sector, and women; a financial system that intermediates savings to those capable of investing efficiently, including microfinance borrowers, women, and the rural sector; a funded, defined-contribution pension system that will promote saving in the short run and, supplemented by a tax-financed scheme to assure a minimum pension, will secure adequate, universal pensions in the long run; capacity building focused on developing a positive institutional environment progressively more able to implement the policies listed above; protection of property rights and a regulatory environment that effectively protects workers' rights and the environment.

Before making other recommendations, the report stresses the importance of domestic institutions for growth. Thereby the report endorses the "institutional stance," the thesis that prosperity is primarily determined by the quality of institutions.

An emphasis on institutions also appears in John Rawls's *The Law of Peoples*. As he insists, the causes of the wealth of a people, and the forms it takes,

> lie in their political culture and in the religious, philosophical, and moral traditions that support the basic structure of their political and social institutions, as well as in the industriousness and cooperative talents of its members, all supported by their political virtues. I would further conjecture that there is no

society anywhere in the world—except for marginal cases—with resources so scarce that it could not, were it reasonably and rationally organized and governed, become well-ordered. (1999b, 108)

Partly based on this view, Rawls rejects redistributive duties among peoples beyond duties of assistance to "burdened" societies, nonaggressive societies lacking appropriate traditions, resources, or technology. That duty seeks to enable societies to develop their own institutions and thus shape their development.

This chapter marks a turning point. We now consider the first ground with a global scope, which is also the first nonrelational ground. Broadly egalitarian principles of justice apply within states, in virtue of the special relationship among their members. But what principles apply globally? Are there none, as statists think? Are they by contrast strong principles, if different from those that hold in states? If they are somewhere in the middle, what exactly do they require, and do they require more of rich countries than those are doing now? In light of how chapter 2 argued for broadly egalitarian principles within states and what chapter 3 said about the significance of relations for the derivation of principles of justice, it is implausible to expect that nonrelational grounds deliver broadly egalitarian principles. But we can expect that some principles of justice apply outside states. Let us start our investigation by considering what, if anything, follows from our *common humanity* as a ground of justice.

Our common humanity leads to an account of human rights, which in turn generates a duty of assistance in building institutions. The principle associated with this ground is that human rights so understood be realized. This chapter integrates four themes, sufficiently distinct to be treated separately but intertwined because each contributes to the characterization of common humanity as a ground. Part I explores the institutional stance on development. Part II develops the notion of a "conception of human rights." Part III offers such a conception built around the idea of common humanity and connects that conception to the institutional stance. It is at this point that I argue that claims of common humanity generate a duty of assistance in building institutions. Finally, part IV engages Simon Caney's (2005) version of nonrelationism to argue that certain more expansive views of the role of common humanity in a theory of global justice are implausible. This chapter is in part 1 of this book because it contains this discussion of nonrelationism, a view that contests the normative importance of state membership as I have developed it. I divide this chapter into different parts to make it easier to return to relevant sections later. Parts I and II of the chapter introduce material that part III puts to immediate use, but that also resurfaces in later chapters.

Here I note two things. First, this chapter does not exhaust the claims of common humanity. Such claims also enter into our discussion of humanity's collective ownership of the earth in part 2 of the book. But that theme is nonetheless not most plausibly understood as a development of the idea of a distinctively human life. For that reason, but also because of the richness of its implications, I discuss collective ownership in another part of the book. Second, whereas in terms of what I call a conception of human rights the view on human rights presented in this chapter passes for such a conception, chapters 7 and 11 argue for a conception of human rights as membership rights in the global order. The present conception will be integrated into that conception (in a manner that will become clear later). That later conception is the view of human rights that I propose in this book. The point of this chapter is to some extent negative: nonrelationists exaggerate the role of the idea of a distinctively human life for global justice, and I discuss the implications of that idea at this stage of the book's argument to make that point.

2. Section 2 of part I explains the institutional stance, and section 3 explores some consequences of the view that this stance provides the content of a duty of assistance we have in virtue of our common humanity. The discipline to which we must look for an assessment of the institutional stance, development economics, is an evolving field shaped by disagreements. In the 1950s and 1960s its focus was on governmental planning. Later it was on market ideas, summed up in the "Washington Consensus." The consensus stressed fiscal discipline, trade liberalization, privatization, deregulation, and secure property rights. Later, institutional quality was added, including corporate governance, anticorruption measures, independent central banks, social safety nets, and poverty reduction. Disagreement persists about whether the goal of development is growth, assuming this solves other problems eventually, or whether we should think of development in terms of several goals (as captured, e.g., by the UN's Human Development Indicators); how precisely indicators such as life expectancy, school enrollment, infant mortality, and malnutrition relate to income; and whether there is a single best recipe for development.[2]

The debate about why some societies are poor and volatile and others wealthy and stable dates back at least to Adam Smith's *The Wealth of Nations*. This debate has gained sophistication through econometric techniques that permit the testing of broad hypotheses about causes of growth against cross-country data. Three major views have emerged, one of them being the institutional stance:

Geography: Prosperity is primarily determined by factors such as location, climate, resource endowment (including soils), disease burden, and thus agricultural productivity, the quality of human resources, and transportation costs.[3]

Integration: Prosperity is primarily determined by world market integration.[4]

Institutions: Prosperity is primarily determined by the quality of institutions, such as stable property rights, the rule of law, bureaucratic capacity, the existence of appropriate regulatory structures to curtail at least the worst forms of fraud, anticompetitive behavior, graft, and the quality and independence of courts, but also the cohesiveness of society, the existence of trust and social cooperation, and thus the overall quality of civil society.[5]

One may find it odd to ask which theory wins. Prosperity depends on many factors, including those championed by these theories, mixed with history and human choices. Factors relevant for growth affect each other. Countries with stable institutions can more easily integrate their economy globally, and successful integration facilitates their maintenance. Landlocked countries and those far from markets have difficulty trading. The absence of debilitating epidemics favors stable institutions, but institutions also advance capacities to control diseases. Resource abundance, by contrast, can foster rent-seeking institutions ("resource curse"). Not only do these factors influence each other but prosperity itself, the *explanandum*, affects factors that supposedly cause it. It may be *because* a country is wealthy that it has good institutions, benefits from trade, or can control diseases—not vice versa. Still, questions about deep causes that are not outcomes of feedback processes are meaningful. Econometrics investigates how much cross-country variation the three views above can respectively explain.

The challenge for the institutional stance is to show that institutions are genuinely causally efficacious, to resist proposals that growth causes good institutions, not vice versa, or that institutions arise only because of favorable geographic factors. Only recently did econometric results suggest that the causality of Institutions was crucial. A key contribution, building on earlier work, is Rodrik, Subramanian, and Trebbi (2004), who show that institutions trump everything else: once institutional effects are determined, Integration has nothing left to explain, and Geography little. Moreover, institutional quality significantly affects market Integration, and vice versa, and Geography affects institutional quality. It is mostly channeled through impact on institutions that Geography and market Integration matter without undermining the causal efficacy of Institutions.

"There is now widespread agreement among economists studying economic growth that institutional quality holds the key to prevailing patterns of prosperity around the world," says Rodrik (2007). "Rich coun-tries," he explains,

> are those where investors feel secure about their property rights, the rule of law prevails, private incentives are in line with social objectives, monetary and fiscal policies are grounded in solid macroeconomic institutions, idiosyncratic risks are appropriately mediated through social insurance, and citizens have civil liberties and political representation. Poor countries are those where these arrangements are absent or ill-formed. Of course, high-quality institutions are perhaps as much a result of economic prosperity as they are its cause. But however important the reverse arrow of causality may be, a growing body of empirical research has shown that institutions exert a very strong effect on aggregate incomes. Institutions are *causal* in the sense that a poor country that is able to revise the rules of the game in the direction of strengthening the property rights of entrepreneurs and investors is likely to experience a lasting increase in its productive capacity. (184)

I adopt the institutional stance. I thereby adopt an empirical stance in the growth debate, conceding that arguments that depend on it are sub-ject to revision in light of possible changes in the evidence. But let me be clear that dependent on this stance in part III will not be arguments for principles of justice or arguments at the level of deriving general duties from them but arguments at the logically still later stage of deriving spe-cific duties or prescriptions from a general duty. The institutional stance lets us specify the content of duties in virtue of common humanity better than we otherwise could. But we must be aware of the limitations of that stance. First, the social sciences can explain only what the world was like in the past. Their results can only marginally inform policy choices re-garding measures that have not yet been tried. Social science results do not show, for instance, why we should not make massive transfers to the poor, regardless of whether they help with institution building. Second, these results are statistical and may not speak to specific countries. So it is important that country studies confirm that institutions "that provide dependable property rights, manage conflict, maintain law and order, and align economic incentives with social costs and benefits are the founda-tion of long-term growth" (Rodrik 2003, 10).

To illustrate, we may consider Botswana (Acemoglu, Johnson, and Rob-inson 2003), a tropical, landlocked country with negligible agriculture in a politically precarious location. At independence, Britain left 12 kilome-ters of roads and a poor educational system. Known for its devastating HIV rates, Botswana suffers from high inequality and unemployment. Officially a democracy, it has yet to see a functioning opposition. Some 40 percent of Botswana's output draws on diamonds, recalling the resource curse. But Botswana is a growth miracle. Between 1965 and 1998 it had an average yearly growth rate of 7.7 percent, and in 1998 its average per-capita income was four times the African average. Rule of law, property rights, and contract enforcement work. The government is efficient and relatively free of corruption. Indigenous institutions encourage partici-pation and constrain elites. Institutional quality and good policies have allowed for success against the odds.[6]

One might object that the three aforementioned theories endorse *explanatory nationalism,* fallaciously reducing development to domestic causes. States and individuals, says Pogge (2002), react to incentives set by the global order, which may affect institutional quality. Inquiries com-mitted to explanatory nationalism cannot detect the impact of the global order. But the institutional stance does not commit this fallacy. While those theories collect data on a country-by-country basis, this is an orga-nizational device that does not address any *causes* of institutional perfor-mance. To the extent that the global order (or an oppressive past) causes bad institutions, this, alongside geographic factors, must be considered in the execution of a duty of assistance.

3. According to North (1990), institutions

> are the humanly devised constraints that shape human interaction. In conse-quence they structure incentives in human exchange, whether political, social, or economic. Institutional change shapes the way societies evolve through time and hence is the key to understanding historical change. (3)[7]

Institutions can emerge and persist only if most individuals support the "rules of the game." This is so especially for institutions that cannot be effectively created by governmental fiat (as, say, market-regulating insti-tutions can), such as a constitution guiding generations through disputes, a legal system enforcing property rights and contracts, as well as a cul-ture of trust, shared understandings of what are reasonable benefits from and sacrifices imposed by cooperation, commitment to the common good, and other hallmarks of civil society. Call the view that institutions requir-ing broad domestic support matter especially for prosperity the *Authen-ticity Thesis*. This thesis is safe within the confines of the institutional stance: there can be a "stable structure to human interaction" only if most people cooperate. Often all external aid can contribute otherwise is ana-lytical work, identification or training of internal reform champions, or technical assistance.[8]

The institutional stance (plus the Authenticity Thesis) generates three *prima facie reasons* against development assistance. These reasons constrain a duty of assistance in building institutions. The first is that assistance may well be ineffective: what is needed cannot be "imported." The (re-)building of institutions ("nation building") can only evolve from within. The second is a paternalism concern: outsiders inevitably shape institutions in their own image. The third is that the stability of institutions may be undermined if those whose participation maintains them rely on outside support. The institutions might collapse once the support is withdrawn.

Each reason must be suspended to justify assistance. One reason for suspending all three is if, contrary to the statistical support for the institutional view, in some cases persistent poverty turns on factors that the institutional stance captures inadequately. But even to the extent that institutions are crucial, each reason *can* be overruled. Contrary to the first and third, it may be possible to offer the needed help. Contrary to the second, paternalism may be grotesquely irrelevant in the face of death and starvation. However, while each case requires much more empirical analysis, development is not primarily a matter of transferring resources. I argue below that there *is* a duty to aid the global poor, a duty of assistance in institution building. These prima facie reasons constrain that duty.

PART II. CONCEPTIONS OF HUMAN RIGHTS

4. The discussion of the institutional stance in part I of this chapter and the upcoming discussion of conceptions of human rights merge in part III. Section 4 introduces the notion of a human right, as well as the notion of a *conception* of human rights. Section 5 further elaborates on the terms introduced in section 4 and submits that we should be pluralists about conceptions of human rights since none offers the single most plausible set of answers to crucial questions about human rights.

Human rights are rights that are invariant with respect to local conventions, institutions, culture, or religion. The language of human rights focuses on abuses committed by those in positions of authority: of two otherwise identical acts, only one might violate human rights, namely, the one that amounts to an abuse of authority. This point also appears in Pogge (2002), who says that human rights

> can be violated by governments, certainly, and by government agencies and officials, by the general staff of an army at war, and probably also by the leaders of a guerilla movement or of a large corporation—but not by a petty criminal or by a violent husband.... Human-rights postulates are addressed, in the first instance at least, to those who occupy positions of authority within a society (or other comparable social system). (57–58)

The reference to domestic violence points to a problem: what if, say, violence against women is structural? As for instance Mill argued in *The Subjection of Women* (2006), society can exert its own tyranny. When violence against women is entrenched, it seems to makes sense to say that women's human rights are violated. More generally, at least certain non-state actors need to be taken seriously as human rights violators.

But there is a difference between, say, thefts committed by petty criminals and thefts that are part of abusive patterns of government behavior or otherwise expressions of socially entrenched or violently enforced oppression. The difference consists in their effect on, or the extent to which these scenarios express, one's status in society. Pogge (2002) says that "human rights are, then, moral claims on the organization of one's society" (64). But how many violent husbands must there be for wife beating to be about the organization of society? Let me simply assume that we can sensibly distinguish between structural problems and individual aberrations. I take the *concept* of human rights to refer to rights (vis-à-vis agents who, in virtue of their size, power, etc., can intelligibly be held responsible for this matter) *with regard to the organization of society* that are invariant with respect to local conventions, institutions, culture, or religion.[9]

A host of questions arises about human rights. Why would we hold such rights? Is there a set of features of human beings on which such rights are based? What ought to be their function in the global order, and does this help define what they are? What list of rights arises in this way? Who must do what to realize these rights? Cohen (2006) proposes that human rights have three features: they are universal and owed by every political society to everybody, they are requirements of a political morality whose force does not depend on their expression in enforceable law, and they are especially urgent. Any account of human rights must meet these constraints, as well as two methodological assumptions: fidelity to major human rights documents, so that a substantial range of these rights is accounted for (a criterion that grants that major human rights documents play a significant role in fixing the meaning of human rights talk), and open-endedness (we can argue in support of additional rights).

However, these criteria (which I agree characterize the *concept* of human rights) do not entail commitments with regard to a range of questions about such rights. The function of a *conception* of human rights is to provide a fuller set of answers.[10] A conception consists of four elements: first, a list of rights classified as human rights; second, an account of the basis on which individuals have them (an account of what features make individuals rights holders);[11] third, an account of why that list has that composition, a principle or a process that generates that list; and fourth, an account of who must do what to realize these rights, an account of corresponding obligations. Any full-fledged conception also makes clear both why such a conception is worth having and why the language of rights (rather than goals or values) is appropriately used.

Conceptions often take as their starting point a stance on the first, second, or third component and add the others, which may be trivial (if the basis on which rights are held readily determines these rights, say) or may require argumentative work.[12] These components are logically tied (choices constrain what one can coherently choose for the other components), whereas the fourth raises rather different questions. With which component one begins depends on what one thinks one can defensibly claim about human rights. Conceptions that start with a list are *list-driven*, those that first specify a basis are *basis-driven*, and those that use some principle to generate a list are *principle-driven*. Being "principle-driven" means that such a conception is guided by some idea of what ought to be on the list of rights other than the specification of a basis; the primary example is a specification of their function in international politics.[13]

5. Let us look at some conceptions to illuminate this classification. Beitz distinguishes "orthodox" from "practical" conceptions. Orthodox conceptions are basis-driven. To explain such conceptions, Beitz quotes John Simmons's view of human rights as

> rights possessed by all human beings (at all times and at all places) simply in virtue of their humanity.... [They] will have the properties of universality, independence (from social or legal recognition), naturalness, inalienability, non-forfeitability, and imprescriptibility. Only so understood will an account of human rights capture the central idea of rights that can always be claimed by any human being. (Beitz 2004, quoted from Simmons 2001a, 185)

What renders conceptions *orthodox* is "the idea that human rights have an existence in the moral order that is independent of their expression in international doctrine" (Beitz 2004, 196). To sharpen the contrast with the conception of human rights as membership rights in the global order I start discussing in chapter 7 (which is not orthodox), let me add the phrase "and independent of the existence of political structures." Orthodox conceptions then become a proper subset of basis-driven conceptions, examples being accounts using views of what matters about our common humanity as a basis, such as a Kantian conception of personhood, a logic of moral agency, a view of the distinctively human existence, or claims of self-ownership or need. Being basis-driven, orthodox accounts begin with the second component (that basis), which leads to the third (a principle generating the list), which in turn leads to the first (that list). The fourth component (whose duties?) remains to be settled separately.

One will adopt such a conception if one can defend a view of what it is about humanity that makes us rights holders and turn this into an overall plausible conception. The choice of the first and third component is restricted by the second. The second component may not uniquely fix the list. In disagreements about what shared humanity entails, political practice or views about the function of human rights in global society may help generate a list. But it can only be in a *supplementary* manner that considerations other than those drawing on the basis affect that list. I present such a view below. Rather than appealing to "common humanity," one can develop basis-driven accounts in terms of political structures, starting with a view either on membership in any defensible domestic order, as Scanlon (2003b), Habermas (1999), or Cohen (2004) do, or on membership in the global order, as I do later.[14] Basis-driven conceptions vary enormously.

On a "practical" conception,

> the functional role of human rights in international discourse and practice is regarded as definitive of the idea of a human right, and the content of international doctrine is worked out by considering how the doctrine would best be interpreted in light of this role. (Beitz 2004, 197)

We obtain a conception of human rights by starting with the third component (an account of why the list of rights is what it is), in this case, by assessing what ought to be their *function* in the global order. Thereby we generate a list, thus adding the first component. This is a principle-driven conception.[15] Beitz interprets Rawls (1999b) along such lines, the relevant function being the preservation of a world where liberal and decent peoples prosper. Such an approach is consistent with a range of ways of providing the basis on which rights are held. Different cultures may have different ways of doing so, a view Beitz ascribes to Rawls. A principle-driven conception will be chosen if claims about what generates the list can be made with more certainty than claims about possible bases.

Richard Rorty's (1993) "sentimentalist" view provides a list-driven conception. Rorty dismisses reflections on the basis on which rights are ascribed: "the question whether human beings really have [human rights] is not worth raising" (116). He takes a similar stance with regard to the third component, saying only that the emergence of a human rights culture owes "everything to hearing sad and sentimental stories" (118). The list of rights has emerged through a process of broadening compassion. Rorty focuses on the fourth point (whose duties?) through an appeal to the need for education to enable people to see similarities between themselves and others. He considers the second and third component dispensable: neither helps explain why we endorse human rights.

There is unlikely to be a single most plausible conception of human rights, a single most plausible set of answers to the questions to which such a conception offers answers. Coherent answers support each other, with disagreements between conceptions occurring along different dimensions. The universality captured by the idea of human rights allows for different elaborations. This should be unsurprising: human rights discourse is too amorphous to allow for a uniquely best such conception. Nor would such pluralism be problematic. Different conceptions may help "to command reasoned support and to establish a secure intellectual standing" for human rights (Sen 2004, 317).[16]

Let me end this section by clarifying the relationship between the concepts of human right and natural right. *Human rights*, again, are moral rights that are invariant with respect to local conventions, institutions, culture, or religion. *Natural rights* are moral rights whose justifications depend on natural attributes of persons and on facts about the nonhuman world. The force of these rights can be recognized by all reasonable people independently of the provisions of positive law. All natural rights will be invariant in the sense required by the *concept* of human rights. Yet once we specify a *conception* of human rights, we must clarify the relationship between natural rights and human-rights-according-to-that-conception. Some such conceptions do not classify human rights as natural rights. On a Beitzian practical conception, for instance, human rights would not depend on *local* conventions, but no justification of the sort needed to establish natural rights appears. So human rights then are not natural rights. As opposed to that, according to the conception in part III below, human rights are natural rights. But only those natural rights are human rights that are needed to protect the distinctively human life. In chapter 6 we encounter natural ownership rights, which are natural rights but not human rights according to the conception developed in part III.

In chapter 7 we encounter the conception that I advance in this book and that integrates the conception from part III (as we will see in chapter 11). According to my conception, human rights are membership rights in the global order and thus associative rights (rights that hold in virtue of membership in particular associations). As I explain later, global responsibilities are derived from different *sources*. The distinctively human life is one such source, as is collective ownership of the earth. So while human rights in my conception indeed are associative rights, some human rights have their logical foundation in natural rights. But other sources generate human rights that have no such foundations but instead essentially appeal to features of the human world to that end. According to my conception, all natural rights give rise to human rights, but not all human rights are derived from natural rights.

PART III. COMMON HUMANITY AS A GROUND OF JUSTICE

6. Sections 6 and 7 introduce the idea of a distinctively human existence and explore how to develop it into a conception of human rights. Section 7 returns to the institutional stance: that conception of human rights generates a duty of assistance in building institutions. I now survey different ways of developing a basis-driven conception using common humanity as a basis. Our goal ultimately is to find principles of justice associated with common humanity. The distribuenda are the things to which individuals are entitled in virtue of the rights that register as human rights on this conception.

At the core of any such approach there will be a view of what counts as a *distinctively human life* (which gives content to the idea of common humanity) and the insistence that such a life is *valuable*. As James Griffin (2008) explains:

> Human life is different from the life of other animals. We human beings have a conception of ourselves and of our past and future. We reflect and assess. We form pictures of what a good life would be—often, it is true, only on a small scale, but occasionally also on a large scale. And we try to realize these pictures. This is what we mean by a distinctively *human* existence.... And we value our status as human beings especially highly, even more highly than even our happiness. This status centers on our being agents—deliberating, assessing, choosing, and acting to make what we see as a good life for ourselves. (32)[17]

Attempts to develop a conception of human rights from this starting point must address especially these two matters: first, we must explain *just what* it is about the distinctively human life that generates rights. We must explain the *basis* in this basis-driven conception. Second, we must show that features of the distinctively human existence lead to human rights, that is, to *rights* rather than goals or values, and to *human* rights according to the concept adopted from Cohen (2006). Much work has been done on both questions. While claims of common humanity generate a theory of human rights (common humanity being the basis), they do not do the kind of work for global justice that nonrelationists claim they do.

One approach to the first matter is a revitalized natural law tradition, developed for instance by Finnis (1980). A commitment to natural law in this tradition involves an objective theory of a good life that typically includes basic goods, such as health, knowledge, or friendship. Another response gives a central role to dignity and its connection to freedom and reason, often referring to Kant. Also enlisting dignity, Griffin (2008) argues that the crucial feature of a distinctively human life is "normative agency": "what we attach value to, what we regard as giving dignity to human life, is our capacity to choose and to pursue our conception of a worthwhile life" (44).

Amartya Sen and Martha Nussbaum champion capabilities as the relevant feature, stressing values like freedom, empowerment, or choice (Sen 1985, 1987, 2004; Nussbaum 2000, 2006). David Miller (2007) bases a conception of human rights on the significance of "basic needs," "the conditions that must be met for a person to have a decent life given the environmental conditions he faces" (184). Such needs are tied to ideas of the necessary, unimpeachable, or inescapable. They include but are not exhausted by "food and water, clothing and shelter, physical security, health care, education, work and leisure, freedoms of movement, conscience, and expression" (184).[18]

Although we need not select one of these approaches over the others, section 7 returns to this subject. For now let me proceed to the second matter, how features of the distinctively human existence lead to human rights. One way of establishing what rights people have is via a Kantian self-consistency approach, according to which an agent falls into a contradiction with himself when not treating others in a manner that involves respect for rights. Alan Gewirth (1978, 1984) has made self-consistency central to his derivation of human rights. However, many philosophers have become doubtful of the enterprise of deriving substantial prescriptions from self-consistency. An alternative is to appeal to ideas about what we can reasonably expect of each other and to insist that such considerations are strong enough to generate rights. The difference lies in what error in practical reasoning one makes by disregarding rights.[19]

Approaches that proceed in this second way (as Griffin, Miller, Sen, or Nussbaum do) begin with an appeal to the normative significance of the feature of common humanity that they stress. Brock (1998b) explains that "if the needs are not met, we are unable to do anything much at all and certainly are unable to lead a recognizably human life" (15). Griffin (2008) states that it is "the mere possession of this common capacity to identify the good that guarantees persons the protection of human rights" (46). Miller (2007) insists that basic needs are both morally urgent and of universal reach, and thus generate rights (197).[20] O'Neill (1986) argues that the needy are unusually prone to coercion and that it is a matter of respect for their autonomy not to let people fall into such a situation. Similarly, Goodin (1985) argues that we ought to protect those who are vulnerable to us *because* they are vulnerable. He thinks that in many familiar cases, the best explanation for the presence of duties is vulnerability.[21]

The question becomes *just how* an appeal to the significance of features of the distinctively human life establishes *rights*, rather than goals or values. One response is to introduce limitations on the range of conditions under which this appeal creates rights, and thereby to contain implausible implications. Griffin (2008) talks about "practicalities," empirical insights into the limits of human understanding and motivation that ensure that normative agency does not ask too much of individuals.[22] Miller (2007) offers several limitations on what can be demanded on behalf of needs satisfaction, such as limits imposed by what human agency cannot provide at all, what cannot be demanded of others, and what could be provided only if the needs of others were violated to whose satisfaction these others have a claim (186–90).

Yet this strategy of *limiting unsatisfactory implications* provokes the question of why these features whose significance is made central should have a sufficient grip on others to generate rights *at all*. Pursuing this strategy is like being told, in response to a request for directions, how to avoid going too far while one is still unsure the direction is right. Still, crucially, nothing more need or can be said to show that individuals have rights. Scanlon (2003a, 2003b), for one, thinks of an argument for rights as involving an empirical claim about how individuals behave or how institutions work in the absence of particular assignments of rights; a claim that this result would be unacceptable, based on valuations of consequences in a way that takes into account considerations of fairness and equality (as appropriate); and a further empirical claim about how the envisaged assignment of rights will produce a different outcome. Within this approach, which I adopt as an account of rights, one can articulate ideas about needs or normative agency and their importance, and then indeed also block implausibly strong implications. But after *all this* is said and done, Scanlon submits, and plausibly so, there is nothing *more* to say to address the question whether such an argument *really* delivers rights. We have reached the limits of what a theory of rights can deliver.

David Wiggins (1987) offers a slightly different response to the challenge of why this kind of approach could generate rights. Wiggins argues (within the confines of a theory of needs) that needs must be met for us to be able to maintain any social morality. If somebody is denied what is vitally needed, she has reason to withdraw support from society.[23] The first reply emphasizes that respect from others is the appropriate response to certain features of our common humanity, whereas this second one stresses what reactions are appropriate for those who are mistreated. A response of the sort Wiggins presents is also open to defenders of other

views about just what it is about our distinctively human existence that
generates rights.

7. Section 6 has sketched the contours of a conception of human rights
based on the idea of common humanity. What should be clear now is
how broadly anchored in familiar positions is the intellectual support for
the thesis that the implications of common humanity are much more
limited than nonrelationists propose. But we must pursue the matter further. First, to obtain a *principle* that generates a list of rights, we must
explain in more detail what facets of our distinctively human life generate
rights. Second, we must assess what duties apply to whom, given this
basis and principle. As far as the first matter is concerned, the answer will
vary depending on which of the proposals reviewed above we adopt. If
we endorse the distinctively human life as a basis, it may, for instance, be
considerations of both agency and needs that generate rights to protect
such life.[24] However, what is crucial for our purposes is that for *any* of
the candidates, it will be hard to specify a reasonably determinate list of
rights (and to specify the *principle* that generates it).

As far as agency is concerned, for instance, we must ask at what level
to protect individuals to ensure they can exercise agency. Slaves can exercise some agency, which is why they are acquired. But is the agency dimension of a distinctively human life sufficiently protected if slaves are
sheltered from more cruel forms of violence?[25] As far as the needs approach is concerned, it is possible to conceive of even basic needs at different levels. In their influential work on needs, Doyal and Gough (1991)
distinguish fundamental needs (physical health, mental competence to
choose and deliberate) from intermediate needs (which spell out what is
required to satisfy fundamental needs: nutritional food, clean water, protective housing, a nonhazardous environment, appropriate health care,
security in childhood, significant primary relationships, physical security,
economic security, appropriate education, safe birth control, and safe child-
bearing). One can ask whether what is *needed* for a distinctively human
life is protected sufficiently if satisfaction of fundamental needs is guaranteed. The capabilities approach too leads to such a question since we can
identify certain basic capabilities as especially urgent.

A general difficulty in identifying a list of rights emerges. I have identified facets of a distinctively human life that supposedly generate rights.
For this approach to generate natural rights (which human rights are on
this conception), the basis must apply to all human beings, and must permit reasonably precise und uncontroversial inferences to duties of others.
However, if there are competing interpretations of the level at which to

protect agency, needs, or capabilities to allow for a distinctively human life, we should accept one that generates the *weaker* set of rights. Otherwise one could reasonably object (and so make the relevant rights controversial and, crucially, render doubtful their status as *natural* rights), based on the availability of a weaker interpretation, which *exhausts* the argumentative force of the starting points, that too many duties are imposed. To be sure, the mode of reasoning I use here (and one more time in chapter 6) essentially turns on the account of natural rights in part 2 of this book. It does not apply more generally.

This difficulty arises about the *lower* boundary of required protection. That boundary matters for disagreements with those who doubt that the idea of the distinctively human life does much work at all. However, the opponents envisaged here are not such skeptics but nonrelationists. What matters therefore is the *upper* boundary of protection that we can base on the idea of the distinctively human life. So let us suppose we can solve the problems concerning the lower one. Presumably this would generate a basic list of rights protecting the physical and mental integrity of each person, and make sure each person can at least get by. We reach the upper limit of a list we can derive from such an approach once we reach rights for which we cannot argue by reference to what it takes to protect the distinctively human life but whose defense essentially requires references to associations (features of membership that are not closely tied to the distinctively human life)—and requires such references not just for specific assignments of duties but also for establishing entitlements *in the first place*.

As far as the UN's Universal Declaration of Human Rights is concerned, drawing merely on the protection required for the distinctively human life, we cannot obtain rights associated with liberal democracy, as opposed to other forms of governments; the secular state, as opposed to other forms of political organization; or the value of equality, as opposed to other forms of distribution or status. In none of these cases does the significance of the distinctively human life establish the required difference. No matter what proposal we adopt for what precisely matters about that kind of life, such a life is available to those who do not live in a liberal democracy or a secular state or do not enjoy a status of equality. Trying to derive the protection of such values from the distinctively human existence hopelessly overextends that idea.

This sketches how far we can push the idea of common humanity to construct a conception of human rights. Thereby this also sketches how far we can go thinking of common humanity *as a ground of justice*. The principle associated with that ground is that the distribution in the global population of the things to which people have human rights is just only if everyone's rights are satisfied (and thus only if everyone has enough of these things to lead a distinctively human life). One might say it is not obvious that if there are human rights to X, it follows that their violation is an injustice, that is, that there is a corresponding principle of the form "the distribution of X in the global population is just only if everyone has X." For instance, statists need not deny there are human rights, and yet they deny there are global principles of justice. So they object to this move. But I agree with nonrelationists to the extent that I count common humanity as a ground, one whose scope includes all of humanity and whose principle I just stated. What nonrelationists have to say for their approach (see chapter 1) succeeds to the extent that it warrants an inclusion of common humanity (as well as collective ownership of the earth, see chapter 6) as one ground in a theory of global justice. It does not succeed to the extent that it argues for stronger principles associated with this ground and to the extent that it denies there are relational grounds (a matter to which part IV of this chapter returns).

Since I have not pursued the argument far enough to offer a list of rights, I cannot specify the distribuenda with more concision. Pursuing that argument further, however, is not required to assign common humanity a suitable place within a theory of global justice and would generate a host of questions that are peripheral to our inquiry. (The distribuenda are not the human rights themselves. Natural rights are equally distributed, and a deviation from that distribution is logically impossible.) The principle associated with common humanity is not concerned with relative economic standing, and the list of rights secured by that principle is shorter than the list that applies within a liberal state. In that sense, this principle is weaker than the principles that hold within a state. Nevertheless, this principle demands *much* more than what the world manages to deliver.

Let us turn to the question of what duties the principle of justice that I just stated creates. Who has what obligations to make sure the distribution in the global population of the things to which people have human rights is just? The general answer to this must be that, for everyone (individual or institution), the *general* obligation is to do whatever the individual or institution can (within limits) to bring about or keep a just distribution. To proceed from here, Jeremy Waldron plausibly suggests that rights are "best thought of not as correlative to one particular duty ... but as generating successive waves of duty, some of them duties of omission, some of them duties of commission, some of them too complicated to fit easily under either heading" (1993b, 25). We must ask, then, what *specific* obligations or prescriptions for actions follow for individuals and institutions, and specifically states, in any given context. For both, we can distinguish actions relating to the part of the distribution within their own state and to the part lying outside. The primary bearer of duties imposed by the need to protect an individual's distinctively human life is her state, given the significance of states for individuals. For states, we can distinguish actions aimed at ensuring that the rights of their citizens are satisfied and actions aimed at ensuring that the rights of outsiders are satisfied. If the state is wealthy enough and satisfies its obligations under the stronger principles that apply only within states, the human rights of its citizens will automatically be satisfied.

That leaves us with specific obligations to help those outside the state. The most plausible way of thinking about such obligations is in terms of a duty of assistance in ensuring that (in this case *other*) states effectively can, and are organized such that relevant forces are motivated to, provide such protection. A sensible way of thinking about such duties is in terms of assistance in building institutions, and here we can enlist the results of part I above. Good institutions provide the background for civil and political rights and are essential for economic growth. By an instrumental argument, assistance in building institutions provides at least some of the content for a duty actors outside a person's state have to protect her distinctively human life. I say "at least some" because such a duty is not exhaustive. Sometimes assistance in building institutions is not called for but nevertheless duties arising from common humanity apply, such as in cases of natural disasters that require immediate help. Moreover, people may need short-term help, which must be provided before any efforts in strengthening institutions can flourish. Still, assistance in building institutions is the most sensible investment in the future of troubled countries. Therefore, this duty of assistance is the crucial obligation implied by the conception of human rights we have explored in this chapter.

The problem of limits applies to the general duty, to do what one can, within limits, to secure a just distribution. In each context, what one can do, within the limits, will be different. Specifically, how much of a sacrifice do individuals, states, or other organizations have to make to satisfy a duty of assistance? Sometimes the duty of assistance will be very demanding, but sometimes no duty applies because what requires doing outsiders cannot do (see section 3). It is often difficult to assess whether a duty of support in institution building applies and is demanding, or whether it does not apply because some of the reasons against assistance hold. Brian Barry (1982) concludes his discussion of this vexing question by stating, appropriately, that

> there is no firm criterion for the amount of sacrifice required to relieve distress. This does not mean that nothing can be said. I think it is fairly clear that there is a greater obligation the more severe the distress, the better off the potential helper would still be after helping, and the higher the ratio of benefit to cost. What is indefinite is where the line is to be drawn. (225)

Barry's statement speaks to short-term assistance, but the point applies with even greater force to a duty of assistance in building institutions. Generally, there is a considerable *boundary problem* as far as the limits of our duties are concerned that derive from the idea of the distinctively human life. It is hard to delineate the precise implications of that idea. One aspect of this problem is that it is hard to draw inferences from statements about, say, needs to the conclusion that, as a matter of justice, specific actions are required. Such arguments are strongest when they do not rely exclusively on claims of need but integrate considerations not drawn from the idea of common humanity (see chapter 12 for an illustration). This boundary problem is an intrinsic feature of attempts to assess what follows from the idea of common humanity. At the end of chapter 15 we obtain some more insight into the nature of this duty of assistance. However, the question of how much, and precisely what, is owed in virtue of our common humanity will remain rather intractable.

PART IV. CANEY'S NONRELATIONISM

8. Part IV engages with particular nonrelationist efforts to derive much further-reaching conclusions from common humanity. The opponent is Simon Caney (2005). Combining our discussion in part III with the results of the earlier chapters allows us to rebut Caney's version of nonrelationism. Without an account of a distinctively human life, it is hard to see why demands of justice apply at all. A relation among citizens, after all, is a relation among human beings. But while internationalism recognizes common humanity as one ground of justice, it is misguided to think that common humanity is the only such ground, or that principles of the sort I have argued apply within states hold in virtue of common humanity. Caney holds that the principles that apply based on this ground are the kind of principles that I argued apply only within states. Since he develops this view in a manner I believe many nonrelationists find appealing, I engage with his view by way of completing my account of common humanity as a ground.

Rather than a self-declared nonrelationist, Caney is a self-declared cosmopolitan. A cosmopolitan's central claim about justice, says Caney, is that, fundamentally, all persons should be included within the scope of its principles. Cosmopolitans recognize, however, that these principles may sometimes be realized best if people comply with special duties (2005, 105)—but "we have yet to see a persuasive argument to the effect that there are special duties of justice to fellow-nationals" (270). Caney's strategy is to identify a moral argument of sorts and to argue that that argument appeals to properties of persons that apply globally. Therefore its conclusion applies to all human beings. Limiting such arguments to particular groups means to commit what Caney, following Black (1991), calls the "fallacy of restricted universalism": "A distributive theory, that ascribes rights and claims on the basis of certain universal attributes of persons, cannot at the same time restrict the grounds for those claims to a person's membership or status within a given society" (2005, 357). Attempts to derive principles of justice from universal attributes that nevertheless are supposed to be limited to certain groups (e.g., compatriots) commit this fallacy.

Caney's chapter 3 applies his strategy to civil and political liberties. He concludes that the rationale for many civil and political rights entails that they apply universally. Thereby Caney argues for what he calls the "the scope$_1$ claim": "the standard justifications of rights to civil and political liberties entail that there are *human* rights to these same civil and political liberties" (66). The scope$_1$ claim holds, says Caney,

> because the standard arguments for civil and political rights invoke a universalist "moral personality." That is, the relevant aspect of persons is the right to be subject to principles to which they can reasonably consent (for contractarians), or their use of moral language (for Habermas), or their humanity and status as persons (for deontologists), or their ability to lead a fulfilling life (for perfectionists). As such, it would be incoherent to adopt any of these lines of reasoning for a particular right and then ascribe that right only to other members of one's community. (77)

His chapter 4 applies this strategy to the scope$_2$ claim: "the standard justifications of principles of distributive justice entail that there are cosmopolitan principles of distributive justice" (107). The scope$_2$ claim entails that "the very logic that underpins most domestic theories of justice actually implies that these theories of distributive justice should be enacted at the global, and not (or not simply) the domestic level" (107; see also 116). So "borders are not of fundamental moral importance" (265).

9. Below I address Caney's reasoning for his scope$_2$ claim, but let me start with his attacks on relationism. Both times the point is that he derives too much from common humanity while neglecting the relevance of relationships for justice. To review the strategies in support of relationism from chapter 3: first, without appeal to relations, we cannot grasp how duties transcend a basic level; second, human beings have reason to value relations, which bears on the applicability of justice. Caney resists these arguments:

It is hard to see why economic interaction has any moral relevance from the point of view of distributive justice. [...] Consider a world with two separate systems of interaction that have no contact but are aware of each other and suppose that one of them is prosperous whereas the other is extremely impoverished. Compare, now, two individuals—one from the prosperous system and the other from the impoverished system—who are identical in their abilities and needs. The member of the prosperous system receives more. But it is difficult to see why—concentrating on any possible and reasonable criteria for entitlement—this is fair. *Ex hypothesi*, she is not more hard-working or more gifted or more needy. In all respects they are identical (bar one, namely that one is lucky to live in the prosperous society and one is not) and yet an institutionalist approach confers on one more benefits. (2005, 110)[26]

I offer four responses. First, in light of the arguments in chapter 2, Caney's considerations become question begging (or anyway misleading, if they tempt us to deny the moral relevance of membership). Caney envisages two people identical up to features that are morally irrelevant. Yet according to relationism, as well as according to my pluralist view, membership matters morally even if it has arisen in a manner for which individuals deserve no credit. Moreover, my pluralist view is driven by the idea that one must constructively establish distributive entitlements with reference to relevant grounds of justice. Common humanity is one such ground. However, we can derive only so much from that starting point; part 3 explores "how much." A related, second response is that the inferences from "X is not deservedly held" to "X is illegitimately held," and to "others have a duty to ensure X is not longer so held," fail. What is problematic also—and this is the third response—is the sheer idea that individuals have a similar makeup but are differently situated. "To ask why I am to submit to the power of the state," says T. H. Green in his *Lectures on the Principles of Political Obligation*, "is to ask why I am to allow my life to be regulated by that complex of institutions without which I literally should not have a life to call my own"(1941, 122). The influence of one's immediate environment on personal identity is so profound that Caney's thought experiment does not apply.

A fourth response is that relationists, too, can accommodate considerations of arbitrariness and thus absorb some of the thrust of the nonrelationists' stance by offering their own account of the significance of their competitors' guiding idea.[27] They can respond to the arbitrariness of the conditions of birth by first pondering what, and how much, people have in common in virtue of sharing the relevant relation (say, membership in a state). Relationists then assess how participation in that relation may invalidate claims based on morally arbitrary features. I have discussed this topic at the end of chapter 2, but to illustrate, I recall Rawls's argument against the Natural Liberty conception of his second principle of justice (*Theory of Justice*, secs. 11–14).

Natural Liberty (capitalized to denote a principle) is a competitor to the second principle as Rawls ends up formulating it. According to Natural Liberty, equality of opportunity requires that positions of influence ought to be formally open to all according to talent (as opposed to Rawls's more demanding *fair* equality of opportunity), and material inequalities ought to be arranged efficiently (as opposed to Rawls's more demanding difference principle). The extended Rawlsian account of shared membership in a state shows how much people have in common in virtue of such membership. It is against this background that it becomes plausible to say that only if morally undeserved features (such as talents and circumstances) can be harnessed for social advantage ought they to bestow personal advantage. So relationists and internationalists can accommodate the intuition that the moral arbitrariness of the conditions of birth stands in a tension with their generating special claims. Nonrelationists make too much of it.[28]

10. Finally, let me address Caney's case for the scope$_2$ claim. While some principles of justice apply globally, I deny that the "logic that underpins most domestic theories of justice actually implies that these theories of distributive justice should be enacted at the global, and not (or not simply) the domestic level" (Caney 2005, 107; see also 116). Internationalism is not subject to this claim. The protection of a distinctively human life only takes us so far (see section 7 for "how far"). We must appeal to relations to derive additional rights and duties. Chapter 2 shows how membership in states matters for justice. The condition on which the fallacy relies, that rights are ascribed on the basis of universal attributes, does not hold for the relevant principles.

Appeals to the distinctively human life alone fail to license the derivation of principles beyond what I argued above. Nor do they license Caney's proposals that "persons of different nations should enjoy equal opportunities: no-one should face worse opportunities because of their nationality" and that "everyone, without discrimination, has the right to equal pay for equal work" (122–23). However, these may still be rights people have everywhere against their *respective* governments (and limited in scope to their country) because nowadays just about everybody lives in a state.

Let me conclude. This chapter has integrated four themes, distinct enough to be treated separately but intertwined because each contributes its share to an account of common humanity as a ground of justice: the institutional stance on development, in part 1; the notion of a conception of human rights, in part 2; the conception of human rights built around the idea of common humanity, in part 3; and finally, in part 4, an engagement with Caney's nonrelationism, to argue that his more expansive understanding of common humanity in an account of global justice is implausible.

We are now also well prepared for later discussions of human rights in chapters 7, 11, 12, and 13. Those chapters discuss my conception of human rights as membership rights in the global order, which integrates the conception in this chapter (the distinctively human life being one source from which membership rights are derived). We have in any event not exhausted the claims of common humanity. Such claims also reenter in part 2, which discusses collective ownership of the earth as a ground of justice. But that theme is not most plausibly understood as a development of the idea of a distinctively human life. For that reason, and because of its far-reaching implications, I discuss collective ownership in a separate part of the book, a discussion to which we turn next.

PART 2

Common Ownership of the Earth

CHAPTER 5

Hugo Grotius Revisited

Collective Ownership of the Earth and Global Public Reason

1. In part 1 of this book we encountered two grounds of justice, one relational (membership in states) and one nonrelational (common humanity). Part 2 explores another nonrelational ground: humanity's collective ownership of the earth. The distribuendum is the resources and spaces of the earth. We discuss principles that regulate this distribuendum in chapters 7–10. Chapters 5 and 6 address foundational questions. Although common humanity has received more attention than collective ownership, it is reflection on collective ownership that turns out to be philosophically more fruitful. Like common humanity, it will not get us as far as nonrelationists might hope, but it yields interesting results about a range of topics.

Considering collective ownership of the earth a ground of justice means revitalizing and secularizing an approach central to seventeenth-century political philosophy that has never again reached as much prominence. Hugo Grotius, Thomas Hobbes, Samuel Pufendorf, John Locke, and others debated how to capture the ownership status of the earth and the conditions under which parts of the Global Common could be privatized. Except for the recent revival of left-libertarianism, this approach has been almost invisible since the Rawlsian renaissance of political philosophy. Nonetheless, this approach is present in international law, where for forty years the term "common heritage of mankind" has been applied to the high seas, the ocean floor, Antarctica, and outer space.[1] It is unsurprising that ideas of collective ownership would play such a prominent role in the seventeenth century. European expansionism had come into its own, so questions of global reach entered political thought and needed to be addressed from a standpoint that was nonparochial (not essentially partial to one of their viewpoints) as far as European powers were concerned. At the same time, appealing to God's gift of the earth—as reported in the Old Testament—was as secure a starting point as these troubled times permitted.[2]

Although that debate took the biblical standpoint that God had *given* the earth to humankind, some protagonists, such as Grotius and Locke, thought this matter was also plain enough for reason alone to grasp. Indeed, the view that the earth originally belongs to humankind collectively is plausible without religious input, as chapter 6 shows. We have much to gain from revitalizing this idea. What is at stake is ownership of, as John Passmore put it, "our sole habitation ... in which we live and move and have our being" (1974, 3), or in Henry George's words, of "the storehouse upon which [man] must draw for all his needs, and the material to which his labor must be applied for the supply of all his desires" (1871, 27). Or, as Hannah Arendt said in *The Human Condition*, "The earth is the very quintessence of the human condition, and earthly nature, for all we know, may be unique in the universe in providing human beings with a habitat in which they can move and breathe without effort and without artifice" (1958, 2).[3]

To illustrate the significance of humanity's collective ownership, suppose the population of the United States shrinks to two, but they control access through border surveillance mechanisms. Nothing changes elsewhere. Surely these two should permit immigration since they are grossly underusing their area. We can best explain this view by the fact that all of humanity has claims to the earth.[4] Chapter 8 addresses immigration from the standpoint of humanity's collective ownership of the earth. Topics this approach also illuminates include human rights (chapter 7), duties toward future generations (chapter 9), and duties arising from climate change (chapter 10). Today we face not only problems of a global reach but problems that put our planet itself in peril. It is only appropriate to find a suitable place in moral and political philosophy for theorizing humanity's claims to the earth.

This chapter reacquaints readers with the idea of humanity's collective ownership by discussing the work of Hugo Grotius (1583–1645). Like no other work in the philosophy of international relations, *De Jure Belli ac Pacis Libri Tres (DJB)*, *Three Books on the Law of War and Peace*, published in 1625, makes world ownership central to relations among both individuals and political entities (as well as those between individuals and such entities). Like no other work in the history of political thought that discusses property, *DJB* addresses questions of global scope. *De Jure Belli* seeks to do so in a way that develops a standpoint of what one may call *global public reason*, a standpoint from which positions are to be justified by way of giving reasons that are acceptable to people of different moral or political backgrounds. Grotius does not offer anything like a grounds-of-justice approach, but he does explore a range of questions of global scope from a standpoint combining natural law and collective ownership, and thereby illustrates the fruitfulness of exploring the idea of humanity's collective ownership of the earth. My own account of Common Ownership in chapter 6 is a secularized version of his view. Grotius also inspires my discussion of duties from climate change in chapter 10, and of a human right to pharmaceuticals in chapter 12. Other chapters, too, return to Grotius, who will be an even more important interlocutor from now on than Rawls was in part 1.

Section 2 of this chapter explains how reflection on collective ownership enters Grotius's work. Section 3 explores how Grotius introduces his views on natural law. Section 4 discusses how he introduces the collective ownership status of the earth. Section 5 explores how, according to *DJB*, a morally legitimate system of private ownership law could develop against the background of persisting natural collective ownership rights. Section 5 is pivotal because it is there that I say most about how Grotius uses humanity's collective ownership to constrain what people may do with resources and spaces. Section 6 explains that Grotius's earlier work approached the questions of section 5 somewhat differently. Section 7 offers a proposal for resolving the tension between the two accounts, one that throws additional light on how Grotius thought about collective ownership. Section 8 concludes.

Let me add two points of clarification. First, as I explained in chapter 4, *natural rights* I take to be rights whose justification depends on natural attributes of persons and facts about the nonhuman world. The force of these rights can be recognized by all reasonable people independently of the provisions of positive law. Justifications of natural rights do not exclusively involve conventions or institutions that hold within or among groups, nor do they exclusively involve any transactions, such as promises or contracts. Natural rights may in principle include rights whose justification *also* involves transactions or agreements, but such transactions and agreements must be of a sort that does not undermine the universal acceptability of the rights thus generated. As moral rights, natural rights stand in contrast to (moral) transactional and (moral) associative rights. Mine is a broad notion of natural rights, which contrasts with narrower notions that tie natural rights to theology or a conception of practical reason. It is so broad, in fact, that it may sometimes be debatable whether a right is best understood as a natural right or as a moral transactional right or a moral associational right.

Precisely what duties natural rights imply must be worked out for given proposed rights, but in principle, all human beings could be duty bearers. Transactional and associative rights hold only among those involved in the transaction or belonging to the association. Transactional rights may arise from promises or contracts and associative rights from membership in particular associations, as, for instance, rights of citizens do. Natural, transactional, and associative rights are three kinds of moral rights that stand in contrast to legal rights (which may or may not replicate some of the moral rights). Moreover, natural, transactional, and associative moral rights can all be articulated within T. M. Scanlon's account of rights that I adopted in chapter 4.[5] What I said about the characteristic features of these types of rights pertains to the second part of how Scanlon understands a rights claim, namely, the reasoning given about why a situation without rights would be unacceptable.

Natural law can be defined in a manner parallel to natural rights, except that we are now talking about moral prescriptions rather than rights of individuals. In the broad sense in which I use these terms, they cover both Grotius's understanding of natural law and the rights that emerge from the divine gift of the earth, and so the components of the theory with reference to which he assesses the legitimacy of legal property regimes. I explain as much as we need of Grotius's theory, but the notion of natural right I use in the remainder of this book is the one I just repeated.

Second, the subject of part 2 of this book is original ownership. Asking about original ownership is not asking about a certain period but about whether the resources and spaces that exist independently of human activities are owned in a sense that is prior to moral claims individuals or groups have to resources based, say, on first occupancy or the mixing of labor with resources, as well as prior to any kind of legal claims they may have. For Grotius, original rights also have a temporal aspect: only original ("ancient") rights have existed *since creation*. Since Grotius offers an account of the divine gift that, in the understanding of his time, actually occurred, temporal aspects naturally surface. The revitalization of this discourse must purge it not merely of its religious aspect but also of this historical aspect. I leave Grotius's temporal references without additional comments when we encounter them.

2. Grotius is mostly remembered for a distinct theory of international relations. This theory revolves around the idea of an international society in which states are taken for granted and motivated by self-interest. Nonetheless, states are also subject to moral constraints.[6] Grotius's magnum opus, *De Jure Belli*, explores when war could or ought to be waged and what constraints apply to its conduct. Early in book I, Grotius explains that his concern is with "differences of those who do not acknowledge one common Civil Right whereby they may and ought to be decided" (I.1.I). The causes of war that "most men" agree are justifiable are "Defence, the Recovery of what is our own, and Punishment" (II.1.II.2). This statement is followed by an investigation of what properly and exclusively is "our own," our *suum*, an inquiry to which much of book II is devoted. Since "defense" often protects what is one's own, and "punishment" occurs if people take what is not theirs, *ownership* is central to war and peace. To address differences among those who do not share a civil law Grotius

combines an account of natural law with one of *collective ownership of the earth*, and thereby accounts for each person's *suum*.

Grotius had discussed the questions of *DJB* before, in *Mare Liberum* (*ML*), *Free Sea*, published in 1609. This book was a version of the twelfth chapter of a larger work that was lost until the nineteenth century, and then appeared as *De Jure Praedae Commentarius* (*DJP*), *Commentary on the Law of Prize and Booty*. (I often use the abbreviations *DJB* and *DJP*; readers may want to remember that *DJB* stands for *De Jure Belli* by recalling that "B" is for *bellum*, the Latin word for war, as in "belligerent.") *De Jure Praedae* addresses moral and legal questions about the capture by the Dutch of a Portuguese merchantman in the Straits of Singapore. This incident occurred when colonization and trading had already been raising questions about the conditions under which natives could be displaced and how Europeans should relate to them to begin with; what actions could establish the priority of claims among Europeans to territories or trade privileges; and what sort of control over the seas could be legitimately exercised. To see how open these questions were I note that *ML*, which argues that even coastal waters were collectively owned, was followed by John Selden's *Mare Clausum*, *Closed Sea*. Selden argued that the seas could be owned, and that England owned much of its surrounding waters.[7]

Central to those questions, for Grotius, was the question of who could legitimately make what sort of use of parts of the earth, as well as of its resources and wildlife. The answers needed to take account of natural rights and take individuals seriously as co-owners of the earth. Grotius licenses intervention and displacement of indigenous people in response to violations of natural law and prescriptions that derive from original ownership of the earth, which include unacceptable use of collectively owned resources (e.g., refusing to let others pass, *DJB* II.2.XIII.2), as well as atrocities like cannibalism or piracy (*DJB* II.20.XL.3; see also II.25. VIII). Author of spirited defenses of Christianity (see, e.g., Grotius 1819), Grotius believes that Christians owe each other special consideration (*DJB* II.15.X and II.15.XII; but see *DJP*, chap. 13). However, "the factor of religious faith … does not cancel the natural or human law from which ownership has been derived" (*DJP*, 308). Non-Christians, too, are co-owners of the earth. Grotius does *not* license interference merely in response to wrong beliefs (*DJB* II.22.IX; *ML*, 18), or for refusals of commerce with Europeans (*ML*, 18, 14–15).

Whereas Hobbes thought wars arise precisely because people do what they are allowed to, Grotius believed wars could be avoided if only people adhered to what they were permitted to do. For this to be true, what each person is allowed to do must be acceptable to others. The theory

Grotius develops—combining his views of natural law and of collective ownership—is a standpoint of what nowadays we may call *global public reason,* one from which positions are to be justified by way of giving reasons people of different moral or political backgrounds could accept.

3. Both *DJP* and the later *DJB* start with reflection on what it is for individuals to have rights and obligations, and both offer an account of what natural rights individuals have. In *DJP* Grotius states that

> since God fashioned creation and willed its existence, every individual part thereof has received from Him certain natural properties whereby that existence may be preserved and each part may be guided for its own good, in conformity, one may say, with the fundamental law inherent in its origin (21)

and then lists six laws of nature: it is permissible to defend one's life; it is permissible to acquire what is useful for life; no one should inflict injury on others; nobody should seize what has been acquired by others; evil deeds should be corrected, and good deeds should be recompensed (23–29). Once they enter civil society, individuals must also protect others, and contribute to what the community needs (37). These laws seem to entail at least a thin version of the thesis that people own (have rights of use to) the earth. Nonetheless, as we see in section 4, Grotius also introduces an account of collective ownership provided by a divine gift. The overall picture of entitlements emerging from this list of natural laws in conjunction with collective ownership of the earth is then brought to bear on changing socioeconomic circumstances.

In the later *DJB*, Grotius asserts in response to Carneades (an ancient skeptic whom Grotius enlists as interlocutor) that humans are distinguished by a "Desire of Society, that is, a certain Inclination to live … in a Community regulated according to the best of [their] Understanding" (*Prolegomena* (P), VI; see also P, VIII). This sociability is the "Fountain of Right" (P, VIII). The basic rights Grotius mentions here include

> the Abstaining from that which is another's, and the Restitution of what we have of another's, or of the Profit we have made by it, the Obligation of fulfilling Promises, the Reparation of a Damage done through our own Default, and the Merit of Punishment among Men.

Both works assert that respect for property is essential for acceptable human living arrangements, and for peace. Society exists for the protection of the *suum* (*DJB* I.2.I.5). Natural right, property, and peace must be theorized together.

The skeptic is brushed aside more than he is answered. If the concern is that there is no justice, Grotius responds that there is. Justice consists in the design of society in accordance with the rational nature of those who live in it, which includes the preservation of natural rights (see *DJB* I.1.III.1). If the concern is that it is folly to be just, Grotius responds that it is not. That human beings display sociability, if only in the limited sense of pursuing peaceful arrangements, is taken for granted. Grotius sees human beings as driven by both a desire for self-preservation and a need of society. He assumes that considerations of right and long-term expediency are in harmony. Grotius also formulates prescriptions for relations among nations, prescriptions that are meant to express everybody's best interest (*DJB* P, XVIII). In response to the worry that strong states have no reason to accept any prescriptions, he points out that even the strongest sometimes need assistance and thus have an interest in maintaining a system where rights are respected (*DJB* P, XXIII and XXVIII; see also P, XIX).[8]

In the earlier *DJP*, the law of nature is based on God's will; in *DJB*, God continues to be the lawgiver, or "Author of Nature" (*DJB* I.1.X.1), but cannot change its content (*DJB* I.1.X.5): that content would be the same (as Grotius says in the famous *etiamsi-daremus* passage in P XI) *if there were no God.*[9] Natural right as the "Rule and Dictate of Right Reason" (*DJB* I.1.X.1) can be known either by "a priori" reasoning in accordance with the law of nature, or "a posteriori," by observing what people commonly agree on (I.I.XII; see *DJP,* 25). The second approach accounts for Grotius's extensive surveys of opinions on questions he investigates.

Grotius's view is new for holding that rights are in some ways like possessions individuals own and can forfeit.[10] He distinguishes among several meanings of *iura*, rights, one of which conceives of a *ius* as "a moral quality of a person, making it possible to have or to do something correctly" (*DJB* I.1.4). A *ius* is a "faculty" or an "aptitude" (depending on whether it is perfect or imperfect) of the person, something a person *has*, rather than something an action or a state of affairs *is* when it is in accordance with the law.[11] Whereas earlier theorists spoke of "the right" or "what is rightful," Grotius stresses powers and entitlements of the person who "has rights." But natural rights do not protect against governmental authority if they have been surrendered under appropriate conditions, nor do they provide guarantees against slavery (*DJB* I.3.8.1, II.5.XXXII). Rousseau would later complain that Grotius "spares no pains to rob the people of all their rights and invest kings with them" (*Social Contract*, 2, 2; see also 1, 2 and 1, 4).

4. Let us now see how Grotius introduces the idea of collective ownership of the earth in *DJB*. The *suum* appears early in *DJB* I, where we learn that

"our Lives, Limbs, and Liberties" would still be considered "properly ours" if property per se had never been introduced (I.2.I.3). A sphere of what is ours exists prior to property arrangements. We may consume resources provided by nature, but there is no natural right to more than that (e.g., to accumulate things). Much of book II gives an account of how natural use rights are justly extended through acts of the will. The *suum* emerges through the interaction among persons with natural rights who *also* share ownership of this planet. As Grotius explains, making reference to Genesis (1:26 and 9:2–3; see also Psalm 24:1):

> Almighty GOD at the creation, and again after the Deluge, gave to Mankind in general a Dominion over Things of this inferior World. *All Things*, as *Justin* has it, *were at first common, and all the World had, as it were, but one Patrimony*. From hence it was, that every Man converted what he would to his own Use, and consumed whatever was to be consumed; and such a Use of the Right common to all Men did at that time supply the Place of Property, for no Man could justly take from another, what he had thus first taken to himself; which is well illustrated by that Simile of Cicero, *Tho' the Theatre is common for any Body that comes, yet the Place that every one sits in is properly his own*. And this State of Things must have continued till now, had Men persisted in their primitive Simplicity, or lived together in perfect Friendship. (II.2.II.1)

So the earth was *given* to humankind in common.[12] As for the entitlements generated thereby, Cicero's image is telling: There are only liberty rights to seats (the freedom to take an unoccupied seat), no claim rights (no entitlement that a seat be kept), but while the liberty is exercised, while the seats are taken, one may not remove people forcefully. Samuel Pufendorf, in his *De Jure Naturae et Gentium* (*DJNG*) IV.4.V, would later ask: How can a mere corporeal act prejudice the faculty of others without consent? Grotius explains how: consent is not needed because interference with this liberty right violates natural law. However, what Grotius has said up to this point about natural rights to resources is bound up with primitive circumstances (see Salter 2001). Agreement, or adjustment (see below), is needed for further-reaching rights to property (e.g., rights to recover things one has cultivated).[13]

Grotius resorts to a theistic construction in a work that also famously states that "all we have now said would take place, though we should even grant, what without the greatest Wickedness cannot be granted, that there is no God, or that he takes no Care of human Affairs" (*DJB* P, XI). However, one should not overstate the extent to which Grotius attempts to detach his foundations from Christianity. Immediately after stating the thought I just quoted Grotius qualifies its importance:

the contrary of which appearing to us, partly from Reason, partly from a perpetual Tradition, which many Arguments and Miracles, attested by all Ages,
fully confirm; it hence follows, that God as being our Creator, and to whom
we owe our Being, and all that we have, ought to be obeyed by us in all Things,
etc.

Also, early in book I of *DJB,* Grotius introduces a classification of law
that includes a distinction between natural and volitional law. Volitional
law may be divine or human (see Onuma 1993, chap. 2). God's word is
divine volitional law. While God does not determine but merely states the
content of *natural* law, he may or may not issue *additional* commands.
God chose to give the earth to humanity, but did not have to do so. Natural law articulates a standpoint for settling disputes among those outside
of a common civil law because it applies to human beings as such. One
cannot claim territory because "the Possessor should be a Wicked Man,
or have false Notions of GOD, or be of a stupid Mind" (*DJB* II.20.IX),
unless such people are "entirely destitute of the Use of Reason" (*DJB*
II.20.X.1). Still, although people are not accountable for not having received God's revelations (*DJB* II.20.XLVII.4), the *suum* is fixed by reference to a theory that incorporates the revelation of the earth's being a
divine gift.

Nonetheless, Grotius does not think that it is only through revealed
religion that we know about the original ownership of the earth. In the
Jurisprudence of Holland (written roughly at the same time as *DJB*) Grotius discusses ownership of the earth differently. After chapter 1 introduces the distinction between natural and positive law in a way similar
to how *DJB* distinguishes between natural and volitional law, chapter 3
states that "it is a proverbial saying that by the law of nature all things
are common." There are different ways in which human beings can know
about original ownership: *DJB* emphasizes divine revelation, whereas the
Jurisprudence emphasizes the intuitiveness of this idea.[14]

5. Originally, nobody could claim a *persistent exclusive* right to material
objects: I can eat an apple, but I have no right against others not to seize
apples that I stored. Next, Grotius explores how a *morally legitimate* system of private ownership law could develop against the background of
persisting natural collective ownership rights. Given the collective ownership thesis, how can the fact that much of the world is privately owned in
law be morally legitimate? At first sight, *DJB* and *ML* offer rather different accounts of how private ownership could legitimately emerge from
collective ownership, the differences concerning questions that loomed

large for seventeenth-century writers. But these differences matter less than it seems. The reasoning required to make that point reaches back to my point that Grotius was developing a form of global public reason. This section continues to discuss *DJB*. Section 6 addresses *ML,* and section 7 seeks to resolve the tension between the accounts. It is in this section that I can say most about how Grotius constrains what people can do with the resources and spaces of the earth.

De Jure Belli and *Mare Liberum* both associate the transformation of collective ownership into legitimate private ownership with problematic developments. One feature of the original state of simplicity was that people were "rather ignorant of the Nature of Vice" (*DJB* II.2.II.1). Such a simple state could not last, and was replaced with one where people "applied themselves to various Arts.... The most antient Arts were those of Agriculture, and Feeding Cattle" (*DJB* II.2.II.2). Alongside these changing socioeconomic arrangements what originally is held in common is divided ever more through *agreements,*

> either expressly as by a Division; or else tacitly, as by Seizure. For as soon as living in common was no longer approved of, all men were supposed, and ought to be supposed, to have consented, that each should appropriate to himself, by Right of first Possession, what could not have been divided. (II.2.II.5)

The end of Grotius's account is marked by quotes from Cicero and Quintilian, references we also find in *ML:*

> 'Tis no more, saith Cicero, than what Nature will allow of, that each Man should acquire the Necessaries of Life rather for himself than for another. To which may also add that of Quintilian, If it be so established, that whatever has fallen to the Share of a Person for his Use, properly belongs to him; surely whatever we possess by a lawful Title, can never, without Injustice, be taken from us?[15]

This finishes the main discussion of the emergence of private property in *DJB*.[16] Let me add two points. First, in *DJB* II.2.III, the chapter after the one we discussed, Grotius explains that nobody can have property rights in the sea. The sea is big enough for everybody's use: changing socio-economic circumstances do not call for a new property regime. Second, in both *DJB* and *ML*, first occupancy is central (for *DJB*, see II.5, but also II.3.1, II.3.IV.1, and II.8.VI). In II.8.VI, Grotius introduces a plastic for-mulation, remarking that "the beginning of Possession is joining Body to Body, and this in Moveables is done usually by the Hands; but in Im-movables, by our Feet." People realize that adjustments are necessary, and accept them. First occupancy is the mechanism though which the changes occur.[17]

How can Grotius's stance on original ownership accommodate demands of those who are absent when first occupancy occurs? One thing to notice is that, in *DJB,* Grotius does not regard future generations as rights holders:

> he who is not yet born, can have no right, as that Substance which is not yet in Being has no Accidents. Wherefore if the People (from whose Will the Right of Government is derived) should think fit to alter that will, they cannot be conceived to injure those that are unborn, because they have not as yet obtained any Right. (II.4.X.2)

Still, restrictions on private property exist. Rights created by first occupancy are constrained. *DJB* II.2.VI.1 ends by emphasizing that "the Rules of Natural Equity" matter (see also II.3.VI, where we read that those who originally introduce private property do so intending to deviate as little as possible "from the Rule of natural Equity"), which is followed by a discussion of cases of necessity:

> From whence it follows, first, that in a case of Absolute Necessity, that antient Right of using Things, as if they still remained common, must revive, and be in full Force: For in all Laws of human Institution, and consequently, in that of Property too, such cases seem to be excepted. (*DJB* II.2.VI.2)

This right of necessity is no matter of charity (II.2.VI.4). It restricts what property rights could have been reasonably intended at the time of inception. The right of necessity itself is restricted. It can only be invoked if other means have been exhausted: if the actual owners do not need the property; and if restitution is made later, where possible.[18]

Original ownership offers only limited natural rights to begin with. Equity does not entail any sort of redistributive measures to make sure everybody *benefits equally* from the introduction of a system of private ownership (see also II.2.IX). Nonetheless, original ownership has far-reaching implications as far as appropriation is concerned. It is part of this right of necessity that in a just war, refuge can be taken in a neutral country. In addition, there are limitations to property rights that do not seem to be rights of necessity but restrictions on what individuals can rightfully claim as theirs in the first place: others may avail themselves of the right of innocent profit (e.g., sail on rivers), and even demand passage over land to trade with others (II.2.XI–XIII). While those whose lands are involved may take precautions, or levy reasonable charges, granting this right is mandatory (II.2.XIII.3). People may rest ashore to recover from a journey (II.2.XV.2), and may seek "a fixed Abode" (II.2.XVI.2) if persecuted at home as long as they abide by the laws of the host. Products must be made available at reasonable prices if producers do not need them (II.2.XIX). Even the right to marriage ought not be denied, women apparently being part of the common stock (II.2.XXI).[19]

Finally, consider immigration (including immigration that is unwelcome to the original inhabitants), which illustrates not only how potentially far-reaching Grotius's view is but also how its planks may stand in some tension:

> And if there be any waste or barren Land within our Dominions, that also is to be given to Strangers, at their Request, or may be lawfully possessed by them, because whatever remains uncultivated, is not to be esteemed Property, only so far as concerns Jurisdiction, which always continues the Right of the antient People. (II.2.XVII)

Those who accept local law cannot be refused if they wish to settle on waste land. Regarding the colonization of the Americas, the implication of this passage and its surrounding text is that Europeans cannot force their way in if their goal is to bring civilization. But neither can their desire to settle on waste land be refused entirely, and they *could* force their way in if it is.[20] However, now the following is confusing:

> We may now proceed to those Things which may become a Property, but are not so yet. Of this Kind are many desert and uncultivated Places, some Islands in the Sea, wild Beasts, Birds, and Fish. But here are two Things to be remarked, one is, that a Country is taken Possession of, either in the Lump, or by Parts: The former is usually done by a whole People, or by him who is their Sovereign; the latter by the particular Persons of which the People is composed, but yet so that it is more common to assign to every one his Share, than to leave each Portion to the first Occupant. But if, in a Country possessed in the Lump, any thing remains unassigned to private Persons, it ought not therefore to be accounted vacant; for it still belongs to him who first took Possession of the Country, whether King or People; such as Rivers, Lakes, Ponds, Forests, and uncultivated Mountains. (II.2.IV)

Foreigners cannot presume that "Beasts, Fish, and Birds" (II.2.V) are there for the taking. So, on the one hand, civil law restricts the possibilities of acquiring things that seem unappropriated. On the other hand, peaceful settlers cannot be kept from barren land. So when is forced immigration appropriate? This problem arises for Grotius's view that whole peoples can appropriate, or individuals in charge of them. While Locke can assess whether a state uses more space than it ought to by looking at how individuals expand their labor, Grotius holds a broader view of what counts as occupation and what counts as land where a civil law is in force. The solution may be to approach the subject of what counts as occupation with an open mind: that others are not doing what we would do with their land does not mean it is "unoccupied." But this matter also shows that Grotius does not always offer clear advice.[21] What is crucial, however, is that original collective ownership rights constrain appropriation. Private property arrangements are legitimate only if these constraints are respected.

Let me describe what I have argued in this section in terms of a terminology that I introduce in chapter 6. Grotius thinks that original ownership rights provided by the divine gift include a liberty right to appropriate materials, but also an elementary claim right against others to let some such appropriation take place, and an immunity right, a right not be subject to economic and political conditions under which the goals that are supposed to be secured by these rights can no longer be secured. It is on account of the discussion in this section that I think Grotius held something rather close to the view that in chapter 6 I call Common Ownership.

6. I have discussed *De Jure Belli* first because that book is Grotius's main work. The earlier *De Jure Praedae* does not offer an account of how humanity came to own the earth. *De Jure Belli* takes collective ownership for granted. In the *Prolegomena* Grotius mentions only that since

> God fashioned creation and willed its existence, every individual part thereof has received from Him certain natural properties whereby that existence may be preserved and each part may be guided for its own good, in conformity, one might say, with the fundamental law inherent in its origin. (21; see also 24)

Moreover,

> of those things which nature had brought forth for the use of man she would that some of them should remain common and others through every one's labor and industry to become proper. (ML, 6)

Here too Grotius considers this early stage a golden age (21).[22] *Mare Liberum* also explains the process by which things became "proper." Again we read that early on, there exists only a right to use. But *ML*'s account of what happens next does *not* turn on agreement:

For seeing there are many things the use whereof consisteth in abuse, or for that being converted into the substance of the user they admit no use after, or because by use they are made worse for use, in things of the former kind, as meat and drink, a certain propriety appeared not severed from use. For this is to be property, so to appertain to any that it cannot also be another's, which afterwards by a certain reason was derived to things of the latter kind, to wit, garments and chattels or movables; which being so, all immovable things—to wit, fields—could not remain undivided, although the use of them consists not simply in abuse, yet the use thereof was procured by reason of some abuse, as ploughed fields and orchards of fruit trees for food, pastures also for raiment, but they could not in common suffice for the use of all people. Property being found out, there was a law set down which should imitate nature. For, as in the beginning that use was had by corporal application whence, we said before, property had his original, so by the like application it seemed good they should be made the proper goods of everyone. That is that which is called occupation by a word most aptly applied unto those things which before were indifferent. (ML, 22–23)

This seems to be a rather different account from *DJB*. Grotius distinguishes between two stages. In the first, use creates special relationships between things and users. Sometimes *use* amounts to consumption, thus to *abuse*: apples I eat are no longer left for others to use similarly. A form of private ownership becomes inseparable from use. At the second stage Grotius explains that something similar happens in other cases. The passage speaks of "a certain reason," "ratio." People realize the value of assigning objects to individuals: occupation often changes objects of use. Buckle talks of the "logic of historical situations" (1991, 14). "The original principle—the use right sanctioned by the natural law of self-preservation" —he explains,

is adapted and interpreted to meet the exigencies of particular factors and situations (such as the limited re-usability of some things, and pressures caused by limited amounts of usable land) as they come to bear. The "logical process" [i.e., the "ratio"] is a process of reasoning conducted from within a historical situation, about that situation: i.e., a process which will stand in need of revision as new situations arise. (15; see also 23)

Instead of compacts *modifying* collective use, in this account private ownership arises through *natural extensions* of use, without any reference to agreements.

Grotius again completes this discussion with references to Cicero and Quintilian. He apparently meant to discuss the same development on both occasions. At the end of both passages, he discusses the limitations of appropriation, especially as far as the *seas* are concerned (in *ML* beginning at the bottom of p. 24, in *DJB* at the beginning of II.2.III.1). The centrality of occupation as the basis for private ownership becomes clear here too.[23] Since the seas cannot be occupied they cannot be claimed. Even if occupation were possible, it would be unacceptable because the seas can be gainfully used without excluding others. In terms of the approach in *ML,* the point is that no need naturally arises to exclude people from access to the seas; in terms of the agreement approach in *DJB,* nobody would reasonably endorse an agreement to that effect.[24]

7. It is peculiar that Grotius would offer two accounts of the origins of private property of which only one stresses agreements. If he changed his mind about this subject, he would have done so in a pivotal matter for the property discourse of his time. Defending the view that the earth was given to Adam in private, Robert Filmer—the pivotal figure in the property discourse of the seventeenth century, and a much underappreciated thinker—insists that those who argue that everything is originally owned collectively face a dilemma: either private ownership is illegitimate because private rights are usurping collective rights (politically unacceptable); or the terms of God's donation can vary by agreement (intellectually disreputable).[25]

On the face of it, advocates of collective ownership had to tackle the second horn. Needed was an account that would allow for private ownership to arise without assigning too large a role to agreements. Pufendorf made agreements central nonetheless.[26] To this Filmer objected (*Patriarcha,* 1949, 262–74) not merely that it rendered divine gifts changeable but also that consent had not, and practically speaking could not have, occurred. Since only universal consensus would render it legitimate, private property is then illegitimate. Locke thought that no relevant agreements could have been adopted (II, 28). Another possibility would be to present a consensus-based account of private property that shows why this route is not so problematic after all. So indeed, it seems to matter *greatly* whether or not one adopts a consensus-based approach.

However, there is an interpretation that minimizes tensions between Grotius's two accounts. This takes us back to my point that he was offering a peculiar and primitive version of a standpoint of global public reason. Grotius's starting point is God's gift. This leads to a "peculiar" understanding of such a standpoint because of this connection to a religious starting point; and to a "primitive" version because all that is developed from there is the idea of collective ownership. Nevertheless, Grotius uses this idea to offer a standpoint from which to settle disagreements among those who do not share a civil law, in conjunction with his account of natural law. Originally, everybody has a nonpermanent use right to every-thing. Whereas Hobbes thought the most basic insight one could make uncontroversial was that everybody had a right to self-preservation, Grotius started with several laws of nature spelling out what individuals have a right to in ways meant *to be reasonable for everybody*. Grotius is guided by solidaristic assumptions and a view of humanity as susceptible to moral motivation.[27] He traces that standpoint throughout socioeco-nomic changes, to which the *suum* must be adapted. Individuals cannot help but consent to all this, or can be taken to have consented, as Grotius stresses in *DJB*. Still, the normative validity of the process derives from the fact that certain property arrangements are reasonable given certain postulates of natural law, the original ownership status of the earth, and the changes that have occurred.

Whereas in the earlier account we find the idea that a certain form of ownership is inseparable from use (*ML,* 88), in the later one we find the idea that original collective use served the same purpose as private own-ership. In the former account there is no room for agreements to play an important role. Yet the point in both accounts is that the earth belongs to everybody. It is left to the will of men to develop this status, in ways that make sense of the original equity. As Buckle (1991) says, private property

> stands in no special need of justification, since it is a social institution devel-oped to serve the same purpose as the necessary purpose served by the uni-versal original use right. In the light of this perspective, how property comes about can be regarded as a matter of only moderate importance: what matters is just that it comes about as a natural response to circumstances generated when human beings abandoned their original life of primitive simplicity. (43)

What is crucial for the resolution of the tension is that it is not essential how property arrangements emerge, which is the point about which the accounts differ. Grotius's strategy for assessing the legitimacy of private property is not, for instance, to investigate what actions in the world (i.e., agreement, labor, occupation) may generate natural private ownership rights, and then, in a second step, to ask whether ownership *law* as it has developed is consistent with those, and, if it is, to conclude that it is legitimate.

What Grotius asks instead to assess the legitimacy of private property is whether property arrangements serve the society's socioeconomic pur-poses in a reasonable way while remaining consistent with original own-ership rights. Property arrangements must offer reasonable adjustments to new circumstances. There is room for social criticism if property ar-rangements fail to make sense of the original moral equality. Since Gro-tius does not make consent basic, Filmer's worry that there is no location one can visit where such consenting occurred loses its bite. Finally, the divine gift is changed only in the sense that it is adjusted to different settings. Grotius endorses an account of the emergence of private ownership that does not encounter the problems that arise for conventionalists like Pufendorf.[28]

8. Richard Tuck (1979, chap. 3) explains that Grotius's view on original ownership linked earlier "scholastic" and "humanistic" theories. The scholastics thought there was a natural "dominium" much like dominium (ownership provisions) in the civil law. The status of the earth could be understood in terms of such ownership. The humanists argued that nobody had rights under a prelegal natural order. There was no continuity between the civil law and ownership provisions in prelegal orders. Grotius introduces a unique kind of ownership rights to the earth, which becomes possible because, pace the humanists, prelegal man is a subject of rights. But pace the scholastics, his ownership rights differ from rights in the civil law, but could be termed "dominium" *by similitude* with civil law provisions. *Mare Liberum* is self-consciously aware of the lack of apt terminology:

> We are to know, therefore, in the first beginning of the life of man, dominion [i.e., *dominium*] was another thing and communion differing from that which they are now. For now dominion [*dominium*] publicly properly signifieth that which so appartaineth unto one that after the same manner it cannot be another's, but we call that common whose propriety is conferred among many with a certain fellowship and agreement excluding the rest. The defect of tongues hath enforced to use the same words in a thing which was not the same. And so these names of our custom are referred to that ancient law by a certain similitude and resemblance. That, therefore, which at that time was common was no other thing than that which is simply opposed unto proper. (20–21)

Grotius struggled to formulate an ownership status different from what the civil law considers ownership.[29] It would be for his sympathetic critic Pufendorf, in *DJNG*, published in 1672, to provide a suitable term and thus clarify what Grotius meant:

> The Term Communion is taken either negatively, or positively. In the former manner things are said to be common, as consider'd before any Act or Agreement had declared them to belong to one rather than to another. In the same sense, things thus consider'd are said to be No Body's, rather negatively, than privately, i.e., that they are not yet assign'd to any particular Person, not that

they are incapable of being so assign'd. They are likewise term'd *res in medi quibusvis expositae*, Things that lie free for any Taker. But in the positive Signification of the Word, common Things differ from Appropriated only in this Respect, That the latter belong to one person only, the former to many Persons together, though in the very same manner. To proceed, *Property or Dominion, is a Right, by which the very Substance, as it were, of a Thing, so belongs to one Person, that it doth not in whole belong, after the same manner, to any other.* For we take *Dominion* and *Property* to be the very same. (IV.4.2)

Pufendorf not only used "communion" where Grotius used "dominium." He also distinguished positive from negative communion, endorsing the latter and ascribing it to Grotius (although he thought Grotius sometimes got confused about the distinction). "Positive" communion is what chapter 6 reintroduces as "joint" ownership, which involves a process of co-owners deciding jointly about what to do with what they own collectively. "Negative" communion (Grotius's view, what chapter 6 reintroduces as common ownership) formulates an idea of the relationship between human beings and the world that is less demanding while still capturing the idea that the earth is *for* the use of human beings. As Buckle (1991) says about both positive and negative communion, "in using the world for their own ends, human beings are not strangers (or trespassers) on a foreign soil. They are at home" (95)—in a world that God gave them in common.[30]

The details of the ownership status of the earth are far from obvious even among those taking their cues from Genesis. Robert Filmer insisted that for Christians "to dream either of a community of all things, or an equality of all persons, is a fault scarce pardonable" (262). Instead, God gave the earth to Adam in private ownership, who bequeathed it to his heirs. This view circumvents the need to show how private property could have arisen. Grotius's view of the divine gift made no sense to Filmer since it ascribed to God a deed that conventions were supposed to alter. Debate ensured from here: Pufendorf defended Grotius arguing that Adam could not have had private ownership without anybody else around.[31] Alongside Filmer, Selden rejected negative communion, but endorsed positive communion among Adam and his sons. Locke took Filmer seriously enough to devote his *First Treatise* to refuting him.

Like Grotius in the *Jurisprudence* appealing to a "common saying" (*De Cive* 1.10), Hobbes argued for positive communion without biblical references. He claimed that "nature hath given all to all, from whence we understand likewise, that in the state of nature, profit is the measure of right."[32] Hobbes's view too, which, according to *Leviathan*, includes a right to one another's bodies, was rejected by Filmer (*Patriarcha*, 241). For Filmer there could be no such right, given the status accorded to Adam.

How to interpret the divine gift was the crucial issue in the central theme of seventeenth-century political thought.[33] Chapter 6 reveals that characterizing original ownership is nontrivial also in the secularized version of this approach.

Let me conclude. In his 1825 *Lectures on the History of Philosophy*, Hegel began his short discussion of *DJB* by stating that "no one reads [it] any longer, although it was extremely influential" (1990, 179). Several decades earlier Rousseau had written scornfully that the "science of political right is yet to be born, and it is to be presumed that it never will be born. Grotius, the master of all our learned men in this matter, is only a child and, what is worse, a child of bad faith" (1979, 458). The work of this "child of bad faith"—which indeed should be read—is nevertheless an excellent point of reference for explaining how collective ownership of the earth can help us think through questions of global reach, and how the challenge of characterizing this ownership status itself generates important philosophical questions. This chapter has demonstrated the wealth of applications of the idea of humanity's collective ownership of the earth.

Grotius wrote at a time when many questions of global scope first arose, and when just what "sovereign" states were allowed to do still needed to be settled. Nowadays sovereignty has become problematic, and we must reconsider what states rightfully can do. Now there is, if anything, even more of a need than in Grotius's time for a nonparochial standpoint from which to settle questions of global reach. However, while Grotius took non-Christians seriously as natural rights holders, he wrote for a readership that accepted the book of Genesis. It is first of all that part of his thought that we must reconsider for original ownership of the earth to factor into our investigation of the grounds of justice. Chapter 6 recreates this standpoint without theology. In the remainder of the book, I repeatedly return to Grotius for inspiration.

CHAPTER 6

"Our Sole Habitation"

A Contemporary Approach to Collective Ownership of the Earth

---

1. Alongside others preoccupied with collective ownership of the earth, Grotius held that God had *given* the earth to humankind in common. In his eighteenth-century treatise on English common law, William Blackstone considered this donation "the only true and solid foundation of man's dominion over external things, whatever airy metaphysical notions may have been started by fanciful writers upon this subject" (1979, 3). But the view that the earth originally belongs to humankind collectively is plausible not only without "airy metaphysical notions" but also entirely without religious input. To ask about "original" ownership is to ask whether ("original" or "external") resources that exist independently of human activities are owned, in a sense prior to the moral claims individuals or groups have to resources based, say, on first occupancy or the mixing of labor with resources, as well as prior to any kind of legal claims they may have. Original collective ownership rights would be natural rights that human beings have with regard to what John Passmore called "our sole habitation ... in which we live and move and have our being" (1974, 3), regardless of when and where they are born. This chapter explores from a secular standpoint the view that the earth belongs to humankind collectively. I offer a view on the ownership status of the earth that I call Common Ownership.

We inquire about materials that exist independently of human contributions (air, soil, raw materials such as minerals, coal, water), but also about how biophysical factors such as climate endow regions with value for humans. It is the earth *as a whole* that is collectively owned. Inferences from there to ownership of parts of the earth are nontrivial, a subject explored in chapter 10. Natural ownership rights speak to raw materials and spaces only, not to what we have made of them. But artifacts use up resources too, and the distinction between what "is just there" and what humans have shaped is blurred, say, for land human beings have wrested from the sea. Chapter 8 explores this topic.[1] When Grotius wrote, land was central to the economy. When Marx wrote, attention had shifted to the means of production in industrializing societies. Maybe we now live in the "age of access" and must understand basic economic parameters ("paid-for experiences"; Rifkin 2000) yet differently. So it is important to be clear that what is originally owned is three-dimensional space of differential usefulness for human purposes, regardless of its era-dependent economic relevance. I exclude wildlife from collectively owned resources, but including it would be conceptually unproblematic.

I talk about "collective ownership" generically, capturing the idea that, in some sense to be explicated in more detail, humanity as a whole owns the earth. In this chapter we encounter different developments of this idea, different *conceptions* of collective ownership. States may adopt vastly different systems of ownership, explicating what forms of control, benefits, or exclusion owners may have, as well as differing ideas about who can own what and how. Some states have insecure property rights, are unable to enforce rights, or cannot control access to their territory. Some indigenous peoples may reject ideas of ownership entirely. Still, humanity's collective ownership formulates a standing demand on all groups to occupy the earth in a manner that respects the equal status of all individuals with regard to original resources.

Blackstone famously remarked that nothing

> so generally strikes the imagination, and engages the affections of mankind, as the right of property; or that sole and despotic dominion which one man claims and exercises over the external things of the world, in total exclusion of the right of any other individual in the universe. (1979, 2)

Species of collective ownership that constrain this "sole and despotic dominion" are bound to be controversial (although, as we noted, Blackstone himself endorsed the idea of humanity's collective ownership through divine donation). So let me address a typical reductio through which some seek to ridicule collective ownership. Can anybody sensibly claim, asks Murray Rothbard, that a newborn Pakistani baby has claims to a plot in Iowa that Smith just transformed into a field?[2] As soon as we consider such implications of collective ownership, says he, we realize its implausibility. Smith has claims on the strength of his efforts. The baby has none. However, collective ownership does not require that every nugget of gold found on the ocean floor be divided among all humans, or each drop of oil extracted from the Arabian Peninsula. That the baby has claims on a par with Smith's is consistent with Smith's not having to vacate *that* land (the baby does not have a claim to each object) and with Smith's not having to *vacate* that land (the claim may be satisfied through compensation, cohabitation, etc.). A detailed view of collective ownership remains to be established, but it is not so easily shown to be absurd.[3]

I assume throughout that, globally, and modulo our ability to find sensible allocation mechanisms, there is enough to satisfy everybody's basic needs. In a world that is wildly at odds with that assumption (e.g., the post-apocalyptic world in Cormac McCarthy's harrowing novel *The Road*), much moral thought must be reconsidered. The plausibility of claim rights to external resources is not undermined by the existence of emergency situations (e.g., shipwrecks) where claims to noninterference may not hold.

Section 2 introduces collective ownership as well as some of its conceptions, especially Common Ownership. Section 3 offers an initial defense of collective ownership and of Common Ownership. Section 4 explores what work Common Ownership does in an engagement with libertarianism. Section 5 defends Common Ownership against objections in terms of the value of the environment. Sections 6 and 7 explore two alternative conceptions of collective ownership and develop objections to them. Section 8 relates the results of this chapter back to our overall inquiry into global justice. Sections 9 and 10 illustrate how Common Ownership enters into debates in the philosophical literature. Section 9 shows that one version of left-libertarianism (Otsuka 2003) is incoherent. Section 10 shows that one of Pogge's (2002) arguments for the claim that the global order harms the poor, fails. While those two sections will be of interest mostly to specialists, subsequent chapters explore a range of topics from the standpoint of collective ownership that are of broad philosophical interest.

2. An entity may have roughly four types of ownership status: *no* ownership; *joint* ownership—ownership directed by collective preferences; *common* ownership—the entity belongs to several individuals, each equally entitled to use it, within constraints; and *private* ownership. Common ownership is a right to use something without a right to exclude other co-owners. If the Boston Common were held *in common* when it was used for cattle, a constraint could have been to bring no more than a certain number, a condition supported by respect for others and a concern to avoid the tragedy of the commons. If Bostonians held the Common *jointly*, each use would require the consent of every other co-owner. Joint ownership ascribes to each owner rights as extensive as private ownership rights, except that others hold the same rights. (The most plausible view on duties to nature must be factored in; see section 5.)

The difference between common ownership and no ownership emerges clearly if we ask how to generate natural *private* property. To that end, No Ownership would require a theory of *acquisition*. The crucial issue is how to generate rights and duties constitutive of the property at all, one important question being whether this process is subject to moral constraints. Right-libertarians deny this (see section 4). But such a denial does not follow from No Ownership. One may argue that, while resources are originally unowned, acquisition requires consideration of others ("provisos"). Common Ownership would require a theory of *privatization*, the crucial issue being how to derive private ownership from a bundle of rights and duties constituting common ownership. Private ownership derives either from a contract, or in a way that renders contracts superfluous. (I speak of "appropriation" when staying neutral between acquisition and privatization.)

"Joint Ownership" and "Common Ownership" in capital letters are names of conceptions of collective ownership and hence views about ownership specifically *of the earth*. In lowercase letters, "joint ownership" and "common ownership" are general forms of ownership. Again, I say that humanity "collectively" owns the earth if what matters is merely that in some recognizable sense, humanity as a whole owns the earth. Section 3 gives more content to collective ownership. I use the term "Equal Division" for the conception of collective ownership that corresponds to private ownership. According to Equal Division, each of altogether n human beings has a claim to a $1/n$ share of original resources. Joint Ownership, Common Ownership, and Equal Division are the three conceptions of collective ownership that I explore. No Ownership too will be discussed below, or more specifically, its uses within libertarianism. Political philosophers in the seventeenth century debated how to interpret God's gift. We need a similar debate about these conceptions. There may well be other conceptions. As Rawls (1999c) defends his principles not against *every* objection but against several relevant alternatives, I defend my preferred conception, Common Ownership, against a short list of competitors.

Let me elaborate on Common Ownership some more. Its core idea is that all co-owners ought to have an equal opportunity to satisfy basic needs to the extent that this turns on collectively owned resources. This formulation, first, stresses an equality of status; second, it insists that the equality concerns opportunities to satisfy basic needs (there being no sense in which co-owners are entitled to an equal share of what is collectively owned, let alone to support in getting such a share, any more than co-owners of the Boston Common had such claims); and third, it does so (only) insofar as such needs require collectively owned resources.[4] In the standard Hohfeldian rights terminology, common ownership rights include liberty rights, accompanied by what Hart (1982) calls a "protective perimeter" of claim rights (171). To have a liberty right is to be free of duties to the contrary. Co-owners are under no duty to refrain from using resources. However, were co-ownership reducible to such rights, a Hobbesian state of nature would arise in which everybody was allowed to interfere with anything. Some might legitimately be deprived of everything. Common Ownership guarantees minimal access to resources by adding a protective perimeter of claim rights, similar to how Grotius argued that individuals may take from nature what they need to survive, and others are not allowed to interfere. (This demand of noninterference is limited to appropriations necessary to satisfy a person's basic needs.) There might be further-reaching natural rights with respect to these resources, including exclusive rights to bits of the earth arising from such actions as occupation, consent, and so on. And there will be positive law that regulates access to resources in legal systems. In cases of a conflict, natural common ownership rights have priority.

Property arrangements of the positive law may be conventions where access to resources plays little immediate role for most people. A necessary condition for the acceptability of such conventions—to make sure of the aforementioned priority—is that the core purpose of the original rights is still met. That purpose is to ensure that co-owners have the opportunity to meet basic needs. Grotius, too, recognizes something like this, by imposing limitations on property conventions. In Hohfeldian terminology, co-owners have an *immunity* from living under political and economic arrangements that interfere with their having such opportunities. So the right involved in common ownership is no simple use right but a more complicated disjunctive right either to use (in the narrow sense) resources and spaces to satisfy one's basic needs or else to live in a society that does not deny one the opportunity to satisfy one's basic needs in ways in which it otherwise could have been done through original resources and spaces. In chapter 7 this immunity takes us to human rights.

Hobbesians might say that individuals may rationally agree to live under conditions that fail to offer guarantees that are called for by the aforementioned immunity. But given the basic nature of the needs at stake, individuals would normally make such agreements only under duress. The unstated premise of this objection seems to be that if we accept a natural right to X, then we cannot consistently accept living arrangements that do not guarantee X. But that is false: we may reasonably settle for less if we believe it is the best we can get.[5]

We can now also see a difference between common ownership of the earth and common ownership of the Boston Common. Bostonians had rights to use the common for purposes other than basic needs satisfaction. But such purposes reflected shared cultural understandings of how it was appropriate to use land. Since I wish to construct a set of natural ownership rights, I limit their content to what would be acceptable to every reasonable person. Therefore I talk about basic needs satisfaction. I recall also the Iowa farmer-Pakistani baby challenge discussed earlier. Common Ownership includes no right to use whichever resources and spaces a person chooses to satisfy her basic needs. This right is only a right to access some (sufficient) bit.

3. I argue for Common Ownership in several stages. I explain first why one should find collective ownership of the earth plausible. Since Common Ownership captures a minimal conception of collective ownership, the argument for collective ownership also takes us to Common Ownership. The challenge is to explain why stronger conceptions, and conceptions of some prominence (Joint Ownership, Equal Division), are implausible. In between, I further delineate its content by exploring what work Common Ownership does in the debate about libertarianism, as well as by assessing objections on behalf of the value of the environment.

One might insist that "ownership" is misleading in this context. After all, natural ownership rights are detached from the complex set of rights and duties that the civil law delineates under the heading of property law (Honoré 1961). But first of all, I am talking about collective ownership of the earth because I am concerned with claims to resources and spaces. Second, there is a connection between natural collective ownership rights and property law, parallel to the connection between Rawls's principles of justice and judicial decisions. Like Rawls's four-stage sequence (1999c, sec. 31), which begins with the Original Position, then proceeds to the constitutional, legislative, and finally to the judicial stage, I begin with the abstract viewpoint of collective ownership, develop conceptions of it, and could (but do not) proceed to assessing civil law prescriptions in light of the most plausible conception.[6]

I introduce three claims to establish that (and the sense in which) humanity collectively owns the earth. Conceptions of collective ownership (of which Common Ownership is one) spell out precisely what this means. The first claim is that the resources and spaces of the earth are valuable to and necessary for all human activities to unfold, the most important of which is to secure survival. This claim remains true as long as human life is earth-bound and accounts for the relevance of inquiries about original ownership. It also makes sure that references to remote galaxies do not lead our inquiry ad absurdum. What is meant is not that *all* resources are necessary for *each* human activity to unfold. What is meant is that the earth is humanity's natural habitat, a closed system of resources everybody needs for survival. If space travel expands humanity's habitat, we may have to reformulate this first claim. The other claims speak to the expanded space, too. The idea of a "common heritage of humanity" has been applied to outer space. More problematic than the outer limits of what is collectively owned is why we should accept that the relevant space includes the *whole* earth. Why could not people in Japan or New Zealand say they, but *only* they, collectively own their islands? A reply— to show that what is collectively owned is the whole earth—must wait until section 4.

The second claim is that the satisfaction of basic human needs matters morally, and matters more than any environmental value (such as protecting the biosphere). I elaborate below on the reference to environmental values. Whereas the first is descriptive, this claim (like the next) is normative. Without such an assumption we cannot illuminate the appropriateness of talk about *claims* in this context. Chapter 4 discusses the normative significance of the distinctively human life. The satisfaction of basic needs ("the conditions that must be met for a person to have a decent life given the environmental conditions he faces"; Miller 2007, 184) is morally as significant as life itself. I wish to make maximally uncontroversial claims that lead to a universally acceptable, nonparochial standpoint to adjudicate questions of global reach and generate a set of natural rights. I mean by "basic needs" merely Doyal and Gough's (1991) fundamental needs: physical health and a mental competence to choose and deliberate. The first claim is also true broadly for "human activities." However, such a broad claim is unsuitable for deriving claims of universal reach.

The third claim states that, to the extent that resources and spaces have come into existence without human interference, nobody has claims to them based on any contributions to their creation. This claim merely states a straightforward implication of the nature of the resources whose ownership status is at stake. The matter is nonetheless significant. Since nobody has such claims, nobody can have claims to resources that draw on accomplishments of *others,* either, as I may be entitled to an inheritance if I am the designated beneficiary of somebody else's accomplishments. We may take social primary goods as an example. No new-born baby has done more than another to create such goods, but others have. For entities whose form of existence depends on human interference, it is not generally true that of any two individuals, neither has a stronger claim to them. The only way of denying this is to insist that no manner of being involved with the way in which an entity comes into its form of existence generates claims to it.[7] This I take to be false. Maximally uncontroversial is that to resources and spaces that have come to exist without human interference nobody has claims in terms of accomplishments that are privileged over those of others. No statement about (human-made) artifacts is as uncontroversial.[8]

While the first and third claim also hold for animals (as does, arguably, the second, for some animals), I assume that humans stand in moral relations to each other that differ from their relations to animals, if only because the distinctively human life differs in important ways from the life of animals. Nothing turns on claiming that animals are inferior. I explore original ownership to assess redistributive claims humans make *on each other.*[9] So the first claim explains why there can be claims *to original re-*

sources and spaces of the earth. The second makes clear how *claims* of some sort arise here. The third insists that such claims *cannot be constrained by reference to the accomplishments of others.* In a nutshell, all human beings have some kind of claims to original resources and spaces that cannot be constrained by reference to what others have accomplished. I said I would talk about collective ownership generically, capturing the idea that, in some sense to be explicated in more detail, humanity as a whole owns the earth. That sense has now been established and is contained in the summary sentence I just provided.

But the three claims I have discussed also take us to Common Ownership. We can sum up our account of Common Ownership as follows: first, each person, independent of her actions, has a natural right to use original resources and spaces to satisfy her basic needs, and second, in conflicts with any further entitlements with respect to these resources, this natural right has priority. The realization of common ownership rights may involve either the right to use original resources and spaces of the earth or else the right to live in a society that does not deny one the opportunity to satisfy one's basic needs in a way in which it otherwise could have been done through the use of original resources and spaces. The liberty, claim, and immunity rights constitutive of Common Ownership are entailed by my three claims. Common Ownership offers a way of making precise the idea of collective ownership of the earth that the three claims establish. It does so by proposing a minimally demanding set of rights.

4. Let us see what work these claims do in a discussion of libertarianism. This discussion further clarifies Common Ownership. Left-libertarians hold that agents are self-owners but that natural resources are owned in some egalitarian manner. As opposed to that, right-libertarianism's *differentia* is the denial of any but at most a minimal moral account of ownership of external resources.[10]

There are various ways of endorsing such a denial. Jan Narveson seems to deny that any compensation is due for acquiring original resources.[11] Such right-libertarians may recognize constraints on appropriation. But they either think these constraints are nonmoral, such as requirements that first occupancy extend only to what occupiers can meaningfully occupy; or else grant that the constraints are moral but minimally so, in the sense that one is morally permitted to acquire things only for which one can claim first occupancy and where first occupancy is nonmorally constrained by meaningful occupation. Others deny that objects of appropriation are "external." Israel Kirzner (1978) argues that until a resource has been discovered, *it has not*, in the sense relevant to the rights of access and common use, *existed at all.*[12] Although left-libertarians often count

Nozick (1974) a right-libertarian, right-libertarians attack even his weak proviso that permits acquisition of unowned resources only if it makes nobody worse off.[13]

Right-libertarians endorse versions of No Ownership as a view of original ownership. No Ownership holds that there are no natural duties not to use original resources and (apart from a minimal original liberty) no natural rights to use resources either. Theorists like Narveson add the provision that through actions such as occupancy, people can unilaterally acquire natural rights to external resources. Theorists like Kirzner deny that any additions are needed to conceptualize appropriation. They insist that discovery changes the nature of the objects to such an extent that no *original* resources are appropriated. This view strikes me as bizarre.

One might think No Ownership is the default view on original ownership. Otsuka (2003), for one, does, since "in the absence of any such belief that the earth was previously owned by some being who transferred this right of ownership to humankind at the outset, it is reasonable to regard the earth as initially unowned" (22, n. 28). But as Wenar (1998) notes, No Ownership possesses no such character if we accept any natural rights at all (as Otsuka does [2003, 3–4], and as I do too). Since (a) views on collective ownership other than No Ownership are not entirely implausible to begin with and (b) there are no circumstances where no rights hold, No Ownership loses its default status.

Generally, No Ownership can be developed in three ways. First, no provisions for appropriation are added. Second, provisions for unilateral appropriation are added that do not require consideration of others. And third, unilateral acquisition is constrained through "provisos," conditions that do require consideration of others. Nozick, for one, endorses a proviso:

> You may acquire previously unowned land (and its fruits) if and only if you make nobody else worse off than they would have been in the state of nature in which no land is privately held but each is free to gather and consume food and water from the land and make use of it.[14]

Otsuka (2003), too, endorses a proviso:

> You may acquire previously unowned worldly resources if and only if you leave enough so that everyone else can acquire an equally advantageous share of unowned worldly resources. (24)

I do not discuss the first possibility. I distinguish between No Ownership without provisos (meaning now the second possibility) from No ownership with provisos. No Ownership without provisos is what I will now take right-libertarianism to mean, and No Ownership with provisos is one version of left-libertarianism.

Let us explore No Ownership without provisos. European conquerors in the sixteenth century claiming for their king all land between Atlantic and Pacific would not meaningfully occupy anything. Right-libertarians can recognize constraints of meaningful occupancy much as somebody who condones lying might insist that communication requires linguistic structure. (They might even agree that these are minimal moral constraints.) An objection to restricting constraints on acquisition in this way might insist that it is inappropriate for accidents of space and time (namely, those that create opportunities for unilateral acquisition) to determine property holdings, certainly if this process is supposed to lead to rights resonating through the ages.

No Ownership might create a situation in which some people's opportunity to satisfy basic needs is not ensured. Defenders say that that would be so not because needs lack moral significance but because of morally impeccable actions of others. However, the reasoning that led to Common Ownership enters now. It is the third claim above—that to the extent that resources and spaces exist without human interference, nobody has claims to them based on contributions to their creation—that does important work here. All human beings have some kind of claims to original resources and spaces that, crucially for present purposes, cannot be constrained by what others have accomplished either in the present or in the past. If basic needs satisfaction is morally significant and the resources required to that end exist independently of human accomplishments, then all human beings must have an opportunity to make ends meet.

Nobody can be reasonably asked to accept a situation where she cannot satisfy her basic needs because the required resources and spaces are integrated into other people's activities (beyond what those need to satisfy their basic needs). Theories of appropriation must be limited accordingly, and right-libertarianism fails to do so. One can press against defenders of No Ownership without provisos that they unacceptably disregard a notion of even *minimal human solidarity*, an acknowledgment of minimal entitlements everybody has to opportunities to acquire resources, to the extent that such resources are needed to satisfy basic needs. Morally (otherwise) impeccable behavior of others cannot overrule the significance of such opportunities (which is why I talk about minimal *solidarity*). The utmost failure of such solidarity is the refusal to share the earth with others altogether. It is in such terms that Hannah Arendt—who thinks that "the earth is the very quintessence of the human condition" (1958, 2)—characterizes the nature of crimes against humanity. Most egregiously, so the author of *Eichmann in Jerusalem* tells us, the Nazis "wished to make the entire Jewish people disappear from the face of the earth" (1963, 268).

Common Ownership is a better way of thinking about original ownership than No Ownership without provisos. Let me add some additional points of clarification. To begin with, I have yet to respond to somebody who denies that the shared space of humanity is the *whole* earth. The view that it is not the whole earth that is collectively owned implies that one may deny support or entry to some even in light of the complete absence of opportunities to satisfy basic needs. However large we make the local area to which we restrict ownership, there are possible futures in which, for instance through natural disasters, that area could not support the needs of those within it. To cover for such cases, each person must have rights to the whole earth. If people have rights only to local resources, duties relating to people's basic needs (i.e., duties to provide the relevant opportunities) would be distributed too narrowly, namely, only among fellow locals. Minimal solidarity must apply to *all* of humanity.[15]

One might wonder whether an analogous argument would not after all extend the rights to the whole universe. The whole earth might face disasters, too. However, for now we face a situation in which natural disasters might well annihilate our planet, but none in which humanity's habitat is larger than this planet. One way of comprehending the idea that outer space is a natural heritage of humanity is in terms of its potential for being subject to natural ownership rights should space travel expand humanity's habitat. It should be noted that while common ownership rights are natural rights, they are not human rights according to the conception from chapter 4. According to that conception, human rights are rights needed to protect the distinctively human life. *In principle,* the distinctively human life is not earth-bound, although it is for the foreseeable future. We should distinguish between theorizing about the distinctively human life and theorizing about what contingently but enduringly is our natural habitat now.

Common Ownership has some strength. Nonetheless, it captures a minimal version of collective ownership. The claims I made in support of collective ownership should be acceptable across cultures. Natural rights are rights every reasonable person should be able to accept. We must therefore limit ourselves to minimally demanding starting points. Reasonable people can reject conceptions proposing a stronger set of ownership rights than Common Ownership because Common Ownership exhausts what we can make of the claims about original ownership that everybody should reasonably accept. My argument for Common Ownership as the preferred conception rests partly on this claim, and partly on objections to competing conceptions.

I have so far limited my discussion of No Ownership to versions without proviso. Alternatively, defenders of No Ownership may accept a proviso. Depending on the proviso, they would adopt either a theory identical in what it permits and forbids to one of the conceptions in this chapter or a different theory. As I am in the process of arguing, among those conceptions Common Ownership is most plausible. As we saw, we should reject conceptions proposing a stronger set of ownership rights than Common Ownership. Since, moreover, no proviso would be of interest that formulates restrictions that leave people unable to satisfy basic needs, no separate discussion of No Ownership with provisos is necessary.

5. Presumably, some would reject Common Ownership by doubting whether *ownership* aptly captures our relationship to the natural world. Walt Whitman praised animals, by way of contrast with humans, by emphasizing that "not one is demented with the mania of owning things" (sec. 32 of "Song of Myself," Whitman 1961). Yet crucially—and this is indeed a decisive point to note as far as the plausibility of my revitalization of the collective ownership approach is concerned—collective ownership is a view about the relationship among human beings that can readily integrate plausible accounts of environmental values.[16] While the civil law often permits us to destroy objects, collective ownership does not per se entail the permissibility of wanton destruction, nor does it commit us to ascribing merely instrumental value to nature. Valuing nature intrinsically, as sublime or awesome, as providing a context in which human life obtains meaning, and even as sacred, is consistent with my view. Again, parallel to Rawls's four stages connecting the Original Position with judicial decisions, I begin with the abstract standpoint of collective ownership, develop a conception of it, and could proceed to assessing civil law prescriptions in light of the most plausible conception. Considerations about the value of nature matter at that last stage. Only then can we settle conclusively what can be done with resources.[17]

The idea that humanity owns the earth has done its share in the history of human chauvinism. But my secularized understanding of collective ownership does not presuppose the arrogance associated with a reading of the Bible that subjects the creation to the human will, an attitude that emerges, for instance, in Calvin's view that God took six days to create the world in order to demonstrate to human beings that everything was prepared for them. In that way my approach differs from its seventeenth-century predecessors, many of whose advocates accepted this stance.[18]

Not all manners of capturing the value of nature are consistent with collective ownership. To reflect this point, I have formulated the second claim that supports collective ownership as follows: The satisfaction of basic human needs matters morally, and matters more than any other environmental value (such as protecting the biosphere). Aldo Leopold's credo ("A thing is right when it tends to preserve the integrity, stability, and beauty of the biotic community. It is wrong when it tends otherwise"; 1949, 224–25), is inconsistent with any version of collective ownership. Leopold suggests that eventually we will find "owning land" as revolting as "owning people." This "land ethic," later developed by Callicott (1989) and others, moves outside *enlightened anthropocentrism*, the view that all values must be values to human beings and on a human scale, which, however, does not mean instrumental values or values of human flourishing exhaust their range. Enlightened anthropocentrism (which I think is the correct view of the value of nature) recognizes that answers to environmental questions "must be based on human values, in the sense of values that human beings can make part of their lives and understand themselves as pursuing and respecting" (Williams 1995, 234).[19]

Outside of such a view also stands arguably the "biospheric egalitarianism" of the deep ecology movement inspired by Arne Naess (1989), according to which all living things, including plants and ecosystems, have value in their own right.[20] It may so happen that humans care more about each other than about other entities, but biospheric egalitarians consider it human chauvinism to give any morally privileged status to human projects (Routley and Routley 1980). According to Locke, "The Earth, and all that is therein, is given to Men for the Support and Comfort of their Being" *(Second Treatise*, 1988, sec. 26). And indeed, minimally this idea, stripped of theology and human arrogance, must be acceptable within approaches to the question of how to value nature for humanity's collective ownership of the earth to be plausible.

The idea that there is moral significance to the satisfaction of basic needs and that this significance at least *tends* to overrule environmental concerns conflicts only with rather extreme forms of environmental ethics. It is not the case that any human need must prevail, say, even if the Grand Canyon must be destroyed to meet it. As Frances Kamm (2007) writes, "Sometimes the remarkableness of something or its uniqueness calls for more protection than does something else's having moral status" (230). The potential for conflict increases if we understand the priority given to beings with a subjective good (especially humans) as including a further-reaching priority for the good life of such beings beyond the satisfaction of needs. Required would be a considerable priority for the good of such beings, although none that holds that this sort of good trumps all other considerations. I endorse a priority statement of this strength (to avoid trivialization in the clarification of the relationship between collective ownership and environmental ethics), although this plays no role in subsequent arguments that deploy Common Ownership.[21]

6. Let me defend Common Ownership against two competing conceptions of collective ownership, Joint Ownership and Equal Division. I con-

sider first Joint Ownership. To support this view, one needs a theory of what it is about individuals that requires such a high standard of justification for each use of collectively owned assets. Defending Joint Ownership, James Grunebaum (1987) takes the notion of *autonomy* to imply that each use violates a person's autonomy unless she approves.

A first response might be that this use of autonomy overstates its normative weight. The notion of autonomy captures a vision of persons controlling their destiny to some extent. The limited control over one's destiny demanded by the value of autonomy might imply that one should have some control over one's immediate environment, but not over the rest of the world. However, what is really troublesome is that if each person must *be asked* about any use of the collective property, she must also *ask* about any such use. So others can veto uses that satisfy basic needs. Joint Ownership would not give people the claim right that Common Ownership acknowledges. So Joint Ownership violates autonomy by expecting each person to get everyone's consent before she can satisfy her basic needs.

Perhaps I have not offered the best view of Joint Ownership. Joint Ownership, one might say, should not be conceptualized at the level of acquisition (which is where my objection applies). Instead, this view captures the idea that we must justify the acquisition of resources to each other. This could be done by modeling an original position where all parties are joint owners and seek to agree on principles under which all may acquire without unanimity in particular acts. In the original position, this is to ask what permissions it is reasonable both to give and to receive.

Let us grant all this. But Common Ownership would then emerge from such deliberation. As we noted in chapter 2, an "original position" is an expository device to capture factors relevant to collective decisions. Rawls's *Theory of Justice* is the contemporary *locus classicus* for the application of this device. Given the nature of the state, we must decide which features of individuals give them just claims to primary goods. In each case, this must be carefully argued in light of the factors characterizing shared membership in the state as a ground of justice. In the original position where deliberators are concerned with one state, deliberators know all and only those features of themselves that entitle them to primary goods. Were we to construct a similar device here, we could only help ourselves to the claims leading to collective ownership, of which, after all, Common Ownership and Joint Ownership are competing conceptions.

Suppose the question arises of whether, say, intelligence and strength make it acceptable for some to acquire more resources than others. One might incline to answer negatively because of the morally arbitrary nature of these features. But this will not do. Let us consider again the parallel to the state. Strength and intelligence should have a limited effect on one's distributive shares because such assets are morally arbitrary. Pressed *why* this arbitrariness matters, we could say that everybody, weak or strong, intelligent or simple-minded, is subject to the state (an artificial structure) and offer the considerations discussed in chapters 2 and 3 when we explored the normative peculiarity of the state. However, crucially, when discussing resources and spaces, we can offer no such elaboration to support duties among all co-owners beyond what Common Ownership prescribes. As long as the exercise of intelligence or strength does not keep others from satisfying basic needs, there is nothing morally problematic about this exercise. Unlike in the case of the state, no *additional* considerations are available when discussing resources and spaces to explain why certain kinds of arbitrariness would be problematic.

What enters here is a point made before: whenever somebody offers a stronger interpretation of collective ownership than Common Ownership, a sensible response is that Common Ownership exhausts the claims supporting collective ownership. As reasonable persons can reject stronger claims in support of collective ownership, they can also reject stronger conceptions of it. So no stronger conception delivers *natural rights* (rights every reasonable person should accept). Therefore, as a way of setting up certain deliberations, Joint Ownership does not conflict with Common Ownership as a view about how co-owners should relate to each other. Common Ownership would be chosen in the original position that accompanies Joint Ownership so understood.

7. Let us consider now Equal Division as defended, for instance, by Hillel Steiner (1994). Equal Division gains plausibility from the idea that there is a (figurative) heap of resources to which each person has an equal claim. However, the idea of "dividing up" such a heap presupposes an ability to assign values to sets of resources to render them comparable. This could be done in ways that either do or do not draw on human practices. The second manner of doing so is ruled out from the start. Such an approach would involve evaluations made from something like a divine standpoint, or a standpoint of the universe. Regardless of whether it is plausible for anything at all, such a standpoint holds no plausibility for an assignment of values to original resources. These assignments would have to be made in a way that draws on human practices.

To assign such values, one would need to find some way of assessing an *aggregated* value for the overall heap of resources. This would be complicated because we would have to assess not only the property values of two-dimensional spaces but the overall usefulness of three-dimensional regions for human purposes. But let us ignore the complexity of this enterprise. What is crucial is that defenders of Equal Division need a uniquely most plausible way of assessing the value in question, one that everybody could reasonably accept. The aggregate value of the overall heap of resources would in particular draw on valuations of raw materials. However, many materials acquire value only through activities that require social contexts. How valuable, say, oil, uranium, or silicon is depends on what people can and want to do with the substance. So it depends on what technology is available that requires these materials; on how people choose to integrate it into their lives; and on what specific property rules determine what they can do with resources and technology.

These matters not only vary across societies, they are not the sort of thing for which there would be a single most plausible arrangement that everybody could be expected to respect. One might say that, at least for those entities for which there is a world market value, we should use that value, and find some way of assigning values to those entities not priced in this way. However, world market prices have arisen from different ways of valuing entities in local contexts and merely reflect their differential impact on overall demand. Such prices cannot provide what defenders of Equal Division need to determine which resource bundles have equal value.[22]

One might wonder whether the problem could be solved through an auction mechanism of the sort used by Ronald Dworkin (1981, 2000). Dworkin envisages a scenario in which a group of shipwrecked people enter an auction with the same number of shells to bid for resources. Participants calculate their demands at every price and submit the results to an auctioneer. The auctioneer sets the prices so that the demand across participants equals the amount of the goods. All shells are spent, and all goods clear. What individuals can acquire arises from how much others value the goods. But as Dworkin is aware, the applicability of this device presupposes facts about what kind of technology is available, how people choose to integrate it into their lives, and what rules determine what they can do with resources and technology. Dworkin's device therefore does not provide what defenders of Equal Division need.[23]

One might also object that I fail to do justice to Steiner (1994). Steiner aims to distribute *freedom* equally. He seeks to do so via two derivative principles of original ownership: self-ownership of persons and equal ownership of original resources, captured in terms of Equal Division. Equality of resources (equality of the current exchange value of individuals' current total holdings) is supposed to be *indicative* of equality of freedom. But we again encounter the problem that the value of any set of resources and spaces depends on preferences and judgments about what types of actions can be performed, as well as on the level of technology that generates those. These things indeed change over time in response to scientific advancement and cultural shifts. None of this is a problem if Steiner's view is appropriately limited in its application, as Dworkin's auction mechanism is limited to people who have much in common as far as scientific advancement and cultural parameters are concerned. But we cannot thereby establish Equal Division as a way of generating natural original ownership rights.

8. Centuries after Grotius and Locke, Bertrand Russell stated in "A Free Man's Worship" that a major component of an atheist's worldview was the realization that the world was not made for us (1919, 52). That a nuanced defense of humanity's collective ownership is available without insisting that the world was made for us is no small matter. (That is so even though philosophers like Grotius may not have thought divine revelation to be the only way of knowing about this ownership status.) Common Ownership, a rather minimal way of understanding what collective ownership amounts to, is its preferred conception. The following chapters develop its consequences.

Our findings contrast with the broadly egalitarian results with which I started to develop my pluralist view on the grounds of justice in part 1. As such a ground, collective ownership differs enormously in its implications from shared membership in a state. While the density of the relations of shared membership in a state creates strong principles of justice, there is little to say by way of formulating starting points that generate natural ownership rights. Within an intensely shared and jointly maintained social world, egalitarian pressures are considerably higher than for the natural world (but also, as we will see in part 3 of this book, higher than for those parts of our social world that are less intensely shared). We find that the following principle of justice is associated with collective ownership: The distribution of original resources and spaces of the earth among the global population is just only if everyone has the opportunity to use them to satisfy her or his basic needs, or otherwise lives under a property arrangement that provides the opportunity to satisfy basic needs. This principle is the pivotal result of part 2 of this book.

Much as in the case of human rights explored in chapter 4, one might say that it is not obvious that if there are natural ownership rights to X, it follows that there is a corresponding principle of justice. The response is the same: I agree with nonrelationists to the extent that I count humanity's collective ownership as a nonrelationist ground. Nonrelationism succeeds to the extent that it warrants an inclusion of common humanity and collective ownership as grounds in a theory of global justice. The considerations in support of collective ownership, I take it, also support my claim that pluralist internationalism should register collective ownership as a ground.

We have not yet addressed how advocates of Common Ownership should think about privatization. They could accept further-reaching natural rights with respect to these resources, including exclusive rights to bits of the earth arising from such actions as occupation, consent, and so on. Common Ownership merely states a set of natural rights people have regardless of actions they may have performed. Such a theory of privatization could not interfere with basic needs satisfaction, as I argued No Ownership without provisos might. This leaves space for a theory that falls short of such implications. I do not pursue this subject further here (though chapter 8 has more to say about it) except to remark that I doubt that strong natural ownership rights can plausibly be added to Common Ownership. Perhaps certain actions unilaterally generate rights that everybody should reasonably accept. But even if so, it would be hard to see how one could bequeath entitlements to people who have not performed the action in question.

One might *still* wonder if we do not plainly *need* some conception stronger than Common Ownership to give fair consideration to those bearing the consequences of appropriation. As an example, let us consider two groups of shipwrecked people on an island. One group occupies most of it, leaving just enough to the other group to satisfy basic needs. According to Common Ownership, this may not be unjust, which might seem counterintuitive. But Common Ownership does not demand of those left with little to acquiesce. As far as original ownership is concerned, they are justly entitled to taking holdings if the others do not use them to satisfy basic needs. Neither side commits an injustice, as far as those rights are concerned, either by appropriating much more than others or by not accepting this result. Nor would they in that sense commit an injustice if either side defended the exercise of their rights with force, if the force was limited to what was necessary to this defense. This analysis also applies to the thought experiment (in chapter 5) of the two people who control access to the United States via sophisticated border surveillance. They would not do anything unjust in terms of Common Ownership, but neither would others if they tried to dismantle the surveillance to enter the country.

While this seems right as far as natural ownership rights are concerned, we can also ask under what circumstances could both sides be *reasonably expected* to waive their liberty right to resources within, or entry to, a certain portion of three-dimensional space. Under what conditions could they not only attempt to control entrance to an area, but expect outsiders to accept exclusion? As concerns the group that occupies most of the island, we should say this: while it would not be unjust to exercise liberty rights in this way, it would be reasonable for the group to waive its rights, but unreasonable to expect others to suspend efforts to enter. Chapter 8 explores this matter systematically. For now the point is that Common Ownership does give appropriate consideration to individuals who bear the consequences of appropriation. It does so by allowing not only for judgments of "just" and unjust" but also for judgments in terms of what exercises or waivers of rights it is or is not reasonable to expect.

9. To conclude, I explore two of its implications to illustrate what kind of work Common Ownership does. Both illustrations refer to debates in the philosophical literature and can be safely skipped on a first reading. One implication is that a prominent version of left-libertarianism is incoherent.[24] Michael Otsuka (2003) combines a libertarian understanding of personhood with a broadly egalitarian view of original ownership, a version of No Ownership with provisos. However, my interest in Otsuka now concerns his manner of combining a *libertarian* understanding of personhood with *any kind* of view on the appropriation of external resources that requires consideration for others.

In this view of personhood, individuals have a right of self-ownership, which Otsuka understands as a conjunction over two rights (2003, 15):

1. A very stringent right of control over and use of one's mind and body that bars others from intentionally using one as a means by forcing one to sacrifice life, limb, or labor, where such force operates by means of incursions or threats of incursions upon one's mind and body (including assault and battery and forcible arrest, detention, and imprisonment).
2. A very stringent right to all of the income that one can gain from one's mind and body (including one's labor) either on one's own or through unregulated and untaxed voluntary exchanges with other individuals.

However, granting a "very stringent right to all of the income that one can gain from one's mind and body" is anathema to those endorsing the minimal solidarity involved in the acceptance of Common Ownership. One natural ownership right is an immunity from living under arrangements where an equal opportunity to satisfy basic needs is not realized. Once we endorse minimal solidarity, it does not matter as categorically as Otsuka assumes how we enable others to meet basic needs. One may still defend limits on redistribution, but would not take a rejection of redistribution as far as Otsuka.[25] As a view combining ideas of a common ownership of resources with ideas of personhood such that nobody is required to aid others, left-libertarianism is incoherent.

We would not need to argue for the superiority of Common Ownership over other conceptions if we could read this superiority off theological premises. We would then have to make no other commitments to exclude No Ownership, and we would be free to adopt views on personhood independently, or read those off theological premises, too. But outside of theology we must ask with regard to both our conception of collective ownership and our view of personhood why one would want to endorse *those* rather than plausible competitors. Otsuka's view brings the reasons required to maintain these views separately into a tension. Defenders of No Ownership with a proviso, such as Otsuka, wish to ensure nobody is *at a disadvantage* through other people's acquisitiveness. Disagreement remains about what proviso to adopt, and thus how to think about advantage. But why care about disadvantaging others at all? Kirzner and Rothbard have no qualms about disadvantaging people, insisting nobody is *entitled* to not being so treated. The reasons for endorsing any kind of proviso conflict with the reasons for endorsing the second bit of Otsuka's right to self-ownership. No unified stance endorses both.[26]

10. Another implication of Common Ownership concerns an argument in Thomas Pogge (2002) that the global order wrongfully harms the poor:[27]

> *Uncompensated Exclusion*: The better-off enjoy ample advantages in the use of a single natural resource base from whose benefits the worse-off are largely, and without compensation, excluded.

This view succeeds *only* if the natural resource base belongs to humankind collectively. Unless those barred from enjoying a share of resources have a legitimate claim, no violation occurs through unilateral appropriation. In light of Common Ownership, Uncompensated Exclusion is plausible only if one takes a particular viewpoint within the debate about the sources of prosperity we encountered in chapter 4.

Common Ownership implies that co-owners who unilaterally use resources do not owe compensation *merely* because others fail to do the same, or *merely* because they exploit particular resources that others do not find where they live. However, adversely affected parties have a valid complaint if they do not have what access they need to satisfy their basic needs. This would mean either that they are illegitimately prevented from using resources or otherwise harmed in the sense that their interests are thwarted by unilateral acquisition in a manner contrary to their status as co-owners. As far as the first condition is concerned, it has become rare that some societies keep others from extracting resources, or that countries own extraction facilities in colonies. Moreover, many of the poorest countries are resource-rich. This leaves us with the second condition.

We seek to identify a way in which interests are thwarted in a manner inconsistent with people's status as co-owners that can be ascribed to the global order rather than to specific countries. The most plausible way of spelling out Uncompensated Exclusion in that sense is that the global order wrongfully harms the poor because the relative economic standing of countries within it is fixed by the fact that some possess more useful resources than others, although humankind owns those resources collectively. Such a disadvantage for some through unilateral exploitation by others is said to inflict a wrong because all are co-owners.

We can readily rebut Uncompensated Exclusion by sticking to the notion of injustice delivered by Common Ownership. Common Ownership embodies such a minimal understanding of collective ownership that an injustice occurs only if individuals are prevented from satisfying basic needs to the extent that this turns on external resources. In section 8, however, we encountered a different way of inquiring about the compatibility of certain actions or states of affairs with Common Ownership, namely, to ask about the conditions under which individuals could reasonably be expected to waive their liberty rights. That is the kind of inquiry we are now conducting.

Implicit in my way of spelling out Uncompensated Exclusion is

Resource Significance: Resources are crucial for countries' wealth.

Unless Resource Significance holds, Uncompensated Exclusion fails to show that the global order harms by wronging co-owners. Resource Significance is not a necessary condition for the success of the harm claim made by Uncompensated Exclusion if we adopt either Joint Ownership or Equal Division; but it is if we adopt Common Ownership. Recall now these views about the sources of prosperity from chapter 4:

> *Institutions:* Growth and prosperity depend on the quality of institutions, such as stable property rights, the rule of law, bureaucratic capacity, the existence of appropriate regulatory structures to curtail at least the worst forms of fraud, anticompetitive behavior, graft, and the quality and independence of courts, but also the cohesiveness of society, the existence of trust and social cooperation, and thus the overall quality of civil society.
>
> *Geography:* Growth and prosperity are primarily determined by factors such as location, climate, resource endowment, disease burden, and thus agricultural productivity, the quality of human resources, and transportation costs.
>
> *Integrations:* Growth and prosperity are primarily determined by world market integration.

If Integration holds, a country's wealth level does not crucially turn on resource endowment. A country may offer to the market what it has a comparative advantage to do, which may be tourism, manufacturing, or services. A similar argument holds for Institutions. Arguably, only Geography supports Resource Significance. So one must endorse Geography for Uncompensated Exclusion to show that the global order wrongfully harms the poor. The institutional stance that I adopted in chapter 4 implies that Uncompensated Exclusion fails.

CHAPTER 7

Toward a Contingent Derivation of Human Rights

1. Chapters 7–10 discuss various topics from the standpoint of Common Ownership: human rights, immigration, duties to future generations, and duties arising from climate change. In preparation, and with the benefit of our discussion in chapter 6, this chapter begins by exploring the role that reflection about original ownership can play in political philosophy. The remainder makes a connection between collective ownership of the earth and human rights.

Let me elaborate on three themes to help illuminate the nature of our subsequent inquiries and thus the philosophical interest in collective ownership. To begin, there are two reasons why we should explore the relevance for moral argument of the contingent fact that every satisfaction of a human need depends on some use of the resources and spaces of this planet. First, such reasoning adds in important ways to what we can derive from the significance of basic needs alone. Recognizing the significance of basic needs does not readily deliver conclusions about precisely what is demanded of people. We saw in chapter 4 that inquiries about duties in virtue of basic needs—and duties in virtue of common humanity more generally—face a *boundary problem*. It is hard to assess not only how imposing these duties are but also, and more important now, *precisely what their content is*. Integrating the aforementioned contingent fact allows us to add specificity. This should be plausible enough: we have *more* to work with than merely the significance of human need.

The second reason is that we increasingly confront problems that concern our use of the earth as such, or that affect us not as members of certain communities, but as inhabitants of the earth. Climate change is the obvious example of such a problem. For instance, the preamble of the 1992 United Nations Framework Convention on Climate Change begins by acknowledging that "change in the Earth's climate and its adverse effects are a common concern of humankind." But we must also think here of certain threats to all life on earth, threats that in our planet's approximately 4.5 billion years of history have indeed materialized and, during certain periods, massively affected all existing life. Asteroids that are traveling somewhere in outer space might collide with the earth. When such asteroids are detected far in advance, we might be able to take measures to change their trajectories. However, efforts at detecting such objects and at changing their trajectories would require (or in any event would considerably benefit from) coordinated efforts. If larger asteroids do hit the earth, the consequences might be (and in the distant past may have been) apocalyptic and lead to the extinction of many, most, or conceivably all forms of life. Other threats to the basic conditions of life that make the existence of humankind possible include massive volcanic eruptions that are discontinuous with the kind of eruptions that has occurred in the last several thousand years, as well as solar storms that might have unprecedented effects on the earth's magnetic field and thus cause massive disruption to all major means of communication. These storms would travel from the sun to the earth too fast and with too much force for us to intercept them. But within limits it is possible to prepare for such events. The same is true for massive volcanic eruptions.

What these problems have in common is that they do confront us as inhabitants of this planet with the planet's current climate conditions, so friendly to the ongoing existence of human life. There were good reasons why theorizing collective ownership was pivotal to political thought in the seventeenth century. After all, at that time humanity had to confront political and economic questions that were of genuinely *global* reach. Such problems we continue to encounter. But in addition, we also have a much higher degree of scientific awareness of dangers that threaten the stability of the conditions that make our existence on this planet possible to begin with and that thus compel us to recognize common concerns we have as inhabitants of the earth. So it does indeed behoove us to theorize collective ownership, and to theorize it separately especially from the distinctively human life.

The second and related theme on which I would like to elaborate concerns the relationship between inquiries into collective ownership and inquiries into the nature of moral discourse. Much contemporary moral and political philosophy reflects on rather foundational matters that have *no* clear-cut implications for relatively concrete issues in the domain of justice or elsewhere ("what ought to be done about such and such?"). To be sure, philosophical inquiry can the more readily present concrete policy advice the more decidedly it is biased toward the status quo and the more willingly it takes its cues for what is right and wrong from observing what is widely believed. And these are precisely the kinds of concessions that philosophers normally are, and should be, unwilling to make. Nonetheless, my approach involves relatively less abstract characterizations of different grounds of justice and so is more likely to have at least somewhat more concrete implications than inquiries into the nature of moral discourse. This is true especially for collective ownership of the earth.

The idea that individuals are owners of sorts (even for a very abstract idea of ownership) has no priority as a *fundamental* characterization of moral agency over ideas of persons as self-governing or self-authenticating sources of claims, or as possessing basic moral powers, and so on. But not only do such ideas often fail to have reasonably concrete implications (as we noted for the significance of basic needs); given the *elementary* nature of the premises deployed in defense of Common Ownership, we can also be more certain of the adequacy of an account of original ownership than of the success of broader characterizations of moral discourse. We can be more certain of that success *even though* it comes with challenges of its own.[1]

Third, in light of what I said about this second theme, let me distinguish between two kinds of inquiry. First, we can ask what principles of justice follow from Common Ownership, and what obligations follow in turn from those. We started to do this in chapter 6. This line of inquiry is most central to this book. Second, we can also ask whether there are any weaker demands that apply to individuals as co-owners, short of obligations of justice. Let us say that anything that can reasonably be expected of us is a "demand of reasonable conduct." "There is a demand of reasonable conduct on person P to perform action A" is then equivalent to "P can be reasonably expected to do A," as well as to "It would be unreasonable for P not to do A." Obligations of justice are demands of reasonable conduct, and particularly stringent ones, but they are not the only ones. While it must be explained why considerations are reasonably acceptable, beyond what I say about the grounds of justice I do not offer foundations to illuminate the nature of such acceptability (which would be foundations of moral discourse as such). Many of my arguments in such contexts will be driven by what fits best with intuitions about demands of reasonable conduct when those are applied to problems that we can frame within the ownership approach and that substantively turn on collective ownership.

Within discussions about the relationship of being co-owners, "right" and "wrong" are used in a capacious sense: actions may be right in the sense of just (required by obligations of justice) or in the sense of "what (only) can reasonably be expected," and similarly for wrong. Chapter 9 introduces an account of right and wrong in terms of legitimate expectations within relationships. Among those who stand in the relationship of sharing a ground of justice (such as collective ownership), such legitimate expectations may include both demands of justice and other demands of reasonable conduct. The possibility of distinguishing between inquiries about justice and inquiries about reasonable acceptability among those who stand in the relationship of sharing this ground increases the fruitfulness of the standpoint of Common Ownership.[2]

Grotius too occasionally mentions an idea of equity beyond what we can capture in terms of just and unjust by reference to original ownership. There is room for social criticism if private property is not arranged in a manner that takes seriously the original moral equality. Also, Grotius endorses several laws of nature, in addition to the divine gift of the earth. I differ from Grotius in the following ways. First, I offer arguments in support of collective ownership that dispense with theology. Second, I do not offer an account of the laws of nature to embed my inquiry into a larger moral framework. Instead, I have offered an account of the distinctively human life as a basis for human rights.

Let me preview the results of the upcoming chapters. In chapter 6 we found the following principle associated with collective ownership: the distribution of original resources and spaces of the earth among the global population is just only if everyone has the opportunity to use them to satisfy her or his basic needs, or otherwise lives under a property arrangement that provides the opportunity to satisfy basic needs. That principle is the pivotal result of part 2 of this book. This chapter presents another principle associated with collective ownership: the distribution of original resources and spaces of the earth among the global population is just only if everyone's membership rights in the global order are satisfied. That principle derives from the principle in chapter 6 given the existence of the global order.

In chapter 9 we encounter an additional principle of justice: the distribution of the original resources and spaces of the earth across different generations of human beings is just only if everyone has the opportunity to use them to satisfy her or his basic needs, or otherwise lives under a property arrangement that provides the opportunity to satisfy basic needs. Chapter 9 develops a framework that makes it possible to consider future generations explicitly and presents two future-directed obligations of justice. Finally, in chapter 10 we find that, as an obligation of justice, regulating access to the absorptive capacity of the earth is required to make sure the basic climate conditions of the earth are preserved. This obligation follows from the principle in chapter 6 in light of the particular nature of the absorptive capacity.

We also encounter several demands of reasonable conduct. My proposal for immigration in chapter 8 formulates conditions under which it would be reasonable for co-owners to refrain from entering certain regions, even though they would violate no duties of justice by doing so. Chapter 9 argues for a principle of intergenerational equality: each generation can be reasonably expected to leave a nondeclining stock of natural capital behind. Finally, chapter 10 argues that access to the absorptive capacity of the earth ought to be regulated by a *fair-division scheme*. It is an obligation of justice that access to that capacity be regulated, and it is a demand of reasonable conduct that such regulation be done by a fair-division scheme.

2. The remainder of this chapter links three ideas: collective ownership of the earth, membership rights in the global order, and human rights. Collective ownership leads to a conception of *associative* rights for whose protection there is a global rather than merely national responsibility. It is appropriate to think of rights thus derived as human rights, which leads to a conception of human rights as membership rights in the global order. Section 2 explains why certain responsibilities apply at the level of the global order to make its imposition acceptable to co-owners. Section 3 changes perspectives and explains why such responsibilities correspond to rights of individuals against the global order. I explore what rights we can obtain in this way. Natural ownership rights are the logical foundation of these associative rights. Section 4 introduces the idea of membership in the global order, as well as the corresponding notion of membership rights. The rights in section 3 are such rights. Membership rights in the global order provide us with a basis-driven conception of human rights. Sections 5 and 6 explain why it makes sense to think of such rights as human rights and illuminate the nature of this conception. In this chapter, then, I start developing the conception of human rights that I propose in this book. In chapter 11 we see that the conception from chapter 4 can be integrated into that conception.[3]

One topic on which this chapter has little to say is how to distribute global responsibilities among different entities in the global order. My emphasis is on the state. While non-state actors can also violate human rights, I neglect this subject here. Chapter 11 returns to these matters. Section 7 reconnects our discussion to the subject of justice and introduces another principle associated with collective ownership. Section 8 offers a case study in how to apply the machinery I have introduced. Our question is whether inhabitants of disappearing island nations have a human right to relocation. Finally, sections 9 and 10 provide an additional motivation for the importance of Common Ownership to political philosophy, drawing on Rawls's *Political Liberalism*. This discussion involves an analogy between Rawls's principles of justice and my conception of human rights.

To begin the discussion, let us note that the imposition of a system of states that divides up the world's resources and spaces must be reconciled with Common Ownership. First, each state imposes a complex system of political and economic relationships that determines what original resources individuals can access. Second, a system of states imposes a pattern of ownership whereby groups claim (group-specific) collective ownership for certain regions. Co-owners are excluded from exercising rights with regard to much of what is collectively owned. In virtue of the concentrations of power that it includes, a state system can readily violate rights of co-owners, first by undermining their opportunities to satisfy basic needs where they live, and second by impeding their ability to relocate.[4]

Common Ownership grants individuals an immunity right against living under political and economic arrangements that interfere with *those subject to them* having opportunities to satisfy their basic needs. The arrangement to which individuals are subject is not merely the state in which they live but the global order. Each state, in virtue of its access to their bodies and assets, might deprive individuals of opportunities, but so, crucially, might other states, by refusing them entry if they cannot satisfy basic needs where they live. When individuals cannot satisfy basic needs where they live, other states that could provide this ability but refuse would not merely fail to offer aid, they would deny them the opportunity to satisfy needs. If there are multiple states that a needy person might reach, no single state refusing entry would deny the opportunity to satisfy needs. Each state merely eliminates one option from the set. But *collectively* they deny the opportunity to satisfy basic needs.

One might say that individuals who are threatened where they live do not generally have an opportunity to seek entry elsewhere, and therefore such states would indeed merely fail to aid those people. But this underdescribes the extent to which a state system based on inviolability of territory contributes to such predicaments. Were our world no longer committed to such principles and were rich states more inclined to admit people whose ability to make a living is threatened in their country of origin, organizations would spring up that specialized in making sure people reach such destinations. People would pledge future income to purchase such services, or charitable organizations would help.

The point noted in the preceding paragraph also responds to the following objection: "The argument above identified two ways in which the state system threatens the ability of co-owners to satisfy basic needs, first by the threat that their own state will interfere, second by the threat that other states will stop them from moving somewhere else. One can readily see why obligations relating to the latter threat (concerning matters of immigration) are global responsibilities, but why should obligations relating to the first threat be?" The response is that people would indeed more readily leave places where they cannot satisfy basic needs if we did not live in a world that severely limits such moves. The two scenarios— people being threatened at home and being unable to move elsewhere— are closely related. Or might also object as follows: Suppose we own a boat together and somebody interferes with your use of it. This would not mean I have to stop that interference or else let you use the boat when I am entitled to use it. But this is a wrong comparison. If we own the boat in common and this situation arises, *and we are all in the boat*, you would have to give me refuge as long as the boat does not capsize.

Ownership rights are pre-institutional. Guarantees must be given to co-owners that institutional power will not be used to violate their status. Responsibilities must be allocated at the level of the state system per se, as collective responsibilities, rather than resting exclusively with individual states, and then only with regard to their citizens. Let me recast the conclusion of this section in terms of rights of individuals. The flip side of the obligations to individuals on the part of institutions that we just discussed is a set of rights of individuals vis-à-vis the global order. Their logical foundation is that they can be derived from natural ownership rights in conjunction with contingent facts about how the world works. We can note already that these rights must be *associative* rights of sorts—rights that hold because individuals live within a particular association, the global political and economic order.

3. So let us change perspectives and think about the matter at hand from the standpoint of rights of individuals. To this end, we envisage individuals with common ownership rights who live under the global order. We then ask what protection they must have for their status as co-owners to be preserved. A necessary condition for the acceptability of property conventions (which I take to be sufficiently inclusive to capture the existence of state boundaries) is that the core purpose of original liberty and claims rights is met, to preserve the ability of co-owners to meet basic needs. This leads to two fundamental guarantees that states and other powerful organizations owe to individuals, guarantees whose realization is a global responsibility: first, they must ensure that their power does not render individuals incapable of meeting basic needs; second, they must create opportunities for them to meet basic needs. I assume that such opportunities are assessed vis-à-vis standards of "normal species functioning," as found in the normative literature on health care (e.g., Daniels 1985). Assessing what amount of opportunities individuals must have to satisfy basic needs by way of reference to what it takes to reach standards of normalcy, we can avoid complications from the fact that handicapped people can make only limited use of opportunities. Such guarantees neutralize the dangers that the global order poses for individuals' co-ownership status.

Let us first discuss the demand that states and other powerful organizations not render individuals incapable of meeting basic needs. On a narrow reading, this generates only a very small set of rights: basic rights to life (a right not to be killed) and bodily integrity. Occasional nonincapacitating torture, say, or arbitrary arrests without grave consequences are consistent with such protection. Yet according to a broader reading, rights provide more *robust* protection. We should adopt this broader view. After all, we are assessing what set of associative rights should protect a bundle of natural rights of vital importance, rights needed to ensure individuals can meet basic needs. But in the pre-institutional scenario where these rights hold, no agent is as powerful as the state. It is in light of the power of states and of the importance of the rights that are at stake that control mechanisms must be imposed especially on states to ensure that the individuals' status as original co-owners prevails. The permanence and reliability of that protection matter critically.[5]

On this broader reading, co-ownership status is not preserved merely if it so happens that states do not render individuals incapable of meeting basic needs. States must be *bound* to refrain from doing so. Their power must be limited so that they cannot simply elect to become abusive. Adding ideas of robustness responds to the nature of the state as a powerful agent, one that (generically, ignoring phenomena such as failed states) is not only overwhelmingly more powerful than individuals but is organized in complex ways that might generate abuse in many forms. Rights provide limited protection against this possibility. Still, ensuring that individuals are *robustly* protected in light of the dangers posed by the state system requires such constraints, although we cannot achieve perfect protection.

On this view of what it is to preserve the co-ownership status, the set of rights we can derive from the demand that political and economic organizations not render individuals incapable of meeting basic needs is obviously larger than on the narrow reading. Precisely which rights this reasoning delivers, however, is much harder to assess. Robust protection of individuals can be obtained in two ways. First of all, one can empower the individuals themselves so that they can hold powerful entities accountable. Second, one can constrain the exercise of power so that powerful entities do not develop practices that readily become abusive. Much social scientific and historical investigation is needed to fix a precise list. What is plausible, however, is that to the rights to life and bodily integrity (which on this broader reading we must also understand more comprehensively) we must add individual liberties (e.g., freedom from forced labor, freedom of conscience, freedom of expression and association, freedom of movement, and freedom to emigrate), as well as political rights (e.g., to accountable representation) and due process rights (e.g., to a fair trial).

In addition to ensuring that the power of states and other organizations is not used to render individuals incapable of meeting basic needs, such organizations must provide opportunities for individuals at least to meet basic needs. Everybody must have the opportunity to enjoy a minimally adequate standard of living as far as food, clothing, and housing are concerned. Property conventions that provide for exclusive rights of access might make it impossible for individuals to satisfy basic needs through original resources. To make this acceptable to co-owners, they must have other ways of doing so. Here, too, a broader understanding of rights suggests itself, at least in societies with sophisticated economies that make it difficult to satisfy needs without actively participating in society. An elementary right to education and a right to work, understood as a right not to be excluded from labor markets, can be supported within such societies (see also chapter 13). Such rights constitute robust protection of rights to food, clothing, and housing.

4. Chapter 4 discussed the concept of human rights and introduced the notion of a conception of such rights.[6] I also explored there a conception based on the idea of a distinctively human life. This chapter has begun work on another conception, also basis-driven, the basis being *membership in the global order*. Human rights as membership rights in the global order are derived from different *sources*, one of which is collective ownership of the earth. Recall that orthodox conceptions do not appeal to contingencies other than laws of nature, general facts about human nature, or the fact that certain beings are human. A conception of human rights in terms of membership in the global order uses contingent facts more freely (by way of enlisting features of an empirically contingent but relatively abiding world order). This conception is basis-driven but is not orthodox.

Let me elaborate on this idea of membership in the global order. Chapter 1 showed that it makes sense to talk about a global order that includes but is not reducible to actions of states; has arisen through a history of interferences; has generated institutions charged with global problem-solving; and continues to evolve. Two things matter now. First, the major actors within this system are *interconnected*, influencing each other's trajectory through political and economic interaction as well as through legal or cultural channels. The way in which states have spread, and the fact that now most of the land masses are indeed governed by states, rather than other possible and historically existent structures that have been replaced as part of the spread of European forms of organization, strikingly testify to such influence. Moreover, today, events and decisions elsewhere shape the incentives and prospects of governments, companies, and other agents. This is true also of large powers, as shown by the extent to which fear of terrorism guides current U.S. foreign policy.

Second, there is a point to speaking of "membership rights" in this order. Being a member means to live on the territory covered by it and to be subject to those bits of this interlocking system of jurisdictions that apply to one's situation. Nothing more is meant by membership. Today all humans are members in this broad sense. Membership rights in the global order are rights held vis-à-vis that order. Enough structures to render the term "global order" applicable, as well as an accompanying capacity for coordinated action, is a condition for the existence of rights held within that order. Indeed, there is enough structure because of the existence of organizations that are designed for, and concern themselves with, global problem solving (as indicated by names such as World Trade Organization or World Bank). Here we may think of the world population as contained in a large set, and of the global order as captured by relations among its elements. All citizens of a country stand in one such relation, all persons whose countries are in the WTO in another, and so forth. Membership rights in this order are rights persons hold qua members of this set with those structures imposed, where differentiations matter for the assignment of responsibilities.

Talk about membership might cause concerns. One might worry that membership rights will not apply to everybody. What, say, of North Korea? However, individuals are co-owners of the earth and are therefore at least potentially constrained by the imposition of the state system even if they do not feel the constraints. They are therefore members in my sense. Involvement with organizations of global reach, especially inclusion in these organizations of the countries where individuals live, is not required for membership in the global order. The existence of such organizations serves to rebut the objection that there is insufficient structure for talk of membership rights to apply.

Alongside Thomas Pogge (2009), one might nonetheless worry that my conception at least triggers unwelcome debates about who precisely is a member. (Would Palestinians be members? Would it not be tempting for some to press that question?) Membership language lends itself to political manipulation. However, first, *natural* rights individuals hold qua humans enter this account, namely, qua ownership rights. Moreover, in chapter 11, when we explore other sources of membership rights in the global order, I integrate the idea of a distinctively human life as a source into my conception. Second, for *any* basis it is possible, and politically expedient for some, to doubt that some people are properly regarded as human rights holders. In the sixteenth century, when European intellectuals processed the conquest of America, Francisco de Vitoria had to address the view that Native Americans could not hold rights because they could not govern themselves. Natives, he originally wrote in 1532,

> have order in their affairs; they have properly organized cities, proper marriages, and overlords, laws, industries, and commerce.... They likewise have a form of religion, and they correctly apprehend things which are evident to other men, which indicates the use of reason. (*De Indis*, 1991, q.1, a. 6; 1991, 250)

Vitoria's opponents used phenotypic and cultural differences to argue that some were not human "in the right away" to hold rights. Centuries later, Jorge Luis Borges's short story "Deutsches Requiem" has a Nazi officer reflect on his life on the eve of his execution. "Nazism," he believes, "is intrinsically a *moral* act, a stripping away of the old man, which is corrupt and depraved, in order to put on the new" (Borges 1998, 231). What underlies this thought is the view that some persons have obtained levels of physical, mental, and cultural perfection compared to which others merely pass as depraved. Alleged inferiors could not appeal to the idea of human rights to seek protection from their oppressors because, like, allegedly, the American natives, they would not be human "in the right way."[7] The potential for such approaches and debates arises since complex assumptions about what it is to be human factor into a conception of human rights that turns on the idea of a distinctively human life. In light of my thin understanding of membership in the global order, it is certainly *no easier* to trigger such debates about that idea.

Let me elaborate on the distinctions among "source," "basis," and "ground." "Ground" relates to principles of justice, while the other two terms relate to conceptions of human rights. Within such conceptions, asking about a *basis* means asking about what features turn individuals into rights holders. The conception I am now exploring is basis-driven, the basis being membership in the global order. But membership rights can be derived from different *sources*. They vary in nature, but each generates rights that do not merely apply to individuals where they live but are global in reach. (To wit: there are rather different ways in which matters may be of global urgency and take on the form of a right, which are the defining features of this conception of human rights.) So the basis of this conception is actually a disjunction over different sources. Sources, too, are bases, given how Chapter 4 defines the term. But they are bases that are most plausibly understood as being integrated into another basis in this disjunctive way. This chapter discusses only collective ownership. Chapter 11 explores additional sources, one of which is the distinctively human life.

5. But why would it be plausible to think of such membership rights as *human rights*? Drawing a connection between collective ownership and human rights, although mediated through membership in the global order, might seem rather odd. However, lest one think this approach is excessively capitalist or materialist, misses the spirit of the human rights movement, or obviously mislocates the concern behind human rights, I recall here that at stake is ownership of "our sole habitation ... in which we live and move and have our being" (Passmore 1974, 3).

Many will think a conception of human rights must focus entirely on what it means to hold rights in virtue of being human. The conception in chapter 4 did just that. However, this is not the only way of developing the concept of a human right. During the drafting of the Universal Declaration of Human Rights, the UNESCO sent a questionnaire to intellectuals around the world. Political scientist Quincy Wright began his response by saying, "Human rights suggest rights which are alike for all human beings" (1949, 143). This apt formulation suggests that it is not necessary to understand human rights as rights individuals have "in virtue of being human." Instead of referring to the source of validity of human rights ("in virtue of being human"), the term "human" could refer plainly to the scope of application of the idea of "human rights."[8] Understanding human rights as membership rights in the global order is one possibility of thinking of them that way, and in chapter 11 I argue that the conception based on the idea of the distinctively human life should be integrated into this conception.

There are distinctive virtues to approaching human rights the way I do here. One concern about human rights is the problem of parochialism, the question of how such rights can plausibly be of global reach and justify actions also against societies whose culture does not support those rights, or impose duties on those who had no role in causing the problem at hand. The way of connecting collective ownership, human rights, and membership in the global order that I develop here shows why talk about *rights* (rather than values or goals) is appropriate, and locates a nonparochial source of human rights in plausible and elementary starting points.

The defining feature of human rights in my conception—which is not already part of the concept of human rights—is that such rights are important moral demands (which assume the form of rights) against authority as it applies to individuals in their immediate environment and that are at the same time also *matters of urgent global concern*. For a right to X to be a human right, it cannot just be a right vis-à-vis the person's own state but must also be a right vis-à-vis the global order, and the global order must have obligations that go distinctly beyond mere nonviolation. To put it in terms of duties, for a right to X to be a human right, it must involve duties (beyond nonviolation) on the part of entities in the global order other than a person's own state. Chapter 11 offers a view about how to think about the division of obligations among different entities in the global order, and different sources of human rights explain different ways in which something can be of global concern.

To argue that X is a human right, what is required in a first, preliminary step is that X be shown to be a matter of importance in the affected agents' immediate environment, and then, second, that a genuinely global concern can be established. (It is hard to imagine that anything could be of global concern for which one cannot take that first step, and often that step will be obvious; but what is constitutive of X's being a human right is the second step.) In the process one must also show why what is at issue is appropriately captured *as a right*. Collective ownership is one source from which we can obtain such global relevance.[9]

Contrast this with Joshua Cohen's (2004, 2006) conception of human rights in terms of membership rights in a political society. Cohen's notion of membership is that

> a person's good is to be taken into account by the political society's basic institutions: to be treated as a member is to have one's good given due consideration, both in the processes of arriving at authoritative collective decisions and in the content of those decisions. (2006, 237–38)

Human rights then are rights individuals hold in their respective communities to be assured of inclusion. In my conception some rights that ensure inclusion in political communities are the global order's responsibility, but via additional argument. For individuals everywhere to have a claim to something vis-à-vis their respective community is insufficient for this to be a claim of urgent concern to people everywhere and to global institutions. The difference between these kinds of membership captures an ambiguity that permeates human rights talk (and whose existence supports pluralism about conceptions of human rights), namely, whether such rights in the first instance apply *to each individual* or else are *of global relevance*, with accompanying responsibilities for entities other than a person's own state that go beyond nonviolation. If one considers the first stance primary, the challenge becomes to explain to what extent others far away should have responsibilities regarding all these rights; if one considers the second stance primary, the question becomes how much of fundamental importance to persons can be incorporated.[10]

My conception recognizes the normative importance of global interconnectedness, an increasingly tightly structured world in which humans influence each other in ways beyond the possibilities of earlier ages. The emergence of a global order within which it makes sense to speak of membership rights marks a crucial change in world history, a process that has created new entitlements of people vis-à-vis each other. Contemporary human rights culture is *not simply* the continuation of trends with a far older pedigree, including the natural rights tradition, which reaches back to medieval jurists. But it is *also* that, and my conception recognizes this by giving pride of place to natural rights (ownership rights), as well as by endorsing the idea of a distinctively human life as another source of rights (see chapter 11). It should also be noted that rights could become of global concern only because they have long been of concern in other contexts where authority is exercised. Persons did have at least some of those rights before there was a global order, but not in virtue of membership in it.

6. Questions about the "fit" between the conception of human rights as membership rights in the global order and the rights in the UN's Universal Declaration and other human rights instruments are premature. This chapter looks only at one source of membership rights. Nonetheless, since we are exploring the plausibility of the connection between human rights and collective ownership, let me pursue this question just for this source. The fundamental guarantees states owe to individuals generate two sets of rights—liberties and political rights, on the one hand, and social economic rights on the other, broadly speaking—that together go far in securing human rights as they are ordinarily conceived. However, there are limits to the fit between the Universal Declaration and the rights we can derive from this source. Many of the rights in the declaration that do not register in this account can be derived as rights of citizens in a state, given the account of shared membership in chapter 2. People have these rights *everywhere qua citizens*. But this is insufficient to make them membership rights in the global order, and thus *human rights*.

To decide whether X can be derived from Common Ownership, we must explore whether states could robustly protect individuals' ability to meet basic needs without endorsing X. Again, assessing whether a state that does not endorse X would also be prone to violating common ownership rights may involve social scientific investigations and historical judgments (since it involves assessing causal mechanisms). The verdict may well be tentative. What is safe to say is that this approach will not deliver rights associated with liberal democracy, the secular state, or the value of equality (which are also beyond the scope of what we could derive from the idea of a distinctively human life). These rights belong squarely to the realm of the *rights of citizens*.

As far as social and economic rights are concerned, this approach will not deliver a right to work as a right to be treated in certain ways at the workplace or to join trade unions, let alone a right that the state provide employment, or one to periodic holidays with pay, a right to education directed at personality development (rather than ability to participate in the economy), or a right to enjoy the arts and to share in scientific advancement. A human right to even basic health care is also hard to justify from this source. Access to such care does not turn on access to original resources as much as access, say, to food or shelter does but instead rests more on access to artifacts and human ingenuity. The rights mentioned in this paragraph are not needed to neutralize the state system's ability to interfere with individuals' co-ownership status. There is too little entitlement in that status to begin with.

Let us discuss a problematic scenario to show what is at stake. Suppose rights to life and bodily integrity are robustly protected, even though no additional rights apply to everybody. Let us consider a form of slavery that (perhaps for religious reasons, and thus enduringly) is tightly regulated so that slaves suffer no bodily harm. They must be taken care of, but nonetheless are kept *as* slaves. This example explores a logical possibility that creates difficulties for my account, but whose features are stipulated to serve that purpose. In the *extremely unlikely* case that protection in such a scenario is robust, it would not be counterintuitive to say there should be less international concern with this case than otherwise.[11] In any event, while other sources from which one may derive human rights do turn this matter into a global concern (see chapter 11), collective ownership does not.

Or consider a human right to democracy (understood broadly enough that it does not include a commitment to rights I earlier argued cannot be accommodated by this conception). One might say a right to democracy should not be a human right in the view I develop because nondemocratic states might ensure individuals can meet basic needs. But can they do so *robustly*? A right to representation emerges more readily than a right to democracy. However, a problem of demarcation arises with any basis- or principle-driven conception. In light of the extent to which a human right to democracy is disputed, it is unsurprising that it is the kind of right that emerges in a gray zone in my approach. A right to democracy must, of course, also be discussed from the standpoint of other sources of membership rights.

Since I regard membership rights in the global order as human rights, one might worry about the fact that rights derived from the demand that political and economic organizations not render individuals incapable of meeting basic needs have an *instrumental* status. However, this derivative status does not show that we can say nothing else about their importance. (We can deploy the machinery from chapter 2 to argue for such rights as citizens' rights.) It is their status *as* membership rights in the global order, and so the claim that these rights are *global concerns,* that receives an instrumental justification. It is unproblematic that some membership rights emerge as supremely important, whereas others obtain their status as rights instrumental to the realization of supremely important rights. These rights would be instrumental not only to the realization of needs but to the acceptability of states.[12]

7. This chapter has linked three ideas: collective ownership, membership in the global order, and human rights. I have begun to introduce a basis-driven conception of human rights (the conception this book proposes), membership in the global order being that basis. The set of such *associative* rights is partially generated by natural ownership rights, collective ownership being one source of those rights. The presence of political and

economic structures requires guarantees to ensure original ownership rights prevail. Membership rights provide these guarantees. Since it is the global order that poses this threat, rather than merely the states in which individuals happen to live, responsibility for these rights is located at the global level (with accompanying differential responsibilities), given that there is enough structure to the global order for it to be meaningful to say that individuals hold rights in virtue of being members in the global order. Naturally, we must ask whether there are other ways of deriving membership rights, other *sources* of such rights. Chapter 11 does so. This part 2 of the book inquires only about collective ownership.

Let me reconnect our discussion to global justice. In a world of states that reserve the right to keep people from entering, respect for Common Ownership rights *as a matter of justice* entails collective responsibilities. Pluralist internationalism registers the following principle as associated with collective ownership as a ground: the distribution of original resources and spaces of the earth among the global population is just only if everyone's membership rights are satisfied. This principle follows from the pivotal one in chapter 6 ("The distribution of original resources and spaces of the earth among the global population is just only if everyone has the opportunity to use them to satisfy her or his basic needs, or otherwise lives under a property arrangement that provides the opportunity to satisfy basic needs") *given* the existence of the global order. At the level of duties, we obtain: human rights understood as membership rights in the global order (to the extent that we can derive them from collective ownership) ought to be realized.

This new principle of justice that I just derived applies globally (contra the statists), but it is not as egalitarian as principles that hold within states, and not as egalitarian as globalists or nonrelationists would like. I am not claiming that, were there no global order, there would be a right to an institutional order to ensure basic needs were met. Common Ownership cannot generate such a right. My derivation of human rights is contingent in the sense that I presuppose the existence of a global order and assess the impact of this fact given Common Ownership.

8. To apply my conception of human rights, let me explore whether inhabitants of disappearing island nations have a human right to relocation.[13] Straddling the equator, the nation of Kiribati consists of thirty-three coral atolls spread over 3.5 million square kilometers in the Pacific. Rising sea levels and salination caused by climate change might make the islands uninhabitable. As a consequence, Anote Tong, Kiribati's president, proposed scattering his people of about 100,000 throughout the world.[14] Other small-island and low-lying coastal countries face similar problems.

In 1990, many such countries formed the Alliance of Small Island States (AOSIS), one of whose purposes is to articulate concerns about climate change. The main thrust of their interventions has been to insist on the urgency of climate change mitigation, rather than the sort of adaptation advocated by Tong. But his proposal was cautiously endorsed in the Niue Declaration on Climate Change in 2008.

That inhabitants of Kiribati ought not be left to drown is morally over-determined. Still, it is illuminating to see precisely what reasoning bears on this matter, and specifically how it engages my conception of human rights. Again, states and other powerful organizations must offer guarantees to neutralize the dangers imposed on co-owners by the global order. One such danger is that the existence of states limits opportunities to move elsewhere if individuals cannot make a living where they are located. If areas are lost to sea-level rise, there is no longer a way of respecting the troubled party's co-ownership rights by helping the inhabitants make a living in their current location. The only way of respecting these rights is to permit immigration. For Grotius, rights of necessity prevail over property arrangements. In the present view, the rights of "submerged" people take precedence over the preferences of others to keep migrants out.

So there is a human right to relocation. It even includes a demand on host countries to put new immigrants in a position to make a living. Whether my approach supports Tong's wish for his people to move to the same location we cannot know without further investigations that reveal which countries over- or underuse three-dimensional spaces (to use terms developed in chapter 8). If countries underuse their resources and spaces to such an extent that the whole population can be admitted, Tong's people have such a claim vis-à-vis those countries. However, such a claim has a weaker status than the basic claim of each to emigrate somewhere. The latter is a question of human rights and justice, the former a matter of demands of reasonable conduct. But it is possible also that one country may accept them all as a way of discharging its required contributions to climate change adaptation (see chapter 10).[15]

9. Let me conclude this chapter with a different topic. Now that I have offered a derivation of membership rights in the global order, we can see the relevance of the ownership standpoint in a new way, in a manner that draws on John Rawls's *Political Liberalism*. Published about twenty years after *A Theory of Justice*, *Political Liberalism* takes a constitutional democracy as given and develops ideas implicit in it, deriving principles of justice from ideas implicit in its political culture. The ownership perspective allows us to see a parallel situation at the global level. Just as it is implicit in constitutional democracies that individuals are considered free

and equal citizens, so it is implicit in the global order that individuals are seen as co-owners. And just as principles of domestic justice make states acceptable to such citizens, so human rights make the global order acceptable to co-owners. The rest of this chapter develops this parallel.

Moral theories, we can say, drawing on Bernard Williams (2005c), must adopt a view of persons that is either factual or normative. A liberal theory may, empirically, see persons as autonomous choosers. But opponents (say, fundamentalists) see persons differently, say, as creatures of divine grace whose fates are ill-understood as resulting from autonomous choice. It seems practically impossible to settle this dispute. Alternatively, a theory may treat individuals *as* persons with certain capacities for purposes of the theory but defend that view without appeal to facts. Then we "need to identify a place in the world, a practice, which will give the set of concepts a grounding in reality. This is what Rawls does when he identifies something like this [a liberal conception of personhood] as the discourse of modern democratic states" (Williams 2005c, 21). This "grounding in reality" is the starting point from which to argue for the theory at hand. Rawls's view of personhood is supposed to be plausible only to those accustomed to democratic practices, citizens who see each other as free and equal (Rawls 1993, 19–20). But proceeding in this way has the advantage of formulating principles that do speak to the persons who are involved in the relevant practices.

What is characteristic of the global order is that groups make claims to resources and spaces by excluding others. With most of the land of the earth divided up, "control of territory is the essence of a state" (Malanczuk 1997, 75). John Ruggie (1998), for one, thinks territoriality has given way to "postmodern" states characterized by declining territoriality. Indeed, seeing the global order *only* as a system of territorial states would ignore many recent developments. Nonetheless, much control of access remains with states. The global order *is* a system of territorial states. While this might change eventually (if, e.g., Wendt [2003] is right that a world state is inevitable), it is the most fundamental fact about the way we live now (see chapter 15).

In the minimal sense of maintaining exclusionary practices, a *commitment to property* is de facto implicit in the global order. Since within organized groups individuals either are themselves property holders or are not, it is also de facto implicit in the global order that individuals are seen as *either* property holders themselves *or* otherwise as members of groups that can hold property, mediated through community practices. (Below I elaborate on the optical metaphor of individuals being "seen" in a certain way; "individuals are seen by the global order as X" should for now be considered synonymous with "there is a commitment to X in the global order.") This disjunctive statement is a platitude. It is precisely its platitudinous character that makes the idea that a commitment to exclusionary practices is implicit in the global order a good starting point for reflection. It should be noted that I do not merely talk about practices that are *officially sanctioned* by international law. The fact that such law is primarily concerned with states rather than with individuals and thus does not *endorse* individuals as property holders is irrelevant. What matters is what sort of practices of control over resources humans have adopted in their relations with each other, and thus what happens *within* the global order.

Collective ownership formulates a standing demand on all groups that occupy the earth to do so in a manner that respects individuals' equal status with regard to resources. As I will explain, this delivers a sense in which it is implicit in the global order that individuals themselves are seen as property holders. First of all, individuals are de facto seen as property holders in the disjunctive sense stated in the preceding paragraph. In a next step, crucially, collective ownership allows us to engage the ownership practices of the global order. By a reference to collective ownership we can argue that the idea of individuals as co-owners captures an *idealization* of a role that persons actually occupy, the one described in those disjunctive terms. In other words, the disjunction describes people's actual role with respect to (positive legal) ownership, and Common Ownership states what their role *ought* to be. Individuals have a moral status as co-owners that must be respected even where individuals are not themselves seen as property holders. Therefore, it is also implicit in the global order that individuals themselves are seen as property holders—in the sense that the idea that individuals are co-owners idealizes a role they de facto occupy. Collective ownership articulates an *internal critique* of actual practices by identifying an idealization of a role that individuals occupy.

10. More elaboration is needed on the parallel I started to develop. How similar is the sense in which it is implicit in the global order that individuals are co-owners to the sense in which it is implicit in constitutional democracies that individuals are free and equal citizens? Again, the idea that individuals are co-owners is an idealization; empirically it might be false that individuals are respected as co-owners in any plausible sense. But it is an idealization we ought to care about in virtue of the considerations supporting collective ownership. Moreover, the idealization emerges from, and speaks to, our practices. Indeed, something much like these considerations supports the claim that it is implicit in the culture of constitutional democracy that persons are seen as free and equal citizens in *Political Liberalism*. As Rawls explains,

the conception of the person is worked up from the way citizens are regarded in the public political culture of a democratic society, in its basic political texts (constitutions and declarations of human rights), and in the historical tradition of the interpretation of those texts. For these interpretations we look not only to courts, political parties, and statesmen, but also to writers on constitutional law and jurisprudence, and to the more enduring writings of all kinds that bear on a society's political philosophy. (1993, 19–20)

Individuals are not *empirically* free and equal. Instead, there are practices accompanied by moral ideas about citizenship. It is within those ideas—which refer to persons in idealizing ways—that individuals are *seen as* persons with certain powers. But there is also a connection between these ideas and the practices that individuals engage in so that, again, it makes sense to say that being persons with such powers is an idealization of the role that individuals actually occupy in domestic democracies.

One might worry that what we can say about co-ownership is much less than what Rawls says to substantiate the idea that individuals "are seen" as free and equal. Many political practices and historical precedents support that passive voice optical metaphor in the case of citizenship. However, there does not seem to be a counterpart to the authority of constitutions and court judgments in the case of co-ownership: there do not seem to be any "raw materials" to which we could draw attention to delineate the idealizations involved, parallel to how we can look to domestic constitutions and constitutional adjudication to see how a liberal conception of personhood is rooted in political practices. Indeed, in the ownership scenario the idealization is supported in a much thinner manner: we start with a platitude that characterizes individuals as co-owners (that they are de facto seen as *either* property holders themselves *or* otherwise as members of groups that hold property) and subject that platitude to an internal critique to reach the idealization that individuals themselves are seen as co-owners. In the domestic context, as Rawls states, "the conception of the person is worked up from the way citizens are regarded in the public political culture of a democratic society." The internal critique is the manner of this working up in the case of co-ownership.

In addition to the aforementioned platitude we can also work up the idea of individuals as co-owners from important documents of the global order. Joint Article 1.2 of the International Covenant on Civil and Political Rights and the International Covenant on Economic, Social and Cultural Rights states a right of all peoples to "freely dispose of their natural wealth and resources." According to Article 21 of the African Charter on Human and Peoples' Rights, "peoples shall freely dispose of their wealth and natural resources. This right shall be exercised in the exclusive interest of the people. In no case shall a people be deprived of it."[16] UN General Assembly resolution 1803 (XVII) of December 14, 1962, discusses the "the right of peoples and nations to permanent sovereignty over their natural wealth and resources," insisting that it "must be exercised in the interest of their national development and of the well-being of the people of the State concerned." Finally, Article 1 of the UN Declaration on the Right to Development," adopted as Resolution 41/128 of December 4, 1986, talks of a human right to development that includes "the exercise of [peoples'] inalienable right to full sovereignty over all their natural wealth and resources."

So there are relevant raw materials in addition to the platitude that draws on the plain existence of exclusionary practices. Nonetheless, the public culture of global political life is much thinner than that of constitutional democracies (a theme to which I return in chapters 17 and 18). Therefore, it is unproblematic that we can say *less* (than in the case of citizenship) to substantiate the idea that individuals are seen by the global order as co-owners. An account of human rights, say, cannot be nonparochial *unless* its support draws on a *thin* set of practices.

An objector might also find a disanalogy between the two cases since the notion of an internal critique of exclusionary practices appears to have no domestic counterpart. The working up of ideas from practices seems to mean something different there. However, Rawls acknowledges that democracies contain *associations* (1993, 40–43; 1999c, sec. 79). There could exist (and historically there have existed) forms of democracy that regard members of some associations as more entitled to power than others. (We need only think of democracies where voting power depends on wealth, and where the wealthy are more or less loosely organized in associations.) It takes, and historically has taken, an internal critique to obtain a culture in which individuals are seen as free and equal. Such a critique could insist that differences in voting power not follow criteria that are irrelevant in light of other commitments contained in the political culture. So there is room for the idea of an internal critique domestically, too.

It is implicit in the global order, then, that individuals are seen as co-owners, similar to how it is implicit in constitutional democracies that they are free and equal citizens. Co-ownership emerges as an idealization of roles that individuals actually occupy, much as free and equal citizenship emerges as such an idealization. To take the next step, these idealizations make it the case that both human rights and principles of domestic justice regulate practices in which persons are engaged. Just as principles of justice emerge by way of justifying the basic structure to citizens, human rights as I have derived them from Common Ownership emerge as part of a justification of that order to co-owners.

So the ownership approach can claim the methodological advantage that Williams captured for *Political Liberalism*. The fact that an ideal of a political role for individuals is implicit in political and economic practices allows us to find a grounding in those practices for distributive or other normative principles that speak to persons who share those practices (citizens or co-owners). This connection to such practices helps us see those principles or rights as justifiable to such persons. Human rights guarantee that the global order is acceptable to co-owners, parallel to how principles of domestic justice make states acceptable to such citizens. That the ownership approach lets us develop this parallel makes an additional case for its philosophical fruitfulness.

CHAPTER 8

Proportionate Use

Immigration and Original Ownership of the Earth

1. Most debates about immigration concern policies of specific nations. What is "best" for a country turns on conflicting cultural, political, or economic views, and what is beneficial from any such viewpoint for one segment of the population might not be for others.[1] But most stances regard immigration as a privilege and fail to ask about duties to would-be immigrants. We now explore whether the physical aspect of immigration provides constraints on immigration policy.[2] The fact that the earth is originally collectively owned must affect how communities can regulate access to what they occupy. In the nineteenth century, Henry Sidgwick's *Elements of Politics* anticipated this thought:

> I do not think that the right of any particular community to the exclusive enjoyment of the utilities derived from any portion of the earth's surface can be admitted without limit or qualification, any more than the absolute exclusive right of a private landowner can be admitted. The rigor of this right has hitherto been mitigated, in modern states generally, by the practical allowance of free immigration; but if this should ever be sweepingly barred, I conceive that the right of exclusion would be seriously questioned in the case of states with large tracts of waste land suitable for cultivation; and that some compromise would have to be found necessary between the prescriptive rights of the particular state and the general claims of humanity. On the one hand, no well-ordered community could reasonably be required to receive alien elements without limit or selection; on the other hand, an absolute claim to exclude alien settlers adequately civilized, orderly, and self-dependent, from a territory greatly under-peopled, cannot be justified on the principle of mutual non-interference. (2005, chap. 15.4)

Immigration nowadays is "sweepingly barred." But the idea that original ownership must affect how communities can regulate access is surprisingly hard to develop. This is due in no small measure to the fact that the ownership standpoint should not focus on surfaces, as Sidgwick or authors like Grotius and Locke held. Moreover, much relevant empirical work is unavailable. However, the concept of original ownership delivers a moral viewpoint from which to think about immigration, one that shows that immigration is not exclusively a matter for any state to regulate according to its own interest.

The establishment of exclusive political structures is consistent with Common Ownership. As chapter 7 argued, there is a collective responsibility at the level of the global order to make sure all people can meet basic needs. It is part of my proposal that the response required to scenarios in which individuals cannot satisfy basic needs is to make sure they can do so where they live, rather than permit immigration for that reason. This chapter assumes that basic needs are satisfied. The question of

what immigration polices countries ought to adopt if this condition fails, [...], and thus if many actors do not act in accor[...] [th]erefore becomes the kind of question of noni[...] largely omits.[3] It is important to keep in mind [...] [immi]gration is part of the overall approach to global [...] [n]ationalism develops.

[...] [consider]ed the hypothetical case of the U.S. population [...], those two controlling borders by electronic [...] [viol]ate the obligations of justice that follow from [...] prohibiting immigration, nor do others by seek[ing...] [...] [any]body's ability to satisfy basic needs is threatened. [...] [coul]d not reasonably expect others to refrain from [...] [ri]ght to enter U.S. territory. As opposed to that, it [...] [permissib]le conduct that they let others exercise their lib[...] [th]ere is an asymmetry when it comes to demands [...] But if they do admit immigrants, is there some [...] [coun]try reverses and the Americans face no demand [...] [th]at they let more people in, whereas outsiders face [...] stop trying to enter?

Generally, once the earth falls into separate units, we can ask what those units must be like and what they must do for each other, so that co-owners can be expected to comply with exclusion from units to which they do not belong. Section 2 of this chapter offers an account of *relative over- and underuse* of original resources to answer that question. Sections 3–6 address worries and questions. Section 7 compares my account with other approaches to the physical aspect of immigration. Section 8 offers a brief glance at illegal immigration into the United States, using a parallel to the civil law notion of "adverse possession" to argue that, under certain conditions, illegal immigration is morally unobjectionable.[4]

2. How should we make sense of the idea that co-owners are *overusing* resources (and so need not admit more people to be able to expect compliance with their immigration policies) or are *underusing* them (so have to)? One might think of developing this idea in terms of population density. However, areas with the same population density differ dramatically: one may consist of arable land with an evenly spread population, another may consist mostly of desert with a population crowded into small fertile areas. One may harbor lots of minerals, another be depleted of them; one may be adjacent to the sea, another landlocked. An approach in terms of population density is not suitable for our purposes. We need a measure that evaluates a region's overall usefulness for human activities.

For any state S the desired measure would deliver a measure V_S of the value of the collectively owned resources on S's territory, including the biophysical conditions determining the usefulness of this region for human purposes (e.g., climate, location on the globe, vegetation, topography, etc.). To assess the extent to which S's territory is used, one would divide V_S by the number P_S of people in S. V_S/P_S is the *per-capita use rate* of commonly owned resources on S's territory.[5] V_S/P_S includes noncirculating resources (which are not literally used), such as unmined minerals and unextracted oil (suitably discounted). Below we discuss situations in which a society is in no position, or has chosen not, to extract resources feeding into its use rate. The point is to have a measure of what is at a society's disposal, broadly speaking, actually and potentially, a measure of a stock that takes into account how readily that stock could be transformed into a flow of resources, rather than a measure only of the current flow.

The territory of S is *relatively underused* (or, simply, underused) if V_S/P_S is bigger than the average of these values across states (so that the average person uses a resource bundle of higher value than the average person in the average country). It is *relatively overused* (or, simply, overused) if this value is below the average. If V_S/P_S is above average, co-owners elsewhere have a pro tanto claim to immigration, in the sense that underusing countries cannot reasonably expect others to comply with immigration policies until such claims are satisfied. It is then a demand of reasonable conduct that the state permit immigration. (I discuss the "pro tanto" character of this claim below.) If a country is not underusing, others can be reasonably expected to accept its immigration policies (if nothing is independently problematic about them).

Immigration will be permissible until the values of V_S/P_S are rather close to each other across all states. Individuals would then populate the earth in proportion to the overall usefulness of its regions for human purposes. The intuitive fairness of this way of sharing the collectively owned resources and spaces provides the basic argument in support of this way of approaching immigration. This chapter elaborates both on my proposal and on the nature of the basic argument in its support.

Global coordination is required for sensible implementation. Underusers can relinquish territory, allowing for the founding of other political entities, or admit more people. Prudential *and* moral reasons then speak against keeping immigrants permanently outside the political community. The world's population may agree that underusers pay others off. However, underusers could not reasonably do so if those others—who, after all, are co-owners of original resources and spaces—*prefer* immigration. In this regard, ownership of the earth indeed is much like ownership in legal systems. Suppose A and B participate in a car-sharing scheme. B may not sell the car and leave some of its value on A's table without A's consent. A owns a share in the use of the car, not a monetary equivalent.[6]

To be sure, internal to states, individual claims to access to commonly owned resources are not always acknowledged. What is the difference between internal defection and external demands for entry that allows paying off those interested in the former, but not those interested in the latter? In the internal case, much more is at stake for states. Acting on such preferences would undermine their functionality, which would give states much stronger reasons not to do so than what they could muster to deny requests for immigration (although some request for secession are legitimate). Granting requests to immigrate has no such consequences, especially if states can exercise discretion in admissions. States may also spread out required changes in their immigration policies to preserve their functionality. Only a commitment to the legitimacy of states could warrant this sort of concern for their functionality. Parts 1 and 4 of this book support such a commitment.

Since we want to say that one region is taken up to a larger or smaller extent than others, all-things-considered comparability is essential, which is most straightforwardly accomplished by a one-dimensional measure, something like the aggregated world market price. We are looking for the value of original resources and spaces in a country, not of its artifacts. Specifically, world market prices would reflect the usefulness of entities for human purposes in light of limitations on availability. Such prices would also reflect technological constraints. Suppose we discover minerals far underground but lack extractive technology. Such resources would enter in a discounted way. Resources that happen not to be in flow but are part of the stock to which a country controls access should not create *much* pressure regarding immigration. But they should create *some*.

Objectors might argue that little of the world's resources is nationalized, that securitization of resources is increasing, and that barriers to direct foreign investment and ownership of these securities are decreasing. In what sense, then, can the population be said to be underutilizing the three-dimensional space a country occupies, given that many entities within this space trade on the global market and might be controlled by anybody in the world? This problem is structurally parallel to the problem of resources that are difficult to access. Difficulties of access come in degrees, which is why their value must be discounted in an assessment of the value for human purposes of the three-dimensional space in question. The extent to which control from the outside keeps the population of a country from using resources and spaces varies similarly. So discounting again is the correct response.

Some of the required pricing will be novel: biophysical factors shaping the usefulness of locations for human purposes are not normally priced. Humanity has had no trouble attaching price tags to ever more entities. However, reflections on prospects to broaden the U.S. National Income and Product Accounts (measuring activities in the U.S. economy) to include activities and assets not tied to market transactions and thus not captured in those accounts have revealed difficulties in doing so. Of note, *no such measure is in use.* The closest approximation that I know of is a method developed by the UN Food and Agriculture Organization and the International Institute for Applied Systems Analysis, which offers an inventory of land resources and an evaluation of their biophysical potential, the so-called *agro-ecological zones methodology.* However, we can turn neither to economists for well-established methods of extending pricing in this way nor to biophysical scientists for strong candidates for such a measure. All I can do now is explore the conceptual possibility of such a measure, formulate desiderata, and contrast mine to other proposals that assess demands to entry.[7]

3. One might question the possibility of measuring over- or underuse meaningfully.[8] Resources and spaces that came into being without human help often are subsequently altered by human activity. The Netherlands became prime land through the polder dikes. Previously, the area was a wasteland by any indicator assessing the value of original resources. Similarly, eradicating diseases such as malaria changes the value for human purposes of whole regions. The problem is widespread: most farmland, for example, has been improved in some way, even if merely by removing rocks or trees.

How should we think about what to include and exclude in calculating underuse and overuse? The case of the Netherlands also shows that one cannot dismiss the relevance of this question by arguing that only in regions that have a high usefulness for human purposes prior to any human additions can ingenuity increase that usefulness in a way that makes a difference to questions of immigration. The Netherlands, with its high population density, would presumably emerge as a highly overused area relative to the value of resources with human inventiveness factored out, a task we must leave to the biophysical sciences and the ingenuity of econometricians. Can a case be made that, perhaps in time, the value of products of human ingenuity should be included when we measure underuse and overuse?

Suppose a generation has passed: the added value is there, but the current generation did nothing to create it. Is it reasonable for this generation to continue to block immigration even if it is enjoying a higher total value of (the now enriched) original resources per capita than everyone else (and thus is underusing)? For this new generation, the added value is like the unimproved value in that it was lucky enough to be born into the enjoyment of it. The Dutch could admonish outsiders to add value to other resources. However, those outsiders could respond that such a demand would be unfair because the contemporary Dutch did not have to do so. The Dutch could reply in turn that it is still reasonable for them to block immigration: although they did not create the added value, their predecessors could make their contributions only given their cultural background. What made polder dikes possible was national unity and stability within which the required skills could flourish. It is because of social, legal, or political conditions that people can improve common resources, or invent things for which resources are necessary *enablers*.[9]

So the reason why the legacy of their predecessors should belong to the current generation of Dutch is the following two-stage argument: First, if commonly owned resources could be improved and other entities invented only because of the culture in which their predecessors participated, *others* have acquired no claim to the value thereby added to the common stock. They have not been relevantly connected to this process. Second, the contemporary Dutch are relevantly tied to that process. They are the contemporary participants in a culture that made earlier achievements possible and maintains them. Moreover, their predecessors presumably wanted *them* to benefit from these achievements. Considerations about what is owed to the dead were applied by Ridge (2003) to reparations for past injustice. Similar considerations hold for inheritance. It is thus up to the current generation of Dutch to regulate this legacy, and others have no claim to immigration based on it.[10]

But we can easily create doubts about the strongest version of the view I ascribe to the Dutch: that contemporary Dutch people have claims to *all* the value their predecessors added and that it is reasonable for this new generation to continue to block immigration even if they are enjoying a higher value of original resources per capita than everyone else. One source of doubt is that this argument makes it appear as if the Dutch had made their accomplishments in isolation, even though those were made in interaction with others. To the extent that such interaction was voluntary (and thus presumably rewarded appropriately), it does not generate claims by others. To the extent that it was not, it might generate claims to compensation, which, however, is orthogonal to my concerns.

A second source of doubt is more relevant. Regardless of how deserving of the added value the Dutch predecessors were, their acts cannot generate claims that resonate through the ages to the exclusive benefit of relatively few. That outsiders (had they been allowed in) *could*, and in due course *would*, have added the increased value might not undermine the claims of those who did so. But it does weaken the claims of their *offspring*. The point is similar to the objection to first-occupancy theories of acquisition: first-comers can legitimately claim land. Their accomplishments prevent others from doing the same, but that does not undermine desert-based claims they have because of their accomplishments. But such occupation cannot entitle their offspring to exclude others. Like the original value improvers, their heirs bar others from making those same accomplishments. Unlike them, the heirs are tied to the accomplishments only by being offspring of those who made them.

This argument casts doubt on the view that the relevance of national culture for the predecessors' ability to add value to commonly owned resources creates special entitlements for that culture's current participants. But it is a big step from there to the conclusion that with time, this added value becomes sufficiently like external resources for all of humanity to have an equal claim to it. Thus, neither can the Dutch claim that the features of their culture necessary for the value added by their predecessors to commonly owned resources entitle them to all that value, nor is it plausible that all such value turns into common property because others would have provided it, too. We are pointed to some intermediate view on whose details it is hard to be clear. We confront a bewildering array of counterfactuals whose truth and relevance are difficult to assess. Let me briefly state what seems like an intuitively plausible, if incomplete, view.

Common resources improved by technology or by other means should be counted as common when that technology or those other means *have become readily available*. Polder dikes should be so counted. The value of common resources should be measured in a manner that incorporates the impact of commonly available technology and other human factors that others could (and in due course would) have provided. But artifacts, ideas, practices, and other things for which external resources have been mere enablers should not be counted as common. The value of the Dutch economy beyond the value of improved common resources should not be so counted. Some arbitrariness in drawing the line is inevitable. Drawing a distinction, say, between choice and circumstance (a distinction central to much recent discussion about domestic justice) also encounters this problem. In any event, implementing my proposal requires global coordination. Precisely what counts as common may have to be left to a political process.

Intervention (deforestation, pollution) might also lower the value for human purposes of certain resources. Following the same argument, the offspring of those who caused the damage are not responsible for it. They do not have to allow for more immigration than demanded by the current per-capita use rate because the value of the resources occupied by them is lower than it would be had certain mischief not been done.

4. Chapter 6 rejected Equal Division as a conception of collective ownership because there is no measure of equal shares of resources that would give defenders of Equal Division what they need. However, section 2 introduces a measure of proportionate use that seems to be suitable to precisely this end. A consistency concern rears its ugly head. Yet there is a difference between my discussion of Equal Division and what I do with the measure of relative use. As a conception of collective ownership, Equal Division requires an account of equal shares for it to be *coherently defined*. But a measure of proportionate use serves a purpose different from *defining* a conception of collective ownership: to explain when persons can reasonably be expected not to disregard immigration restrictions. The question about reasonable acceptability of compliance with immigration policies arises *as a political question*. Questions about global value commitments also arise in this way. Humans have irrevocably encountered each other and must negotiate value commitments regardless of whether one can set some values apart as uniquely most plausible. Similarly, people seek to move, so questions about conditions under which we can expect people to accept exclusion *simply arise*, and require an answer.

It is only because this measure of over- and underuse is political that I could say, in a pragmatic spirit, that "all-things-considered comparability is essential, which is most straightforwardly accomplished by a one-dimensional measure." In a political context it is also important to come up with something that all involved parties could reasonably accept. But since questions about immigration *simply arise,* the standards of success differ: it is asking too much to make the viability of this approach depend on the availability of a uniquely most plausible measure obtained by ex ante reasoning. As opposed to that, the very coherence of Equal Division depends on the availability of such a measure.

Since the question about reasonable acceptability of immigration policies arises here as a political question, one might wonder about cases in which a population values resources in terms of a nonstandard measure (perhaps religiously motivated) that is distant from the approach used to assess overall usefulness of regions for human purposes. According to their own measure, they do not underuse their region, although according to the official one they do. Do others have a claim to entry? For the immigration problems our world faces, this question is only moderately relevant. Most emigrants wish to enter countries that are integrated into world markets and find assessments of resources in terms of prices acceptable. Two things in addition should be noted. First, permission to immigrate does not entitle one to do as one pleases. Even if we address demands of reasonable conduct with regard to immigration by valuing resources a destination country wishes to exempt from valuation or by using a measure it rejects, its worries can be addressed through other protective measures. Like other people, immigrants may not be allowed to bring certain resources into circulation or practice certain activities in particular regions. Second, if problematic cases do not involve primary immigration destinations, one may also accommodate exceptions in the use of a measure of usefulness for human purposes, in the same way in which liberal states accommodate religious practices if this does little harm.

5. Legitimate use, an objector might say, is not numerically proportionate use but has a purpose: the development of communities with certain features. The proposed measure, the objector continues, develops that perspective inadequately. "Arguments from preservation" insist that states should accomplish goal X, which, however, they cannot accomplish without immigration constraints. Candidates include the preservation of a culture or its purity, an economic or technological standing (human and physical capital, a wage structure that can be preserved only by regulating markets), or a political system (where, e.g., moderate inequality may depend on keeping the numbers of unskilled workers low). While such arguments often draw on self-interest, we may read them as insisting that there is independent value to preserving X. According to this objector, demands to immigration must somehow engage arguments that assess the moral weight of such goals, rather than proceed in terms of over- and underuse.

One can criticize such arguments on internal and external grounds. Doing the former means to suggest X conflicts with immigration constraints devised to protect X. Suppose a liberal democracy imposes immigration barriers so that wages do not fall on relatively low-wage labor markets because immigrants increase labor supply. If one were to argue that such constraints conflict with the ideals of liberal democracy, one would criticize a preservation argument on internal grounds. Criticizing preservation arguments on external grounds is to suggest that preserving X is not worth the costs of imposing constraints. An external criticism of the argument just stated would be to insist that such a policy causes too much misery abroad.

However, preservation arguments generally do not give proper weight to collective ownership. A culture shared only by two people with a vast territory might be worth preserving in some sense, but others could not reasonably be expected to waive their rights to enter. What resources are used *for* should enter the discussion, but only in a supplementary manner. The earth must be shared among all human beings. My proposal, in conjunction with the other components of my approach to global justice, offers a vision of how to do so that should be reasonably acceptable to all co-owners. Groups that claim more resources and spaces for their culture than they should reasonably occupy infringe on others illegitimately.

To illustrate how preservation arguments might relate to considerations drawing on collective ownership, we may consider the "White Australia" policy. "White Australia" stands for an immigration policy that was in place for much of the twentieth century. Its goal was to exclude nonwhites. Arguments from preservation minimally require a showing that the society as a whole would be too densely packed, or would not attract "the right sort of people," to allow for the continuation of the respective project if there were more immigration. But immigration into underpopulated areas is often compatible with maintaining the national project. Normally, land within a society is not uniformly populated. There often are relatively underpopulated areas, such as the American Great Plains, the Canadian northlands, or the Australian outback. The White Australia policy did claim more territory than was acceptable. For that reason, "White Australia could survive only as Little Australia" (Walzer 1983, 47).

However, the White Australia policy was impermissible also because Australia was never purely white. Aborigines could have launched a preservation argument of their own, insisting they are not properly respected in a state that asks obedience of them while admitting only whites. On the other hand, had Australia been purely white at some point, had Australians desired to keep it that way, and had they limited their territory proportionately, White Australia would have been acceptable, but not enduringly so. Australians would have traveled and invited visitors, students, or business partners for longer stays. Some would have wanted to ask foreigners to stay, to share their lives with them. Only unacceptable constraints could have prevented this development. A morally acceptable Little White Australia would have been short-lived.

Generally, countries have some discretion to choose applicants. (I can now spell out the point from section 2 that outsiders have a pro tanto claim to immigration on underusers.) Countries with strong social systems are entitled to select immigrants with professional credentials, countries with demographic problems to choose young people, and culturally homogenous countries to prefer applicants who share much of its culture. Countries also have some discretion to channel immigrants to particular regions—to less populated areas, say, although immigrants tend to take their port of entry as the default location to settle. Canada, for instance, seeks to place immigrants in rural areas.[11] It is acceptable to make admission conditional on a prior declaration by would-be immigrants to settle in certain regions. One would have to think carefully about what sanctions could legitimately be imposed were immigrants to renege on their commitments, but tax penalties would certainly be acceptable.

However, discretion in choosing immigrants is limited. Other things being equal, since the guiding idea of my proposal is proportionate use, applicants from overusing countries have priority. Also, immigration policy should integrate the duty of assistance in building institutions from chapter 4 (which is a duty of justice that has precedence in cases of conflict). Just how it should do so is a difficult empirical question. Sometimes immigration supports development because it decreases population pressure or generates remittances. But there is also a "brain drain" problem if those who leave are valuable for development and their departure creates no commensurable benefits.

6. One might worry that my proposal sets perverse incentives. One way of not underusing resources is to waste them, another is to increase one's population. From a global standpoint, a sustainable population size is needed, which is inconsistent with unconstrained population growth. Such growth, however, seems to be in a country's interest if it wants to stop immigration (or bar reasonable demands to permit immigration). Similarly, environmental policies need to be adopted that do not worsen climate change and pollution. But it seems to be in a country's interest to deplete its resources, if it wants to stop immigration. However, as far as waste is concerned, states can reasonably be expected not to engage in such actions—a claim that will be borne out in chapter 9, when we explore what to say on behalf of the idea of intergenerational equity with regard to commonly owned resources.

What we can say now, however, is that the impact of perverse incentives will be minimal because it will be difficult for states to do much of what the incentives encourage them to do, or there will be other, opposite incentives on states as well. Some of what factors into an assessment of under- or overuse cannot be depleted (e.g., location in a climate zone). Moreover, countries that deplete resources face a problem, namely, resource depletion. As Jared Diamond (2005) argues, governments have often adopted unwise resource-related policies, under circumstances when they must have been able to anticipate their harmful consequences. Diamond submits that the vested interests of elites undermined their motivation to prevent damage that would have affected future generations more than themselves. But recording such phenomena is rather different from being worried about governments deliberately adopting certain policies *in order to* block immigration.

The population decrease facing Germany, Italy, or Japan is exemplary of this argument. These countries have trouble adopting policies to increase their population, although this is in the current generation's interest. It is hard to imagine that liberal democracies, at least, could adopt policies that would motivate couples to have children as a means of preventing immigration. Individuals would perceive future immigration as a less immediate threat than a decrease in old-age benefits, so if the threat of the latter is not enough to motivate them to procreate, worries about immigration are unlikely to do so. To the extent that worries about perverse incentives are credible nonetheless, global contracts are needed. Such contracts would assess how many immigrants each country should take, and include provisions to undermine perverse incentives. One could base such arrangements on populations in a given year, or on estimates of population sizes at a future date.[12] A country's duty to accept immigrants is not entirely a function of its own conditions but turns on averages across countries.

A related worry is that immigration into rich countries exacerbates environmental burdens. Rich countries should not increase the number of those partaking of unsustainable consumption and production patterns. Yet the transformation of economies into more sustainable operations must occur alongside suitable immigration reforms. Just as states could not reject demands to immigration based on the fact that more immigration requires changes in social policy, environmental duties do not provide states with a legitimate reason to neglect its duties vis-à-vis immigration.[13]

7. Let me compare relative over- and underuse as a device for assessing demands to entry with two other such measures. First, there is an absolute notion of overpopulation, discussed by Michael Dummett (2001, chap. 4; 2004). Such a measure decides on entry by asking whether a region can support more people. More needs to be said about what counts as supporting. Is it enough if more people could survive? Or must countries be able to support more people at the same standard of living as their current population enjoys? But no matter how we answer these questions, nobody disrespects my status as co-owner, or violates any demands of reasonable conduct, by denying me entry to regions that are relatively overused even if they could accept more people without collapsing physically. I can then be expected to move elsewhere.

Or suppose that the earth were much more crowded, and no area could support more people. By Dummett's absolute test, every country is overused and none need admit immigration. But by my relative test, some might: if the value of resources per capita was still different in different countries, there could still be countries that were relatively underused. We can reasonably demand of others that they admit us even if they are in dire straits if we are worse off. A reasonable distribution of burdens from immigration shares them out *proportionately*. In particular, this idea of proportionality should integrate the equal ownership status that individuals *do* have with regard to original resources and spaces but do not have with regard to other sources of wealth. Such an idea, in turn, is captured by relative under- and overuse.

Eric Cavallero (2006) observes that countries are subject to emigration and immigration pressure. Some are under *positive pressure*: on balance, proportionately more people want to immigrate than emigrate— proportionately, that is, in a manner that factors in differences in population size. Other countries are under *negative immigration pressure*: on balance, more people want to leave. Cavallero proposes that countries under negative pressure have claims to aid. Countries under positive pressure must permit immigration or give aid to decrease pressure by making it appealing for people to stay where they are. ("Want to immigrate" refers to hypothetical preferences, stipulating that immigration is feasible.) Cavallero assesses immigration pressure assuming that visa applications are feasible and means for relocation are provided. For Cavallero, immigration pressure indicates *inequality of opportunity*. Countries with positive pressure tend to offer better opportunities than countries with negative immigration pressure. A legal system should not create bars to equal opportunity based on arbitrary traits such as nationality. International law allows states to restrict immigration. Unless those restrictions are balanced by improving opportunities in worse-off countries, this creates bars to equal opportunity on the basis of nationality.

Cavallero's argument is driven by the "cosmopolitan premise," that "ongoing institutions of international law should not systematically disadvantage anyone on the basis of involuntary national citizenship or national origin" (2006, 98). However, the starting point should be a slightly modified premise, that "ongoing institutions of international law should not systematically disadvantage anyone *in a morally unacceptable way* on the basis of involuntary national citizenship or national origin." We can then enlist the results of part 1 of this book. Morally arbitrary disadvantages are not always unacceptable. Not every disadvantage on the basis of one's nation of birth is problematic. Global equality of opportunity is not morally required.

While my account tracks neither actual nor hypothetical preferences, my concern is to explore reasons why countries face demands of reasonable conduct to accept immigrants. To the extent that wealth has arisen on bases other than commonly owned resources, my approach does not generate entitlements or reasonable demands to entry to share wealth. My proposal is as far as we can go if we start with Common Ownership. To go further we would need to offer a parallel argument about common ownership of "nonoriginal" wealth (i.e., artifacts). I do not think such an argument is available.

8. I conclude with a brief glance at illegal immigration to the United States.[14] Gertrude Stein wrote in 1936, "In the United States there is more space where nobody is than where anybody is. That is what makes America what it is" (1995, 45–46). In terms of my approach to immigration, that statement might well describe a problem. Although the relevant measure of proportionate use is decidedly not population density, I now use it as a very crude guide. In 2007, Germany and the UK had a population density of about 600 per square mile; for Japan it was 830, for the Netherlands 1,200, and for Bangladesh a striking 2,600. In the United States it was 80. Population density varied by state, but only in Massachusetts, Rhode Island, and New Jersey did it surpass 800. In cities it was different yet again: New York had about 26,000 inhabitants per square mile, and eight other cities were above 7,500. London had about 11,000, Tokyo 33,000, and Paris 52,000 people.

It takes extensive policy changes to accommodate large numbers of immigrants, but if one merely ponders these numbers, the United States critically underuses resources. If so, and assuming this evaluation will not need to be revised if we obtain better ways of assessing underuse, illegal immigrants (in any event, those from overusing countries) cannot reasonably be expected to refrain from seeking entry. Immigration reform should create a state of affairs in which illegal immigrations could reasonably be expected to stay away. One could not resist this conclusion by pointing out that many new immigrants would want to settle in the same few, overused locations. It is a matter of social policy (which would have to be adjusted accordingly) to solve this problem.

But even if illegal immigration is in that sense not wrong from the standpoint of collective ownership, perhaps it is wrong in another way. Perhaps the laws of morally acceptable states (including immigration policies) should be respected even if the state goes astray. However, the usual reasons why laws ought to be obeyed *qua laws* (rather than because they are morally required) only address members of the society. To those, one may say that their ongoing presence or participation in economic, social, or political life establishes a tacit acceptance of the country's law. Fair-play arguments might apply. Perhaps some people, such as naturalized citizens, have explicitly accepted the laws. But none of this gives would-be illegal immigrants reasons not to break laws that bar them *from entering* if they wish to participate in the society while abiding by its laws.

Let me offer an argument in support of legalizing illegal immigrants who are in the country *regardless* of whether U.S. immigration policy is reasonably acceptable as a whole. My argument draws on the civil law notion of adverse possession. This term refers to the open occupation of property by people who do not own it, assuming the owners know of the situation and do not challenge it. If the situation persists for a certain period, civil law allows ownership, or aspects of it, to pass to the occupiers. Like a knowing but noncontesting owner, the United States presumably underoccupies its space and has created niches for illegal immigrants. They are a mainstay of parts of the economy. Illegal immigration, in the aggregate, occurs in a manner and on a scale that is known to the public. Such immigrants hold jobs, have licenses, and participate in society in many ways. The United States falls short of what in principle it *could* do to enforce immigration laws. A moral form of adverse possession has taken hold. Among co-owners, this situation creates pressure to facilitate adjustment of status for illegal immigrants.

This glance at illegal immigration into the United States completes this chapter. As far as Common Ownership is concerned, considerations of justice do not take us far in formulating a moral evaluation of immigration policies. However, we can ask about conditions under which such policies are reasonably acceptable among co-owners, and thus about the conditions under which the liberty right to entry should reasonably be waived. This chapter has formulated a response to this question in terms of over- and underuse of resources. It is a demand of reasonable conduct that states accept my immigration proposal, but they are not required to do so as a matter of justice. But in that case, illegal immigration would be neither unjust nor deserving of condemnation from the standpoint of reasonable acceptability.

CHAPTER 9

"But the Earth Abideth For Ever"

Obligations to Future Generations

1. Generations of humans occupy the earth successively. Earlier generations' eagerness to shape the future in their own image has greatly helped later comers. Throughout history, many societies have also recognized duties toward future generations. However, earlier mistakes might cost later generations dearly.[1] Human beings have long been able to undermine their chances of survival in their surroundings, but, as Rachel Carson writes in *Silent Spring*, "Only within the moment of time represented by the present century has one species—man—acquired significant power to alter the nature of his world" (1962, 5). It is sometimes even said that we live in a new geological era, the Anthropocene. This term—which includes the Greek word for human being—characterizes the period in which humankind has surpassed the rest of nature in its impact on the structure and function of the earth system. Until the next asteroid or perhaps a massive sun storm hits the earth, it is likely to be people more than other forces that determine the future of all known life. And indeed, the debates about sustainability and climate change reflect the fact that humans' increased ability to shape their environment imposes considerable risks on the future. Contemporary societies routinely must address what to do about front-loaded goods, goods that largely benefit the present but for which later generations must pay.[2] (Think of the lifetime of greenhouse gases in the atmosphere.) Inquiries about duties toward future generations are urgent.

So far we have exclusively considered principles concerning a population at a given time, and associated obligations concerning such people. But in this chapter, our main questions are the following: Are there principles of justice that we can derive from Common Ownership and that regulate distribution among generations? If so, what duties follow from those principles for people living now, and their institutions? And are there additional demands of reasonable conduct with respect to future generations that arise from Common Ownership? The first part of the title of this chapter is from the Bible, Ecclesiastes 1:4 (American King James Version): "One generation passeth away, and another generation cometh, but the earth abideth for ever." Alas, we can safely assume the earth will not actually abide *forever*. In this regard, Shakespeare's Prospero must be right:

> And like the baseless fabric of this vision,
> The cloud-capp'd tow'rs, the gorgeous palaces,
> The solemn temples, *the great globe itself*,
> Yea, all which it inherit, shall dissolve,
> And, like this insubstantial pageant faded,
> Leave not a rack behind.
>
> *Tempest*, Act 4, Scene 1, 151–56 (italics added)

But we can also safely assume that there will be future generations. To be sure, the question of whether there are duties to future generations arises in principle for any ground of justice. This matter merits further investigation beyond what I can do now.

If one makes collective ownership as central as Hugo Grotius did, one has to assess the moral status of future people eventually. Grotius dutifully does so but, as chapter 5 noted, dismisses the matter:

> He who is not yet born, can have no right, as that Substance which is not yet in Being has no Accidents. Wherefore if the People (from whose Will the Right of Government is derived) should think fit to alter that will, they cannot be conceived to injure those that are unborn, because they have not as yet obtained any Right. (*DJB* II.4.X.2)

Grotius does not think *successive* generations *collectively* own the earth. People who are already dead or not yet alive do not count as co-owners now but they had (will have) their turn when they were (are) alive. Future people own what is left to them. And indeed, the ownership approach does not generate strong duties to future generations. However, it does deliver some such duties, and so the account I develop now differs from Grotius. As climate change raises its own issues, I discuss it separately in chapter 10.[3]

Much philosophical energy has been invested into addressing skepticism about intergenerational morality. Most commonly, this skepticism has been cast in terms of our ability to wrong or harm future generations. Actions at earlier stages affect the composition of future generations. In one way of thinking about what it means to wrong or harm people, actions that are among the conditions of X's existence cannot wrong or harm X. Given the significance of these concerns, I use a response strategy to this skepticism to frame my discussion of future generations within the ownership approach. A disadvantage of proceeding this way is that it adds an extra step: we approach the quest for principles of justice that apply across generations via an account of wronging that is designed to meet such skepticism. But the (to my mind decisive) advantage is that thereby a response to this skepticism—which we must address one way or another—is built into my approach to obligations to future generations.

The account of wronging that I adopt is Rahul Kumar's (2003). In Kumar's view, wronging consists in violations of legitimate expectations in relationships. For a given relationship, the question becomes what the *source* of legitimate expectations is (what generates duties), and then what their *contents* are.[4] The source of expectations in the relationship between parents and children is that children generally exist because of an act of will of at least one parent. Part of the content of these expectations could be not to let the child suffer serious harm the parents could prevent without substantial burdens for themselves. We can utilize this approach to explore the nature of our relationship with future generations understood as a relationship among generations of co-owners, and characterize the legitimate expectations they have of us by identifying the source and contents of these expectations. Some of these turn out to be principles of justice, whereas others are (mere) demands of reasonable conduct.

Section 2 introduces Kumar's account. Section 3 discusses ways of characterizing our relationship with future generations that have nothing to do with the ownership approach. I explore these accounts to show how hard it is to say anything about obligations to future generations at all, and thereby to generate appreciation for the deflationary account that the ownership approach provides. Sections 2 and 3 are preliminary, and it is only in section 4 that I can start discussing our main questions. The ownership approach offers a partial account of the sources of legitimate expectations of future generations. (It does not address duties arising from a shared cultural legacy.) Constitutive of the morally relevant relationship among generations is merely that they successively occupy the same space to whose creation no individual has contributed more than any other. An *asymmetrical capacity to shape the natural world* is the source of future generations' legitimate expectations. This account does not let us say as much about duties to future people as one might have hoped. But that much at least we can safely say.

Once we have identified their *source* (section 4), we can explore the *contents* of these expectations (section 5). Current generations must not take undue advantage of their ability to shape the earth for future generations. First—and this continues our discussion in chapter 7—earlier generations must leave behind institutions within which future people can exercise human rights if earlier generations can satisfy their own basic needs. Second, to the extent that current institutions make plans or adopt policies that affect future generations, such measures must consider the ability of future generations to meet basic needs. If we use resources for more than satisfaction of needs, we must ensure that future people can at least satisfy their needs.

We must ask whether the second obligation requires only that future generations be able to meet basic needs somehow, or whether it requires the preservation of actual resources and spaces. That question leads to the debate about sustainability, which we pursue in sections 6 and 7. It turns out that the second obligation does require the preservation of actual spaces and resources. However, common views about sustainability also include a commitment to intergenerational equality that we must assess independently (section 8). There are parallels between my inquiries about immigration and future generations: the former inquires "horizontally" about use of the earth within one generation, whereas the latter inquires "vertically" about its use across generations. The concept of "strong sustainability" offers a vertical parallel to proportionate use. Like proportionate use, strong sustainability, including intergenerational equality, formulates demands of reasonable conduct, in this case for successive generations. Section 9 briefly considers what we can say about duties to future generations that share membership in a state.

Duties to future generations are puzzling because the existence of future people depends on present actions and because relations that usually render principles of justice and demands of reasonable conduct applicable (contracts, cooperation, coercion) do not extend across generations. The ownership approach is not marred by these problems. Its key contribution is to illuminate a moral relationship in which *all* human beings, no matter when and where they live, stand with each other vis-à-vis original resources. Within the account as we have developed it so far, we have to assess the relevance of the fact that persons live at different times.

2. Following Derek Parfit (1984), philosophers have spent much energy on the *nonidentity problem*. That problem, to paraphrase Friedrich Schiller, is the hollow lane through which accounts of what is owed to future generations must come. If different genetic makeups generate different identities, the composition of future generations depends on minor behavioral variations. If its conception had happened at even a slightly different time or under different circumstances, the child's genetic makeup would be different. Major historical events affect many people, and so affect who will be alive in the future. Moreover, in a widespread way of thinking about what is involved for action A to harm person X, the following is true: if A had not happened, X would be better off. Let us assume that being alive for some period of time is generally better than not being alive at all. Since many who will be alive in the future will not exist if governments adopt different policies (those being the kind of event that

affects who will be alive in the future), it seems such policies cannot harm them, unless, perhaps, those policies condemn them to lives not worth living at all. If, say, we take measures to mitigate climate change (to reduce emissions), different people will be alive than if we adapt (take measures to live with the changes). If different measures should have been taken, this error does not seem to harm future people. If being harmed is a necessary condition for being wronged, they will not be wronged either. These results seem counterintuitive.

Skepticism about our ability to harm and wrong future people can be broadened into skepticism about *obligations* to them. If one can have obligations, then it is possible to violate them. If one violates an obligation to a person, then one harms or wrongs her. So if one can neither wrong nor harm future people, there can be no obligations to them either, especially no obligations of justice. There is no need for us to discuss these matters in detail. But we do need an account of wronging that does not make it conceptually impossible to wrong future generations (in which case I say the account "meets the nonidentity problem"). Drawing on T. M. Scanlon (1998), Kumar (2003) offers an account that satisfies that criterion and provides a suitable apparatus with which to approach the question of what we owe future people.

According to Kumar, wronging "requires that the wrongdoer has, without adequate excuse or justification, violated certain legitimate expectations with which the wronged party was entitled, in virtue of her value as a person, to have expected her to comply" (2003, 107). What can be legitimately expected depends on the relationship. There can be wronging without anybody being harmed in the sense that her interests have been thwarted, as when somebody is oblivious that, for a second, she is being threatened by a car over which a drunk driver momentarily loses control. There is something wrong with failing to exercise due diligence even if no harm is done (and even if, unbeknownst to the driver, the pedestrian has waived his right to safety). Or we may consider a case that Parfit (1984) discusses. Somebody who was born to a fourteen-year-old takes offense at teenage motherhood being criticized. He insists that his life is worth living, although his first years were hard. This man retrospectively waives any right to being born under different conditions. However, this waiver does not rebut the objection to his mother's giving birth: "The objection must be that, if she had waited, she could have given to some other child a better start in life" (365).

What matters for legitimate expectations is not that individuals of a psychophysical identity (*this* or *that* person) stand in a relationship. What matters is that people of certain "types" do. "Types" are normatively significant sets of characteristics, roles persons play in relationships. In parent-child relationships one type is that of a parent and one is that of a child. Being a parent entails characteristics that generate legitimate expectations. In teacher-student relationships one type is that of a teacher and one is that of a student. A wrongs B if A does not meet legitimate expectations that B has against her within a relationship in which A and B embody certain types. A teacher might have a duty to order books for a course (Baier 1981). If she fails to do so (without adequate excuse), she wrongs her students because her role (type) requires such an act. She commits a wrong regardless of whether it matters to the students whether they can get the books in time, and regardless even of whether anybody takes the course. She wrongs the students because people of their type, too, are subject to expectations. To satisfy these expectations, they need those books.

Let us consider again the parent-child case: Parents are causally involved in the creation of children, which, where intercourse is optional, involves interventions of the will. Suppose parents omitted precautions that would have spared a newborn a handicap. The precautions would have delayed intercourse, and so the child's psychophysical identity would have been different. Depending on how one conceives of harm, *that* (handicapped) child would not be harmed because *it* would not exist otherwise. However, it is a legitimate expectation on being a parent to take care of the child's needs, which includes saving her from handicaps at minor costs. We may or may not want to say the child was harmed, and the child may or may not regret that it was conceived; but the child was wronged because the parents violated legitimate expectations within parent-child relationships.

This account of wronging meets the nonidentity problem because legitimate expectations do not arise as a function of harm done but as a function of roles that individuals occupy (the types). It is not true that no act that is among the conditions of a person's existence can wrong her. One might object that Kumar's view revolves around the idea of persons actually interacting in certain capacities. (After all, he means for his approach to be a *contractualist* account, a point on which I will not elaborate.) The relevant *relationships* could then not hold between past and future generations. But we are free to adopt a broad notion of a relationship (and need not worry whether committed contractualists can readily accommodate such a notion) as a kind of interconnectedness among people, one whose details we need to specify and within which we can formulate legitimate expectations. We can then say that present actions wrong future generations without worrying that the composition of these generations depends on those actions. Below I identify first the source and then the content of legitimate expectations of future generations. That exercise clarifies the nature of that relationship: co-ownership across generations.

One might also worry that this account does not ease concerns with regard to the applicability of rights talk to nonactual people. Whatever concerns one might have with regard to *rights* along such lines carry over to *legitimate expectations*. But the advantage of this account is not that it replaces rights talk with talk about legitimate expectations. The point is that an account in terms of expectations within relationships renders the ability of X to wrong Y by doing A independent of whether Y was around when A was committed and of whether Y's existence depends on A. It may or may not make sense to say that Y has rights or expectations before he is around. But as soon as he is, he may complain about failures of X in virtue of her participation in this relationship.

Kumar's account allows us to eliminate two forms of skepticism about moral relations with future people. The first is that future people cannot be wronged by actions that are necessary conditions of their existence. A second form is that we cannot be in a relationship of *mutual advantage* with future people.[5] But Kumar's account does not presuppose the implied view of justice as mutual advantage. That Humean circumstances of justice do not hold among generations does not keep us from formulating legitimate expectations among them.

In chapter 7, I used the terms "right" and "wrong" in a capacious sense: actions may be right in the sense of "just" (required by obligations of justice) or in the sense of "what (only) can reasonably be expected," and similarly for actions that may be considered wrong. Among those who stand in a relationship, such as by sharing a ground of justice, legitimate expectations may include both demands of justice and other demands of reasonable conduct. As far as the relationship among generations of co-owners is concerned, this chapter delivers both principles of justice and demands of reasonable conduct. If their precise nature does not matter, I simply talk about legitimate expectations.

3. "From the standpoint of a higher economic form of society," Karl Marx wrote in *Capital*,

> private ownership of the globe by single individuals will appear quite as absurd as private ownership of one man by another. Even a whole society, a nation, or even all simultaneously existing societies taken together, are not the owners of the globe. They are only its possessors, its usufructuaries, and, like *boni patres familias*, they must hand it down to succeeding generations in an improved condition. (1972, chap. 46, 776)[6]

This statement opposes Grotius's view of the matter. For Marx, each generation has an obligation to the next to hand down this planet in an improved condition; for Grotius, there are no duties to future generations. But precisely what creates legitimate expectations of future generations of any sort? What is the *source* of such expectations? To set the stage for the account that emerges from the ownership approach, I first explore some other views of how to think about the source of such expectations. The ownership approach provides a rather sobering account of what ties generations together. Thus, readers might ask, "Why not think about future generations in some other way?" I seek to preempt such questions by showing that it is difficult to derive obligations to future generations in other ways. Thus, there is reason to value what we can obtain from Common Ownership. Like section 2, this section is a preliminary to the main business of the chapter.

As we noted, what generates legitimate expectations in parent-child relationships is that engendering children generally involves acts of the will. Such acts create helpless beings whose lives might be miserable. Rawls seeks to assess duties to future generations based on a different fact, namely, that people care about their children. Individuals in the Original Position are presumed to be heads of families. Since the flourishing of these children is interconnected, their future becomes a public good.[7] So the parent-child model suggests two explanations of why we might have duties to future generations: because we are causally responsible for there being future generations; or because we care about all our descendants in the way we care about our children.

But arranged marriages and similar cases aside, from the standpoint of grandparents and more remote ancestors, the conception of children *just happens*. It does not engage their will. Moreover, many grandparents love their grandchildren; people may feel a biologically triggered attachment to the future of their genes; and without people's sexual activities their more remote offspring would not exist. But none of these points is of the right sort to create legitimate expectations of future generations. Not only does the moral relationship among generations differ remarkably from parent-child relationships, but *biological lineage* fails entirely to establish duties among generations.[8]

A second candidate for such a source is that earlier comers have an independent duty to bring later generations into existence and thus have a duty to procreate. Hans Jonas (1984) offers a transcendental argument for such a duty. He argues that we cannot deny there ought to be future generations without running into performative contradictions. We act *purposefully* by objecting this way; but the reason why humanity ought to be preserved is its ability to act purposefully. By denying a duty to continue the existence of humanity, one exercises the property in virtue of which it is true that humanity ought to have a future (155). This argument fails. By objecting, somebody may endorse her own purposeful nature, and be committed to endorsing that nature for herself. Nothing follows, however, for an endorsement of the need for humanity to survive through another generation and beyond in virtue of its overall purposefulness.[9]

A different argument for a duty to preserve humankind as long as possible stresses the value that this would generate. Contradicting the Mephistophelean dictum that "everything that comes into being deserves to perish" (Goethe, *Faust*, ll. 1339–40), Gregory Kavka (1978) argues that there are moral reasons for wanting humankind to survive. First, human life is generally a good thing for those who possess it. Second, the continuation of humanity's artistic and intellectual accomplishments matters.

James Lenman (2002) raises some plausible objections to Kavka's position. He grants there is tremendous value to human life (the joy of individuals at being alive, objective accomplishments). But the sheer fact that there is value to X's existence does not imply that, at any given time, one should maximize the number of versions of X. This is true also if X is human life. Therefore it is also implausible that it matters in itself for how long humanity extends. (One may say the universal of being human has already been instantiated.) Nor is there a narrative of humanity that will be disrupted in the same way in which a premature death disrupts a life (an analogy suggested by Kavka). We have a good understanding of the stages of a person's life, and somebody who dies young has not passed through all of them. But no such stages exist in the development of humankind. Lenman also points out that appeals to the value of biological diversity do not help his opponents since humanity decreases diversity. "The Age of Mammals," writes H. G. Wells in his *Outline of History* with subtle irony, "culminated in ice and hardship and man" (1920, 49).[10]

On behalf of Kavka, one might respond as follows. Drawing on Ronald Dworkin (1993), we can distinguish "incremental value" from "inherent value" or "sanctity." Even if we doubt there is reason to maximize the number of things with sanctity, there is reason to maximize the number of things with incremental value. Human life has sanctity, but accomplishments have incremental value. That point provides an instrumental reason for maximizing the number of humans: more humans presumably create more accomplishments. Since earlier accomplishments pave the way for later ones, the optimal distribution of brilliant minds is not for them to exist simultaneously. Nor is it for them to stretch out as thinly as possible. We obtain the optimal distribution if we make sure that there are enough (but not too many) humans living at any given point in time. So we have a duty to preserve humanity for as long as possible.

But this attempt to salvage Kavka's argument fails. Great accomplishments harbor potential for great misery. "He that increaseth knowledge, increaseth sorrow," according to that book of the Bible from which I took the title of this chapter, Ecclesiastes 1:18. Technological and organizational achievements made the world wars and Auschwitz possible. "The end of the State," writes the Polish poet Czeslaw Milosz, describing the days when German and Soviet troops divided up Poland, "was marked by a chaos that could occur perhaps only in the twentieth century" (1981, 150). The value from more accomplishments does not offset the higher risks of suffering. Lenman is right after all: we have no duty to keep humankind in existence for as long as possible. Future generations are likely to exist, but there is no duty to bring them into existence that could be a source of their legitimate expectations of us.

Let us consider a different way of arguing that we have duties to future generations (and that they have legitimate expectations of us). Perhaps we form part of an intergenerational chain involving past and future. Legitimate expectations of future people pertain to duties *we* have to our ancestors (to maintain their cultural achievements) and that future people can expect us to meet. Baier (1981) argues that "past generations have rights against us, that we not wantonly waste or destroy what they made possible for us to have, not intending it for us only" (180). Baier enlists Edmund Burke's idea of an intergenerational community and Hume's claim that we see ourselves "plac'd in a kind of middle station betwixt the past and the future" (178). In this view, we have duties to past generations to maintain their achievements. Members of future generations (like anyone else) can legitimately expect us to live up to those duties. So those duties to past generations are the source of legitimate expectations of future generations.

However, little should depend on actual ancestral intentions. Earlier generations often had no altruistic intentions about their legacy. Self-aggrandizement loomed large in the creative acts of our ancestors, as did a desire to see improvement in their own lives. Even where gratitude is appropriate, we honor our ancestors best by developing their legacy, which might mean respecting their accomplishments by moving beyond and replacing them. Still, we should not readily demolish things that have stood the test of time, especially if many generations have approved of them. Considering future generations is helpful, too, to constrain our judgment. (Would they want us to replace that Baroque church with a modern structure?) But there are reasons why innovations would pass such scrutiny, primarily that, after careful deliberation, we think we actually *can* do better.[11]

Should we improve the collective legacy as a whole, even if we eliminate specific things? Is there a duty "to leave 'as much and as good' of the public goods previous generations have bequeathed" (Baier 1981, 176)? (I am talking about cultural accomplishments, not the natural environment.) Pace Marx, it strikes me as indefensible that we would have an obligation to leave the planet in an *improved* condition.[12] Moreover, if our collective legacy deteriorates, it is rarely salient that duties *to future generations* were neglected. The large-scale destruction of cultural legacy (which is what such deterioration often amounts to) normally accompanies so much misery that violations of future people pale. Our reflections deliver a nonfrivolity condition, that each generation take care of its legacy and develop it wisely. A standard against which to measure "wise" development is that intermediate generations have not opted to replace certain ancestral achievements.

4. The one source of legitimate expectations of future generations we have been able to identify emerged from a discussion of *cultural accomplishments*. What about natural spaces and resources? Does Common Ownership lead to legitimate expectations of future generations?[13] It does, and my next goal is to show how. We can now address the main questions posed in the introduction. In chapter 6 I identified several claims in light of which I formulated collective ownership and supported Common Ownership as its preferred conception. These claims delivered the following view: that all human beings have some kind of claims to original resources and spaces that cannot be constrained by reference to what others have accomplished applies to *all* human beings *regardless* of when they live. This view, like all the claims leading up to it, does not mention the temporal status of individuals. To delineate legitimate expectations of future people within the ownership approach, we must ask how to accommodate the fact that individuals live at different times. While discussing the cultural world we explored the *source* of legitimate expectations and their *content* simultaneously. Now I divide these steps and begin with the source of legitimate expectations future people have within the ownership approach.

Two points should be noted, in addition to the fact that none of the claims that supported collective ownership mentions the temporal status of individuals. The first point is a reply to an objection. Those who agree with Grotius might say that future people need not, and cannot, be taken seriously as owners. There is no X that successive generations own *together*. Instead, for each generation j there is an Xj (resources j collectively owns). Xj emerges from Xj − 1 through the cumulative impact of generation j − 1. But this objection endorses an erroneous view of what we commonly own. The domain of the ownership relation is not merely a set of materials that can be removed from the common pool so that the next generation owns whatever is not consumed. That domain is the three-dimensional space *within* which humans make a life. Resources and spaces are located, consumed, shaped, left waste or intact, and so on, within this domain. The domain is likely to be left to the next generation in some shape. There *is* something that successive generations own together: the earth, whose ongoing existence for now is necessary for humanity's survival. This point might seem trivial, but it rebuts one way of thinking about ownership across generations.

Second, the formulation of expectations of future people must take a certain form. Only the living can *exercise* rights. Future people can factor into decision processes *only* as beneficiaries. For instance, Hurka (1993, 36) suggests that the ownership standpoint pushes toward mitigating climate change rather than adaptation, because we must take future people seriously as individuals with claims to resources. But to that end one has to show that the best way to *benefit* future people is to mitigate climate disruption. So far we have said nothing to show this. In chapter 8 we saw that co-owners have claims to actual resources and spaces and can be paid off only if they agree, not based on an argument that this would be an appropriate way of benefiting them. However, for future generations what we need, and all we need, precisely is a discussion about how best to benefit them. Perhaps one answer is that we should adapt to climate change.

We have noted three points: none of the reasoning that supported collective ownership mentioned the temporal status of individuals; there is something successive generations own *together*, the earth itself; and future people can be taken seriously as co-owners only as beneficiaries. Future people are co-owners now, although their status is special in this way. We can now assess how to accommodate the fact that individuals live at different times and determine the source of legitimate expectations of future generations. Humankind spreads over generations, occupying the same three-dimensional space. (The Sermon on the Mount notwithstanding, it is at least not merely the meek who inherit the earth; New Testament, Matthew 5:5.) Except for the duties derived above regarding the preservation of the cultural world, *all* that constitutes the moral relationship among them is that they (a) are humans who successively occupy the earth, (b) can expect that there will be generations after them, and (c) can expect that those generations will need resources for survival, without having done more than anybody else to create these resources to begin with.

What is characteristic of this relationship is an *asymmetrical capacity to shape the earth*—the fact that *earlier* generations can leave the earth in the shape in which *subsequent* ones find it. This capacity is the source of legitimate expectations future generations have of earlier comers (insofar as Common Ownership is concerned). It is because of the three points above that it is appropriate to consider this capacity the source of legitimate expectations. The first point forces us to see that there exists a duty-generating relationship among generations. The second reveals a domain with regard to which there can be intergenerational duties. The third shows that we must capture future people's passivity in this relationship. To think of the asymmetrical capacity to shape the earth as a source of duties is sensible as much as it is sensible to think of the involvement of the parents' will with the existence of children as such a source.

What matters is that earlier generations *do* have the capacity to shape the earth as later generations will find it, rather than that the latter cannot reciprocate. Suppose future generations could degrade resources through backward causation. We would then still have a duty not to take undue advantage of them. They would have a parallel duty not to take undue advantage of us. This capacity differs from vulnerability, explored by Robert Goodin (1985). Future generations are vulnerable to us in ways in which we are not to them. Perhaps future people can do things for us (as O'Neill [1993] argues), but their expected deeds can benefit us only through our *beliefs* (e.g., that they will preserve our memory). Asymmetrical capacity captures a broader idea: later generations are vulnerable, but also must be taken seriously as co-owners. One may ask with regard to each ground of justice how to think about future generations. Vulnerability might matter greatly when we discuss future generations with regard to common humanity. But collective ownership allows us to go beyond what we can say based on common humanity alone, and to that extent makes our conclusions more secure.

5. We are developing an account of duties to future generations in terms of legitimate expectations within a relationship. The relevant *relationship* is that among subsequent generations of co-owners. The *source* of expectations is the asymmetrical capacity to shape the earth. Mine is a deflationary account of duties to future generations, but being able to say this much is no small feat in this difficult terrain. Next I explore the *content* of these expectations in two steps. This section formulates one abstract obligation that captures the content of these expectations and gives rise to two more specific obligations.

The general obligation giving content to legitimate expectations of future generations is that the former can expect of the latter not to take *undue advantage of this asymmetry*. Since there is a domain that successive generations own together; since among any two individuals, no matter in which generation they respectively live, neither has done more to create original resources; and since future generations can only be taken seriously as co-owners in a passive way, it is reasonable to ask earlier generations not to take undue advantage of this asymmetry. *Undue* advantage taking occurs first of all if earlier comers use resources without trying to make sure that future people, too, can exercise their ownership rights once they are alive.

To spell out what it means to make sure that future people, too, can exercise ownership rights once they are alive, let us recall from chapter 7 that human rights are membership rights in the global order that in turn partly derive from collective ownership. Guaranteeing these rights is a global responsibility because they are potentially threatened not merely by a person's state but also by the unwillingness of other states to grant entry if the person lives under an abusive government. If there continues to be a global order, individuals continue to have membership rights. Future people can legitimately expect the current generation to leave behind institutions within which they can exercise membership rights, if that generation is in a position to leave behind such institutions. Various earlier arguments support this obligation. First, the current generation is obligated to ensure that their institutions respect human rights. Second, the preservation of institutions realizing human rights is a paradigmatic case of a scenario in which the *cultural accomplishments* of earlier generations ought to be preserved. So the present discussion merely adds support to duties we have already recognized.

The second of the two more specific obligations that capture the idea that no undue advantage should be taken is closer to the core of collective ownership, and introduces an obligation we have not already established. This obligation states that to the extent that within current institutions plans are made or policies adopted that affect future generations, those generations (both the next one and subsequent ones) can expect that such planning makes sure that their ability to meet basic needs is preserved, to the extent that this depends on original resources and spaces. There is no such duty if people cannot satisfy their needs, but if they use resources to build a life in which they can do more than merely satisfy basic needs, they ought to enable later-comers to do at least that much. We are not merely obligated to leave behind institutions within which this could be done *in the future*, but future concerns must already be integrated now. The prevalence of front-loaded goods makes this a significant obligation.[14]

One might wonder why I am adding "to the extent that this depends on original resources and spaces." Since we can take future owners seriously only as beneficiaries somebody might argue that we benefit future people most by finding ways of satisfying needs that do not turn on resources and spaces. So we should add "to the extent that this depends on original resources and spaces *or on substitutions thereof* that have been made better to meet needs that previously were satisfied by access to original resources and spaces." However, sections 6 and 7 show that we must in fact preserve the resources and spaces of the earth, thus vindicating my formulation.

Before turning to that discussion, let us reconnect to the overall argument in part 2 of this book. Given the existence of the global order, the two obligations I just stated, like the more abstract one from which I derived them, capture obligations that correspond to a principle of justice. That principle states that the distribution of the original resources and spaces of the earth across different generations of human beings is just only if everyone has the opportunity to use them to satisfy their basic needs, or otherwise lives under a property arrangement that provides the opportunity to satisfy basic needs. That principle in turn follows from the pivotal principle in chapter 6 ("The distribution of original resources and spaces of the earth among the global population is just only if everyone has the opportunity to use them to satisfy her or his basic needs, or otherwise lives under a property arrangement that provides the opportunity to satisfy basic needs") once we explain how to take future generations seriously within a theory of justice—which we do through the approach in this chapter, which has led to an account of the source and contents of legitimate expectations of future generations.

6. Is the second obligation then best understood as requiring that future persons be able to meet basic needs *somehow*, or do they have legitimate expectations regarding the preservation of *resources*? To answer this question, we take a look at the debate about *sustainability*. "The idea of sustainability is a distinctly modern notion," as Dale Jamieson (2002) explains, "closely tied to the schizophrenia of modern life that simultaneously persecutes nature while trying to protect it" (327). A starting point for the sustainability debate is the 1987 Brundtland Report, *Our Common Future*, which stressed the urgency of fostering growth while paying attention to global equity and environmental concerns. "Sustainable development" is explained there as "development that meets the needs of the present without compromising the ability of future generations to meet their own needs" (World Commission on Environment and Development 1987).[15]

Let us distinguish weak from strong sustainability.[16] *Capital* is whatever forms the capacity to provide utility; *natural capital* is the capacity of nature to provide humans with utility (those parts of nature that fail to do so being disregarded), such as resources, plants, ecosystems, or species; *man-made capital* includes infrastructure such as roads or machines; and *human capital* includes knowledge and skills. Adopting either form of sustainability means insisting that the future be integrated into decision making. Being committed to *weak sustainability* means insisting on a nondeclining stock of total capital; being committed to *strong sustainability* means insisting on a nondeclining stock of (some forms of) natural capital. (This is a rough understanding; below I distinguish "strong" from "absurdly strong" sustainability.) It is by insisting on a *nondeclining* stock that we obtain a commitment to intergenerational equality as a lower boundary. Since practically the point of the sustainability debate is to limit consumption (which renders an increase of the stock unlikely) I assume that a commitment to a nondeclining stock is effectively a commitment to intergenerational equality.

According to weak sustainability, all forms of capital are substitutable for each other, and the preservation of anything in particular is not required. Future people cannot complain as long as they are no poorer in total capital. In contrast, the most common version of strong sustainability identifies some forms of natural capital as significant, or "critical" (to make clear that, say, obscure species of beetles do not deserve preservation, a point that presupposes, controversially, that we have a sufficiently good understanding of ecosystems to consider the extinction of such species "noncritical"). So even if future people are richer in terms of overall capital, they can complain if this wealth comes at the expense of such capital. Neumayer (2003) distinguishes two variants of strong sustainability. The first thinks of the maintenance of (normally critical) natural resources in terms of their overall value. Within the domain of such resources, substitutability holds, but not otherwise. Increases within that domain offset depletion, but man-made capital does not. More whales may offset damage to the ozone layer, but human inventions do not.[17]

The other variant of the natural stock approach insists on preserving a certain physical stock without referring to the value of the environment for human ends. Defenders deny the viability of a standpoint that assigns some natural capital a special status while assessing nature in terms of such a value. This variant is "absurdly strong" (Holland 1997, 1999); from now on I use "strong sustainability" only for the first variant). In this view, nature receives insufficient protection if it is considered capital. This does not mean nothing can be used, but use would be constrained in ways that do not appeal to the value of stock for human purposes. One constraint might be to use renewable resources only to the extent that their stock does not deteriorate, and nonrenewable resources only if we invest into functionally equivalent ones, to ensure that regenerative capacities and environmental functions remain intact.[18]

7. Weak, strong, and absurdly strong sustainability all incorporate views about whether (and which) resources ought to be preserved. Which of

these views should we adopt to obtain the best understanding of what the second obligation in section 5 requires? One might think the ownership approach *obviously* rejects weak sustainability. This is implied by Hurka (1993, 36), who suggests that future people must be taken seriously as claimants of *resources*. However, any argument for an alignment between ownership approach and a view on what should be preserved must adopt a view on how best to benefit future owners. Once the earlier thought of future people *as beneficiaries* is in sight, we see that we cannot simply assume that the view on what must be preserved that is most readily aligned with the ownership approach is the view advocated by strong or absurdly strong sustainability rather than that advocated by weak sustainability. The case must be made with care. I offer three arguments to show that weak sustainability fails to capture how future people ought to benefit. These arguments do not select between strong and absurdly strong sustainability.

To begin, I recall that the amount of commonly owned resources under the control of a country affects how much immigration the country should permit. At least some transformations into other forms of capital, however, diminish the amount of resources with regard to which we make immigration-related judgments. When Norway extracts North Sea oil and channels the earnings into investment funds, it might not diminish the value of the global stock of capital. Nonetheless, it might thereby transform common materials into something that only belongs to Norway. Since such substitution affects demands of reasonable conduct with regard to immigration, it should not be entirely straightforward. Strong and absurdly strong sustainability adopt a view on what should be preserved that creates normative objections to such a transformation. Weak sustainability makes it too easy to remove materials from the common stock.

The other arguments appeal to the value of nature. The second refers to the instrumental value of natural resources, insisting that weak sustainability does not optimally secure the future of humanity. Of concern are biodiversity losses, loss of ecosystems or life-support systems such as the global climate and the ozone layer, and soil erosion. We must ask to what extent protecting these assets requires the nonsubstitutability of natural resources, and how to assess opportunity costs from giving a special status to such resources. Neumayer (2003) insists that "the combination of the distinctive features of natural capital with risk, uncertainty and ignorance suggest the conclusion that there are good reasons for the non-substitutability of specific forms of natural capital" (124). These features are that those forms of capital (global life-support systems, biodiversity) provide for elementary life functions better than any replacements ever could, that we have no practical way of replacing them, and that it is hard to know which elements of our environment will matter. So there is a strong rationale for caution about depleting natural capital. Although weak sustainability can address these points to some extent, explicit attention to natural resources through nonsubstitutability does a better job capturing an appropriate conservativeness regarding these resources.[19]

The third argument draws on the noninstrumental value of nature. Chapter 6 adopted *enlightened anthropocentrism*, the position that values ultimately must be values on a human scale. This view is compatible with valuing nature intrinsically, as sublime or awesome, or as providing a context in which human life obtains meaning. Not only is this stance consistent with Common Ownership, it also gives us reason to think that the specific way in which we ought to benefit future people is by preserving resources. Those ways of valuing nature support the preservation of the natural environment.

This section began by noting that different versions of sustainability formulate views about whether (and which) resources ought to be preserved, and by asking which of them we should adopt. We can conclude that we should reject weak sustainability. I recall here the second obligation in section 5: to the extent that within current institutions plans are made or policies adopted that affect future generations, those generations (both the next one and subsequent ones) can expect that such planning makes sure their ability to meet basic needs is preserved, to the extent that this depends on original resources and spaces. The preservation of the *stuff,* of natural resources and spaces, matters. So we should understand that obligation as requiring the preservation of actual resources and spaces to the extent needed for the satisfaction of basic needs, rather than as requiring merely the preservation of a stock of capital to that end (a stock within which resources or spaces are substitutable for other forms of capital).[20]

8. The views on sustainability in sections and 6 and 7 include a commitment to intergenerational equality (preservation of a nondeclining stock). Should we endorse such equality? As far as Common Ownership is concerned, resource depletion is not *unjust* if it is consistent with the two obligations in section 5. One might object that it matters that we are dealing with an unknown number of generations. We can safely assume that future people will want to have children. But if we do not preserve resources, some generation might be unable to have children who can sustain themselves. Yet it would not *now* be *unjust* to exercise one's rights and help bring about a situation in which future people ought not repro-

duce, as they ought not if their offspring cannot sustain themselves. Again, there is no duty to bring future people into existence.

Chapter 8 noted that there was nothing unjust about groups claiming disproportionate parts of the earth. With regard to the relationship among generations, Common Ownership again does not license strong conclusions about what is unjust, which leads to the worry that we might owe future generations too little. However, as with immigration, we can inquire how much of what is collectively owned each generation can consume in a way that would be reasonably acceptable to all generations. The present discussion offers a vertical account—over time—parallel to the horizontal account of immigration. One difference is that, at any given time, there is a knowable number of people, whereas we do not know how many generations there will be. We cannot determine intergenerational duties via ideas of *proportionate* use as in the immigration case. If we knew how many generations were ahead, we would not have to bequeath a nondecreased stock, only enough for each generation to live above a threshold. But we do not know how many generations there will be. So no proposal that captures a demand of reasonable conduct for each generation can allow for a decrease between generations of the stock of natural resources.

Intergenerational equality is a sensible response to this situation. Strong sustainability, including its commitment to intergenerational equality, emerges as a proposal for reasonable conduct successive generations should accept, much like proportionate use in the immigration scenario. In support of this proposal we can indeed enlist the point that future generations are likely to have offspring. (We could not use this to argue that exercising ownership rights in the present would be unjust.) However— and this explains why that proposal is only "much like" the immigration proposal—this reasoning entails only a readily defeasible commitment to intergenerational equality. One reason for waiving it is if a temporary decline in resources generates improvements for remote generations. Another is if one generation is in an exceptionally good position to transform resources into technological advancements (say, because of scientific breakthroughs) or finds itself in dire need of resources (say, because of natural disasters). But within such limits, intergenerational equality is a demand of reasonable conduct—and a result we obtain in addition to the earlier principle of justice.

9. What I argued concerning injustice and unreasonableness vis-à-vis future generations applies at the level of humanity and has no immediate implications for particular countries. However, one can in principle

inquire about duties to future people with regard to *any* ground of justice —a matter that, again, merits further investigation beyond what I can do now. (I say one can "in principle" inquire about this matter because we have seen in this chapter how hard it is to say anything about obligations to future generations.) By way of concluding, let us take another look at shared membership in a state. A helpful reference point is de-Shalit (1995), who argues in a communitarian manner that a person's self is constituted by an intergenerational community. The "self is not totally confined within the barriers of its own physical existence" (124).[21] De-Shalit thinks membership in such communities generates duties.

To avoid intergenerational communitarian commitments, we can recast the fact that our community shapes our selves, and so generates duties to contemporaries in the community, in terms of the profound importance of the basic structure (see chapter 2). The community of the future might well continue to live in that same basic structure. Thus, people at that time will have duties to each other much like the duties contemporaries have toward each other. By preserving or developing a particular basic structure rather than another, we shape the basic structure in which future people will find themselves. This point by itself is a source of obligations toward future generations. I do not explore this matter in detail, but one point matters. The basic structure generates attitudes and policies that preserve the environment for future generations. For that reason, my arguments for obligations to future generations *at the level of humanity* also apply at the level of the basic structure *for given countries*. A demand of reasonable conduct is that each generation arrange the basic structure in such a way that it generates environmental policies in accordance with strong sustainability.

Let us conclude. While Marx overstated the point, saying, "like *boni patres familias*, they must hand it down to succeeding generations in an *improved* condition" (1972, chap. 46, 776; italics added), the current generation can be expected to act as trustees for future generations. This chapter has spelled out what this means. Some of the duties that this generation has to future generations concern the preservation of climate conditions hospitable to human life. That topic, however, also raises questions of conventional distributive justice (i.e., distribution at a given time), as well as questions about the ownership status of one part of the earth, to wit, the atmosphere. I therefore discuss climate change separately, in chapter 10.

CHAPTER 10

Climate Change and Ownership of the Atmosphere

1. Naturally occurring greenhouse gases, such as water vapor, carbon dioxide, and methane, form a thermal blanket that traps sun energy inside the atmosphere and thereby makes the earth inhabitable in the first place. However, in recent centuries human activities have greatly increased greenhouse gas concentrations. Considerable quantities of carbon dioxide have resulted from burning fossil fuels (coal, oil, and gas, which generate most of the world's energy) and from deforestation. Increasing evaporation of water amplifies the warming effects of these gases by causing larger greenhouse effects than combustion and deforestation alone. The result is global climate change.

On average, global surface temperatures have risen by about 1.25 degrees Fahrenheit over the past 150 years. Most of the increase has occurred since 1970. Other actual or likely consequences of increasing greenhouse gas concentrations include changes in patterns of precipitation, thawing of the permafrost, melting of glaciers, sea-level increases, and changes in the frequency and intensity of storms. Depending on the location, risks for humans caused by climate change include decreases in the availability of water and in the productivity of farms, forests, and fisheries; a prevalence of oppressive heat and humidity; an increase in the range and frequency of diseases and pests; greater damage from storms, floods, droughts, or wildfires; and decreasing biodiversity. The speed of these changes is troublesome even where otherwise they might be welcome.

The Intergovernmental Panel on Climate Change concluded that most of the increase in average temperatures is very likely due to increases in man-made greenhouse gas concentrations.[1] There are three options: to let these changes happen and suffer the consequences (an option I do not consider), to mitigate climate change (reduce its pace and magnitude), or to adapt (reduce the impacts of climate change). Possible mitigation pathways include reducing greenhouse gases (through changing energy use, reforming agricultural practices, or limiting deforestation) and using geoengineering to remove gases from the atmosphere or create cooling effects to offset heating. Possibilities for adaptation include developing crops resistant to climate change, strengthening public health defenses, improving flood control and drought management, building barriers against sea-level rises, or avoiding development in at-risk areas.

Chapter 9 presented two obligations of justice concerning future generations: First, future people can legitimately expect that the current generation will leave behind institutions within which they can exercise membership rights, if that generation is in a position to leave behind such institutions. Second, to the extent that within current institutions plans are made or policies adopted that affect future generations, those generations can expect that such planning makes sure their ability to meet basic needs is preserved, to the extent that this depends on original resources and spaces. In addition, strong sustainability turns out to be a demand of reasonable conduct. Those obligations entail that climate change policy must have top priority in policy making, and the demand of reasonable conduct entails that mitigation play an important role in our response strategy. The preservation of resources and spaces matters. However, these results tell us nothing about how burdens from mitigation and adaptation should be distributed. This chapter explores what we can learn from the standpoint of collective ownership about how to distribute these burdens specifically among states. To that end, I explore the ownership status of the atmosphere.[2]

We face questions about the distribution of these burdens only if actions that trigger climate change constitute a wrong. Otherwise climate change would just be among the events that render independently existing duties applicable (which it *also* is). But the nature of this wrong cannot lie simply in the fact that climate change thwarts people's interests. Competitive markets do so, too, but no wrong might occur. One way of characterizing the wrong done through climate change is to argue that the ownership status of the atmosphere is incompatible with certain patterns of greenhouse gas emissions. One way of developing that theme in turn is to regard the atmosphere, as Singer (2002a) does, as a "global sink" whose use must be regulated.

Singer, among others, thinks of such regulation in terms of an equal per-capita approach: each person has an equal claim to pollute. The distribution of burdens from climate change can then be derived by assessing which entity has so far polluted more (or less) than it should. This approach has some intuitive plausibility, and it is not only among philosophers that it has reached some prominence: the Indian government, for one, has taken this stance. However, this way of developing what the ownership approach has to say about burdens from climate change is flawed: we own the earth *as a whole*, not the atmosphere *in particular*. Common Ownership does not imply that any nugget of gold on the ocean floor must be shared out among all of humanity. But then neither does the atmosphere have to be shared out in that manner. So we must think carefully about what it means for ownership *of the atmosphere* (and thus for the moral assessment of patterns of greenhouse gas emissions) that humanity owns *the earth*.

Section 2 of this chapter returns to Grotius's discussion of freedom of the seas. In his day, ownership of the seas was fiercely disputed, but today his response to that controversy can be fruitfully applied to our equally contentious problem of ownership of the atmosphere. Section 3 discusses ownership of *parts* of the earth systematically from the nontheological standpoint of Common Ownership. Grotius distinguished parts of the earth that could legitimately be appropriated to the exclusion of others from those that should remain in common. But there is a third, intermediate status: for some regions, private appropriation may not be acceptable, but some other sort of regulation of use may be. Different goods provided by such parts of the earth could then be regulated differently, depending on the nature of the good. Section 4 argues that the atmosphere has that status. Moreover, regulation of access to the *absorptive capacity* of the atmosphere (its capacity to absorb greenhouse gases in a way that preserves basic climate conditions, one good provided by that part of the earth) is required by *justice*. It is then a *demand of reasonable conduct* that such regulation be done in terms of ideas of fair division. So, like chapter 9, this chapter combines an inquiry in terms of justice with one in terms of reasonable conduct.

The remainder of this chapter explores ways of thinking about a fair division of burdens. Section 5 rebuts the equal per-capita approach. Sections 6 and 7 explore the importance of past emissions for this distribution. I reject the proposal that a principle of accountability for historical emissions ought to guide the distribution of burdens. Common Ownership thus helps rebut two initially plausible approaches to this matter. In both cases, the theory of the different sorts of ownership status of parts of the earth from section 3 offers guidance. Section 8 sketches a proposal for this distribution. The main virtue of that proposal, except for its prima facie plausibility, is that it is a consistent extension of results obtained from the ownership standpoint. These results are mostly negative, but in the search for a solution to a fair-division problem, demonstrations of weaknesses of prima facie plausible contenders make significant contributions. After all, a successful proposal brings relevant criteria that bear on the problem into reflective equilibrium. More discussion is required to defend my proposal. Still, even those of its elements that do not follow from collective ownership presuppose that climate change (a) is a moral problem (b) whose burdens ought to be divided fairly. Casting climate change as such a problem is a major contribution of this standpoint.[3]

Let us consider an objection to the claim that we should assess the ownership status of the atmosphere to determine the distribution of burdens from climate change. If those burdens arise because of damage to goods in which we have ownership rights, this objector says, we do not need to know who owns the objects used for the interference. Suppose A uses a car to run over B's fence. We need not settle who owns the car to know who must fix the fence. In the case of climate change, we already know who owns, say, the crops that fail because of climate change. Therefore, inquiries about who owns the atmosphere are superfluous.

The car is used for the unmediated infliction of harm. In the climate change scenario, however, climate change affects the crops, but emissions cause the change. Instead of one occurrence, as in the car case, we have two occurrences related as cause and effect: emissions and atmospheric changes. We need not know who owns the car because the fact that it is used to inflict harm is obvious and salient. If the car is intentionally driven into the fence, the wrongness of the harm is clear. But in the climate change case, emissions are causally once removed from the harm whose wrongness is at issue. We should inquire about ownership of the atmosphere to see if this way (greenhouse gas emissions, the first occurrence) of affecting the medium that does harm (climate change, the second) is right or wrong. To this inquiry there is no parallel in the car case since there is no relevant distinction between two occurrences. The car case does not contradict the idea that we should investigate the ownership status of the atmosphere.[4]

2. Grotius thought God had given the whole earth to all humans in common. But he also thought that under certain conditions at least parts of the earth could be privatized, so that some people could legitimately exclude others. But was this true of all the earth? In particular, was it true of the seas? Grotius concluded that it was not. He also hinted that it might not be legitimate for the air either: "The same might be alleged of the Air too, could we put it to any Use" (*De Jure Belli* II.II.III.1). But nowadays we *can* put "the Air" to use. This chapter applies what we learn from Grotius's account of the seas to "the Air" to derive lessons for distributional questions about climate change. But let us first recall why he does not think privatization could be legitimate for the seas.

According to *De Jure Belli*, people realize that adjustments to original ownership are necessary in response to changes in their living conditions. But the sea is big enough for everybody's use. Thus no such adjustments are needed. In *Mare Liberum* we read that a form of private ownership becomes inseparable from use since use changes objects and certain kinds of use can only be made by relatively few people. Private ownership arises through natural extensions of use. Grotius insists that, physically, the seas *cannot* be occupied. So no natural extension of use can generate private ownership. Even if possible occupation would be unacceptable since people can benefit from using the seas without excluding others.

Today we can monitor and patrol the sea by air and water. Differences between the ability to occupy land and water have become a matter of degree. Nor is it still true that use by one party leaves intact what others can do with the sea: that is so for ships traveling through the seas, but not for fishing or seabed exploitation. In the nineteenth century, Sidgwick realized that Grotius's argument was no longer valid for fisheries (2005, 228). Grotius's reasons for thinking that the seas cannot legitimately be privatized no longer hold.[5] At a more abstract level, Grotius offers a plausible view, which, however, no longer applies to the seas. What is durable in his ideas is that, first, given a certain state of technology, the original purpose of ownership rights (that individuals can meet basic needs, to the extent that that turns on original resources and spaces) can be preserved in the case of the sea without new property arrangements, and second, if ownership rights can be preserved in this way, they ought to be, so that no new arrangements should be made, barring technological change.

Behind that idea lies a sensible conservative principle of occupation. It can be acceptable to occupy parts of the earth by excluding people. Such exclusion will presumably occur, but unless there is a good reason to exclude people, they should not be excluded. In this sense, collective ownership, though consistent with occupation under certain conditions, imposes obstacles to it. These constraints are aspects of an overall coherent development of the idea of collective ownership. The founding of communities (normally accompanied by political and economic arrangements that benefit from privatization) is a reason for exclusion—Grotius takes no issue with the existence of states. The burden is on those who wish to legitimize appropriation. As he saw it—in light of the technology of his age, as we may now add—that burden could not be met for the sea.

3. We must ask whether within my version of Common Ownership too a distinction becomes available between parts of the earth that can legitimately be privatized and parts that cannot. Provided no one's ability to satisfy basic needs is threatened, it is consistent with justice that people try to exclude others from areas of the resource in question, and it is equally consistent with justice that those others ignore those attempts and try to enter. We cannot reproduce Grotius's distinction in terms of justice. But we can draw some distinctions between parts of the earth in terms of demands of reasonable conduct.

Parts of the earth may have three different sorts of moral ownership status, capturing different demands of reasonable conduct with respect to privatization. First, parts of the earth can be owned in accordance with conventions allowing occupation to the exclusion of others. Second, parts of the earth can remain in common ownership, there being a demand of reasonable conduct against attempts to regulate these parts. These two sorts of status appear in Grotius: the seas either could be appropriated or had to be left in common. But *in addition*, parts of the earth may be governed by conventions to regulate access to and use of particular elements of the space in question (and there is a demand of reasonable conduct to provide such regulation), but none focusing *on occupation to the exclusion of others*. Such conventions may include different regulations for different goods, and may leave access to some goods unregulated. As far as the seas are concerned, fisheries and seabed resources may be regulated, but the ability of ships to travel through may not.

Under what conditions does reasonable conduct demand of co-owners to accept these forms of ownership? States can reasonably expect others to accept borders and thus immigration policies only if those policies abide by proportionate use. But that analysis presupposed there was nothing unreasonable *in principle* about the fact that regions could be occupied to the exclusion of others. This chapter broadens our analysis by asking if for some parts of the earth it would be unreasonable under any circumstances to expect others to accept appropriation or to appropriate anything in the first place. I first ask this question generally, and then section 4 proceeds to the atmosphere.

Grotius focused on the seas, but regions for which it is unacceptable to impose conventions allowing for appropriation to the exclusion of others also include "the skies" (the atmosphere), the airspace above the land and sea masses, as well as Antarctica. After technological changes have triggered human interest in these regions, each has become a subject of international law. The term "common heritage of mankind" has been applied to these areas (as well as to outer space, which is not in the domain to which our discussion about collective ownership currently applies).[6] Within my nontheological approach, we can regain Grotius's conservative principle of occupation. This principle provides guidance to the conditions under which co-owners may reasonably be expected to refrain from entering certain regions. Again we can say that, presumably, parts of the earth will be used by some to the exclusion of others; nonetheless, there is a burden on those who seek to show that specific parts can be occupied in such a way that others can be expected to stay away, to demonstrate under what conditions that is so. A clear case in which this burden is met is the founding of communities that would not function properly without excluding people.

There may, however, be strong reasons not to subject certain parts of the earth to appropriation. Susan Buck (1998, chap. 1) distinguishes among different categories of goods according to two criteria, excludability and subtractability. Goods may allow more or less readily for users to exclude others. Moreover, use by some prevents similar use by others to more or less considerable degrees because it subtracts value from the entity in question.[7] Put in these terms, a clear case for leaving areas in common is if the following obtain: first, the area does not lend itself to the founding of durable communities (presumably because human beings cannot easily survive there owing to, say, the temperature or a lack of oxygen), and second, the goods that this area provides are characterized by low degrees of excludability and subtractability. For such areas, nobody can be expected to respect conventions deviating from common ownership, and there is a demand of reasonable conduct not to try and privatize bits of such areas (or regulate their use).

At some stage, these conditions were satisfied for each of the areas regarded as mankind's common heritage, trivially so while lack of technology made their use impossible. These areas still do not lend themselves to the founding of communities, the existence of Antarctic research stations, submarines, or planes notwithstanding. But for many goods, technological progress has made exclusion easier, and new ways of exploiting goods create a higher degree of subtractability. Changes apply differently to these areas, and took effect first with regard to the goods provided by the seas, prompting Grotius to write *Mare Liberum*. Although he argued that the seas should be left in common, he did so because others were then arguing for the opposing view. If deviations occur from the clear case for leaving areas in common, we must reconsider the status of the respective parts of the earth.

Grotius might well have been right about ownership of land and sea for his own time, although his views about the sea no longer withstand scrutiny. Technological change may create a situation where the reasons why areas should remain in common no longer apply. Appropriation to the exclusion of others may then be acceptable. Or we may need conventions beyond the original rights without permitting exclusion, if *neither* the clear case for leaving areas in common *nor* a case for the founding of durable communities applies. It would then be unreasonable to expect others to accept occupation. But it would be unreasonable, too, if unrestricted liberty rights persisted. For such areas, we need different norms of access to the goods provided by that part, depending on their nature.

4. The skies are a paradigmatic case of a part of the earth for which co-owners could not reasonably be expected to waive their rights in favor of exclusive appropriation. There is no demand of reasonable conduct on

people to accept it if others tried to privatize bits of the skies, and there is a demand of reasonable conduct not to do so. Nor would it be reasonable for everybody to retain the unrestricted exercise of their rights.

Different conventions should be adopted for different goods provided by the skies. Before the invention of airplanes, the skies played little practical role in human affairs. This invention, however, created a new good: airspace control. Because of the possibility of aerial bombing, such control is precious. It is highly subtractable, and technological advancements have increased possibilities for exclusion. The norm quickly emerged that control of airspace above a country belongs to it.[8] For airspace above the high seas, access is not restricted in this way. Although the skies *as such* should neither be legitimately appropriated to the exclusion of some nor be left in common ownership, this convention pertaining to this particular good is supported, as a demand of reasonable conduct, by whatever arguments support the moral acceptability of states to begin with (see chapters 15 and 16 on that subject).

Another good provided by the skies is the *absorptive capacity* of the atmosphere, its ability to absorb greenhouse gases in a manner that preserves basic climate conditions. That capacity is highly subtractable: there are limits to how much greenhouse gas human beings can emit in total without climate change, and with increasing emissions we are approaching that limit. Unlike airspace, it is a good of low excludability: greenhouse gases disperse uniformly in the atmosphere. What damage they cause does not depend on where they are emitted. How should we regulate access to this good?[9]

Absorptive capacity is a peculiar good. Like airspace control, it is provided by the skies, and thus by a part of the earth that, as such, should neither be legitimately appropriated to the exclusion of some nor be left in common ownership. At the same time, there is great moral urgency to regulating access to the absorptive capacity. A collapse of the climate conditions under which human life flourishes may easily make it impossible for individuals to meet basic needs. That *regulation be provided* for this good to make sure individuals can meet basic needs is a requirement of justice associated with collective ownership. Given the nature of the absorptive capacity, this point follows from the obligation in chapter 9 that, to the extent that within current institutions plans are made or policies adopted that affect future generations, those generations can expect that such planning makes sure their ability to meet basic needs is preserved, to the extent that this depends on original resources and spaces.

Two strands of argument merge here. One is that the absorptive capacity is a good provided by a part of the earth (the skies) for which co-owners cannot reasonably be expected to accept exclusive appropriation, while at the same time it would also be unreasonable for everybody to retain the unrestricted exercise of their rights. The second strand is that regulating access specifically to the absorptive capacity is required as a matter of justice. Justice requires that access be regulated so as to stop catastrophic damage from climate change. This requirement (and thus the second strand of argument) by itself does not preclude, say, privatization of the skies (whatever that might mean for the case of the atmosphere's absorptive capacity).

The first strand raises the question of how we should regulate access to the absorptive capacity. Relevant for assessing how we should regulate this particular good provided by the skies are the economic importance of emissions and the absorptive capacity's subtractable and nonexcludable nature. Nobody can reasonably be expected to accept regulation that permits privatization of this good (again, whatever that might mean practically). Nor would it be reasonably acceptable that access be regulated in accordance with bargaining power. To be sure, airspace control can legitimately be regulated by norms that respectively exclude some. However, not only is airspace control a good of high excludability, there is also no parallel here to the support for that kind of regulation that arguments for the moral acceptability of states provided. In the present case, reasonable conduct requires an appropriate *fair-division* scheme.[10]

What principles of dividing burdens from climate change are fair, given that regulation is morally required? This question takes up the remainder of this chapter and leads to theories of fair division. Such theories deal with the arbitration of competing claims, which may not always literally "divide" anything, but may also regulate access. A well-known difficulty is that there is often a lack of salience for any solution under the typical circumstances calling for fair-division solutions, conditions of persistent disagreement. Rarely does any one solution stand out as head and shoulders better than any other. The search for a solution to a fair-division problem often involves an exploration of several prima facie plausible criteria. Ultimately a proposal brings the relevant criteria into reflective equilibrium. Criteria that factor into a successful proposal look more plausible in light of weaknesses of competing criteria. The demonstration of such weaknesses is often essential to this quest for fair-division solutions. It is this kind of contribution that the standpoint of collective ownership makes to the search for a fair distribution of burdens from climate change.

Considerations of collective ownership rebut two common approaches to regulating access to the absorptive capacity. The first is the idea that each person has a claim to an equal per-capita share of the atmosphere, the second is a principle of accountability for historical emissions, at least those versions that find fault with past emitters or endorse no-fault-based liability.[11] In sections 5–7, my assessment of these approaches discusses burdens from climate change in a narrow sense, burdens that follow from "regulating access to the absorptive capacity," one form of mitigation. But the proposal in section 8 (which goes beyond what we can establish in terms of collective ownership) considers burdens in a broader sense, burdens that follow from overall responses to climate change (mitigating, adapting, or some mix thereof).

5. Let us begin with the per-capita approach. Singer (2002a) and others have asserted that humanity collectively owns the absorptive capacity. Singer advocates a per-capita view as the principle of distribution pertaining to this good. Each person should be allowed to consume (or "access") the absorptive capacity to the same degree. Each person should be allowed to bring about the same volume of emissions. One may implement this approach via a "cap-and-trade" system. We would choose a global limit, each country obtaining an amount of permissible emissions (its "cap") based on population size. Countries that wish to pollute more must purchase additional rights. One way of assigning caps is that each person since, say, the Industrial Revolution has the same entitlement. We must then determine how much pollution that involves in light of bearable greenhouse gas concentrations.[12] As Vanderheiden (2008) states in support of this view, "The atmosphere presents a rare example of a pure public good, where no one has a valid claim to larger shares of the good than anyone else" (225).[13]

Still, we must reject this approach. The discussion of the different kinds of ownership status that parts of the earth may have shows there is no ex ante reason to think an equal per-capita approach is appropriate to the absorptive capacity. Note three points. First, chapter 6 rejects the Equal Division conception of collective ownership, which views collective ownership as entailing, for each person, a claim to an equal share of resources. According to Common Ownership, no such claims arise. So no support for the equal per-capita approach comes from a commitment to Equal Division as conception of collective ownership, or from any intuitions that draw on its plausibility.

Even if Equal Division were the preferred conception of collective ownership, it would not entail that the *absorptive capacity* should be equally divided. Views about collective ownership do not immediately license conclusions about how parts of the earth must be shared out. The idea that humanity collectively owns the atmosphere will be plausible only to those who endorse collective ownership of the earth. After all, there is nothing distinctive about the atmosphere that would restrict collective ownership to it. Therefore, if the argument in Singer (2002a) is driven by Equal Division (and it is easy to see why it would get intuitive support that way), it is the sort of move to which right-libertarians have argued that defenders of collective ownership are committed, only for those same right-libertarians to insist that this very move amounts to a reductio ad absurdum of collective ownership. Chapter 6 discussed this matter, the move in question being the inference from the claim that the earth is collectively owned (in a certain way) to the claim that each part of it is so owned.[14] However, as we noted, and this is the second point, collective ownership *of the earth* does not imply that any particular object on or part of it must be divided up. This inference especially does not hold for the absorptive capacity. It is because this inference fails that we had to discuss the ownership status of parts of the earth the way we did. What is wrong with the right-libertarian reductio is also wrong with Singer's argument.[15]

The third point is this. One might think our discussion of the absorptive capacity should proceed as did the discussion of immigration in chapter 8. Common Ownership does not entail that, as a matter of justice, we should adopt an equal division of pollution permits, just as it does not entail that, as a matter of justice, portions of the commonly owned three-dimensional space ought to be used proportionately. Still, proportionate use makes for reasonable acceptability of borders: reasonable conduct demands of outsiders respect for the immigration policies of countries that use a proportionate share of commonly owned spaces and resources. One might argue similarly for a Singerian equal per-capita approach. Once such an approach is adopted, co-owners can be expected not to exercise liberty rights in a contrary manner.

However, there are considerable differences. In the immigration scenario we needed a measure of the usefulness of three-dimensional regions. Such regions not only constitute complex bundles of goods, they represent the whole portion of commonly owned space a country claims for itself. In light of the significance of states, such portions of collectively owned space have a privileged status that makes the acceptability of immigration arrangements dependent on proportionate use. But this is different from claiming that proportionate (equal per-capita) use of one good is the principle that ought to guide the distribution of burdens from climate change. Absorptive capacity is a significant good. But so are others, such as water or fertile land. Once we acknowledge that we can so divide up commonly owned resources or spaces, we cannot block a slippery slope toward the right-libertarian reductio.

We should also note some implausible implications of the equal per-capita approach. Countries would obtain allocations regardless of how this affected their economy, how they used them, what importance they had for people's lives, and whether they reduced emissions. Some of these concerns could be resolved by clever allocation and trading mechanisms.

But the overall picture that emerges is this. The three points capture difficulties in attempts to argue from Common Ownership that we should adopt the equal per-capita approach. We are hard-pressed to identify positive reasons for doing so given that Common Ownership is the preferred conception of collective ownership. We have also encountered problems with the implementation of the equal per-capita proposal. These issues would be innocuous if there were an ex ante entitlement to an equal share of pollution. But precisely that thought encounters the difficulties spelled out in the three points above.

6. "Everyone has the same claim to part of the atmospheric sink, at least as a starting point for discussion," says Singer (2002a, 35), "and perhaps, if no good reasons can be found for moving from it, as an end point as well." But we have articulated good reasons for moving from it. Let us next consider the idea that past emissions ought to be taken into account when we regulate such access. We may call this the "principle of historical accountability," in contrast to the "principle of equal per-capita allocation." As I argue in section 7, "past emissions" are best understood as emissions before 1990, though nothing in this section hangs on that choice of date. The point of the proposal is that it should matter, when we regulate access, that industrialized nations have already consumed some of the absorptive capacity. I ultimately adopt only a highly qualified version of the idea that past emissions should matter for the regulation of access.[16]

The following considerations are often taken to support the view that, contrary to the principle of historical accountability, past emissions should be *disregarded*. First, past emitters, at least in earlier stages of industrialization, did not and (in any relevant sense) could not know that greenhouse gases might have catastrophic effects. Nor could they know that fossil fuels would long remain essential: their emissions became problematic only because economies continued to depend on such fuels. Second, it is unclear who caused what damage. Nor is it clear who should be accountable: should it be only states, or also companies or individuals?[17] Third, the benefits of industrialization spread across the world. Developing countries now benefit from inventions made during earlier industrializations that used inferior technology.[18] Moreover, countries other than those in which most emissions occurred have benefited from those emissions via trade, as well as via the spread of technology and scientific understanding, whose development was possible only in industrialized societies.[19]

I grant that the second point fails: one cannot block demands for integration of past emissions into future-directed regulation on the strength of difficulties in assigning responsibilities. Granting this makes my argument more difficult (since I ultimately accept only a highly qualified version of the principle of historical accountability), so I do not dwell on it. There has been much controversy about the third point. Shue (1999) responds that developing countries have paid for the benefits they obtained. Singer (2002a) insists that in the United States, most goods and services are for domestic consumption. However, quality of life has improved since the Industrial Revolution in terms of longevity, child mortality, and literacy. These benefits cannot be detached from industrialization and have been of global reach despite their differential effects. Still, not all past emissions are such that everyone has benefited from them. Although, as, say, Polanyi's *Great Transformation* argues, and Zola's *Germinal* illustrates, it would be wrong to think that early emitters benefited much from their emissions (since those were miserable times), it is still true that with respect to at least some past emissions, the emitters benefited but the rest of the world did not. So the third point cannot be used to dismiss the relevance of past emissions.

What is crucial for determining the relevance of past emissions is therefore an assessment of the first point (that past emitters could not know about the problematic consequences of pollution). But a preliminary objection to the relevance of this point must be considered. Tort law sometimes endorses *strict liability*, accountability without fault. Could this notion not allow us to hold people accountable for past emissions, even though nobody was at fault then? But strict liability must overcome a strong presumption of unfairness. Minimally, it should not apply without the affected individuals being aware of it. Only then can they choose whether to participate in the relevant activities. Therefore, strict liability should not apply where people lacked the background understanding to act in certain ways.[20]

So, *did* past emitters violate any of the obligations of justice or demands of reasonable conduct that follow from Common Ownership? Our discussion of the ownership status of the atmosphere can help us answer this question. That discussion also allows us to evaluate the behavior of our ancestors. According to Common Ownership, in addition to areas subject to appropriation by occupation to the exclusion of others, there are areas that should be left in common, or else be governed by conventions that go beyond common ownership without allowing for appropriation. The moral ownership status of these areas depends on the available technology, and might change in time. What changes especially is whether co-owners can be expected to waive liberty rights either because private occupation is appropriate or because access to the respective parts should be regulated by norms other than those allowing for appropriation. In Grotius's time, co-owners could not be expected to waive rights to the seas. But advances in, say, fishing and seabed exploitation have created a situation in which they can be expected to accept principles regulating access to these goods. The same is true for the absorptive capacity.

Section 4 showed that it *now* is a violation of justice for states to leave access to the absorptive capacity unregulated. What is crucial, however, is that technology in early stages was *already* such that a new regime of access to that good was required as a matter of justice. The volume of emissions even then, made possible by new technology, had made the absorptive capacity highly subtractable. Early emitters violated obligations of justice when permitting unrestricted emissions. Still, they could not know about the problematic consequences of pollution. We arrive at a familiar distinction. We often appeal to what individuals, subjectively speaking, had reason to do by way of assessing when to blame or excuse them. But we think of requirements of justice differently, in terms of what, all things considered, or objectively speaking, people ought to do.

So, while it did violate obligations of justice not to adopt conventions of access to the absorptive capacity to limit emissions, a set of conditions of *maximally excusatory force* applies to early emitters. The standpoint from which we can say earlier decision makers violated obligations of justice sets aside their scientific limitations. We cannot blame people for failing to regulate access to the absorptive capacity. "Attempts to apply fault-based standards are virtually guaranteed to become embroiled in more or less irresolvable controversy about historical explanations," says Shue (1996, 16). "Yet never to attempt to assess fault is to act as if the world began yesterday." We can assess fault, but although there was wrongdoing in the past, there was no blameworthy fault. The world did not begin yesterday, and this approach in terms of Common Ownership allows us to articulate the thought that what justice requires with regard to the absorptive capacity, and what people could reasonably be expected to know, has evolved.

7. To continue our discussion of the principle of historical accountability, let us ask, what is the relevant date before which emitters should not be blamed for emissions? Gosseries (2004) mentions various sensible dates, among them 1896 (the publication of an article by Svante Arrhenius on the greenhouse effect, "the first warning of global warming" [Neumayer 2000, 188]), 1967 (the publication of the first serious modeling exercise on the matter), 1990, and 1995 (the publication of the first two IPCC reports).[21] An advocate of historical accountability, Eric Neumayer (2000) thinks it was not before the mid-1980s that the public and decision makers became aware of the greenhouse effect. The 1992 UN Framework Convention on Climate Change too sets a plausible date. The years of the

publication of the third and fourth IPCC reports (2001, 2007) are also possible, as both reports added clarity to climate change issues.[22]

The crucial question is at what time decision makers could have been expected to know, specifically, the *dangers* of climate change. By this standard, 1990 is the latest sensible date: the 1990 IPCC report already absorbed a body of insights gathered over years. Any choice of date will trigger the objection that if countries cannot be blamed for emissions prior to year X, they cannot be blamed for having committed themselves, over generations, to lifestyles that essentially involve massive emissions. Come year X, they were locked into certain patterns. However, if year X is fixed as the latest possible year, this objection loses its force.

In light of the relevance and visibility of the 1990 IPCC report, and of persistent doubts that a choice of date other than the latest sensible one would inevitably create about what decision makers may have been expected to consider, 1990 is also a sensible choice, *provided* the proposal for the distribution of burdens acknowledges reasons other than rectification of wrongful past emissions as reasons for which disadvantaged countries can demand aid. The importance of 1990 can then make us neglect the fact that it is the *latest* sensible date. Put differently, if the only aid available to poor countries on the correct proposal was from past emitters in virtue of blameworthy emissions, then the later we moved the date, the less aid poor countries would get, and so we would have to worry about choosing the latest sensible date rather than, say, the earliest. However, earlier chapters showed there is a duty to help states realize human rights, and thus help them create conditions under which the realization of these rights is possible, as well as a duty of assistance with building institutions. One sensible way of making good on these duties is the sharing of technology and other support to mitigate or adjust to climate change. It is because of these independently existing duties that also affect the distribution of burdens from climate change that the choice of the latest sensible date before which emissions are not blameworthy is not too worrisome.

Our discussion of historical accountability has reached three conclusions. First, past emitters violated obligations of justice. Second, they cannot be blamed for their emissions, nor are they strictly liable for them. Third, defining past emitters as emitters before 1990 depends on the assumption that the proposal for the distribution of burdens acknowledges reasons other than rectification of blameworthy past emissions as reasons for which disadvantaged countries can demand aid in dealing with climate change. My proposal for the distribution of burdens is informed by these points, and adopts only a highly qualified version of historical accountability. Collective ownership offers a language of right and wrong

with regard to use of parts of the earth that has entered the reasoning leading to these conclusions.

8. Sections 5–7 have discussed burdens from climate change (and their
distribution) in a relatively narrow sense, namely, burdens that follow
from "regulating access to the absorptive capacity," which is one form of
mitigation. Now I consider burdens in a broader sense, to wit, burdens
that follow from whatever overall response we take to climate change.
The proposal will in fact distinguish between burdens from adaptation
and burdens from mitigation. What I have argued so far draws on Common Ownership directly (except for the argument for 1990 as the cutoff
year). The results only partially determine how to regulate access to the
absorptive capacity. The proposal I am about to make integrates our findings, but also goes far beyond them. The proposal is tentative. I wish to
show how to extend our results to a plausible overall proposal for distributing the burdens from climate change.

As we noted, a common way of addressing a fair-division problem is
to explore the strength of various initially plausible criteria and to make
a proposal that brings the relevant criteria into reflective equilibrium.
One way in which a proposal gains plausibility is through the relative
weakness of criteria that are not integrated. So arguments demonstrating
such weaknesses are essential steps in this process. Our findings about
the equal per-capita principle and the principle of historical accountability constitute such demonstrations (and in that sense partially determine
how to regulate access to the absorptive capacity): the former should not
be integrated into a proposal for a distribution of burdens from climate
change; the latter should be integrated, but in a way that respects the results summarized at the end of section 7. Any plausible overall proposal
is constrained thereby, which is one way in which the ownership approach contributes to the search for such a proposal. Another way, I recall, is by showing why climate change is a moral problem whose burdens
we must divide fairly. Various duties for which I have argued earlier apply
especially to climate change. Again, one way of making good on these
duties is the sharing of technology and other support to mitigate or adjust
to climate change.

The proposal that I am about to make and that respects these constraints integrates ideas about who is able to pay ("ability to pay" principle) and ideas in term of current per-capita emissions ("polluter pays"
principle). Although we cannot derive these principles from collective
ownership, their applicability presupposes that climate change is a moral
problem whose burdens must be divided fairly. The focus on polluter
pays and ability to pay principles is sensible partly because of the weak-

nesses of other approaches, especially the approaches we have explored. But partly this focus is sensible also because these principles are plausible by themselves. As far as the polluter pays principle is concerned: climate change occurs because there are emissions, and they do damage. Who produces them must matter *somehow* to the distribution of burdens (albeit in a way that takes into account whether the polluters were blameworthy). One may wonder, however, why ability to pay bears on the problem at hand. As a matter of justice, the ownership status of the earth requires that access to the absorptive capacity be regulated. All co-owners *share* this responsibility. Reflection on how to divide the resulting burdens then leads us to the ability to pay principle. That principle receives support from, for example, Shue's (1999) point:

> When some people have less than enough for a decent life, other people have far more than enough, and the total resources available are so great that everyone could have at least enough without preventing some people from still retaining considerably more than others have, it is unfair not to guarantee everyone at least an adequate minimum. (541)

In addition to the principles that have been mentioned (per-capita equality, past emissions, polluter pays, ability to pay), few others even ought to be considered. The willingness to pay principle asks those to shoulder the burdens who are most willing to pay, where willingness expresses the extent to which they expect to be harmed. Since this principle disregards causal involvement and capacity to deal with the problem, it should enter any overall proposal at best in a very limited way. My proposal integrates it in just such a way, in the sense that not all burdens from climate change count as burdens that should be distributed at the global level.

The principle of comparable burdens and the view that the size of the land area should trump have nothing to contribute once the ability to pay principle and the consumer pays principle are integrated. A common approach is grandfathering, which takes emissions of a certain year as given and asks countries to reduce by a fixed percentage of those earlier emissions. Yet this criterion merely offers political expediency. Finally, in competition with a polluter pays principle there is a consumer pays principle, according to which consumers should pay for emissions required to produce the goods they consume. Yet this is implausible if producers sell voluntarily. Producers control emissions, buyers do not. One might say that if buyers act voluntarily, they control emissions by creating demand. But they only do so mediated through actions of producers. Perhaps it is implausible to say about very poor countries that they "control" emissions since they normally have very limited choices in what they can put on the world market. However, as long as those countries need not contribute to a solution to climate change, the consumer pays principle is unacceptable.[23]

Let me now consider burdens from adaptation and mitigation separately. Suppose that advice needs to be given concerning a global treaty that distributes burdens from climate change from now on, for a fixed overall level of acceptable future emissions. Mitigation concerns future emissions only, and so (I contend) past emissions are (largely) irrelevant to the problem of how to distribute the resulting burdens. Adaptation, however, is (necessarily) adaptation to the results of past emissions, and so past emissions and associated questions about culpability and wrongdoing become relevant to the question of distributing burdens. Among burdens from adaptation we can distinguish burdens arising because of emissions that occurred after people became blameworthy (i.e., after 1990) and those from emissions that occurred before. Obviously, we can separate these emissions merely for the sake of analysis. Yet we seek principles that guide treaties regulating emissions and possibly also transfers, by offering an idea of what it means to treat people as equals from the standpoint of collective ownership. The path from there to allocations or penalties is thorny, and involves political and economic considerations beyond the scope of this inquiry.

As far as burdens from adaptation are concerned, countries that did not take considerable measures to reduce emissions *after* 1990, the wealthy ones anyway, have a duty to compensate those that have been harmed because of this, with a priority on the poorer ones. Such compensation could include financial or technological aid. To the extent that adaptation becomes necessary because of emissions before 1990, no such duty applies. The fact that past polluters did commit *a wrong* enters this proposal (see below, where I discuss costs from mitigation), although in a smaller manner than if they owed compensation. Costs of adaptation that arise because of emissions after an agreement has been concluded do not factor into my proposal. There are no international obligations merely because some countries are in less temperate zones, beyond a general duty of aid (or other humanitarian duties) and specific obligations that arise, say, because of trading. Similarly, not all costs of climate change should trigger redistribution. At the same time, the overall level of acceptable future emissions could be fixed in a way that considers the resulting costs of adaptation. And as we noted in chapter 7, inhabitants of countries that will be inundated have a human right to relocation. Climate change will also change the relative usefulness of locations for human purposes and thus bear on what claims to immigration to other countries are reasonably acceptable.[24]

Next, let us consider the burdens of mitigation. The goal here is to assess which countries need to make how much of a sacrifice, compared to business-as-usual trajectories (trajectories as they would be without climate change). This is where the polluter pays and ability to pay principles enter. The states that should modify their production are those that, in terms of per-capita wealth, can best afford changes (ability to pay) and those that on a per-capita basis emit most (polluter pays). These principles must be combined. Michaelowa (2007) plausibly groups countries into categories depending on a combined index, weighing both criteria equally. The amount of reduction for which a country is responsible, by reducing its emissions or by getting others to do so, is a function of this index. A country would be the higher on this ranking the higher its per-capita income and the higher its overall emissions. Many countries would not incur obligations because they rank too low.

We should supplement Michaelowa's proposal in such a way that for roughly equal index levels, countries ought to make more sacrifices if they have benefited from past emissions. No blame would be assigned for these emissions. Still, benefiting from them amounts to free riding on *ill-gotten* gains, and their presence should make a difference somewhere. This is the only way in which emissions from before 1990 appear in my proposal. Historical accountability indeed enters only in a highly qualified way.[25]

We can sum up this proposal as follows:

Suppose there is a fixed overall level of acceptable future emissions:

Burdens from adaptation

    Adaptation that becomes necessary because of emissions that occurred after 1990 but prior to the conclusion of a climate treaty: Countries that did not take considerable measures to reduce emissions after 1990, the wealthy ones anyway, have a duty to compensate those that have been harmed because of this, with a priority on the poorer ones. Since it will be impossible to assess specifically which kinds of adaptation become necessary because of these emissions, at the practical level this duty will generate an obligation for the offending countries to transfer money and technological aid, at a negotiable level, to countries that need to take measures to adapt.

    Adaptation that becomes necessary because of emissions that occurred before 1990 or after the conclusion of a climate treaty: No action is required.

Burdens from mitigation

    States must assess which countries need to make how much of a sacrifice, compared to their business-as-usual trajectories, so that emissions stay below the overall acceptable level.

    States that should modify their production are those that, in terms of per-capita wealth, can best afford changes (ability to pay) and those that on a per-capita basis emit most (polluter pays). The amount of reduction for which a country is responsible, by reducing its emissions or by getting others to do so, is a function of a ranking of countries in terms of a combined index of these criteria (both being weighted equally). A country would be higher in this ranking the higher its per-capita income and the higher its per-capita emissions.

For roughly equal index levels on this list, countries ought to make more sacrifices if they benefit from past emissions.

This proposal brings into reflective equilibrium the morally relevant considerations for regulating access to the absorptive capacity of the atmosphere. The ownership approach depicts the problem of finding a proposal for such regulation as a fair-division problem, rules out one prima facie plausible approach (equal per-capita division), and highly qualifies the relevance of another (historical accountability). I have not explored alternative ways of completing this partial answer to the question of the distribution of burdens that I derived from Common Ownership. Nor have I assessed how these considerations enter into an overall climate change policy. There is a moral concern not only with the distribution of burdens but also with making sure measures that respond to climate change are taken at all. Considerations such as environmental impact, flexibility over time, and compliance also matter. Fairness considerations must fit appropriately into such proposals. But I hope to have shown how the ownership approach contributes to the search for a plausible distribution of burdens from climate change.

We have reached the end not merely of our discussion of the implications of the ownership approach for climate change but also of our exploration of humanity's collective ownership of the earth as a ground of justice. Section 1 in chapter 7 contains a summary of the results of chapters 7–10 that readers may wish to consult again. These chapters, I hope, have rehabilitated an old idea and shown how it can be fruitfully applied to a range of modern problems. I have also used that idea to show that, contra the statists, certain principles of justice apply globally. However, contra the globalists and nonrelationists, none of these principles sanctions redistribution at a level comparable to what the difference principle calls for within states. Part 3 turns to international political and economic structures.

PART 3

International Political and Economic Structures

Human Rights as Membership Rights in the Global Order

1. So far we have developed pluralist internationalism by considering what principles of justice hold within states, in virtue of relations shared by their members, and what principles hold globally, in virtue not of specific relations or institutions but of more fundamental features of all human beings, such as their sharing a distinctively human life or living on a particular planet. Part 3 now continues the development of my pluralist view by considering what principles apply globally in virtue of specific relations and institutions that now hold in a globalized era among people around the world.

We have already done preliminary work on this question. Part 1 of this book asked whether the relations that now hold globally are sufficiently similar to those within states to make it true that Rawlsian principles of justice hold globally. I argued there that they are not: relations that hold globally are significantly "thinner" than those within states. Rawlsian principles hold only within states. I also gave a prima facie case for a positive result, that contra the statists, who hold that *no* principles of justice apply globally, some weaker principles are likely to hold globally in virtue of those thinner relations. I did not attempt then to identify those principles. Part 2 considered what principles follow from the fact that people are co-owners of the earth, in conjunction with the contingent fact that we inhabit a world with multiple states and global institutions. Thereby I arrived at a conception of human rights as membership rights in the global order. The principle that emerged was, roughly, that it is unjust if any of these rights are not realized for any member of the global order.

Part 3 builds on that earlier discussion of the global order as a ground in two ways. First, I broaden my conception of human rights beyond Common Ownership. I offer a general schema for arguing that, given the existence of certain global relations, there is a human right to X—which is ipso facto a general schema for coming up with specific principles of justice grounded in membership in the global order, principles of the form "it is unjust if any member of the global order lacks X." I employ my schema in some specific cases, arguing that there is respectively a human right to essential pharmaceuticals, work, and leisure. Thinking of membership in the global order as a ground of justice recognizes that the earth is covered by a system of states and that there are international organizations that seek to be of global reach.

I also consider a specific aspect of the global order, the existence of the trading system, which is associated with some distinct principles of justice concerning the distribution among states of gains from trade. The international agreements that legally structure trade create incentives, render economic interaction predictable and enforceable, and so affect the fate of billions who make a living through their ties to the trading. Different agreements could have been adopted. Nowadays, "For a society to be integrated effectively into the world economy, its government must belong to the WTO, which in turn requires accepting a large number of quite intrusive rules" (Buchanan and Keohane 2008, 27). The WTO concerns us in chapter 18. For now, let us merely note that its treaty is a "single undertaking": members cannot choose which bits to endorse. The trading system is part of the global order. So are states, but particular principles apply to them nonetheless. In virtue of the different points mentioned in this paragraph, involvement with the trading system is a ground of justice. In the case of "membership in the global order," the distribuenda are the things to which membership rights generate entitlements. In the case of "involvement with the global trading system," the distribuenda are gains from trade. Theorizing about these two grounds presupposes the existence of the grounds discussed in parts 1 and 2. Nonetheless, the existence of the structures that constitute the global order and the trading system makes it plausible to think of those as grounds of their own.

The remainder of chapter 11 resumes the discussion of human rights and thus of membership in the global order. Chapter 12 explores whether there is a human right to essential pharmaceuticals, and chapter 13 explores whether labor rights are human rights. The discussion of subjection to the trade regime, the fifth ground, begins in chapter 14 with an exploration of duties from trading and some principles associated with that ground. Chapter 18, in part 4, completes our discussion of trade by assessing the WTO.

Let me clarify two points. First, I use the terms "source" and "basis" in specific ways. Within conceptions of human rights, I talk of the *basis* on which persons have rights. This chapter develops a basis-driven conception, the basis being membership in the global order. Membership rights are derived from several *sources*. These sources vary considerably in nature—providing us with a deeply pluralistic theory of human rights—but each generates rights that do not merely apply to individuals where they live but are global in reach. So the basis is a disjunction over different sources. Sources are bases in the sense in which chapter 4 defined the term. But they are bases that are best integrated into a plausible conception of human rights in this disjunctive way, in combination with other sources. I return to this subject when I explain why I do not advocate a conception based solely on the idea of a distinctively human life. Common Ownership is a ground of justice and a source of membership rights within a basis-driven conception of human rights whose basis is membership in the global order. Such membership is both a ground of justice and the basis for a conception of human rights. Common humanity is a ground of justice, but also one source of membership rights. I have also used it as a basis for (what we may now call a preliminary) conception of human rights in chapter 4. The close connections between these terms (ground, basis, source) show that the organization of the material in this book is inevitably somewhat artificial and that the usefulness of categorizations is limited (which is especially apparent in this part 3). In any event, global duties are often overdetermined.

Second, I recall here that chapter 4 adopted T. M. Scanlon's account of rights. Arguments for rights involve an empirical claim about how individuals behave or how institutions work without rights, a claim that this result would be unacceptable, and a further empirical claim about how the envisaged assignment of rights would produce a different outcome. We have made little use of the details of this account and have mostly omitted discussion of the first and third components, the most important point being that there is an appropriate understanding of rights in the background. But we can understand the sources within my conception as articulating ways in which scenarios are unacceptable, and involve responsibilities, *at the global level*. For a right to X to be a human right, it must be a right vis-à-vis the global order as such, and involve obligations on the part of entities in the global order other than a person's state.

2. Where truth is being spoken to power nowadays, appeals to human rights tend to be used, rather than the language of Marxism, critical theory, modernization or dependency theory, or alternative moral languages, like that of justice or plainly of rights and duties other than "human" rights.[1] "Human rights is the idea of our time, the only political-moral idea that has received universal acceptance," writes the legal scholar Louis Henkin, perhaps with some exaggeration, while "the suspension of rights is the touchstone and measure of abnormality" (1990, xvii–xviii). But indeed, human rights talk has become the common language of emancipation.[2]

Chapter 4 argued that the idea of common humanity generates a conception of human rights based on the idea of a distinctively human life (an idea that is in any event better understood as contributing a source to the present conception). Chapter 7 introduced another basis-driven conception that regards human rights as membership rights in the global order. That conception is the view of human rights this book proposes. Collective ownership is the only source of such rights I have so far discussed. But once we reach membership rights starting from collective ownership, it behooves us to reverse the direction of inquiry to assess *how else* to derive such rights.

Membership in the global order is a ground because the political and economic arrangements in which we live generate demands of justice at the global level. Connecting this idea to human rights does not mean to deny the importance of the world wars or the Holocaust for the actual emergence of human rights practices. ("The last war not only took the lives of scores of millions of people. Without intending to, accidentally, the last war also shattered the great palace of culture of European morality, aesthetics, and custom. And humankind drove back to gloomy caverns and icy caves in their Rolls-Royces, Mercedes, and Moskviches," writes the Polish novelist Tadeusz Konwicki in *A Minor Apocalypse* [1999, 7]). Instead, it is to stress the moral relevance of global structures within which we can sensibly speak of membership rights. Legal scholar Mary Ann Glendon (2001) aptly calls the Universal Declaration of Human Rights "a declaration of interdependence ... of people, nations, and rights" (174). The presence of these structures allows us to identify sources of global rights and duties.

The conception from chapter 7 regards human rights as *associative* rights, rights individuals hold in virtue of belonging to an association. Natural rights so far enter qua ownership rights, collective ownership of the earth forming one source of membership rights. Whether human rights have pre-institutional origins or not depends on the source. By construction, since we discuss membership in the global order, this approach shows how certain moral concerns are of global reach. At least as far as chapter 7 developed it, this approach shows why the language of rights, rather than goals or values, is appropriate here. Chapter 6 showed that, at least for collective ownership as a source, the foundations of human rights are simple and obvious.

The principle of justice associated with common humanity is that the distribution in the global population of the things to which human rights (understood as rights protecting the distinctively human life) generate entitlements is just only if everyone has enough of those things to lead a distinctively human life. The principle associated with membership in the global order is that the distribution in the global population of the things to which human rights (understood now as membership rights) generate entitlements is just only if everyone has enough of those things for these rights to be realized. Since membership rights derive from different sources, that second principle is equivalent to one replacing the phrase "these rights" with a conjunction of the sort "rights derived from source X1 and rights derived from X2, etc." The distribuenda depend on the sources. Both the principle associated with common humanity and the one associated with membership in the global order generate a duty of assistance in building institutions via an instrumental argument.

Sections 3–6 of this chapter discuss other sources of membership rights. Sections 7 and 8 explore responsibilities, spelling out the idea that the addressee of human rights is the global order as such. I discuss what it means to hold rights within that order, rebutting the objection that there could be no plausible conception of human rights as membership rights in that order because there is no sense in which individuals *hold* such rights. I will not offer a list of rights. Doing so would involve case-specific investigations of normative and empirical matters far beyond what I can do here. I limit myself to some case studies, as well as to assessing what kind of argument is available given a particular source of human rights. My main reason for developing a conception of human rights here is to show what role human rights play in a theory of global justice.

3. In my conception, human rights involve a genuinely global, rather than a universal but respectively local, responsibility. There is then a clear difference between *human rights* and the *rights of citizens*. Not every wrong, not even every rights violation, creates an undifferentiated duty for everybody, even for every political entity in a position to do so, to help provide a remedy. My conception captures nothing like the attitude of Father Zossima in the *The Brothers Karamazov*, that "everybody is responsible for everything and everybody" (chap. 41). The human rights practices that have emerged partly through governmental activities (the Universal Declaration of Human Rights and other human rights instruments), partly through domestic and global civil society movements, frequently focus on the beneficiaries of human rights. Notoriously underspecified are, in particular, duties across borders. Human rights practices are *demand-side* focused, whereas my approach is *supply-side* focused, making global responsibilities central (Beitz 2009, chap. 5). Therefore we will inevitably encounter discrepancies when assessing whether global responsibilities accompany demands in the language of human rights.

To argue that X is a human right, X must first be shown to be a matter of importance in the agent's immediate environment (i.e., in one's interaction with some authority, often, but not necessarily, a government), and then that X is a global concern. For a right to X to be a human right, it cannot just be a right vis-à-vis the person's own state but must also be a right vis-à-vis the global order, and the global order must have obligations that go distinctly beyond mere nonviolation. It is hard to imagine that anything could be of global concern for which one could not take that first step. Introducing such a two-stage procedure creates some flexibility in articulating sources of membership rights. For instance, for sources that involve natural rights (common ownership and the distinctively human life), the demonstration that indeed we are talking about a natural right addresses both steps simultaneously—to the extent that all human beings could then in principle be addressees. However, let us recall the boundary problem from chapter 4: it may be unclear *how much* and *precisely what* protection of the distinctively human life requires. In cases that trigger such doubts, one may first argue that the right in question indeed is a right against the immediate environment (perhaps drawing on considerations of social justice), and then explore how to establish a global concern with the matter at hand. Chapter 12 offers such an argument.

Distinguishing these two steps also makes it possible adequately to articulate the importance of enlightened self-interest and global interconnectedness for the derivation of moral rights. To wit: the moral nature of the derivation may be shown in the first step, and enlightened self-interest or interconnectedness could then demonstrate the global concern. In any event, constitutive of X's being a human right is the second step. This discussion must also reveal why the matter at hand is aptly captured *as a right*. The formulations "being of global concern," "being a global responsibility," "being important at the global level," and "being globally urgent" I use interchangeably; the point is to establish a responsibility at the global level for the realization of something that has the form of a right. To put it in terms of duties, for a right to X to be a human right, it must involve duties (beyond nonviolation) on the part of entities in the global order other than a person's own state.

Sources of membership rights may be *substantive* or *procedural*. As far as substantive sources are concerned, something can be globally urgent in at least three ways: first, on account of enlightened self-interest; second, in virtue of global interconnectedness (understood as shared causal responsibility); and third, for moral reasons that do not turn on interconnectedness (so understood). That third category includes considerations of common ownership as well as considerations of the distinctively human life. So I distinguish altogether four substantive sources. Sections 3 and 4 discuss these substantive sources. Sections 5 and 6 explore procedural sources. There are international concerns that assume the form of rights without thereby being membership rights in the global order. Here we may consider the concerns addressed by private international law (regulating private relationships across borders). Those do not register as human rights since they are demands against private persons, with authorities acting as mediators or enforcers. Other treaties capture the coordination of moral concerns vis-à-vis authorities, such as minor International Labour Organization treaties. Those fail to meet the urgency standard. A precise limit to what counts as urgent is impossible to draw, but in this regard there is nothing unusual about my conception.

Let me begin our exploration of the substantive sources with the third category since we are already familiar with it. Chapter 7 discussed Common Ownership. Chapter 4 treated common humanity (or the distinctively human life) both as a ground of justice and as a basis for a conception of human rights. However, common humanity also contributes a *source* of membership rights. Human rights deriving from the distinctively human life as a basis are *natural* rights, rights whose justification depends on natural attributes of persons and facts about the nonhuman world and whose force can be recognized by all reasonable people independently of the provisions of positive law. For natural rights, all human beings could in principle be duty bearers, regardless of the conditions under which we live: therefore, the protection of the distinctively human life is of global urgency, and today the global order is the obvious addressee of these rights.

Common ownership rights are natural rights, too. In that case, we have derived membership rights by asking what protection individuals need for their status as co-owners to be maintained. Under the global order, the ability of co-owners to meet basic needs must be preserved. We obtain a set of *associative* rights against the global order through an instrumental argument, by exploring how to preserve, in a robust manner, the core purpose of natural ownership rights under the conditions of the global order. For the distinctively human life as a source we must again ask what protection individuals must have for that life to be preserved within the global order. But now the set of natural rights whose contours chapter 4 sketched is coextensive with the set of associative rights against that order. No additional instrumental argument is needed that would generate a set of associative rights that is not coextensive with the natural rights. What is required for the protection of co-ownership status depends on the conditions under which human beings live on this planet. What is required for the protection of the distinctively human life is invariant with regard to such conditions. Therefore we only needed one chapter (chapter 4) to develop the distinctively human life as a source but two (chapters 6 and 7) for common ownership of the earth.

While natural rights apply to human beings regardless of the presence of political structures, such structures affect the assignment of responsibilities. Distant individuals could have no duties of any practical relevance vis-à-vis each other before they were economically or politically connected. (What is characteristic of human rights in my view is that they cannot just be rights vis-à-vis the person's own state; the global order must have obligations pertaining to those rights that go distinctly beyond mere nonviolation.) Chapter 4 discussed the subject of responsibilities to some extent, and this chapter does as well. So, while the set of natural rights needed to protect the distinctively human life is coextensive with the set of associative rights needed for that purpose under the global order, only the latter set comes with a fine-grained assignment of responsibilities made possible by an economically and politically interconnected world that contains entities of different sorts (individuals, countries, international organizations, corporations, etc.). The discussions in chapters 4 and 7 revealed that the range of associative rights in the global order needed to protect the distinctively human life and that of associative rights needed to protect original co-ownership robustly have major overlaps. This should be unsurprising, given the significance of human needs in the ownership approach.

So, much like chapter 7 (which was explicitly conducted in terms of that view), chapter 4 can be seamlessly integrated into my conception of human rights. And now I can also explain why this book does not advocate the earlier conception. The protection of the distinctively human life is of global urgency because natural rights in principle impose duties on everybody regardless of the conditions under which we live. But a major motivation for proposing my conception is the recognition that there are *other ways* in which something could be of global urgency. And even in the case of natural rights, the presence of the global order bears on the assignment of duties. This gives us good reason to acknowledge the importance of the global order for the kinds of claims human beings have against each other. For these reasons, I prefer thinking of the distinctively human life as a source rather than a basis for a free-standing conception of human rights.[3]

4. Let us explore the two remaining substantive sources. To begin with, something may be of global urgency on the strength of mutual *enlightened self-interest*. There are two aspects to entity E's enlightened self-interest. First, there is self-interest as seen in the long run. Second, enlightened self-interest includes the realization of moral interests or concerns that apply to E, for instance the realization of certain rights for which E is responsible if E is a state. Let me illustrate the distinction for the state. A state acts to advance its enlightened self-interest in the former sense paradigmatically, by securing peace and stability. Only in a politically stable situation can a state function properly. A state acts to advance its enlightened self-interest in the latter sense if it creates a regional or global environment of the sort required for it to discharge its (independently established) obligations, either to its citizens or to people elsewhere.

For enlightened self-interest to be a source of membership rights, it must be the enlightened self-interest *of individuals* (since sources are bases). But the connection between the enlightened self-interest of states and that of individuals is tight. For instance, it is in an individual's long-term interest to live in a country that discharges its state functions properly. Therefore, regional and global stability is in her long-term interest. Contrary to Marxist visions of class struggle, the economic long-term interests of individuals coincide with that of a just state that distributes the social product in a way that is to everybody's benefit. As far as the second sense of enlightened self-interest is concerned, we merely need note that the obligations of states are the obligations of their citizenry. At this stage we need no additional explanations of personhood, to obtain a better understanding of the selves whose interests are at stake. We have already said much about the distinctively human life, as well as about citizenship—except that now we are interested not in morally appropriate reactions to different kinds of moral status but in what self-interest makes it rational to do.

For this source, one would have to show that certain matters give rise to rights domestically (the idea of human rights being a moral one), and a self-interest argument would then show why this matter is of global urgency. The second step would reveal why it is in the enlightened self-interest of people in countries X1, X2, etc., that people in Y have certain rights realized. This also means that, strictly speaking, enlightened self-interest is not by itself a source: the source is enlightened self-interest *plus* the considerations needed for the first step. The same is true for interconnectedness, below. To elaborate on how this source might operate using the first sense of enlightened self-interest, it may be necessary for the preservation of peace that authority be exercised in certain ways (or, phrased differently, preserving the peace would be very difficult unless authority was exercised in certain ways), perhaps because unchecked governments will also be abusive vis-à-vis others, or create negative externalities (refugees, etc). ("Necessary," "very difficult without": the closer we come to necessity, the stronger an argument we produce.) Concerns about peace, and the impossibility of limiting certain evils to domestic affairs, were motives behind the formation of the League of Nations and what limited recognition human rights had then. Such concerns also triggered more expansive efforts to incorporate human rights in a framework of institutions, declarations, and treaties after World War II. The phrase "justice and peace in the world" (acknowledging the ties between justice and peace) occurs early in the Preamble of the Universal Declaration of Human Rights.[4]

And indeed, troubled states are a global liability. They spread refugees and draw others into conflicts. Financial crises are internationally transmitted. Drug trafficking, illegal immigration, arms trade, human trafficking, money laundering, and terrorism must be fought globally because the networks behind them often operate globally. Disease control is a global problem as much as environmental sustainability is. Conversely, development delivers gains from trade, and from cooperation in science, culture, business, or tourism. In 1940, H. G. Wells, British intellectual and advocate for a declaration of human rights, wrote, "In only a week of years, as we have seen, a terroristic gangsterism can develop from backstreet outrages to a savage and dangerous assault upon the peace of mankind" (1940, 109–10). Martin Luther King overstated the matter in his Letter from a Birmingham Jail, insisting that "injustice anywhere is a threat to justice everywhere" (1963, 79). Nonetheless, enlightened self-interest is a powerful way of showing that something is globally urgent.

Globalists might wonder whether we could not follow a similar process to show that Rawlsian principles of justice apply globally after all. We could take state membership to establish a right against one's state to live in a place where the difference principle holds; and argue that as a matter of enlightened self-interest, states must see to it that the difference principle applies globally. So it is a human right that the difference principle holds globally. However, the premise about self-interest is (contingently) false. States have an enlightened self-interest in regional and even global stability, and more generally in the preservation of their ability to discharge their state functions. They also have an enlightened self-interest in the creation of an environment in which they can satisfy their obligations. But in our world, none of this requires that the difference principle hold globally, or in all countries. The wording above was "necessary/very difficult without," and that strict standard is not met here. Of course, the realization of any demands against one's government will be easier if global expectations are such that those demands are satisfied. But this does not show that enlightened self-interest entails that something is of global concern. After all, such a judgment involves an assignment of duties. But since a proliferation of duties may well not be in the duty bearers' enlightened self-interest, we must indeed insist on that strict standard.

Let us proceed to another substantive source, *interconnectedness*. Something may be globally urgent because of a causal responsibility on the side of the global order for the problem for which the right is supposed to be the solution. That problem has been caused by economic and political integration, by processes of globalization. In this case, too, we must capture the relevant concern in terms of features of individuals to identify a source of membership rights. The relevant feature is that individuals are participants in, or in any event subject to, the global economy and the global political system. In these capacities, to a degree that varies considerably, persons are involved with or affected by economic transactions and political processes that tie distant individuals around the world. In this case too, what matters is that a *right* is established. The second step of the argument in this case would reveal the sense in which the global order as such is causally responsible for certain problems for people in Y for which an assignment of rights would be the solution, as well as the sense in which this imposes obligations on people in countries X1, X2, etc. Here I emphasize the difference from enlightened self-interest. In the case of self-interest, the second step would reveal why it is either in the long-term interest of people in countries X1, X2, etc., that people in Y have certain rights realized (I am thinking paradigmatically of stability concerns) or else necessary for their ability to make good on certain obligations that people in X1, X2, etc., have independently.

In support of the claim that interconnectedness is a source from which to derive global membership rights, I turn again to the ideas of the global order and membership in it introduced in chapters 1 and 7. Major actors in the global order influence each other through political and economic interactions, as well as through legal, cultural, and other channels. Today, events and decisions elsewhere shape the incentives and prospects of governments, companies, and other agents. H. G. Wells captures the relevance, and the novelty, of interconnectedness nicely:

> The abolition of distance and the overwhelming development of power in the world during the past century have rendered uncoordinated political and economic controls more and more monstrously wasteful and destructive. They have to be brought together under a collective direction, a political and economic world order, or our race will blunder to complete disaster. (1940, 59)

Like enlightened self-interest, interconnectedness is not by itself a source: strictly speaking, the source is interconnectedness *plus* the considerations needed for the first step. While enlightened self-interest and interconnectedness indeed draw on different considerations to establish a global urgency, they often apply jointly. To illustrate this, let us revisit the discussion in chapter 7 of a case where rights to life and bodily integrity are robustly protected but other rights are not. We saw that benign slavery is consistent with the rights derived in chapter 7, in the very unlikely case that its benign nature is robust. So Common Ownership does not generate a human right against benign slavery.

However, let us consider the following argument drawing on enlightened self-interest and interconnectedness. To begin with, considerations about membership in states show that individuals have a claim against their state for protection against benign slavery as well. The increasing intensity of transnational interactions creates opportunities, and triggers demand, for human trafficking and thus modern-day slavery. Millions are smuggled across borders and kept in bondage to work in the sex industry, or in private households, or in sweatshops. Since in any given country (especially in those that are major destinations of, and create demand for, human trafficking) individuals have a right to protection against enslavement, it is in every country's enlightened self-interest to combat human trafficking. Otherwise the number of de facto slaves *in their midst* will increase. Regions where even the most benign form of slavery persists (alongside other regions where certain groups are held in contempt and kept in dependency) are among the likely origins of such trafficking. The combination of enlightened self-interest and interconnectedness supports a human right not to be enslaved in any way.

To conclude our discussion of substantive sources, I note that such sources apply differently. Collective ownership and common humanity apply to everybody and support the same rights from each person's standpoint. Enlightened self-interest and interconnectedness also apply to everybody. This should be clear for enlightened self-interest, but it is also true for interconnectedness. Everybody is at least subject to the global order, although not everybody can sensibly be said to participate in it. However, since people's circumstances vary considerably, enlightened self-interest and interconnectedness may well support different rights from different persons' standpoints. Their implications for human rights will be less clear-cut for those two sources than for common humanity and collective ownership.

5. One way in which concerns can become common within a political structure is for them to be regarded as such by an authoritative process. We can enlist *procedural* sources to argue that human rights express membership "as the global order sees it." Jointly, substantive and procedural considerations constitute a standpoint of global public reason assessing matters of global concern. It is not that certain issues become *problematic* only in virtue of such a process but that they are thereby endowed with global urgency. Populations and governments may declare matters of global urgency in this way because they wish to "lock themselves in," to bind future governments to contribute to the realization of certain rights.[5] Another reason is plain moral solidarity.

Procedural sources are on a par with substantive sources as far as their ability to generate membership rights is concerned. However, one reason why the availability of procedural sources is significant is that there will often be doubts about precisely what rights substantive sources generate. Given the conceptual constraints on that notion, there are limits to what any kind of process could declare a human right. Presumably the range of plausible candidates will be limited to cases where substantive sources seem inconclusive. Needless to say, there can also be authoritative procedures to put global administrative law in place, which falls short of the urgency of human rights.

How should we characterize authoritative processes that generate membership rights (and hence involvement with such a process as a procedural source of human rights)? To answer this question, we must first appreciate why it is plainly hard to assess what counts as such a process. To that end, I first look at what authority the process may have had that led to the Universal Declaration of Human Rights. Difficulties in seeing the authoritativeness of that process are exacerbated for processes needed to establish membership rights in the global order. For those entail global duties, whereas the Universal Declaration is uninformative on the subject of who must do what. The second way of illustrating the difficulties in assessing what counts as an authoritative process is by looking at what processes count as authoritative *domestically*. To that end we turn to an account of deliberative democracy.

In the eyes of many, the Universal Declaration fixes human rights discourse. Charles Malik, Lebanese philosopher and diplomat, one of its drafters, introduced the document to the UN General Assembly on December 9, 1948, pointing

> each country to places in the Declaration where it could either find its own contributions or the influence of the culture to which it belonged. The Latin American countries had brought to the process the ideas and experiences gained in preparing the Bogotá Declaration on the Rights and Duties of Man. India had played a key role in advancing the nondiscrimination principle, especially with regard to women. France was responsible for many elegancies in drafting. The United Kingdom and the United States had shared the wisdom acquired in their long experience with traditional political and civil liberties. The Soviet Union, with broad support from many quarters, had championed the newer social and economic rights in the interest of "improving the living conditions of the broad masses of mankind." The importance of remembering that rights entail duties had been emphasized by participants from China, Greece, Latin America, the Soviet Union, and France. Many countries had contributed to the article of freedom of religion and rights of the family. Due to the immense variety of its sources, the Declaration had been constructed on a "firm international basis where no regional philosophy or way of life was permitted to prevail." (Glendon 2001, 164–65)

Charged with drafting a declaration acceptable to members of diverse backgrounds, the UN's Commission on Human Rights started deliberating in January 1947. This project triggered plenty of debate, reactions, and correspondence worldwide. A painstaking endeavor to find widely acceptable formulations, its work involved political tussles as well as philosophical debates. Remarkably diverse by contemporary standards, the commission was chaired by Eleanor Roosevelt and included Malik, the Chinese Renaissance man Peng-Chun Chang, the French judge René Cassin, and the Indian reformer Hansa Mehta, among others, and was also advised by the Canadian legal scholar John Humphrey, director of the Human Rights Division of the UN Secretariat.

The international relations scholar Martin Wight (1966) argues that the pursuit of the good life is confined to small communities. As opposed to that, in exploring relativism Bernard Williams (2005a) points out that a new "we" must be "negotiated" (69) when cultures encounter each other. Pace Wight, since human beings have irreversibly encountered each other, they *must* negotiate a common life, a "we," beyond coordinating survival. The Universal Declaration emerged from such negotiations, taken literally. After the declaration was written, work began to formulate legally binding treaties. Lauren (2003) sums up the declaration's impact:

> In a period of fifty years the world witnessed a veritable revolution in the process of transforming visions of international human rights into reality. Never before in history had there been so many achievements in extending rights, setting standards, protecting rights through binding treaties and covenants, promoting rights through education and the media, enhancing rights through advisory services in the field for those who suffered, and expanding activities to break the former culture of impunity. Together they helped millions of people gain their independence and assisted unknown numbers of others by preventing abuses, securing freedom from torture or prison, acquiring access to monitoring bodies and humanitarian aid, and obtaining national and international legal protections for their rights. In addition, they inspired national constitutions, regional intergovernmental organizations, and states to use the observance or violation of human rights by others as a criterion for their policies. In almost every one of these endeavors, reference was made to the Universal Declaration of Human Rights as customary international law and the power of its vision to change the world. (269–70)

Still, it is disputable how much authority the framing process itself had. It is also disputable how much authority the broad ostensible acceptance of human rights generates. As far as the first point is concerned, in 1948 the UN had about one-third as many members as today. Large parts of the world were colonized. Although the drafting committee was indeed remarkably diverse, Western traditions dominated. Unsurprisingly, several non-Western participants, too, had a Western education. Critics assert that

The white human rights zealot joins the unbroken chain that connects her to the colonial administrator, the Bible-wielding missionary, and the merchant of free enterprise.... Thus human rights reject the cross-fertilization of cultures and instead seek the transformation of non-Western cultures by Western cultures. (Mutua 2004, 51)

As far as the ostensible acceptance of the declaration is concerned, Jeremy Rabkin (2005) argues that its nonbinding nature permitted states to endorse it without being committed. The apparent success of "this talkfest"

encourages the very misplaced belief that there is genuine consensus when there is not. And this misplaced belief encourages ventures that go wildly beyond what the actual international community is actually able to sustain, igniting or exacerbating very serious conflict. (164)[6]

Political reality offers explanations of the ostensible success of human rights *other than* the commitment of self-declared supporters. Rabkin's skepticism is confirmed by findings about governments' compliance with human rights treaties they have signed. Countries might sign up to increase their reputation without intending to reform. On the other hand, (Thomas) Risse (2000) insists that disingenuous support may generate "argumentative self-entrapment" (32). States might merely be paying lip service but gradually be drawn into supporting human rights. Still, the point on which Rabkin rightly focuses is that expressions of support do not settle the extent of the declaration's authority. That worry adds to the concern that the drafting process was not of the right sort to ensure that people worldwide ought to accept the declaration because of it. Such worries, in turn, only begin to capture the challenge for authoritative acceptance of human rights since we must then show an acceptance of global responsibilities.[7]

The second way of seeing difficulties in assessing procedures as authoritative is to ask what procedures are authoritative *domestically*. While the first discussion explored a process at the international level and thus showed why we must be careful in identifying an authoritative process at that level, the second provides an example of the right sort of process, but one that pertains to another domain and is hard to transfer. Joshua Cohen (1997a) offers an account of deliberative democracy that explains why democracy is a value. Deliberation is crucial: "outcomes are democratically legitimate if and only if they could be the object of a free and reasoned agreement among equals" (73).

The following conditions characterize such deliberation. First, participants are free: they are bound only by the results of this deliberation, and are in a position to take the fact that something emerged through deliberation as sufficient reason for compliance. Second, citizens present or criticize reasons. Decisions are made based on such reasons, not based on self-regarding preferences. The emphasis is on the "making" of decisions: we care about what outcome actually emerges from the process, not what outcome ought to have emerged (given the available reasons). Third, parties are formally and substantially equal. They are formally equal since the rules of the deliberation do not single out specific people to create advantages or disadvantages for them. They are substantially equal because "the existing distribution of power and resources does not shape their chances to contribute to deliberation, nor does that distribution play an authoritative role in their deliberation" (74). Fourth, deliberation aims to reach rational consensus, to find reasons persuasive to all committed to acting on the results. Absent consensus, one should use majority rule.

Such a process, or an institutional approximation, is needed domestically to obtain an authoritative procedure. The reference to institutional approximations matters because decision making may be authoritative also outside of direct democracies. What is crucial is that "at the heart of the institutionalization of the deliberative procedure is the existence of arenas in which citizens can propose issues for the political agenda and participate in debate about those issues" (Cohen 1997a, 85). Procedures that satisfy these conditions presuppose substantive values of inclusion and equality (Cohen 1997b). Their authoritativeness depends on how they embody such values.

6. For authoritative acceptance of *global* responsibilities we must go through such a process once domestically, for each state, and once globally. Procedures cannot by themselves generate duties for states not involved in them; however, involvement is not necessarily governmental—in some cases authoritarian governments might not speak for their people but some other entity does. Authoritative acceptance of global responsibilities presupposes domestic mechanisms to empower governments (or conceivably other entities) to consent to global duties, as well as international structures within which countries can authoritatively accept duties. In both cases, the value of institutions depends on how they approximate the ideal procedure. We must identify approximations that make plausible *both* that duties have credibly been undertaken *and* that these are indeed duties of global reach.

As far as credible acceptability of duties is concerned, one might wonder how it would even be possible to approximate in *international* affairs the conditions under which imposing decisions on citizens is plausible. How could Mozambique or Laos be substantially equal as participants in global affairs to France or Japan? However, political scientist Harald Müller (2007), for one, argues that the domestic does not differ dramatically from the international case. Jürgen Habermas (1992) shows how his theory of communicative action (developed in Habermas 1981) can identify conditions under which *domestic* institutions allow for approximations of communications that let citizens reach agreement. Müller thinks something similar applies internationally.

One could think of such an approximation along three lines. First, international law guarantees equality of states. Power differentials are not neutralized, but mitigated because the notion of state sovereignty gives each state reason to appeal if its interests are disregarded. Second, practices such as reciprocity or differential treatment for poor countries have the same effect. Both mechanisms create a positioning of the burden of proof. For instance, the United States had to justify why it rejected the Kyoto Protocol aimed at stabilizing greenhouse gas emissions. Third, negotiations among states are commonly conducted (more or less) publicly and assessed in terms of generally acceptable norms. Violations may cause a loss of reputation or isolation. So once a distinction between ideal situation and approximation is available the two-stage ideal of deliberation is not useless for assessing international affairs. Domestically too, differences in wealth, education, or talents pose obstacles to substantive equality. To conclude Müller's reasoning: obstacles at the international level are *bigger,* but not so much that the theory applies only domestically.[8]

However, this reasoning only shows that it is not impossible that there would be authoritative processes at the global level. The characteristics of international politics that Müller identifies are insufficient to give us the credible approximation we are looking for. They do not resolve the concerns raised by Rabkin. I am unsure what a complete answer to the first challenge is (that duties are credibly undertaken), but one criterion of success is that international inequalities in power do not essentially factor into an explanation as to why countries accept duties. The three points identified by Müller cannot reassure us that such inequalities do not play this role.

As far as the second matter is concerned (that duties are of global reach), one must be careful not to mistake processes that lead to the acceptance of human rights standards domestically for processes that ipso facto endorse duties of global reach. Important work has been done to identify civil society processes that show why and how societies accept human rights standards, processes explored in particular under the heading of vernacularization, the translation of human rights norms into local practice (Merry 2006; Goodale and Merry 2007). While such mechanisms may show that we need not be skeptical about the authenticity or relevance of certain governmental commitments to human rights, they would not readily show that there is a commitment *to global membership rights*, with accompanying duties of *global* reach. It is one thing to show that a government is committed to respecting human rights domestically, another to show that it is also committed to promoting human rights elsewhere.

To be sure, there are some recent examples of proposed duties of global reach. To begin with, one may think of the "responsibility to protect." This notion captures a state's responsibility to prevent genocide and other massive violations, as well as the international community's responsibility when states fail in this regard.[9] Second, there is the principle of universal jurisdiction, whereby states claim jurisdiction over certain criminals regardless of their relation to them (Steiner, Alston, and Goodman 2007, 722ff., 1161ff.; Reydams 2004). Finally, one may think of the International Criminal Court, which prosecutes individuals for genocide, crimes against humanity, war crimes, and the crime of aggression (Steiner, Alston, and Goodman 2007, 1291ff.; Broomhall 2003).

Yet in light of the difficulties involved in getting duties of global reach credibly accepted, the best we can say is that the duties involved in these efforts are accepted by countries that have explicitly endorsed them *as* such duties and whose authenticity in making international commitments cannot be doubted along the lines articulated by Rabkin. In any event, there is currently no good example of an actual *membership right* in the global order (with accompanying duties of global reach) that has been accepted through authoritative processes both domestically and internationally. This is only something to look forward to in the future. Nonetheless, at least conceptually, procedural sources are an important component of my account of human rights.

This completes our discussion of sources of membership rights in the global order. Proposed rights may receive support from any or all sources, and their strength may vary. A critical discourse can occur if proposed rights fail to receive support from all sources. Conclusive support from one source is enough to establish a human right. Insufficient support from other sources then illuminates its disputed nature but does not undo its status as a human right. Conversely, insufficient support from one source absent inquiries into others only defeasibly establishes that X is not a human right. Its ability to account for contestation and pluralism confers additional plausibility on my conception.

7. I am developing a basis-driven conception of human rights. I have described the basis (a disjunction over various sources) and the process that generates the list of rights that emerges in this view (derivation from sources). But we also must address the assignment of responsibilities, the

fourth component in a conception. Here I recall that for a right to X to be a human right, it must involve duties (beyond nonviolation) on the part of entities in the global order other than a person's own state. Sections 7 and 8 illuminate what it means to hold rights within the global order to ensure my conception cannot be rejected because there is no plausible way of so "holding" rights. We must explain what the global order's being the addressee of human rights involves for entities in it. Still, stressing that the global order itself is the addressee means to emphasize, for instance, that states—carrying the main burden—do not merely have duties to their citizens. States must do *their share* in a global scheme of dividing up responsibilities.[10]

Duties do indeed not merely apply to states. That thought also occurs in the preamble to the Universal Declaration: "every individual and every organ of society, keeping this Declaration constantly in mind, shall strive by teaching and education to promote respect for these rights and freedoms." What this amounts to for entities within the global order depends on their nature. All entities in the global order—including individuals— have the duty to "refrain" from human rights violations. (The terms I use to characterize the nature of the duties of different entities appear in quotation marks; from Nickel [1993] I adopt the terms "refrain," "protect," and "provide.") Since human rights are held against those in positions of authority, we must be careful in assessing what obligations individuals as such have in this context. Individuals ought to refrain from violating human rights in two senses. First, they should not do the kind of thing against which the rights protect, not because they are held against individuals but because the weight of reason that establishes that these rights are held against those with authority *also* creates a duty for individuals not do the sort of thing against which the rights protect. Second, individuals should comply with reasonable measures that those in positions of authority take to protect human rights. Given the urgency that characterizes human rights, this much seems plausible as a duty of individuals as such.

States provide the immediate environment in which people's lives unfold. The primary responsibility for realizing human rights thus lies with states. States must "protect" and "provide" human rights to their citizens. They must not only refrain from violating rights, they must also protect individuals within their jurisdiction from abuses by third parties. When it is in the nature of the rights in question—here we may think of social and economic rights—states must provide them in the first place. Since human rights as membership rights in the global order are a global responsibility, states must also "assist" *other* states with the realization of such rights in their (the other states') jurisdiction if the other states are incapable of doing so themselves. They must "interfere" if other states are unwilling to maintain an acceptable human rights record. Such duties of assistance and interference are held alongside other states, and may well be exercised through international organizations. Since states have these duties of assisting and interfering, they must also "record" the human rights performance of other states, especially those with which they interact regularly (e.g., through trade).

International organizations, too, must "assist" states in discharging duties, and "interfere" if states are unwilling to maintain an acceptable record. They have the additional responsibility of "supervising" the human rights records of states, in any event in the domain of their activities (e.g., the WTO in the domain of trade). Businesses too have duties, especially transnational corporations with great impact on societies. A 2008 UN report plausibly distinguishes between a duty of states to "protect" human rights and that of businesses to "respect" them (Ruggie 2008; see also Ruggie 2007). Transnational corporations should be accountable for human rights without being directly under the purview of international law, with its ensuing complications. States must set appropriate incentives. Companies should be legally obligated to adopt due diligence standards to ensure human rights are respected. Responsibilities for human rights are differential.

To the extent that human rights cannot be currently realized, they are *manifesto rights* (Feinberg 1973). Thinking of them as membership rights means considering them moral demands that apply where it makes sense to raise such demands, or else to create conditions under which it does.[11] The teleological character of my view already surfaced in chapter 9, when I argued that Common Ownership implies a duty to bequeath institutions within which future people can realize human rights. Some framers of the Universal Declaration also self-consciously created a teleological document. Chilean delegate Santa Cruz said that "if the Declaration were to be adjusted only to existing conditions it would not achieve a very useful purpose" (Morsink 1999, 162).[12]

If a state is in a position to realize human rights but chooses not to, intervention may be appropriate, ranging from political and economic pressure and support for the opposition to military action. Amartya Sen (2004) illuminates the differential nature of responsibilities involved. Recognizing human rights implies

> an acknowledgement that if one is in a plausible position to do something effective in preventing the violation of such a right, then one does have an obligation to consider doing just that. It is still possible that other obligations or non-obligational concerns may overwhelm the reason for the particular action in question, but that reason cannot simply be brushed away as "none of one's

business." Loosely specified obligations must not be confused with no obligations at all. (340–41)

8. Let me elaborate on the differences between the global order and states as far as membership is concerned, as well as on the connection between membership and rights held in virtue of that status. Chapter 2 noted how Leibniz explains that princes of the Holy Roman Empire are sovereign in virtue of having immediate day-to-day power to rule. The emperor's authority is higher, but he can enforce it only through war. Suppose individuals have certain rights in virtue of being subject to the emperor, and other rights in virtue of being subject to the prince. The analogy between this situation and the situation of people today who are citizens of a state and members of a global order is this: in both cases there are rights held independently of citizenship that must be enforced in ways other than through state mechanisms.

Suppose the emperor wishes to enforce some rights but is opposed by a prince. While nobody ceases to hold those rights, the emperor may find it wise to suspend enforcement. Such cases illustrate two points: First, rights individuals hold in virtue of being subjects of the emperor *rather than* in virtue of being subjects of the prince involve the kind of enforcement that is at the emperor's disposal *rather than* that at the prince's. Second, it will often be plausible to suspend enforcement: the costs of war are high. But since enforcement of the sovereign's will may be suspended too, the difference is one of degree. To illustrate, a New York City Police Department policy prohibits shooting at moving vehicles "unless deadly force is being used against the police officers or another person present, by means other than a moving vehicle."[13] Suppose that enforcing some right held within the United States in a particular instance requires shooting at a moving vehicle (to stop robbers from escaping), but no such deadly force is used. Enforcement may then be suspended. Many a sensible prince would agree with such a policy.

Onora O'Neill (2005) argues that, since human rights are not tied to duties of specific agents and to specific enforcement mechanisms, talk about human *rights* is a misuse of language. One might sidestep that worry, she says, by considering human rights to be aspirational. Yet not only is this a cynical reading of the Universal Declaration (granting, as it seems to, that we are negligent about realizing rights), but it breaks with a common view of rights as associated with duty bearers. We would accept, then, that where human rights are unmet, nobody is at fault, is accountable, or owes redress. O'Neill sees this tie between rights and duties held by somebody charged with enforcement as an "exceptionless logical point."

To the extent that O'Neill does make a logical point, we can preserve it. Membership rights in the global order have a duty holder (that order). However, similar to rights individuals hold in virtue of being subject to the emperor, human rights are not held in virtue of citizenship but in virtue of membership in the global order. This point has two important implications. First, in the global order, membership rights currently often are "aspirational" in the logically unproblematic sense that one can only progressively realize them. We can distinguish between "strict" human rights, whose more or less immediate realization can be expected, and "aspirational" ones, which can be realized only progressively (but also *must* be so realized). This distinction will vary by state, change over time, and be contested. What has bearing on the distinction is both resource limitations and political obstacles. A person's state must protect her rights, strict and aspirational ones, as appropriate. The international community has a duty to defend strict rights by intervening as appropriate if the government fails. The global order must aid governments that need assistance, and intervene as appropriate if countries refuse to make efforts toward realizing aspirational rights.

We are used to rights that hold within *states*. But it is not true that those are rights (among other reasons) because they are readily enforceable. It is the other way around: they are readily enforceable because state power is of a certain nature. It is also because of the differences between states and the global order that it might be problematic for rights guaranteed by constitutions to be manifesto rights, although this is less problematic for human rights. In addition, discussion about *accommodation* is needed in the case of the global order as much as in domestic scenarios. Sometimes recognizing that "they do things that way" should preclude intervention. O'Neill is right about the link between rights and duties. But we ought not have too narrow a view of what that entails.[14]

Second, who the enforcement agents are, and what they should do, remains to be developed in detail. As René Cassin, a drafter of the declaration, said about that document twenty years after its passing, "Now that we possess an instrument capable of lifting or easing the burden of oppression and injustice in the world, we must learn to use it" (1968, 6). But there is progress: the sheer articulation of human rights standards is an expression of global concern. Human rights are a source of moral progress partly *because* discourse about them creates a situation where the question of on whom duties fall *must* be worked out.

Let us conclude. This chapter has explored membership in the global order as a ground of justice. The associated principle is that the distribution in the global population of the things to which human rights—membership rights in the global order—generate entitlements is just only if everyone has enough of them for these rights to be realized. Human rights are rights that are accompanied by responsibilities at the global level. To demonstrate that there is a human right to X we require a showing of urgency at the global level, rather than wherever people live (the state level). While chapter 7 introduced one source from which to derive such membership rights in the global order (collective ownership), this chapter has explored what other (substantive and procedural) sources there are. A genuinely pluralistic theory has emerged, one that acknowledges different reasons why global responsibilities may be assigned: because of our common humanity, which generates demands that are ill-understood as applying only among those who share certain political and economic structures; because we collectively own our planet; because we are involved in global political and economic processes; because of mutual enlightened self-interest; and because of an authoritative process.

We have also illuminated what it means to hold rights within the global order, rebutting the objection that there could be no plausible conception of human rights as membership rights in that order because there is no sense in which individuals *hold* such rights. Responsibilities for their realization are differentiated. Chapters 12 and 13 further elaborate on my conception of human rights, and thus also further illuminate membership in the global order as a ground of justice. Chapter 12 explores whether there is a human right to essential pharmaceuticals. Chapter 13 explores whether labor rights are human rights.

CHAPTER 12

Arguing for Human Rights

Essential Pharmaceuticals

1. Legally speaking, there arguably is a human right to vital pharmaceuticals, such as those on the World Health Organization's list of essential medicines. However, while lawyers explore what such a right amounts to practically or, say, whether it conflicts with the Agreement on Trade-Related Aspects of Intellectual Property Rights (TRIPs), our concern is to explore whether philosophical approaches deliver a human right to pharmaceuticals, specifically, whether my conception of human rights as membership rights in the global order does (according to some source that it recognizes).[1] This is a case study of how to apply my conception to questions of the sort "Is there a human right to X?" Chapter 7 included one such study, chapter 13 offers another. These studies engage a broad range of topics—naturally so, because diverse problems may be of global concern. Within the human rights movement, the UN's Universal Declaration of Human Rights and other major human rights documents are meaning fixing: there is a human right to X if and only if some major document says so. But a philosophical conception must be open-ended. We must explore whether there is such a right to X for each X about which this claim sensibly arises, and it must be possible to add new rights.

Yes, there is a human right to essential medicines. However, we must carefully assess what kind of right it is. My argument does not deliver a right that essential pharmaceuticals be affordable for everybody, or that pharmaceutical companies focus research-and-development efforts on such drugs rather than on minor ailments that trouble mostly the rich. Instead, what is owed to people across the world is that the regulation of intellectual property generally, and of vital pharmaceuticals especially, not recognize far-reaching private rights, beyond what it takes to compensate inventors and set incentives for future inventions.[2]

Most of this chapter explores what sort of private property rights in ideas it is legitimate for a legal system to recognize. Only in the final section do I use those results to answer the human rights question. I draw on material from my discussion of common ownership of original resources. I do not *derive* my conclusions from that discussion but explore an *analogy* between original ownership and ideas. The right I eventually derive does not emerge from common ownership but from the distinctively human life.

As far as common ownership is concerned, I do not draw on the arguments presented in chapter 6 but on my discussion of Grotius in chapter 5, specifically (as in the discussion of the atmosphere in chapter 10) on his account of ownership of the seas. I talk about Grotius because of the plausibility for the domain of ideas of the considerations he introduces for limiting ownership to the seas, considerations that do much work in my argument.

Just as there is a Global Common, the set of ideas may form an Intellectual Common. Section 2 develops this parallel. What claims to controlling the use of ideas there can be then must be assessed in light of the point that ideas originally belong to a Common. This general approach has drawn on chapter 5 of John Locke's *Second Treatise of Government*, a discussion so influential in theorizing property that Drahos (1996) assigns it "totemic status" (41). However, rather than Locke, my revitalization of the ownership standpoint draws on Grotius. So I also develop this analogy to the Intellectual Common by way of engaging with Grotius, which generates more restricted intellectual property rights than Locke-inspired approaches. (I explain later why it should indeed be Grotius rather than Locke who provides inspiration here.) Section 3 addresses arguments for more extensive rights than are forthcoming in my approach. If there is an Intellectual Common, claims to more extensive rights are implausible. Strikingly, a similar rebuttal of arguments for more extensive rights is available even if there is no Intellectual Common. Section 4 makes that case. We obtain a general argument against the legitimacy of private intellectual property beyond compensation and incentive setting wherever intellectual property is regulated. Ontological assumptions in support of an Intellectual Common made along the way ultimately drop out.[3] Therefore, I will ask readers tentatively to accept some strong positions on the ontology of ideas without offering much argumentative support for them.

With my general argument concerning the possibility of private intellectual property in place, we have yet to assess whether there is a *human right* to vital medicines. There is, in the sense that such pharmaceuticals ought to be regulated at the global level and private rights to them should be constrained, as stated before. We can tie the availability of essential medications to the protection of a distinctively human life as a source of membership rights in the global order. However, we must be careful to establish a global concern for the availability of such medications. Pharmaceuticals, after all, must be provided, and put together in the first place, through somebody's labor. They would not be available at all if it were not for somebody's ingenuity. In chapter 4 we encountered a boundary problem for attempts to derive rights and duties from the idea of a distinctively human life. For the reasons just mentioned, a possible right to essential pharmaceuticals is located at this boundary. Section 5 offers two ways of showing why there is a global concern with essential pharmaceuticals, enlisting the earlier results of this chapter. Within my conception, there are other ways of approaching the question of whether there is a human right to essential pharmaceuticals. However, an approach that helps itself to considerations of intellectual property offers a powerful way of supporting such a right.[4]

2. I begin by considering what sort of private property in ideas it is legitimate for legal systems to recognize. I first ask whether Grotius's argument against private ownership of the seas can be applied to ideas. As chapter 10 shows, freedom of the seas is no longer called for on Grotius's own terms. However, his reasoning in support of freedom of the seas bears not only on the atmosphere but also on a different domain, the domain of ideas, including scientific, musical, literary, or other artistic works and inventions, as well as images, names, symbols, or design patterns. How people can exploit ideas economically is regulated by intellectual property law, which includes patents, copyrights, and trademarks. Transferring Grotius's considerations as to why the seas should remain unappropriated to this domain entails restrictions for the domain of ideas.

Like land, the seas were originally given to people in common. Those arrangements should be kept unless there are good reasons to change them. Grotius thought there were good reasons in the case of the land, but good reasons against doing so in the case of the seas. He offers three reasons why the seas should remain unappropriated: first, anybody's use of the seas is consistent with everybody else's similar use; second, everybody benefits from leaving the seas unappropriated; and third, the seas cannot be occupied. Grotius concludes there are no legitimate private property rights to the seas.

Let us explore whether these arguments transfer to the realm of ideas. First, parallel to how Grotius argues that the use of the sea is consistent with everybody's use of it, Thomas Jefferson classically made this point for ideas:

> If nature has made any one thing less susceptible than others of exclusive property, it is the action of the thinking power called an idea.... Its peculiar character ... is that no one possesses it the less, because every other possesses the whole of it. That ideas should be freely spread from one to another over the globe, for the moral and mutual instruction of man, and improvement of his condition, seems to have been ... designed by nature.... Society may give an exclusive right to the profits arising from them, as an encouragement ... to pursue ideas which may produce utility, but this may or may not be done, according to the will and convenience of the society, without claim or complaints by anybody.[5]

There is a point to private property in things like apples: only one person can make certain uses of them. As Grotius insists with regard to the seas and Jefferson with regard to ideas, there is no point to private property rights in those. Gains for occupiers do not depend on excluding others unless we are talking about profits accrued *from exclusion*.

Second, *Mare Liberum* argues that everybody benefits from leaving the seas free, appealing to its relevance for trade. Not only does use of ideas not subtract from their usefulness for others, it adds to it, by stimulating intellectual activities that inspire yet more such activities. *Everybody* benefits from a situation where ideas are unappropriated (given that anybody's use does not interfere with everybody else's). Only a few benefit, respectively, if social and legal norms protect appropriation. Were we to change intellectual property arrangements now, not everybody might benefit from these changes: those who were previously allowed to appropriate ideas *might* not. ("Might not": they would gain the use of everyone else's ideas, although they would lose exclusive use of their own.) However, I argue from an ex ante standpoint from which we must assess what individual rights there should be in the first place.

Now let us consider Grotius's third point, that the seas cannot be occupied. In certain ways of understanding what it is to occupy something, that is true of ideas as well. One can keep ideas secret, or distract people from them, but one cannot do anything to an idea to keep it from being independently grasped. One cannot do anything parallel to how, in the case of land, "the beginning of Possession is joining Body to Body" (Grotius, *De Jure Belli ac Pacis* II.8.VI). A body A's being joined to B decreases space for C to be joined to B. Such joining may affect the object itself in ways that make it impossible for others to do the same, or create a situation where others could join the object the same way only by first removing some who did so earlier. But a mind's grasping an idea decreases no other mind's capacity to do so and creates no reason for other minds not to do so: nobody can establish a privileged claim to an idea to the rightful exclusion of others. Of course, even if one cannot unilaterally do anything to or with an idea that has such an effect, one can "occupy" ideas in the sense that there could be (and are) social and legal norms of intellectual ownership, such as patent law and copyright law. But such "occupation" is possible *only* through such norms, which require of non–rights holders to renounce the option of using ideas even though such use is consistent with everybody else's doing the same. This observation raises the question of why anybody should accept such norms, which takes us back to the other two considerations against privatization.

Grotius's arguments seem to apply to the realm of ideas. But how would we obtain the first part of the argument, which delivers the presumption against privatization? One way of arguing for such a presumption is to show that there is an Intellectual Common in the same way in which there is a Global Common. That there is an "Intellectual Common" means that, morally speaking, everyone has some sort of equal claim to every idea. That thesis produces a presumption in favor of preserving that equality when it comes to laws concerning the use of ideas, and thus against private intellectual property rights (which by their nature enshrine unequal claims). I do not draw stronger conclusions from the Intellectual Common thesis than this presumption against private intellectual property. Ultimately, I do not rely on such an Intellectual Common at all.

One way of arguing for an Intellectual Common is to defend ontological *realism* about objects of intellectual property law. Such realism denies that scientific, musical, or other artistic works are "products" of the mind. Instead, they exist outside the realm of either material or mental objects. They belong to a (Fregean) "third realm" of nonmental, supersensible entities, distinct from both the sensible external world and the internal world of consciousness. There is, then, no invention, refinement, or any other human *contribution* to these entities.[6] By assumption, objects in that realm exist prior to human activities. Nobody has a claim to them that draws on her contributions to their existence.

To be sure, even defenders of such realism concede that sometimes there are special reasons that defeat the general presumption against private intellectual property rights. First, individuals may fairly claim *compensation* for investments in making ideas accessible, compensation that may take into account their opportunity costs. Second, consistent with the argument for limitations on private rights is for societies to *set incentives* to stimulate creativity. However, I argue below that that presumption excludes, or anyway offers heavy resistance to, considerations supportive of benefits or private intellectual property rights for inventors for reasons other than compensation and incentive setting.[7] "Excludes or offers heavy resistance to": it is hard to establish conclusively that *only* fairness-based compensation and a society's right to set incentives overcome the presumption against private intellectual property rights according to the view we are presently assuming. However, certain considerations commonly entertained in the literature do not overcome that presumption.

Let me make three points by way of providing further explanations. First, let me say more about the term "presumption" and thus about the logic of my argument. The Intellectual Common thesis (backed by ontological realism about ideas) creates a presumption against private intellectual property rights by rendering *salient* the initial thought that there should be no special claims to ideas. After all, in this view it is not because of human contributions that ideas exist. The thought that this presumption renders salient—resistance to private property rights—is fortified by additional arguments provided by the three Grotian considerations. However, reflection on the need for compensation and incentives shows that the initial thought must also be revised. But crucially, additional arguments for private intellectual property rights must be weighed against the case against private intellectual property rights (i.e., the Intellectual Common backed by ontological realism plus the three Grotian points).[8]

Second, recognizing compensation and incentive setting as reasons for creating private intellectual property rights leaves much potential for disagreement about how far-reaching the rights are that these arguments create, a point I do not pursue but must acknowledge. Judge Frank Easterbrook articulates it as follows:

> A patent gives the inventor the right to exclude competition for 20 years, and thus to collect an enhanced price for that period. Is 20 years too long, too short, or just right? No one knows. A copyright lasts the life of the author plus an additional period that Congress keeps increasing in response to producers' lobbying. What is the right length of a copyright? No one knows. A trademark lasts forever (or at least for as long as the product is made, and the name does not become generic in the public's mind). A trade secret (such as the formula for Coca-Cola, or the source code of a computer program) lasts as long as the developer can keep the secret. Are these durations optimal? No one knows. How much use, and by whom, should be permitted without compensation under the fair use doctrine? No one knows. (2001, 406)

Easterbrook's comment is too open-ended: compensation and incentives do not require the most extensive unlimited eternal property rights imaginable. Nonetheless, his comment does highlight that there will be a range of views on how to fill those categories.

Third, the contrast between Locke and Grotius here is striking. Locke produced an account of collective ownership of the earth, and then explained how things can be privatized. He took little (if any) interest in a possibility that loomed large in Grotius, that there was good reason for co-owners not to accept privatization of certain parts of the earth. However, it is to *those* parts that the realm of ideas is analogous. Therefore we should indeed turn to Grotius rather than Locke for the analogy between the Intellectual Common and the Global Common.

3. Let us consider arguments for more extensive rights to private intellectual property than what compensation or incentives require. For now, I assume an Intellectual Common, as well as realism about ideas. One argument for more extensive rights is that protecting inventions does not make anybody worse off. Inventions, as argued by Robert Nozick, would not exist without the inventor.[9] Jeremy Waldron (1993b) replies that one might well be made worse off by inventions. Suppose I am dying of a disease for which there is no cure yet. Suppose somebody finds one, but that cure is inaccessible to me. Then I die knowing I can be cured. Yet while this reply goes a long way toward answering Nozick, the issue is moot if realism about ideas is true. Consider the following excerpt from an influential 1907 textbook by economist John Bates Clark that Waldron quotes to illustrate Nozick's view (a view capturing an attitude opposite Jefferson's):

> It is as though in some magical way [a patent holder] had caused springs of water to flow in the desert or loam to cover barren mountains or fertile islands to rise from the bottom of the sea. His gains consist in something which no one loses, even while he enjoys them.[10]

Crucially, however, if realism is true, the person who made the water flow hit on something that was standing under a presumption against privatization. That person should receive compensation, but cannot demand *additional* rewards based on the fact that nobody is worse off.

However, my rebuttal might seem implausible, at least for achievements that appear utterly disconnected from the societal state of knowledge. To make this point, Becker (1993) refers to Jorge Luis Borges's story "Pierre Menard, Author of the Quixote," about a linguist devoted to rewriting *Don Quixote* (Borges 1998, 88–95). Menard endeavors to mimic Cervantes's mindset at the time of writing his masterpiece and to reproduce it, not from memory but *from scratch*. The reason why this is absurd—in ways in which it is not absurd that Scott and Amundsen simultaneously raced toward the South Pole, or that Newton and Leibniz invented calculus at about the same time—is that Cervantes's achievements seem so essentially tied to the functioning of *his* mind that even somebody who knows precisely what he knew would write a different novel.[11]

To defend the view that, still, there should be no private rights beyond compensation and incentive setting, one might insist that *anybody* who makes a discovery benefits from the labor of predecessors, no matter how big a leap to the invention. Moreover, the social context determines the usefulness of, or appreciation for, an invention (Hettinger 1989). But the main reply to the point of the Borges story remains that if *indeed* realism is true, there will be more or less demanding discoveries, but no inventions.[12] The ludicrous nature of efforts to recreate the *Quixote* does not rebut this point, any more than we could rebut the idea that Edmund Hillary and Tenzing Norgay first reached, and in that sense *discovered*, the summit of Mount Everest by reference to everybody else's inability ever to do so again (in the case, say, of a disease permanently damaging the physical potential of human beings right after their success). Some discoverers may be held in great awe. Their abilities might be so immense that, owing to high opportunity costs, they receive high compensation. They might in fact be the only human beings capable of making the discoveries in question. Nonetheless, they have no *inventors' claims* and cannot *thereby* press for private rights beyond what they are entitled to as compensation and rewards promised to set incentives.

Similar considerations apply to Child's (1990) argument that there are infinitely many ideas: inventors never diminish the stock. They bring something into our world in a way that makes nobody worse off but some better off.[13] But these matters too are moot if realism is true. Whether "removing" ideas from a common stock diminishes its size and thereby makes anybody worse off has no bearing on our inquiry. Waldron (1993b) helpfully advises us to think about property rights from the standpoint of those who are supposed to comply with them. If realism is true, we need not even appeal to social value to make it reasonable to resist compliance with demanding private rights *beyond* what is covered by compensation and incentive-setting.

4. Realism about abstract objects is not outlandish. However, I have not merely assumed that basic ideas or plots, foundational themes or literary motives are elements of the realm of nonmental supersensory objects but rather that the objects of patents and copyrights themselves are such elements: the detailed ideas behind finished scientific inventions, completed copyrighted poems, particular drawings, and so forth. I have assumed realism about entities that bear a producer's distinct touch (and thus have located such entities in the Intellectual Common). Patent law is concerned "with the meaning and the characteristics of inventiveness and creativity, seeking to identify the locus of true innovation" (Lachlan 2005, 107). Strong realism makes such lawyerly efforts look peculiar.[14] A weaker form places only basic components into the third realm and into the Intellectual Common, but thereby weakens the presumption against privatization that we obtain in this way. However, I argue now for a conclusion much stronger than that private rights are limited under the assumption of strong realism about ideas, namely, that we should restrict private rights to compensation and incentive setting *regardless* of whether we endorse strong realism.

We may consider a very different but similarly extreme characterization of objects of intellectual property. Suppose there is no Fregean third realm, no Intellectual Common, no presumption against privatization.[15] Suppose ideas are not discovered but created. We now have a presumption in favor of private property rights potentially much beyond what compensation and incentive setting license. By assumption, there is nothing more to the ontological status of ideas than that they arise from a person's consciousness. Ideas are inextricably interwoven with the mental activities of their creators.

But although we now have a presumption in favor of private property rights, we must ask about the acceptable *reach* of these rights. Crucially, and perhaps surprisingly, the three Grotian considerations against privatization reenter by way of delineating the reach of acceptable property rights. These considerations were that gains do not depend on excluding others, that leaving ideas unappropriated benefits everybody, and that ideas cannot really be occupied. Earlier, these considerations ensured that the presumption against privatization can generally not be overcome. Exceptions were fairness-based compensation and consequentialist considerations in favor of incentives for invention. Now these considerations reenter, by limiting the extent of the rights for which there is that presumption. These considerations once again ensure that we consider the standpoint of those expected to comply with regulation, and once again entail a limitation of private property rights to what we can obtain via appeals to fairness and incentive setting.

So the Grotian considerations lead to the same conclusion regardless of whether we assume strong realism about ideas or a strongly subjective view according to which ideas are products of the mind, although they enter in very different ways. Since I have used the ontological assumptions to generate presumptions about the legitimacy of private property rights, we can also say that the Grotian considerations lead us to the same conclusion regardless of what sort of presumption (against or in favor of private intellectual property rights) we start with. In one case these considerations enter by reinforcing a presumption against private property rights (in the strong realism approach to the ontological status of ideas). In the other case they enter by limiting the reach of private property rights in a scenario where there is a presumption in their favor (in the subjective approach). In the first case, fairness-based compensation and incentive-based rewards appear as revisions of a presumption against private property rights (one that the Grotian considerations fortify). In the second, they appear as substantive ways of developing a presumption in favor of private intellectual property rights, rights that the Grotian considerations limit to what we can obtain from fairness-based compensation and incentive-based rewards.

However, so far we have operated with two strong views on the ontology of objects of intellectual property. Strong realists eliminate the contribution of human creativity, whereas antirealists overstate its role. This suggests an intermediate view, which according to Shiffrin (2001) would

> locate only the subject matter and materials of intellectual products in the commons, for example, facts, concepts, ideas, propositions, literary themes, musical themes, and values. Authors discover these things and their interconnections. They make them publicly accessible by expressing them, often, in unique ways. (159)[16]

As Shiffrin also remarks, the proper characterization of the metaphysical nature of objects of intellectual property law may not be in terms of a view "in between" the extreme views. The proper view may be a domain-specific hybrid that holds that the appropriate characterization varies across different objects of intellectual property law. In any case, the argument for limiting private rights to compensation and incentive setting applies throughout. The same results follow regardless of whether we have a third realm of ideas or whether ideas are human creations. The ontological assumptions made along the way drop out now. We can state what from now on I call the "main result" regarding the possibility of private intellectual property rights:

> The ontological status of intellectual products has to be characterized *to some extent* in terms of components readily placed into a third realm, and *to some extent* by appeal to human creativity. (One of these extents may vanish.) So *to the extent* that we must appeal to something in that third realm, the considerations for that case apply; *to the extent* that we are talking about products of the human mind, the considerations for that case apply. Either way, the respective argument generates the same constraints on what private rights are reasonably acceptable. Therefore, these constraints apply to the whole range of intellectual property.

To use a mathematical analogy: I have offered an argument for two extreme cases, and shown that the same argument also holds for the intermediate cases that can be understood as "convex combinations" of the extreme cases. We could now also formulate a corresponding result that omits the ontological assumptions and instead proceeds in terms of presumptions either against or in favor of private intellectual property rights.

By way of comparison, let us consider Shiffrin's (2001) strategy. Shiffrin postulates an Intellectual Common even on the subjective view of the ontology of ideas: "Creations could become part of the common—available equally to all—when their nature did not require exclusive use, to symbolize the equal moral status of individuals" (164). Shiffrin replaces metaphysical arguments for the Intellectual Common with moral arguments in its support (which are much like the three Grotian considerations). Drawing on Locke, she argues (the "first" view mentioned is the one stipulating an independent existence of ideas, the "second" is hers as just sketched):

> Locke's writings do not directly develop the foundations of the common property presumption. But there is reason to favor the second understanding. It, unlike the first, reflects the themes that initially animate Locke: the emphasis on equality, the connection between equality and common ownership, and reasoning about property in light of its nature—that is, in light of what is necessary to make full and robust use of it. The qualities of intellectual property strongly engage these Lockean themes—especially the facts that exclusive use is generally unnecessary for its proper use and that, to the contrary, its full

exploitation commonly depends on nonexclusive use. These features generate moral reasons to regard intellectual products as part of the intellectual common, even if they are pure authorial creations. (164)

I have argued that the considerations against privatization play different roles depending on the metaphysical status of ideas, but that we arrive at the same constraints on intellectual property regulation regardless of whether there is an Intellectual Common. The divergence between Shiffrin's strategy and mine, therefore, is about how to characterize the work done by the considerations against privatization.

5. So is there a *human right* to vital medicines? To show that there is, we must show first that access to pharmaceuticals is a matter of importance in the affected agents' immediate environment, and then establish global urgency. I take it that the preliminary step can easily be met. I also take it that in that way, we can establish that what is at stake here is a right. It lies in the nature of essential pharmaceuticals to be a matter of such importance, in light of the strong connections between health and social justice.[17] What is more problematic, however, is to establish a genuinely global concern with a right to essential medicines. Perhaps such a right is best understood exclusively as a right of citizens in their respective community rather than a human right. If indeed it is a human right, its source would presumably be the distinctively human life. But as we noted in section 1, it is doubtful whether that kind of life really requires such a right for its protection, with its accompanying global responsibilities.

Given that there are such doubts, the results of this chapter provide assistance. Let me offer two arguments for a human right to essential pharmaceuticals. According to the first, the conclusion that the regulation of vital medicines is a matter of urgent global concern emerges in three steps. First, our reflections on intellectual property entail that a certain domain of such property should be regulated globally. This domain includes ideas with regard to which it makes sense to speak of discovery and an Intellectual Common. For any two human beings, it is true that neither has done more than the other to create the entities in that domain. There is a case for *global* (at least *globally harmonized*) rather than *country-specific* regulation of property in this domain. Second, pharmaceuticals are in this domain because they draw on physiochemical properties of molecules. Such properties are among the entities for which strong realism is most plausible. Third, within the domain of those ideas with regard to which this case for global regulation is plausible (i.e., those that are in an Intellectual Common), entities immediately tied to basic needs present an especially plausible and urgent case. This includes the ideas behind vital medicines.

There is, thus, an urgent global concern with the regulation of vital pharmaceuticals. Our main result then entails a human right to essential medicines, in the sense that it is owed to people around the world first to regulate intellectual property in such medicines globally, and second to regulate it without far-reaching private rights. We can indeed tie the availability of essential medicines to the protection of a distinctively human life as a source of membership rights in the global order. Again, what is obvious is the connection between human need and essential pharmaceuticals. The present argument addresses the doubts about whether there is a *human right* based on this source. It does so by establishing a global concern via considerations of intellectual property. The argument for a human right to essential medicines cannot succeed entirely by appeal to the relevance of essential pharmaceuticals for human life. Of course, considerations of intellectual property by themselves have nothing to do with the distinctively human life. I have offered an auxiliary argument that becomes relevant only because it is doubtful whether there is a human right to essential medicines.

However, my argument endorses realism about the contents of the ideas behind pharmaceutical patents. It would be unfortunate if the case for a human right to essential pharmaceuticals depended on this endorsement. Fortunately, another argument also establishes an urgent global concern with the regulation of vital pharmaceuticals. There currently is intellectual property regulation at the global level. The Agreement on TRIPs is part of the WTO treaty and determines minimum standards for many forms of intellectual property regulation. Also specifying enforcement and dispute resolution mechanisms, the Agreement on TRIPs remains the most comprehensive international agreement on intellectual property. But not only is there this kind of intellectual property regulation at the global level, it is also true that *interconnectedness* makes it inevitable that some intellectual property regime or other (possibly merely a rather loose one) is in place regardless of whether there is a particular treaty (such as that on TRIPs) governing that regime.

Our main result applies to the current global intellectual property regime. There ought to be no intellectual property regulation (not only but *especially*) globally that grants rights beyond what we can obtain via compensation and incentive setting. The redistributive effects of the Agreement on TRIPs have generated much controversy, one concern being that the agreement's provisions redistribute money from developing countries to copyright and patent owners in developed countries by imposing provisions on countries that would otherwise have weaker laws in this domain. Since private rights ought to be limited in this way, and since it is implausible that either would generate duties for very poor countries, the Agreement on TRIPs should not impose burdens on them. This means at least that people in poorer countries ought to be free to make generic drugs. Economic analysis is needed to substantiate this claim, but presumably the wealth differential between rich and poor is so large that compensation and incentives for the pharmaceutical industry are unlikely to depend on markets in such countries.[18]

The first argument responded to the observation that it was doubtful whether the distinctively human life would generate a human right to essential pharmaceuticals, and offered an auxiliary argument that turned on the metaphysical nature of the ideas behind intellectual property rights. This second one draws on both the distinctively human life and on interconnectedness as sources of human rights, and does not need an auxiliary argument beyond what these sources supply. Whereas the first argument identifies a reason *in favor of* global regulation of a certain sort, the second identifies a reason *against* regulation of a certain sort.

While the second argument proceeds without an auxiliary argument that does not turn on sources of membership rights, there is a sense in which the second argument is weaker than the first. There is a philosophical gain from the ontological assumptions backing the first argument. After all, that second argument applies only once some global intellectual property regime or other exists. However, since there is global regulation now, and since interconnectedness makes it inevitable that some property regime or other is in place regardless of whether there is a particular treaty governing that regime, both arguments have identical implications. Neither generates a claim against anybody to invent medications that are not yet available. But neither does either dispute private property rights that are justifiable by considerations involving incentives and fair compensation. It may not be a human rights violation if some people cannot afford essential pharmaceuticals.

Both arguments entail that it is owed to people around the world that intellectual property generally and vital pharmaceuticals in particular not be regulated in a way that recognizes far-reaching private rights (beyond what is justifiable in terms of incentives and fair compensation), especially at the global level. In that sense—but as far as this chapter is concerned, *only* in that sense—is there a human right to essential pharmaceuticals. In terms of justice, our result is this: the distribution of intellectual property rights granted by various laws globally is just only if no one has more extensive private rights to ideas relating to essential pharmaceuticals than is needed to compensate that person or entity for developing these pharmaceuticals or to provide incentives for future developers. Respect for the distinctively human life creates strong reasons to devise market mechanisms that make sure that everybody can afford essential pharmaceuticals. But such efforts go beyond what is required by the human right this chapter has established.

CHAPTER 13

Arguing for Human Rights

Labor Rights as Human Rights

1. Labor rights appear in the Universal Declaration of Human Rights and are covered by the International Covenant on Economic, Social, and Cultural Rights.[1] In its 1993 Vienna Declaration, the UN insisted that "all human rights are universal, indivisible and interdependent and interrelated" (Article 5). As far as the UN is concerned, labor rights are human rights, as much as any other rights identified in the Universal Declaration. Yet labor rights are the first to be questioned in philosophical inquiries, notoriously so Article 24, which addresses "rest and leisure," "reasonable limitations of working hours," and "periodic holidays with pay." Allen Buchanan (2004), for one, says that "in some extreme cases, such as the notorious right to holidays with pay, it is pretty obvious that they are not necessary for a decent human life, though they may make for a better life for many people" (129). Sidney Hook (1980) thinks of that same right as "mirth-producing" (92). I discuss labor rights (specifically, rights to work and leisure) as another case study of how to apply my conception to questions of the sort, "Is there a human right to X?"

In light of the persistent skepticism confronting the idea of labor rights as human rights, it behooves us to look at the historical development that brought labor rights into the declaration. Section 2 of this chapter does so. Section 3 articulates objections to their presence there. The remaining sections explore whether we can derive labor rights from the various substantive sources of membership rights in the global order that we distinguished in chapter 11. There is, of course, a human right to be able to meet basic needs at the subsistence level. One difficulty in the upcoming discussion is to argue specifically for labor rights given that there is such a right. After all, one might think that of global concern is only whether individuals can satisfy basic needs. Versions of the right to work and the right to leisure indeed are human rights. Common humanity as a source does not take us far, but common ownership, enlightened self-interest, and interconnectedness converge: according to these sources, a right to work is a human right when understood as a right against the state obstructing labor markets, a right to minimum wages, and a right not to be fired for frivolous reasons. There is no human right to work qua right to full employment, nor is there such a right to "just and favorable conditions of work" (Article 23 of the Universal Declaration), or to form labor unions. There is a human right to leisure in the sense that working hours should be limited so that workers can recuperate from the strains of work. But there is no global concern for a right to leisure strong enough to guarantee paid holidays. Stronger rights to work and leisure may well be (and I think are) rights of citizens, but they are not human rights.

2. At a conference in 1847, the Communist League decided to publish its principles. The result was the *Communist Manifesto* of 1848, drafted by Marx and Engels. The league was an international organization, and the *Manifesto* addresses problems of global scope:

> The bourgeoisie has through its exploitation of the world-market given a cosmopolitan character to production and consumption in every country. To the great chagrin of Reactionists, it has drawn from under the feet of industry the national ground on which it stood. All old-established national industries have been destroyed or are daily being destroyed. They are dislodged by new industries, whose introduction becomes a life-and-death question for all civilized nations by industries that no longer work up indigenous raw material, but raw material drawn from the remotest zones; industries whose products are consumed, not only at home, but in every quarter of the globe.... The bourgeoisie, by the rapid improvement of all instruments of production, by the immensely facilitated means of communication, draw all, even the most barbarian, nations into civilization. (McLellan 1977, 248–49)

Solutions, too, must be of global scope: according to Marx and Engels, what is distinctive about communists is that "in the national struggles of the proletarians of the different countries, they point out and bring to the front the common interests of the entire proletariat, independently of all nationality" (McLellan 1977, 255). The *Manifesto* famously concludes with the battle cry, "Working Men of All Countries, Unite!"

The *Manifesto* is not primarily about rights. The emancipation Marx and Engels sought was expected to come through changing the economic structure, which supposedly would create a communist society that would allow persons to develop their true humanity, their "species-being." Years later, Marx's *Critique of the Gotha Program* emphasized that he did not seek to realize certain rights. He dismissed that program for containing "nothing beyond the old democratic litany familiar to all; universal suffrage, direct legislation, popular rights, a people's militia, etc." (McLellan 1977, 611). Instead, in a higher phase of communist society ... after labor has become not only a means of life but life's prime want; after the productive forces have also increased with the all-round development of the individual, and all the springs of co-operative wealth flow more abundantly—only then can the narrow horizon of bourgeois right be crossed in its entirety and society inscribe on its banners: from each according to his ability, to each according to his needs! (McLellan 1977, 615)

Understanding emancipation in terms of an increase in rights would merely have cemented old structures that had to be overcome.

Many in the working class movement, however, did not share Marx's aversion to the language of rights, or his view that emancipation could not occur within the socioeconomic confines of contemporary societies. The Gotha Program itself belonged to a unified German socialist party oscillating between a revolutionary and a reformist orientation. Ultimately the reformists won, and the socialists became Germany's largest party. Internationally, the reformists demanded labor rights. By the end of World War I, the labor movement had become impossible to ignore. Morsink (1999) quotes the World Federation of Trade Unions as arguing that the war had been won partly because of "the active help of the working class and as a result of its sacrifices" (169). Moreover, assistance to trade unions in defeated countries had been a major factor "in the spread of democracy in the political, social, and economic domain." They also added a reminder that unorganized labor might pose a threat. The Treaty of Versailles codified the concern for labor rights internationally (regarding workers' pay, benefits, working conditions, and the way in which those are negotiated) and founded the International Labor Organization (ILO), a permanent organization involving governments, employers, and workers to coordinate progress in the realization of labor rights.[2]

The labor movement had reacted to the pitiful working conditions created by the Industrial Revolution. As the Manifesto illustrates, there had been an international dimension to the causes of that state of affairs as well as to plausible remedies: *international* capitalism was perceived as the problem.[3] Working conditions are affected by the conditions on relevant markets. If markets are international, so are the problems they affect. For instance, better benefits and pay mean higher labor costs. Other things (such as productivity) being equal, higher costs entail a competitive disadvantage and make it harder for labor to obtain better conditions. Hence, nineteenth century labor advocates worried about what happened elsewhere but not only out of class solidarity or altruism. On the side of governments and employers, a desire for coordination arose from fear of disorder as well as from the worry that lower labor standards elsewhere would undercut prices.

The ILO was later incorporated into the UN, which endorsed labor rights in the Universal Declaration:

Article 23

1. Everyone has the right to work, to free choice of employment, to just and favorable conditions of work and to protection against unemployment.

2. Everyone, without any discrimination, has the right to equal pay for equal work.

3. Everyone who works has the right to just and favorable remuneration ensuring for himself and his family an existence worthy of human dignity, and supplemented, if necessary, by other means of social protection.

4. Everyone has the right to form and to join trade unions for the protection of his interests.

Article 24

Everyone has the right to rest and leisure, including reasonable limitation of working hours and periodic holidays with pay.[4]

But as Leary (1996) explains, although workers' rights are human rights,

the international human rights movement devotes little attention to the rights of workers. At the same time, trade unions and labor leaders rarely enlist the support of human rights groups for the defense of worker's rights. A regrettable paradox: the human rights movement and the labor movement run on tracks that are sometimes parallel and rarely meet. (22)

Alongside the antislavery movement and the women's liberation movement, the Red Cross, and other humanitarian or emancipatory efforts, the labor movement was one of the more issue-specific movements that helped prepare the stage for human rights.[5] Still, human rights organizations often show little interest in labor issues, while labor organizations do not see themselves closely aligned with the human rights movement.

Nonetheless, labor rights are noted in the Universal Declaration of Human Rights, and these historical remarks illustrate two points. First, the declaration addresses concerns with regard to which both historically and in recent memory much had gone wrong. Second, the solutions required international coordination. This is clear with regard to the articles that deal with civil and political rights as well as with judicial procedure, all of which the Nazis had disregarded virulently. They first committed violations at home, and subsequently at a larger scale in the countries they overran. By mentioning peace in addition to justice and liberty in its preamble, the declaration makes clear that, although the concerns addressed there must be addressed within countries, they affect others too by jeopardizing peace. Mutatis mutandis, these points apply to Articles 23 and 24. The connection between justice and peace also appears in the preamble of the International Labour Organization's charter. To use R. H. Tawney's term, most people now live in "acquisitive societies," or in societies that aim to become so. All these societies are, one may say, acquisitively interconnected. Since the Universal Declaration reacts to evils that have occurred in recent memory and require international solutions, the regulation of societies' acquisitive activities has a strong prima facie claim to be counted as part of the "common standard of achievement" that, according to its preamble, the declaration set out to capture.

3. Nevertheless, labor rights have attracted doubts about their status *as* human rights. Let me discuss three influential objections. The *nature-of-rights objection* has been prominent in the discussion of social and economic rights. Regardless of how we think of the moral urgency of the issues behind labor rights, we should not think about them in terms of *rights*. Talking about a right to something involves an identifiable addressee with a relevant connection to the holder. In light of this point, Bernard Williams (2005a) formulates the following worry for labor rights:

> Nobody doubts that having the opportunity to work is a good thing, or that unemployment is an evil. But does it mean that people have a right to work? The problem is: against whom is the right held? Who violates it if it is not observed? ... Even if governments accept some responsibility for levels of employment, it may not be possible for them to provide or generate work, and if they fail to do so, it is not clear that the best thing to say is that the rights of the unemployed have been violated. I think that it may be unfortunate that declarations of human rights have, though for understandable reasons, included supposed rights of this kind. Since in many cases governments cannot actually deliver what their peoples are said to have a right to, this encourages the idea that human rights represent merely aspirations, that they signal goods and opportunities which, as a matter of urgency, should be provided if it is possible. But that is not the shape of a right. If people have a right to something, then someone does wrong who denies it to them. (64)

If there is a right and it is not satisfied, Williams seems to be saying, then someone has done wrong. If someone does wrong, then that agent has the power to make it the case that the right was satisfied. But no one has the power to make it the case that everyone has the opportunity to work.[6] The main premise of this argument, a supposed conceptual truth about rights, is similar to that of Onora O'Neill's argument I introduced in chapter 11 (although she concludes there are no human rights at all, not specifically none concerned with work). A right's being "in principle enforceable" in O'Neill's argument presumably implies that someone has the power to bring it about that the right is satisfied. So both arguments link rights to someone's having the power to make sure the right is satisfied. My response is the same in this case. Human rights can be aspirational. Therefore the relevant duties are to do what one can to bring about their satisfaction. In some cases, specific agents have duties toward the immediate provision of certain rights. In other cases measures must be taken so that rights can be satisfied in the future. It is possible for rights to be unsatisfied and yet for nobody to have done anything wrong.

The second objection is the *inferior urgency objection*. This argument proceeds as follows: If X is a human right, then it is no less urgent than any other human right. Labor rights are less urgent than some other rights that everyone accepts are human rights (e.g., certain political or civil rights, or perhaps a right to subsistence). Therefore, labor rights are not human rights. Cranston (1973) argues that social and economic rights fail the test of "paramount importance" (67). It is "a paramount duty to relieve great distress, as it is not a paramount duty to give pleasure." It would be a "splendid thing" if, say, everybody had periodic holidays with pay. Yet it would not be as serious a deficiency if such rights were not realized as if civil and political rights were disregarded. This objection does not deny that labor rights have *some* urgency. But, it claims, among morally urgent issues, one needs to differentiate. This kind of objection is not committed to regarding *all* civil and political rights as especially urgent (and as human rights), and might grant that a right of subsistence, too, is of paramount importance, so that *some* social and economic rights are human rights: but *not* the rights in Articles 23 and 24.

I agree that labor rights are not of "paramount importance." A conception that considers labor rights human rights delivers a list that does not *only* include rights of "paramount importance." My conception limits human rights to matters of urgent global concern but need not endorse the idea that all human rights are of *equal* (namely, *greatest*) urgency. The considerations in chapter 7 and 11 that make plausible why mine would be a conception *of human rights* in the first place outweigh the insistence that human rights be limited to those of greatest urgency.

A third concern is a *cultural imperialism* objection, which insists that counting labor rights as human rights expresses such imperialism. Western societies took specific developmental trajectories, including industrialization and its accompanying history of labor relations. There were important similarities in the central problems through which the major countries involved in this history went. As Macklem (2002) explains,

Although they aspire to the level of universal principle, many of the recommendations and conventions promulgated by the ILO speak most directly to the industrial histories of those states responsible for their formulation. When these states participated in the formation of the ILO, mass production was the dominant form of productive relations and the main object of their attention. The era of mass production was a period of rising unionism, standardized employment relations, direct state involvement in a wide range of economic activities, and various forms of social corporatism. (617)

Labor rights provided a coordination device to ensure every country abided by certain norms so that nobody obtained an advantage from violations (see also Macklem 2005). However, counting labor rights among "common standards of achievement" applicable to countries that have evolved differently is unreasonable in terms of "fit": asking developing countries to adopt social and economic standards before their trajectory takes them there means asking them to endorse norms that do not suit their stage of development. We can put the objection as follows. If something is a human right, then it must be appropriate to demand of all countries (now) that they satisfy it. It is not appropriate to demand of all countries that they satisfy labor rights; it is only appropriate to ask this of countries at a certain stage of development. Therefore, labor rights are not human rights. This objection specifically concerns labor rights, rather than articulating a general resistance to human rights.

But I recall again that some human rights can be aspirational. In many contexts this will be true for labor rights. It might not be appropriate to demand of all countries that they satisfy labor rights *now*, but only to demand of them that they do so eventually. And that, in turn, is appropriate for developing countries if we expect them to, or at least hope that they will, pass through the same stages of development eventually.

4. Although we could formulate responses to these objections rather briefly, this was so because chapters 7 and 11 have done much work that we could readily apply. However, we have not yet shown that labor rights are human rights according to my conception. To set the stage, let us distinguish various interpretations of the right to work and the right to leisure.

Understood minimally, a right to work is a liberty right, and thus is like the right to marry, which means only that the state will not obstruct marriage in certain ways (e.g., by prohibiting interracial marriages). A right to marry does not require states to assist people whom nobody wishes to marry, nor does it require states to stop individuals from obstructing the marriages of others in ways that are not otherwise offensive. According to such a minimal understanding, a right to work requires of states only that they not obstruct employment prospects in certain ways (other than by making sure basic rules that define employment relationships are respected, ranging from prohibitions of child labor to regulation that requires specific qualifications of people who enter certain lines of work).

On more demanding readings, more aspects could be added: a right to work could require that the state help people find jobs, or facilitate job creation; or that the state itself create jobs. A right to work could be an outright claim right. Such a right could also require that the state make sure employees are treated fairly, which may involve specifications concerning workplace safety, an insistence on equal treatment (as well as equal pay for equal work), an insistence that wages suffice to maintain a certain kind of life, or the provision that unions are acceptable. Article 23 of the Universal Declaration of Human Rights articulates a much more extensive understanding of a right to work than the minimal understanding. However, the UN insists that the right to work not be understood as a claim right (General Comment No. 18, adopted on November 24, 2005, UN Economic and Social Council).

A right to "rest and leisure" also comes in different versions. On a minimal understanding, such a right merely entails a limitation of hours below the threshold of physical exhaustion. Daily working hours would be limited, and presumably there would periodically be a day off. Versions of such a right differ in terms of how much time they give off, and for what reasons. Understood more extensively, a right to leisure could require that daily or weekly working hours be limited more than what is required to avoid physical exhaustion, or that time off be given in relatively short intervals (one or two out seven days, or more); or that time remain for pursuing other interests, such as participation in religious observation or other customs (which may entail that a number of days be set aside as holidays annually); or that more extended periods of time be given for such purposes, or for recreation (vacations). A very strong understanding of the right to leisure incorporates into wage relationships that employers, or the state, continue to pay workers for extended amounts of time set aside for recreation (paid vacations).

Article 24 captures an extended understanding of the right to leisure by talking about "reasonable limitation of working hours and periodic holidays with pay." The Universal Declaration recognizes the significance of leisure for human beings not merely by recognizing this right in the first place but also by placing it in a separate article, rather than listing it alongside the right to work.

5. To determine whether rights to work and leisure are human rights, we must explore whether we can derive such rights from the different sub-

stantive sources we have distinguished. One source that does not take us far is common humanity. To see this, we notice how Nickel (2007) argues for the view that labor rights should be counted as human rights. We can imagine a world, he says,

> in which economic problems have been solved, in which automation, central-
> ized production, and free services make it unnecessary for most people to en-
> gage in economic activity except as consumers and householders.... If such a
> world were to emerge, and be reliable and sustainable, people would not need
> all the basic economic liberties.... But we are still in a situation in which most
> adults need to make an economic contribution. (128–29)

Nickel is right about all of this, but telling for present purposes is that it is indeed *most* adults who need to make an economic contribution—whereas by far not all of them do. Indeed, the distinctively human life is not necessarily a working life. Basic needs must be satisfied, but not necessarily through work. Those who think of paradise as a place where food and pleasure are provided effortlessly do not envisage a form of life that deviates from the distinctively human life. Those who believe that satisfactory work is an essential part of the flourishing human life—of our "species-being," as Marx put it—are ill-advised to insist that those who do not work cannot lead a distinctively human life. The distinctively human life generates a right to work only under specific conditions, when the preservation of that life requires it. But then the right to work instantiates some other, more basic, right and does not require independent justification.

Let me continue with Common Ownership as a source. At the core of Common Ownership there is a natural right to access to original spaces and resources of the earth to satisfy one's basic needs. As chapter 7 argued, Common Ownership entails two fundamental guarantees that states and other powerful organizations must give, and whose realization is a global responsibility: they must ensure that their power does not render individuals incapable of meeting their basic needs, and they must provide opportunities for individuals to lead lives at least at subsistence level. Such guarantees neutralize the dangers imposed on the co-ownership status by the global order. It is the second guarantee that matters now. Property conventions that provide for exclusive rights of access might make it impossible for individuals to satisfy basic needs through original resources. To make this acceptable to co-owners—that is, so as not to violate their core natural rights—states must make sure individuals have other ways of doing so. This move does not generate an extensive list of rights, and in itself it does not generate a right to work in even the weakest form of a protection from exclusion from labor markets. After all, states may guarantee subsistence by providing welfare.

However, chapter 7 could derive more rights by adding contingent premises about how the world works. The core thought was that states are (as a matter of fact) more likely to live up to their core obligations reliably and robustly if they also guarantee various other rights (and if other states do what they can to get them to do so as well). In this way we could generate a longer list of rights. Can some form of the right to work or right to leisure be derived this way? I think it can: we can derive a right not to be excluded from labor markets, to receive minimum wages to meet basic needs, and not to be fired for frivolous reasons, but not a right to employment or a right to certain workplace conditions or a right to form unions. Similarly, we can derive a right to enough leisure time to recuperate from the strains of work but not a right to paid vacations. At least for advanced economies where basic education is crucial for success in any line of work, we can also derive an elementary right to education, understood not as a right to the development of one's personality but as a right to being equipped with the basic prerequisites for participation in the labor force.

To argue for this claim, I must show that the rights I specified do emerge from this source and that no stronger versions of the rights to work and leisure do. States must provide opportunities for individuals to lead lives at least at subsistence level. One way of discharging this obligation is to provide people with sufficient supplies to satisfy basic needs. Presumably the state could not do so for its whole population but could do so for certain groups that it chooses to exclude from labor markets. To argue from the state's obligation that I just restated for a right to work is to argue that a state must not discharge its obligations in the way I just sketched. Presumably it would not be sensible for states to keep individuals off labor markets and instead provide them with supplies, rather than permit them to earn money and pay taxes on income. Governments have often been politically motivated to exclude parts of the population from markets. But it would be peculiar if they subsequently paid them social security monies. After all, the former would be motivated by hatred or some other form of strong aversion, whereas the latter would be motivated by benevolence or the recognition of basic rights.

The peculiarity of such a situation would not entail that there is a right not to be so treated. But crucially, a scenario in which a society discriminates against a group by excluding it from labor markets cannot be counted on to provide that group's means of livelihood on an ongoing basis. Such a combination is possible but not *robust,* in light of the plainly conflicting motivations on which exclusion from labor markets and provision with supplies would be based. The risk is too large that such obstruction of employment would be merely an early stage of a development that would lead to worse. In this way we can derive a right to work understood as a right against the state obstructing employment possibilities. We can also derive a right to minimum wages that would make sure basic needs can be met, and a right not to have employment terminated for frivolous reasons (e.g., the capriciousness of employers, which would make one's ability to satisfy basic needs too insecure). Similarly, we could derive a right to leisure understood as a right to the limitation of working hours so that workers may recuperate from work.

To see whether stronger versions of the right to work and the right to leisure can be derived, we must ask whether robust protection of the purpose of original ownership rights requires a right to employment, a right to "just and favorable" conditions at the workplace, a right to form unions, a right to extended periods of vacation, and so on. A proper treatment of this question calls for social scientific and historical investigation. However, a sensible guess is that we cannot press this reasoning further than we have. On the face of it, it is implausible that people's ability to meet basic needs cannot be protected robustly unless such extended versions of the rights to work and leisure hold. Any doubts weigh heavily because we seek to derive rights that carry global responsibilities.

One objection to my reluctance to extend the argument further (specifically to a claim right to employment) is that employment is an *inherently* more robust form of satisfying basic needs than social security. Those who make their living through gainful employment possess a kind of self-sufficiency that those lack who depend on social security for their livelihood, and who are thus exposed to the government's whims and woes. As far as the robust protection of basic needs satisfaction is concerned, it is thus preferable to impose obligations on governments to make sure people have jobs rather than merely to provide social security. What is true is that someone who holds a job that is subsidized or created by the government has at least some chance of finding new employment should the government terminate its support. But someone who lives off welfare might become increasingly unqualified for gainful employment. However, for one thing, this point would not suffice to impose an obligation on states to create jobs as long as they provide social security. Moreover, if jobs exist only because governments subsidize or create them, they provide no more self-sufficiency than social security.[7]

6. Common Ownership has delivered a right to work understood as a right against the state obstructing employment possibilities, as a right to minimum wages to make sure basic needs can be met, and as a right not to be fired for frivolous reasons. We could also derive a right to leisure

understood as a right to the limitation of working hours so that workers can recuperate. What about the two remaining substantive sources, enlightened self-interest and interconnectedness?

The general form of arguing for human rights is a two-stage process: we must show that the matter at hand generates an important demand against authority in the agents' environment, and then that the issue is of urgent global concern, and thus that there are associated obligations also on other states or international institutions. We do not need to go through this two-stage procedure when dealing with natural rights (or clear cases of natural rights that, unlike the case in chapter 12, do not trigger the boundary problem). Therefore, we did not go through this procedure for the two sources we already addressed. But for enlightened self-interest and interconnectedness we need to do so.

Let us first identify the concerns that make labor rights important items on the agenda of domestic politics. The moral concern behind (or what I call the generic case for) labor rights is that everybody ought to be able to have a share in the productive system of her society. After all, this productive system is a conventional system with which participants are expected to comply and in which they are otherwise subject to coercive measures. The extended Rawlsian account of shared membership in states is salient here: chapters 2 and 3 explored the nature of shared membership in a state as ground of justice. Not everybody works for a living. Nonetheless, while a right to work is not essentially connected to the distinctively human life, it is so connected to citizenship in modern states. Citizens are expected to comply with quite a range of expectations, as spelled out in chapters 2 and 3. Labor rights guarantee that, in return for compliance, citizens can participate in economic life in ways that respect their status. Whether they do so is a separate matter. But for most adults, paid work indeed is the source of livelihood, and they spend much of their time earning the money on which to live and raise families. Employment is also a crucial source of self-esteem for those who make their living through wage relationships.

So rights to work and leisure are readily shown to be rights of citizens. The generic case creates duties for states to ensure *at least* that nobody is systematically excluded from employment, that workers can meet basic needs through wage relationships and are treated in certain ways in their workplace, and that working hours are limited. We need not decide whether stronger versions of the right to work (e.g., one according to which the state must provide employment) or of the right to leisure (e.g., one to paid vacations) are morally preferred. Presumably, the rights of citizens go further than what I just stated, but according to enlightened self-interest and interconnectedness (which here converge with common ownership), it is not a matter *of urgent global concern* whether each person has employment, enjoys just and favorable working conditions, or has paid vacations.

Let us turn to enlightened self-interest and interconnectedness, then, starting with the former. Assuming that a country recognizes some forms of rights to work and leisure, is it in that country's self-interest that other countries recognize such rights, too? Initial reflection on this question can draw on reasons Marx and Engels discussed in the *Manifesto* and that later motivated the creation of the International Labour Organization. Labor conditions in one country affect its competitiveness, and so also the competitiveness of others, on the world market. Mutual self-interest played an important role in the process that led to the formation of the International Labour Organization: it was in no country's interest to be at a competitive disadvantage if others could benefit by exposing their workforce to unfavorable working conditions.

But we must be careful in assessing precisely what enlightened self-interest establishes when it comes to work and leisure. To be sure, the presumption is that we are talking about the enlightened self-interest of states as a whole. The motivation specifically of the *Communist Manifesto* was to make sure workers across different countries would see themselves as *the* working class rather than as members of particular countries. Suppose we think of enlightened self-interest as the long-term interest of a state, and suppose that, pace the communists, principles of domestic justice make sure the economic long-term interests of different groups are reasonably well aligned. (It turns out that if we think of A's enlightened self-interest as capturing what is necessary for the realization of A's moral obligations, the same considerations enter that we are about to discuss.)

One might think it is not in country A's long-term interest that country B respect a right to work, in the minimal sense of not obstructing access to labor markets, and a right to leisure, in the minimal sense of limiting work hours. Presumably B's competitiveness will not rise but fall if it discriminates against parts of its workforce and does not provide opportunities for its workers to recuperate. Not excluding people from the labor force and letting them take holidays make the labor force bigger and more productive, and so improves competitiveness in B. If A and B compete, it is precisely because it actually is in B's long-term interest to respect minimal rights to work and leisure that it does not seem to be in A's. On the other hand, better working conditions are costly, and perhaps some of them reduce competitiveness—at least vis-à-vis similarly situated competitors. If so, it is indeed in A's long-term interest that B improve the conditions under which its workforce labors (and it would then also be easier for A to meet its own obligations toward its workers).

But long-term interest should be understood less competitively. Quite plausibly, it is in A's long-term interest to help B build an emancipated and well-educated population to maintain a sophisticated economy, an economy that in turn can engage in ultimately mutually beneficial competition with A. It is not necessarily in the short-term interest of any government of B that such a population emerge, but that is a different matter. Labor rights promote the emergence of such a population. I cannot even begin to address the empirical issues, but this understanding of self-interest seems to offer much support for labor rights as human rights. Most plausibly again, we find that this support is for a right to work understood as a right against the state obstructing employment possibilities, a right to minimum wages to make sure basic needs can be met, a right not be fired for frivolous reasons, and a right to a limit on working hours so that workers can recuperate. Further-reaching aspects of the right to work and the right to leisure do not seem to bear on the long-term self-interest of outsiders. Their dealings with the state in question are sufficiently fostered through rights to work and leisure as I have delineated them and would not recognizably benefit from additional aspects of these rights.

As discussed in chapter 11, the general point that it is in the interest of countries that others respect rights because countries with oppressed people are unstable and potentially a threat (war, illegal immigration, etc.). That consideration, too, provides support for labor rights as human rights, and does so in combination with considerations that draw on interconnectedness. So let us turn to that one remaining source of human rights.

7. Using interconnectedness as a source, we can argue as follows. X is a human right if X is a right for people locally, vis-à-vis their own state, and the problem for which that right is supposed to be a solution is caused by economic and political integration, by processes of globalization. As far as the right to work and the right to leisure are concerned, the generic case for labor rights takes care of the first step. What about the second?

The problem to which rights to work and leisure are supposed to be the solution is, first of all, the problem of finding gainful employment to make ends meet, and second, to work under bearable conditions. In an interconnected world, these problems take on a particular form, namely, to find gainful employment on labor markets, or anyway in economies, that are increasingly shaped by processes of globalization. Ever more ways of making a living, one way or another, depend on transnational processes and interactions. Most straightforwardly, this would be because workers are involved in production processes or the provision of services that are integrated into global markets, markets that involve structured and repeated exchanges according to rules that are codified by domestic and international law, and that determine incentives of governments, industries, and individuals in participating countries. Individuals might produce things for export, use parts that have been imported, provide services for industries that do either, or provide services for people in or from other countries. In addition, many people work abroad, at least temporarily, and send remittances home.

Even people who are not connected to transnational processes in these ways might be affected by such processes because they work in sectors indirectly affected by the flourishing of sectors that are so connected. More work might be available in such sectors when work is being vacated by people who move to export-oriented industries (or less work, if the export business is struggling and people seek to change jobs). If working conditions or employment prospects are abysmal, people might drift off into the many forms of international crime that flourish through increasing interconnectedness, such as drug trafficking or human trafficking.

To appreciate the global nature of labor conditions, let us also briefly talk about the WTO, which chapter 18 discusses in detail. The WTO treaty is concerned not only with traditional trade in goods, it also includes agreements on services, intellectual property rights, and investment measures, as well as agreements on, for instance, sanitary barriers to trade. Agriculture and textiles were absent from the WTO's predecessor treaty but are part of the WTO's mandate. The WTO also deals with policy harmonization, and thus enters the domain of domestic decision making. The Agreement on TRIPs, for instance, mandates national regulatory standards.

It is thus evident that the working conditions of many people across the globe are affected by transnational processes. To recall, the problems to which rights to work and leisure are supposed to be the solution are, first, the problem of finding gainful employment to make ends meet, and second, the problem of working under bearable conditions. To the extent that possibilities for this kind of employment are shaped by processes of globalization, this problem indeed is global in nature. Obviously, people are affected by these processes very differently, and to very different degrees. As chapter 11 noted, this is a general feature of both enlightened self-interest and interconnectedness as sources of membership rights in the global order. A judgment needs to be made whether in spite of such differential involvement in the matter at hand, considerations drawing on interconnectedness suffice to establish a global concern. As far as labor conditions are concerned, both the significance of this matter and the extent to which it involves the global population support that conclusion.

So interconnectedness too delivers a right to work and a right to leisure. Again we must ask what forms of these rights we obtain. For interconnectedness the question becomes, precisely what problem has been caused by global political and economic processes? Interconnectedness affects employment prospects. Therefore it makes sense to say that the global order caused a problem to which labor rights are the solution, the problem of finding gainful employment with bearable working conditions. So we readily obtain the rights we have already established through common ownership and enlightened self-interest: a right to work understood as a right against the state obstructing employment possibilities, as a right to minimum wages to make sure basic needs can be met, and as a right not be fired for frivolous reasons, as well as a right to a limit on working hours so that workers can recuperate.

But here, too, it would be hard to push this reasoning further. We would make too much of the impact of global political and economic processes on domestic labor conditions if we tried to cast the problems to which, say, a right to just and favorable conditions of work, a right to join unions, or a right to paid vacations are appropriate responses as problems caused through processes of globalization. This reasoning would overreach then. Interconnectedness does not apply here with much precision. Therefore it is sensible to limit the rights we support in this way to rather constrained ones. In any event, this reasoning does support the conclusions we have already reached.

Let us conclude. Limited rights to work and leisure can be derived from common ownership, enlightened self-interest, and interconnectedness. The right to leisure poses a particular challenge. Michael Walzer (1983), for one, rightly rejects "periodic holidays with pay" as a human right because it is unnecessarily specific (196). He insists that such holidays take a partisan stance in favor of vacations as opposed to festivals for which time is given off (see also Waldron 1993b, 12f). Indeed, to the extent that we can demonstrate a global concern with a right to leisure, such a concern is tied to leisure as recuperation from work. However, it is difficult to assess how much leisure is needed to that end. The versions of the two rights we have been able to derive fall short of what is listed in Articles 23 and 24 of the Universal Declaration of Human Rights. A case can be made that the rights listed therein are rights of citizens, but in stronger versions than what I have argued, the right to work and the right to leisure do not register as human rights.

CHAPTER 14

Justice and Trade

1. Part 3 of this book develops pluralist internationalism by exploring what principles of justice apply globally in virtue of the specific relations among people that hold in an increasingly interconnected world. Chapters 11–13 have investigated one way in which global relations anchor such a principle, by being the basis for human rights. Let us now change tracks and consider what justice requires for international trade. This involves us in two separate problems: first, what follows about trade from the human rights–oriented principles we have already encountered, and second, whether any new and distinct principles of justice arise out of the fact that we live in a world of multiple states where there is trade across borders.[1]

Standard economic theory teaches that trade benefits all countries involved, at least in the long run, and if the country is taken as a whole. (Some people *within* states might lose out.) If country A is better at producing cheese than wine, it should obtain wine by trading cheese. If the reverse is true for B, B should trade wine for cheese. A has a *comparative advantage* in cheese and B in wine, even if A is better at producing both. While there are other reasons for trade liberalization, this insight, going back to David Ricardo's 1817 *Principles of Political Economy*, underlies international economics. Trade theory supports free trade: barriers like tariffs and quotas obstruct mutually beneficial transactions. Countries should undo them, even unilaterally.

I do not address economic arguments for or against free trade. Instead, what concerns us is, what does *justice* require when it comes to trade? Does it require free trade? Or does it require of states any of the trade-restricting measures that supporters of free trade oppose, such as subsidies or tariffs? In fact, this inquiry delivers some principles that constrain trade from the standpoint of justice. These principles apply within states but are associated with grounds other than shared membership in states. This chapter discusses both relations within states *and* relations among states, and so straddles parts 1 and 3 of this book. While chapter 18 in part 4 discusses the WTO as an institution, my concern now is with norms of trade.

Export subsidies—governmental payments to producers for exporting products—appear prominently in debates about what justice requires when it comes to trade. Particular controversy surrounds agricultural subsidies in rich countries. The subject of subsidies preoccupies us for several sections since it serves as a useful organizing theme for a range of considerations bearing on what justice implies for trade. Section 2 provides some information about the economics of subsidies. Section 3 assesses how a principle of global justice we have already encountered—that human rights be realized—bears on subsidies. In conjunction with widely held but not conclusively established empirical premises, that principle entails a duty for developed countries to drop trade barriers for developing countries (including subsidies).

The remaining sections explore whether there are any independent principles of justice having to do with the distribution of gains and losses from trade, both among and within states. Sections 4–6 stay with the subject of subsidies and explore what arguments are available in support of those who ask their government for subsidies. Claims to governmental support succeed under certain circumstances, but no principle of justice specifically supports claims *to subsidies*. As far as the identification of additional principles of justice is concerned, sections 4–6 are unsuccessful.

Section 7 addresses a different question, which does lead to an independent principle of justice concerned with trade. One might say country A need not be concerned with harm done to those in B who are involved in the trade between A and B. But subjection to the international trade regime is a ground of justice, and a principle associated with it is that the distribution of gains from trade among countries is just only if no country enjoys gains that come "at the expense" of people involved in the trade. This does not mean other countries have obligations whenever trading occurs at somebody's expense. But there are international obligations if those who are thus affected are victims of human rights violations, either because of the trade or independently. It is worth pointing out that the principle we find associated with subjection to the trade regime as a ground of justice—like the principles associated with membership in the global order—is considerably weaker than the Rawlsian principles that apply domestically. By way of concluding, section 9 reflects on how talk about *justice* maps into talk about *fairness*. After all, while I seek to integrate reflection on trade into a theory of global justice, discussions about normative aspects of trade often appeal to fairness.

2. Let us turn to subsidies. Alongside antidumping measures, export subsidies are common forms of protectionism. "Dumping" occurs if goods are sold at less than "normal" (WTO) or "fair" value (U.S. language). Antidumping duties make imported goods more expensive, to help domestic industries. These measures are the primary fairness topics covered by WTO regulations (which constrain both). Also criticized as inefficient,

specifically agricultural export subsidies in the United States, the EU, and Japan are widely seen as serving the rich at the expense of the poor. According to Wolf (2004),

> total assistance to rich country farmers was $311 billion in 2001, six times as much as all development assistance, indeed more than the GDP of Sub-Saharan Africa. In 2000, the EU provided $913 for each cow and $8 to each Sub-Saharan African. The Japanese, more generous still, though only to cows, provided $2,700 for each one and just $1.47 to each African. Not to be outdone, the US spent $10.7 million a day on cotton and $3.1 million a day on all aid to Sub-Saharan Africa. (215)

Wolf concludes that "the priorities shown here are obscene."

Export subsidies benefit domestic producers but harm domestic consumers because there are fewer goods on that market, and so prices rise. While redistributing wealth, subsidies also cause "deadweight losses," distortions arising because restrictions motivate producers to produce more and consumers to consume less.[2] Moreover, subsidies harm producers abroad by lowering world market prices (if subsidies are large enough). Ipso facto, subsidies benefit consumers elsewhere. Agricultural subsidies benefit net food-importing countries, which in 1999 included forty-five of the forty-nine least-developed countries (Panagariya 2003, 22). Yet by harming the producers abroad, subsidies might also harm consumers in those countries by undermining their chances of working for such producers, and so by negatively affecting their job prospects.[3]

Subsidies create winners and losers, as would their removal. The expiration of the Multi-Fiber Agreement (which had regulated textiles markets for decades) benefited China. Similarly, removing subsidies might give some countries an advantage in agriculture and cause others to alter what they produce. Yet as it is hard to predict which countries would make the shift—only retrospectively do we see that the Multi-Fiber Agreement supported its beneficiaries against China—liberalization might not benefit the countries on whose behalf it is demanded.

Still, consequentialist considerations support the case for trade liberalization, although the strength of this support is a matter of debate. According to Anderson (2004, 550), estimates of gains from liberalization range from $254 billion annually ($108 billion for non-OECD countries, 1995 dollars) to $832 billion ($539 billion for non-OECD countries, 1997 dollars). (These are estimates of *full* liberalization, not merely by rich countries, which primarily benefits their consumers.) As Anderson and Martin (2006) have said, "Freeing all merchandise trade and eliminating agricultural subsidies are estimated to boost global welfare by nearly $300 billion a year by 2015. Additional gains would come from whatever productivity effects that reform would generate" (11). They add that 45 percent of the gains would go to developing countries, more than their share of global GDP.

Such estimates depend on the predictive model, and specifically on what assumptions they make about what will happen to production patterns in different countries when subsidies expire. The degree of variation here is astounding. Hertel and Keeney (2006) provide significantly lower estimates of the benefits from trade liberalization. They estimate that eliminating agricultural subsidies and liberalizing trade in goods and services would lead to gains of $151 billion, $34 billion for developing countries. Others claim that the importance of removing especially agricultural subsidies has been exaggerated (e.g., Birdsall, Rodrik, and Subramanian 2005) and that other programs would produce much higher gains (especially a work permit program that generated remittances that could be put to work immediately in the home economy of the guest workers).[4]

3. Justice demands that human rights be realized. This principle implies a duty of assistance in building institutions. Also, as noted in chapter 4 (and again in chapter 11), there is a boundary problem with regard to this duty: it may be unclear *how much* and *precisely what* is required by such a duty. As far as an assessment of subsidies from the standpoint of justice is concerned, the central empirical problem is to determine which trade policies of developed countries would help developing countries build institutions. The central moral question is whether, in light of the boundary problem, adopting such policies is required of developed countries. Empirical findings on the relevance of trade can make only a prima facie case for certain trade policies.

Links between trade and growth and between growth and other goals— such as the UN's Millennium Development Goals, mentioned in chapter 4—make a strong case for helping developing countries join markets. Alas, controversial empirical matters are central to this argument. It is indeed only *to the extent that* trade is tied to these purposes that it bears on the satisfaction of duties to developing countries. (Of course, it is only to the extent that trade matters for growth and other goals that subsidies pose a moral problem.) How plausible is this link? At least in a broad range of circumstances, trade theory recommends liberalizing trade since doing so benefits participating countries. Much of the evidence seems to support this view. Many economists think trade liberalization is necessary, though insufficient, for fast growth—insufficient because absent credible policies, enforceable contracts, and other hallmarks of stability, openness cannot trigger sustainable growth.[5]

Yet there is disagreement about just how important trade and liberalization are for development, as I noted in section 2, when I recorded the considerable differences in the estimation of benefits from trade liberalization. Therefore, there is corresponding disagreement about how much *priority* to put on reducing trade barriers rather than on exploring alternative solutions. Those who think institutions are essential for development stress domestic reform. They fear that too much attention paid to trade will distract from the reforms that are really needed and perhaps initiate measures that do not help the problems they are supposed to solve, and thus are not worth the sacrifices that accompany them. These disputes make it hard to reach a verdict about the importance of the termination of subsidies for development.[6]

There is another complication. Suppose the relevance of trade for development is strong enough to warrant the claim that developed countries should abolish trade-distorting subsidies, especially in agriculture. Yet such subsidies also lower prices for net food-importing countries. If the relevance of trade for development makes it compelling to abolish subsidies, this is because of the *aggregative* importance of trade, not because abolishing subsidies would immediately and positively affect each country. Initially, net food importers will be worse off. Gains from the discontinuation of subsidies must be redistributed to countries that suffer. This will cause political problems because the gains are widely disseminated.

This recalls the moral question of whether, in light of the boundary problem, adopting trade policies that foster development is required of developed countries. Again, empirical findings on the relevance of trade make only a prima facie case for certain trade policies. By way of anticipating a consideration that we encounter systematically in chapter 15, let us note that there is a compensatory aspect to duties based on common humanity (including the duty of assistance in building institutions). So in many cases in which doubts arise if certain measures are required on behalf of common humanity, we should decide *in favor of so counting them*. The matter at hand offers a good illustration of how to make use of that consideration. The countries that would benefit from such measures frequently are those that may well have been disadvantaged through a colonial past.

What we can conclude, then, is that *to the extent* that trade does matter for development—and thus if the required empirical premises, which are widely held but not conclusively established, do indeed hold—the principle of justice that human rights be realized and the entailed duty of assistance in building institutions do imply that trade policies should be adopted that foster development, including the suspension of subsidies. This result applies not just to agricultural subsidies but to all domains where export subsidies are trade distorting and where such distortions hamper development.

One might object as follows. Investments in infrastructure, education, and health, environmental standards, decisions about interest rates, and so forth affect the prospects of producers not only at home but elsewhere, too. Should, say, the United States create an inferior infrastructure so that Africa can become more competitive? Or suppose a government can aid an industry by investing either in research and development or in export subsidies. Except for efficiency, why would the government not be indifferent between these measures? Two points can be noted in response. First, it would be wrong to assume that if country A excels at X, such excellence automatically disadvantages those who are not equally good at X. While A's excellence will prevent some from doing business that otherwise may be able to, it also creates opportunities for people elsewhere to do things that otherwise would have been impossible for them.

But second, competition will indeed not only have beneficiaries. What is peculiar about subsidies is that states generally adopt them *after* they have already provided favorable conditions for economic advancement. That is, these countries have already taken measures to make sure their industries put out products that are competitive on the world market. Subsidies are paid to make sure that products sell on the world market even though they are not competitive otherwise. There is a striking unfairness to a setback in competitiveness that is inflicted on others simply through a transfer to competitors of money that is not even linked to attempts to improve performance. One can find fault with such measures without finding fault with measures taken to enhance competitiveness.

It should also be noted that developing countries themselves subsidize domestic producers. It is in the logic of my argument that it applies between two groups of countries such that one has duties of aid to the other. It does not apply among developed countries or among the least-developed ones. There will be a gray zone where it is unclear what duties countries have toward each other, consisting of economies that are neither among the developed nor among the least-developed countries. The most important case is what developed countries should do vis-à-vis least-developed countries.

4. So far we have explored how familiar principles of global justice bear on trade. Let us explore whether there are any independent principles that have to do with the distribution of gains from trade, both among and within states. Sections 4–6 continue to be concerned with subsidies. But we now ask how to argue for subsidies from the standpoint of those who wish to receive them. Let us consider three such arguments. First, some

may have an actual claim against the government to be put in a position to continue in a line of work that has become unprofitable. Second, the political community as such may have a prerogative to indulge in certain products and, say, to pay subsidies if this is what it takes to keep farmers in business—even though payments harm farmers abroad. And third, perhaps subsidies should be paid because the community as a whole has moral commitments that require the protection of members who unilaterally suffer from these commitments. Domestic producers could make such an argument if their competitiveness suffers because they must comply with higher labor standards than are used abroad, and if these standards are implied by the community's moral commitments.[7]

I started the discussion about subsidies in section 2 by looking at agricultural subsidies. Which of these three arguments is adduced in political debate depends on what kind of production process is at stake. Agriculture generates very different issues from, say, steel production. Nonetheless, we must explore all three arguments to see what kind of case in support of subsidies is available, and whether such a case delivers a principle of justice. Let us begin by considering the argument that some may have a claim against the government to continue in a line of work that has become unprofitable. Governmental support for domestic producers whose occupational choices are frustrated can take many forms, such as unemployment benefits or aid to enter other lines of work. For claims specifically to export subsidies to succeed, the government must be liable for occupational choices and their consequences to such an extent that individuals are entitled to protection from foreign competition, and are so entitled only because otherwise they could not continue in that line of work.

One might think everybody is in the labor market at her own risk (except that a social system provides basic safeguards) and for her own sake (except that she must help maintain the basic structure through taxes). People acquire skills, and keep most of the gains. If demand dries up or the price those skills command goes down, the state owes them only protection against hardship. This view is implicit in the political economy of liberal market economies, as in the United States. However, there is another variety of capitalism, the coordinated market economy, where states plausibly owe more than such protection. Indeed, different varieties of capitalism are consistent with the enlarged Rawlsian framework of membership in states from chapter 2, in much the same way in which various property regimes are (Rawls 2001, secs. 41–42).

Versions of capitalism are characterized by institutional complementarities: one set of institutions operates effectively only (or more effectively) if accompanied by other institutions. This applies especially to ownership arrangements and labor markets. Coordinated economies have rigid labor markets, markets that encourage employees to acquire specialized skills, rewarding them with job security. Other factors that shape the political economy complement such markets. Participants in coordinated economies have a different relationship to the state than those in liberal economies. The following assessment of labor markets in Germany and Japan is useful:

> Social constraints and opportunities ... typically enforced by social institutions, define the legitimate place and the possible range of market transactions and markets in the economy-cum-society in which they take place. By circumscribing and thereby limiting the role of markets, they typically "distort" them, for example by shielding desirable social conditions from market fluctuations. (Streeck and Yamamura 2001, 2)

By actively promoting specialization, the government participates in its citizens' professional decisions. The risk that accompanies specialization, if occurring in response to how labor markets are framed, is justifiable to citizens only if the state offers guarantees beyond protecting against hardship if they fail.[8]

One might object that individuals must always make choices in light of legislation. There is nothing special about legislation that determines the basic setup of labor markets. Yet this objection runs together too many legislative acts. Suppose I am Swedish and make life choices based on Swedish liquor laws. As far as legislation is concerned, I am left with many alternatives, namely, those that do not engage liquor laws. (My life as it is might not make it easy for me to make such choices. I might be a scion of a liquor-selling family, but that is not a matter of legislation but something about my life.) Suppose I am Japanese and must decide whether to invest in certain skills and find that labor markets make it irrational not to specialize somehow. Short of emigrating or accepting failure (unemployment), I cannot escape from this choice. So laws like those that shape the setup of labor markets differ from just any law that affects choices.

In liberal economies, individuals can specialize or not, accepting risks with each decision. Since the system is prepared to deal with workers who lack specialization and may need additional training, even those who specialize and fail might have an easier time switching sectors than in coordinated economies. In liberal systems, too, states "subsidize" individuals; they provide the infrastructure that enables individuals to live and pursue goals, ranging from education to roads. Yet support for unprofitable lines of work is beyond the limits. But even in coordinated economies one may doubt whether individuals have claims against the state to make it possible for them to continue in a line of work. Of course, especially for well-trained people who have spent all their life in one niche, the costs of

change might be forbidding and would include not only monetary investments, for instance for additional training (which the state may cover),
but also the psychological difficulty of adjusting to a new environment.
In coordinated economies, these considerations strongly support claims
to governmental assistance. However, even under the most favorable conditions for this kind of argument to succeed, we can only show that if
their life choices end in frustration, employees generically have a claim
to a high level of governmental support.

Individuals have a claim based on the risk they are encouraged to take
in coordinated economies. The state may aid them through generous unemployment insurance, early retirement packages, or additional training.
But states are under no obligation to make sure people can simply continue in their chosen line of work. No claim to this kind of support is
forthcoming, let alone a claim of justice. In particular, it is not the case
that, in coordinated economies, gains from trade must be distributed in
such a way that people can continue in their line of work. The state may
help people who are negatively affected by trade by helping them leave the
export sector altogether.

5. Now that we have explored the individual claims–based argument in
support of subsidies, let us turn to the collective preference–based argument. For instance, the French might consider redistribution and deadweight losses acceptable to continue the production of baguette from
French grain, Camembert from French cows, or foie gras from local ducks.
Far from honoring a duty, they might have a collective preference for
home-grown products and be willing to pay for them.

To be sure, preferences for home-grown products can be realized without trade distortions. For instance, farm products can be transformed
into (or be remarketed as) gourmet products. Higher prices for "French"
products would keep farmers in business if consumers paid for such quality. (Once subsidies are removed, French products become less expensive
at home, but more expensive abroad. Other producers then enter the
French market and beat the prices of French producers. So those go out
of business unless they create a market for gourmet products.) The existence of subsidies indicates that the government thinks this preference
should be maintained through its authority, not consumer choices. But
this way of upholding a collective preference would have to outweigh
claims of farmers in developing countries. That, in turn, would be acceptable only if trade had little to do with development, much less than what
is empirically plausible.

However, a stronger argument for state action on behalf of home-
grown products stems from more weighty values than food preferences.

The preservation of food may be part of the preservation of the French culture or countryside. Or perhaps it is part of a strategy of making sure France can survive emergencies. Supporters might claim that without government support, these goals fall prey to collective action problems. Still, even such claims for governmental action must come to terms with the relevance of trade for development. Since as a matter of justice, poverty alleviation bears more weight than cultural preservation, attempts at preservation ought not be trade distorting (assuming, again, the appropriate relevance of trade for development). Concerns about security are another matter. However, these concerns would be met if countries kept in business a limited number of farmers with the required know-how, and in addition preserved a share of their lands for possible farm use in the future. Not much of an argument in support of broadly based export subsidies emerges this way.

6. So let us explore a final argument in support of the view that some should be supported to continue in a line of work although markets would not allow it. Suppose legislation for social standards is adopted not merely because it expresses what our practices happen to be but for moral reasons that capture views about how persons ought to be treated. If labor standards abroad differ from those we are collectively committed to, and if domestic producers suffer as a consequence, the harm done should be redistributed among all members of the community. Such redistribution may take the form of export subsidies. In addition, the import of goods produced under conditions of which our community disapproves could be restricted. Both measures help domestic industries. A consideration in support of such measures would also be that, in this way, we avoid setting incentives for future treatment of the relevant sort. If lower labor standards are negatively sanctioned in this way, they might change.

This argument falls short of demanding that one prevent others from treating people badly in ways other than by protecting those in the country who act properly and by refusing to set incentives that would instigate such behavior at home and abroad. The fight against corruption is illustrative. For a long time, many countries treated domestic corruption differently from corruption abroad. Playing along with corruption abroad was not punishable (Eigen 2003). Suppose corruption was prohibited in country A because of moral concerns about the conditions under which people should get ahead. Country A should protect those of its citizens who abide by its norms (for instance, by making sure that those who do not, do not gain advantages thereby) and should refrain from setting incentives for corrupt behavior in B by tolerating that its, A's, citizens become complicit with corruption in B. But A need not take additional measures against B. Or we might consider a case involving animals. Foie gras is duck or goose liver fattened by force-feeding. Some countries have laws against such practices but not against importing foie gras. Suppose A has prohibited force-feeding because of moral concerns for animals. A should refrain from setting incentives for the future production of foie gras by prohibiting imports. But A need not act in other ways to prevent B from producing foie gras.

If legislation of social standards rests on moral reasons, *then* domestic industries deserve protection. Often, however, social standards have been adopted for protectionist reasons, or have arisen from domestic power struggles. Domestic industries then cannot insist on shifting the harm to everybody if competitors abroad benefit from different practices. Only if the intent behind social standards is moral is there an argument to that effect. Let us look at an excerpt from the 1930 U.S. Tariff Act:

> All goods, wares, articles, and merchandise mined, produced, or manufactured wholly or in part in any foreign country by convict labor or/and forced labor or/and indentured labor under penal sanctions shall not be entitled to entry at any of the ports of the United States, and the importation thereof is hereby prohibited.... But in no case shall such provisions be applicable to goods, wares, articles, or merchandise so mined, produced, or manufactured which are not mined, produced, or manufactured in such quantities in the United States as to meet the consumptive demands of the United States.[9]

The protectionist intent is easy to track: the legislators have no qualms about importing goods produced by prison labor if demand in the United States is higher than supply. Import is prohibited only if the United States can satisfy its own demand. So the point is not that there is something morally problematic about using convict labor in this way. But while in this case the protectionist concern is obvious, it will often be hard to tell whether, say, labor legislation has been adopted as a moral view. Generally, identifying collective moral commitments involves both conceptual and practical problems.

At least in Western democracies it is plausible for cases of severe human rights violations that legislation against such acts was adopted for moral reasons. For instance, Western countries have adopted legislation against oppressive governance in virtue of a moral view of personhood, captured as early as in the 1789 Declaration of the Rights of Man and of the Citizen, whose Article II lists resistance to oppressive governance as an end of political associations. So if domestic industries suffer setbacks because competitors benefit from severe human rights violations, it seems they have a claim to the redistribution of the damage thus caused.

Yet this argument, drawing as it does on actual collective commitments and thus ultimately intentions, is not of the right sort to deliver *principles of justice*. What we are getting in this way are pro tanto considerations;

indeed, if we are committed to certain moral views, then those of us who suffer harm from our commitments can make a strong case that their damages be redistributed. But any response to this demand must not violate our duties of justice. In particular, this kind of argument cannot validate export subsidies if such payments violate a duty of assistance in building institutions. This third argument succeeds only within the constraints set by principles of justice (but it does succeed within these constraints).

7. We have found that to the extent that trade matters for development, the principle of justice that human rights be realized and the entailed duty of assistance in building institutions imply that trade policies should be adopted that foster development, including the suspension of subsidies. We have failed to find considerations of justice that support subsidies. But international trade as a ground also generates its own principles of justice. Specifically, I argue for the following principle: the distribution of gains from trade among states is just only if no country enjoys gains that come "at the expense" of people involved in the trade.

One-time trading does not generate a justice relationship, but international trade is a structured and repeated exchange involving markets and bodies of law (domestic and international) that regulate them. This activity is mutually beneficial for the involved countries as a whole. So on both sides, trade that comes at somebody's expense (in the pejorative sense in which the term is intended) generates ill-gotten gains. These gains come *at the expense* of certain people if either (a) their contributions to the production of goods or the provision of services for export do not make them better off (than if they were not producing those goods at all) to an extent warranted by the value of these contributions (and they did not voluntarily accept such an arrangement), or (b) their involvement in the trade has emerged through human rights violations (e.g., they are coerced into working in the relevant industries), or both. The "to-the-extent" addition in (a) ensures that those who lose out may still have complaints even if they gain from trade. Condition (b) ensures they may still have complaints if their contributions are adequately valued.

As far as the justice of international trade is concerned, we are indeed talking about contributions to the production of goods or the provision of services *for export*. Domestic exchanges are covered by principles of domestic justice. There will be a gray area: goods from a certain line of production that are normally purely domestic might on rare occasions go into international trade, or goods for domestic trade may use minor parts that were imported. But these matters are negligible. Various cases are covered in conditions (a) and (b): people who lose out benefit from their work, but not as much as they should; they do not benefit at all; and they are pushed into doing this work through human rights violations. To see why in (a) I have added the qualification "and they did not voluntarily accept such an arrangement," let us take a real-world example. Michael Bloomberg, as of 2012 the billionaire mayor of New York City, works for a symbolic payment of $1. Presumably his contribution to the city does not make him better off to an extent warranted by its value. But we should not say that any economic transactions would occur at the expense of people who have made such decisions.

On the one hand, this principle of justice implies a basic acceptance of the idea that the value of contributions to trade is determined by facts about supply and demand. But on the other hand, this principle seeks to rectify certain distortions that determine what people receive for their contributions. To determine what it means to make people better off to an extent warranted by the value of their contributions we need to make comparisons to the wages of others, either locally or according to otherwise comparable standards. Local comparisons (comparisons within one country) permit us to identify discrimination against particular groups involved with the trade. The reference to "otherwise comparable standards" is meant to cover cases where an oppressive government has a negative effect on how most people benefit from participation in the economy (and so the standard of comparison cannot be domestic), or where powerful countries or corporations exercise power in order to depress the economies in a whole region of this planet (and so the standard could not be regional, either).

Needless to say, what I have said about what it is to be made better off to an extent warranted by the value of one's contributions is an incomplete discussion of a notoriously difficult subject. Much room is left for additional theoretical exploration, as well as for debate in particular cases. Still, it is important to recognize that international trade generates its own principle of justice, to say as much as we can at this abstract level about its contents, and to put this principle into an overall picture of global justice.

International trade is a ground of justice because of its structured nature and significance for people's ability to make a living. International trade is a human creation, and its structure could be devised differently. The statist's insistence that trade is not subject to principles of justice is mistaken. Still, as far as this ground is concerned, people are related to each other merely as fellow participants in the trading system. This ground differs considerably from the relationship of shared membership in states explored in chapters 2 and 3. We have noted how other grounds bear on trading. In addition, individuals are subject to domestic principles of justice. But if we are merely asking about principles that govern trade, we have nothing more to work with than what I stated in this paragraph. In that relationship, nobody should be taken advantage of; gains from trade should not come at anybody's expense. But that is as far as we can go by way of offering a principle regulating the distribution of gains from trade among countries.

One might worry that this principle is either too narrow or too broad. It might be perceived as too narrow because it does not guarantee that participants in trade have enough to make a living. But nothing about trading generates an obligation to make sure that is so. If people's contributions do not warrant returns of that sort, we should not diagnose this as a problem about the justice of the trading. However, other principles of justice already require that people have enough to satisfy basic needs.

One might worry that the principle I stated is too broad and thus too demanding. As far as condition (a) is concerned, trade might come at some people's expense even though they are doing well. We may take as an example a group of engineers in a developing country who, because they belong to a traditionally disadvantaged ethnic group and thus have limited bargaining power, earn only 60 percent of the income of other engineers, but nonetheless earn 500 percent of the national average, and are not otherwise mistreated. Is this an injustice in the trade relationship (assuming those engineers contribute to the production of goods or services for export)?

It is, but such a case nonetheless would not generate international responsibilities. For international trading partners to be responsible for injustice in the trade relationship, the people affected by them must be victims of human rights violations, either because their involvement with the trade constitutes such a violation or because they are independently subject to violations. As part of an overall scheme of assigning responsibilities among entities involved in trading, violations of that principle below this standard should be a domestic responsibility. International trading partners already have a duty to assist or interfere when it comes to human rights violations. But they have that obligation in virtue of being part of the global order, and thus alongside other entities. Being involved in trade with particular violators means they should focus on them when it comes to discharging their share of this duty. Other states ought to help end the human rights violations rather than end their association with violations through trading. In a world where human rights are realized for everyone, it would still be possible for states to enjoy gains from trade at the expense of some people. But remaining obligations to make the trade relationship just then lie with the state in which the people live at whose expense the tainted gains occur.

Suppose trade between A and B occurs at the expense of some people in A whose human rights are violated. One might still be concerned that the principle I have formulated is too broad and imposes too many international obligations. First, B might not benefit *from the violations*: A would sell goods for the same price if no violation occurred, but since violations do occur, a certain subgroup in A pockets extra gains. Second, even if B discontinued trade, the violations would continue because there are other buyers. Suppose France considered discontinuing oil purchases from Nigeria unless Nigeria agreed to reforms. Presumably, Nigeria could sell its oil elsewhere. And third, by way of illustration, a facet of apartheid in South Africa was that nonwhites were losers in trade. Apartheid was not fueled by gains *from trade*. More generally, human rights violations might not have occurred *because* the oppressors sought to gain from trade—the fact that they did could be a "fortunate" side effect for them. But trading partners would then not be sufficiently implicated in the oppression to bear responsibility.

However, the first two scenarios do not show that my principle is too broad. Trading partners are responsible not because they benefit from trade *more* when human rights are violated but because they are connected in certain ways to those whose rights are violated. The fact that demand from elsewhere would uphold the violations does not exonerate those creating the current demand.[10] Let us consider the third point. If trade played a role in the emergence of human rights violations, this fact would offer *additional* support for assigning responsibilities to trading partners. What remains problematic is that trading partners receive ill-gotten gains at the expense of those whose rights are violated even if the prospects of such gains have not caused the violations. The apartheid scenario shows that a diagnosis of injustice does not require that trading partners set incentives in the strong sense that, without trade, those whose rights are violated would be better off. There is a problem already if they do not benefit adequately from their contributions and thus are taken advantage of in this way.[11]

8. Our inquiry has led to two main results. First, we have found that, to the extent that trade matters for development, the principle of justice that human rights be realized and the entailed duty of assistance in building institutions imply that trade policies should be adopted that foster development, including the suspension of subsidies. I have also argued in support of an independent principle (the only principle we have found that is associated with subjection to the international trade regime as a ground of justice) that the distribution of gains from trade among states is just only if no country enjoys gains that have come at the expense of people involved with the trade, where these gains occur *at the expense* of certain people if either (a) their contributions to the production of goods or the

provision of services for export do not make them better off (than if they were not producing those goods at all) to an extent warranted by the value of these contributions (and they did not voluntarily accept such an arrangement), or (b) their involvement in the trade has emerged through human rights violations, or both. Chapter 18 completes our exploration of the trading system by discussing the WTO.

Discussions about normative aspects of trade often concern *fairness*. So I should explain how fairness and justice map into each other.[12] Like justice, fairness is concerned with the distribution of burdens and benefits. One can assess such distributions in multiple ways: one may ask which one maximizes welfare, inflicts the least harm, or best satisfies external goals. Yet fairness, like justice, is concerned with *what people are owed*. Let us call demands that people have because they are owed something *stringent claims*. Unlike justice, fairness does not necessarily aim at satisfying stringent claims per se but at their *proportionate* satisfaction. Suppose we are all owed a medication, and the more we take of it, the more we recover. No considerations other than medical need enter, and the needs are equal. Nobody can complain of unfairness if her claim is not fully satisfied if all are satisfied equally. So there are two ways for a distribution to be fair: either everyone's stringent claims are fully satisfied, or they are not, but they are nonetheless (un-)satisfied proportionately (in the example, this means (un-)satisfied to an equal degree).

This notion of fairness generates various questions. First, what are the bases for stringent claims? Second, if stringent claims arise on different bases, how should we compare them? Third, what does it mean to satisfy claims made on different bases "in proportion"? The language of fairness applies broadly, and to specific issues as well as to rather abstract ones. Often, discussions about fairness concern distributions of particular goods, such as inheritances, offices, medications, or kidneys, as well as burdens, such as taxes, layoffs, or household chores. Or such discussions may concern the process governing such distributions. Fairness in trade is more abstract than many such scenarios, but similar issues arise.

Chapter 1 also talked about "stringent" claims when introducing distributive justice. The core meaning of fairness concerns the *proportionate* satisfaction of *those* especially stringent claims. In addition to this core meaning, fairness talk may be pragmatic, or context dependent. Individuals may draw on many considerations to support stringent claims, to tax relief, a corner office, exemptions from service, rewards, and so on. I call these claims pragmatic or context dependent, however, because they can be overruled by considerations of justice. This extended use reflects the fact that the extreme weightiness pertaining to justice is associated less consistently with fairness. Fairness can be less "weighty" than justice in the extended use; nonetheless, when it involves the same especially stringent claims—as it does in the core use—it is equally "weighty."[13]

So fair distributions may not be just, for two reasons: first, fairness can apply to distributions where the subject matter is not substantial enough for justice to apply (since the stringent claims involved are not the right sort of especially stringent claims), and second, justice requires the full satisfaction of stringent claims whereas fairness requires only their proportionate satisfaction (or nonsatisfaction). A situation in which everyone's right to free speech is equally violated might be fair, but not just. But a just distribution is also fair: if people's stringent claims are fully satisfied, they are satisfied proportionately. Conversely, if a distribution is unfair (and is one to which justice applies), then it is also unjust; but if a situation is unjust, it may not be unfair (as in the free speech example). *Principles of fairness,* stating what distributions are fair, are either principles of justice or else say what it means for different stringent claims to be satisfied in proportion.

To the extent that fairness applies to trade, those affected through the distribution of trade-related burdens and benefits have claims *on different bases.* The discussion in this chapter has reflected that fact. Some people have demands on their government since trade worsens their situation vis-à-vis others', possibly undermining their status as free and equal citizens. People elsewhere might have complaints about that country's policies if those deprive them of income, or on the basis of common humanity. The basis of their claims differs from that of people in that country. The bases of stringent claims regarding trade are some of the grounds of justice, shared membership in a state, membership in the global order (with the different sources that such membership involves, understood as basis for a conception of human rights), and subjection to the trading system itself. Principles of fairness in trade either are principles of justice as it applies to trade (and thus the principles of justice rehearsed at the beginning of this section are such principles) or else they are principles that state how stringent claims regarding trade that arise on different bases are satisfied in proportion.

Sections 4–6 attempt to articulate stringent claims regarding trade based on shared membership in states. While we saw that some of these claims succeed in the sense that they support redistributive measures within states, and so must bear on the trade policy of states, they do not amount to claims of justice. Thus they carry less weight than the claims of justice that can be made based on human rights concerns or based on subjection to the trading system itself. The result of this inquiry in sections 4–6 could therefore itself be summed up in a principle of fairness in trade that describes the relative weight of the different claims we considered.

To conclude, my account of fairness allows us to respond to an argument that applying fairness to trade is conceptually muddled. Fairness is often tied to the image of "leveling the playing field," which suggests a requirement of the equalization of certain conditions, whereas trade thrives on differences.[14] It is because A and B differ in their productive abilities that they trade. So how could ideas about leveling apply here? Yet such leveling is tied to the notion of *equality of opportunity*. In a typical usage, John Roemer (1998) explains that one prevalent conception of equality of opportunity

> says that society should do what it can to ... level the playing field among individuals during their formative periods, so that all those with relevant potential will eventually be admissible to pools of candidates competing for positions. (1)

On my account, the idea of leveling the playing field does not generally apply to fairness. There is a link between the leveling metaphor and fairness only if fairness, in particular cases, requires equality of opportunity—which is not the case across states.

PART 4

Global Justice and Institutions

CHAPTER 15

The Way We Live Now

1. I have finished presenting my account of the grounds of justice (except that chapter 18 will revisit our discussion of trade, by looking at the WTO). In the course of developing pluralist internationalism I have explored five grounds: shared membership in states, common humanity, humanity's collective ownership of the earth, membership in the global order, and subjection to the global trading system. According to the vision of the just world that this approach proposes, broadly Rawlsian principles apply within states. Globally, everyone has access to original resources and spaces, or is provided with other means to satisfy her basic needs. A list of human rights is realized for everybody (including the right to essential pharmaceuticals and labor rights, as defended in chapters 12 and 13). No state enjoys gains from trade that have come at anyone's expense. Each generation, if in a position to do so, passes on the original resources and spaces in such a condition that the next generation is able to satisfy its basic needs and realize human rights. However, this does not require that the difference principle apply globally. If in addition all (mere) principles of reasonable conduct are satisfied, immigration is permitted into any state that underuses original resources and spaces. The burdens of climate change are fairly divided among states, guided by ability to pay and polluter pays principles. No generation passes on to the next a smaller stock of resources and spaces than it has inherited itself (if it is in a position to do otherwise).

I conjecture that realizing these principles would go a long way toward eliminating poverty and reducing inequality. In a just world, the mutual benefits of economic interaction could come to full fruition. Countless gifted individuals would no longer have to focus on securing bare survival. Yet what is also true is that a just world could plainly be as unequal as ours (across countries, that is, not within countries). The poor would be richer, but the rich could be richer, too. Ours is not a just world—though not in virtue of inequality but in virtue of widespread human rights violations, and thus in virtue of the state of the worst-off falling below a minimum threshold. Also, in a just world as I envisage it, there could be much more inequality than in different views of a just world, for instance one in which the difference principle applied globally.

These results might strike some readers as wrongheaded. Suppose there is a very rich country where human rights are satisfied but the difference principle is not. Suppose there is another country that is not wealthy enough for the difference principle to apply but where human rights are satisfied (though barely so). Suppose everyone in the wealthy country is richer than everyone in the poor country. Internationalism implies that the only injustice in this scenario may be within the rich country. There is no injustice in the relative situations of the countries. But the response to any worry this scenario might create is straightforward: our inquiry has not delivered principles that condemn this scenario per se.

Kok-Chor Tan (2004) points out that "in a world marked by stark international inequality, it is implausible that citizens of richer countries may show greater concern to compatriots without simultaneously undermining the ideal of universal equal respect" (157–58). In a very unequal world, that is, the realization of any principles of justice may be in jeopardy. Let me illustrate how serious this worry is. In *The Culture of Disbelief*, in a context that does not otherwise concern us, the legal scholar Stephen Carter recollects two encounters with teenagers and asks which ones are "the most dangerous children in America" (1993, 204–5). In the first encounter Carter is forced to take shelter from a shoot-out among drug dealers in Queens. In the second he overhears a conversation among girls in a commuter train passing through wealthy Connecticut suburbs. The girls seek to impress each other with the exclusivity of their communities, dropping the names of fashionable people who live there or stop by. One girl mentions that her father owns a store. Another one's triumphant outcry, "Your father has a store?," decides the contest in the second girl's favor. That people in the first girl's neighborhood own stores means it lacks exclusivity.

The dealers are likely to be dead or imprisoned within a few years. It is those privileged teenagers, submits Carter, who are the most dangerous children because of the socially insulated way in which they can advance through life. If their insulation makes them callous toward fellow citizens, as it too often does—and this takes us back to Tan's worry—how much more will it make them callous toward individuals in faraway lands? How would privileged individuals in an unequal world care about any kind of injustice affecting distant individuals? Education, media engagement, political leadership, and much else is needed to make it more likely that people empathize with distant strangers and let these people's plight enter into their election behavior so that governments, in turn, take seriously their obligations toward noncitizens. This is a truly daunting task that must accompany the realization of my vision of justice. It is nonetheless a *much* easier task to accomplish than to abandon states, or to take other measures to reduce global inequality further than my theory would. Tan's worry is serious, but especially globalists or nonrelationists get no mileage from this fact.[1]

From now on, I take internationalism as established, as a view of what a just world would be like. In the rest of the book I consider three main problems that arise out of this view and relate to institutions. One is a problem we have already encountered in previous chapters. What obligations do various institutions have to bring about a just world? In chapter 17 I focus on the state, drawing together the threads of my discussion so far and asking how the various obligations on the state to bring about a just world mesh together. In chapter 18 I begin the task of doing the same for global institutions by focusing on one, the WTO. The second problem arises out of the first. As well as their obligations to bring about a just world, do institutions also have a further obligation to give an account to potential beneficiaries of justice of what they are doing (or not doing) to bring about a just world? In chapter 17 I argue that they do, and consider how the state ought to live up to that obligation; in chapter 18 I consider how the WTO ought to do so. There is, however, a third problem that arises out of my account, and that relates to institutions. It is not one we have already seen, but it is logically prior to the other two. So I consider it now.

According to internationalism, particularly strong principles apply only within states (a topic I discussed in connection with the normative peculiarity of states). Weaker ones are associated with other grounds. The features of the world that create this situation—namely, there are multiple institutions within which immediacy and reciprocity apply, but there are no global institutions with these properties—exist only contingently. But if the state system exists only contingently, then it could cease to exist. If it ceased to exist and were replaced with a world with no states (no institutions within which reciprocity and immediacy applied), then the global principles would be the *only* principles of justice that applied. If the state system were replaced with global institutions in which reciprocity and immediacy held, then the difference principle would apply globally. Crucially, if *in addition* it would be morally desirable for the system of states to cease to exist (in either of these ways), then my theory could not be our ultimate ideal of justice. Instead, that ideal would be the vision in favor of which the state system should disappear.

So we must ask whether we can establish that it would be morally desirable for the state system to cease to exist. Is it true that there morally ought to be no states, or a global state rather than a state system? Answering that question is also relevant to answering the two questions concerning justification posed in chapter 1: whether states can be justified to people excluded from them (say, by immigration control) and whether the whole system of states and global political and economic institutions can be justified to those living under it. If there ought to be no state system, then it cannot be justified.

Chapter 15 considers several arguments that find moral flaws in the way we live now, the system of states. We explore four strategies one might deploy (a) to identify moral flaws of the state system and (b) to use these flaws to conclude that there ought to be no system of states, and thus no global order. (Chapter 1 defined the global order as the system of states plus the set of organizations and other international entities that see themselves as concerned with global problem solving.) Chapter 16 offers a sweeping objection to any attempt to argue toward the conclusion that the state system ought to cease to exist (and formulates this objection in the framework of an account of what it is to *justify* a system of states). So it is unproblematic that chapter 15 inevitably overlooks some arguments to the effect that there ought to be no states. To some of the upcoming arguments we can only respond by appeal to the conclusions of chapter 16. Therefore, these two chapters are closely intertwined. Chapter 16 finds that we are not entitled to conclude there ought to be no states, but neither can we secure a justice-based rationale for their existence. There remains a nagging doubt about whether there ought to be states at all; nevertheless, morally and not merely pragmatically speaking, we ought not abandon states now, nor ought we aspire to do so eventually.

Section 2 of this chapter elaborates on the contingent nature of states.[2] Section 3 explores the argument that what is morally problematic about the state system is the very existence of borders. We discuss various ways of spelling out this objection. The concern is that the existence of borders is inconsistent with the value of freedom, liberal justice, or democracy. This list of values with which borders are allegedly inconsistent is admittedly incomplete. Simone Weil, for instance, has argued (as part of a vehement indictment) that the state "has also turned territorial frontiers into prison walls to lock up people's thoughts" (1971, 123). However, arguments enlisting freedom, liberal justice, and democracy fail to identify flaws of the state system as such.

The remaining three arguments address versions of one particular moral complaint about the state system, that it wrongfully harms the global poor. Section 4 explores an argument from Thomas Pogge (2002) that the global order wrongfully harms the poor by imposing a certain institutional framework, even though an alternative would operate more to their advantage. There is a sense in which the global order, by not doing enough to satisfy the duties of justice that my theory generates, wrongfully harms the poor. The question then becomes whether the rectification of this deficiency requires either a world state or no states, or whether either version of a political arrangement that does away with a state system would do better in the realization of justice. But that question we can answer only if we have a credible idea of what a world without states would look like. Chapter 16 argues that we do not have such an idea. Section 5 assesses the idea that statistics revealing the extent of poverty and inequality by themselves show that the global order wrongfully harms the poor. Such data have some prominence in debates about global justice. It turns out, however, that they do not reveal a moral shortcoming of the global order. This third strategy fails.

A fourth and final way of articulating a moral complaint against the global order, investigated in sections 6 and 7, is that the state system wrongfully harms the poor because developing countries would be much better off today had it not been for the emergence of a state system with its ensuing colonial ambitions. Chapter 16 offers a negative assessment of the meaningfulness of large-scale counterfactuals involved in the benchmark of harm that this argument uses. So the verdict on this argument, too, depends on chapter 16. But in a preliminary step, I explore at least somewhat more tractable claims: that developed countries are better off because they have kept developing countries in a relationship of dependence, and that colonialism has inflicted lasting harm. Indeed, the state system has wrongfully harmed the poor because institutions in former colonies have often emerged from a history in which the range of available options was formed enduringly by concerns other than the well-being of the colonized. But again in light of what we find in chapter 16, this result does not imply there ought to be no states. Much as Anthony Trollope's novel from which I borrow the title of this chapter finds a lot to criticize in mid-nineteenth-century England, so we find much to criticize in the global order. But we do not find that it ought to cease to exist.[3]

2. It is a contingent fact that there are multiple institutions within which immediacy and reciprocity apply, but there is no global institution with these properties. To elaborate, this section draws attention to some historical aspects of the development of states, and of some of the features that inform my account of their normative peculiarity—for the purposes of illustration, specifically some of the features that inform my account of the immediacy of states. States continue to be central to the political organization of humanity. Most people remain citizens of the same state all their lives. This is not to disregard emigrants, asylum seekers, dual citizens, refugees, and stateless persons. However, their numbers are small when compared with those who are none of these.[4] This is also not to disregard states that cannot effectively control their territory, whose boundaries are disputed, or that are not widely recognized (Krasner 1999). Still, the world's political system continues to be shaped by states. Their number has only recently reached its maximum to date.

Yet it is also true that "the modern state is the distinctive product of a unique civilization," as L. T. Hobhouse states at the beginning of *Liberalism*

(1994, 3). States have arisen in response to certain conditions and might disappear in response to others. Historians disagree about why states arose. For instance, Hendrik Spruyt (1994) argues that territorial states, alongside city leagues and city-states, emerged in response to economic changes in the late Middle Ages: "States won because their institutional logic gave them an advantage in mobilizing their societies' resources" (185). Charles Tilly (1990), for one, disagrees, claiming that states succeeded because France and Spain adopted forms of warfare that temporarily crushed their neighbors and introduced a political model that others were compelled to adopt (183).

As well as the existence of states, the extent to which my characterizations of immediacy in chapter 2 apply to different states is contingent. Of note is what James Scott (1998) says about the impact of equal citizenship on post-Revolutionary France:

> For all the advances in human rights that equal citizenship carried with it, it is worth recalling that this momentous step also undercut the intermediary structures between the state and the citizen and gave the state, for the first time, direct access to its subjects. Equal citizenship implied not only legal equality and universal male suffrage but also universal conscription, as those mobilized into Napoleon's armies were shortly to discover. From the heights of the state, the society below increasingly appeared as an endless series of nationally equal *particuliers* with whom it dealt in their capacity as subjects, taxpayers, and potential military draftees. (365)

Scott uses some of the same vocabulary that chapter 2 employed to characterize legal immediacy. The modern state made its society "legible" (2) by initiating reforms to facilitate the execution of state functions such as taxation, conscription, and the prevention of rebellion. The premodern state did not know much about its citizens and their assets, and so could intervene only crudely. But state intervention in the nineteenth century became "more sophisticated and more formidable" (Poggi 1978, 108), contributing to a development that made the relationship between individuals and states immediate.[5]

Robb (2007) documents this development, again for France, today paradigmatically characterized by legal and political immediacy. Until the late nineteenth century, most inhabitants did not speak French comfortably. Newly transferred officials often needed translators. Last names were not universally used. Peasants might not see more people in a lifetime than would fit into a village church. Decades after the Revolution, much of the population lived in settlement patterns that guaranteed isolation and ignorance. State access to bodies and assets was anything but immediate. Merchandise traveled through a maze of back roads, without centralized account keeping. There were no statistics before Napoleon, and no maps of France until the nineteenth century.[6] "They had locally appointed officials," writes Robb, highlighting the limited amount of immediacy,

> an agent to collect taxes and a guard to police the community. But laws, especially those relating to inheritance, were widely ignored and direct contact with the central power was extremely limited. The state was perceived as a dangerous nuisance: its emissaries were soldiers who had to be fed and housed, bailiffs who seized property and lawyers who settled property disputes and took most of the proceeds. Being French was not a source of personal pride, let alone the basis of a common identity. Before the mid-nineteenth century, few people had seen a map of France, and few had heard of Charlemagne and Joan of Arc. France was effectively a land of foreigners. (23)

Slowly, measures were homogenized, land use was stratified, the design of orderly cities was encouraged (to facilitate policing), the use of surnames became universal, and traffic patterns were centralized. Compulsory education offered instruction in a standard language. In the process of such developments within countries (of course, not only in France), risk sharing was collectivized, creating robust and reliable insurance systems.[7] De Swaan (1988) calls this aspect of the emergence of immediacy "comparable in significance to the introduction of representative democracy" (149).

Not everybody thinks of the emergence of immediacy altogether positively. Scott argues that the creation of legal immediacy, in combination with a belief in progress and technology, an authoritarian state, and an incompletely evolved civil society, led to disaster. Porter (1994) submits that one outcome of this process was twentieth-century industrialized warfare, "the most bitterly conflictual of human phenomena but also the most intensely cooperative" (192).

3. As William Blake says in "Auguries of Innocence," "Every night and every morn // some to misery are born. // Every morn and every night // Some are born to sweet delight." Indeed, the existence of states entails that life prospects differ vastly, and are to a large extent decided by birth. Milanovic (2005), for one, shows that inequality among countries is much larger than inequality within countries. Therefore we must interrogate the very legitimacy of borders.

Let us explore whether arguments enlisting freedom, liberal justice, and democracy can identify any moral flaws of the state system. I will consider first the concern about freedom. One way of making the point that national borders unacceptably restrict freedom draws on Amartya Sen and Martha Nussbaum's approach to freedom in terms of "capabilities." Nussbaum offers a list of capabilities central to what she considers a life with dignity. "Bodily integrity" is on her list, of which one instantiation is "being able to move freely from place to place." The challenge is to explain why immigration policies can constrain this capability. This challenge is no artifact of Nussbaum's version. The capabilities approach per se stresses the value of freedom, empowerment, and choice.[8]

Borders do constrain freedom and choice since they keep some people from going where they would like to be. But borders also protect the economic and political conditions that create opportunities for other people. That is why references to freedom occur on different sides in the debate about open borders. A more refined notion of freedom might allow us to make progress but would inevitably introduce controversies of its own. As long as we are not questioning the existence of states as such, the challenge is to identify a comprehensive proposal that defines the conditions under which a state system should be acceptable to all people. Such a proposal would set limits of acceptable demands by appeal to freedom. Internationalism contributes to such a proposal by telling us what justice requires, including what justice (and, respectively, reasonable conduct) requires when it comes to immigration. But crucially, in light of the ambiguous significance of borders for freedom and choice, we cannot appeal to that value to identify a problem with the state system as such.

Some have argued that, owing to liberalism's commitment to moral equality, liberals must reject immigration barriers as plainly *unjust*. Liberalism, Joseph Carens notes, condemns the use of morally arbitrary facts about persons to justify inequalities.[9] Examples include race, sex, and ethnicity. Political communities that treat people differently on the basis of such features are illiberal and unjust. But citizenship seems as arbitrary as any of those. The reasons for which we deny that distributive shares within states should be determined by skin color or sex also commit us to holding that (global) distributive shares should not be determined by place of birth. Carens (1987) compares the existence of states to medieval feudalism. One way of putting the concern is that within a state system, citizens and noncitizens are treated differently—at borders, for example. Thus, such a system—and this is the moral complaint—inevitably provides opportunities for a considerable amount of morally arbitrary behavior.

Carens is correct that moral equality and the value of common humanity cannot expire at borders. But he is wrong in thinking that the irrelevance of sex and race for the determination of distributive shares within states reveals the same irrelevance for shared citizenship. One reason why distributive shares within states should not be determined by skin color or sex is that there is nothing about these features that makes those who have them inherently more deserving of such shares. Moreover, a higher ratio of distributive shares for some based on such factors would not create direct or indirect benefits for others. As opposed to that, the account of shared membership in states in chapter 2 constructively establishes the normative peculiarity of states. That account shows why certain principles hold among those who share a state, and thus demonstrates the relevance of shared membership in a state from the standpoint of justice. Human beings who share a state owe to each other more than those who do not. The fact that shared citizenship arises in a manner for which individuals deserve neither credit nor blame (and in that sense is morally *arbitrary*) does not make it morally *irrelevant*. It is unproblematic that a state system provides opportunities for morally arbitrary behavior as long as that behavior nonetheless tracks what is morally relevant. Border controls do so.[10]

Arash Abizadeh (2008) argues that unilateral border control is inconsistent with a democratic theory of popular sovereignty. When institutions coerce, the coerced must have a say about it; there must be *actual* justification to the demos. It is an essential part of the system of multiple states that there are institutions that coerce people (noncitizens) to whom no such justification is given. These people are coerced, actually or potentially, through the presence of borders. Therefore, the state system—which permits each state to control its borders—ought not to exist, and ought to be replaced with institutions that would give justification to a global demos.[11] Abizadeh argues that the idea of a *bounded* demos of *democratic* theory is incoherent. If we assume a bounded demos, the justification for excluding some from entering the country in question would be required only vis-à-vis those who already belong to the demos, but not to all those affected by it. So a bounded demos cannot democratically legitimize the coercion it exercises.[12]

What kind of legitimization does a demos require? Let us call a set of people constrained by intense cooperative and coercive structures as described in chapter 2 a *potential demos* of democratic politics. Such a demos is "potential" because I have said nothing about the extent to which its members are enfranchised. Coercive and cooperative structures create pressure toward enfranchisement. Enfranchising parts of the potential demos increases the pressure for more complete enfranchisement. Moral arguments demand the transformation of a potential demos into a demos of democratic politics. One might object that this process does not deliver a legitimate demos because it has not been democratically constituted: no vote has determined that this circle of people should be united to the exclusion of others. Yet as long as this demos is internally just and its members endorse its institutions, that is unproblematic.

The objector might reply that this transformation does not properly consider all affected interests. Mexicans who wish to enter the United States never consented to there being an American demos that unilaterally constrains immigration. Yet interests can be considered in domain-specific ways, in ways that take into account the grounds of justice that the relevant people share. To the extent that interests are affected by trade policies, for instance, we should ensure that such policies are fair (chapter 14). But being under such a duty does not mean a demos must enfranchise everybody connected to it through trade. Internationalism ensures that the interests of the Mexicans at the U.S. border are considered, in particular through the proposal on immigration in chapter 8. Other duties apply on the basis of other grounds, and in some cases immigration-related measures may be instrumental to realizing them. Moreover, and crucially, states are required to give account of their efforts to contribute to the realization of principles of justice, as chapter 17 argues. As we will see there, however, it is only within states that such accountability must assume the shape of democratic decision mechanisms. For those who are not members of the state, no *additional* claim to enfranchisement arises.[13]

4. Arguments enlisting freedom, liberal justice, and democracy fail to identify moral failings of the state system as such. So far we have no reason to conclude there ought to be no states. Let us next consider three arguments for the view that the global order, including the system of multiple states, wrongfully harms the poor, and therefore this system should be replaced either with a world state or with no states. More than 20 percent of the world's population live in abject poverty, on less than $1 day, and about 50 percent live on less than $2. Some 25 percent are illiterate. The 2.5 billion people in low-income countries have an infant mortality rate of over 100 for every 1,000 live births, compared to 6 in high-income countries. These numbers testify to an enormous number of human rights violations. As indeed William Blake put it so strikingly in "Auguries of Innocence," "Some are born to sweet delight // Some are born to endless night." Often it is hard to assess why countries are in such dire straits, and how to improve their plight. It is equally difficult to determine why there is an *overall pattern* of radically uneven life circumstances across the world, and thus within a shared political and economic system of multiple states. One can approach that question with analyses of different scopes.

For instance, Paul Collier's (2007) *The Bottom Billion* argues that the pitiful state of the eponymous billion is due to poverty traps (conflict trap, natural resource trap, and traps constituted by being landlocked with bad neighbors and by having bad governance in small countries). An explanation of that scope explains why it is hard for some regions to catch up while others prosper. Gregory Clark's (2007) *A Farewell to Alms*, taking a broader historical perspective, asks why this "Great Divide" between developed and developing world could arise. Before the late eighteenth century, he argues, humanity faced a "Malthusian trap": new technology enabled greater productivity, but its effects were absorbed by population increases. In Britain, however, as disease kept decimating the poor, the more literate and thus more productive sons of the wealthy assumed lower social positions. Downward mobility enabled Britain to escape from this trap.

Covering the period since the last ice age, 13,000 years ago, Jared Diamond's (1997) *Guns, Germs, and Steel* takes a yet broader perspective. He argues that gaps in power and technology originated in environmental differences, amplified by various factors. These factors were primarily differential endowments with crops and domesticable animals, as well as the fact that Eurasia's dominant east–west axis generated a huge area with similar climates within which successful cultures could expand. Subsequently, superior weapons provided military supremacy, European diseases weakened local populations, and centralized governments promoted technological advances and military organization. The vast scope of Diamond's analysis contrasts with that of authors like Collier and Clark, but also with other large-scale approaches "that focus on advanced literate Eurasian civilizations of the last 5,000 years" (24). He mentions Arnold Toynbee's *Study of History*, but the point also applies to Immanuel Wallerstein's world systems approach (Wallerstein 1980), or any other (broadly conceived) Marxist approach to global history. Diamond argues that all these approaches fail to account for the emergence of the observed pattern of radically uneven life circumstances.

These and other social scientific or historical approaches seek to *explain* why parts of humanity find themselves in a distinctly harmful state while others do not. To argue in addition that the poor are being *wrongfully* harmed requires an account of the nature of the wrongs involved. I explore three ways of articulating that the system of multiple states, or the global order, wrongfully harms the poor. "The poor do need help," Pogge (2002, 23) writes, "because of the terrible injustices they are being subjected to." One argument he presents for the claim that the global order wrongfully harms the poor (and the next argument that we will explore) is Shared Institutions. I break it down into several propositions:

Imposition: The better-off impose a shared institutional order on the worse-off (i.e., the global economic and political order introduced in chapter 1).
Feasible Alternatives: There is a feasible alternative institutional order under which radical inequality would not persist.[14]

Implication: The existing institutional order is implicated in the persistence of radical inequality because there is such an alternative.

Extra-Social Factors: Radical inequality cannot be traced to extrasocial factors affecting different people differently.

Pogge (2005b) puts the thrust of this argument as follows:

> Minor redesigns of a few critical features would suffice to avoid most of the severe poverty we are witnessing today. In this sense, we are not far from a global institutional order that would satisfy the minimal human rights standards of justice. (58; similarly Pogge 2007, 30, 52)

Pogge's focus is on poverty, whereas ours for much of part 3 of this book has been on human rights. Since there is a human right to subsistence, we could recast Feasible Alternatives as stating that there is a feasible alternative institutional order under which the current level of human rights violations would not persist.

I accept the Imposition and Extra-Social Factors propositions and focus on Feasible Alternatives (and derivatively on Implication). The Feasible Alternatives proposition apparently makes a weak claim since it does not specify mechanisms through which the global order relegates developing countries to inferiority. One theory that does so is dependency theory, which argues that poor countries at the world economy's periphery cannot develop as long as they are in thrall to rich nations at its center because (as one version has it) prices of primary commodities (their main exports) are bound to fall relative to manufactured goods. Such views carry a heavy burden of proof that Pogge avoids by not making claims about mechanisms.[15] It is because the Feasible Alternatives (and thus Shared Institutions) proposition is weak in this sense that it apparently strongly indicts the state system.

Pogge seems to think "feasibility" is primarily a matter of allocating money to developing countries, money that can and should be provided by the rich. It would take just 1.2 percent of the income of rich economies, $312 billion annually, to bridge the aggregate shortfall of those living on less than $1 per day to the $2 line.[16] Pogge's proposal for raising some of those funds is the Global Resource Dividend, which would tax resource extraction. Other proposals include insistence on the UN-recommended 0.7 percent of GNP as official development aid; taxes on environmentally undesirable activities (carbon use) or socially problematic activities (weapon trading); the Soros proposal to donate "special drawing rights"; and the currency transfer tax ("Tobin tax"), or a more general tax on financial markets, in the style of a value-added tax on financial transactions.[17]

However, the feasible alternatives proposition must be understood from the standpoint of the institutional stance from chapter 4. While Pogge's considerations show that abject poverty will be surmountable *if* closing such a gap is a matter of transferring money, the "if" clause is dubious. Suppose in situation S1 we have the funds to cover the financial shortfall. This is insufficient to create S2, where nobody lives on less than $1 a day. We need reliable ways of distributing funds to individuals who do not simply have bank accounts they can securely access (and to which we could transfer money without interference by local strongmen), as well as an environment in which they could actually spend the money. Both times this involves *institutional* improvements. Similar points apply if one wishes to support medical and educational advancements. For instance, one cannot improve education by building a few schools but must invest in teacher training, books, supplies, family support, and much else—which is not only more expensive but requires a peaceful and stable environment.

That *sustainable* measures for *enduring* change require good institutions has become a guiding insight for many at the intersection of the social sciences of development and its practice. Having funds to close the aggregate *financial* shortfall between S1 and S2 is at best necessary, but it is not sufficient for S2 to be *feasible*. S2 becomes feasible only if appropriate institutional improvements are made. But not only must we not understand "feasible alternatives" as if the provision of funds were sufficient for bringing about an institutional alternative, we must also not understand it as if blueprints for eradicating poverty had long been available but remained unused for lack of willingness to take necessary steps.[18] Development economics remains a discipline with substantial disagreements. The field has seen a sequence of ideas about how to generate fast growth. Over decades of experimentation with different approaches, many countries received substantial shares of GDP as official development aid, often under the condition of implementing what then seemed like the most promising plan to advance development. Nonetheless, poverty and human rights violations persist.

The shared institutions proposition does succeed in making a moral complaint about the global order, but in a sense that takes into account the matters we just discussed. There plausibly are numerous ways of improving the situation of the poor through institutional change that are insufficiently explored and poorly understood. Specifically in terms of the duty of assistance, the manner in which the global order wrongfully harms the poor is by not doing enough to make good on that duty. It should be recalled that this chapter explores strategies one might want to deploy to find moral flaws in the system of states, and then to use these flaws to conclude there ought to be no state system. So the question now becomes whether we have reason to conclude there should be no system of states.

If it is impossible within the state system to take obligations of justice seriously, but it is possible in a world without states or with a world state, then we should conclude there ought to be no states. Much the same will be true if a world without states or a world state makes it much easier to realize justice. But this is a discussion that I cut short now and postpone until chapter 16. The envisaged comparison among a state system, a stateless world, and a world state requires that we have a reasonably good understanding of what a world without multiple states would be like. But as chapter 16 will argue, we do not have such an understanding. Therefore the flaw we have found with the state system does not lead to the conclusion that there ought to be no state system.

5. "The extent of human suffering and premature deaths due to poverty-related causes is not well-known in the West," Pogge (2002, 98) writes, providing information about global poverty and inequality throughout. Indeed, one might think the extent of poverty and inequality by itself reveals that the global order wrongfully harms the poor. But we must ask, what can we actually learn from these data for the question of whether the global order wrongfully harms the poor?[19]

Let me begin with a thought about the role of domestic versus global factors in explaining poverty and inequality. Pogge suggests that one goal of macro-explanations transcending national factors is to explain why so many countries are poor and so few rich (as opposed to explaining the economic status of this or that country). Yet we must be careful with this question. If one considers suicide rates, micro-explanations will not capture the full story; societal factors must be considered. There are two senses in which we can inquire about such factors. First, we may ask non-comparatively which societal factors matter, and second, we may ask comparatively why a country has a different suicide rate than similar countries. These approaches are related (checking on the comparative side helps ensure the noncomparative explanation is complete, checking on the noncomparative side shows to which countries one should compare) but respond to different inquiries.

However, the question "Why are so many countries poor and so few rich?" arises only noncomparatively. We have no sense of "what is to be expected" as we do when countries with similar characteristics have a lower suicide rate than the country under consideration. Plausibly the country with a higher suicide rate "than expected" has good reason to change the relevant factors because something goes wrong in that society that does not go wrong elsewhere. But such reasoning does not apply if we have no sense of "what is to be expected," as is the case for the question of why so many countries are poor and so few are rich. Whatever is wrong with that fact, it is not that there is an obvious gap between what is to be expected and what is the case. The mistaken perception that there is such a gap may contribute to a sense that evils such as poverty and starvation must be attributable to some entity that "does the harming."

Statistics hardly show unambiguously that the global order harms the poor. While indeed, 1.2 billion people in 1998 lived below the poverty line of $1.08 PPP 1993 per day,[20] currently a smaller share of the world population lives in misery than ever before, as measured in terms of any standard development indicator. The progress made over the last two hundred years is miraculous. In 1820, 75 percent of the world population lived on less than $1 a day (appropriately adjusted). Today, in Europe, almost nobody does; in China less than 20 percent do, in South Asia around 40 percent; and altogether slightly more than 20 percent do. The share of people living on less than $1 a day fell from 42 percent in 1950 to 17 percent in 1992. Historically, *almost everybody* was poor. That is no longer true.

It is true that high-income economies include 15 percent of the population but receive 80 percent of income (Pogge 2002, 99). Around 1820, per-capita incomes were similar worldwide, and low, ranging from around $500 in China and South Asia to $1,000–$1,500 in some European countries. So the gap between rich and poor was 3:1, whereas, according to UNDP statistics, in 1960 it was 60:1, and in 1997 74:1. But it is also true that, between 1960 and 2000, real per-capita income in developing countries grew on average 2.3 percent (doubling living standards within thirty years). Britain's GDP grew an average of 1.3 percent during its nineteenth-century economic supremacy. For developing countries, things have been better recently than they were for countries at the height of their power during any other period in history.

The average income per capita in 1950 worldwide was $2,114, while in 1999 it was $5,709 (1990 dollars PPP); for developing countries, income per capita increased from $1,093 to $3,100 during this period. Similar improvements occurred in life expectancy, which rose from forty-nine years to sixty-six years worldwide (from forty-four years to sixty-four years in developing countries), and so has increased more in the last fifty years than in the five thousand years preceding. The literacy rate rose from 54 percent in 1950 to 79 percent in 1999. Infant mortality fell from 156 in 1,000 live births to 54 worldwide. Furthermore, while the UNDP inequality statistics above used international exchange rates, things look different if one uses the purchasing power parity standard. According to such calculations, which account for what money buys in different countries, inequality had risen by 1960 to 7:1 and has since fallen to about 6:1

because of higher growth in the developing world. It is true that aid has often been given for strategic reasons, has declined since the Cold War, and constitutes a tiny percentage of donors' GDP (Pogge 2002, 8).[21] But for recipients the transfers are substantial. In 1993, sub-Saharan countries received on average 11.5 percent of GNP as aid (Zambia received 23.6 percent, Tanzania 40 percent).[22] The Marshall Plan, hailed as the greatest aid program ever, is estimated to have given recipients less than 2.5 percent of their annual GNP (Eichengreen et al. 1992).

What conclusion such statistics warrant depends on the period considered ("sub-Saharan Africa has made progress over a two hundred–year horizon, but not for the last twenty years"), whether one looks at absolute or relative quantities ("the number of abysmally poor has remained unchanged for fifteen years, but their share of the world population decreased"), and whether one looks at individuals or countries ("the median developing country has experienced zero growth over the last twenty years; still, inequality between two randomly chosen individuals has fallen"— because of growth in India and China). Still, what is remarkable is not that so many now live in poverty but that so many prosper, not that so many die young but that so many survive, not that so many are illiterate but that so many can read. If one looks at the last two hundred, one hundred, or fifty years, things have improved dramatically for the poor. The two hundred–year and the fifty-year horizons (roughly speaking) are especially significant. The former captures the period when the Industrial Revolution perfected the division of labor, which led to technological advancements across the board, advances that originated largely in what are today industrialized countries but that worked to everybody's benefit. The fifty-year horizon captures the period in which the global order came into its own.

Historically speaking, the global order seems to have brought tremendous advances. Moreover, advances in medicine and food production are largely due to countries that have shaped that order. As far as we can tell, the global order has benefited the poor. This is so although the *absolute* (as opposed to *relative*) number of people in poverty is higher now than two hundred years ago. But Pogge (2005a), for one, considers it "inappropriate to use percentages for the comparison. The killing of a given number of people does not become morally less troubling the more world population increases. What matters morally is the *number* of people in extreme poverty" (32). Yet our question is not whether a state of affairs characterized by the poverty statistics of two hundred years ago is better or worse than the contemporary state of affairs. We are interested in these statistics to gauge the impact of the global order on human beings. If we assess the difference in impact on students of the quality of teaching between times t1 and t2, we will not be interested in the absolute numbers of students who failed at t1 and t2 if the student population has increased enormously. If the grade distribution remains unchanged, the school's impact is presumably the same as it was on the smaller population. This analogy to the global order is deficient since the number of students is not a function of the teaching system, whereas the global order plays some role in determining population size. Yet this increase itself is the result of advances in technology and hygiene, so the role of the global order in determining population size does not trigger an objection to my argument. Both in my illustration and as far as the global order is concerned, the challenge is to develop a causal account of this impact. Relative numbers at least allow for a sensible hunch. Absolute numbers do not even do that much.[23]

6. Surely, one might say, developing countries are now better off than two hundred years ago—but so were African Americans under Jim Crow compared to antebellum days. (Would my reasoning admonish African Americans to be grateful for Jim Crow?) So this insight does not get us much when we inquire whether the system of states wrongfully harms the poor. Another way of articulating a moral complaint against the global order is that that system does so because its founding put the world onto a historical trajectory that created, or at least considerably contributed to, the current discrepancies in wealth and the current deplorable human rights record in many parts of the world. While developing countries are better off now than they were two hundred years ago, they would be even better off had it not been for the emergence of a system of states with its ensuing colonial ambitions. This is the fourth strategy of identifying a moral shortcoming of the global order that might push us toward the conclusion that there ought to be no state system.

The trouble is that it is impossible to say anything about the counterfactual benchmark of harm in this argument. Chapter 16 offers a negative assessment of the meaningfulness of large-scale counterfactuals about questions such as "what if the state system had never emerged" or "what if colonialism had never occurred." So for this argument, as for the second one above, the verdict depends on our discussion in chapter 16. But as a preliminary step let us explore at least somewhat more tractable claims, such as that developed countries are better off because they have kept developing countries in a relationship of dependence, and that colonialism has inflicted lasting harm.

The view that developed countries are rich because they have kept developing countries in a relationship of dependence was defended prominently by dependency theory, formerly widespread especially in Latin America. Dependency theorists argue that the development and even the internal structure of different parts of the world were primarily determined by their place in the world economy. Decisions about organization at the state level were secondary. This theory comes in different versions, the strongest claiming that the global North has become rich and maintains its wealth at the expense of (and thereby wrongfully harms) the global South. Weaker versions claim some other form of dependency, for instance, that resources from the South become cheaper over time relative to manufactured goods from the North. Development and underdevelopment are different sides of the same coin. Some proponents of dependency theory see themselves as Marxists (e.g., Immanuel Wallerstein or Andre Gunder Frank). Often their work has been tied to earlier Marxist reflection on imperialism. Nonetheless, dependency theory emerged from debates about development economics rather than from attempts to build a Marxist theory of global history—and indeed, not all of its major representatives have seen themselves as Marxists (e.g., Brazil's former president Cardoso has not).

Yet dependency theory has found increasingly fewer followers. David Landes makes this point rather too bluntly by stating that dependency theory and related theories have become incredible to all but "a dwindling group of Marxist historians." One reason why this way of capturing the decline of dependency theory is too flippant is that classical Marxism (as opposed to later versions that intersected with dependency theory) was not committed to the view that development would be uneven across countries. The *Communist Manifesto* famously insisted on the increasing *lack* of differences among countries. Nonetheless, dependency theories have indeed been in decline because they offer a view of the world economy (organized around ideas of a center and a periphery that are connected in ways that are inevitably disadvantageous for the periphery) that has been increasingly hard to reconcile with patterns of development. Judging from the state of this field, dependency theory does not offer a promising strategy to argue that the global order wrongfully harms the poor.[24]

More broadly accepted is the view that colonization has inter alia contributed to the development of the North, owing to capital from the slave trade as well as from cheap raw materials and labor. Investments in colonies were disproportional to the benefits Europeans reaped. Often colonialism contributed to the destruction of the environment and of existing social structures, and thus exacerbated underdevelopment. As the geographer Carl Sauer wrote with regard to early colonialism in the Americas, "In the space of a century and a half—only two full life times—more damage has been done to the productive capacity of the earth than in all of human history preceding." He bemoaned that "the previously characteristic manner of living within the means of an area" was replaced by a "reckless gutting of resource for quick 'profit'" (1969, 147). It is tempting to say that the global order wrongfully harms the poor because colonialism has created disadvantaged countries that have difficulty holding their own in the global order.

Indeed, while it happened, colonialism disrupted lives, killing, mutilating, or enslaving many in the process. But one would need to show that there is *persisting* injustice rooted in colonialism to establish the claim that it is because of the colonial past that the global order wrongfully harms the poor. Historians reach differentiated assessments of the colonial heritage. Fernand Braudel, who is among the greatest historians to have emphasized the role of large-scale socioeconomic factors in the making of history, says:

> Education and a certain level of technology, of hygiene, of medicine and of public administration: these were the greatest benefits left by the colonists, and some measure of compensation for the destruction which contact with Europe brought to old tribal, family, and social customs.... It will never be possible to gauge the full results of such novelties as employment for wages, a money economy, writing and individual ownership of land. Each was undoubtedly a blow to the former social regime. Yet these blows were surely a necessary part of the evolution taking place today. On the other hand, colonization had the real disadvantage of dividing Africa into a series of territories—French, English, German, Belgian, and Portuguese—whose fragmentation has been perpetuated today in too large a cluster of independent states, which are sometimes said to have "Balkanized" Africa. (1987, 134)

Most historians find colonial rule to have been woefully inadequate while it lasted.[25] Yet one need not agree with Niall Ferguson's (2003) largely apologetic approach to at least British colonialism to see that this inadequacy does not show that the legacy of colonialism, all things considered, continues to impose harm that outweighs advances in infrastructure or medicine. At the same time, one does not need to disagree with the starting point of postcolonialism—"that it is possible to understand today's world only by foregrounding the history of colonialism" (Krishna 2009, 3)—to think that we cannot take for granted that colonialism created a world where the essence of the relationship between developed and developing countries *now* is that the former wrongfully harm the latter.[26]

Reflection on colonialism may reveal ways in which the global order wrongfully harms the poor not through contrasting the world-as-it-is with the world-as-it-could-have-become but through inquiries about the path the world *has* taken. But perhaps I have misidentified the relevant feature of colonialism that we need to discuss in this context. Ypi, Goodin, and Barry (2009) argue that duties turning on a colonial past hold now because they were not honored then. Colonizers brought their dependencies into their coercive and cooperative system. In terms of the account of shared membership in chapter 2, the colonized were therefore owed transfers *in the past*. What they were owed then they are still owed. The current claimants are their heirs, in whose estates the original claims continue to accrue interest.

However, this move seems to treat these debts like money that was put in a bank account at some point and since then not only has accrued interest but has been bequeathed to subsequent generations who never touched it. Sher (1980) raises the following concern:

> Where the initial wrong was done many hundreds of years ago, almost all of the difference between the victim's entitlements in the actual world and his entitlements in a rectified world can be expected to stem from the actions of various intervening agents in the two alternative worlds. Little or none of it will be the automatic effect of the initial wrong itself. Since compensation is warranted only for disparities in entitlements which are the automatic effect of the initial wrong act, this means that there will be little or nothing left to compensate for. (13)

On this view, debts from the past are *not* like untouched accounts. Perpetrators are accountable only for automatic consequences of their wrongs, not for the effects of actions of others, which undermines contemporary claims the more strongly the longer ago those actions originated.

Often we can make sense of certain events as automatic effects of recent colonial wrongs. Exemplary here is the Democratic Republic of Congo. A 2002 study of institutional quality assigned Congo/Zaire the lowest score. There is a link between the lack of good institutions, as well as many other troubles the country has had, and the Belgian occupation.[27] The Congo Free State, first the property of Leopold II and later transferred to the Belgian state, was exploited with gruesome recklessness and without providing political or economic structures to prepare for independence. At independence in 1960, the country did not even have a basic network of roads. Tensions on independence day and a mutiny prompted by the conduct of the remaining Belgian officers led to the murder of Prime Minister Lumumba, which inaugurated the Mobutu dictatorship, which led to a civil war of deplorable dimensions. We cannot blame Belgium for the harmful interventions of others. But we can blame it for creating a state incapable of solving collective action problems.

For automatic effects of colonial failings, Ypi, Goodin, and Barry are clearly right. But granting this much endorses their claim only within limits. They may respond that Sher's objection treats the past too much like a sequence of generations that could have readily reconsidered earlier accomplishments to change their path, and that Sher ignores the extent to which momentous decisions locked in later generations. According to theories of path dependency, events at turning points constrain the range of subsequently available institutional arrangements. Had other events occurred (assuming they were realistically possible), the later range of opportunities would have been different. No generation of Congolese can abruptly alter the pernicious parameters that shape their interaction. Crucial events in the past cast long shadows, by creating conditions under which later generations rise and acquire attitudes or inclinations. As we read in William Faulkner's *Requiem for a Nun*, "The past is never dead. It's not even past."[28]

So perpetrators are accountable not only for automatic effects but also for the manner in which their deeds shape future opportunities. Colonial institutions were rarely designed for the benefit of indigenous people. To revisit that analogy, often colonists decidedly were like people who opened an account *and* also created the parameters that shaped the lives and attitudes of future users, as well as the conditions under which they would make withdrawals. The main result of this section, then, is that in former colonies institutions have arisen from a history in which the range of available options was often shaped enduringly by concerns other than the well-being of the colonized.

7. We are exploring strategies one might want to deploy to find moral flaws of the system of states, and then to use these flaws to conclude there ought to be no such system. Like the second strategy, this fourth one has led to a justified moral complaint about the state system. Again, the question arises as to whether we should take this result as a reason to conclude there ought to be no system of states. Before I respond, let me present one implication of our result in section 6.

That result throws additional light on the nature of the duty of assistance in building institutions from chapter 4. The conditions under which this duty applies are not such that disparate and far-flung groups of humans emerge from disjoint histories to encounter each other for the first time. Instead, the status quo to which this duty applies has emerged from an intertwined history, often driven by violence, which has opened into a present of radically uneven life chances. Presumably *some* share of the advantages in which the world's rich indulge would be unavailable to them were it not for past injustice. To that extent, these advantages are ill-gotten. Similarly, to *some* extent the misery of the poor has been caused by pernicious interactions with people from other parts of the world, which resulted in institutions that were not geared toward enhancing the well-being of those expected to comply with them and that continue to cast a shadow.

Past violence has not only produced ill-gotten gains, it has also created difficulties in making good on the duty of assistance. To the extent that past violence constitutes a link between ill-gotten gains and difficulties in satisfying this duty, there is a *compensatory* aspect to that duty. Chapter 4 stressed that it is hard to judge how demanding that duty is. Duties in virtue of common humanity involve a considerable *boundary problem* because we can ascertain their demandingness only in terms of the normative significance of common humanity. It is in light of this compensatory aspect of this duty that in many cases where doubts arise if certain measures are required, we should decide *in favor of so counting them*. That point applies ipso facto to all duties that internationalism generates, to the extent that those create a boundary problem of the sort we identified for the duty of assistance. Chapter 14 has already employed this reasoning.

One might wonder, however, whether I properly capture the magnitude of duties arising from our shared past. Ypi, Goodin, and Barry (2009) make that point by comparing decolonization to divorce: in both cases more successful partners owe transfers as a result of a shared past. Or we may think of African Americans under Jim Crow, who may have claims to reparations or affirmative action to overcome obstacles resulting from enslavement and subsequent discrimination. However, in these scenarios we are talking about demands that arise against a background of persisting cooperative and coercive structures. Couples marry with such structures already in place, and remaining in place if they separate. At a minimum, each person who goes through divorce still has a right to the protection he or she is entitled to *as a citizen*. African Americans under Jim Crow were treated as second-class citizens while being expected to comply with the political and economic system. We must understand the nature of their disadvantage against that background. (So my reasoning does not admonish African Americans to be grateful for improvements of the Jim Crow era over slavery.)

Moreover, guidance for the division of assets at a divorce should come from an assessment of how well-off the partners would likely have been without the marriage. Other arrangements might be in place, but their acceptability would depend on the fact that people should know about them when entering marriage. In cases of colonial history we are often talking about centuries, at least decades. The impact of colonization on individual life trajectories is much harder to assess than that of marriages. Relevantly similar cases are easily available in marriage cases, to draw comparisons: the lives of other individuals in that society. Similarly, the fate of other groups in the same society helps make relevant comparisons in the case of Jim Crow.

Does section 6 provide a reason to conclude there ought to be no state system? We can answer affirmatively only if a world without states or a world state would make it at least much easier to realize justice. We now arrive at the point that we also reached at the end of our discussion of the second strategy. The envisaged comparison between a state system, a world without states, and a world state that an affirmative answer would presuppose requires a reasonably good understanding of what a world without multiple states would be like. Chapter 16 argues that we do not have such an understanding.

Let us conclude. I have argued that no moral complaint arises against the system of states—against the way we live now—because the existence of borders is inconsistent with freedom, liberal justice, or democracy, or because statistics about the global order all by themselves reveal that it wrongfully harms the poor. My responses to the other two strategies depend on arguments chapter 16 has yet to make. In addition to the point that we do not have a reasonably good understanding of what a world without multiple states would be like, we must still argue that large-scale counterfactuals about what the world would be like had a state system never evolved, or had colonialism never occurred, are not meaningful. Let us turn to these tasks.

CHAPTER 16

"Imagine There's No Countries"

A Reply to John Lennon

> Imagine there's no countries
> It isn't hard to do
> > John Lennon, "Imagine"

1. In chapter 15 we began to consider this question: Is there any successful argument for the claim that there morally ought to be no states at all, or just a single, global state, rather than the world of multiple states in which we live now? I explored four strategies one might deploy (a) to identify moral flaws of the state system and (b) to use these flaws to show that there ought to be no such system. This chapter offers a framework for, and then systematically develops, a sweeping objection to any attempt to argue toward the conclusion that, morally speaking, the state system ought to cease to exist and that instead there morally ought to be either no states or a global state. In the process, I also respond to some issues left open in chapter 15 (summarized at the end of that chapter). At the heart of my objection is the claim that John Lennon, in his famous song from which this chapter's epigraph is taken, is wrong. He not only invites us to imagine a world with no states ("no countries") or perhaps a single global state ("the world will be as one," several lines later), he also tells us that it is easy to imagine such a world. But it is not easy. Lennon's is not a dream we ought to join—contrary to what he asks us to do—because we cannot, in any action-guiding way, imagine a world without a system of multiple states.

Globalists or nonrelationists might respond as follows to the question of whether, morally speaking, there ought to be a state system to begin with: "There ought not, but for pragmatic reasons, this is no conclusive reason to dismantle them now." As opposed to that, Kant famously thought there plainly ought to be states. In state-of-nature scenarios without organized power, individuals should found states, as opposed to remaining in that state of nature, but also as opposed to founding other forms of political organization. The answer to the question of whether there ought to be states that I defend is: "There remains a nagging doubt about whether there ought to be a system of states to begin with; nevertheless, morally and not merely pragmatically speaking, the state system ought not to be abandoned now." What is crucial is that we do not understand competing ideals well enough to adopt them as action-guiding at this stage in history. To say "the reason why the state system ought not to be dismantled at this stage is merely pragmatic" dramatically misrepresents the relevance of that point.

I recall here why we are interested in the question of whether it would be morally desirable for the state system to give way to either a world state or a world without states: if there ought to be no system of multiple states, my theory cannot be our ultimate ideal of justice. Instead, that ideal would be the vision in favor of which the state system should disappear. This chapter reflects on epistemic limits of utopian thinking, which constrain what normative stances we can take in the domain of global justice. I seek to reconcile the state's moral relevance with its historical contingency. Falling short of what those hope for who seek to justify states exclusively in terms of rational or moral virtues unique to them, my view disavows any "romance of the nation-state" (Luban 1980). A grand project of modern political philosophy has failed: to establish that there ought to be states without leaving a nagging doubt, a suspicion that there might be no moral or rational reconstruction of the development of states. But it is true also that epistemic considerations do not allow us to establish the sort of view formulated by Henry Sidgwick, that "our *highest* political ideal admits of no boundaries that would bar the prevention of high-handed injustice throughout the range of human society" (2005, 197, italics added). A view that urges us to realize a global regime that is not primarily state-based, or holds that it is only for practical reasons that we should not do so, endorses a "highest ideal" we do not understand well enough to pursue.

My envisaged opponents are not primarily those who actively seek to dismantle the state system now. Hardly anybody seriously calls for such radical change, and I will not entertain this possibility. My opponents are indeed mostly those who respond to the question of whether, morally speaking, there ought to be multiple states by saying either "there ought not, but for pragmatic reasons, this is no conclusive reason to dismantle them now," or "there ought to be (multiple) states." The results of this chapter impose considerable constraints on institutional changes that, for instance, globalists and nonrelationists could reasonably propose, as well as on the kind of evaluation of the global order they can sensibly make. Neither proposals nor evaluations may involve a vision of a world without a multiplicity of states.

We do not understand what a world would be *like* where all state power (except, perhaps, a world state), ranging from border control to maintenance of social insurance, is replaced with other arrangements. We do not understand a world whose distinctive features do not include multiple states. This radical ideal in Lennon's song we do not grasp well enough to pursue. This criticism also applies to those who endorse a stateless world (or a world state) as a long-term ideal, to be reached gradually. Such approaches still presuppose that we understand what we pursue.[1] Wittgenstein went too far stating that philosophy leaves everything as it is (*Philosophical Investigations*, sec. 124). But philosophy should not propose ideals we are bound to understand only poorly.

Our goal, again, is systematically to develop a sweeping objection to any attempt to argue toward the conclusion that the state system ought to cease to exist. The framework within which I do so is that of an account of what it is to *justify* states. Section 2 offers such an account and argues that such a justification *now* indeed is a justification of a state system. I explain the connection between the statements "the state system is justified" and "there ought (not) to be a system of states." To say that "there ought to be a system of multiple states" means that in a scenario without organized political power, individuals morally ought to found states, rather than stay unorganized or organize political power differently.

We are entitled to say "there ought to be states" only if we can conclusively refute *skepticism from below* and *skepticism from above*. Skepticism from below holds that it is not the case that there morally ought to be any forms of organized power, including states. Skepticism from above assumes that there ought to be organized power, but holds that it is not the case that power ought to be organized in multiple states. This is skepticism from above, since the world state and strong supranational structures are among the alternatives. There might be other possibilities, but their unifying feature is that they replace states with *other* coercive structures. We are entitled to say "there ought to be no states" only if we can conclusively establish at least one type of skepticism.

To illustrate how modern philosophy has responded to these forms of skepticism, section 3 looks at three strategies to justify the state to begin with, in Hobbes, Kant, and Rawls. Section 4 explores replies to skeptics from below and concedes that they create a nagging doubt: there might be no moral or rational reconstruction of the existence of states. Since skepticism from below cannot be conclusively rebutted, we are not entitled to say that human beings ought to live in multiple states. If asked whether there ought to be multiple states, we are left with saying either "there ought not, but for pragmatic reasons, this is no conclusive reason to dismantle them now," or, alternatively, "there remains a nagging doubt about whether there ought to be a state system to begin with; however, morally rather than merely pragmatically speaking, states ought not to be abandoned now."

Section 5 excludes the first response. That response is plausible only if we have an action-guiding political ideal that competes with a state system. But we do not. For the same reason, neither type of skepticism can be conclusively established, and we cannot conclude that there ought to be no system of states. So, regarding the question of whether there ought to be a state system, we should be neither theists nor atheists. We should be agnostic. For my objection to any attempt to argue toward the conclusion that the state system morally ought to cease to exist, section 5 is essential.

Section 6 develops a retrospective counterpart to the judgment that certain forward-looking ideals are insufficiently intelligible to be action guiding, thereby supplementing the view in section 5: we also do not understand large-scale counterfactual speculation about how the past might have been different. In addition to the point that we do not understand a world without multiple states, this too is a point we need to establish to close a lacuna in chapter 15. Section 7 concludes. We ought to make our world of states as good as possible rather than aspire to a different kind of political world. There remains a nagging doubt about whether there ought to be a state system to begin with; nevertheless, morally and not merely pragmatically speaking, states ought not be abandoned now. This is my reply to John Lennon. This is also all one can say about the vexing question of whether there ought to be (multiple) states. And we do end up with a sense in which the state system is justified, albeit a rather moderate one.[2]

2. As long as there are states, we can explain how they (or those with relevant properties) differ relevantly from other political entities—as argued in chapters 2 and 3. But this does not imply a duty to found states. Perhaps, all things considered, their emergence has been regrettable, and we should reorganize our affairs. Following Simmons (2001b), to offer a *justification* for X (acts, policies, institutions) is to argue that X is rationally or morally acceptable. We offer justifications if there is opposition, and thus in response to objections. We seek to justify states because we cannot take for granted that human beings live in states simply because it suits their nature. Justifications may include comparative and noncomparative considerations. Entities can be praised for prudential or moral advantages in a manner that does not involve comparisons. They can also be praised vis-à-vis alternatives.[3]

"Justifying the state" cannot mean showing the prudential or moral superiority of *any* state over all *possible* alternatives. It means to show the superiority of *particular* forms of the state over all *relevant* alternatives. Post-Hobbesian political philosophy argued that, under a broad range of circumstances, founding a state—rather than organizing their lives some other way—is what individuals ought to do in non-state situations. The doubts these justifications were supposed to defeat are captured by skepticism from below. They are doubts expressed especially on behalf of those—the philosophical anarchists—who favor living arrangements that lack certain features of states, especially their coerciveness, or who anyway consider organized power illegitimate. The philosophical anarchist has been to modern political philosophy what the moral skeptic has been to ethics.[4]

Debates with anarchists have normally proceeded under the assumption that what was at stake was merely the founding of *one* state. However, more is needed to justify states in an increasingly interconnected world than a rebuttal of anarchistic objections to the founding of any given state. One may be able to say to each individual in isolation that rationally and morally speaking, she ought to join a state. But the overall *system* of states triggers objections of its own. Competition among states generates new security concerns. "Justifying the state" now means justifying a system of states.

But the presence of such a system does not merely entail that we must adjust discussions with the anarchist. Individuals are generally unable to choose their state, and which state they are born into shapes their life prospects. This creates challenges for the justification of states in an era of political and economic interconnectedness. We must justify the state's coercive power also to people excluded from the territory over which it rules, such as would-be immigrants. Objections to a system of multiple states also arise from skepticism from above: skepticism that does not question coercive power per se, but insists that such power should not be organized in a plurality of states. As chapter 1 noted, alternatives to a system of states include a world state, a world with federative structures much stronger than the UN, a world with a more comprehensive system of collective security, one in which jurisdictions are disaggregated, or one in which border control is collectively administered or abandoned entirely. Again, skepticism from below holds that it is not the case that there morally ought to be any forms of organized power, including states. Skepticism from above assumes there ought to be organized power but holds that it is not the case that power ought to be organized in multiple states.

Let us see to what extent we have already justified the state system. The account of the state's normative peculiarity from part 1 can be embedded in such a justification. The discussion of the enlarged Rawlsian account of shared membership shows why living in states is prima facie advantageous. It is, after all, groups of individuals characterized by that account who produce the primary social goods.[5] That account also responds to the objection that no global political system is acceptable that contains entities (a) that do not include all human beings and (b) whose members take themselves to have duties of justice that do not apply to everybody. This objection might arise from globalist concerns that there is no relevant difference between states and certain other structures, especially the global order. Or this objection might develop the nonrelationist stance that, from a standpoint of justice, there is no relevant difference among human beings. Globalists and nonrelationists would not normally insist that states should in actual practice be abolished. But they would press this objection by way of identifying a pro tanto deficiency with the justification of states. By answering this objection, the chapters that develop the state's normative peculiarity form part of a justification of states. To the extent that we have already answered them, the objections to the global order in chapter 15 also find room here.

Yet all this is consistent with saying that the problems arising from the sheer fact that there is organized power outweigh the moral and prudential advantages of a system of states. All this is also consistent with saying that the problems arising from the particular way of organizing power in multiple states outweigh these advantages. All things considered, the state system might still lose the argument when compared to no states at all or, say, a world state as a competing political arrangement of humanity. So an engagement with skeptics from below and above is essential to seeing in what sense, if indeed ultimately any, the state system is justified.

Let me clarify some conceptual links. To say that there ought to be (multiple) states is synonymous with saying that there is a duty to found states if they do not exist yet and to maintain a system of states if it exists. We are entitled to say that there ought to be a state system only if we can conclusively refute skepticism from below and skepticism from above. We are entitled to say there ought to be no such system only if we can conclusively establish at least one form of skepticism. At it turns out, we are entitled to say neither the one nor the other.

If we are entitled to say that there ought to be a system of states, then such a system is justified (and the reasons why there ought to be such a system would provide the arguments with which we can justify states). If we are entitled to say that there ought to be no such system, then it is not justified. However, a state system may be justified even though we are entitled to say neither that there ought to be a state system nor that there ought to be no such system. This would be the case if the following conditions applied: (1) The system of states has certain moral or prudential advantages, certain objections to it can be answered, and, to the best of our understanding, no alternative political system has moral or prudential advantages that outweigh those of a system of states. So we cannot conclude that there ought to be no state system. (2) Nonetheless, there remain nagging doubts about the acceptability of the state system, and we cannot conclude either that there ought to be a system of states. It is in the moderate sense of conditions (1) and (2) that the state system is justified. Neither type of skepticism can be either conclusively established or refuted. Thereby we also find a sweeping objection to any attempt to argue toward the conclusion that the state system morally ought to cease to exist, the objection that completes the discussion we began in chapter 15.

3. Let us look at how three distinguished philosophers respond to skepticism from below and above: Hobbes, Kant, and Rawls. My interest is in their overall strategies. Often taken as the starting point for justifications of the state, Hobbes's *Leviathan* introduces a view of human nature and envisages humans in a situation without any power that reliably protects them. That state of nature abounds in violence and insecurity. Persons who might otherwise be peaceful engage in second-guessing and realize that preemptive aggression is rational, as "there is no way for any man to secure himselfe, so reasonable, as Anticipation; that is by force, or wiles, to master the persons of all men he can, so long, till he see no other power great enough to endanger him" (1991, chap. 13, 87–88).

What ought individuals to do? In addition to forming states, Hobbes considers (a) lying low to avoid conflict and (b) forming smaller defense alliances, less tightly organized than states. Lying low fails because of the rationality of anticipation. Forming smaller groups fails because they are internally unreliable and are in the same situation vis-à-vis each other as individuals are without them. Hobbes's reasoning involves "logical and conceptual analysis combined with empirical observations and probabilistic reasoning" (Kavka 1986, 4). Despite Hobbes's praise for the geometrical method, many empirical assumptions enter, about human psychology and the ensuing interaction among human beings, as well as about the conditions under which this interaction forces a situation in which founding a state seems advisable. The conditions include nonextreme scarcity, a certain population density, people being concerned with reputations, and a capacity for coordinated action.

So for Hobbes, the positive case for founding states is that states solve the security problem that exists in the state of nature. He rebuts solutions to that problem that dispense with coercive structures, thereby addressing skepticism from below. Skepticism from above does not worry him, although his occasional remarks on the matter have given rise to a "Hobbesian" approach to international relations. "In all times," he says,

> kings, and persons of sovereign authority, because of their independence, are in continual jealousies, and in the state and posture of gladiators; having their weapons pointing, and their eyes fixed on one another; that is, their forts, garrisons, and guns upon the frontiers of their kingdoms; and continual spies upon their neighbors; which is a posture of war. (1991, chap. 13, 90; see also chap. 21, 149)

Leviathan never pushes the argument further to support a world state. Although states are in the same situation with each other as individuals are in a state of nature, unlike the life of individuals, their existence is not bound to be "solitary, poor, nasty, brutish, and short" (chap. 13, 89). Wars between states "uphold thereby the Industry of their subjects" (chap. 13, 90), for which "Industry" there was "no place" in a state of nature among individuals (chap. 13, 89). A state of nature makes it all but impossible for individuals to make a living. Wars between states are not equally detrimental. Hobbes never entertains skepticism from above since he does not think the security problem is equally urgent at that level.[6]

Kant diagnoses similar problems in the state of nature. Without coercive authority, individuals "can never be secure against acts of violence from one another, since each will have his own right to do what seems right and good to him" (*Metaphysics of Morals*, sec. 44, 456). Property acquisition is provisionally possible in the state of nature, but rights are insecure and indeterminately circumscribed without "external, public, and lawful coercion" (137). Yet individuals are not merely prudentially advised to join states but *owe* it to, and can force, each other to found arrangements where rational wills can live together harmoniously. As Kant says in *Perpetual Peace*, a "man (or an individual people) in a mere state of nature robs me of any such security and injures me in virtue of this very state in which he coexists with me" (1970b, 98, n.). Not submitting to states is to prefer the "freedom of folly to the freedom of reason," which is "barbarism, coarseness, and brutish debasement of humanity" (103).[7]

Kant's positive case for the state is like Hobbes's except that Kant is less focused on plain physical security. He pays more attention than Hobbes to what the removal of physical insecurity enables persons to do with each other. Moreover, unlike Hobbes, Kant does not rest his case once a system of states is established. More is needed. So Kant takes skepticism from above more seriously than Hobbes. Right cannot prevail among persons in their own state if outsiders threaten their freedom. "Perpetual peace," for Kant, is the "ultimate goal of the whole right of nations" (*Metaphysics of Morals*, 1996, sec. 61, 487). As the seventh proposition in his *Idea for a Universal History with a Cosmopolitan Purpose* states, "The problem of establishing a perfect civil constitution is subordinate to the problem of a law-governed external relationship with other states, and cannot be solved unless the latter is also solved" (1970c, 47). What political arrangements should exist globally, given that states by themselves fail to solve the security problem?

Perpetual Peace proposes a federation of states opposed to war. While Kant thinks of this as the completion of the project begun with states, *Perpetual Peace* insists that states cannot be forced to submit to an international regime.[8] States have a lawful internal constitution and thus do everything individuals are required to do. *Perpetual Peace* assumes that states would reject a world state (1970b, 105), and that this suffices not to recommend one. Religious and linguistic diversity plays a role too in Kant's attitude toward the world state, and he also finds that "governing [a universal association of states] and so protecting each of its members would finally have to become impossible" (*Metaphysics of Morals*, 1996, sec. 61, 487). The purpose of the federation is "[not] to meddle in one another's internal dissensions but to protect against attacks from without" (sec. 54, 483).[9]

Rawls does not discuss any kind of skepticism. *A Theory of Justice* takes for granted that there is some sort of state, and explores just what sort it ought to be. *Political Liberalism* takes even more for granted: it offers a conception of justice for a constitutional democracy whose inhabitants endorse a plurality of reasonable doctrines (1993, xx). Rawls assumes institutions will be coercive, and that individuals care enough about justice to accept coerciveness in its pursuit. Three points are striking: first, how much Rawls takes for granted after centuries of theorizing about the state; second, his assumption that states do much more than solve security problems; and third, how little he says about what is normatively peculiar about states. Rawls apparently thinks modern philosophy has rebutted skepticism from below, leaving to him the design of states. As for skepticism from above, Rawls endorses Kant's views in *Perpetual Peace* (Rawls 1999b, 10). In addition, I recall the discussion of Rawls's political constructivism in chapter 1, which also generates a response to skepticism from above.[10]

4. We are entitled to say there *ought* to be a system of multiple states only if we can conclusively establish that both types of skepticism fail. This section argues that skeptics from below succeed at creating a nagging doubt that there is a moral or rational reconstruction of the existence of states. Therefore, we are not entitled to say there ought to be a system of states.

Some right-libertarians resist the idea that there are no reasonable alternative ways of securing the benefits guaranteed by the state and argue that the state has done more harm than good. Murray Rothbard regards the state as

> the supreme, the eternal, the best organized aggressor against the persons and property of the mass of the public. *All* States everywhere, whether democratic, dictatorial, or monarchical, whether red, white, blue, or brown.... And historically, by far the overwhelming portion of all enslavement and murder

in the history of the world have come from the hands of government. (1996, 46–47)[11]

Libertarians offer models of public choice that do without states, and identify historical societies that realized libertarian ideals. In ancient Ireland and precolonial Africa, people apparently enjoyed adequate security and had sophisticated property arrangements without coercive enforcement.[12]

Even those rejecting Hobbes's claim that just about any state is preferable to non-state arrangements may argue that abusive states were unavoidable in developing political formations that solved the security problem. The suggestion that that problem is solvable without states raises the possibility that history might not be so reconstructable. We face the disturbing prospect that the advantages that life in states has made possible could have been available without states and their coercion apparatus and tendency to make war against each other. All things considered, despite what we have already said toward a justification of a state system, states might merely be tamed versions of entities that arose when, as Nietzsche put it, "some pack of blond predatory animals, a race of conquerors and masters," decided to set "its terrifying paws on a subordinate population which may perhaps be vast in numbers but is still without any form, is still wandering about" (*On the Genealogy of Morality*, 1998, Second Essay, sec. 17).[13]

Doubts about Kant draw on these doubts about Hobbes. Kant never explains, as Simmons (2001b, 140) argues, why we have a duty to live in states rather than a general duty to respect rights. Nor does Kant explain why anybody inflicts an injury by refusing membership in society if others have accepted it and thus solve each other's security problem. Perhaps there is no other way of securing these benefits. But then the doubts about Hobbes reenter. Kant concluded too quickly that alternatives for solving the security problem were unavailable, without duly considering that the state solution generates problems of its own.

We cannot show that it would be irrational or immoral to adopt arrangements other than states. However, maybe we set the standards too high. To argue for anarchy, says Jonathan Wolff (1996),

it is not enough to point out the peculiarity of the state and the difficulties with many of the arguments in favor of it. Rather, in contractualist terms, it has to be shown that reasonable people seeking agreement on the nature of the social world would prefer anarchy to the state.... The defense of the state, we may say, needs only to meet the burden of proof assumed in the civil, not the criminal, courts: not beyond reasonable doubt, but by the balance of probabilities. (115)

Wolff appeals to epistemic standards. As far as Hobbes is concerned, Wolff's point is that agents in a state of nature rationally should found a state. "By the balance of probabilities" states solve the security problem best. As far as Kant is concerned, there should be enough confidence in the success of the moral argument for states, as well as enough abhorrence of the costs associated with omitting the founding of states, to make that case acceptable. Both times anarchists demand too much if they ask for more.[14]

Yet Wolff neglects the breadth of Michael Walzer's (1970) remark that "religion and philosophy have claimed their martyrs, as have family, friendship, and office.... But surely there has never been a more successful claimant of human lives than the state" (77). I recall, too, that political scientist Rudolph Rummel introduced the term "democide" (murder committed by governments) to insist that a "preeminent fact about government is that some of them murder millions in cold blood" (1994, 27). The number of war deaths over the last five centuries has been estimated at 150 million.[15] Ecological problems, too, are often associated with the state system.[16] Once we recognize troubles arising from the interactions among states, and thus broaden the conversation with the anarchist, Wolff's conclusion might not follow. Would it *really* be rational to found states "by the balance of probabilities" rather than try to arrange affairs without creating multiple centers of coercive power? Would it *really* be immoral not to do so, given the limited confidence we should have in arguments for states and the moral costs of founding states erroneously?

The strength of skepticism from below is often underappreciated, especially when we update it in light of the existence of multiple states. I first had to concede that such skeptics create a nagging doubt about the success of a major project of modern political philosophy. Now we also have to grant that even after switching to reflection about epistemic standards, we cannot conclude that skepticism from below fails. Since we cannot refute skepticism from below, we are not entitled to say there ought to be a system of multiple states.

We are left with two answers to the question of whether there ought to be a state system. First, we could say that "there ought not, but for pragmatic reasons, this is no conclusive reason to dismantle them now." That is, we can establish that there morally ought to be no system of states. This means that there are moral reasons to try to get rid of the state system now, but there are practical reasons against this which outweigh them; all things considered, then, we ought not to try to get rid of states now. Second, we could say "there remains a nagging doubt about whether there ought to be a system of states to begin with; however, morally rather than merely pragmatically speaking, states ought not to be abandoned now." I argue next that, crucially, we do not understand well enough what a world without states would be like to judge that, all things considered, it is a better world than a world of multiple states.[17]

We are entitled to say that there ought to be no system of states only if we can conclusively establish at least one type of skepticism. If we do not understand well enough what a world without multiple states would be like, we cannot so establish *either* type. Therefore, we are not entitled to say that there ought to be no system of states. So we cannot respond to the question of whether there ought to be a system of states by saying "there ought not, but for pragmatic reasons, this is no conclusive reason to dismantle them now." To give *that* response presupposes (a) we have an intelligible ideal of a world without multiple states that offers guidance for our political actions, while (b) nonetheless, we refrain from pursuing this course of action because it would be politically or psychologically too difficult to realize that ideal. Absent such an ideal, we must conclude that "there remains a nagging doubt about whether there ought to be a system of states to begin with; however, morally rather than merely pragmatically speaking, that system ought not to be abandoned now." Section 5 makes that case, enlisting the epistemic considerations Wolff sought to enlist to rebut skepticism. Such considerations do not rebut the kind of skepticism that arises in this context, but they do show that such skepticism cannot be conclusively established.

5. In *The Twenty-Year Crisis*, the historian E. H. Carr quotes Karl Marx as making the following claim, in 1853, about utopian thinking versus the importance of preserving the status quo:

> Impotence expresses itself in a single proposition: the maintenance of the *status quo*. This general conviction that a state of things resulting from hazard and circumstances must be obstinately maintained is a proof of bankruptcy, a confession by the leading Powers of their complete incapacity to further the cause of progress and civilization. (1939, 208; Carr provides no Marx reference)

Raymond Geuss has discussed the utopian thinking Marx indirectly praised here. Geuss (2005) argues that "when a theory is widely believed and has come to inform the way large groups of people act, deeply hidden structural features of it can suddenly come to have a tremendous political impact" (35). Referring to the work of Isaiah Berlin, F. A. Hayek, Karl Popper, and J. L. Talmon, his illustration for this phenomenon is Marxism. Theories like Marxism, says Geuss,

> present themselves with a certain prima facie plausibility as theories committed to promoting human freedom.... Nevertheless ... a deeper account of their

political views would reveal hidden authoritarian elements, such as a commitment to a "positive" rather than negative freedom. It was eventually this hidden structural kernel of the theory, not the private motives of its supporters, that had the last word in the real world of politics.... The Soviet Union, as it actually was, was the real content of Marx's "positive" liberty. (36)

Let us consider one (admittedly contentious) way of thinking about the phenomenon to which Geuss draws attention. Recall the following passage from the *German Ideology* (jointly written with Friedrich Engels):

> For as soon as the distribution of labor comes into being, each man has a particular, exclusive sphere of activity, which is forced upon him and from which he cannot escape. He is a hunter, a fisherman, a shepherd, or a critical critic, and must remain so if he does not want to lose his means of livelihood; while in communist society, where nobody has one exclusive sphere of activity but each can become accomplished in any branch he wishes, *society regulates the general production* and thus makes it possible for me to do one thing today and another tomorrow, to hunt in the morning, fish in the afternoon, rear cattle in the evening, criticize after dinner, just as I have a mind, without ever becoming hunter, fisherman, cowherd, or critic. (McLellan 1977, 185; my italics)

So in one of the relatively few passages where Marx illuminates communism, he mentions a crucial matter only in passing, that "society regulates the general production." This point captures a hidden structural feature that did have a tremendous impact. The authors of the *German Ideology* could not anticipate the Soviet Union's five-year plans, Mao's Great Leap Forward, or the measures communist societies would take to squelch opposition as they went about regulating the production. Instead, the paragraph where Marx and Engels assume that such regulation is up to society also envisages individuals happily pursuing multifarious activities, which the authors thought possible only if society took care of background parameters. In his *Main Currents of Marxism* (2005), in particular, the Polish philosopher Leszek Kolakowski has argued that Stalinist Russia was no aberration but Marxism's logical culmination. Even to the extent that Marxist ideas were misapplied, such misapplications evolved from the very efforts to apply the ideas.

The thesis of the inevitability, or faithfulness to doctrine, especially of Stalin's Soviet Union within Marxist theory is engulfed by bitter argument. I recall especially the controversy between the British historian E. P. Thompson (1973) and Kolakowski. Thompson insisted on the existence of Marxist traditions disconnected from Stalin's crimes. Some might say that the regulation mentioned in *German Ideology* is compatible with radical kinds of democracy.[18] But I also recall Geuss's concern that "when a theory is widely believed and has come to inform the way large groups of people act, deeply hidden structural features of it can suddenly come to have a tremendous political impact." Applied to this case, the concern is that Stalinism is one way of developing a recognizable form of Marxism. In the Soviet Union, one development of Marxism had come to inform the way large groups act. One view of what it is for society to regulate the production did have a considerable impact under those circumstances.

At the end of section 4, I noted that unless we possess an intelligible ideal of a world without multiple states that can guide our political actions, we cannot respond to the question of whether there ought to be a system of states by saying that "there ought not, but for pragmatic reasons, this is no conclusive reason to dismantle them now." For *either* sort of skepticism to push us toward that conclusion—for either sort to be conclusively *established*—presupposes the availability of large-scale utopias: utopian visions that either push for abandoning coercive structures altogether or push for replacing the multiplicity of states with a world state or other alternative coercive structures. What is crucial is that, independent of my illustration in terms of Marxism, the point I am borrowing from Geuss can be reinterpreted as a criticism of such utopias.

Large-scale utopias, surely those that envisage redesigning the global political system to such an extent that the state system is abandoned, can only be incompletely theorized. Formal models can fix basic parameters and "predict" what happens by making derivations. However, comprehensive visions of the future inevitably are incomplete in ways that are hard to gauge from experiences with limited scenarios. Once such visions come to guide many people's actions, certain features that could not have been expected to be significant may become significant. Those who dislike certain effects of states might stipulate a world with certain features (free movement, universal equality of opportunity, etc.), as Marx stipulated that "society would regulate the general production." But in both cases, at the time of conception there was (or is) no good understanding of what it would be like to have this vision realized, the difference being that Marxist theories have since been tried.

My point is not to enlist any of the conservative attitudes identified by Hirschman (1991): the perversity, futility, or jeopardy thesis. The first says that purposive action to improve some feature of the political, social, or economic order only exacerbates the condition one wishes to remedy. The second holds that attempts at social transformation fail to "make a dent." The third argues that the costs of change are too high since they endanger previous accomplishments. My point is, instead, that utopian thinking readily involves us in the construction of visions that we do not understand well enough to comprehend what their realization would look like. But utopian thinking can sensibly be action-guiding *only if* we have a reasonable reassurance that changes will not create larger problems than they solve. There can be no such reassurance without a reasonably clear understanding of what the world would be like once those changes occurred. Replacing the current global order with one in which all states are subject to coercive interference by regional or global institutions, or one that does away with states and other coercive structures entirely, is a case in point if ever there was one. Isaiah Berlin once wrote that "utopias have their value—nothing so wonderfully expands the imaginative horizons of human potentialities—but as guides to conduct they can prove literally fatal" (1992, 15). One way in which they can prove fatal is if we do not understand well enough what a world would be like once the utopia is implemented.[19]

The answer to the question of whether there ought to be a state system at all that I have proposed is "there remains a nagging doubt about whether there ought to be a system of states to begin with; however, morally rather than merely pragmatically speaking, states ought not to be abandoned now." Although I have advanced *epistemic* considerations, I put the point as a moral one to emphasize the difference between my view and that of theorists who think we should preserve states merely for *pragmatic* reasons. The magnitude of irresponsibility involved in demanding that the state system be abolished is considerably higher if the correct view is—as indeed it is—that we should continue to live in (multiple) states because we do not understand a competing vision of world order well enough than if the correct view is that we should do so because we do not know how to realize our vision of a world without multiple states. To highlight that thought I say that *morally speaking, we ought not to abandon states now.*

6. So we cannot respond to the question of whether there ought to be a system of states by saying "there ought not, but for pragmatic reasons, this is no conclusive reason to dismantle them now." Absent an action-guiding ideal of a stateless world (except, possibly, a world state), skepticism from above and below cannot be pushed far enough to make that statement. So although neither type of skepticism can be conclusively rebutted, neither type can be conclusively established either. Both types create doubts, but nothing more. We are not entitled to say there ought to be states, but neither are we entitled to say there ought to be no states.

My epistemic argument might seem weakest for the global state alternative: at first glance, a global state seems easier to imagine than a world of no states, or any other arrangement of coercive power than a state system. A global state, one might say, would just be more of what we are already used to (a state), only bigger. And a world state, after all, might in any event strike many as an attractive alternative to the system of multiple states. To the extent that the enlarged Rawlsian account of membership in chapter 2 offers a philosophically attractive political vision, one might wonder why it should not be expanded to all human beings. But the thought that the epistemic argument would apply to a world state with less force than to other alternatives to the state system is illusionary. A global state would then replace all the different power centers that have emerged on this planet, one global power that could interfere with the lives of human beings across the world in much the same way in which now multiple states can interfere with the lives of people respectively under their jurisdiction. The point I have borrowed from Geuss paradigmatically speaks to the kind of political, economic, legal, and social transition that humanity would have to go through to build a world state (or any other global or quasi-global structure that would replace the multiplicity of power centers characteristic of our system of states).

A retrospective counterpart throws additional light on my argument in section 5. As certain ideals about the future cannot be action-guiding, so we should also refrain from certain judgments about the past. Plausibly, history would have been altered had the unpredictable wind over the channel blown differently during attempted invasions of England, famously in 1066, 1588, and 1688.[20] It is sensible to think about how England would have developed had Charles I crushed the Covenanter Rebellion in 1639: there might have been no civil war, or it might have ended differently.[21] And it is sensible too to think about how World War II would have progressed differently had Stalin left Moscow in 1941, scared by German advances.[22] After all, we make causal claims about such events. William might not have defeated Harold in 1066 had he landed much earlier or later so that Harold would not have had to fight him immediately after defeating the Vikings further north. Arguably, the English Civil War could start only because the monarchy was in a particular state, in which it was partly because Charles had reacted in certain ways to the Covenanter Rebellion. Arguably, Stalin's endurance was crucial for the Russian war effort, the assassination of Franz Ferdinand in 1914 had a specific relevance for European history, and the Battle of Gettysburg was a crucial event during the American Civil War, which might or might not have ended differently had Pickett's ill-fated charge been on its way earlier in the day.

Obtaining a good understanding of the matter in question is to be able to assess, first, the extent to which counterfactual outcomes would have been seriously possible (agents came close to deciding differently, or natural events could have occurred differently with high probability), and second, what the occurrence of alternate possibilities would have meant in the near future. But unless history unfolds in patterns that do not much depend on individual actions (in which case counterfactual history is point-less), such reflection is sensible only to the extent that it turns on well-understood incentives and motives of individuals unfolding before the background of social, political, and economic parameters. Such specula-tion is most plausible where it merely involves a few decision makers. Since even small behavioral changes mean that people have different chil-dren (given the volatility of facts about encounters between sperms and eggs), predictions of events that depend on individual decisions are im-possible once we move into the generation following the event about which we think counterfactually.[23] For that reason, historians engaged with counterfactuals normally write articles, whereas a counterfactual account of book length more often than not is meant to be historically informed fiction.

What should we make of the idea that the world would be a better place if states had never emerged, or if colonialism had never happened? Such questions defy sensible answers. It is hard (if not impossible) to as-sess when agents came close to deciding differently, or natural events might readily have occurred in other ways, so that one could say that such occurrences would have prevented these developments. It is equally hard to assess what alternate course would have emerged. Had Europe-ans not colonized Africa, indigenous peoples might have built prosperous civilizations. Or perhaps war would have thwarted such efforts. Accord-ing to Herbst (2000), facts of physical geography in Africa impeded the emergence of powerful states.

When we evaluate counterfactuals, we first assess what the world would be like were the antecedent true. We then resort to cases where some claim similar to the antecedent in fact was true to evaluate whether the conse-quent of the counterfactual will also be true in a world where the ante-cedent is. But in the cases mentioned—what if states had never developed or colonialism had never occurred—doing so is impossible. The point is not that we cannot meet a threshold of reasonable certainty when specu-lating about what the world would look like had these developments never occurred. Instead, we must plead complete ignorance. The uncer-tainty about what many people who, as it happened, were never born would have done; how numerous events would have unfolded that, as it happened, never occurred; how innovations would have changed lives that, as it happened, never took place—such factors (spread over centu-ries) make it impossible to say what things would be like had the past been different.[24]

Researchers in comparative politics heavily employ counterfactual rea-soning. Holding other factors constant, they compare countries, say, in the WTO with similarly situated nonmembers, or a country's period of not belonging to the WTO with its period of belonging. Yet when assessing the global order as such, when asking about the development of the state system per se, we cannot hold other factors constant and judge what the world would be like had the current order not developed. We have only this world to work with. While we can comprehend claims about what the development of Poland would have been had it not joined the EU, we cannot make sense of claims about what the world would be like had the state system not developed.[25]

The reason why we ought to refrain from certain judgments about the past is the same as why we should refrain from supporting certain utopian visions. Insofar as this is plausible for scenarios about the past, and to the extent that it is plausible that the reasoning in both cases is the same, this discussion about counterfactual history supports and supplements what I argued about utopian visions in section 5. (This discussion also closes a lacuna we left in chapter 15.) We ought to refrain from judging the statement that "the world would now be a better place if the state system had not developed" for the same reason why we ought to refrain from passing judgment on the statement that "the world will be a better place, or look such and such, if the system of states is abandoned."

7. Long ago Edmund Burke gave what in hindsight looks like a response to John Lennon. For changes of such a magnitude, Burke says, commenting on the French Revolution,

> the burden of proof lies heavily on those who tear to pieces the whole frame and contexture of their country, that they would find no other way of settling a government fit to obtain its rational ends, except that which they have pursued by means unfavorable to all the present happiness of millions of people.[26]

Burke thought the Revolution reflected an unacceptable conception of politics, to uproot an existing order for abstract ideals. Yet most people would presumably say that, all things considered, it was good that the Revolution occurred (showing that social orders can change, in such a way that a new order eventually commands broader acceptance), and that its condemnation expresses a bad kind of conservatism. People used to be unable to imagine a world without slaves, or one in which women voted; what Europe would be like without Germany and France being archenemies; what an erstwhile autocracy would be like with its subjects democratically empowered, and so forth. Presumably the world is the better for these changes.

"Thought achieves more in the world than practice; for once the realm of imagination has been revolutionized, reality cannot resist," Hegel once wrote.[27] But thought is not easily revolutionized. Hayek (1973) offers what might count as a reply to Hegel: "The sources of many of the most harmful actions are often not evil men but high-minded idealists" (70).[28] It would be impossible to offer an account of what ought to be tried and what not. Much depends on how many follow suit. Discouragement might be self-fulfilling.[29] Nevertheless, we should not follow Lennon and explore what the world would be like without countries. We do not know enough to do so. This claim is true even if Burke was wrong about the French Revolution, and even if we do not fully understand how to distinguish between the two cases. Certain large-scale developments are not the sort of thing on which one can sensibly advise, especially since there is little to learn from smaller scenarios. The success of the French Revolution has little to teach us about the question of this chapter. And contrary to Goodin (2008), domestic democracy has little to teach about global democracy. Nor is there much to learn from the EU about global integration. The circumstances are too specific.

Rawls's (1999b) notion of a *realistic utopia* is useful here (see also Rawls 2001, secs. 1, 4). "Political philosophy," he explains, "is realistically utopian when it extends what are ordinarily thought to be the limits of practicable political possibility and, in so doing, reconciles us to our political and social condition" (11). First of all, a realistic utopia is relative to a time. What is realistically utopian now may differ from what it is generations later. It is not now part of a realistic utopia to dismantle states. What is part of such a utopia are efforts at global problem solving that require coordination among and reform within states, which in due course alter what counts as realistic utopia. Second, a realistic utopia reconciles us with our social world: some aspects of that world we cannot change, at least not now, or we would be ill-advised to change.

Third, a realistic utopia goes much beyond what is politically doable within the next election period. Still, a realistic utopia "must contain principles that members of that society could be brought to accept by reasoned discussion, which means that the principles cannot have implications that those citizens would find abhorrent" (Miller (2008, 46–47). Of course, what people find abhorrent has emerged from a historical development (a theme, e.g., in Nietzsche's *Genealogy*). That we have long lived in states generates resistance to dismantling them. The anarchist Peter Kropotkin lamented,

> What is worse than all I have enumerated, is that the education we all receive from the state, at school and later on in our life, has so vitiated our brains that the idea of liberty itself goes astray and is travestied into servitude. (1943, 9)

Yet even if this is true, it does not undermine what I have argued.

Rawls (1999b) cannot sharply delineate realistic from nonrealistic utopias (20). Nonetheless, anarchism and views of world order that dismantle the state system in favor of other structures (including a world state) are clearly inaccessible. The change they demand is too radical. Nor can we credibly assert that we should gradually approximate this goal because we do not understand the goal itself well enough to aspire at approximation. Pace Lennon, we cannot "imagine" a world without (multiple) countries in ways required for such ideals to be adopted.

Let me conclude. The topic of this chapter is a rather grave one. The association of the existence of states with many evils exerts much pressure on the justification of states. Pogge (2002, chap. 7), for one, insists that the existence of states undercuts peace, security, democracy, the reduction of oppression, and the maintenance of the ecology. Or consider the following striking statement:

> Within certain limits set by military and political power considerations, the modern state may do anything it wishes to those under its control.... In matters of ethics and morality, the situation of the individual in the modern state is in principle roughly equivalent to the situation of the prisoner in Auschwitz: either act in accordance with the prevailing standards of conduct enforced by those in authority, or risk whatever consequence they may wish to impose.... Existence now is more and more recognizably in accord with the principles that governed life and death in Auschwitz. (Kren and Rappoport 1980, 140, quoted in Bauman 1989, 86–87)

The point is that the removal of violence from everyday life that has often accompanied the emergence of states might have occurred at a truly horrific price. The state provides the machinery for the systematic exercise of violence against those who do not belong to it, or against those who are unwelcome in the eyes of an ideology (often a nationalist, religious, ethnic, or racial ideology) that has hijacked that machinery. Exerting violence under the insignia of value, purpose, and power, the state's machinery harbors enormous motivational potential to enlist individuals to do its bidding. The state can use projections of value to inspire individuals to make sacrifices or instigate them to commit atrocities, it may bestow an overarching purpose and meaning on their lives that would otherwise be beyond reach for them, and it may absorb them into projects much larger than what individuals could ever hope to accomplish by themselves. Once an ideology has hijacked the state's insignia, it can readily respond to, and abuse, the quest for meaning that is so characteristic of human beings—after all, as Nietzsche points out at the beginning of the Third Treatise of his *Genealogy*, human beings "will sooner will nothingness than not will at all." Kren and Rappoport (1980) urge us to consider the extent to which life in states as such resembles life in Auschwitz, and thereby submit that such a life is the price to pay for what the state provides. They are going too far, but Auschwitz itself indeed is an egregious symptom of the ensuing potential.[30]

Chapter 17 will show that states are accountable for their contributions to the realization of justice also to noncitizens. The mechanisms and institutions that such accountability requires should go a long way toward reducing the evils associated with states. Nonetheless any argument like the one in this chapter shoulders an enormous burden. Still, it is appropriate to conclude that a system of multiple states is justified in the moderate sense that a prima facie positive case for states is available (i.e., the Rawlsian account of state membership that shows that living in states is prima facie advantageous), that certain objections to it can be answered, and that, to the best of our understanding, there is no alternative political system with moral or prudential advantages that outweigh those of a state system. Drawing on the limits of our understanding of political ideals, my epistemic argument shows there can be no successful argument that would entitle us to say that there morally ought to be no states, or that there morally ought to be a global state. This much we can indeed say on behalf of the way we live now. But it is also all we can say. There remain nagging doubts about its acceptability. We are not entitled to say that there ought to be a system of multiple states.

CHAPTER 17

Justice and Accountability

The State

1. We have seen that that there are no successful arguments to the conclusion that there ought to be no states or that there ought to be a global state. We have therefore repelled a worry (articulated at the beginning of chapter 15) that my theory only spells out what justice requires in a world with an institutional structure (multiple states) it would be better to be rid of. Instead, my theory spells out what justice requires given an institutional structure that is morally justified in a moderate sense and to which we cannot clearly imagine an alternative. Rather than trying to abolish the state system, we should bring about the satisfaction of all principles of justice within it. So let us turn to the other two questions about justice and institutions that arise within pluralist internationalism and that I posed at the start of chapter 15. What obligations do various institutions have to bring about justice? And do they have a further duty to give an account of their action (or inaction) on justice to the populations who would benefit, and if so, how should this accounting be done? This chapter focuses on the state. I consider which principles states ought to be concerned about and in what order of priority. After giving a general argument that all institutions ought to be accountable for what they do in pursuit of justice, I start exploring how the state might best live up to its obligation to be accountable. Chapter 18 continues with that subject.

To capture what states ought to do in pursuit of justice, section 2 introduces the notion of one ground being embedded in another. Since states are embedded in other grounds, principles not tied to shared membership in states also apply to states. Section 3 offers a list of principles that apply to the state. Section 4 offers some additional reflection on this list. Sections 5 and 6 explore the notion of accountability and assess whether agents are accountable to those in the scope of principles toward whose realization they have duties, and what such accountability implies. Justice has not always been understood as involving accountability *to* those in this scope: to the extent that the Psalmist's King David violated a duty by sending Uriah to certain death in battle in order to facilitate his affair with Uriah's wife, David believed he owed an account to God ("against thee, thee only, have I sinned"), not to those in the scope of relevant principles (including Uriah). Outside theology, those within the scope of principles of justice are obvious candidates to whom duty-bound agents are accountable. Still, we must argue for this point (and its institutional implications) with care.

Sections 5 and 6 distinguish different forms of accountability and argue that agents with duties toward realizing principles of justice are accountable to those in their scope. This point matters greatly for an assessment from the standpoint of justice of institutions, states as well as international institutions (and the relationship between them). Section 7 shows, however, that it is inherently difficult for democracies to prioritize the pursuit of justice if it concerns noncitizens, and to be accountable to them. This result highlights the difficulties involved in determining the institutional context in which governments ought to give accounts to noncitizens. One radical proposal, which I rebut in section 8, is that we ought to build global democratic institutions. Yet while actual global democracy is not appropriate to that end, international institutions (short of global democratic institutions) must play an essential role in helping with the realization of justice and in providing structures for states to give account. Chapter 18 shows in detail how that may work for at least some principles of justice, with the WTO providing the setting in which states may give account at least for their efforts toward realizing some principles of justice. Section 9 briefly concludes.

2. Every agent and institution has the duty to do what it can, within limits, to bring about the necessary conditions of just distributions, as described in principles of justice. The first task when asking how institutions (or indeed any entity with obligations of justice) ought to contribute to justice is to ask, for *which* principles do they have this obligation to do what they can, within limits, to bring about justice? The second question is, what is the priority ranking of those principles for this institution? A final question (but one we do not discuss) is, what specific actions are required of a given institution to discharge its duties of justice?

When talking about priority among principles, I do not have in mind that from the standpoint of the universe, achieving justice is more important in some distributions than in others. Such a standpoint generates no priority ranking among the principles of justice. But we can ask whether for a given agent or institution charged with trying to bring about justice there is a priority among these principles. Institutions have particular purposes (that other entities may or may not also have), have limited time and resources, and have more power and competence to influence things in some areas than in others. They may plausibly also have their very own concerns of justice that would not stand out from the standpoint of the universe but to which entities may show partiality in their execution of their general duty to do what they can to bring about justice. I assume that all principles of justice can be satisfied at once within a world of multiple states. Given this assumption, the problematic aspects of granting this kind of partiality especially to states are much less troublesome than they otherwise would be.

Let us say that ground G is *embedded* in H if the individuals in the scope of G are also in the scope of H. I introduce this notion to answer the question, for which principles of justice does an institution (in this case the state) have corresponding obligations? I respond as follows. First, we find the ground G most closely linked with the institution (in this case, the ground of state membership). A ground is "linked" with an institution if the operations of the institution are primarily directed at, or most directly affect, the people in the scope associated with that ground. For instance, the operations of a state (or its government) are primarily directed at members of that state.

We ask then what principles are associated with that ground, where a principle is associated with a ground if it either arises from the ground in the familiar way (e.g., as the Rawlsian principles arise from the ground of state membership) or arises from another ground in which the first ground is embedded. So this sense of a principle's being associated with a ground is broader than what we are familiar with. Then we apply this rule: An institution has duties corresponding to all principles associated (in the broader sense) with the ground linked to the institution. This approach to deciding which principles an institution has duties to try to bring about is more restrictive than the view that entities with obligations of justice are responsible for all principles. States, for instance, have no obligations relating to Rawlsian principles in other states or, say, principles applying to people on another planet.

Shared membership in a state is embedded (given that there is a global order and a trade system) within common humanity, collective ownership of the earth, membership in the global order, and shared subjection to the trade system unless the respective country does not participate.[1] In parts 1–3 of this book, we found that the following principles are associated with these grounds. In other words, what follows is a list of the principles for which states have corresponding obligations apart from those that arise from shared membership in a state:

1. *Common humanity:* The distribution in the global population of the things to which human rights (understood as rights needed to protect the distinctively human life) generate entitlements is just only if everyone has enough of them to lead a distinctively human life (and thus if those rights are satisfied).

2. *Collective ownership:* The distribution of original resources and spaces of the earth among the global population is just only if everyone has the opportunity to use them to satisfy her or his basic needs, or otherwise lives under a property arrangement that provides the opportunity to satisfy basic needs.

3. *Membership in the global order:* The distribution in the global population of the things to which human rights (understood as membership rights) generate entitlements is just only if everyone has enough of these things for these rights to be realized.

4. *Trade:* The distribution of gains from trade among states is just only if no country enjoys gains that have come at the expense of people involved with the trade, where these gains occur *at the expense* of certain people if either (a) their contributions to the production of goods or the provision of services for export do not make them better off (than if they were not producing those goods at all) to an extent warranted by the value of these contributions (and they did not voluntarily accept such an arrangement), or (b) their involvement in the trade has emerged through human rights violations, or both.

The result in (1), regarding common humanity, has actually been subsumed under membership in the global order. I list it separately because common humanity is nonetheless a ground of justice. Below, when I state an order of priority for states, I merely talk about membership rights and make no special mention of common humanity. The principle concerning membership rights that derive from collective ownership, however, is covered by the general formulation in (3). A list of principles associated with ground G (in the broader sense) is (by definition) incomplete until we know in which grounds H it is embedded and what principles are associated with H (in the narrow, familiar sense). A full statement of principles in G must also determine priorities among principles associated with H vis-à-vis those associated only with G. Inquiries about principles associated (narrowly) only with G are preliminary: we must revisit them once we know the principles (narrowly) associated with H.

In a key scene in Alexander Solzhenitsyn's disturbing *In the First Circle*, his protagonist, Innokenty Volodin, explains his desperation about Stalinist Russia, and does so in a manner that illustrates the geometrical intuition behind one ground being embedded in another:

"You see this circle? That's our country. That's the first circle. Now here's the second." A circle with a larger diameter. "That is mankind at large. You would think that the first forms part of the second, wouldn't you? Not in the least! There are barriers of prejudice. Not to mention barbed wire and machine guns. To break through, physically or spiritually, is well-nigh impossible. Which means that mankind, as such, does not exist. There are only fatherlands, everyone's fatherland alien to everyone's else." (2009, 314)

The grounds-of-justice view, especially the idea of shared membership in a state being embedded in common humanity as a ground, offers a vision of a world where Volodin's view does not apply. Mankind does exist, and generates obligations.

3. Let us return to Rawls to see how the list of principles I just presented must be modified when we add in the principles we have been assuming hold for states. We have assumed that something like Rawls's principles hold domestically:

1. Each person has the same indefeasible claim to a fully adequate scheme of equal basic liberties, which scheme is compatible with the same scheme of liberties for all.
2. Social and economic inequalities are to be arranged so that they are both (a) attached to offices and positions open to all under conditions of fair equality of opportunity and (b) to the greatest benefit of the least advantaged.

Let us recall also that Rawls begins with a more general conception of justice:

All social values—liberty and opportunity, income and wealth, and the social bases of self-respect, are to be distributed equally unless an unequal distribution of any or all of these values is to everyone's advantage. (1999c, 54)

The general conception allows for inequalities with regard to all social primary goods. Yet in the statement of the two principles, Rawls gives priority to the first, and within the second, to the first clause. Such prioritizing becomes reasonable only once circumstances allow for effective realization of the liberties in the first principle (1999c, sec. 26). As long as concerns for survival dominate, people can permissibly give priority to making sure they survive over satisfying basic liberties. They may well be prevented from realizing a political system capable of protecting liberties. Exempting any goods from trade-offs is then not required, and possibly even inappropriate. The stage of development at which the general conception gives way to the two principles (the stage at which concerns about survival no longer dominate) is also the stage at which principles associated with grounds other than shared membership in a state ought to be integrated into the formulation of principles that define governmental responsibilities (including a statement of priorities among the principles).

Rawls (1999c) writes that a complete statement of the difference principle (2(b) above) integrates a just savings principle, which regulates how much should be left for future generations (258). He also states (1999b, 106–7) that a duty of assistance and a just savings principle are natural duties that "express the same underlying idea." Freeman (2007a) argues in light of these passages that

> the duty of assistance to burdened peoples, to meet their basic needs, is to be satisfied, like the just-savings principle, before determining the distributive share of the least advantaged in one's own society under the difference principle. Rawls then seems to afford the kind of importance to meeting basic human needs worldwide that moderates claims of distributive justice within a society. (309)

The idea seems to be that the difference principle, fully formulated, includes a clause to set aside some resources whose distribution has not yet been regulated by the first principle and the first part of the second principle.[2] In my terminology, this is an effort to present a list of principles that does not merely include those that apply in virtue of shared membership in a state but also those associated with grounds in which shared membership in a state is embedded.

I address the question of how to combine (and apply to the state) principles associated with different grounds only at this stage largely because this book has more or less discussed one ground at a time. The proposed rank-ordering of principles as they apply to the state not only will be controversial, it is not readily amenable to conclusive argumentation to exclude alternative orderings. This point applies both to the rank-ordering of the principles themselves and to the relative priority, if any, among components of a principle. G. A. Cohen (2011) addresses the general problem this way:

> Philosophers sometimes end their articles by saying this sort of thing: it is a task for future work to determine the *weight* of the consideration that I have exposed. But nobody ever gets around to that future work. Many wish they could, but nobody knows how to do it. (205)

My point about the lack of conclusive arguments to support my ordering reflects the nature of a pluralist theory. I do wish I could come around to future work that says more on this point. But indeed, I cannot. Yet we can say at least the following: like other entities, states (i.e., their populations) have their own concerns of justice that do not stand out from the standpoint of the universe but to which they may show partiality in their execution of the duty to do what they can to bring about justice. Many states are destitute. But the richer states are extraordinarily powerful entities and can shoulder a broad range of duties of justice. Nonetheless, even the most demanding understanding of what can reasonably be expected of them must acknowledge that resources and abilities are limited. In light of these points, and drawing on our results throughout, I submit the following list of principles of justice that ascribe obligations to states, in order of priority (which reflects my own considered judgment):

1. Within the state, each person has the same indefeasible claim to an adequate scheme of equal basic liberties, which scheme is compatible with the same scheme of liberties for all.
2. (a) The distribution in the global population of the things to which human rights (understood as membership rights) generate entitlements is just only if everyone has enough of them for these rights to be realized. (b) The distribution of original resources and spaces of the earth among the global population is just only if everyone has the opportunity to use them to satisfy her or his basic needs, or otherwise lives under a property arrangement that provides the opportunity to satisfy basic needs.
   (Principles 2(a) and 2(b) are at the same level of priority.)
3. Within the state, each person has the same indefeasible claim to a fully adequate scheme of equal basic liberties, which scheme is compatible with the same scheme of liberties for all.
4. Social and economic inequalities are to be arranged so that they are both (a) attached to offices and positions open to all under conditions of fair equality of opportunity, and (b) to the greatest benefit of the least advantaged.
   (4 (a) has priority over 4 (b).)

The discussions of the components of this list in earlier chapters provide an extended commentary on their meaning and implications, especially for items 2 (a) and 2 (b), which have a rather complex background, and also have implications with regard to future generations. Two grounds do not appear: common humanity and subjection to the trade regime. The implications of common humanity are subsumed under 2 (a). To the extent that trade creates obligations for states pertaining to other states, they too are subsumed under 2 (a). To the extent that trade creates domestic obligations, they are subsumed under principle 4. This does not mean that trade does not generate demands of justice; it merely means that the principles on this list are sufficiently general to absorb these demands to the extent that they apply *to states*. The trade-related principle of justice will be present explicitly once we talk about the WTO.

Rawls's first principle appears in two versions. Principle 1 omits the word "fully." States need not help improve the fates of noncitizens if circumstances do not allow them to realize a *broadly adequate* scheme of equal basic liberties for their citizens, but this scheme does not need to be *fully* adequate before obligations to help improve the fates of others apply. If citizens of a state are in a position to enjoy a broadly adequate scheme of equal basic liberties, the duties generated by principle 2 have greater importance than the provision of a *fully* adequate scheme of equal basic liberties. A certain level of deficiency in the realization of Rawls's original first principle should not discourage states from doing their share for obligations under principle 2. Principle 3 restates Rawls's first principle, including the word "fully," to capture his own prioritizing of his principle over his second principle (my principle 4). While the state system per se is justifiable (in the moderate sense explained in chapter 16), principle 2 requires *considerable* policy changes vis-à-vis the status quo (see section 4 of this chapter). That principle also requires additional reflection on how to distribute burdens among states and other entities in the global order.

In addition to principles of justice (and the corresponding obligations of justice), part 2 of this book also offers some demands of reasonable conduct regarding immigration policies (chapter 8) and intergenerational equality (chapter 9):

(α) *Immigration:* If the territory of state S is relatively underused, co-owners elsewhere have a pro tanto claim to immigration.

(β) *Intergenerational equality:* Each generation can reasonably be expected to leave a nondeclining stock of natural capital behind (*strong sustainability*).

(γ) *Absorptive capacity:* Regulation of access to the absorptive capacity of the atmosphere ought to be done in terms of ideas of fair division.

It is an obligation of justice (one that we derived from collective ownership) that regulation of access to the absorptive capacity be provided that leaves basic climate conditions intact so that basic needs can continue to be satisfied. Item γ supplements that obligation with a demand of reasonable conduct. Chapter 10 proposes a fair-division scheme. Again, the point at which Rawls's general conception gives way to his two principles is the point at which principles associated with other grounds ought to be integrated into a full statement of principles that apply domestically. Plausibly, principles that capture reasonable expectations would only be integrated at a later stage of development, when countries can be expected to contribute to the creation of a mutually acceptable global order. Those principles should then get priority over principle 4, which is concerned with the relative standing of citizens *vis-à-vis each other* and regulates inequalities that remain after the preceding principles have been realized.

Those demands of reasonable conduct should be discharged—and resources redirected accordingly—before the remaining primary goods are regulated entirely in terms of domestic priorities.

The next stage is to spell out the actions required of particular states in pursuit of justice. As far as the duties of justice are concerned that we have introduced in this book, I recall here that states have a duty of assistance in building institutions, and that there are obligations that the current generation leave behind institutions within which future generations can exercise membership rights, and that to the extent that within current institutions plans are made or policies adopted that affect future generations, those generations can expect that such planning makes sure their ability to meet basic needs is preserved. But we can say little in the abstract about what these duties imply for particular states. What actions count as "doing what one can within limits to help bring about justice" depends on the circumstances of a given state.

4. Aristotle used the term *endoxa* for beliefs that are widely accepted among those who have thought carefully about the matter at hand. The grounds-of-justice approach preserves many endoxa about global justice. Nonetheless, thinking about justice in this way has significant implications that push beyond such endoxa, implications that become clear now that we can detect the obligations that apply to states.

Governments must not only be governments of, by, and for their people. We must assess governments in terms of how they foster the realization of all principles that apply to them, including those that do because membership in a state is embedded in other grounds. Governments are trustees of the earth on behalf of future generations. If their people can satisfy basic needs, governments must ensure that future generations can do the same. If their people are well-off, governments ought to help ensure that future generations are, too. As a matter of justice, governments are guardians of membership rights in the global order and partly responsible for the realization of a duty of assistance toward the poor. To the extent that past violence has created difficulties in satisfying this duty, there is a compensatory aspect to this duty. This aspect implies that in many cases when doubts arise as to whether certain measures are required, we should decide in favor of so counting them. Governments must also assume responsibility for a just trade system, considering the interests of those who live elsewhere. Governments must do their share to foster the flourishing of humanity.

The grounds-of-justice approach dilutes the contrast between domestic and foreign policy. To ensure acceptability of the global order, governments can reasonably be expected to assume responsibility for a globally even-handed (and to some extent harmonized) immigration policy, and to guarantee that humans can live on this planet in accordance with the idea of proportionate use from chapter 8. Ensuring acceptability also requires the implementation of a climate change policy, for instance as sketched in chapter 10. Governments must not neglect duties with regard to immigration, climate change, or future generations even if (given *current* policies) discharging such duties threatens disproportionately to affect disadvantaged segments of society. Social policy must be reformed, then, and especially domestic tax codes must be adjusted accordingly. Inheritance taxes and other taxes targeting the increasingly large share of the very wealthy in rich countries' economies are particularly suitable sources of income that could help with discharging international duties. Governments must think of matters of domestic and global justice together rather than in isolation, and with distinct priority for domestic matters.

To illustrate, let us consider just two implications of this way of thinking about governments. According to Articles 54 and 56 of the German Basic Law, the president, chancellor, and federal ministers take the following oath:

> I swear (or affirm) that I will dedicate my efforts to the well-being of the German people, promote their welfare, protect them from harm, uphold and defend the Basic Law and the laws of the Federation, perform my duties conscientiously, and do justice to all. So help me God.

This oath mentions justice owed to everybody. Nonetheless, it overwhelmingly prioritizes duties toward Germans. The oath of the president of the United States is equally focused on those who were in a position to elect him (Article 2 of the U.S. Constitution), requiring of him or her "to the best of my ability, preserve, protect and defend the Constitution of the United States." These oaths are representative of the oaths taken by heads of states or governments around the world, the German oath being unusual in its mention of "justice to all." They should be reformulated, or interpreted appropriately, to include duties of justice toward noncitizens.

A second illustration comes from Article 2 (7) of the UN Charter:

> Nothing contained in the present Charter shall authorize the United Nations to intervene in matters which are essentially within the domestic jurisdiction of any state or shall require the Members to submit such matters to settlement under the present Charter.

The phrase "within the domestic jurisdiction of any state" should be interpreted in such a way that violations of duties of justice, including those that apply to people outside states, are not protected, and are not exempted from appropriate outside interventions.

5. But are these the only obligations of states that relate to justice? I argue next that there is a further type of obligation, an obligation to give an account for what one is doing to live up to the other obligations of justice. That result will inform the remainder of this chapter and chapter 18. For that result to be sufficiently sharp, however, we need an analysis of the notion of accountability as well, which this section provides.

For any entities A and B that are capable of having obligations, A is *accountable* to B for activities in domain Δ if and only if A (in some sense, morally or legally) owes B an actual justification for A's activities in Δ. In that case, A and B stand in an *accountability relationship*. The emphasis on actual reason giving is essential to accountability. If A has a duty to B in some domain, A does not automatically owe B an actual justification of A's activities in that domain. For cases in which we want to say that an actual justification is owed, we must argue for that view separately.

Whether A succeeds in fulfilling its obligation to give an actual justification depends on A alone. However, what B does matters to the further question of what is required for accountability to be *effective*. An accountability relationship is *effective* if and only if the following conditions apply:

Regarding A, the account giver: A (a) has the physical and intellectual ability to defend its actions in domain Δ, and (b) can be responsive to sanctions B may impose if A falls short of B's expectations on actions in Δ (or to rewards, if A meets or exceeds expectations).

Regarding B, the account recipient: B (c) has the knowledge and competence to judge A's actions in domain Δ, and (d) can impose sanctions to penalize A if A falls short of B's expectations on actions in Δ (or to reward, A if A meets or exceeds expectations).

The existence of such "knowledge and competence" entails the existence of standards of performance that apply to Δ. I do not include any conditions on the appropriateness of B's actions (i.e., that B not demand anything unreasonable from A) or on the form or quality of A's justification. Such conditions are not part of the idea of accountability. If (a), (b), (c), or (d) fails, accountability is *ineffective*. Accountability relationships can be more or less effective. The flaws might depend on either A or B, or both, and might be matters of knowledge or ability, as well as of the impact of the sanctions. Ways for accountability to be ineffective include its being exercised rarely, or merely as an all-things-considered (rather than a fine-tuned) judgment, as in democratic elections. An accountability relationship may be ineffective also simply because A or B is not sufficiently well organized or constituted.

An accountability relationship between A and B is *intermediate* if A is accountable to B and B acts on behalf of entity C, such that B is accountable to C for B's activities in domain Δ. A may or may not be accountable to C, and the standards by which B should judge A may be shaped by B's being accountable to C. The relationship is *ultimate* if it is not intermediate. Often agents are intermediately, and more or less effectively, accountable to relatively few overseers, who are ultimately, but less effectively, accountable to a larger group. Examples include hierarchical structures in companies, where employees are intermediately and often effectively accountable to supervisors while managers are ultimately accountable to shareholders. Yet shareholders might only have a periodic and unfocused influence, and therefore the managers are not effectively accountable to them. Democratic governance is another case. Within bureaucracies, employees are intermediately and effectively accountable to supervisors. Ultimately, the government (which includes cabinet members who are supervisors in certain areas) is accountable to voters. But voters often are not knowledgeable and sanction only rarely, and then only in an all-things-considered manner.

We can initially distinguish two different possible origins of A having an account-giving obligation to B, and will soon be interested in a third. (Asking about "origins" means to ask in virtue of what there is a duty to give account; it is not a historical question.) First, A and B may stand in an accountability relationship because A is an agent and B a principal that delegates tasks to A. The origin of A's obligation is whatever constitutes their principal–agent relationship (e.g., promises or contracts). Hierarchies in bureaucracies often work like that, as does fiscal authority between funding agencies and recipients, as do supervision relationships among institutions. Such relationships may be ultimate or intermediate, and more or less effective. Second, there may be independent norms in accordance with which A must perform. B's presence qua account recipient serves an instrumental (not norm-generating) purpose. The origin of A's obligation then lies in A's duty to abide by or implement these norms. Such norms may be substantive (prescribe goals) or procedural (prescribe processes). Supervision among institutions may be like this. Ethics boards supervising compliance with norms whose validity does not depend on their authority fit here as well. Legal responsibility too is often like this: one contracting party may take another to court, and that party is accountable to the court for breaches. (Assume the laws exist independently of the courts, as in civil law traditions.)[3]

Accountability may be symmetrical: A may be accountable to B, and B to A, for actions in Δ. It is easy to see how this could be when the origin of accountability lies in independent norms. (Accountability does not have to be organized this way when its origin lies in independent norms, but unlike in the principal–agent case, which by its nature is asymmetrical, we can readily see how it *could* be.) To illustrate, let us consider Cohen and Sabel's (1997, 2005) notion of a deliberative polyarchy. What makes deliberative polyarchy *polyarchic*

> is its use of situated deliberation within decision making units and deliberative comparisons across those units to enable them to engage in a mutually disciplined and responsive exploration of their particular variant of common problems.... Polyarchy addresses a dual problem: (1) comparable problems, arising in different settings, need solutions appropriately tailored to those settings, and (2) solutions in each setting need to be subjected to the pressure of deliberative comparison with solutions adopted in the others so that all reflect understanding of what was done elsewhere, and why. (2005, 780–81)

Captured through a process in which decision-making units explain their reasons *to each other*, accountability here involves only procedural norms of problem solving. Such relationships may be quite effective: concerned with similar problems, both entities may be well organized and possess competence, and underperformance may be sanctioned through public criticism, termination of funding, or disrupted careers. Cohen and Sabel suggest that such accountability is suitable to (and notice it in) international organizations like the EU.

6. We can now move from this general account of accountability to the question I posed in the introduction to this chapter, that is, whether agents with obligations to help bring about principles of justice are accountable for what they do (or do not do) to those in the scope of the principles. We reach this question by asking whether we can add a particular third way for accountability relationships to arise. Do agents with duties to contribute to the realization of principles of justice owe actual account giving, in some way, to those in the scope of these principles? (More specifically, in what follows we will be interested in the *moral* obligations of *institutions*.) If we limit ourselves to secular arguments for this proposition—"agents with duties to help bring about a just world also have a duty to offer an actual justification to the relevant population"— the answer is affirmative. I will give two arguments for that view.

First, there is an argument from respect. If people in the scope of principles were mere recipients, the fact that they are moral agents would not be taken seriously enough. One might think such an argument is available for any instance of somebody's having a duty, and so implausibly exclude the possibility of duties for which one does not owe actual justification. But to begin with, let us recall from chapter 1 the stringency of duties of justice. Second, let us note that duty bearers might err in executing duties (because of flawed information, cognitive mistakes, or motivational failures). Since errors in performing especially stringent duties are very serious, the prospect of errors in executing such duties requires that duty bearers offer reasons for choosing their course of action and subject them to scrutiny.

Such errors would be "serious" in the sense that the stringency of a duty resonates in the gravity of the error involved in not doing one's share in the satisfaction of that duty. Moreover, the stringency of duties of justice is also—often, though not always—reflected in the badness of the consequences for the person to whom the duty is owed when it is not satisfied. These considerations show why duty bearers should give account for how they go about their tasks. What is special about duties of justice has been exhausted at this point. But we can add that reasons—since they must be given—should be given to those in the scope of the relevant principles (or agents acting on their behalf). *Their* stringent claims are at stake. For duty bearers to give reasons to people *other than* those in the scope of such principles would without cause belittle the people in the scope of the relevant principles.[4]

The second argument for why it is plausible that duty bearers should be accountable to those in the scope of relevant principles is instrumental. Effective accountability ensures that the manner in which duty holders act is under scrutiny *on behalf of* (not necessarily *by*) those whose stringent claims are at stake. If duty bearers must give reasons to those whose claims are at stake, chances increase that justice is done. The prospect of giving a justification motivates agents to do their best for fear of embarrassment or sanctioning, and makes it unlikely that the agent will simply forget. Moreover, the justification gives the relevant population more leverage to compel agents to do their duty.

While this claim—that if duty bearers must give reasons to those whose claims are at stake, chances increase that such justice is done—might sometimes be defeated, it is very plausible. Hume called justice "the cautious, jealous virtue" (1975, 184). Justice is jealous "since it decrees each person's due, and we are jealous of our due, resent being denied it, and are apt to compare it with what others are getting" (Baier 2010, vii–viii). Those who stand to gain have reason to ensure that they do. Those who stand to lose have reason to ensure they are not burdened more than they ought to be. For the two reasons stated in the preceding paragraph, account giving makes it considerably more likely that both purposes are met.[5]

These arguments establish a loose tie between the holding of duties and accountability to those in the scope of relevant principles. This connection is "loose" since my arguments cannot deliver conclusions about the kind of accountability involved. My arguments do not entail effective accountability since those in the scope of principles might be unable to do their part. Nor, for instance, do my arguments license us to exclude intermediate accountability as one way of making good on the respect owed to the relevant people. Yet my arguments do entail that accountability should be *as effective as reasonably possible* given the circumstances under which account giving must occur. This is clear for the instrumental argument, which works the better the more effective account giving is—but by the same token, my claim also holds true for the argument from respect.

One implication is that if accountability is ultimately owed to an unorganized group, there is normative pressure to create an entity to which others are intermediately and effectively accountable and which itself owes an account to the population as a whole. That entity acts on behalf of the unorganized group, receives justifications from the relevant agents on its behalf, and in turn gives account to the global population in whichever ways remain possible, if only by publishing widely accessible accounts of its activities and by being open to debate. The link between justice and accountability does much work in this chapter and in the next.

7. Section 6 shows that those with duties of justice also have a duty to give account for how they go about realizing justice. What is the best way for states to discharge their justice-related accountability obligations? To approach that question, I argue first that, from the standpoint of accountability, domestic politics is peculiar. On the one hand, it is straightforward to establish how governments ought to account for domestic justice, namely, through democratic elections. On the other hand, it is precisely the fact that domestic justice is tied to democratic accountability that leads to a problem for the state's ability to give account to noncitizens.

Principles of justice that apply in virtue of shared membership in states hold because human beings live together under certain conditions. Crucially, the same conditions that generate principles of justice *also* make democracy the most appropriate form of governmental accountability within states. According to Dahl's (1989) plausible vision of democracy, democratic government must offer its participants possibilities for effective involvement. Participants must have adequate and equal opportunities for placing questions on the agenda and for giving reasons for endorsing one outcome over others. They must have equal opportunities to express a choice that is equal in weight to that of any other citizen. To approach collective choices with enlightened understanding, participants need adequate and equal opportunities to reach decisions. Dahl defends his conception by appeal to the values of freedom, personal development, and opportunities to satisfy urgent political concerns. However, he does not think these considerations support democratic government for just any group, but only for groups characterized by a particular understanding of a *demos* of democratic politics.

Below I say more about what such a demos is. What matters now is that these considerations in support of democracy apply straightforwardly to those jointly involved in the intense form of cooperative and coercive interaction characteristic of the enlarged Rawlsian account of membership. So we find a ready answer to the question of how governments ought to give account for what they do about domestic justice. A clear route leads from *principles of justice* that apply in virtue of shared membership in a state to a certain mode of *accountability* toward those in their scope. That route goes through what Habermas (1998) calls their *co-originality*. The particular character of shared membership in states takes us both to especially demanding principles of justice and to a highly demanding accountability mechanism.

Periodic elections confirm or replace governments. In representative democracies, governmental accountability frequently is intermediate (to parliaments). Ultimate accountability to the people is often ineffective. But in light of the co-originality of principles of domestic justice and democratic accountability, it should be unsurprising that there is much more to democratic accountability than the elections themselves. There is an intricate division of power among organizational layers within democratic states that seeks to realize a range of moral goals while keeping governance functional. Citizens encounter a state machinery that can be overwhelming and forbidding; is characterized by legal and political immediacy, as depicted in chapter 2; and may require heavy sacrifices. Still, that machinery is charged with protecting its citizens and with enabling them to build a life. Under favorable conditions, citizens grow up with some engagement with the political processes (which also makes accountability make effective). As we know since Tocqueville's *Democracy in America*, the role of elections in public life, and the activities of account giving during the campaigns that precede them, mirror a country's political culture. While their co-originality establishes a link between domestic justice and democratic accountability, the extent to which elections generate a process of *effective* account giving depends on this political culture.

Alas, this very link creates problems once we recognize that shared membership is embedded in other grounds that add to the list of principles by which governments ought to abide. A government that is democratically accountable to its citizens for domestic justice has strong incentives to neglect other duties. The problem is not merely that the dynamics of electoral politics—the ability and willingness of political parties to make promises they can realize only by neglecting other duties—might *occasionally* interfere with other values. The real problem is that voters are preoccupied with their own concerns. Politicians cater to these preoccupations, running the risk of being penalized in elections if they fail to do so. This normally implies a high degree of political inward-directedness.

To the extent that domestic politics seeks to realize justice, efforts focus on domestic principles. The problem we have detected concerns both the pursuit of justice as far as it involves noncitizens and the state's ability to give account to them. (There is no reason to think that nondemocratic governments do better on this score.) Again, from the standpoint of accountability, domestic politics is peculiar: domestic principles of justice are tied to democracy as the appropriate form of accountability. Yet not only do governments have other duties, they are also accountable to those in the scope of other principles of justice. Thus the fact that governments are accountable in this way for principles of *domestic* justice creates a challenge for finding accountability mechanisms related to *other* principles of justice.

8. Some principles associated with grounds in which shared membership in a state is embedded have all of humanity in their scope. But governments have a disincentive to give account to people other than their own citizens. Would not therefore *global democracy* be the appropriate accountability mechanism? Note that we do not reach the topic of global democracy because we are exploring what would be the best way for *global institutions* to give account to the global population, in parallel to democratic accountability within states. We are considering global democracy as a way *for states* to account for their contributions toward the realization of principles whose scope includes noncitizens. For instance, the global population might elect representatives who would be ultimately accountable to them while states would be intermediately accountable to them. Another, more demanding possibility would be that noncitizens join citizens in having voting rights with respect to the government of each state. Each government would be ultimately accountable to the world population.

According to Dahl, control over the agenda of collective decision making lies with the demos of democratic politics. That demos includes all adult members of the relevant group except transients and persons with severe mental defects. For their adult members to qualify as a demos, a group must be clearly bounded, must desire to have political autonomy and a democratic process, and must not violate other people's rights by having this process. Consensus among them must be higher than among people within other feasible domains. The benefits of creating a democratic unit must outweigh the costs.

Crucially, there is no *global* demos. Therefore it is inappropriate to employ global democratic institutions for states to give account for their contributions to justice. According to Dahl, demoi are defined in a way that involves demarcation from those who do not belong to it. So there simply could be no global demos. While that definitional problem can be solved, there could not plausibly be a global demos without a public even roughly similar to a domestic public. Yet as Robert Keohane (2006) puts it succinctly, a global public would require

> a large "imagined community"—people who share a sense of common destiny and are in the habit of communicating with one another on issues of public policy. The fate of the European constitutional treaty shows that even in the European Union, such a sense of common destiny is not yet widespread. (77)[6]

Without a global public, there is no global demos for which democratic institutions would be appropriate. So arguments for democratic mechanisms do not speak to the global case, and thus do not tell us how states ought to be accountable to the global population. Of course, civil society across nations is organized in multifarious ways. It is appropriate to talk about a *global civil society* (Kaldor 2003). In an increasingly interconnected world, many individual relationships are transnational in nature. A plentitude of charities, development organizations, faith-based organizations, professional associations, business associations, and advocacy groups draw on membership across many countries, even around the world. But a global civil society falls far short of being a global demos.

The ideas behind democracy apply to all human beings. But they have institutional implications only for appropriately organized groups. Such reasoning is familiar from part 1. Moreover, Dahl (1999) considers democracy unsuitable for global governance for another reason. As it is, citizens have little control over foreign policy within democratically governed countries. It is improbable that they could have such control over international organizations. Dahl regards such organizations as bureaucratic bargaining systems on which the democratic machinery does not bear.

Nonetheless, in recent decades much work has been done to explore whether some kind of democratic governance would be appropriate or required outside of states. Democracy, we are told, should become post-national, international, plurinational, multinational, transnational, global, or cosmopolitan.[7] Such approaches produce objections to my claim that democratic accountability is not an appropriate way for states to discharge their accountability duty to noncitizens. So, by way of contrast to Dahl, let us consider "cosmopolitan democracy," a view advocated in one form or another by theorists such as David Held (1995, 2004), Daniele Archibugi (2008), Mary Kaldor (2006), Patrick Hayden (2005), Richard Falk (1995), and Simon Caney (2005). Cosmopolitan democrats do not generally seek to abandon states. They think of states as units within a multilayered governance system. That system includes intergovernmental institutions whose members are states, as well as cosmopolitan institutions that are ultimately accountable to all human beings on a "one citizen, one vote" basis. World citizenship and national citizenship would coexist in a system of autonomous but complementary units. Representation in the UN and elsewhere should be strengthened. Transnational civil society and especially nongovernmental organizations (NGOs) should participate in governance.[8]

The aforementioned theorists argue for cosmopolitan democracy for a number of reasons: an appropriate consideration of the interests of all involved requires global democracy; democracy has bestowed more benefits than other forms of governments in domains in which it has been tried (city-states, territorial states), and there is reason to think that this will be true at the global level; international society is already thickly institutionalized, and individuals increasingly have multilayered identities, corresponding to economic globalization. These potentially overlapping identities provide the basis for participation in global civil society. In due course, states will "wither away," the demoi of domestic politics submitting to the global demos. Crucially, cosmopolitan democrats might say that the current absence of a global demos does not affect their argument. A global demos does not need to precede global democratic institutions. Instead, their creation may help with the formation of such a demos. More plausibly, gradual reform toward global democratic institutions would also gradually lead toward a global demos.

Cosmopolitan democrats are partly right. On the one hand, justice requires accountability, and requires it to be as effective as reasonably possible. Given the disincentives that democratic domestic politics creates for governments to pursue justice if it concerns only noncitizens, account giving to noncitizens is not sensibly placed into a domestic institutional framework. It is as far as these matters are concerned that the cosmopolitan democrats are correct. They are also correct that the absence of a global demos does not settle the question of how account giving should occur that does not merely address fellow citizens. But on the other hand, our results from chapter 16 imply that we should not now aim for the kind of fundamental change involved in creating a global demos. These results critically supplement the point that there currently is no global demos. Perhaps states will wither away, and we must then reconsider what counts as realistic utopia. But saying *that* is different from now urging reforms designed to create a global demos. We must find ways of holding states accountable for such matters, short of presupposing or aiming for a global demos.[9]

The results of chapter 16 and this chapter, put together, give us a good sense of where to look for acceptable accountability mechanisms, and thereby provide the transition to chapter 18. It is international organizations or other entities of global administrative law that most plausibly create the context in which states give account to noncitizens for their contributions to justice. These entities would be transnational or even global in nature but would neither presuppose nor seek to bring about a global demos. In one way or another, they would critically involve states, or at least respect their presence. At the same time, giving account within such entities is different from, and considerably more effective than, simply giving account to other states directly, without an institutional framework that structures the relevant activities and could impose sanctions. Similarly, giving account within such entities is more effective than giving account to NGOs that cannot enlist the sanctioning power of states. When we think about the design of such entities, we must be aware that centuries of learning about democracy teach little for global institutions. Those must go through a learning process that is entirely their own.

9. Let us conclude. What obligations do various institutions have to bring about justice? And do they have the further duty to give an account of their action (or inaction) on justice to the populations who would benefit? If so, how should this be done? These are the questions this chapter has been concerned with in regard to the state. To capture what states ought to do in pursuit of justice, I have introduced the notion of one ground being embedded in another. Since states are embedded in other grounds, principles not tied to shared membership in states also apply to states. I have offered a list of these principles and reflected on how the implementation of that list in political practice would affect the world.

Next we turned to the subject of accountability. I have offered a proposal of what accountability is and argued that agents are accountable to those in the scope of principles toward whose realization they have duties. As far as my account is concerned of how states should best discharge their obligation to give an account to the global population of what they do about justice, this chapter offers the negative part of my answer (that this should not involve global democracy) and a mere sketch of a positive part (that the account giving of states should occur in international organizations or perhaps other entities of global administrative law). Chapter 18 develops that part for certain principles of justice and for the WTO as such an organization. But chapter 18 also deals with the WTO in its own right, as an international organization that has obligations of justice and must account for what it does in their pursuit.

CHAPTER 18

Justice and Accountability

The World Trade Organization

1. In chapter 17 we saw that it is international organizations or other entities of global administrative law that can most plausibly provide the context in which states give account to noncitizens of their contributions to justice.[1] Chapter 17 left it at a mere sketch of that point. One goal of this concluding chapter is to explore whether a suitably reformed version of the WTO could help states fulfill their obligation to give an account of what they do to realize the various principles of justice, to the extent that those principles are concerned with or bear on trade. But the WTO is not merely of interest because it could be a venue for states to give account. What is needed in the development of pluralist internationalism now is work that applies the grounds-of-justice approach to international institutions and other forms of global rule making. To participate effectively in the global economy, governments must arguably belong to the WTO. But membership subjects countries to intrusive rules affecting the well-being of billions of people. Discussing the WTO is thus a suitable way to begin such work, and so also an appropriate way of ending this book.

I first look at the WTO from the standpoint of justice, and then turn to accountability. That is where we return to what I still owe from chapter 17, but also ask how the WTO itself ought to give account. Section 2 provides some more background information about the WTO. Much as we asked about the state, we must ask about the WTO what its duties are with regard to the realization of principles associated with different grounds. Section 3 explores what principles of justice apply to the WTO. As in the case of the state, principles other than those emerging from subjection to the trade regime apply to the WTO because the trade system is embedded in other grounds. This point creates a large mandate for the WTO as an agent of justice, at least to the extent that trade instruments are effective ways of bringing about justice. That in turn is an empirical issue that for the most part is beyond the scope of this book.

Section 4 explores some questions about what the WTO should do in pursuit of justice. First of all we must ask whether its very existence helps or impedes the realization of principles it must help realize. If it impedes their realization, then we ought to abolish the WTO. But there is a justice-based rationale for the existence of a global trade organization. The question becomes how to improve the current WTO. The problems that arise from within my theory for the WTO must be problems with regard to its ability to satisfy its obligations of justice. The sheer fact, for instance, that some countries benefit more from the WTO than others does not register as such a problem. Nonetheless, there are a fair number of such problems. Section 4 sketches a few. Next we turn to accountability. Section 5 returns to the unfinished business from chapter 17 to explain how *states* ought to account for their contributions to justice, for instance to fairness in trade. The WTO should be reformed to provide the setting within which states can do so. Section 6 explains how the WTO itself ought to give account. Section 7 sharpens my argument by suggesting that there is no justice-based rationale for a global development agency. Section 8 concludes.

2. "The necessities of traveling and trade," George Bernard Shaw writes in his *Intelligent Woman's Guide to Socialism and Capitalism*,

> and the common interest of all nations in the works and discoveries of art, literature, and science, have forced them to make international agreements and treaties with one another which are making an end of "keeping to ourselves," and throwing half bricks at foreigners and strangers. (1928, 157–58)

Today, many of these "agreements and treaties" that put an end to the "keeping to ourselves" are administered by the WTO. In 2010 the WTO had 153 members, representing more than 95 percent of world trade, and 30 observers, most seeking membership. The WTO came into being in 1995 under the Marrakesh Agreement, replacing and expanding the General Agreement on Tariffs and Trade (GATT) that had existed since 1947. While the GATT had dealt only with tariff barriers for trade in goods, other matters had become pressing over time (trade items other than goods, such as services; concerns that bear on trade, such as sanitary standards; and types of protection other than tariffs). The WTO treaty—sometimes referred to as a Global Trade Constitution (e.g., Charnovitz 2002, 377)—also includes agreements on services, intellectual property, and investment measures, as well as agreements on, for instance, sanitary barriers to trade. Agriculture and textiles, though absent from the GATT, are part of the WTO's mandate.[2]

In contrast to the GATT, the WTO is an institution, with a staff of more than six hundred and headquarters in Geneva. The organization is governed by a biannual ministerial conference, a general council responsible for administration, and immediately by a director-general appointed by the ministerial conference. Compared to the World Bank and the IMF, the WTO has few staff. Its major concern is to facilitate negotiations. The WTO is often described as a "member-driven" organization. The members themselves negotiate and implement agreements.

Members commit themselves to nondiscriminatory trade practices, using a *most-favored nation rule*: products made in one member country should be treated no less favorably than like products (very similar products) made in any other (with few and clearly specified exceptions, such as preferential treatment for developing countries). A favorable status for one member with regard to some product applies to all. Members also accept a principle of *national treatment* for foreign goods, to treat them no less favorably than national ones: domestic taxes or similar measures must not be levied differentially on domestic and foreign goods. In addition, the WTO applies a principle of reciprocity, which ensures that countries do not unilaterally benefit from nondiscrimination but offer equivalent market access. It is hard to apply this criterion to developing countries since they often lack the market shares required to respond in kind if developed countries open markets to them.

The WTO also deals with policy harmonization, and to that extent it enters the domains of domestic decision making. Most striking is the inclusion of the Agreement on Trade-Related Aspects of Intellectual Property Rights (TRIPs), which we encountered in chapter 12. The WTO tackles issues that classical arguments for free trade do not cover. TRIPs, for instance, mandates national regulatory standards, as well as means of enforcing them. Lawrence (1996) calls the model of integration followed under the GATT "shallow integration," distinguishing it from the "deep" integration that requires harmonization. The GATT exempted developing nations from many duties ("special and differential treatment"), but their concerns were absent from negotiations, notably agriculture and textiles. The inclusion of those concerns in the WTO, alongside the treaty's "single-undertaking" character—the fact that all members must accept the treaty as a whole—has ended this second-class status. But the WTO's single-undertaking character also means that new members cannot, for instance, excuse themselves from TRIPs.

If one member accuses another of violations, and if negotiations fail, the first can request adjudication. The dispute settlement mechanism permits retaliation via trade-related measures. Retaliation can occur across issues and so can be deployed in ways that hurt. The GATT allowed losing parties to block decisions. WTO rulings can only be rejected unanimously. Compared to the GATT's, the WTO's dispute settlement mechanism is considerably strengthened.

From the standpoint of economic theory, the WTO's existence may seem puzzling. (It may seem puzzling already if one thinks that some, but perhaps not all, of the things that countries must do when joining the WTO would be beneficial for them to do anyway.) According to trade theory, it would be beneficial for one country to remove barriers to imports even if other countries did not reciprocate. So why has a system of treaties been necessary to ensure that everyone does it? Why in particular do trade agreements describe removing barriers as a "concession" by a country, if doing so is advantageous? The answer is that it is easier for governments to sustain the commitments necessary to obtain the benefits of such arrangements (e.g., to overcome domestic resistance driven by special interests that might lose when trade barriers are reduced, even though the country as a whole benefits) if they have promised to do so in an international agreement. Moreover, as Narlikar (2005) explains,

> if countries have some mechanisms of binding themselves and each other to commitments in tariff reductions, the risk of retaliatory trade war ... is reduced. Herein lies the logic of multilateral trade liberalization. An international trade organization establishes rules of reciprocity on a generalized basis across three or more countries, and thereby multilateralizes reciprocity. By monitoring and enforcing these rules, the multilateral trade organization guards against cheating and defection by member countries. (5)

3. What duties of justice does the WTO have? To answer this question, we can use the approach from section 2 of chapter 17. I recall here that every institution has the duty to do what it can, within limits, to bring about the necessary conditions of just distributions. To answer the question of what duties the WTO has, the first step, in my pluralistic theory, is to ask, which of the various principles does the WTO have a duty to do what it can, within limits, to try to realize? As for states, we must ask whether there is a ground most closely linked with the WTO. This is (obviously) shared subjection to the global trading system. Chapter 14 discussed principles of justice (or fairness) in trade. States have obligations to bring about this kind of justice, and so does the WTO. In fact, the relationship between the WTO and this principle is parallel to that between states and the Rawlsian principles. In chapter 17 we noted that this principle of justice in trade drops out of the list of principles that apply to *states*—not because trade does not generate demands of justice but because the principles on that list are general enough to absorb them. But given the policy domain for which the WTO has been put in place, that is not the case here. Next we ask in which other grounds that ground is embedded, and are directed to collective ownership of the earth, membership in the global order, and common humanity. We conclude that the relevant principles with regard to which the WTO has obligations are those associated with these four grounds.

These results contradict views that limit the WTO to trade liberalization. Nonetheless, the extent to which the WTO must be guided by principles associated with those other grounds is bounded by what trade can achieve, which is an empirical question. Still, just as states cannot limit themselves to duties in virtue of shared membership, the WTO cannot ex ante limit itself to trade regulation.[3] One striking consequence of the result that the WTO has duties to realize principles that have all of humanity in their scope is that the WTO has obligations to the citizens of nonmember countries as well as to those of member countries.

The WTO is already officially concerned with more than trade or efficiency. The preamble of the Marrakesh Agreement talks about "reciprocal and mutually advantageous arrangements directed to the substantial reduction of tariffs and other barriers to trade." Yet these goals should be pursued "with a view to raising standards of living, ensuring full employment and a large and steadily growing volume of real income and effective demand," as well as with a view to ensuring that "developing countries, and especially the least developed among them, secure a share in the growth in international trade commensurate with the needs of their economic development."[4] Limited as it is, moral language appears in the WTO's mandate. This language ought to include justice.

We can make another argument to assess what duties the WTO has when it comes to justice. Entities that are empowered by states and whose activities affect the satisfaction of the obligations to which states are subject ought to assist states with their duties. In virtue of having been founded by and receiving power from states, such entities are subject to demands of justice that apply to states, namely, those with regard to the domain for which they were founded. Therefore, the WTO ought to help states realize obligations *they* have in virtue of being involved with the trade system. What is important to note is that this implication also concerns *purely domestic* obligations of trade.

We have yet to discuss how the WTO ought to be accountable, which adds demands on the organization. However, a commitment to *justice* ought to be added to the moral commitments in the mandate. Most important, given the set of principles of justice that internationalism advances, the WTO must have a human rights–oriented mandate. Since the view of human rights that I have defended implies a duty of assistance in building institutions, the WTO also has a development-oriented mandate that derives from this human rights–oriented mandate.

4. Let us consider how the WTO should be transformed. The first question we need to answer is whether its very existence helps or impedes the realization of the principles in whose realization it ought to assist. But if no trade organization with global aspirations had been founded yet, it would be the case that we ought to found one now. We saw in chapter 17 that the realities of domestic politics prove obstacles to governments taking seriously duties of justice pertaining to noncitizens. Therefore, there should be *transnational* entities whose member governments both coordinate and account for efforts to realize principles whose scope is not limited to fellow citizens. Because of the *global* nature specifically of trade, such coordination and account giving with regard to trade-related matters should not occur in regional entities. They should take place in a global trade organization. And because there is a system of multiple states, we readily find a justice-based rationale for the existence of the WTO: the existence of such an organization makes it more likely that justice will be done as far as trade is concerned.[5]

But it may be the case that this organization ought to be very different from the current WTO. To see what is at stake, I note what Michalopoulos (2002) considers the benefits of WTO membership. First, membership strengthens domestic institutions for the conduct of trade. Such strengthening is required prior to accession to the WTO. Second, membership improves the ease and security of access to export markets. Third, membership provides access to a dispute settlement mechanism for trade issues. The second point throws light on what is involved in *not* being a member. Not being in the WTO means that members, especially large countries with market power, may impose tariffs when times are bad, and one cannot demand change if the policies of members frustrate one's prospects. The second and third points illuminate how the WTO creates certainty in the trade rules, which is generally advantageous for weaker countries. As Narlikar (2005, 7) says, "if a country is small and weak, its international economic life without an international trade organization would be 'nasty, brutish, and short.'"

But crucially, saying that there are benefits to joining the WTO *as it is,* and even saying that these benefits provide conclusive reasons for joining, is consistent with saying that joining a different global trade organization would be better still, for some or all countries. Actors incur differential opportunity costs from participating in the trade system. Powerful players can impose terms on weaker ones that have no realistic alternative to joining the organization largely as it is. Indeed, saying that there are these benefits to joining is also consistent with saying that for many states, joining the WTO as it is now, or not joining at all, is a choice between the Scylla of subjection to unwanted and perhaps unreasonable norms and the Charybdis of isolation.[6]

On the other hand, there is a problem for my theory if (and only if, with the exception of accountability issues) something about the WTO makes human rights less likely to be realized, future generations more likely to be ignored, tainted gains from trade more likely to be enjoyed, and so on. The problem for my theory arises only if the institutional design of the WTO leads to violations of principles of justice that generate obligations for the institution. It is not problematic by itself, for example, if some countries benefit more within the WTO than others. The specific questions that arise include the following: Does joining the WTO make it more or less likely that a country that does not respect human rights will come to do so? What could the WTO do differently to make it more likely (or even more likely)? What does the WTO do, and what could it do, to reduce the number of states enjoying the sort of tainted gains from trade that are the focus of the principle of justice in chapter 14? To what extent is trade policy designed to help discharge the duty of assistance in building institutions?

These questions raise issues beyond what I can sensibly discuss here. Let me only mention a few matters, mostly drawing attention to problems rather than offering solutions. One crucial issue is the lack of power for poor countries in rule making. From the standpoint of justice, this is a problem because it creates a high risk that WTO policies will not have the best interests of the global poor in mind, including their interest in having justice realized. According to Hoekman (2002), the WTO's member-driven nature strains some national delegations: "Many countries have no more than one or two persons dealing with WTO matters; a large minority has no delegations in Geneva at all" (47–48). Barton et al. (2006) plainly doubt the WTO's member-driven character, insisting that "the reality of a complex organization supported by an educated and sophisticated staff is not entirely consistent with this image" (212). Both assessments draw attention to the problem that many decisions are made by informal blocks of powerful nations that meet frequently (and so work in a manner that would overstretch the resources of smaller members) and enjoy the assistance of a sophisticated staff—a practice accompanied by a lack of transparency and predictability for those excluded from the caucuses. Officially, the WTO is a one-member, one-vote organization, its decisions being consensus-based (consensus designating absence of disagreement). But since many members are effectively excluded from influence, WTO procedures favor the powerful.[7]

A related matter is that poor countries face difficulties maneuvering the dispute settlement system. The system is generally highly regarded. According to Barton et al. (2006), the WTO's process

> is by far the most effective international dispute settlement process. Although it is natural that some of its decisions and processes are criticized, few would say that it is not a basically fair process or that there has been corruption. The system uses high-quality decision makers, has the power to enforce a signifi-

cant and specific body of international law, and has control over a trade sanction that seems to be of just the right strength both to be politically acceptable and to generally induce compliance. (210)[8]

Yet the system depends on compliance. Suppose powerful countries fail to comply, and in response smaller countries wish to retaliate through trade sanctions. But such retaliation is of little use for countries without an impact on world market prices; they cannot harm or benefit other countries through trade measures. Monetary compensation would sometimes be preferable for smaller countries. Moreover, since participation requires staff and expertise, countries are not equally able to benefit from the system.[9]

Underrepresentation of the poor, asymmetrical capacities to take advantage of the system, and the informal exercise of power are widely acknowledged problems. Narlikar (2005) characterizes the WTO in terms of an unsustainable discrepancy between "extreme legalization, particularly in the enforcement of its rules through the dispute settlement mechanism, on the one hand, and an inordinate reliance on de facto improvisation in the making of those rules, on the other" (42; see also Narlikar 2009). There are various ways of defending the WTO from those charges. To facilitate the participation of poor countries, the WTO offers variable transition times. International donors and nongovernmental organizations (NGOs) aid developing countries with capacity building. In 2001, the Advisory Centre on WTO Law opened in Geneva. Moreover, proposals to render enforcement of WTO rules independent of economic power have long been around, such as the proposal to allow *coalitions* of countries to take responsibility for enforcement.[10] Developing countries themselves have sought better ways of coordinating and articulating stances. But these defenses cannot dispel the worries. Since the same worries—which call for more empowerment of the poor—also arise for accountability, I return to this subject below.

Another crucial question is to what extent, or in what ways, deep integration is suitable to discharging the duty of assistance in building institutions. One concern is that policy harmonization constrains the freedom of poor states to take measures that might aid development. For instance, harmonizing commerce infrastructures deprives countries of the flexibility to protect themselves with tariffs during crises. At one end of the spectrum of views on the advisability of such harmonization, Rodrik (2007) proposes to regard the WTO as "an organ that manages the interface between different national practices and institutions" rather than as "an instrument for the harmonization of economic policies and practices across countries" (215). He finds no convincing evidence associating trade liberalization with subsequent growth ("while global markets are good for poor countries, the rules by which they are being asked to play the game are often not," 240). Stiglitz and Charlton (2006) concur. Considering countries in Latin America and East Asia, they argue that

> it is inappropriate for the world trading system to be implementing rules which circumscribe the ability of developing countries to use both trade and industry policies to promote industrialization. The current trend to force a narrow straightjacket of policy harmonization on developing countries is simply not justified by the available evidence. (17)

This negative take on deep integration would require fairly radical reform to redesign the WTO so that it stops requiring deep integration as a condition of membership.[11]

At the other end of that spectrum we find, for instance, Barry and Reddy (2008), who explore ways in which the WTO could help implement a link between trade and labor standards. Such linkage is desirable because it creates incentives for governments to improve labor standards. Rights to trade would be conditional on the promotion of labor standards. Thus, deep integration is useful, and should be used, for the promotion of human rights. My argument about which principles of justice apply to the WTO supports such a linkage proposal. More generally, my argument supports proposals to make rights to trade conditional on the promotion of human rights and the eschewing of tainted gains from trade—but only if there is no empirical argument leading to the conclusion that doing so would backfire and would make these goals less likely to be realized rather than more.

A final issue concerns accession. Negotiations about joining the treaty are often arduous and asymmetrical. Each member can impose conditions (*beyond* the treaties), but the applicants are generally in no position to do so. However, the WTO has obligations to nonmembers, in virtue of having duties that correspond to principles that have all of humanity in their scope. Since countries cannot afford to stay away, one straightforward way of filling these obligations with content is to insist that existing members not use the accession process to their advantage.[12]

5. Let us turn to accountability. States in particular ought to give an account to potential beneficiaries about what they are doing in pursuit of justice. In chapter 17, I did not finish answering the question of how states should do this when the account is owed to noncitizens, or indeed to all humanity. Global democracy does not provide a mechanism through which states ought to do so. Account giving to NGOs by itself does not offer a solution since such organizations cannot make account giving ef-

fective, for want of available sanctions and rewards. Nor should states give accounts to other states outside a framework that could appropriately organize and direct their powers to sanction and reward. International organizations, especially those whose members are states, could do so, and so provide the most plausible location for states to give account to noncitizens.

Among those, the organization devoted to regulating trade is the natural candidate within which states ought to account for their pursuit of fairness in trade, as well as for the realization of other principles that can be effectively pursued via trade instruments. Governments should participate in the WTO partly as account givers, partly as recipients qua representatives of their people. Within WTO structures, governments should explain how they seek to realize justice, subjecting themselves to scrutiny by other governments, WTO staff, and plausibly also NGOs or independent experts. (NGOs may already attend WTO ministerial conferences.) States would be intermediately accountable to the WTO (which would be utilized to achieve effectiveness) but would ultimately be accountable to the global population. To be accountable to the WTO would mean to be accountable to other states organized within the WTO, but also to WTO staff and suitable NGOs.

For instance, for the principle of justice in trade—that the distribution of gains from trade is just only if no country enjoys gains that have come at the expense of people involved with the trade—states should have to give periodic reports on whether or not their benefits from imports or exports are tainted in this way. WTO expertise should help determine what kind of gains would count as tainted. NGOs and independent experts may also help with the problem that many governments do not represent their people. Care must be taken that NGOs increase the effectiveness of account giving rather than that of special interests.[13]

Effective account giving requires that the recipients be in a position to pass informed judgment and impose sanctions. This takes us back to the subject of empowerment of poor members. Such empowerment is essential (to make sure the WTO takes seriously its duties in pursuit of justice, and to make sure effective account giving occurs) and is the crucial element of my proposal for how to think about the state's accountability to those in the scope of principles that are not associated with membership in a state (to the extent that these are tied to trade). Poor countries must have standing in the WTO. At least, they must be properly represented. This requires financial and logistical support, which richer members must provide. As we saw chapter 17, it is a duty of justice to make account giving as effective as reasonably possible.

Account giving ought to occur within both adjudication and rule-making processes. However, increased empowerment would complicate dispute settlements and negotiations. Narlikar (2009) writes that transparency, to the extent that there has been more of it, has decreased the WTO's efficiency. Not only does increased empowerment (which presumably here involves increased transparency) entail taking longer to reach agreement, but inefficiency may decrease commitment to the process. The problem is bigger for rule making (negotiations) than for dispute settlement, which involves only a relatively few actors each time. As far as adjudication is concerned, empowerment means that all members can equally take advantage of the WTO machinery. But what are the institutional implications of such empowerment for the rule-making process?

Narlikar (2005) argues that the only way of overcoming inefficiency in making decisions (which she discusses with regard to a situation prior to additional empowerment) is to create an executive board. Any such proposal leads to the inevitably controversial question of how that board would be composed. Another proposal is to adapt the deliberative-polyarchic structure Cohen and Sabel (2006) detect in the EU (see chapter 17). As a matter of justice, the WTO has a human rights–oriented mandate, and derivatively a development-oriented mandate. What this amounts to depends on how trade regulation is best used to that end, which is an empirical question that goes beyond what I can do here. Similarly, accountability requires that WTO members be empowered to participate effectively, but what this means practically is a matter of institutional design we cannot settle from within the grounds-of-justice approach. In any event, the accountability mechanisms must be strong enough to have access to effective sanctions even against powerful countries. And that, of course, is a target that is not easy to reach.

Some might worry that if international organizations can sanction governments, there is a cost to the value democracy (see Dahl 1999). But domestic democracy is normatively constrained through principles of justice other than those associated with shared membership, as well as through accompanying accountability mechanisms. The "costs" incurred by such implications of a theory of justice are therefore acceptable.[14] But these alleged costs are in any event not too cumbersome. After all, pluralist internationalism does not imply that the WTO should give votes to countries depending on population size any more than it implies that there ought to be global democracy. Nor does it support the determination of detailed trade policies by majority rule among countries. Keohane and Nye (2003) are correct that it would be a category mistake to seek to make the WTO genuinely democratic. The trade system falls short of the thick structures that characterize states. A weaker set of principles of justice applies within this system. What kind of accountability is required also reflects these differences.

6. We have discussed what principles apply to the WTO, and the ways in which the WTO should be the setting in which states account for their contributions toward fairness in trade and other principles of justice. This leads to the question of how the WTO itself should give account. As an institution with obligations of justice, the WTO also has obligations to give account to the relevant populations (in its case, the population of trading states and the global population of individuals). As the organization that provides the setting for the accounts given by states to the population of trading states and the global population, the WTO in turn owes an account to those on whose behalf it is working.

For each state giving account for what it does in pursuit of justice the account recipients are other states, suitable NGOs, and the WTO staff. One reason why states need the WTO as a setting in which they can give account is because it is impossible to have effective accountability directly with an unorganized global population. One might wonder whether the WTO itself can have an effective accountability relationship with the global population. We should not introduce an additional organization to this end (which would have to be accountable in some other way as well). Instead, the WTO's account giving should be to governments, to the extent that those represent their populations. The chief administrators of the WTO should explain to government representatives (including representatives of nonmembers) how the organization contributes to the realization of principles that have humanity as a whole in their scope, or, for the principle of justice concerning trade, the population of trading states.

Since the WTO is a member-driven organization, however, and since those members are mostly states, we should make sure the WTO's account giving is not limited to states. Otherwise such account giving would be too much like talking to oneself (except for the nonmembers). To make account giving as effective as is reasonably possible, it should include also NGOs. Equally sensible would be the development of a deliberative polyarchy among the WTO and organizations like the World Bank and the IMF. The creation of a think tank to provide expertise may also help make account giving effective and help explore how trade-related measures can assist in the pursuit of justice.

7. To sharpen my discussion of the WTO, let me contrast my case for a global trade organization with that for a global development agency, such as the World Bank.[15] For the same reasons as in the trade case, states should coordinate efforts to satisfy their duty of assistance, as well as the relevant account giving, in the framework of transnational entities. (Let us assume now that we are talking about the non-trade-related aspects of

duties of assistance.) However, there is no reason why a *global* organization ought to be charged with these purposes, or why there should be a single biggest or otherwise most distinguished such institution. As chapter 4 noted, several different views on how to go about satisfying a duty of assistance exist. There is considerable disagreement on how best to help developing countries. Even within the institutional stance, various approaches persist about how to do so. Plausibly, the overall aid efforts would be more successful if they were more dispersed—or even more dispersed, since organizations other than the World Bank are already in the business of devising development projects. It is unlikely that one global organization could embrace a range of approaches to how best to achieve development and more likely that separate organizations could do so.

There is, then, no justice-based rationale for a world development agency similar to the one we encountered for a trade organization in section 4. What then should we make of the existence of the World Bank? One unconvincing response is that we should not seek a justice-based rationale for its existence; rather, we should think of the World Bank *as a bank*, a voluntary effort to contribute to economic improvement around the world. On the other hand, every institution has the duty to do what it can, within limits, to bring about the necessary conditions of just distribution, as described in principles of justice. Moreover, the World Bank is too important an agency for development for us not to assess it from the standpoint of justice. And there is, after all, a duty of assistance in building institutions that is implied by my theory of human rights. Insofar as such an entity already exists, it should be reformed in such a way that it consciously is the global institution that coordinates efforts to satisfy that duty and provides a setting for states to give account of their efforts in its pursuit.

Similar reform proposals as we discussed for the WTO then apply to the World Bank. Implementing these proposals would change its character considerably. It would mean, for instance, an endorsement of human rights as membership rights in the global order. (The World Bank does not currently use a human rights framework, fearing it is too political.) Moreover, such reforms would involve a shift away from the responsibility of the governance structure to the countries that provide the funds and dominate the board. That structure should be responsible to those to whom assistance is owed. In a nutshell, either there should be no single organization of such breadth, depth, and influence in development to begin with, or else—and because this institution already exists, this seems the better course to pursue—the organization ought to be reformed (parallel to how the WTO ought to be reformed) to be the single most distinguished institution in charge of coordinating efforts to realize a duty of assistance while *also* providing the setting in which states account for their efforts to that effect.

8. Let us conclude. Entities in global administrative law ought to be utilized to hold each state accountable to noncitizens in the scope of a principle of justice which states have an obligation to try to realize. The WTO specifically should be utilized to hold states accountable to the extent that their duties turn on trade. Additional inquiries about institutional design are needed to make sure accountability is effective. What is required, in any event, is a strengthening of the representation of poor countries, as well as measures that ensure that the perspective of the people is considered even if their governments do not represent them. Measures to strengthen the representation of the poor require efforts that would change the WTO substantially.

Inquiries into what we ought to do to realize justice may call for new institutions. For trade, there already exists an institution we can charge with some relevant tasks. The WTO is only one of the organizations whose role we must reconsider in light of what pluralist internationalism requires. And formal organizations are only one among several kinds of entities in global administrative law whose role in the realization of justice we must either reconsider or explore in the first place. Cicero finished section 41 of the first book of *De Officiis* with "De iustitia satis dictum"—*enough has been said about justice*—though he went on to say much more about justice in later parts of the work. Let me end this book in the same spirit. Enough has now been said about justice. And much more work remains to be done.

Notes

1. For Hegel, see the preface to *Elements of the Philosophy of Right* (1991, 21). Regarding *De Cive*, see Skinner (1989).

2. The term "scope" does not do much independent work. "Not much": grounds do not always uniquely fix the scope. Yet once the grounds are fixed, disagreement about the scope should be relatively minor, of the magnitude of a dispute about who exactly counts as a citizen, given that this matter is largely fixed through legal rules.

3. *Metaphysics of Morals,* Doctrine of Right, sec. 49.E.I (Kant 1996, 473). Hume says that "No virtue is more esteem'd than justice, and no vice more detested than injustice" (1978, 577). Adam Smith begins his *Lectures on Jurisprudence* by pointing out that the "first and chief design of every government is to maintain justice" (1978, 5).

4. (1) Grounds differ from *circumstances* of justice, but the difference becomes clearest within a view that acknowledges multiple grounds. "The circumstances of justice obtain," explains John Rawls (1999b), following David Hume, "whenever persons put forward conflicting claims to the division of social advantages under conditions of moderate scarcity" (110). So both circumstances and grounds tell us "when demands of justice apply," but do so in different senses. Circumstances of justice are those living conditions of human beings under which *any* principles of justice apply *in the first place.* If we live under these circumstances, the grounds specify *which* principles apply to *which* people. See also Barry (1978; 1989c, 152–69). (2) Walzer (1983) offers a theory of "spheres" of justice. His point is that there is a set of distinct spheres for different goods valued by society that have their own distributive principles. Justice requires that the distribution of goods in each sphere must be independent of the distribution in other spheres. That idea is orthogonal to my approach since Walzer talks about the distribution of goods within a society. Shared membership in a state is a ground of justice, and I assume that something like Rawls's two principles holds for domestic societies (see below). The debate with Walzer is located there. Forst (2002) talks about "contexts of justice." Offering a view that is meant to be intermediate between liberalism and communitarianism, he distinguishes among four conceptions of person and community that correspond to four normative contexts (the conceptions of the person being the ethical person, the legal person, citizenship, and the moral person). Justice within one society provides a suitable unity to these contexts. This approach, too, is orthogonal to mine, for the same reason that Walzer's is (except that Forst is further away from discussing actual distribution).

5. Fleischacker talks about distributive rather than social justice. For a discussion of different concepts of justice across the history of philosophy, see Raphael (2001).

6. In contrast is a description of the workings of divine justice on the Day of Resurrection in the Qur'an: "The earth will shine with the light of its Lord; the Record of Deeds will be laid open; the prophets and witnesses will be brought in. Fair judgment will be given between them: they will not be wronged and every soul will be repaid in full for what it has done. He knows best what they do" (39:69–70).

7. (1) I also apply the terms "(non-)relationist" or "(non-)relational" to grounds as adjectives. I use the term "relationship" sufficiently broadly for relationists and nonrelationists to register as offering different accounts of the (by stipulation, for now, unique) justice relationship. The term "relationship" does not differentiate between relationists and nonrelationists. (2) Whether a relation is essentially practice-mediated may be ambiguous. A case in point is the relation of being co-owners of the earth, discussed in part 2 of this book. But that question does not matter deeply because internationalism transcends the distinction between relationism and nonrelationism. For the same reason, there is no need to explain in detail what is meant by "practices," other than that practices amount to patterns of behavior that involve rule following and are governed by mutual expectations. (3) Nothing here should create a prejudgment in favor of a relational or comparativist view of justice, a view that contrasts, for instance, with a sufficientarian understanding. The distinction between relationism and nonrelationism occurs at the level of *grounds* of justice, not at the level of *principles*.

8. Miller (2007, 32–33) reminds us that "arbitrary" sometimes means "undeserved" and sometimes "should make no difference." Differences in needs are undeserved but should make a difference. The manner in which I have introduced nonrelationism above seeks to characterize this position in a way that avoids pitfalls from this ambiguity. See also Nozick (1974, 227): That a fact is arbitrary from a moral point of view "might mean that there is no moral reason why the fact ought to be that way, or it might mean that the fact's being that way is of no moral significance and has no moral consequences. Rationality, the ability to make choices, and so on, are not morally arbitrary in this second sense." Nonrelationists are concerned about avoiding arbitrariness in Miller's and Nozick's respectively first senses. Tan (2004) captures the nonrelationist's concern with arbitrariness: "At the foundational level of deliberation about global justice, impartiality requires that we do not allow people's nationality to influence our views of what people's baseline entitlements are. This is what the cosmopolitan ideal of impartial justice calls for. A person's nationality, a mere accident of birth, cannot by itself be a reason for giving her greater consideration at the foundational level" (158; see also 27–28 and 159–60). For similar statements, see Pogge (1989, 247) and Moellendorf (2002, 55–56, 79).

9. For an attempt to keep the term "cosmopolitanism" useful by employing it in various senses, see Miller (2007, chap. 2), Scheffler (2001b), and Tan (2004, chap. 3). Will Kymlicka (2002) (following a suggestion by Ronald Dworkin) claims that all plausible political theories populate an "egalitarian plateau." Plausible theories of domestic justice define "the social, economic and political conditions under which the members of the community are treated as equals" (Kymlicka 2002, 4).

10. (1) If this is not intuitive, let me explain how internationalism is "between" those standard views. For set S the power set PS of S is the set of all subsets of S, including the empty set and S itself. Suppose M is a subset of S. Suppose we have the following subsets of PS: first, the subset that contains only M; second, a subset that contains M, S, and some other subsets of S that all include M; and third, the subset of PS containing only S. That second subset is "in between" the first and the third in the sense that each member of the second is contained in the one member of the third, and the one member of the first is contained in each member of the second subset. One standard view thinks only persons who share a state are in the scope of principles of justice. The other thinks all human beings are. The grounds-of-justice view distinguishes among several grounds. One such ground is shared only by those who jointly belong to a state, some others (common humanity, membership in the global order, collective ownership of the earth) by all of humanity, yet another by at least most of humanity (subjection to the trading system). In terms of the set-theoretic illustration, S is all of humanity, and M is all individuals in some country. Other sets would be formed by respectively those individuals who are in the scope of some principles of justice. The state is the smallest unit to which principles of distributive justice apply, and principles that apply among those who do not share a state always either include all or none of those who do. (2) Some of my terminology draws on Sangiovanni (2007). However, my usage deviates from his. For instance, globalism, on my account, is a relationist view. Wolff (2009) articulates the need for a "layered" view of justice at the global level, focusing on differences among norms of cooperation; see also Armstrong (2009). (3) For this terminology to demarcate differences at a fundamental level, I assume a nonconsequentialist background theory. We would then, e.g., not assume that social welfare provides the background theory in terms of which distributive justice is developed, as in Hume or Mill. Instead, social welfare is a competing value against which one must delineate justice, as in Rawls. (4) Internationalism transcends relationism and nonrelationism in *two* ways: by arguing that there is more than one ground *and* by arguing that these grounds may be either relationist or nonrelationist. There is logical space for pluralist relationism and pluralist nonrelationism, views that agree with internationalism in asserting a plurality of grounds but argue that these grounds are all either relationist or nonrelationist. (Perhaps the later Rawls, with his distinction between domestic and international public reason, is a pluralist relationist.)

11. Johann Gottlieb Fichte's treatise *Der Geschlossene Handelsstaat* (*The Closed Commercial State;* Reiss 1955, 86–126) offers a peculiar response to globalization. Published in 1800, Fichte's book argues that countries ought to transform themselves into exclusive entities without trade connections to other countries. They may even go to war to create a territory in which autarky can be developed. Afterward, only scientists and artists may interact with people elsewhere. Since countries would be self-contained, they have no reason to go to war. In a Fichtean world, no grounds of justice other than shared membership in a state (and perhaps common humanity) are salient.

12. Bull (1977, chap. 10) also adds a disarmed world, a system of states characterized by more solidarity, one of many nuclear powers, one of ideological

homogeneity, a system of isolated states, and a new medievalism. Finer (1997) offers an overview of what government has amounted to over the millennia. Mann (1986/1993) addresses the sociology of power, including the state. Vincent (1987) discusses many of the questions that arise about the state from a historical and social science perspective.

13. Rawls's way of making justice *central* to an assessment of institutions has a counterpart at the level of personal virtue in the Old Testament. When Solomon worries about his aptitude for kingship, he asks God for the ability to administer justice; see Kings 1:3. Geuss (2005, chap. 1) insists that modern political philosophy attaches no salience to justice.

14. Discussed mainly in section 15, primary goods gain most mileage from objections to utilitarianism's stance that *aggregate* happiness be *maximized* (see secs. 5 and 29). Yet the "equality-of-what" debate shows that, first, one can endorse welfare as currency while rejecting its *maximization*, and second, the prima facie range of currencies also includes Dworkin's "resources," Arneson's "opportunities for welfare," Cohen's "access to advantage," or Sen's "capabilities"—and thus currencies that could as well be used to resist utilitarianism. See Dworkin (1981, 2000), Arneson (1989, 1990b), Cohen (1989), and Sen (1985, 1993).

15. "Something like them": I introduce two principles that guide the choice of a distribuendum; from there we get no knock-down argument to the precise formulation of social primary goods that Rawls uses. A currency is "subjective" if the satisfaction of principles of justice formulated in terms of that currency must be verified at least in part by reference to claims either about mental states or about the correspondence of states of the world to mental states. Examples are welfare defined in terms of experiential states and welfare defined in terms of the satisfaction of desires or long-term plans. A currency is objective if it is not subjective. Thanks to Robert Hockett for joint research into the foundations of primary goods.

16. For a discussion of publicity in Rawls, see Larmore (2003); see also Williams (1998).

17. (1) For the relevance of the fact that principles of justice can be used in deliberations, see Rawls (1999c, 114). To some extent, Dworkin's resources and Sen's capabilities satisfy these constraints. Dworkin's resources, however, were designed without attention to the guidance constraint, whereas Rawls emphasizes the affinities between capabilities and primary goods (Rawls 2001, 168). So my argument supports other currencies *to the extent* that they display the same virtues as primary goods. (2) See also Arneson (2008) for a nonrelationist take on the issues discussed here. The relationism–nonrelationism distinction also bears on the question of how to assess the relationship between justice and other moral concepts. For instance, freedom may be conceptualized as limiting the range of goods society distributes, or alternatively, in terms of individual liberties, be counted among the goods that society distributes. Thinking of justice as the most important virtue of institutions, as Rawls does, requires that we see it as encompassing values such as equality and liberty rather than as competing with them. Nonrelationists proceed differently. (3) G. A. Cohen (2008) objects both to the content of Rawls's principles (that they license too much inequality) and to their metaethical

status as derived through the device of the original position (conditions under which Rawls assumes principles of justice are chosen). Cohen's metaethical concern is that Rawls's device forces him to take seriously considerations as bearing on justice that should not matter that way (e.g., considerations of publicity). Therefore, says he, Rawls cannot appropriately distinguish *justice* from *social regulation*. If so, I cannot help myself to Rawls's principles as I do in this book. But that dispute is orthogonal to my account. For any answer to the question of what counts as grounds, we must reassess how to arrive at principles of justice to see what to make of a possible distinction between justice and social regulation. This response is admittedly superficial. Any account of what is meant by "grounds of justice" that explores in detail the ways in which such grounds are norm-generating is likely to involve the very metaethics that is at issue between Rawls and Cohen. I will not pursue that matter.

18. See Freeman (2007a, chaps. 8, 9). I distinguished inquiries into global justice from inquiries into international justice in a way that classifies Rawls's *Law of Peoples* as an inquiry into international justice. Rawls does talk about a basic structure of the Society of Peoples (1999b, 61–62). So it seems that for him, all principles of justice presuppose some kind of a basic structure, whereas *distributive* justice presupposes the particular kind of basic structure present in a state.

19. Wenar (2006) responds to critics who think *Law of Peoples* is incoherent with Rawls's earlier work (Caney 2002). Crucially, both in the domestic and in the global case Rawls draws on ideas implicit in the public political culture. Rawls believes "that humans should be coerced only according to a self-image that is acceptable to them," which means in particular that "since 'global citizens' cannot be presumed to view themselves as free and equal individuals who should relate fairly to each other across national boundaries, we cannot legitimately build coercive social institutions that assume that they do" (Wenar 2006, 103). Wenar rightly uses this observation to explain why Rawls did not advocate global egalitarian ideals of a sort that, say, Beitz (1999) and Pogge (1989) found natural as an extension of his domestic principles.

20. One may object that on my wider understanding of distributive justice, at least Rawls's duty of assistance to burdened societies would count as a duty of distributive justice. That is plausible, but Rawls does little to explain why such a duty would apply at all. One purpose of recognizing different grounds is to make sure the argumentative work that connects grounds with principles is actually done.

21. As is common in philosophical texts, I capitalize the names of certain positions or conditions. I do so to remind the reader that although these concepts tend to be used in a broad sense (and may also appear in my own text in a broad sense), they stand for a specific and well-defined position or condition in the given context.

CHAPTER 2

1. For the Leibniz essay, see Leibniz (1864). On the Treaty of Westphalia, see Krasner (1993), Dickmann (1959), and Gross (1948).

2. Strictly speaking, state membership per se is not the ground. The ground is *whatever it is* about life in states that makes it the case that some principles apply only within states. This could in principle (and, on the account I offer, actually does) turn out to be something only contingently associated with membership in states as they have been historically understood.

3. Principles are (fully) egalitarian if in some sense they prescribe an equal socioeconomic status for each person in their scope. (Let us assume we are only talking about theories that agree that each person in the scope of principles of justice has equal political status, to avoid clumsy formulations.) Principles could then be more or less egalitarian depending on the degree to, and the ways in, which they permit inequality in that status. One way in which principles may be less egalitarian than others (or less than fully egalitarian) is by not counting among the distribuenda all goods that contribute to socioeconomic status. Another way is by not taking offense at particular sources of inequality (they may not be concerned with inequalities arising from genetic differences but only with those arising from social privileges), or by finding inequalities acceptable if they serve certain purposes (as Rawls does by accepting inequalities that benefit all, including the least advantaged). A third way in which principles may be less egalitarian than others is to prescribe distributions that are not concerned with relative socioeconomic status at all, but only with absolute status (e.g., sufficientarian principles). Principles are broadly egalitarian if they are either fully egalitarian or else are less than fully egalitarian in ways that I sketched but still forbid some inequalities in socioeconomic status.

4. I disregard differences between citizenship and permanent residency and speak of shared membership in states. Membership is a fluid concept, also because of temporary residents and illegal long-term residents. Difficult questions arise. Some people may have less than full citizenship status, which by itself is unproblematic. People's dealings with a certain state, after all, may require presence in the state, which must be legally regulated but does not call for permanent residency. Such people's involvement with the state may change in time, and so they may become gradually naturalized. Difficulties arise when people break the rules of getting integrated into the state and thereby trigger the question of whether this should undo their membership status altogether. Difficulties also arise when partial citizenship status is symptomatic of injustice; see Blake (2002).

5. Morris (1998) lists the following features of the state: continuity in space and time; transcendence (the state does not coincide with the persons of the ruler or the ruled but is a distinct entity), political organization (the state consists of a separate set of institutions that are formally coordinated and relatively centralized), authority (the state is sovereign, hence the ultimate source of authority in its territory), and allegiance (the state expects and receives loyalty from its inhabitants) (46–47). Simone Weil remarks laconically, "It would be difficult to give an exact definition of the State. But it is, unfortunately, only too obvious that the word stands for something very real" (1971, 115).

6. The distinction between "ideal" and "nonideal" theory has recently come up for much discussion. I help myself to Rawls's understanding of the distinction. Ideal theory assumes, first, that "(nearly) everyone strictly complies with … the

principles of justice" (Rawls 2001, 13). Second, ideal theory assumes favorable circumstances (e.g., Rawls 1999c, 216), including economic and social background conditions. Economic and social conditions must not preclude the realization of political ideals, such as a just society. The envisaged ideal must be a "realistic utopia" and so must remain feasible (see chapter 16). Ideal theory helps itself to basic facts about human psychology and does not ask of people what they could comply with only with overwhelming difficulties. To that extent Rawls, like Rousseau in his *Social Contract,* takes men as they are and laws as they might be. "Ideal" theory should not be understood as depicting a community of angels. Conflicts of interest remain prevalent, and occasional transgressions are to be expected. This point matters below when I argue that legal and political immediacy (hence the presence of coercion) is part of ideal theory. Nonideal theory assesses what ought to be done under conditions when either or both of the assumptions of ideal theory are not satisfied. Ideal theory provides guidance for nonideal theory by offering visions of the society we are aiming for. Principles of justice in the first instance are designed for ideal circumstances. But they also apply under nonideal circumstances, in the sense that ideal theory guides nonideal theory. What can be expected of individuals under nonideal circumstances is a difficult subject that has begun to attract attention. See Simmons (2010) for Rawls on ideal theory; for discussion, see also Stemplowska (2008) and Swift (2008). For a dissenting account of nonideal theory, see Sen (2009).

7. Note how Bentham captures legal immediacy in his *Principles of International Law:* "That sovereign then, who has the physical power of occupying and traversing a given tract of land, insomuch that he can effectually and safely traverse it in any direction at pleasure, —at the same time, that against his will another sovereign cannot traverse the same land with equal facility and effect, —can be more certain of *coming at* the individual in question, than such other sovereign can be, and therefore may be pronounced to have the afflictive power [power of hurting somebody] over all such persons as are to be found upon that land—and that a higher afflictive power than any other sovereign can have" (1962, 542).

8. In *Plyler v. Doe* (457 U.S. 202 [1982]), the U.S. Supreme Court held that illegal immigrants were protected by the Constitution because they were included among those "subject to the jurisdiction" of (in this case federal) states. One could say that this judgment states that illegal immigrants too stand in a relationship of immediacy with the government.

9. More generally, the rights I have in mind here are those captured by Rawls's first principle (2001, 44): "freedom of thought and liberty of conscience; political liberties (e.g., the right to vote and to participate in politics) and freedom of association, as well as rights and liberties specified by the integrity (physical and psychological) of persons; and finally, rights and liberties covered by the rule of law." The relevant rights are moral rather than legal rights. Otherwise, states would feature the property of legal immediacy by definition. I take Rawls to be talking about moral rights that should become legal rights.

10. These attributes are conceived in terms of two *moral powers,* the capacities for a sense of justice (to understand, apply, and act from principles specifying fair terms of social cooperation) and for a conception of the good (autonomously

to conceive, revise, and rationally pursue an ordered set of ends characteristic of a person's conception of a worthwhile life). Persons are equal in the sense that each is capable of engaging in cooperation over a complete life as one among many citizens. Persons are free (autonomous) in that they regard themselves and one another as holding conceptions of the good, and as entitled to claims upon their institutions to advance those conceptions if those accord with justice.

11. This section follows Blake and Risse (2008).

12. "Social Unity and Primary Goods" (1999a, 371); see also "Fairness to Goodness" (1999a, 284), "Reply to Alexander and Musgrave" (1999a, 241), "A Kantian Conception of Equality" (1999a, 261), and "Justice as Fairness: Political Not Metaphysical" (1999a, 407). Criticisms of Rawls's treatment of responsibility have triggered much of the constructive work political philosophy has done after Rawls's *Theory*. One may think of Cohen (1989), Dworkin (1981, 2000), Arneson (1989, 1990b, 2008), and Roemer (1996). These writers are sometimes called *luck-egalitarians* (see Anderson 1999; Scheffler 2003), but their concerns are more aptly emphasized by calling them, following Arneson, *responsibility-catering egalitarians*.

13. This is an oversimplification, if a useful one; see Gellner (1983, chaps. 5, 7) for discussion. See also Couture, Nielsen, and Seymour (1998) and McKim and McMahan (1997). There is also a cultural nationalism, as defended by Tamir (1993) and Miller (1995).

14. We can contrast both versions of nationalism with Sieyès's 1789 account of a nation that captures the spirit of my own approach: A nation is "un corps d'associés vivant sous une loi commune et représentés par la même legislature"—"a body of associates living under a common law and represented by the same legislature" ("What is the Third Estate?," Sieyès 2003, 97).

CHAPTER 3

1. My discussion of statism draws on Risse (2006).

2. The relevance of coercion as a basis for duties of justice was also stressed by Miller (1998). Blake (2001) responds to Goodin's (1988) proposal to base such duties on cooperative relationships.

3. Threat involves a lack of voluntariness. So this scenario captures a situation in which one's remaining in a situation that involves a threat is itself voluntary. This sort of situation is of sufficient interest in the present context for us to treat it explicitly.

4. One might say that, even in this case, exit is not as easy as it should be for a decision to remain in a given state to be truly voluntary. The choice offered is only among different regimes that will presumably share certain features. To make a decision to stay truly voluntary, we must add the possibility of leaving the whole ensemble of political structures altogether. We can readily supplement our scenario in this way. But then the objector might say that demands of justice no longer apply because now membership is like membership in a club. One can resist this move by pointing out the many ways in which living in a society is not like being

in a club after all. But the larger point in response to this sort of inquiry is one about the origins of our intuitions about such matters, which I discuss below. Our intuitions do not serve us well to identify necessary conditions for the demands of justice to arise.

5. See, e.g., Rawls (1993, 3, 12, 40, 68, 136, 301; 1999b, 26). Cohen (2008, 132ff., 146 ff.) discusses whether Rawls's basic structure is defined as coercive.

6. One might say that Threat cannot go with the negation of Nonvoluntariness because Threat always involves a form of nonvoluntariness. But the easy-exit scenario described above, which did involve Threat and the corresponding form of nonvoluntariness, also involved voluntariness in a recognizable sense.

7. Both graded and pluralist internationalism deny that for any two individuals, principles of justice either apply or do not apply. Both hold that there are different grounds on which different principles apply. Two individuals could share one ground but not another. However, both forms of internationalism hold that for any ground and for any two individuals, it is true that these individuals either share or do not share that ground. Sharing of grounds *does not admit of degrees*. (This follows from my point in chapter 1 that the grounds determine the scope of principles of justice.) Suppose one wants to say that member states of the EU are characterized by higher degrees of reciprocity than the EU as such. One would have to say that the relation in which individuals stand by virtue of being members of the EU is of a certain nature (which may exhaustively amount to a certain degree or kind of reciprocity), whereas the relation in which individuals stand by virtue of being citizens of a member state is also of a certain, presumably different, nature (which again may exhaustively amount to a certain degree or kind of reciprocity). I would still talk about *two* grounds, rather than one of which one may partake in degrees. However, grounds can stand in the sort of relationship captured by graded internationalism. Some of the principles associated with one ground can be weakened versions of principles associated with another ground. So the formulation "admitting of degrees" does apply to graded internationalism, but not at the level of individuals partaking of grounds. But I recall here that the criteria of statehood come in degrees. This seems to entail that partaking of grounds also *somehow* comes in degrees. But in response to scenarios like that, I say that particular grounds approximate *the reality in states to different degrees*. There are more general ways in which one could formulate the graded/nongraded and monist/pluralist distinctions and combine them with substantive commitments regarding the grounds of justice. But more general distinctions are not useful here.

8. Scheffler speaks of relationships, but in chapter 1 I fixed the terminology in such a way that "relationship" remains neutral with regard to relationism and nonrelationism.

9. See Sreenivasan (2000) for this reading of Rousseau.

10. Beitz means *distributive* justice throughout. Unlike Rawls, he does not reserve the term "distributive justice" for states while thinking that, nonetheless, some duties *of justice* apply globally.

11. For a discussion of attempts to limit the applicability of justice to domestic scenarios (and the claim that they all fail), see Abizadeh (2007).

12. Being a member of the global order means to live on the territory covered by it and to be subject to those bits of this interlocking system of jurisdictions that apply to one's situation. By now all human beings are members in this sense. Chapters 7 and 11 develop an account of human rights as membership rights in the global order. At this stage, I talk about such membership loosely.

13. The difference principle is "comprehensive" because it is concerned with citizens' overall social and economic status. Chapter 4 argues that a duty of assistance is also demanding. But such a duty is both less demanding and less comprehensive than principles of justice at the domestic level in the sense that it ceases to apply once a society can reach the required standards by itself.

14. (1) See Lu (2006) for the history of the idea of world government. For Kant's view, see Kleingeld (2004). For a defense of a world state, see Cabrera (2004). Hoeffe (1999) guardedly defends a world state, a decentralized world republic based on subsidiarity. (2) One might say that Blake (2001) can be enlisted to provide a positive strategy to argue for maximally egalitarian pluralism. After all, Blake gives an argument from coercion to broadly egalitarian principles, without making anything of the fact that coercion is present globally. However, Blake does not ask how to justify to autonomous agents the presence of coercion per se. He asks how to justify the presence of coercion in light of the fact that individuals share a certain kind of relationship. For instance, he emphasizes that the state regulates most property. We would be led on a path toward a pluralist picture of grounds of justice once we sought to transfer his case to the global level. The first order of business would then be to characterize the differences between states and other political and economic structures. (Mutatis mutandis, the same point applies to the idea of reusing Nagel [2005] here.)

CHAPTER 4

1. The Millennium Development Goals (originally scheduled to be reached by 2015) are: to cut in half the proportion of people living in extreme poverty; to achieve universal primary education and gender equality in education; to accomplish a three-fourths decline in maternal mortality and a two-thirds decline in mortality among children under five; to reverse the spread of HIV/AIDS and to assist AIDS orphans; to improve the lives of 100 million slum dwellers. See the UN site for a progress report: http://www.un.org/millenniumgoals/index.html. For the panel report, see http://www.un.org/reports/financing/ (last accessed October 2010).

2. For an introduction, see Helpman (2004). Uncertainty about development strategies suggests humility in approaching the subject; see Rodrik (2007, 5–6). Banerjee (2007) agues that aid is often given without any solid evidence on what kind of aid works. See also Easterly (2008).

3. See Diamond (1997), Gallup, Sachs, and Mellinger (1998), and Sachs (2001, 2003).

4. See Frankel and Romer (1999) and Sachs and Warner (1995). Policymakers from the World Bank, the IMF, the WTO, and the OECD frequently argue that integration into the world economy is the way to prosperity.

5. See North (1990), Landes (1998), Hall and Jones (1999), Easterly and Levine (2003), Acemoglu, Johnson, and Robinson (2003), and Rodrik, Subramanian, and Trebbi (2004). For a skeptical response, see Glaeser et al. (2004). The importance of domestic institutions is also discussed in the IMF's 2003 *World Economic Outlook,* chapter 3.

6. Another good example is Vietnam; see Pritchett (2003). Freeman and Lindauer (1999) argue that economic success in Africa depends on institutional quality. Van de Walle and Johnston (1996) concur.

7. Rawls (1999c, 47–48) defines institutions similarly. One concern about a stance developed with such a broad definition of institutions is that the thesis that "growth depends critically on institutions" becomes too unspecific. However, this concern arises with regard to the practical impact of the institutional stance more than within the confines of our current debate. What matters about the three views above is that Geography traces growth to environmental influences, Integration traces it to what one society "does jointly with others," and Institutions to "what individuals in one society do with each other."

8. The "emergence" and "persistence" of institutions must be separated more than the account above suggests. It may well be possible for outsiders to force the emergence of institutions that would not otherwise have emerged but that then can be maintained by the indigenous population. (An example here is the imposition of democratic structures in Japan after World War II.) Still, situations in which outsiders can impose institutions in this manner tend to be (rare) cataclysmic moments.

9. The German poet Gottfried Benn begins his 1933 defense of National Socialism as follows: "I recently read in a newspaper that in a waiting room in one of the new Prussian ministries a sign with the following contents was posted: 'One does not go in pursuit of selfish concerns to where a new state is being built.' Excellent! That means where history is speaking, individuals have to be silent. This is the concrete form of the new idea of the state" (1933, 11; my translation). This attitude toward the relationship between the state and its citizens is opposite in spirit to what I take to be the point of human rights.

10. For the distinction, see, e.g., Rawls's *Theory of Justice,* sec. 1.

11. One should think broadly about the term "features of individuals" to include bases formulated purely in terms of a distinctively human existence and bases that talk about membership in particular associations.

12. "Will often": nothing turns on this classification being exhaustive, or on the claim that any conceivable view on human rights can be accommodated. (There may well be conceptions of human rights that are not "driven" by any one component, and the work of Onora O'Neill promotes a responsibility-driven conception; see O'Neill [1986].)

13. Bases specify features of individuals in virtue of which human rights are held. In basis-driven accounts, that basis also gives rise to a principle that generates the list, but there can be principle-driven accounts that do not make use of any basis at all, or that consider the principle rather than any basis as authoritative for what human rights are (e.g., Beitz's, discussed below). One may wonder whether basis-driven conceptions are a subspecies of principle-driven ones, namely, those where the answer to the question of why the list is what it is makes reference

to features of individuals. But the point of talking about basis- or principle-*driven* conceptions is to identify that component of the conception that is epistemologically preferred, i.e., that provides the intellectually most secure starting point. However, it is sometimes a matter of controversy whether an account is basis-driven or principle-driven. I suggest below that Griffin's (2008) personhood theory is basis-driven. However, Tasioulas (2010) argues that Griffin distinguishes the basis on which human rights are held (i.e., normative agency) from the principle that generates them (not just the protection of one's status as a normative agent but also its exercise in various valuable ways). It becomes then debatable which of these "drives" the theory.

14. Beitz does so too, but his is best understood as a list-driven conception. He takes human rights practice as authoritative and searches for philosophical underpinnings for it (which differentiates him from Rorty [1993]). Beitz's view is developed most fully in Beitz (2009).

15. Practical conceptions in Beitz's sense are principle-driven. I cannot think of an *interesting* case of a principle-driven conception that is not practical. Raz (2010) also holds a practical conception.

16. For Sen's understanding of human rights, see also Sen (2009, esp. chap. 17).

17. For reflection on the idea of common humanity and a distinctly human existence, see Williams (2005b, sec. 1). See also Feinberg (1973, 94). For a dismissive approach to the idea of human equality, see Schmitt (2008, chap. 17, sec. 2.1). The following account of common humanity by Simone Weil is noteworthy: "'You do not interest me.' No man can say these words to another without committing a cruelty and offending against justice.... At the bottom of the heart of every human being, from earliest infancy until the tomb, there is something that goes on indomitably expecting, in the teeth of all experience of crimes committed, suffered, and witnessed, that good and not evil will be done to him. It is this above all that is sacred in every human being" (1986, 50–51).

18. (1) On needs, see also Wiggins (1987), Brock (1998a, 1998b), Reader (2006b, 2007), Thomson (1987), Braybrooke (1987), and Doyal and Gough (1991). Although needs have particular moral force, they do so only if the being whose needs are in question has a status that renders its needs relevant. (As Simone Weil says in *The Need for Roots*, "When the beggar said to Talleyrand, 'Milord, I've got to live somehow,' Talleyrand replied, 'I don't see that that is necessary.' But the beggar himself saw the necessity for it all right" [1971, 150].) An account of the distinctively human life is necessary to support claims of need. (2) Nagel (1995), drawing on Kamm (1996), characterizes rights as providing a moral status of inviolability. This way of characterizing rights allows us to say that any violation inflicts harm on *all* rights holders by diminishing this status. I explore how to derive rights from the idea of a distinctively human life, whereas Nagel and Kamm characterize their function in moral discourse.

19. I assume that disregarding what someone else reasonably expects of us is an error in practical reasoning. These approaches to rights can be connected in different ways to thinking about practical reasoning more broadly, depending on how one relates one's understanding of inconsistency or unreasonableness in reasoning to views about reasons. The literature on practical reasoning is rarely

concerned with rights, however. For a discussion of themes in that literature that makes for straightforward connections to inquiries about rights, see Forst (2007, chap. 1). The discussion above could become more fine-grained through a more systematic integration of the practical reasoning literature. The natural law approach is accompanied by a third way of establishing what rights people have. It is then a matter of proper inquiry (much as the discovery of laws of physics is) to identify what rights people have.

20. In the *Myth of Sisyphus,* Camus writes that "the absurd is born of this confrontation between the human need and the unreasonable silence of the world" (1955, 21). This statement has a striking resonance when one ponders the moral significance of basic needs.

21. Perhaps I misrepresent Griffin's (2008) take on rights. In chapter 6, he argues that valuing something is to see it under a general description. From there the inference seems to be that it would be unacceptable to deny certain claims of others merely because they are others (assuming that what is at stake is something we have reason to value). But if one asks what mistake somebody makes who refuses to give others proper consideration, the reply must point to an inconsistency. But then one wonders why Griffin insists on the differences between his view and Gewirth's (4; see also 135).

22. Raz (1984) makes clear that, although rights are tied to significant interests, not just any such interest will do, and adds that a special argument is needed to show when it is. He does not explain, however, how to distinguish successful from unsuccessful arguments. Raz (2010) criticizes Griffin for moving from "moral significance" to "rights" without adding a successful argument to bridge this gap.

23. Kant's *Lectures on Ethics* alludes to a similar argument: "We are obliged to be moral. Morality implies a natural promise: otherwise it could not impose any obligations upon us. We owe obedience only to those who can protect us. Morality alone cannot protect us" (1981, 82).

24. Needs, as Thomson (1987) reminds us, are as important as the quality of the person's life. At the same time, the emphasis on a distinctively human life makes it more straightforward to explain why there is something *of value* that deserves protection. Reader (2006a) insists that many criticisms of the basic needs approach are misguided. Sen (1997, chap. 20) provides an extensive discussion of the basic needs approach. Alkire (2002, chap. 5) argues for a "reconciliation" between the basic needs approach and the capabilities approach. See also Alkire (2006) and Griffin (2008, 90).

25. A point Raz (2010) makes against Griffin (2008).

26. See Moellendorff (2002, 79) and Tan (2004, 158) for similar thoughts.

27. Sangiovanni (2007) also discusses how to accommodate ideas about arbitrariness within relationism.

28. (1) See the related discussion in Scheffler (2003, esp. sec. 3). (2) Internationalism also can respond to Scheffler's (2001b) "voluntarist" and "distributive" objections. The former proceeds as follows: Associative duties (duties arising in virtue of practice-mediated relations) can be burdensome to those who bear them. Why should they have to bear such burdens unless they have consented? The distributive objection applies to all obligations that do not apply to all human

beings. Any such obligation A has to B may work to the detriment of C. The obligations of wealthy Americans to help poor Americans before poor foreigners work to the latter's detriment. Internationalists can respond to the voluntarist objection by referring to the significance of shared membership in states. They can respond to the distributive objection that some ways of creating disadvantages are legitimate. (3) Moreover, my pluralist view can respond to a discontinuity worry in Murphy (1998): "We are to imagine that a remote community not yet involved in any external trade or otherwise affected by global institutions, would make no claims of justice on us, but that as soon as we begin to trade with them, thus including them in the world economy, something like the difference principle would suddenly govern our relations—requiring the immediate establishment (or extension) of institutions of taxation and transfer. I find it incredible that the application of the ground rule of economic interaction could have this much moral significance." Some such objection holds for all versions of relationism. Internationalism, however, generates less discontinuity.

CHAPTER 5

1. For "common heritage of humankind," see Attfield (2003, 169–72), Malanczuk (1997, 207–8), and Cooper (1994, chap. 3); see also Buck (1998). The Charter of Principles of the World Social Forum describes the organization as "an open meeting place for reflective thinking ... by groups and movements ... committed to building a planetary society directed towards fruitful relationships among Mankind and between it and the Earth" (http://www.wsfindia.org/?q =node/3, accessed September 5, 2010).

2. See Buckle (1991) and Tuck (1999) for these discussions. I talk about "collective ownership" generically, capturing the idea that, in a sense to be explicated in detail, humanity as a whole owns the earth. Chapter 6 introduces different conceptions of what it means to own the earth collectively. I champion a conception I call Common Ownership. Common Ownership is pretty much what Grotius had in mind, but I argue for it differently.

3. In a speech at American University in Washington, D.C., in June 1963, President John F. Kennedy said the following: "For in the final analysis, our most basic common link is that we all inhabit this small planet." This quotation is set in stone in a column at the entrance to the John F. Kennedy Memorial Park in Cambridge, Massachusetts.

4. One might argue that the best explanation for our intuition in this thought experiment is that produced materials should not be underused, which in the example continue to exist. Gabriel Wollner has suggested an example that makes the same point without triggering this difficulty: Imagine two tribes living in two valleys separated by mountains such that each tribe's living space is confined to its valley. The few members of the first tribe live lavishly on hunting and gathering in their resource-rich valley. Members of the second, much bigger tribe manage to get along in their valley, which provides just enough deer, roots, and berries to ensure a minimally decent life. After heavy rainfall a mudslide opens a passage

from one valley to the other. Learning about the resources of the other valley, the second tribe claims that, as a matter of justice, each tribe should have access to both valleys. (See chapter 5 of Wollner's PhD dissertation, "Egalitarianism with a Human Face," University College London, 2010.)

5. In this view, arguments for rights involve an empirical claim about how individuals behave or how institutions work in the absence of particular assignments of rights; a claim that this result would be unacceptable; and a further empirical claim about how the envisaged assignment of rights would produce a different outcome.

6. (1) For translations, I use the Liberty Fund editions (Grotius 2004, 2005, 2006; see references). For the Latin original of *De Jure Praedae* (*DJP*) and *De Jure Belli* (*DJB*), I use Grotius (1712) and Grotius (1868). I use customary references for *DJB* of the sort I.X.1.I, which is the first subsection in the first section in the tenth chapter of the first book. *De Jure Praedae* and *Mare Liberum* (*ML*) I quote by page; when I quote *ML* separately, the reference is to the separate edition of that work rather than to the chapter of *DJP*. Occasional Locke references take the form "II, 20," which is section 20 in the *Second Treatise of Government*. (2) Bull (1990) distinguishes five features of a Grotian view of international society: centrality of natural law; universality of the natural commonwealth; importance assigned to individuals and non-state groups; solidarity in the enforcement of rules, and absence of international institutions. See Tuck (1979, 1999), Kingsbury and Roberts (1990), Haakonssen (1985), Stumpf 2006), and Cavallar (2002) for historical discussions. There is some debate about whether Grotius deserves the title "father of international law," as opposed to Vitoria, Gentili, and Suarez; on this, see the conclusion in Onuma (1993). A related debate concerns the status of *DJB* in the history of political thought. See Schneewind (1998, 78ff.) for a discussion of Grotius's importance in the history of ethics and Korsgaard (1996, 7–30 passim) for a discussion of Grotius's views on the obligatoriness of natural law. For Grotius's views of ownership, see Buckle (1991).

7. (1) Tuck (1999, chap. 2) says that before Grotius, the general view was that states could claim jurisdiction over neighboring seas. See Boucher (1998, chap. 9), Keene (2005, chap. 4), and Haakonssen (1996, chap. 1) for the historical context. See Pagden (1982) for a discussion of the initial reaction of Spanish intellectuals to the discovery of the New World. (2) Questions arise about the relationship between *DJB* and *DJP*. In footnote 17 to his introduction to *DJB*, Tuck writes, "Even as the *De Jure Belli ac Pacis* was being printed, Grotius was thinking about a new edition in which the work would appear alongside *Mare Liberum* and his essay on the Dutch constitution, *De Antiquitate Batavicae Reipublicae* of 1610 (Briefwisseling, 2:426). He clearly did not suppose then that *DJB* had superseded the earlier work. *De Jure Belli* did appear together in an Amsterdam edition of 1632, though this may not have been authorized." Still, there are developments between *DJP* and *DJB*; see Tuck (1979, chap. 3). For a discussion about how much *DJB* deviates from *ML* as far as freedom of the seas is concerned, see Yanagihara (1993, 154 and references).

8. Cavallar (2002) offers an account of the tensions in Grotius. The worry is not merely that considerations of natural right are squared with considerations of

expediency, but also that Grotius integrates a host of pragmatic considerations, cases where might makes right. For instance, extended exercise of sovereignty renders originally unjust conquest legitimate, and states approve the status quo at the end of wars (*DJB* III.20.XI–XII, III.6.II).

9. See Tuck (1999, 100–102) on how Grotius changed the details about the relationship between God and natural law in *DJB* as compared to his earlier writings.

10. See Schneewind (1998, 78ff.).

11. See also, e.g., Haakonssen (1985, esp. 240). For the different notions of *ius* (law, right, rights), see Onuma (1993, chap. 2). See also appendix 1 in Olivecrona (1971) and chapter 1 in Stumpf (2006).

12. (1) The Qur'an echoes this idea of the earth being a divine gift to mankind to some extent, speaking of the creator who "spread out the earth" for human beings (see 2:22; see also 2:29 and 55:10). Yet the Qu'ran is more commonly concerned with emphasizing God's creation and his control over everything, rather than a divine gift of the earth. (2) Book VIII of Milton's *Paradise Lost* recounts the divine donation as follows: "Not only these fair bounds, but all the earth // To thee and to thy race I give; as lords // possess it, and all things that therein live, // or live in sea, or air, beast, fish, and fowl" Milton (Milton 2000, bk. VIII, vv. 339–41). Interestingly, Maimonides' *Guide for the Perplexed* does not discuss the divine donation at all, not even in chapter XXX of part II, which is devoted to the beginning of Genesis (Maimonides 2007, 212–18). Apparently he did not think the Perplexed would much care about this theme. Maimonides does, however, make a reference to Leviticus 25:23–24: "The land shall not be sold for ever," God explains there, "for the land is mine; for ye are strangers and sojourners with me. And in all the land of your possession ye shall grant a redemption for the land." See Maimonides (2007, 340). For a discussion of the Jewish tradition that drew on this passage and its influence on European political thought in early modern times (which owes much to Maimonides), see Nelson (2010, chap. 2).

13. Waldron (1988, 162–67) identifies two worries that arise about the idea of property in prelegal situations: precision and security. These problems do not arise in very primitive property systems.

14. Locke, I, 28 and I, 86, also thought it was both revealed and self-evident that the earth belonged to humanity.

15. For Grotius, the subject is always *occupation* as opposed to *discovery*, whose centrality was also defended at the time (Yanagihara 1993, 151).

16. This subject is revisited, under the subject of first occupation, at the beginning of chapter 3 of book II; in chapter 2, as he leads up to the discussion of necessity; and in chapter 3 in the context of the discussion of ownership of the sea, which is taken up in chapter 2 but then left, and resumed only in II.2.VII.

17. Occupation can be done also by a whole people or by a sovereign (*DJB* II.2.IV, II.3.XIX, II.8.IX.1, II.9.IV). That peoples occupy spaces as individuals do appears also in *DJP*, pp. 320 and 328.

18. Pufendorf criticizes Grotius for this right of necessity. See Pufendorf, book II, chapter VI.6. See Salter (2005) for discussion. Salter argues that Pufendorf fails to offer a coherent alternative.

19. Tensions arise. For instance, in cases of emergencies, the issue becomes how rights of necessity square with the right to resistance; see Yanagihara (1993). See also Tuck (1979, 78–81).

20. For ideas about *res nullius,* see Tuck (1999), Pagden (2003), and Tierny (1997). On the distinction between jurisdiction and property in Grotius, see Tanaka (1993) and Yanagihara (1993).

21. Compare Vattel (1805, 94) (bk. I, chap. VIII, sec. 81), who was concerned with similar problems: "There are [those] who, to avoid agriculture, would live only by hunting, and their flocks. This might, doubtless, be allowed in the first ages of the world, when the earth, without cultivation, produced more than was sufficient to feed its few inhabitants. But at present, when the human race is greatly multiplied, it could not subsist, if all nations resolved to live in that manner.... Thus though the conquest of the uncivilized empires of Peru and Mexico were a notorious usurpation, the establishment of many colonies on the continent of North American may, on their confining themselves within just bounds, be extremely lawful. The people of these vast countries rather over-ran than inhabited them." This passage from Vattel was quoted in a speech in the U.S. Congress on May 24, 1830, in a debate concerning the proposal to remove Native Americans beyond the Mississippi (see *Debates in Congress: Part II of Volume VI; Register of Debates in Congress, Comprising the Leading Debates and Incidents of the First Session of the Twenty-First Congress,* Washington, DC: Gales and Seaton, 1830).

22. The same is true for Locke; see Waldron (1988, 165).

23. On the importance of occupation, see *ML,* pp. 24, 34. On p. 116 we read that, if things cannot remain common, they become the property of the first taker, both because the uncertainty of ownership cannot otherwise be avoided and also because it is equitable that a premium be put on diligence.

24. Grotius does not think collective ownership requires collective institutions. He rejects a world state, a proposal he ascribes to Dante (II.22.XIII.1). Grotius endorses the existence of states, whose authority he thinks rests on consent. About states, see P XVII, II.20.XVI, and *DJP,* p. 158.

25. See Waldron (1988, 148–57).

26. See Pufendorf IV.4.4 and IV.4.5.

27. The idea of universal fellow feeling appears in important passages: *DJB,* P XIV, states that we all stem from the same parents; see also *DJP,* pp. 305, 364, 434, 453. On natural equity, see *DJP,* p. 501.

28. For references to equity, see *DJB* II.2.X.2, II.11.XIII, II.11.XIX, *DJP,* P 686. See also pp. 28, 583, 1231, 1457, 1472 P 583.

29. *ML,* p 22, says there originally was universal and indefinite dominion (*dominium*); see also *ML,* p. 85.

30. See also *ML,* pp. 95, 91. Locke says, "The Earth, and all that is therein, is given to Men for the Support and Comfort of their Being" (II, 26; see also I, 86).

31. Locke reacts to that point too: I, 40 and II, 4. See Pufendorf, *DJNG* IV.4.4.

32. Why does Hobbes not discuss all this in terms of the book of Genesis? The answer to this must lie in his attitude to Christianity; see Martinich (1992).

33. See Tully (1980, chaps. 3, 4) for seventeenth-century property discourse. The theistic framework also shapes Henry George's reasoning, in the nineteenth century: "If we are all here by the equal permission of the Creator, we are all here

with an equal title to the enjoyment of his bounty—with an equal right to the use of all that nature so impartially offers. This is a right which is natural and inalienable; it is a right which vests in every human being as he enters the world and which during his continuance in the world can be limited only by the equal rights of others. There is in nature no such thing as a fee simple in land. There is on earth no power which can rightfully make a grant of exclusive ownership in land. If all existing men were to unite to grant away their equal rights, they could not grant away the right of those who follow them. For what are we but tenants for a day? Have we made the earth that we should determine the rights of those who after us shall tenant it in their turn? … Though his titles have been acquiesced in by generation after generation, to the landed estates of the Duke of Westminster the poorest child that is born in London today has as much right as his eldest son" (1926, 137).

CHAPTER 6

1. Natural collective ownership rights as I conceive of them also do not speak to the human gene pool. Genes are transmitted through actions of individuals. They do not exist independently of human activities. Steiner (1994, 1999) argues that germ-line genes are effectively natural resources and subject to rent payments. Bovenberg (2006, chap. 3) transfers Grotius's reflections on the freedom of the seas to the case of the human genome, parallel to how I will transfer these reflections to intellectual property in chapter 12.

2. Rothbard (1996, 35). Hospers (1971, 65) makes a similar point.

3. (1) Some think outside a theistic framework collective ownership is *meaningless* (Narveson 2001, 73). What leads to this view are concerns about what exactly is owned and who owns, and to a larger extent concerns about the sort of ownership relation that can apply to humanity per se. These worries are addressed in what follows. One may say ownership presupposes that some people are excluded; "humanity," that is, cannot be an owner unless there is a class of non-owners. This class would consist of animals or extraterrestrials. ("Arriving on earth, E.T., like other extraterrestrials before and after him, found himself sadly excluded from what is collectively owned by humankind.") Yet ownership, in the limit case of humankind as an owner, loses this feature. (2) For discussions of how considerations of original ownership enter discussions of the legitimacy of private property, see Waldron (1988), Munzer (1990), Christman (1994), Penner (1997), and Harris (1996). See Becker (1977) and Reeve (1986).

4. Equality of opportunity is exhausted by the liberty, claim, and immunity rights I am about to introduce. For the Hohfeld terms, see Jones (1994, chap. 1), Edmundson (2004, chap. 5), or Wenar (2005).

5. On Grotius's understanding of rights—rights being individual possessions—it is possible to surrender even minimal rights. A better way of conceptualizing rights is to regard them as reasons, some of which may still apply even if the person whose situation is at stake might wish to forfeit them. While I take much inspiration from Grotius, I part company in particular when it comes to the ontology of rights.

6. Risse (2004b) did not develop collective ownership in this way. Following Christman (1991), there I understood "ownership" to consist of a set of rights and duties: First, we have the right to possess, use, manage, alienate, transfer, and gain income from property. Derivative of these are rights to security in ownership, transmissibility after death, and absence of term (specifying absence of temporal limitations on ownership). In addition, there are the prohibition of harmful use, residuary character of ownership (laws specifying rules of ownership in cases of lapsed interest), and liability to execution in case of insolvency. However, collective ownership of natural resources and spaces is much weaker.

7. I talk about a "form of existence" to make room for the fact that raw materials are used by humans and receive a certain shape then. The particular form of existence of clay may be that of a statue.

8. Beitz (1999, 136–43) discusses principles of justice as they apply to external resources, concluding that "the natural distribution of resources is a purer case of something being 'arbitrary from a moral point of view' than the distribution of talents" (140). See Pogge (1989, 250–53) for critical discussion.

9. For discussions about what is morally special about human beings, see Singer (1993, chaps. 2, 3), Arneson (1999), and Gosepath (2004, chap. 2.5). Most plausibly, as far as extensions of moral considerations to animals are concerned, we would be talking about higher animals. An intriguing question (my flippant reference to E.T. notwithstanding) is whether we should count extraterrestrials as co-owners, should they emerge. In the 2008 science fiction *The Day the Earth Stood Still,* a representative of alien species arrives to assess whether humanity is capable of preserving the earth's rare and thus invaluable life-sustaining capacities. I think such species would have claims.

10. See Vallentyne and Steiner (2000a) for contemporary contributions and Vallentyne and Steiner (2000b) for historical ones.

11. See Narveson (2001, 82–85).

12. For a similar view, see Paul (1987, 230). In an article that belongs to another corner of philosophy, Bittner (2001) criticizes the idea that we ever create anything. Rothbard (1974, 1996) stresses creation less than Kirzner. Objects must belong to somebody, and whoever has "added" to them has a stronger claim than others.

13. See Nozick (1974, 178–82).

14. For discussion, see Nozick (1974, 174–82). In this formulation, I follow Otsuka (2003, 23).

15. We may compare the treatment of this matter in section 62 of Kant's *Metaphysics of Morals,* the Doctrine of Right: "The rational idea of a *peaceful,* even if not friendly, thoroughgoing community of all nations on the earth that can come into relations affecting one another is not a philanthropic (ethical) principle, but a principle *having to do with rights.* Nature has enclosed them all together within determinate limits (by the spherical shape of the place they live in, a *globus terraqueus*). And since possession of the land, on which an inhabitant of the earth can live, can be thought only as possession of a part of a determinate whole and so as possession of that to which each of them originally has a right, it follows that all nations stand *originally* in a community of land, though not of rightful community of possession (*communion*) and so of use of it, or of property in it;

instead they stand in a community of possible physical *interaction (commercium)*, that is, in a thoroughgoing relation of each to all the others of *offering to engage in commerce* with any other, and each has a right to make this attempt without the other being authorized to behave toward it as an enemy because it has made this attempt" (1996, 489); see also the Doctrine of Right (1996, sec. 13, 414–15), as well as *Perpetual Peace,* the discussion of the Third Definitive Article (1970b, 106). The role of the spherical nature of the earth in Kant's theory of property in the Doctrine of Right is difficult to determine. The relevant passages in the *Metaphysics of Morals* are brief, and as, for instance, Flikschuh (2000) argues, Kant's political philosophy in general and his appeal to the spherical nature of the earth in particular are heavily involved with his metaphysics. Roughly speaking, Kant proceeds as follows: Each person has a right to freedom (i.e., not to be subject to another's will). In virtue of this right, each person is entitled to take up some space on earth. But in virtue of the spherical and thus limited nature of the earth, human beings potentially or actually encounter each other. In virtue of these facts (right to freedom, spherical nature of the earth), all humans form a community with the (sole) obligation of regulating property acquisition. To that community Kant ascribes a collective will that is charged with this regulation, and that has to do so in a way acceptable to all persons. (This community must be postulated for there to be personal property at all, the necessity for which follows from the right to freedom.) But since then regulation of property acquisition would capture the will of all, nobody would acquire anything (and subject others to obligations) through unilateral acts. So Kant offers an alternative route to collective ownership of the earth. On Kant's account and on mine, what must follow is the kind of discussion I conduct under the heading of "conceptions of collective ownership." Kant does not address these matters. For a discussion of the differences between Grotius and Kant on original ownership, see Flikschuh (2000, chap. 5, sec. 2). On Kant, see also Byrd and Hruschka (2010, chap. 6, secs. 2–4) and Kersting (1984, 113–54).

16. Common Ownership captures claims and liberties *directed at* other human beings. The corresponding duties may not be all-things-considered duties, which in turn would also take concerns about nature or animals into consideration. See Sreenivasan (2010) for the distinction I just made.

17. A classic starting point for reflection on nature is Mill (1874). For an overview of theories about the value of nature, see Krebs (1999). Wiggins (2000) emphasizes that nature is "sublime and awesome," and that our valuing it thus must have an impact on our attitudes toward it. Goodin (1992) defends the view that the value of nature lies in the fact that it provides a context for our lives to find meaning. What is crucial about this context is that humans have not designed it.

18. One can read the biblical story in different ways; see White (1967) and Passmore (1974, chaps. 1, 2). For the reference to Calvin, see Passmore (1974, 13). An alleged letter from Indian Chief Seattle to U.S. President Pierce from the 1850s takes a different view of ownership of the earth: "The earth does not belong to man; man belongs to the earth.... All things are connected like the blood which unites one family. Whatever befalls the earth, befalls the sons of the earth. Man did not weave the web of life: he is merely a strand in it. Whatever he does to the

web, he does to himself" (Weiss 1988, 1). References to this letter circulate widely among activists, and appear frequently in the literature. For an account of what we actually know about this text and its origins, see Kaiser (1987).

19. See also Wiggins (2000, 7–8).

20. "Arguably": perhaps even deep ecology is reconcilable with collective ownership. Naess (1984) says that "humans have no right to interfere destructively with nonhuman life except for purpose of satisfying vital needs" (266). But we also read that "Ecosophy, as I conceive it, *says yes to the fullest self-realization of man*" (270; emphasis in original). Using ownership language, Naess (1989) writes, "The Norwegian people or the Norwegian state does not own Norway. The resources of the world are not only resources for human beings. Legally, we can 'own' a forest, but if we destroy the living conditions for life in the forest, we are transgressing the norm of equality" (175). But also: "The principle of biospheric egalitarianism defined in terms of equal rights, has sometimes been misunderstood as meaning that human needs should never have priority over nonhuman needs. But this is never intended.... Human beings are closer to us than animals, but there is no unsatisfied need driving the food cosmetic industry.... The dimensions of peripheral needs of humans must be compared with vital needs of other species, if there is a conflict" (170–71). While there might be a way of rendering collective ownership consistent with this outlook, there is more of a commitment to the moral importance of beings with a subjective good (in particular humans) in the ownership approach than deep ecology is likely to be comfortable with.

21. Freeing the idea of collective ownership from its theological context also allows us to respond to a way of ridiculing the idea that the earth exists for the sake of human beings. John Muir, patron saint of the environmental movement, writes, "But if we should ask these profound expositors of God's intentions, How about those man-eating animals—lions, tigers, alligators—which smack their lips over raw man? Or about those myriads of noxious insects that destroy labor and drink his blood? Doubtless man was intended for food and drink for all these? Oh, no! Not at all! There are unresolvable difficulties connected with Eden's apple and the Devil. Why does water drown its lord? Why do so many minerals poison him? Why are so many plants and fishes deadly enemies? Why is the lord of creation subjected to the same laws of life as his subjects? Oh, all these things are satanic, or in some way connected with the first garden" (Muir 1916, cited in Gruen and Jamieson 1994, 24). My view does not lead to such absurdity. Yet neither is my view committed to a caretaking attitude associated with some understandings of the divine creation, captured for instance by the idea of a great chain of being (where nothing is created in vain). See Lovejoy (1957), and for some discussion, Sagoff (2008, 201).

22. (1) See also Mack (2009, sec. 5) for difficulties with determining which resource bundles have equal value. Miller (2007, chap. 3) rejects equal entitlements to resources as a principle of global equality since "the idea of global equality of resources remains indeterminate in the absence of a non-arbitrary way of determining resource values" (61). Although Miller thinks his argument has further-reaching implications, it is an argument (only) against Equal Division, very similar

to mine. (2) A supportive consideration for my argument against Equal Division is this: Suppose we have fixed a context for which we know what technology is available that requires certain materials; we know how people integrate such technology into their lives; and we know what rules determine what people can do with resources and technology. How valuable particular resources would be nonetheless depends *differentially* on the activities of different people. Not everybody would contribute equally to the practices that make materials valuable. This observation would sit uneasily with the claim that the particular manner of valuing resources used in this context should be employed to divide up a figurative heap of resources. (3) If one particular measure for evaluating resource bundles were picked although many materials only acquire value through activities that require social contexts, the claim that all human beings have an equal claim to the spaces and resources of the earth in terms of *that* measure would simply be unfounded.

23. But see Brown (2009, chap. 7) for an attempt to reconstruct Dworkin's auction for the global level. Brown envisages an emergency evacuation of the earth after a crisis that some people from all cultures survive. After arriving on an inhabitable planet smaller than the earth, they use Dworkin's auction device to divide up the land. Brown's proposal for how to adjust Dworkin's device seems to function well as a political proposal (much as my immigration proposal in chapter 8 does), but does not solve the problem we are discussing now.

24. This discussion follows Risse (2004b).

25. Christman (1991, 1994) argues, from an egalitarian perspective, for a conception of ownership that excludes precisely that second bit of Otsuka's right to self-ownership.

26. Vallentyne, Steiner, and Otsuka (2005) insist that coherence should not be required because "there is a very significant difference in the moral status of agents ... and natural resources" (209). This response is unsatisfactory.

27. This discussion follows Risse (2005b). This section introduces comparisons among countries and to that extent anticipates the inquiry of chapter 8.

CHAPTER 7

1. A debate about how to characterize moral discourse has loomed large in the recent German discussion. See Tugendhat (1993), Gosepath (2004), and Forst (2007). Forst (2007, chap. 2) discusses various other approaches to acceptability to reasonable persons.

2. (1) One may wonder whether the difference between demands of justice and (mere) demands of reasonable conduct is just one of degree. Mere demands of reasonable conduct may imply duties, but not duties of justice. But there are, for instance, imperfect duties of beneficence. Those are duties of sorts, but they do not need to be fulfilled on every suitable occasion. Moreover, these duties would be outweighed by duties of justice in cases of conflict. One would violate such a duty nonetheless if one never acted kindly (unless for some odd reason one constantly found oneself in situations where obligations of justice outweighed obli-

gations of beneficence). In that sense the difference between demands of justice and mere demands of reasonable conduct is a matter of degree. That difference involves a structural component too, though, because justice, in my approach, is conceptualized through grounds of justice. To back up the claim that X is an obligation of justice, then, one must tie X to a ground and thereby back up the claim that the matter at hand is of the required stringency. In this way we end up with a rather broad notion of a moral right as corresponding to obligations. That is somewhat unsatisfactory because then imperfect duties could also correspond to rights. Indeed, if there is a duty of beneficence that is imperfect and weaker than duties of justice, no individual whose circumstances could give one an occasion to be kind has a right to such kindness. Nonetheless, collectively humanity does have such a right. That point in turn merely reflects the fact that I have indeed violated an obligation if I have never acted kindly. (2) One might also wonder whether all (mere) demands of reasonable conduct are imperfect rather than perfect. As far as the logical space is concerned that I have carved out for the notion of mere demands of reasonable conduct, duties could well be perfect but nonetheless weaker than the especially stringent duties of justice. I have introduced this (intuitively and theoretically plausible) notion to make room for duties that are weaker than duties of justice. However, there is no need to develop this theory of reasonable conduct more than I do here. Doing so would require adding more foundational moral theory than would be sensible to include in the project this book is engaged in. The present question is therefore the kind of question to which I am unable to provide an answer.

3. Sections 2–6 of this chapter draw on Risse (2009a).

4. I suppress the distinction between property and jurisdiction. Paying attention to it would merely make the formulations clumsier. What matters is that jurisdiction and sovereignty are forms of collective control at the exclusion of others; within each of the units thus demarcated, the property regime is subject to that unit's regulation (where conceivably that regulation itself is subject to constraints —and where in turn this formulation should be understood broadly enough to be able to accommodate even a Lockean view as defended by Simmons [2001a], where sovereignty derives from individual ownership).

5. The importance of the robustness of the protection of individuals is emphasized by the republican tradition; see Pettit (1997). What is crucial for the addition of rights that make protection robust is that we are talking about basic needs. This approach does not lead to a proliferation of rights (such that, for any right whatsoever, we need to add rights against the state to make sure the state cannot violate the original right).

6. The concept of human rights is characterized by three features: they are universal and owed by every political society to everybody; they are requirements of political morality whose force does not depend on their expression in enforceable law; and they are especially urgent. Any account of human rights must meet these constraints, as well as two methodological assumptions: fidelity to major human rights documents, so that a substantial range of these rights is accounted for (a criterion that grants that major human rights documents play a significant role in fixing the meaning of human rights talk), and open-endedness (we can

argue in support of additional rights). A conception of human rights consists in four elements: first, an actual list of rights classified as human rights; second, an account of the basis on which individuals have them (an account of what features turn individuals into rights holders); third, an account of why that list has that particular composition, that is, a principle or a process that generates that list; and fourth, an account of who has to do what to realize these rights, that is, an account of corresponding obligations. Any full-fledged conception also makes clear both why such a conception is worth having and why the language of rights (rather than, say, goals or values) is appropriately used when we talk about "human rights."

7. A widely used manual for the National Socialist youth organization (*Vom Deutschen Volk und Seinem Lebensraum,* Brennecke 1938) starts by pointing out that the "basic pillar of the National Socialist worldview is recognition of the inequality of human beings." The manual also explains that those belonging to the allegedly superior race cannot press their rights either; they must promote Nazi causes.

8. See also Geuss (2003, 140).

9. My statements about the defining features of human rights talk about "importance" and "urgency." Here I use these terms interchangeably. I use different terms to distinguish between the two steps involved.

10. In my view, individuals are members of the global order anyway, and membership rights are necessary precisely *because* that order imposes dangers on *its members.* Membership rights *ensure* appropriate inclusion but do not *constitute* inclusion. Someone still *counts as* included in a community if her membership rights are not upheld. In Cohen's view, it seems someone only *counts as* included if her membership rights are upheld.

11. Here we may consider a historical example. The Code Noire, passed by Louis XIV in 1685, defined the conditions of slavery in the French colonies, including Haiti. While the code threatened slaves with strict punishment for certain offenses, it also offered them some protection against abuse, and required that their masters take care of them in old age and sickness. As one historian of Haiti remarked, the whites did not abolish the code, "they simply ignored it" (Girard 2005, 25). Slavery in Haiti did not lend itself to such regulation. Indeed, it would be an unlikely scenario in which slavery could be regulated robustly.

12. Vernon (2002) offers an account of *crimes against humanity* that bears some resemblance to my account of human rights. The political arrangements human beings have made on this planet (especially the system of states) have been made as if they sought to institutionalize mutual indifference. Vulnerabilities are addressed at the level of communities, especially states. In light of this, communities (especially states) are guilty of a distinctive kind of wrong if they do not merely fail to protect human beings within the realm of power but direct their power systematically against the persons they are supposed to protect. Such violations constitute a deliberate perversion of the rationale of the state system as such. For this reason, systematic violations of this sort are rightly called crimes against humanity. An international responsibility is tied to this type of violation. Vernon distinguishes between human rights violations and crimes against human-

ity: the standpoint of human rights is individualized, whereas crimes against humanity take a more macroscopic view. See also Vernon (2010), which argues that the exclusiveness of given societies can be justified only if they are prepared to offer assistance to other societies.

13. This section follows Risse (2009d).

14. The proposal was made, e.g., during a talk at Harvard University in September 2008; see Alvin Powell, "Island Nation President Plans for Extinction," *Harvard University Gazette*, September 25, 2008 (www.news.harvard.edu/gazette/2008/09.25/13-kiribati.html). See also "Statement by His Excellency Anote Tong, President of the Republic of Kiribati, General Debate of the 63rd Session of the UN General Assembly, September 25, 2008" (www.un.org/ga/63/generaldebate/pdf/kiribati_en.pdf), and Maryanne Loughry and Jane McAdam, "Kiribati—Relocation and Adaptation," *Forced Migration Review* 31 (October 2008): 51–52 (www.fmreview.org/FMRpdfs/FMR31/51-52.pdf).

15. One might wonder whether duties toward the people of Kiribati could not be discharged by receiving them as refugees. However, as Blake (2002) argues, partial-citizenship arrangements are morally unacceptable if they are either exploitative or contribute to an unjust global order. Accepting these people merely as refugees would be impermissible at least in light of the first condition: since sea-level rise is inevitable, inhabitants of Kiribati have no viable alternative to emigrating. So the ownership approach entails that immigration is permissible, but it is on the strength of considerations against partial citizenship that immigrants can insist on admission to full membership.

16. The principle of ownership by the people is also enshrined in constitutions. For example, (what is now) Article 111 of the new Iraqi constitution proclaims, "Oil and gas are owned by all the people of Iraq in all the regions and governerates" (http://confinder.richmond.edu/admin/docs/Iraqi_Constitution_Final_-_30_JAN_06.pdf). See also Arato (2009, 235–36).

CHAPTER 8

1. As George Borjas (2001) puts this point for the United States: "Current immigration policy benefits some Americans (the newly arrived immigrants as well as those who employ and use the services the immigrants provide) at the expense of others (those Americans who happen to have skills that compete directly with those of immigrants). Before deciding how many and which immigrants to admit, the country must determine which groups of Americans should be the winners and which should be the losers" (xiv). Borjas counts immigrants among the beneficiaries, but does not count rejected would-be immigrants among the losers. Peter Brimelow (1995) calls immigration "a luxury for the US" (259), implying there is no obligation to outsiders on this matter. Roy Beck (1996) expresses outrage at the U.S. government for accepting more immigrants allegedly to keep wages low; no question is raised about the entitlements of would-be immigrants.

2. (1) Some countries offer support for immigrants (e.g., language instruction), but none takes extensive redistributive measures to give them much credit

for being latecomers. (2) Some have argued that borders are an economic oddity since returns to labor depend on one's country (Anderson and van Wincoop 2004). This view was also defended by Adam Smith and Milton Friedman. Immigration is then a solution to an impediment of the market, one that should follow naturally now that constraints on the movement of services, goods, and capital are lifted more and more. However, such a view is justified only if little can be said for the validity of borders, which in turn must be assessed through an inquiry into original ownership. (3) I ignore two groups that may demand access. The first is individuals with a morally overwhelming case for entry *independent* of any right to immigration based on original ownership; the second consists of those with an overwhelming case for rejection. It is unclear how to draw the contours of these groups, but moral questions about immigration per se arise about people who belong to neither. I assume this third group is nonempty. (4) David Miller (2005) rejects standard arguments for open borders, his main point being that the alleged rights grounding such a demand do not correspond to duties of others. The standpoint of collective ownership, however, shows how such duties can be generated. Nevertheless, the (culture- and population-size-driven) reasons for exclusion that Miller favors can be reproduced from the standpoint of collective ownership, except that the culture-based argument must be qualified.

3. See Cullity (2004) and Murphy (2000) for proposals regarding compliance under nonideal conditions.

4. (1) This chapter draws on joint work with Michael Blake (Blake and Risse 2007, 2009; Risse 2008, 2009c). (2) To illustrate that much is at stake, let us consider an argument by John Winthrop (1588–1649), first governor of the Massachusetts-Bay Company. In a document setting out the reasons for colonizing Massachusetts, Winthrop refers to the divine gift in Genesis I:28: "The whole earth," he says, "is the Lord's garden, and He has given it to the sons of men with a general commission.... Why then should we stand striving here [in England] for places of habitation ... and in the meantime suffer a whole continent as fruitful and convenient for the use of man to lie waste without any improvement?" Once his reasons for colonization are stated, Winthrop entertains some objections. The first asks why settlers would be allowed to enter land that others have occupied for so long. "As for the natives of New England," he responds, "they enclose no land, neither have any settled habitation, nor any tame cattle to improve the land by, and so have no other but a natural right to those countries. So as if we leave them sufficient for their use, we may lawfully take the rest, there being more than enough for them and us" (Winthrop 1869, 1:309–12; spelling adjusted). Winthrop is right that, as a matter of justice, immigration could not be denied if the immigrants "leave [the original inhabitants] sufficient for their use." But considerations of reasonable acceptability should determine how the space could be shared.

5. Let us think of P_S only in terms of counting people. It would be possible to extend this assessment to certain forms of animal life if one has independent reasons for being inclusive in this way.

6. (1) For the relevant aspects of property, see also Ellickson, Rose, and Ackerman (2002). (2) Hillel Steiner (1992) also explores immigration from the stand-

point of collective ownership (being a defender of Equal Division) and argues that countries can elect to exclude people from immigration if they pay compensation. (3) Ideas about over- and underuse of parts of the earth also played a role in the expansionist policies of Nazi Germany, as well as of wartime Italy and Japan. Hitler's *Mein Kampf* (Hitler (1941)) treats at length the subject of "living space," *Lebensraum,* for the German people; see volume 1, chapter 4, and especially the notorious chapter 14 in volume 2 (see Jäckel 1981, chap. 2). The idea of *Lebensraum* also features prominently in a manual for the instruction of members of a Nazi youth organization, whose title has been translated as *Nazi Primer* but literally is "Of the German People and Its Living Space" (*Vom Deutschen Volk und Seinem Lebensraum*). Carl Schmitt (1941) devoted a treatise to the idea of "space" in international law. However, no philosophical view suffers only because some of its implications *also* appear in an intellectually untenable approach. Collective ownership contradicts Nazi ideology. To the extent that Nazi ideology integrates ideas about over- and underuse, these ideas are distorted by their assimilation into a racist-supremacist approach, in much the same way in which other moral ideas are so distorted (see Haas 1988 and Koonz 2003). It is because of its racist starting points that Nazi ideology licensed conquest as a method of acquiring the space to which the Nazis thought Germans were entitled. Moreover, Nazi ideology grants a central role to an agrarian lifestyle and conceptualizes the value of parts of the earth much more in terms of the value of agricultural land than I do. Finally, Nazi ideology, much like Fichte's political philosophy, mentioned in chapter 1, rejects trade as a way of meeting needs and supports conquest also for that reason. For a discussion of Japanese ideology in this context, see Dower (1986, chap. 10).

7. Sometimes the task of philosophy is to argue that something is needed for which the work must be done in the sciences. For efforts to broaden national economic accounting beyond market activities, see Nordhaus and Kokkelenberg (1999), as well as Abraham and Mackie (2005). For the agro-ecological zones methodology, see the IIASA website, http://www.iiasa.ac.at/Research/LUC/GAEZ/index.htm?sb=6 (accessed May 2010).

8. The discussion in the following paragraphs draws on correspondence with Bill Clark (Harvard University), Guenther Fischer (International Institute for Applied Systems Analysis, Laxenburg, Austria), B. L. Turner (Clark University), Thomas Parris (ISciences, LLC, Ann Arbor), Robert Kates (Harvard University and Initiative on Science and Technology for Sustainability), and Eric Lambin (University of Louvain). Many thanks to them. See Nordhaus and Kokkelenberg (1999) and Abraham and Mackie (2005) for discussion of ways to account for activities and assets not immediately tied to market transactions.

9. External resources are enablers in trivial ways: the realization of ideas involves materials in some form, and at any rate, external resources provide the background against which human life unfolds.

10. The more one emphasizes the relevance of the background culture for the value added by the predecessors, the more pressure there will be to discount the claims of outsiders, but the more pressure there will also be to let all participants in the national culture benefit adequately from the inheritance. We are getting

an argument for a sizable inheritance tax in this way. For inheritance, see Haslett (1986).

11. On the question of why immigrants settle in urban areas, see Cohen (1996). More than 94 percent of Canadian immigrants settled in urban areas in the 1990s; in response, the government created "nominee programs" to offer expedited residency to skilled immigrants willing to settle in underpopulated areas. See James McCarten, "Rural Areas Suffer Lack of Diversity: Immigration to Cities Leaves Countryside Starved for Skilled Labor, Census Figures Show," *Vancouver Sun,* January 22, 2003, B5.

12. Such a move is standard in relevant discussions; see, e.g., Singer's (2002b) discussion of allocating emission permits on a per-capita basis. Miller (2007, chap. 3.4) objects to the idea that individuals ought to have an equal share of resources by pointing out that this would create conditions in which states with responsible policies would in time have to accept conditions favoring countries with irresponsible policies. Such worries can be addressed through the adoption of global standards in environmental and population policy that consider the conditions in which countries find themselves.

13. One might also wonder about the impact of the so-called *resource curse* on my proposal. For many less-developed countries, natural resources have become an obstacle to prosperity. The resource curse afflicts countries that derive a large portion of their income from exporting extractive resources such as oil, natural gas, or diamonds. Some are prone to authoritarian governments in ways that are arguably connected to their dependence on extractive resources: authoritarian regimes can readily increase their power by exploiting such resources. Such countries are also at a higher risk of civil conflict. Rebel groups can sustain armies by occupying certain regions and exploiting their resources. Third, such countries often exhibit lower rates of growth, partly because they are vulnerable to the first two problems, but also because resource-dependent economies are vulnerable to growth-retarding economic effects (see Ross 2001, 2003; Collier and Hoeffler 1998; Le Billon 2001; Sachs and Warner 2001; Rodriguez and Sachs 1999; Auty 2001; Lederman and Maloney 2006; Humphreys, Sachs, and Stiglitz 2007). Social scientists debate the nature of the resource curse—assessing to what extent natural resources are "curse or destiny," see Lederman and Maloney (2006)—but let us assume there is such a problem. My immigration proposal is not much affected by this phenomenon. First, to the extent that the curse is brought on poor countries because of the manner in which international economic interactions sets incentives, or at any rate to the extent that changes in international economic interactions could change the effect of the resource curse, making such changes is a straightforward application of the duty of aid from chapter 4. International economic interactions, as argued, for instance, by Wenar (2008), should then be modified in a way that ensures the curse no longer strikes. Second, let us recall that the measure needed for assessing relative over- and underuse is one of the overall value for human purposes of portions of three-dimensional spaces, rather than one specifically pertaining to resources. However, the resource curse might lower the value for human purposes of certain regions. Thereby, then, the presence of the resource curse generates pressure on other countries to accept more immigrants from countries affected by the curse.

14. This section follows Risse (2008). The parallel between immigration and adverse possession is also explored in Shachar (2009, chap. 6).

CHAPTER 9

1. (1) Fix a generation at 100 years, with an arbitrary starting point, today. The "current" or "our" generation consists of everybody who is alive at some point during the next 100 years. The 100 years capture a period individuals can still regard as affecting them and their children, as well as a period that is affected by what they and their children do. Everybody alive during the preceding 100 years belongs to the "last generation," everybody alive during the subsequent 100 years to "the next generation," and so on. "Future generations" are those from the next generation onward. Everybody alive now belongs to at least two generations unless they were born today, everybody who died yesterday does not belong to the current generation, and since individuals might become older than 100, they might belong to up to three generations. Some implications of this fixation are counterintuitive (and I am using the term mostly in the sense of "birth cohort"), but we only need some way of fixing what is meant by future generations that makes clear that those are not immediately affected by what we do now. (2) Diamond (2005) discusses societies that collapsed. Often these societies were backwater and isolated, but not always. In all cases, environmental issues mattered to their demise.

2. See Gardiner (2001, 2006). Epstein (1992) argues that future generations are best helped by the present generation leaving things to the market to ensure that people can bequeath wealth.

3. Whether future generations have *rights* has been widely debated. Steiner (1983), defender of the choice approach to rights (according to which a necessary condition for the possession of rights is the ability to choose), concurs with Grotius. Feinberg (1974), who endorses the interest theory (according to which possession of rights turns on having interests), allows that future people who will exist have contingent rights. Beckerman and Pasek (2001) argue that our relationship to future generations cannot be assessed in terms of rights, but still think we have obligations to them. Golding (1980) thinks we do not share a moral community with distant generations. De George (1984) holds that we do not owe anything to future generations; Eliott (1979) offers a rebuttal. Partridge (1990) argues that it is problematic to attribute rights to future people, Baier (1981) that it is not. Kavka (1978) rebuts skepticism about what future people will want: we know there are some basic needs they will have. Barry (1989b) doubts that asymmetries between generations can be properly integrated into ethical theories. See also Gosseries (2008a) for these themes.

4. Elsewhere I talk about sources of membership rights in the global order. These uses of "source" are distinct.

5. Dissenting voices on this point include de-Shalit (1995) and O'Neill (1993).

6. Henry George, nineteenth-century American political economist and advocate of the view that land belongs to all of humanity, captures a similar thought concerning future generations: "If all existing men were to unite to grant away

their equal rights, they could not grant away the rights of those who follow them. For what are we but tenants for a day? Have we made the earth that we should determine the rights of those who after us shall tenant it in their turn? The Almighty, who created the earth for man and man for the earth, has entailed it upon all the generations of the children of men by a decree written upon the constitution of all things—a decree which no human action can bar and no prescription determine" (1926, 137).

7. See Rawls (1999c, 111). See Hubin (1976), Barry (1978, 1989b), Gosseries (2001), Gaspart and Gosseries (2007), and Caney (2006a) for discussion. Passmore (1974) takes the same view on the source of our obligations to future generations (see chap. 4).

8. See also Jonas (1984, 4.1–3). Daniels (1988) points out that the duties of children to parents are not symmetrical to the duties of parents to children. Parents made a choice in having children, but children never had a choice. Daniels cannot find a convincing moral account of obligations of children to parents, so he thinks about what it is like to live a life prudentially, and uses that as a basis for the distribution of resources among generations.

9. Krebs (1999, 126) makes the same point. When we discuss reasons to bring future people into existence, or to "keep humanity in existence," we explore reasons to do so *for as long as possible,* not *indefinitely.* We can safely assume that humanity goes extinct eventually. We are asking whether there is something to be regretted if humanity goes extinct sooner rather than later, over and above harm for the immediately affected generation.

10. See also Wilson (1993, 272).

11. In the Burkean spirit, Auerbach (1995) argues we ought to act toward future generations in such a way that they are most likely to honor the commitments and build on the traditions of their ancestors.

12. Gaspart and Gosseries (2007, sec. 3) argue that we would not even *be allowed* to bring about such an improvement, out of justice to the least well-off members of the current generation.

13. For differences between the natural and the cultural world, see also Gosseries (2008b, 67).

14. Obviously, one important discussion to have here is about who has to do what with regard to this obligation. Above I focused on policy makers. But an individual armed with radioactive material, say, could do much damage felt by later generations. Moreover, while the obvious duties in this area relate to the state in which a generation passes on the earth's resources and spaces, one generation can also affect the next generation's ability to satisfy basic needs by determining its size. So duties with regard to population size must be included here.

15. Another common definition of sustainable development is "improving the quality of life while living within the carrying capacity of supporting ecosystems"; see Jacobs (1999, 23). For discussion, see Dobson (1998, chap. 2). For a critical discussion of the usefulness of the notion of sustainability, see Beckerman and Pasek (2001, chap. 5); see also Jamieson (2002). Attfield (2003, chap. 5) is a good introduction to sustainability. As Barry (1999) puts it, "the core concept of sustainability is … that there is some X whose value should be maintained, in as far as it lies within our power to do so, into the indefinite future. This leaves it open

for dispute what the content of X should be" (101). Jacobs (1999) captures some central ideas in the debate about "sustainable development:" (1) environment-economy integration: combining economic growth and environmental protection in planning and implementation; (2) futurity: concerns about the impact of current activities on future generations; (3) environmental protection: a commitment to reducing pollution and environmental degradation and to efficient use of resources; (4) equity: a commitment to meeting basic needs of the poor, as well as equity between generations; (5) quality of life: the recognition that well-being does not reduce to growth; (6) participation: the recognition that sustainable development requires the political involvement of all stakeholders. These ideas shape debates about topics such as the degree of required environmental protection, how much emphasis to put on equity issues, the importance of participation, and how broad a set of topics to cover under "sustainability."

16. See Neumayer (2003, 21), who himself credits the distinction to Pearce, Markandya, and Barbier (1989).

17. According to Solow (1992), sustainability "is an obligation to conduct ourselves so that we leave to the future the option or the capacity to be as well off as we are. It is not clear to me that one can be more precise than that" (506). As an example of failure, he lists Britain's using up North Sea oil without providing anything in exchange. See also Solow (1986). As Neumayer (2003, 23) emphasizes, weak sustainability is rooted in neoclassical economics, but is different in important ways. The rooting comes through the idea of substitutability, and the difference from taking the future seriously. Strong sustainability is disconnected from neoclassical economics. A main proponent of strong sustainability is Herman Daly. Following Mill, Daly endorses a steady state economy, stressing improvements in the quality of life. See Daly (1995, 1996) and Daly and Cobb (1989).

18. Just as Holland asks, "how could one not think that nature deserves a little protection in its own right," Pearce (1998) asks back, "How could one not see the massive opportunity costs that arise from giving the sort of protection to nature that defenders of absurdly strong sustainability demand?" See Norton (2005, chap. 8). Weak and strong sustainability support different reasoning about climate change. As Neumayer (2003, 37) points out, within the substitutability paradigm, reasoning like this (from Schelling 1995) makes sense: "If offered a choice of immediate development assistance or equivalent investments in carbon abatement, potential aid recipients would elect for the immediate." Substitutability supports an adaptation strategy to climate change: we should try to become as rich as possible to have means to adjust to new environmental conditions. Without substitutability, such reasoning is less plausible.

19. E. O. Wilson (1993) refers to biodiversity as "our most valuable but least appreciated resource" (281). For what is involved in the loss of biodiversity, see p. 347. Wilson (1984) develops the theme that humankind cannot flourish apart from the rest of the living world under the name of "biophilia." Perhaps supporters of weak sustainability can accept this argument as a matter of policy. However, we are then talking about decidedly *long-term* policies. There is no recognizable difference between a view that supports weak sustainability as a matter of principle but endorses the considerations above as a matter of policy and one that supports strong sustainability as a matter of principle and policy.

20. (1) One might worry that the ownership approach only enters into the formulation of the first argument. But that approach led to the position that future owners need to be integrated *as beneficiaries*. That move is borne out by these three arguments. One might also wonder whether it is indeed as a matter of justice that resources and spaces must be preserved. Why not say that considerations of justice establish a demand to make sure future people can meet basic needs, but that the additional conclusion about resources and spaces captures a demand of reasonable conduct? However, that conclusion does not *add* a substantive requirement. It merely explicates what it means to take future people seriously as beneficiaries. (2) For ways of valuing nature, see Krebs (1999, pt. 2). See also Eliott (1997) and Tribe (1976).

21. O'Neill (1993) makes a related argument in terms of a proper understanding of well-being.

CHAPTER 10

1. Established in 1988 by the World Meteorological Organization and the United Nations Environment Programme, the Intergovernmental Panel on Climate Change (IPCC) is charged with assessing the risks of climate change caused by human activities. For the background about climate change, see IPCC (2007a, 2007b, 2007c). IPCC reports are the canonical source for the state of climate science. Gardiner (2004) provides a survey of the scientific, economic, and philosophical questions about climate change as of 2004. Aldy and Stavins (2007b) provide a summary of the scientific state of the art as of 2007, as well as a survey of possible policy responses.

2. The ownership approach appears, in the context of climate change, in Singer (2002a), Hurka (1993), Grubb et al. (1992), Grubb (1995), Traxler (2002), and Gardiner (2004). Sands (2003, 14) states, "While it is clear that under international law each state may have environmental obligations to its citizens and to other states which may be harmed by its activities, it is less clear whether such an obligation is owed to the international community as a whole." The ownership standpoint shows why there are such moral duties.

3. I do not discuss how much adaptation and mitigation to target. The considerations we explore can be adjusted to speak to any proposal that fixes such goals.

4. Suppose A goes bankrupt because B sells for less. In that scenario, too, we have two occurrences: B's decision to offer goods for a certain price, and the customers' decisions to buy. It is the consumers who cause A's bankruptcy, B's price setting being once removed from that result. An appropriate question is whether B did anything wrong in shaping this consumer behavior. Yet in neither the market case nor the climate change case would a negative answer preclude duties to victims of such practices: as a citizen, A may deserve social security, to which B must contribute, and similarly for victims of climate change.

5. For more recent developments of the law of the seas, see Malanczuk (1997, chap. 12).

6. See Buck (1998) for the background to the term "common heritage of humanity"; see also Attfield (2003, 169–72).

7. We can combine these criteria in four different ways, which, according to Buck, render particular property arrangements appropriate (also for parts of the earth): If there is little difficulty in excluding others, and if use subtracts from the value of the goods, a private property regime suggests itself. If there is little difficulty in excluding others, but use does not subtract from the value of the goods, a toll regime suggests itself. If there are difficulties in excluding people, and use diminishes value, a common pool regime suggests itself. If there are difficulties in excluding others, and use does not diminish value, the goods should be kept public. These distinctions map onto the threefold distinction among different sorts of ownership status introduced above: the private property regime corresponds to the ownership status that allows appropriation to the exclusion of others, the public goods regime to the status that denies the appropriateness of property conventions beyond the original common ownership rights, and the toll and common pool regime to the ownership status that allows conventions that go beyond the original ownership rights without focusing on occupation to the exclusion of others. For discussion of public goods and common pool regimes from an institutional perspective, see also Ostrom (1990) and Bromley (1992). Buck's (1998) discussions about Antarctica, the open seas, the atmosphere, and outer space show how complex the legal history of all this is.

8. See Buck (1998, chap. 5). Talk about airspace control as a subtractable good is a stretch, but it should still count as sensible usage. One may say that it is intrinsic to the concept of control that it is highly subtractable *whatever* its object. But this point does not pose a problem for my discussion.

9. "Accessing" this good in the first instance means to release greenhouse gases, but, say, geoengineering to remove emissions from the atmosphere counts as well. My description of the absorptive capacity as a good provided by the skies is not quite accurate. Forests, for instance, also contribute to the absorptive capacity. But forests are located in particular countries. So countries with large forests may well deserve some credit toward their required emissions reductions, or may use the planting of forests as one way of contributing to such reductions.

10. This point objects to those (e.g., Posner and Weisbach 2010) who think national self-interest should carry considerable weight in assessments of climate agreements. Self-interest can carry such weight if we are looking for agreement regarding airspace control. But if we ask about the absorptive capacity, relevant is not what is mutually rational but what burdens states can be expected to bear.

11. (1) Shue (2001, 450) thinks it is "slightly odd" to treat the absorptive capacity as a vital resource but does it anyway because it is, as he says, a necessity, and an increasingly scarce one. Buck (1998, 125–28) is reluctant to talk about a common pool regime in the case of the atmosphere (a property regime she thinks should apply for goods of low excludability but high subtractability). Her point is that atmospheric resources are not analogous to resources in other domains (fisheries, seabed resources) and that therefore this terminology does not apply. Clean air, for instance, does not lend itself to ideas of "resource flow." Instead, we should think about the atmosphere in terms of a regulatory regime charged with the regulation

of externalities. But these considerations should be unproblematic for our discussion. Within the literature that Buck (1998) is part of, a common pool regime has a specific meaning. Thus its applicability to the atmosphere may not be straightforward or sensible. Similar problems may arise with regard to the absorptive capacity (not a term Buck uses), but nevertheless, within the approach we have adopted, we can say everything we want to say about absorptive capacity and its regulation. (2) For fair-division methods, see Young (1995) and Brams and Taylor (1996). For difficulties in applying fair division, see Risse (2004a). (3) Grubb et al. (1992) discuss various ways of allocating emissions—by area, GDP, population, etc. But their goal is to offer a politically realistic solution. None of those methods meets that test. See also Grubb (1995) and Traxler (2002). Neumayer (2000, 187) states, "That emission rights should be allocated on an equal per-capita basis and that historical differences in emissions should also be accounted for is ... the shared view of almost every scholar and policy maker from the developing world."

12. Or one may think of the distribution in terms of current populations. Variations are conceivable: one could index population sizes to a year before which actors could be expected to combat pollution. Or one could index to a future year, to avoid perverse incentives for population policy or accommodate countries with young populations.

13. Jamieson (2001) also advocates the equal per-capita proposal, as does Baer (2002); see also Athanasiou and Baer (2002).

14. See Rothbard (1996, 35). Hospers (1971, 65) makes a similar point.

15. Singer (2002a) argues for his approach on pragmatic grounds, suggesting that this would let industrialized countries off lightly compared to their accountability for past emissions. Frankel (2007) dismisses this idea as unrealistic, but in turn is criticized by other contributors to Aldy and Stavins (2007a) as being unrealistic, Frankel being a defender of an international institutional framework with emissions quotas.

16. One version of the equal per-capita approach can be developed in terms of historical per-capita assignments, but one can take historical emissions into account without endorsing an equal per-capita approach. Historical accountability is also known under the name "natural" or "ecological debt"; see Gruebler and Fujii (1991), Smith (1991), Simms (2005), and Neumayer (2000). According to the 2007 IPCC mitigation report, there was a 70 percent increase in greenhouse gas emissions between 1970 and 2004, 24 percent between 1990 and 2004 (3). Marland, Boden, and Andres (2006) report that "since 1751 roughly 305 billion tons of carbon have been released to the atmosphere from the consumption of fossil fuels and cement production. Half of these emissions have occurred since the mid 1970s."

17. See Caney (2006a, 2006b, 2010) for a discussion of these difficulties. Following Houghton (2004, 150), he illustrates the problems of ascribing amounts of harm to climate change by explaining that, say, sea levels in Bangladesh would have risen to some extent anyway, because of soil erosion.

18. This should be kept in mind in reference to statements such as this in Neumayer (2000): "To ignore historical accountability would mean to privilege those who lived in the past in the developed countries and to discriminate against those who live in the present or will live in the future developing countries" (188).

19. There has been a good deal of discussion of historical emissions. See Shue (1996), (1999), Gardiner (2004), Caney (2006a, 2006b), Grubb et al. (1992), Gosseries (2004), and Singer (2002a).

20. On strict liability, see Murphy and Coleman (1990, 126–30). My discussion above is admittedly rather quick in resolving a complicated dispute.

21. Singer (2002a) discusses 1990 as a plausible year, but indexes his equal per-capita approach to 2050.

22. See also Simms (2005, chap. 2) for the history of the discovery of climate change.

23. What is true also is that the more inelastic the good and uncompetitive the market, the more costs to polluters are passed on to consumers. The more elastic the good and competitive the market, the more polluters have an incentive to reduce costs, including the costs of emission permits. For a large share of emissions, the polluter is the consumer. Most electricity production for consumer use is produced in-country. So perhaps not much turns on whether polluters or consumers pay.

24. Caney (2010) proposes a qualified version of the polluter pays principle that holds that "persons should bear the burden of climate change that they have caused so long as doing so does not push them beneath a decent standard of living." However, he also argues that the polluter pays principle cannot cover all aspects of the problem (nonanthropogenic climate change, emissions of the poor, and past emissions—"the Remainder"). This leads to a second principle: "the duties to bear the Remainder should be borne by the wealthy but we should distinguish between two groups—(i) those whose wealth came about in unjust ways, and (ii) those whose wealth did not come about in unjust ways—and we should apportion greater responsibility to (i) than to (ii)." This is similar to what I propose. By way of contrast, Panayotou, Sachs, and Zwane (2002) argue that each country should make sacrifices to the extent that it has contributed to the problem and be compensated to the extent that it suffers from the problem. They argue that countries in temperate zones will be net payers, and countries in tropical zones will be net recipients.

25. Gosseries (2004) argues that if one considers ignorance an excuse, one would condone an unacceptable form of transgenerational free riding. (What he calls *inter*generational free riding is free riding of one generation on another within the same community, whereas transgenerational free riding is free riding of one generation in one community on another generation in another community.) Baer (2006), too, argues that there is something problematic about contemporaries benefiting from harmful activities in the past.

CHAPTER 11

1. On this hegemonic role of human rights talk within emancipatory discourses, see Kennedy (2004).

2. Less enthusiastically, Moyn (2010) calls human rights "the last utopia": an idea that became significant largely based on failures of earlier utopias, and did so mostly in the 1970s. One aspect of using the term "human" rights is that this

phrase creates empathy: the concerns behind these rights are potentially *everybody's*. This thought is captured nicely in a line from the play *The Self-Tormentor* by the Roman playwright Terence that is sometimes quoted in this context: "Homo sum, humani nihil a me alienum puto" (I am a man, I consider nothing that is human alien to me). Worth mentioning here also is a statement famously made to Oliver Cromwell during the Putney Debates about a new constitution for England: "Really, sir, I think that the poorest he that is in England hath a life to live as the greatest he" (Macdonald 1984, 21). By way of contrast is an entry in the diary of Hans Frank, under whose command of the so-called General Government the Nazis committed exceptional atrocities in Poland: "Humanity is a word one dares not use" (Davies 2003, 86).

3. Griffin (2008) explores the connection between the distinctively human life and the notion of dignity. "Dignity" does not denote anything that could not as well be stated without using the term. The term is applied in confusingly many contexts, creating an illusion of unity among rather distinct issues. Nonetheless, it is helpful for my theory to make contact with that notion, to avoid the impression that my theory is more revisionist than it is.

4. Article 1, section 2, of the German Basic Law also makes the connection between human rights and peace. Hitler's *Mein Kampf* mentions the idea of human rights explicitly as a source of resistance to his racist program (vol. 2, chaps. 2, 14).

5. Moravcsik (2000) argues that such reasoning is behind the adoption of the European Convention on Human Rights, but this reasoning works only if countries worry about the future acceptance of rights.

6. See Kennedy (2004) for some considerations as to what might be problematic about the apparent consensus on human rights; see also Mutua (2001). Nickel (2002) explores whether the current human rights system is a global governance regime, and what that would entail.

7. (1) Statistical analyses of cross-country data sets have spread pessimism about compliance with human rights treatises; see, e.g., Hathaway (2002). On the other hand, qualitative, case study–based inquiries have identified mechanisms through which human rights documents and organizations could make a difference in domestic politics. Domestic opposition may challenge governments to abide by rules they have ostensibly accepted. International organizations may contribute to a process of "naming and shaming," or may provide logistic support or training. Eventually the government can no longer ignore these pressures, and first must engage the activists politically, and then make changes. Social scientists have found such success stories in, e.g., Eastern Europe and Central America; see Risse, Ropp, and Sikkink (1999). Making sense of these divergent findings is an area of ongoing research; see, e.g., Simmons (2009), whose findings dispute Rabkin's skepticism. (2) See Koh (1997) on the point that states obey international law to increase their legitimacy. A striking illustration of moral language being used without reflecting moral commitments comes from John Maynard Keynes's assessment of the negotiations in Paris in 1919. To accommodate Woodrow Wilson, the Treaty of Versailles had to be cast in moral language, although everybody else understood that doing so expressed no serious commitment to the values ostensibly endorsed: "Thus instead of saying that German-Austria is prohibited from

uniting with Germany except by leave of France (which would be inconsistent with the principle of self-determination), the Treaty, with delicate draftsmanship, states that 'Germany acknowledges and will respect strictly the independence of Austria, within the frontiers which may be fixed in a treaty between that State and the Principal Allied and Associated Powers; she agrees that this independence shall be inalienable, except with the consent of the Council of the League of Nations,' which sounds, but is not, quite different" (Keynes 2004, 94f). Keynes goes on to list several other such cases. See also Evans (2001, chap. 1).

8. There has been a debate about the use of Habermas's theory in international relations; see Hellmann, Wolff, and Zürn (2003) and Niesen and Herborth (2007). Deitelhoff (2006) offers a reconstruction of the negotiations that led to the International Criminal Court, identifying "islands of conviction" that can be described as successful moral discourses within a world of power.

9. These "responsibility to protect" ("R2P") principles were developed by the International Commission on Intervention and State Sovereignty (established by the Canadian government) in the December 2001 report, *The Responsibility to Protect*. Some of the relevant provisions were reaffirmed by the UN Security Council in 2006, in its Resolution 1674. See Steiner, Alston, and Goodman (2007, 839ff.), Cooper and Kohler (2009), and Bellamy (2009).

10. I do not discuss how actual burdens should be distributed among actors within the global order. For this question, see Miller (2001) and references therein.

11. For a discussion of human rights as manifesto rights, see Beitz (2009, chap. 15). Buchanan (2004) talks about an "application indeterminacy" of human rights. One of three factors that constitute this indeterminacy is that "because at present most if not all societies fall far short of adequately protecting human rights, institutionalizing them is to a large extent a remedial process, a matter of reforming or eradicating those institutions that facilitate the violation of human rights. But these defective institutions will vary across societies, so implementation must vary accordingly" (181).

12. On the teleological nature of human rights, see also Beitz (2001, 277–78).

13. As reported in the *New York Times,* November 30, 2006, in the New York Region section.

14. (1) See Beitz (2009, 164–67). (2) In the biblical book of Job, Job considers possibilities of contesting God's harsh treatment of him. "If it is a matter of justice," Job says, "who will summon him?" (9:19). One way of reading this is that the relationship between Job and God cannot be one of justice because nobody could summon God and thus enforce any just treatment that God may owe Job. In the spirit of my argument above, such an understanding of justice is too limited. Job may have a complaint in terms of justice even though nobody can summon God.

CHAPTER 12

1. Hestermeyer (2007) sums up the state of the art in the legal debate; see also Toebes (1999). Sell (2003) discusses the background to TRIPs and the history

of intellectual property arrangements. See Maskus and Reichman (2005a) on developments in intellectual property protection at the global level. The WHO's list of essential medicines is at http://www.who.int/topics/essential_medicines/en.

2. (1) The latter sort of right draws on considerations that are not specific to intellectual property. Exercising such a right merely entails that individuals can demand rewards that legal structures have given them reason to expect. Societies may always promise rewards beyond what individuals otherwise have a right to. (2) My argument interacts effectively with work on incentive setting for the pharmaceutical industry; see Kremer and Glennerster (2004), Love and Hubbard (2007), and Pogge (2008a, 2008b).

3. Reed (2006) applies Grotian ideas to the gene pool (using an analogy to the sea), but believes these ideas are useful only to Christians. For introductions to the philosophical concerns behind intellectual property law, see Shiffrin (2007). See also Hettinger (1989), Kuflik (1989), and Fisher (2001). For a discussion of these issues specifically with regard to patents, see Sterckx (2005). Lessig (2004) argues for very limited copyrights, kindred in spirit to the present argument. My approach speaks more to patents than to copyrights. Ashcroft (2005) argues in support of states' rights to expropriate property in public health emergencies. Schueklenk and Ashcroft (2002) support a similar conclusion for consequentialist reasons.

4. Buckley and O Tuama (2005) and De George (2005) deal with pricing issues in the pharmaceutical industry. Questions concern what profits are justified, given what risks and difficulties that industry faces, but also given how much they benefit from public subsidies. For a perspective skeptical of the industry, see Angell (2004). See also Cohen, Illingworth, and Schüklenk (2006). Other issues include the question of what areas this industry should invest in, and how to market products. Another question is to what extent regulation of intellectual property causes a lack of access to medication, and what remedies there may be. Maskus and Reichman (2005b) argue that TRIPs has given rise to a transnational system of innovation that could produce powerful incentives to innovate for the benefit of mankind, if developed properly.

5. Jefferson, "The Invention of Elevators" (letter, 1813), quoted in Shiffrin (2001, 138). Wilson (2009) argues against the possibility of a moral right to intellectual property, largely by way of reference to the fact that any one person's use of ideas does not exclude others from making the same use of them (i.e., their nonrivalrousness).

6. Gottlob Frege's 1918 essay, "Der Gedanke: Eine logische Untersuchung" ("The Thought: A Logical Investigation," 1918), is a locus classicus for this view, although I am, for the sake of argument, offering an extreme version of it. See Gideon Rosen's entry on abstract objects at the online *Stanford Encyclopedia of Philosophy*, http://plato.stanford.edu/entries/abstract-objects/. See also Burgess and Rosen (1997). It is also important to mention Popper's theory of reality, which distinguishes among three worlds: World 1 is the world of physical objects and events, World 2 that of mental objects and events, and World 3 the world of products of the human mind. See Popper (1972).

7. The presumption has this effect regardless of what larger strategy of arguing for stronger private intellectual property rights one chooses, e.g., an approach

in terms of natural law, a hypothetical contract between inventors and society, or considerations of distributive justice.

8. Raz (1986, 8–11) helpfully distinguishes among three senses of "presumption in favor of/against something": first, a burden of adducing evidence against the presumed view; second, a "suspension of the normal connection between belief and action," such as in the case of a presumption of innocence; and third, the existence of an unrefuted reason for believing something which is just enough to justify the belief but weak enough also to justify its suspension. Mine is closest to Raz's third sense.

9. Nozick (1974, 178–82).

10. Clark, *Essentials of Economic Theory* (1907, 360–61), in Waldron (1993b, 866). Bainbridge (1992) has a similar view: "The basic reason for intellectual property law is that a man should own what he produces, that is, what he brings into being. If what he produces can be taken from him, he is no better off than a slave. Intellectual property is, therefore, the most basic form of property because a man uses nothing to produce it other than his mind" (17).

11. Becker (1993) also offers an illustration from a scientific context of the phenomenon that achievements are sometimes entirely disconnected from a societal state of knowledge and ability. He refers to the following statement of the mathematician Mark Kac: "'There are two kinds of geniuses, the ordinary and the magicians. An ordinary genius is a fellow that you and I would be just as good as, if we were only many times better.' But for the second kind, 'even after we understand what they have done, the process by which they have done it is completely dark'" (617, n. 22).

12. One might say the arguments I am rehearsing here are appealing precisely because they do not draw on controversial metaphysical assumptions. However, the main result on intellectual property below does not depend on the assumption of realism.

13. See also Moore (1997).

14. For the idea of invention, see Kneale (1955).

15. Paine (1991), a response to Hettinger (1989), captures the competing approaches to intellectual property: "We may begin thinking about information rights, as Hettinger does, by treating all ideas as part of a common pool and then deciding whether and how to allocate to individuals rights to items in the pool. Within this framework, ideas are conceived on the model of tangible property. Just as, in the absence of social institutions, we enter the world with no particular relationships to its tangible assets or natural resources, we have no particular claim on the world's ideas.... Alternatively, we may begin, as I do, by thinking of ideas in relation to their originators, who may or may not share their ideas with specific others or contribute them to the common pool. This approach treats ideas as central to personality, and the social world individuals construct of themselves. Ideas are not, in the first instance, freely available natural resources. They originate with people, and it is the connections among people, their ideas, and their relationships with others that provide a baseline for discussing rights in ideas" (49).

16. Shiffrin argues that the presumption against privatization that comes from the idea of original collective ownership has often been underestimated in Lockean accounts of private intellectual property. In her view, Locke's "mixing" account of

privatization does not provide a foundation for privatization per se but creates a way of assessing which individuals would be allowed to occupy something. Given a presumption against privatization, Lockean accounts of property deliver considerable constraints on the possibility of private intellectual property. For opposing understandings of the Lockean approach to property, see Hughes (1988), Becker (1993), Child (1990), and Moore (1997).

17. For the connection between health and social justice, see Hofrichter (2003) and Wilkinson (1996); see also Barry (2005, chap. 6), Waldron (1993a), and Daniels (1985).

18. (1) This argument does not engage with the moral acceptability of TRIPs in ways internal to considerations of compensation and incentive setting. Maskus and Reichman (2005b) argue that the TRIPs agreement has generated a transnational system of innovation that could produce powerful incentives to innovate for the benefit of mankind if developed properly. Usual arguments supportive of strengthening intellectual property protections even in developing countries include the ability to build local research and development, to attract technology transfers, and to attract foreign direct investment. The economist Joan Robinson once spoke of the "paradox of patents": "The justification of the patent system is that by slowing down the diffusion of technical progress it ensures that there will be more progress to diffuse" (Robinson 1958, 87, cited in Sterckx 2005, 197). As far as TRIPs is concerned, the question is whether the long-term effects in terms of "more progress to diffuse" are big enough to warrant the short-term costs, not merely in terms of "slowing down the diffusion of technical progress" but also in terms of the consequences of this slowdown (e.g., hampered access to medications). (2) One might say one concern behind TRIPs is to undermine drug smuggling, which benefits from the existence of countries without patent protection. However, different policies must solve that problem, rather than overly strong private intellectual property rights that require plausibility independently of such effects.

CHAPTER 13

1. This chapter draws on Risse (2009c).

2. On the history of the labor movement prior to the ILO, see Follows (1951). See also Shotwell (1934). Regarding why there is an ILO, Bartolomei de la Cruz et al. (1996) offer the following answer: "These demands [for international regulation to decrease the poverty in which workers lived] had a humanitarian foundation, but industrialists and governments feared that they would lose out to competitors if they took unilateral protective action which would raise the cost of production in their own countries" (3). Morsink (1999), chapter 5, discusses the background to the Universal Declaration's labor articles.

3. One may say that my discussion presupposes that Marx and Engels offer an accurate assessment of the situation in 1848. On an alternative reading, the Manifesto offers more of a prophecy than an analysis of the situation at that time. Even large parts of Europe, especially Germany and certainly Russia, had

not industrialized in the 1840s. So it might be an exaggeration to speak of a truly international dimension of industrialization and capitalism during that period. But even on such an approach it remains true that the authors of the Manifesto perceived international capitalism as the problem. Arguably, the presuppositions of their vision became a reality in the course of the nineteenth century.

4. By way of comparison, Articles I and II of Part XIII of the Treaty of Versailles prescribe the following: labor is not a mere commodity; a right of association; payment of an adequate wage to maintain a reasonable standard of living; an eight-hour day or forty-eight-hour workweek; a weekly rest of at least twenty-four hours; no child labor; equal pay for equal work; equitable economic treatment of all workers in a country (immigrants as well as nationals); and an inspection system to ensure enforcement. As Alcock (1971, 36) notes, in various respects this regulation fell below what labor representation had demanded.

5. See Lauren (2003, chap. 2).

6. See also Cranston (1973, 66).

7. Arneson (1990a) defends a right to work in the sense that the state has to create jobs. Gewirth (1996, 215) thinks there is a human right "to be effectively able to earn [one's] livelihood through [one's] own productive work."

CHAPTER 14

1. This chapter integrates material from Risse (2007) and Kurjanska and Risse (2008). However, the focus in those articles was on fairness rather than justice, and the discussion was framed in terms of the trade policy of states. See Krugman and Obstfeld (2003) for an introduction to international economics, see Hoekman and Kostecki (2001) on the trading system, and see Trebilcock and Howse (2005) for legal aspects of trade regulation. See Stiglitz and Charlton (2006, chap. 2) for difficulties in applying the idea of comparative advantage to certain scenarios. See Bhagwati (1993) for objections to free trade.

2. As Irwin (2002, 55) reports, the U.S. sugar price is twice that of the world market price. Producers receive about $1 billion annually (42 percent going to 1 percent of farms). The costs of protection amount to $1.9 billion, $0.9 billion being deadweight losses.

3. For net food importers, see Hoekman and Kostecki (2001, 225ff.). The lack of food production in developing countries that are importers (though they have a comparative advantage in labor costs and ought to be able to match global agricultural prices) may already be a result of international price signals (of subsidy-depressed prices), which may provide disincentives for necessary investment in a developing country (see Ingco and Nash 2004).

4. As the *Economist* reported, a World Bank report states that in 2005, immigrants from poor countries were expected to send more than $167 billion back home, which equaled the amount of foreign direct investment and was twice the value of foreign aid that year. Money sent through informal channels may add another 50 percent (*Economist*, November 26, 2005, 116). For the impact of trade on poverty, see Winters, McCulloch, and McKay (2004).

5. See the survey by USITC (1997). See Wacziarg and Welch (2008) and the discussion of the literature in Anderson (2004, 343–44). See also Panagariya (2004). Rodriguez and Rodrik (2000) agree there is a positive relationship between trade and growth but question whether it is due to trade policy rather than to transport costs or demand.

6. See Birdsall, Rodrik, and Subramanian (2005) for that view; see also Panagariya (2005). I am glancing over the details of what it means for trade to be important for development. Trade could be connected merely to growth, but neither trade nor growth might immediately be tied to other development goals. See, however, the UN's *Human Development Report 2003,* and the World Bank's 2004 *World Development Indicators* and references therein, for arguments that growth is relevantly related to other development goals.

7. Throughout, I talk about "higher" and "lower" labor standards. "Higher" standards are not ipso facto morally preferable. I use these terms descriptively, with reference to typical concerns: safety, job security, benefits, the right to unionize, and the like. Loosely, these issues order standards in terms of "weaker" and "stronger."

8. For the varieties-of-capitalism approach to comparative political economy, see Hall and Soskice (2001) and Howell (2003).

9. This is Title 19, U.S. Code, Chapter 4—Tariff Act of 1930; Subtitle II—Special Provisions, Part I—Miscellaneous, Sec. 1307.

10. For discussion, see Thompson (1987, 49–52) and Glover and Scott-Taggart (1975).

11. One might think of fairness in trade in terms of *exploitation.* While the moral significance of Marx's notion of exploitation (taking away of surplus value) depends on the labor theory of value and has suffered accordingly in plausibility, there is no agreement on an alternative understanding. Concerns about exploitation in the context of trade are about unfair advantage taking of sorts. Yet the moral issues underlying these complaints need to be explained more specifically. Therefore I use that term sparingly. For exploitation, see also Sample (2003), Wertheimer (1996), and Goodin (1985). While their proposals differ, they all spell out unfair advantage taking (as does Feinberg [1988, chap. 31]). See also Reeve (1987). For the view that the labor theory of value is an unsuitable basis for the charge of exploitation and that that charge can be motivated differently in a manner appealing to Marxists, see Cohen (1988); see also Roemer (1985).

12. My account of fairness draws on Broome (1999) but differs from his, especially by allowing for different bases on which stringent claims can rest. See Risse (2007) for a slightly more extensive presentation of my account of fairness. Risse (2007) and Kurjanska and Risse (2008) are indeed concerned with fairness, specifically with fairness as it applies to trade policies of states. The main result of those two pieces is the Weak Westphalian View on fairness in trade as it applies to states. However, instead of saying that the effects of trade must be distributed in such a way that no negative rights are violated, as the Weak Westphalian View does, it is better to say more generally that gains from trade should be distributed such that no country enjoys gains that have come at the expense of people involved with the trade.

13. Since there is this pragmatic use, I employ the term "basis" loosely in the context of fairness. Grounds of justice are such bases, some of them being crucial to fairness in trade. This use of the term basis is in principle different from how I use it in the context of conceptions of human rights. "In principle": what counts as a basis in either context may well also be a basis in the other, but the term does its work respectively within different bits of theory.

14. See Burtless et al. (1998, chap. 5).

CHAPTER 15

1. A more general point should be noted. Now that all principles of justice are on the table, one question is whether it would be possible for them all to be satisfied at once. Is the just world I described at the beginning of this chapter possible—logically, physically, psychologically? One version of this question is whether it would be possible to achieve justice (and, in particular, human rights for all) while the system of multiple states exists. Some principles of justice essentially concern distributions involving states (i.e., the Rawlsian principles, but also the trade principles, which deal with a population of trading states). So if they are to be satisfied (other than vacuously, because there exist no entities to which they apply), there must be states (and in the case of trade, multiple states). Thus, if at the same time some of the other principles could *not* be satisfied within the system of multiple states, it would follow that not all of the principles could be satisfied at once. One may have this concern even if one agrees with the argument I develop in this chapter and the next, that we morally ought not abandon the system of multiple states. As my reply to Tan's worry should make clear, I take this problem very seriously to the extent that we are talking about possibility in a psychological sense, or in a manner that concerns institutional design. But we do not have reason to be concerned that the principles this book discusses are not jointly possible in a logical or physical sense, or because their joint satisfaction requires different political arrangements.

2. This chapter draws on (and to some extent revises) earlier work of mine (Risse 2005a, 2005b, 2005c).

3. I am not now concerned with fairness questions about relationships among particular countries, for instance if one country interferes with the affairs of another by forcing a certain development agenda on it, by aiding a repressive regime, or by exercising destructive power. For those topics, see Miller (2010). Much of what Miller argues is complementary to my view, especially his account of Singer's (1972) famous pond case and his discussion of the role of the United States in world politics; see also Miller (1998).

4. Martin (2004, 443) states that "about 175 m people—3% of the world's residents ... —were migrants living outside their countries of birth or citizenship for a year or more in 2000, including 6% classified as refugees." Martin's point is that this is many people; mine is that, comparatively speaking, it is not. Things may change, of course. Attali (2009) makes the following prediction for an era beginning around 2050 at the latest: "Countries will no longer be lived in at any

length by anyone but the sedentary—forced to be there because they are too hostile to risk, too fragile, too young, or too old—and by the weakest, some of them immigrants from elsewhere in search of a more decent way of life" (183). Stateless people received much attention in the important chapter 9 of Arendt's (1975) *The Origins of Totalitarianism.*

5. Elias (1994) puts a positive spin on the creation of legal immediacy: "As long as control of the instruments of physical violence … is not very highly centralized, social tensions lead again and again to warlike actions. Particular social groups, artisan settlements and their feudal lords, towns and knights, confront each other as units of power which—as only states do later—must always be ready to settle their differences of interest by force of arms. The fears aroused in this structure of social tensions can still be discharged easily and frequently in military action and direct physical force. With the gradual consolidation of power monopolies and the growing functional interdependence of nobility and bourgeoisie, this changes" (423). Polanyi's (1957) classic study of the social implications of the market economy in turn argues that this development could become possible only by expansion of the administrative reach of the state, with effects on the lives of the people that were "awful beyond description" (76).

6. For the importance of statistics for the development of the modern state, see Hacking (1990) and Porter (1994). Winichakul (1994) discusses the importance of maps in the formation of a national awareness for the case of Siam (Thailand). Blackbourn (2006) documents the stratification of landscape and its role in state building in Germany, which reflected the process of stratifying society itself.

7. On this aspect of the process, see de Swaan (1988). For the development of states in the nineteenth century in a global perspective, see Bayly (2004). States across the world became increasingly similar during that time.

8. (1) For Nussbaum's list, see Nussbaum (2006, 76). See also Nussbaum (2000). Sen (1980) proposed capabilities as a distribuendum for principles of justice. Later he formulated an approach to development centered on the idea of freedom. See Sen (1985, 1999). (2) For arguments in support of open borders, see Kukathas (2005). Wellman (2008) thinks of freedom of association as an integral part of self-determination and that immigration can be limited by appeal to it. Miller (2007, chap. 8) argues that little is gained from appeals to freedom of association.

9. See Carens (1992, 2003); for related views, see Ackerman (1980), Dummett (2001), Tushnet (1995), Hayter (2000), and Nett (1971).

10. See also Blake (2001).

11. By "demos" I just mean whichever group of people is supposed to carry out democratic procedures. I say more about the term in chapter 17.

12. Goodin (2007) argues similarly.

13. For a discussion of how to determine who should be included in a demos of democratic politics, see Miller (2009).

14. The notion of "radical inequality" is defined as follows: (1) The worst-off are very badly off in absolute terms. (2) They are also very badly off in relative terms—much worse off than others. (3) The inequality is impervious: it is difficult or impossible for the worse-off substantially to improve their lot, and most of the better-off never experience life at the bottom and have no vivid idea of what it is

like to live that way. (4) The inequality is pervasive: it concerns not merely some aspects of life, but most aspects or all. (5) The inequality is avoidable: the better-off can improve their circumstances without becoming badly off themselves (Pogge 2002, 198).

15. I have more to say about dependency theory later in this chapter. How imposing this burden of proof can be is revealed in what Andres Velasco says about attempts to establish dependency theory, which from the start "faced its share of troubles. Armies of graduate students tried to find a positive correlation between expansion in the north and recession in the south, but failed to find it. (Then as now, a boom in the United States and Europe often meant growth for developing countries.) Much less did they manage to prove a *causal relationship* between northern wealth and southern poverty" (Velasco 2002, 44). For such reasons, dependency theory has lost most of its defenders. I return to this subject below.

16. Pogge (2002, 7).

17. Special drawing rights are international reserve assets issued by the IMF; see Soros (2002, chap. 2) for his proposal to donate such rights as development aid.

18. Pritchett and Lindauer (2002) and Easterly (2001) suggest that "big ideas" in development have failed and that there is no general method that guarantees success.

19. Since this discussion is in response to Pogge (2002), I use data also used for the articles (Risse 2005b, 2005c) on which this discussion draws. The contrast between the different views that this chapters develops is very unlikely to be affected by any changes in data in the foreseeable future. Unless otherwise noted, data are from the World Bank's *World Development Report 2000/2001* (2000), the UN's *Report of the High-Level Panel on Financing for Development* ("Zedillo report," 2001), and the World Bank's *World Development Indicators*;(2002); see also Maddison (2001, 265, table B 22). See also Lomborg (2001, pt. 2), especially for different approaches to measuring inequality.

20. Pogge (2002, 98). PPP means "purchasing power parity": the poverty line is fixed at what $1.08 bought in the United States in 1993.

21. See Alesina and Dollar (2000). According to the Zedillo report, official development aid in 2000 was $53.1 billion, down from $60.9 billion in 1992; in 1998, $12.1 billion went to the least-developed countries; 0.33 was the average percentage of GNP contributed as official development aid in 1992, down to 0.22 percent in 2000, contrasted with the 0.7 percent of GNP that is widely agreed.

22. See Van de Walle and Johnston (1996, 20).

23. However, if we were to assess a serial killer, we would presumably look to absolute numbers, and one might wonder why that is. In that case, we are not asking a question of the sort, "what is the impact of system X on a population." What matters is that every life lost is a life intentionally and prematurely disrupted against the victim's will. No further question is salient. If we were exploring why a society produces more serial killers than others, we would again inquire about the impact of a system, and so be interested in relative numbers.

24. For the quotation, see Landes (1998, 381, 429); Bairoch (1993) argues that it was not because of exploitation of developing countries that developed

countries did well. A classic of dependency theory is Cardoso and Faletto (1979). For Marxist approaches, see Gunder Frank (1971) and Wallerstein (1980). See also Amin (1976). For criticism, see Brenner (1977). For an overview (as well as a critical assessment specifically of dependency theories), see Brewer (1990); see also Barone (1985), Callinicos (2009), and Kiely (2010, esp. chap. 2). See Arndt (1987) for an account of dependency theory as part of a discussion of the history of the idea of development. See also Young (2001) and Krishna (2009). Pitts (2010) surveys recent work on empire that bears on political theory and philosophy. She argues that political theory fails to deal adequately with the (problematically) imperial features of the global order. For a positive evaluation of empire and the view that the United States ought to see itself as an empire, see Lal (2004).

25. For some of the recent accounts of the asymmetrical interactions that brought about the current political and economic reality, see, e.g., Curtin (2000), Bayly (2004), Subrahmanyam (2005), or Benton (2001).

26. For a similar assessment to Braudel's, see Wesseling (2004, chap. 8). Fieldhouse (1999, esp. chap. 12) too concurs. For a multidimensional and differentiated assessment of colonialism, see Abernethy (2000, chaps. 16, 17). Frieden (2006) concludes his assessment of the economic consequences of colonialism by stating, "With the exception of cases of outright Leopoldian looting [referring to the Belgian colonization of the Congo] and privileged settler colonies, colonialism was not usually an insurmountable obstacle to economic development" (92–93). He finds that colonialism is one of many factors affecting growth in the developing world and did not always have a negative effect. Headrick (1988) argues that colonies often experienced growth but little actual development because investments went into physical but not human capital. Colonies became modern but remained underdeveloped. Headrick (1981) argues that it is machinery and innovation (and the fascination with them) that is the true legacy of imperialism in colonies, especially in Africa and Asia. For Hobsbawm (1989, chap. 3), the legacy of imperialism lies in the transmission of ideas to minorities of various kinds in the colonies. See Reinhard (1996, chap. 12) for a similar assessment.

27. For institutional quality, see Kaufmann, Kray, and Ziodo-Lobaton (2002). Regarding Congo, see Hochschild (1999) or Freund (1998).

28. For theories of path dependency, see Thelen (1999), Engerman and Sokoloff (2000), and Pierson (2000).

CHAPTER 16

1. (1) As Rawls (1999b) puts the point: "until the ideal is identified … nonideal theory lacks an objective, an aim, by reference to which its queries can be answered" (90); see also Rawls (1993, 285). For discussion, see Simmons (2010). (2) Some readers will think that at least a world state has been conclusively refuted by Kant, and that thus my response to supporters of a world state is gratuitously weak. I discuss Kant below. But for one thing, I develop a particular epistemic approach to assessing the world state. Moreover, my concern is more general: I am concerned with political ideals that do away with any world consisting of multiple states.

2. This view is compatible with endorsing changes locally: in some cases federative structures such as in the EU are appropriate (Morgan 2005), and the case for global cooperation for many issues is overwhelming. The upshot of my discussion agrees with Morris (1998). His chapter 4 explores why there should be states, using game-theoretic modeling and arguments from history. Neither approach delivers a conclusive case for the state, nor does it lead to the conclusion that we ought to try something else. Morris suggests we should try to understand what renders states legitimate, and then make them so.

3. Simmons distinguishes *justification* from *legitimacy*: asking about legitimacy means to ask about what relationship the state needs to have to those over whom it claims the right to rule. A state may be justified because we can defend it as rationally and morally acceptable or even optimal. But it may not have the sort of relationship to certain individuals to give it the right to rule them. (Perhaps a right to rule presupposes voluntary submission.) According to Simmons, a state's illegitimacy is consistent with the subjects still having moral obligations, which sometimes will be the same as political obligations.

4. "Anarchism" has violent connotations, and rightly so. The late nineteenth and early twentieth centuries, for instance, saw a considerable number of actual or attempted assassinations of rulers. One response was the International Conference of Rome for the Social Defense against Anarchists in 1898, following the assassination of Empress Elizabeth of Austria. This conference defined anarchism as "any act that uses violent means to destroy the organization of society." However, *philosophical* anarchists may take a range of attitudes of what *to do* about states.

5. So perhaps instead of saying "We are entitled to say that there ought to be states if and only if we can conclusively refute both types of skepticism," I should say "Given the availability of such a prima facie positive case, etc.," and mutatis mutandis for the negation. However, one may also think of the positive case for states as folded into the responses to the skeptics. So it does not matter how we put it.

6. Williams (1996) argues that problems in the state of nature do not hold in the state of nature among states. Malcolm (2002) argues that for Hobbes, there is no ongoing violence in that second state of nature.

7. Kant references are to the Reiss edition (Kant 1970a) of Kant's political writings. See Habermas (1997) for an introduction to Kant's political philosophy. See also Kleingeld (2004) and Byrd and Hruschka (2010, chap. 9).

8. However, compare *Theory and Practice*, where he says that "even against their will people are forced by the constant wars to enter into a cosmopolitan constitution" (1970a, 90). There is a well-acknowledged problem about how to reconcile Kant's view on the permissibility of coercion to subject individuals to states with his remarks on the voluntary nature of the federation; see Kleingeld (2004). Nonetheless, what remains constant is Kant's concern with skepticism from above.

9. And then there is the cosmopolitan right (172). See also Simmons (2001b, 194).

10. The closest Rawls gets to engaging skepticism from below is his response to Nozick in "The Basic Structure as Subject," in *Political Liberalism* (1993). Yet even that discussion does not argue for coercive institutions vis-à-vis other ar-

rangements. Wolff (1996) offers a reconstruction of what Rawls would or could have said in response to the anarchist.

11. See also Rothbard (1998, pt. 3); for similar views, see Friedman (1973) and Benson (1990).

12. For the Irish case, see Peden (1977). The classical reference for African societies is E. E. Evans-Pritchard's controversial work on the Nuer (Fortes and Evans-Pritchard 1940). Right-libertarians like to enlist support from political anthropologists and take heart in statements like this: "In many societies government simply does not exist" (Lewellen 1992, 1). See Pennock and Chapman (1978) for perspectives on anarchism. Barclay (1982) offers an anthropological look at anarchy. For Africa, see Horton (1985) and Herbst (2000).

13. The sociologist Franz Oppenheimer writes about the state, "The State ... is a social institution, forced by a victorious group of men on a defeated group with the sole purpose of regulating the dominion of the victorious group over the vanquished, and securing itself against revolt from within and attacks from abroad" (2007, 8).

14. The reasoning in this paragraph (as far as it concerns the Kantian moral case) is informed by Eric Beerbohm's unpublished paper, "Nozick's Wager." Beerbohm's concern is with uncertainty in one's moral beliefs. To what extent ought an agent factor into his decision making doubts he has about his moral beliefs? Beerbohm suggests that two things matter: the degree of confidence an agent has in his moral belief (Confidence Consideration) and the amount of the "moral costs" associated with the scenario that his moral belief turns out to be false (e.g., the agent does something that is impermissible; Magnitude Consideration). Such moral costs include everything that is impermissible if his action were permissible. As far as the Kantian argument is concerned, one has to assess its Confidence Consideration in light of the force of the doubts presented above, and the Magnitude Consideration by factoring in everything that would be impermissible if the founding of states had been morally erroneous.

15. See Porter (1994). For the link between the state and wars, see Waltz (1959).

16. Charney (1999) also depicts a bleak picture of state activities: "In total, during the first eighty-eight years of the [twentieth] century, 170 million men, women, and children were shot, beaten, tortured, knifed, burned, starved, frozen, crushed or worked to death; buried alive, drowned, hanged, bombed, or killed in any other of the myriad other ways governments have inflicted deaths on unarmed helpless citizens and foreigners.... It is as though our species has been devastated by a modern Black Plague" (28). See also Bull (1977, 282–84) and Pogge (2002, 183–90). The list of the "world's biggest problems" in Lomborg (2007) includes the following, all of which could be tied to the existence of states: financial instability, lack of intellectual property rights, money laundering, trade barriers, air pollution, climate change; deforestation, land degradation; biodiversity loss; vulnerability to natural disasters; arms proliferation, conflicts, corruption, lack of education, terrorism, drugs, diseases, lack of people of working age, inadequate living conditions of children and women, and hunger and malnutrition.

17. I explain below, at the end of section 5, why I do not put the second option here without appealing to moral considerations: "We cannot establish that there ought to be states or that there ought to be no states. That means that there are

no moral reasons to get rid of states now, but there are practical reasons not to; all things considered, then, we ought not to try to get rid of states now."

18. See, e.g., Avineri (1968, chap. 8), and especially the careful study in Hunt (1974; see also Hunt 1984).

19. Estlund (2008, chap. 14) discusses "utopophobia" with particular reference to his account of democracy. He argues that there is still value even to a "hopeless normative theory" (269). He does not, however, address the sort of problem discussed in the text above.

20. See Russell (1985) for an amusing account of James II's kingship had the winds in 1688 favored him.

21. See Adamson (1997) for this episode of British history.

22. See Montefiore (2004).

23. See Roberts (2004), Hawthorne (1991), Squire (1931), Ferguson (1997), Cowley (2003), and Macksey (1995). See the introduction to Ferguson (1997) for reflections on counterfactual history. Hawthorne engages with philosophical questions about possibility and plausibility in historical understanding.

24. (1) Hawthorne (1991) explains the process in which he came to assess how responses to the Black Death in Europe could have differed and thereby explicates what I just said: "[I have proceeded] by making comparisons, taking 'contrast cases', within Europe itself and extending them. These comparisons consisted simply in looking at the nature, circumstances and effects of actual practical reasonings and their outcomes in action in other arguably relevant circumstances at other otherwise comparable times. The plausibility ... of what might have been depends in part upon what, somewhere, was actually tried. But it does not only depend on this. It also turns on imagining, in the light of what these comparisons suggest, what the relevant agents themselves, as those agents, might have considered and managed to effect" (78–79). (2) Geuss (2005) thinks skepticism about counterfactuals is already a problem at the much more confined domestic level. Geuss (2003) states that much of political theorizing is like telling people who are drowning that the public good requires that they be in a lifeboat (100–101). (3) Even if statements of the required scope could be made about the future ("This is what a world without states as we know them now would look like, etc.") there would be additional worries about implementing such a vision that draw on the idea that "ought implies can." Philosophers take different views about the stringency of this requirement. One extreme view is taken by Griffin, who thinks that the most relevant sense of "cannot" is that something cannot be done by someone in ordinary circumstances with suitable, settled dispositions in a sustainable social order (1996, 90). Elster takes an opposing view: what we ought to do is limited only by biological and physical impossibilities (1985, 201). In the broad sense of historical possibility, says Elster, the principle of ought-implies-can can be turned around: something's being perceived as obligatory might contribute to making it feasible, given its physical possibility.

25. See Diamond and Robinson (2010) for case studies of comparative investigations of historical questions.

26. Quoted in Conniff (1994, 233), from Burke's "Letter to a Noble Lord on the Attacks Made upon Mr. Burke and His Pension."

27. Quoted in Herz (1957, 493), without a reference.

28. Perhaps Max Weber can be taken to formulate an intermediate view between these standpoints, with a twist turning on leadership by distinguished individuals. At the end of "Politics as a Vocation," Weber writes, "Politics is a strong and slow boring of hard boards. It takes both passion and perspective. Certainly all historical experience confirms the truth—that man would not have attained the possible unless time and again he had reached out for the impossible. But to do that a man must be a leader, and not only a leader but a hero as well, in a very sober sense of the word" (Gerth and Wright Mills 1946, 128).

29. Elster (1985, 201).

30. For the themes in this paragraph, see Elias (1994), Bauman (1989), and Giddens (1984).

CHAPTER 17

1. The notion of one ground being embedded in another is defined in terms of individuals. Although one might think it is states rather than individuals that are most naturally in the scope of a trade relation, I would count all individuals who live in states that trade as being in the relevant scope.

2. Rawls (1999c, sec. 44) makes clear that no more savings for the future are required once a society is rich enough to realize the principles of justice. An interesting question is whether, or in precisely what stages, a society would simultaneously be subject to a requirement to save for future generations *and* a requirement to offer assistance to other peoples. Rawls's (1999b) remark that a duty of assistance and a just savings principle "express the same underlying idea" (106ff.) does not necessitate the interpretation in Freeman (2007a) that the duty of assistance and the just savings principle must both be understood as constraints on the formulation of the difference principle as commonly stated, and thus appear, as it were, at the same place in a completed version of the two principles. That discussion merely points out that the duty of assistance and the just-savings principle express the same underlying idea *in certain respects,* namely, that the relevant obligations pertain as long as it takes to realize just societies, but no longer. Nonetheless, I follow Freeman's reading, which strikes me as a sensible answer to the question of how to think about the relative priority of the just savings principle and the duty of assistance vis-à-vis the concerns expressed in the standard formulation of the two principles that I just recapitulated.

3. I use Grant and Keohane (2005) for examples. See also Keohane and Nye (2003). Grant and Keohane (2005) include another possible origin of accountability relationships. A may be accountable to B because A's actions with regard to domain Δ affect B. Organizations that affect people's lives so strongly that they could undermine their ability to make a living may owe an account to those people, in virtue of the urgency of the matters at stake. Another example is market accountability. Investors and consumers react to certain policies of particular countries, or may stop dealing with certain companies depending on their strategies. It might not be correct to say, then, that these countries or companies owe an account to market participants. But it may be in their best interest to act as if they did. How-

ever, below I discuss whether the fact that agents are in the scope of certain principles generates an accountability relationship between them and those who have obligations in terms of these principles. That discussion renders unnecessary an exploration of conditions under which affected interests generate accountability.

4. (1) One might say professors owe students fair grades, but this does not mean students should be empowered to sanction them if they fail their expectations. In this case, particular forms of accountability (students voting on a professor's remaining in office) are ineffective to ensure fairness. Nevertheless, oversight of grading on behalf of students should in principle be there—and it is if students have the possibility of complaining about professorial misconduct to an administrative board and submit evaluations. (2) One might wonder about cases where justice and accountability conflict because one can only be achieved at the cost of the other. Suppose agents can spend a scarce resource either in compliance with justice to the benefit of those within the scope of a principle of justice or to ensure accountability vis-à-vis them. Respect requires that the resource be spent toward justice. Yet granting the priority of the realization of justice over accountability for it does not affect my argument.

5. (1) Perhaps accountability to those in the scope of justice also increases chances that more than justice requires is done, so that then injustice is done to parties with whom an effective accountability relationship is not established. One version of this problem, as we will see below, is that governments have incentives to neglect duties toward noncitizens. However, the response then should be to establish effective accountability relationships with all relevant groups. But what, so the objector might continue, if one *really* cannot do so? Would not in that case the course of action guaranteeing the greatest degree of justice be *not* to have relationships of accountability with *anyone*, rather than having one with some but not others to whom accountability is owed? In such a situation the best might well be the enemy of the good. At the same time, the burden of proof would be very high to show that one *really* cannot establish the relevant accountability relationships in some form (given that much flexibility is involved in what that might entail). (2) The argument from respect and the instrumental argument conflict when those in the scope of principles of justice are less competent to receive accounts from those who are duty-bound than some other group that does so on behalf of those in the scope of those principles. I have no good general response to this problem.

6. See Judt (2006, 796–800) for a discussion that confirms Keohane's point that the EU is not functioning as a state.

7. See Archibugi (2008, chap. 8) for an overview and literature references.

8. My summary captures a quintessential understanding of cosmopolitan democracy. I am not concerned with differences among these authors. Except for Caney, these authors do not approach the subject of global institutions from the standpoint of global justice.

9. See Cohen and Sabel (2005), in particular for the thought that the lack of a global demos shows little. For a discussion of the democracy deficit at the global level, see Keohane and Nye (2003). See also (Thomas) Risse (2003) and Moravcsik (2004, 2008).

CHAPTER 18

1. Kingsbury, Krisch, and Stewart (2005) distinguish five types of globalized administrative regulation: (1) formal international organizations such as the WTO, (2) collective action by transnational networks of cooperative arrangements between national regulatory officials, (3) distributed administration conducted by national regulators under treaty, network, or other cooperative regimes, (4) administration by hybrid intergovernmental-private arrangements, and (5) administration by private institutions with regulatory functions. See also Kingsbury (2008) and Kingsbury and Stewart (2009).

2. See Winham (1998) for the negotiations that led to the WTO. For the political history of the trade system, see Barton et al. (2006). See also Trebilcock and Howse (2005) and Howse (2007). For an introduction, see Narlikar (2005).

3. Petersmann (2001) advocates a human rights approach to WTO law from within a legal framework.

4. For the Marrakesh Agreement, see http://www.wto.org/english/docs_e/legal_e/04-wto_e.htm (accessed September 2010).

5. Note in this context how Keohane (2006) explains why states found international regimes ("clusters of principles, norms, rules and decision-making procedures," 76), especially the WTO (the "closest real-world example" to his model). His "functional" theory (Keohane 1984) asserts that states build international regimes to promote cooperation. Such regimes "reduce transaction costs for states—that is, the costs of making and enforcing agreements. They also alleviate problems of asymmetrical information and enhance the credibility of states' commitments. Their existence can be explained in terms of self-interest; yet the resulting institutions exert an impact on state policies by changing the costs and benefits of various alternatives, and over time have often unforeseen effects" (76). Keohane seeks to *explain* why states found such entities. From the standpoint of justice, these regimes must be *evaluated* in terms of (among other things) how much they contribute to the realization of the state's duties.

6. (1) Barton et al. (2006, chap. 3) point out that most developing countries got little when agreeing to the WTO. "Developing countries accepted this outcome because rejection of the WTO agreements would have made them still worse off" (66) by eliminating guarantees of market access. Offering an evaluation of the WTO treaty, Panagariya (2003) reaches a balanced conclusion, saying that "although the Uruguay Round benefited developed countries more than developing ones, poor nations still gained. First, developing countries liberalized more because they had higher trade barriers to begin with (and remember, in economic terms greater liberalization is a benefit, not a cost). Second, ... developing countries convinced developed nations to commit to dismantling quotas on imports of textiles and clothing. Third, while the Uruguay Round did not enhance developing countries' access to global agricultural markets, it opened the way for future liberalization in this important area" (26). Hoekman and Kostecki (2001, 400) mention disagreement about whether the WTO treaty was generally favorable; studies disagree on implementation costs and TRIPs. Steinberg (2002) says, "Several computable general equilibrium models have shown that the Uruguay Round

results disproportionately benefit developed country GDP's compared to developing countries, and that some developing countries would actually suffer a net GDP loss from the Uruguay Round—at least in the short run" (366). It lies in the nature of such reasoning that claims about how countries have fared under this regime by and large, and over time, may be hard to substantiate. (2) Gruber (2000) asks whether cooperation may not benefit primarily those who have set in motion the process of generating the kind of cooperation that international institutions embody, whereas others may merely participate because they lack alternatives. Differential opportunity costs make it possible for some to impose unfavorable terms on others.

7. See also Stiglitz and Charlton (2006, esp. 167) and Oxfam (2002, esp. 15).

8. Keohane and Nye (2001) come to a similar judgment.

9. See also Wolf (2004, 208). For problems of developing countries in the dispute settlement system, see Shaffer, Mosoti, and Quereshi (2003) and Busch and Reinhardt (2002). See also Delich (2002), Horn and Mavroidis (2003), Narlikar (2002), and Stiglitz and Charlton (2006, esp. 83). Woods (2006) concludes an assessment of the IMF and the World Bank as follows: "Their political structures carefully balanced stakes across those making contributions and those whose representation and cooperation is vital for the organizations to fulfill their mandates. But they evolved—particularly in the 1980s—into institutions increasingly financed by [sic] poor and directed by the rich" (213).

10. There is the Uruguay-Brazil plan to award financial compensation for polices that harm a country's trade (see Dam 1970, 368–73). Lawrence (2003) makes a different proposal for how to bring about compliance without retaliation that is intended to address this concern.

11. (1) Stiglitz and Charlton (2006) state that "the challenge is to design special and differential treatment which gives developing countries flexibility to deal with their development problems and minimizes adjustment and implementation costs, without marginalizing their participation in the global trading system or forgoing the gains from South-South liberalization. To achieve this, all WTO members could commit themselves to providing free market access in all goods to all developing countries poorer and smaller than themselves" (94). Hoekman (2004) suggests dividing the WTO's disciplines into "core" and "non-core." Core disciplines would be accepted by all countries. Developing countries could be permitted to reject non-core rules if that were conducive for development. (2) Chang (2002) shows that now-developed countries have used a broad range of trade policy instruments to facilitate growth.

12. See also Stiglitz and Charlton (2006, 157).

13. NGOs already played an important role at the inception of the Universal Declaration; see Korey (2001).

14. Keohane, Macedo, and Moravcsik (2009) argue that international organizations can enhance the quality of national democratic processes.

15. On the World Bank, see Woods (2006), Berkman (2008), and Marshall (2008). The World Bank is actually a *group* of organizations. But we can neglect the resulting complexities.

Bibliography

Abernethy, David. 2000. *The Dynamics of Global Dominance: European Overseas Empires, 1415–1980*. New Haven, CT: Yale University Press

Abizadeh, Arash. 2007. "Cooperation, Pervasive Impact, and Coercion: On the Scope (Not Site) of Distributive Justice." *Philosophy and Public Affairs* 35: 318–59.

———. 2008. "Democratic Theory and Border Coercion: No Right to Unilaterally Control Your Own Borders." *Political Theory* 36 (1): 37–65.

Abraham, Katharine, and Christopher Mackie. 2005. *Beyond the Market: Designing Nonmarket Accounts for the United States*. Washington, DC: National Academy Press.

Acemoglu, Daron, Simon Johnson, and James Robinson. 2003. "Botswana: An African Success Story." In Rodrik 2003, 80–123.

Ackerman, Bruce. 1980. *Social Justice and the Liberal State*. New Haven, CT: Yale University Press.

Adamson, John. 1997. "England without Cromwell: What If Charles I Had Avoided the Civil War?" In Ferguson 1997, 91–125.

Alcock, Anthony E. 1971. *History of the International Labor Organization*. London: Macmillan.

Aldy, Joseph, and Robert Stavins, eds. 2007a. *Architectures for Agreement: Addressing Global Climate Change in the Post-Kyoto World*. Cambridge: Cambridge University Press.

———. 2007b. "Introduction: International Policy Architecture for Global Climate Change." In Aldy and Stavins 2007a, 1–27.

Alesina, Alberto, and David Dollar. 2000. "Who Gives Foreign Aid to Whom and Why?" *Journal of Economic Growth* 5:33–64.

Alkire, Sabina. 2002. *Valuing Freedoms*. Oxford: Oxford University Press.

———. 2006. "Needs and Capabilities." In Reader 2006b, 229–51.

Amin, Samir. 1976. *Unequal Development: An Essay on the Social Formations of Peripheral Capitalism*. New York: Monthly Review Press.

Anderson, Elizabeth. 1999. "What Is the Point of Equality?" *Ethics* 109:287–337.

Anderson, James, and Eric van Wincoop. 2004. "Trade Costs." *Journal of Economic Literature* 42 (3): 691–751.

Anderson, Kym. 2004. "Subsidies and Trade Barriers." In *Global Crises, Global Solutions*, ed. Bjørn Lomborg. Cambridge: Cambridge University Press.

Anderson, Kym, and Will Martin. 2006. "Agriculture, Trade Reform, and the Doha Agenda." In *Agricultural Trade Reform and the Doha Development Agenda*, ed. Kym Anderson and Will Martin, 3–37. New York: Palgrave Macmillan.

Angell, Marcia. 2004. *The Truth about the Drug Companies: How They Deceive Us and What to Do about It*. New York: Random House.

Arato, Andrew. 2009. *Constitution Making under Occupation: The Politics of Imposed Revolution in Iraq.* New York: Columbia University Press.

Archibugi, Daniele. 2008. *The Global Commonwealth of Citizens: Towards Cosmopolitan Democracy.* Princeton, NJ: Princeton University Press.

Arendt, Hannah. 1958. *The Human Condition.* Chicago: University of Chicago Press.

———. 1963. *Eichmann in Jerusalem.* New York: Penguin.

———. 1975. *The Origins of Totalitarianism.* New York: Harvest.

Arndt, H. W. 1987. *Economic Development: The History of an Idea.* Chicago: University of Chicago Press.

Arneson, Richard. 1989. "Equality and Equal Opportunity for Welfare." *Philosophical Studies* 56:79–95.

———. 1990a. "Is Work Special? Justice and the Distribution of Employment." *American Political Science Review* 84 (4): 1127–47.

———. 1990b. "Primary Goods Reconsidered." *Nous* 24:429–54.

———. 1999. "What, If Anything, Renders All Humans Morally Equal?" In *Peter Singer and His Critics,* ed. Dale Jamieson, 103–29. Oxford: Oxford University Press.

———. 2008. "Rawls, Responsibility, and Distributive Justice." In *Justice, Political Liberalism, and Utilitarianism: Themes from Rawls and Harsanyi,* ed. M. Salles and J. Weymark, 80–107. Cambridge: Cambridge University Press.

Armstrong, Chris. 2009. "Coercion, Reciprocity and Equality beyond the State." *Journal of Social Philosophy* 40 (3): 297–316.

Ashcroft, Richard. 2005. "Access to Essential Medicines: A Hobbesian Social Contract Approach." *Developing World Bioethics* 5 (2): 122–41.

Athanasiou, Tom, and Paul Baer. 2002. *Dead Heat: Global Justice and Global Warming.* New York: Seven Stories Press.

Attali, Jacques. 2009. *A Brief History of the Future.* New York: Arcade Publishers.

Attfield, Robin. 2003. *Environmental Ethics: An Overview for the Twenty-First Century.* Oxford: Polity Press.

Auerbach, Bruce. 1995. *Unto the Thousandth Generation: Conceptualizing Intergenerational Justice.* New York: Peter Lang.

Auty, Richard, ed. 2001. *Resource Abundance and Economic Development.* Oxford: Oxford University Press.

Avineri, Shlomo. 1968. *The Social and Political Thought of Karl Marx.* Cambridge: Cambridge University Press.

Baer, Paul. 2002. "Equity, Greenhouse Gas Emissions, and Global Common Resources." In *Climate Change Policy: A Survey,* ed. S. Schneider, A. Rosencranz, and J. Niles, 393–408. Washington, DC: Island Press.

———. 2006. "Adaptation: Who Pays Whom?" In *Fairness in Adaptation to Climate Change,* ed. Neil Adger, Jouni Paavola, Saleemul Huq, and M. J. Mace. Cambridge, MA: MIT Press.

Baier, Annette. 1981. "The Rights of Past and Future Persons." In *Responsibilities to Future Generations: Environmental Ethics,* ed. Ernest Partridge. New York: Prometheus Books.

———. 2010. *The Cautious, Jealous Virtue: Hume on Justice.* Cambridge, MA: Harvard University Press.

Bainbridge, David. 1992. *Intellectual Property.* London: Longman.

Bairoch, Paul. 1993. *Economics and World History.* New York: Harvester.

Banerjee, Abhijit (with A. Amsden, R. Bates, J. Bhagwati, A. Deaton, and N. Stern). 2007. *Making Aid Work.* Cambridge, MA: MIT Press.

Barclay, Harold. 1982. *People without Government: An Anthropology of Anarchy.* London: Kahn and Averill.

Barone, Charles. 1985. *Marxist Thought on Imperialism: Survey and Critique.* London: Macmillan.

Barry, Brian. 1978. "Circumstances of Justice and Future Generations." In *Obligations to Future Generations,* ed. R. I. Sikora and Brian Barry, 204–48. Philadelphia: Temple University Press.

———. 1982. "Humanity and Justice in Global Perspective." In *Ethics, Economics, and the Law: Nomos XXIV,* ed. J. R. Pennock and J. W. Chapman, 219–52. New York: New York University Press.

———. 1989a. *Democracy, Power, and Justice: Essays in Political Theory.* Oxford: Clarendon Press.

———. 1989b. "Justice between Generations." In Barry 1989a, 494–510.

———. 1989c. *Theories of Justice,* vol. 1. Berkeley: University of California Press.

———. 1995. *Justice as Impartiality.* Oxford: Oxford University Press.

———. 1999. "Sustainability and Intergenerational Justice." In Dobson, *Fairness and Futurity,* 93–117.

———. 2005. *Why Social Justice Matters.* Cambridge: Polity Press.

Barry, Brian, and Robert Goodin, eds. 1992. *Free Movement: Ethical Issues in the Transnational Migration of People and of Money.* University Park: Pennsylvania State University Press.

Barry, Christian, and Sanjay Reddy. 2008. *International Trade and Labor Standards: A Proposal for Linkage.* New York: Columbia University Press.

Barton, John, Judith Goldstein, Timothy Josling, and Richard Steinberg. 2006. *The Evolution of the Trade System: Politics, Law, and Economics of the GATT and the WTO.* Princeton, NJ: Princeton University Press.

Bauman, Zygmunt. 1989. *Modernity and the Holocaust.* Ithaca, NY: Cornell University Press.

Bayly, C. A. 2004. *The Birth of the Modern World, 1780–1914: Global Connections and Comparisons.* Oxford: Blackwell.

Beck, Roy. 1996. *The Case against Immigration.* New York: Norton.

Becker, Lawrence. 1977. *Property Rights: Philosophical Foundations.* Boston: Routledge and Kegan Paul.

———. 1993. "Deserving to Own Intellectual Property." *Chicago-Kent Law Review* 68:609–29.

Beckerman, Wilfred, and Joanna Pasek. 2001. *Justice, Posterity, and the Environment.* Oxford: Oxford University Press.

Beerbohm, Eric. 2010. "Nozick's Wager." Unpublished manuscript. Harvard University, Department of Government, Cambridge, MA.

Beitz, Charles. 1999. *Political Theory and International Relations.* Rev. ed. Princeton, NJ: Princeton University Press.

———. 2001. "Human Rights as a Common Concern." *American Political Science Review* 95 (2): 269–82.

———. 2004. "Human Rights and the Law of Peoples." In *The Ethics of Assistance: Morality and the Distant Needy,* ed. Dee Chatterjee, 193–214. Cambridge: Cambridge University Press.

———. 2009. *The Idea of Human Rights.* Oxford: Oxford University Press.

Bellamy, Alex. 2009. *Responsibility to Protect: The Global Effort to End Mass Atrocities.* Malden, MA: Polity Press.

Benn, Gottfried. 1933. *Der Neue Staat und die Intellektuellen.* Berlin: Deutsche Verlags-Anstalt.

Benson, Bruce. 1990. *The Enterprise of Law: Justice without the State.* San Francisco: Pacific Research Institute for Public Policy.

Bentham, Jeremy. 1962. *Principles of International Law.* In *The Works of Jeremy Bentham.* Edited by John Bowring, 2:535–60. New York: Russell and Russell.

Benton, Lauren. 2001. *Law and Colonial Cultures: Legal Regimes in World History, 1400–1900.* Cambridge: Cambridge University Press.

Berkman, Steve. 2008. *The World Bank and the Gods of Lending.* Sterling: Kumarian.

Berlin, Isaiah. 1981. "Nationalism." In *Against the Current: Essays in the History of Ideas.* Oxford: Oxford University Press.

———. 1992. "The Pursuit of the Ideal." In *The Crooked Timber of Humanity: Chapters in the History of Ideas.* New York: Vintage Books.

Bhagwati, Jagdish. 1993. "Fair Trade, Reciprocity, and Harmonization: The Novel Challenge to the Theory and Policy of Free Trade." In *Protectionism and World Welfare,* ed. Dominick Salvatore. Cambridge: Cambridge University Press.

Birdsall, Nancy, Dani Rodrik, and Arvind Subramanian. 2005. "How to Help Poor Countries." *Foreign Affairs,* July–August.

Bittner, Rüdiger. 2001. "Masters without Substance." In *Nietzsche's Postmoralism,* ed. R. Schacht. Cambridge: Cambridge University Press.

Black, Samuel. 1991. "Individualism at an Impasse." *Canadian Journal of Philosophy* 21 (3): 347–77.

Blackbourn, David. 2006. *The Conquest of Nature: Water, Landscape, and the Making of Modern Germany.* New York: Norton.

Blackstone, Sir William. 1979. *Commentaries on the Laws of England in Four Books,* Facsimile of the First Edition. Vol. 2. Chicago: University of Chicago Press.

Blake, Michael. 2001. "Distributive Justice, State Coercion, and Autonomy." *Philosophy and Public Affairs* 30:257–96.

———. 2002. "Discretionary Immigration." *Philosophical Topics* 30 (2): 273–91.

Blake, Michael, and Mathias Risse. 2007. "Migration, Territoriality, and Culture." In *New Waves in Applied Ethics,* ed. Jesper Ryberg, Thomas Petersen, and Clark Wolf, 153–82. Aldershot: Ashgate.

———. 2008. "Two Models of Equality and Responsibility." *Canadian Journal of Philosophy* 38 (2): 165–201.

———. 2009. "Immigration and Original Ownership of the Earth." *Notre Dame Journal of Law, Ethics, and Public Policy* 23 (1): 133–67.

Borges, Jorge Luis. 1998. *Collected Fictions*. New York: Penguin.

Borjas, George. 2001. *Heaven's Door: Immigration Policy and the American Economy*. Princeton, NJ: Princeton University Press.

Boucher, David. 1998. *Political Theories of International Relations*. Oxford: Oxford University Press.

Bovenberg, Jasper. 2006. *Property Rights in Blood, Genes, and Data: Naturally Yours?* Leiden: Martinus Nijhoff.

Brams, Steven, and Alan Taylor. 1996. *Fair Division: From Cake Cutting to Dispute Resolution*. Cambridge: Cambridge University Press.

Braudel, Fernand. 1987. *A History of Civilizations*. New York: Penguin.

Braybrooke, David. 1987. *Meeting Needs*. Princeton, NJ: Princeton University Press.

Brennecke, Fritz. 1938. *Vom Deutschen Volk und Seinem Lebensraum: Handbuch für die Schulungsarbeit in der HJ*. München: Zentralverlag der NSDAP.

Brenner, Robert. 1977. "The Origins of Capitalist Development: A Critique of Neo-Smithian Marxism." *New Left Review* 104 (July–August).

Brewer, Anthony. 1990. *Marxist Theories of Imperialism: A Critical Survey*. London: Routledge.

Brimelow, Peter. 1995. *Alien Nation: Common Sense about America's Immigration Disaster*. New York: Random House.

Brock, Gillian, ed. 1998a. *Necessary Goods: Our Responsibilities to Meet Others' Needs*. New York: Rowman and Littlefield.

———. 1998b. "Introduction." In Brock 1998a, 1–18.

Bromley, David, ed. 1992. *Making the Commons Work: Theory, Practice, and Policy*. San Francisco: Institute for Contemporary Studies.

Broome, John. 1999. "Fairness." In *Ethics out of Economics*, ed. John Broome. Cambridge: Cambridge University Press.

Broomhall, Bruce. 2003. *International Justice and the International Criminal Court: Between Sovereignty and the Rule of Law*. Oxford: Oxford University Press.

Brown, Alexander. 2009. *Ronald Dworkin's Theory of Equality: Domestic and Global Perspectives*. London: Palgrave Macmillan

Buchanan, Allen. 2004. *Justice, Legitimacy, and Self-Determination: Moral Foundations for International Law*. Oxford: Oxford University Press.

Buchanan, Allen, and Robert Keohane. 2008. "The Legitimacy of Global Governance Institutions." In *Legitimacy in International Law*,. ed. Rüdiger Wolfrum and Volker Röben, 25–62. Berlin: Springer.

Buck, Susan. 1998. *The Global Commons: An Introduction*. Washington, DC: Island Press.

Buckle, Stephen. 1991. *Natural Law and the Theory of Property: Grotius to Hume*. Oxford: Clarendon Press.

Buckley, Joan, and Seamus O Tuama. 2005. "International Pricing and Distribution of Therapeutic Pharmaceuticals: An Ethical Minefield." *Business Ethics: A European Review* 14:127–41.

Bull, Hedley. 1977. *The Anarchical Society: A Study of Order in World Politics*. New York: Columbia University Press.

———. 1990. "The Importance of Grotius in the Study of International Relations." In *Hugo Grotius and International Relations*, ed. Hedley Bull, Benedict Kingsbury, and Adam Roberts, 65–95. Oxford: Clarendon Press.

Burke, Edmund. 1982. *A Vindication of Natural Society: or, a View of the Miseries and Evils arising to Mankind from every Species of Artificial Society*. Edited by Frank N. Pagano. Indianapolis: Liberty Fund.

Burgess, John, and Gideon Rosen. 1997. *A Subject with No Object: Strategies for Nominalistic Interpretation of Mathematics*. Oxford: Clarendon Press.

Burtless, Gary, Robert Lawrence, Robert Litan, and Robert Shapiro. 1998. *Globaphobia: Confronting Fears about Open Trade*. Washington, DC: Brookings Institution Press.

Busch, Marc, and Eric Reinhardt. 2002. "Testing International Trade Law: Empirical Studies of GATT/WTO Dispute Settlement." In *The Political Economy of International Trade Law: Essays in Honor of Robert E. Hudec*, ed. D. Kennedy and J. Southwick. Cambridge: Cambridge University Press.

Byrd, Sharon, and Joachim Hruschka. 2010. *Kant's 'Doctrine of Right': A Commentary*. Cambridge: Cambridge University Press.

Cabrera, Luis. 2004. *Political Theory of Global Justice: A Cosmopolitan Case for the World State*. London: Routledge.

Callicott, J. Baird. 1989. *In Defense of the Land Ethic: Essays in Environmental Philosophy*. Albany: State University of New York Press.

Callinicos, Alex. 2009. *Imperialism and Global Political Economy*. Cambridge: Polity Press.

Campbell, T. D. 1974. "Humanity before Justice." *British Journal of Political Science* 4 (1): 1–16.

Camus, Albert. 1955. *The Myth of Sisyphus and Other Essays*. New York: Vintage Books.

Caney, Simon. 2002. "Cosmopolitanism and the Law of Peoples." *Journal of Political Philosophy* 10:95–123.

———. *Justice Beyond Borders: A Global Political Theory*. Oxford: Oxford University Press.

———. 2006a. "Cosmopolitan Justice, Rights, and Global Climate Change." *Canadian Journal of Law and Jurisprudence* 19 (2): 255–78.

———. 2006b. "Environmental Degradation, Reparations and the Moral Significance of History," *Journal of Social Philosophy* 73 (3): 464–82.

———. 2010. "Climate Change and the Duties of the Advantaged." *Critical Review of International Social and Political Philosophy* 13 (1): 203–28.

Cardoso, Fernando, and Enzo Faletto. 1979. *Dependency and Development in Latin America*. Berkeley: University of California Press.

Carens, Joseph. 1987. "Aliens and Citizens: The Case for Open Borders." *Review of Politics* 49:251–73.

———. 1992. "Migration and Morality: A Liberal-Egalitarian Perspective." In Barry and Goodin 1992, 25-47.

———. 2003. "Who Should Get In? The Ethics of Immigration Decisions." *Ethics and International Affairs* 17:95–110.

Carr, E. H. 1939. *The Twenty-Year Crisis, 1919–1939: An Introduction to the Study of International Relations*. Hong Kong: Papermac.

Carson, Rachel. 1962. *Silent Spring.* Boston: Houghton Mifflin.

Carter, Stephen. 1993. *The Culture of Disbelief: How American Law and Politics Trivializes Religious Devotion.* New York: Anchor Books.

Cassin, René. 1968. "How the Charter on Human Rights Was Born." *UNESCO Courier* 21 (January): 4–6.

Cavallar, Georg. 2002. *The Rights of Strangers: Theories of International Hospitality, the Global Community, and Political Justice since Vitoria.* London: Ashgate.

Cavallero, Eric. 2006. "An Immigration-Pressure Model of Global Distributive Justice." *Politics, Philosophy, and Economics* 5 (1): 97–127.

———. 2010. "Coercion, Inequality and the International Property Regime." *Journal of Political Philosophy* 18 (1): 16–31.

Chang, Ha-Joon. 2002. *Kicking away the Ladder: Development Strategy in Historical Perspective.* London: Anthem Press.

Charny, Israel, ed. 1999. *Encyclopedia of Genocide.* Santa Barbara, CA: ABC-CLIO.

Charnovitz, Steve. 2002. *Trade Law and Global Governance.* London: Cameron May.

Child, James. 1990. "The Moral Foundations of Intangible Property." *Monist* 73: 573–600.

Christman, John. 1991. "Self-Ownership, Equality, and the Structure of Property Rights." *Political Theory* 19:28–46.

———. 1994. *The Myth of Property: Toward an Egalitarian Theory of Ownership.* Oxford: Oxford University Press.

Clark, Gregory. 2007. *A Farewell to Alms: A Brief Economic History of the World.* Princeton, NJ: Princeton University Press.

Clark, John Bates. 1907. *Essentials of Economic Theory, as Applied to Modern Problems of Industry and Public Policy.* New York: Macmillan.

Coetzee, J. M. 2000. *Disgrace.* New York: Penguin.

Cohen, G. A. 1988. "The Labor Theory of Value and the Concept of Exploitation." In *History, Labor, and Freedom.* Oxford: Clarendon Press.

———. 1989. "On the Currency of Egalitarian Justice." *Ethics* 99:906–44.

———. 2008. *Rescuing Justice and Equality.* Cambridge, MA: Harvard University Press.

———. 2011. "Rescuing Conservatism: A Defense of Existing Value." In *Reasons and Recognition: Essays on the Philosophy of T. M. Scanlon,* ed. R. J. Wallace, R. Kumar, and S. Freeman, 203–31. Oxford: Oxford University Press.

Cohen, Jillian, Patricia Illingworth, and Udo Schüklenk, eds. 2006. *The Power of Pills: Social, Ethical, and Legal Issues in Drug Development, Marketing, and Pricing.* London: Pluto Press.

Cohen, Joshua. 1997a. "Deliberation and Democratic Legitimacy." In *Deliberative Democracy: Essays on Reason and Politics,* ed. James Bohman and William Rehg, 67–93. Cambridge, MA: MIT Press.

———. 1997b. "Procedure and Substance in Deliberative Democracy." In *Deliberative Democracy: Essays on Reason and Politics,* ed. James Bohman and William Rehg, 407–37. Cambridge, MA: MIT Press.

———. 2004. "Minimalism about Human Rights: The Most We Can Hope For?" *Journal of Political Philosophy* 12:190–213.

———. 2006. "Is There a Human Right to Democracy?" In *The Egalitarian Conscience: Essays in Honor of G. A. Cohen,* ed. Christine Sypnowich, 226–49. Oxford: Oxford University Press.

Cohen, Joshua, and Charles Sabel. 1997. "Direct-Deliberative Polyarchy." *European Law Journal* 3 (4): 313–42.

———. 2005. "Global Democracy?" *International Law and Politics* 37:763–97.

———. 2006. "Extra Rempublicam, Nulla Justitia?" *Philosophy and Public Affairs* 34 (2): 147–75.

Cohen, Robin, ed. 1996. *Theories of Immigration.* International Library of Studies on Migration, vol. 1. Cheltenham, UK; Lyme, NH: Elgar.

Collier, Paul. 2007. *The Bottom Billion: Why the Poorest Countries Are Failing and What Can Be Done about It.* Oxford: Oxford University Press.

Collier, Paul, and Anke Hoeffler. 1998. "On Economic Causes of Civil War." *Oxford Economic Papers* 50:563–73.

Conniff, James. 1994. *The Useful Cobbler: Edmund Burke and the Politics of Progress.* Albany: State University of New York Press.

Cooper, Richard. 1994. *Environment and Resource Policies for the World Economy.* Washington, DC: Brookings Institution Press.

Cooper, Richard, and Juliette Voïnow Kohler, eds. 2009. *Responsibility to Protect: The Global Moral Compact for the 21st Century.* New York: Palgrave Macmillan.

Couture, Jocelyne, Kai Nielsen, and Michel Seymour. 1998. "Introduction: Questioning the Ethnic/Civic Dichotomy." In *Rethinking Nationalism,* ed. Jocelyn Couture, Kai Nielson, and Michael Seymour, 1–61. Calgary: University of Calgary Press.

Cover, Robert. 1986. "Violence and the World." *Yale Law Journal* 95:1601–29.

Cowley, Robert, ed. 2003. *What Ifs of American History.* New York: G. P. Putnam's Sons.

Cranston, Maurice. 1973. *What Are Human Rights?* New York: Taplinger.

Cullity, Garrett. 2004. *The Moral Demands of Affluence.* Oxford: Oxford University Press.

Curtin, Philip. 2000. *The World and the West: The European Challenge and the Overseas Response in the Age of Empire.* Cambridge: Cambridge University Press.

Dahl, Robert. 1989. *Democracy and Its Critics.* New Haven, CT: Yale University Press.

———. 1999. "Can International Organizations Be Democratic? A Skeptic's View." In *Democracy's Edges,* ed. Ian Shapiro and Casiano Hacker-Cordon. Cambridge: Cambridge University Press.

Daly, Herman. 1995. "On Wilfred Beckerman's Critique of Sustainable Development." *Environmental Values* 4 (1): 49–55.

———. 1996. *Beyond Growth: The Economics of Sustainable Development.* Boston: Beacon Press.

Daly, Herman, and John Cobb. 1989. *For the Common Good: Redirecting the Economy toward Community, the Environment, and a Sustainable Future.* Boston: Beacon Press.

Dam, Lawrence. 1970. *The GATT: Law and International Economic Organiza-tion*. Chicago: University of Chicago Press.

Daniels, Norman. 1985. *Just Health Care*. Cambridge: Cambridge University Press.

———. 1988. *Am I My Parents' Keeper? An Essay on Justice between the Young and the Old*. New York: Oxford University Press.

Davies, Norman. 2003. *Rising '44: The Battle for Warsaw*. London: Penguin.

De George, Richard T. 1984. "Do We Owe the Future Anything?" In *Morality in Practice*, ed. James Sterba. Belmont, CA: Wadsworth.

De George, Robert. 2005. "Intellectual Property and Pharmaceutical Drugs: An Ethical Analysis." *Business Ethics Quarterly* 15:549–75.

de-Shalit, Avner. 1995. *Why Posterity Matters: Environmental Policies and Future Generations*. London: Routledge.

de Swaan, Abram. 1988. *In Care of the State: Health Care, Education, and Wel-fare in Europe and the USA in the Modern Era*. Oxford: Blackwell.

de Wijze, Stephen, Matthew Kramer, and Ian Carter, eds. 2009. *Hillel Steiner and the Anatomy of Justice*. New York: Routledge.

Deitelhoff, Nicole. 2006. *Überzeugung in der Politik*. Frankfurt: Suhrkamp.

Delich, Valentina. 2002. "Developing Countries and the WTO Dispute Settle-ment System." In *Development, Trade, and the WTO: A Handbook*, ed. Ber-nard Hoekkman, Aadiya Mattoo, and Philip English, 71–80. Washington, DC: World Bank.

Diamond, Jared. 1997. *Guns, Germs, and Steel: The Fates of Human Societies*. New York: Norton.

———. 2005. *Collapse: How Societies Choose to Fail or Succeed*. New York: Penguin.

Diamond, Jared, and James Robinson, eds. 2010. *Natural Experiments of His-tory*. Cambridge, MA: Harvard University Press.

Dickmann, Fritz. 1959. *Der Westfälische Frieden*. Münster: Aschendorff.

Dobson, Andrew. 1998. *Justice and the Environment: Conceptions of Environ-mental Sustainability and Theories of Distributive Justice*. Oxford: Oxford University Press.

———, ed. 1999. *Fairness and Futurity: Essays on Environmental Sustainability and Social Justice*. Oxford: Oxford University Press.

Dostoevsky, Fyodor. 2008. *The Karamazov Brothers*, trans. Ignat Avsey. New York: Oxford University Press.

Dower, John. 1986. *War without Mercy: Race and Power in the Pacific War*. New York: Pantheon Books.

Doyal, Len, and Ian Gough. 1991. *A Theory of Human Need*. London: Macmillan.

Drahos, Peter. 1996. *A Philosophy of Intellectual Property*. Aldershot: Dartmouth.

Dummett, Michael. 2001. *On Immigration and Refugees*. New York: Routledge.

———. 2004. "Immigration." *Res Publica* 10 (2): 115–22.

Dworkin, Ronald. 1981. "What Is Equality? Part 2. Equality of Resources." *Phi-losophy and Public Affairs* 10:283–345.

———. 1993. *Life's Dominion: An Argument about Abortion, Euthanasia, and Individual Freedom*. New York: Knopf.

———. 2000. *Sovereign Virtue: The Theory and Practice of Equality*. Cambridge, MA: Harvard University Press.

Easterbrook, Frank. 2001. "Who Decides the Extent of Rights in Intellectual Property?" In *Expanding the Boundaries of Intellectual Property,* ed. Rochelle Dreyfuss, Diane Zimmerman, and Harry First, 405–15. Oxford: Oxford University Press.

Easterly, William. 2001. *The Elusive Quest for Growth: Economists' Adventures and Misadventures in the Tropics*. Cambridge, MA: MIT Press.

———, ed. 2008. *Reinventing Foreign Aid*. Cambridge, MA: MIT Press.

Easterly, William, and R. Levine. 2003. "Tropics, Germs, and Crops: How Endowments Influence Economic Development." *Journal of Monetary Economics* 50 (1): 3–39.

Edmundson, William. 2004. *An Introduction to Rights*. Cambridge: Cambridge University Press.

Eichengreen, Barry, Marc Uzan, Nicholas Crafts, and Martin Hellwig. 1992. "The Marshall Plan: Economic Effects and Implications for Eastern Europe and the Former USSR." *Economic Policy* 7 (14): 13–75.

Eigen, Peter. 2003. *The Web of Corruption*. Frankfurt/New York: Campus Verlag.

Elias, Norbert. 1994. *The Civilizing Process: State Formation and Civilization*. Oxford: Blackwell.

Eliott, Robert. 1979. "Contingency, Community, and Intergenerational Justice." In *Contingent Future Persons: On the Ethics of Deciding Who Will Live, or Not, in the Future,* ed. Nick Fotion and Jan Heller, 157–70. Dordrecht: Kluwer.

———. 1997. *Faking Nature: The Ethics of Environmental Restoration*. London: Routledge.

Ellickson, Robert, Carol Rose, and Bruce Ackerman. 2002. *Perspectives on Property Law*. 3rd ed. New York: Aspen Press.

Elster, Jon. 1985. *Making Sense of Marx*. Cambridge: Cambridge University Press.

Engerman, Stanley, and Kenneth Sokoloff. 2000. "History Lessons: Institutions, Factor Endowments, and Paths of Development in the New World." *Journal of Economic Perspectives* 14:217–30.

Epstein, Richard. 1992. "Justice across the Generations." In *Justice between Age Groups and Generations,* ed. Peter Laslett and James Fishkin, 84–106. New Haven, CT: Yale University Press.

Estlund, David. 2008. *Democratic Authority: A Philosophical Framework*. Princeton, NJ: Princeton University Press.

Evans, Tony. 2001. *The Politics of Human Rights: A Global Perspective*. London: Pluto Press.

Falk, Richard. 1995. *On Humane Governance: Towards a New Global Politics*. Cambridge: Blackwell.

Feinberg, Joel. 1973. *Social Philosophy*. Englewood Cliffs, NJ: Prentice Hall.

———. 1974. "The Rights of Animals and Unborn Generations." In *Philosophy and Environmental Crisis*, ed. William Blackstone. Athens: University of Georgia Press.

———. 1988. *The Moral Limits of the Criminal Law*. Vol. 4, *Harmless Wrongdoing*. Oxford: Oxford University Press.

Ferguson, Niall, ed. 1997. *Virtual History: Alternatives and Counterfactuals.* New York: Perseus.

———. 2003. *Empire: How Britain Made the Modern World.* London: Allen Lane.

Fieldhouse, David. 1999. *The West and the Third World.* Oxford: Blackwell.

Filmer, Robert. 1949. *Patriarcha.* In *Patriarcha and Other Political Works of Sir Robert Filmer.* Edited by Peter Laslett. Oxford: Oxford University Press.

Finer, S. E. 1997. *The History of Government from the Earliest Times,* 3 vols. Oxford University Press.

Finnis, John. 1980. *Natural Law and Natural Rights.* Oxford: Clarendon Press.

Fisher, William. 2001. "Theories of Intellectual Property." In *New Essays in the Legal and Political Theory of Property,* ed. S. Munzer. Cambridge: Cambridge University Press.

Fleischacker, Samuel. 2004. *A Short History of Distributive Justice.* Cambridge, MA: Harvard University Press.

Flikschuh, Katrin. 2000. *Kant and Modern Political Philosophy.* Cambridge: Cambridge University Press.

Follows, John. 1951. *Antecedents of the International Labor Organization.* Oxford: Oxford University Press.

Forst, Rainer. 2002. *Contexts of Justice: Political Philosophy beyond Liberalism and Communitarianism.* Berkeley: University of California Press.

———. 2007. *Das Recht auf Rechtfertigung: Elemente einer konstruktivistischen Theorie der Gerechtigkeit.* Frankfurt: Suhrkamp.

Fortes, Meyer, and E. E. Evans-Pritchard, eds. 1940. *African Political Systems.* Oxford: Oxford University Press.

Frankel, Jeffrey. 2007. "Formulas for Quantitative Emissions Targets." In Aldy and Stavins 2007a, 31–56.

Frankel, Jeffrey, and David Roemer. 1999. "Does Trade Cause Growth?" *American Economic Review* 89 (3): 379–99.

Freeman, Richard, and David Lindauer. 1999. "Why Not Africa?" National Bureau of Economic Research, Working Paper 6942. Cambridge, MA: National Bureau of Economic Research.

Freeman, Samuel. 2007a. *Justice and the Social Contract: Essays on Rawlsian Political Philosophy.* Oxford: Oxford University Press.

———. 2007b. *Rawls.* London: Routledge.

Frege, Gottlob. 1918. "Der Gedanke. Eine logische Untersuchung." In *Beiträge zur Philosophie des Deutschen Idealismus* I, 58–77.

Frieden, Jeffry. 2006. *Global Capitalism: Its Fall and Rises in the Twentieth Century.* London: Norton.

Freund, Bill. 1998. *The Making of Contemporary Africa.* London: Macmillan.

Friedman, David. 1973. *The Machinery of Freedom: Guide to a Radical Capitalism.* New York: Harper-Colophon.

Gallup, John, Jeffrey Sachs, and Andrew Mellinger. 1998. "Geography and Economic Development." *International Science Review* 22 (2): 179–232.

Gardiner, Stephen. 2001. "The Real Tragedy of the Commons." *Philosophy and Public Affairs* 30:387–416.

———. 2004. "Ethics and Global Climate Change." *Ethics* 114:555–600.

———. 2006. "Why Do Future Generations Need Protection?" Working paper, École Polytechnique, Paris.

Gaspart, Frederic, and Axel Gosseries. 2007. "Are Generational Savings Unjust?" *Politics, Philosophy, and Economics* 6 (2): 193–217.

Gellner, Ernest. 1983. *Nations and Nationalism*. Oxford: Blackwell.

George, Henry. 1926. *Progress and Poverty*. New York: Vanguard.

Gerth, H. H., and C. Wright Mills, eds. 1946. *From Max Weber: Essays in Sociology*. New York: Oxford University Press.

Geuss, Raymond. 2001. *History and Illusion in Politics*. Cambridge: Cambridge University Press.

———. 2003. *Public Goods, Private Goods*. Princeton, NJ: Princeton University Press.

———. 2005. *Outside Ethics*. Princeton, NJ: Princeton University Press.

Gewirth, Alan. 1978. *Reason and Morality*. Chicago: University of Chicago Press.

———. 1984. "The Epistemology of Human Rights." In *Human Rights,* ed. E. F. Paul, J. Paul, and F. D. Miller. Oxford: Blackwell.

———. 1996. *The Community of Rights*. Chicago: University of Chicago Press.

Giddens, Anthony. 1984. *The Constitution of Society: Outline of the Theory of Structuration*. Berkeley: University of California Press.

Girard, Philippe. 2005. *Haiti: The Tumultuous History—From Pearl of the Caribbean to Broken Nation*. New York: Palgrave Macmillan.

Glaeser, Edward, Rafael La Porta, Florencio Lopez-de-Silanes, and Andrei Shleifer. 2004. "Do Institutions Cause Growth?" *Journal of Economic Growth* 9 (3): 271–303.

Glendon, Marie Ann. 2001. *A World Made New: Eleanor Roosevelt and the Universal Declaration of Human Rights*. New York: Random House.

Glover, Jonathan, and M. J. Scott-Taggart. 1975. "It Makes No Difference Whether or Not I Do It." *Proceedings of the Aristotelian Society, Supplementary Volumes*, 49:171–209.

Golding, Martin. 1980. "Obligations to Future Generations." In *Responsibilities to Future Generations*, ed. Earnest Partridge. Buffalo, NY: Prometheus Books, 61–72.

Goodale, Mark, and Sally Merry. 2007. *The Practice of Human Rights: Tracking Law between the Global and the Local*. Cambridge: Cambridge University Press.

Goodin, Robert. 1985. *Protecting the Vulnerable: Reanalyzing our Social Responsibilities*. Chicago: University of Chicago Press.

———. 1988. "What's So Special about Our Fellow Countrymen?" *Ethics* 98: 663–86.

———. 1992. *Green Political Theory*. Cambridge: Polity Press.

———. 2007. "Enfranchising All Affected Interests, and Its Alternatives." *Philosophy and Public Affairs* 35 (1): 40–69.

———. 2008. "Global Democracy: In the Beginning." Aboa Center for Economics Discussion Paper No. 30. Turku, Finland: Alboa Center for Economics.

Gosepath, Stefan. 2004. *Gleiche Gerechtigkeit: Grundlagen eines Liberalen Egalitarismus*. Frankfurt: Suhrkamp.

Gosseries, Axel. 2001. "What Do We Owe the Next Generation(s)?" *Loyola of Los Angeles Law Review* 35:293–355.

———. 2004. "Historical Emissions and Free Riding." In Lukas Meyer, *Justice in Time: Responding to Historical Injustice,* ed. Lukas H. Meyer, 355–82. Baden-Baden: Nomos.

———. 2008a. "On Future Generations' Future Rights." *Journal of Political Philosophy* 16 (4): 446–74.

———. 2008b. "Theories of Intergenerational Justice: A Synopsis." *Sapiens* 1 (1): 61–71.

Grant, Ruth, and Robert Keohane. 2005. "Accountability and Abuses of Power in World Politics." *American Political Science Review* 99 (1): 29–43.

Green, T. H. 1941. *Lectures on the Principle of Political Obligation.* Oxford: Longmans.

Griffin, James. 1996. *Value Judgment: Improving Our Ethical Beliefs.* Oxford: Clarendon Press.

———. 2008. *On Human Rights.* Oxford: Oxford University Press.

Gross, Leo. 1948. "The Peace of Westphalia, 1648–1948." *American Journal of International Law* 42:20–41.

Grotius, Hugo. 1712. *Hugonis Grotii De jure belli ac pacis libri tres: in quibus jus naturae & gentium, item juris publici praecipua explicantur : cum annotatis auctoris, ex postrema ejus ante obitum cura : accesserunt ejusdem dissertatio de Mari libero, & Libellus singularis de aequitate, indulgentia, & facilitate : nec non Joann. Frid. Gronovii v.c. notae in totum opus De jure belli ac pacis.* Amstelaedami: Janssonio-Waesbergios.

———. 1819. *The Truth of the Christian Religion in Six Books.* Corrected and Illustrated with Notes by Mr. Le Clerk. Translated by John Clarke. Edinburgh: Turnbull.

———. 1868. *Hugonis Grotii De Jure Praedae Commentarius. Ex Auctoris Codice Descripsit et Vulgavit H. G. Hamaker.* Hagae Comitum: Martinum Nijhoff.

———. 1977. *The Jurisprudence of Holland.* Edited by Robert Warden Lee. Aalen: Scientia.

———. 2004. *The Free Sea.* Edited and with an introduction by David Armitage. Indianapolis: Liberty Fund.

———. 2005. *The Rights of War and Peace.* Edited and with an introduction by Richard Tuck. Indianapolis: Liberty Fund.

———. 2006. *Commentary on the Law of Prize and Booty.* Edited and with an introduction by Martine Julia van Ittersum. Indianapolis: Liberty Fund.

Grubb, Michael. 1995. "Seeking Fair Weather: Ethics and the International Debate on Climate Change." *International Affairs* 71:463–96.

Grubb, Michael, James Sebenius, Antonio Magalhaes, and Susan Subak. 1992. "Sharing the Burden." In *Confronting Climate Change: Risks, Implications, and Responses,* ed. Irving Mintzer, 305–22. Cambridge: Cambridge University Press.

Gruber, Lloyd. 2000. *Ruling the World: Power Politics and the Rise of Supranational Institutions.* Princeton, NJ: Princeton University Press.

Gruebler, A, and Y. Fujii. 1991. "Intergenerational and Spatial Equity Issues of Carbon Accounts." *Energy* 16:1397–1416.

Gruen, Lori, and Dale Jamieson, eds. 1994. *Reflecting on Nature: Readings in Environmental Philosophy.* New York: Oxford University Press.

Grunebaum, James. 1987. *Private Ownership.* New York: Routledge and Kegan Paul.

Gunder Frank, André. 1971. *Capitalism and Underdevelopment in Latin America.* New York: Penguin.

Haakonssen, Knud. 1985. "Hugo Grotius and the History of Political Thought." *Political Theory* 13:239–65.

———. 1996. *Natural Law and Moral Philosophy: From Grotius to the Scottish Enlightenment.* Cambridge: Cambridge University Press.

Haas, Peter. 1988. *Morality after Auschwitz: The Radical Challenge of the Nazi Ethic.* Philadelphia: Fortress Press.

Habermas, Jürgen. 1981. *Theorie des Kommunikativen Handelns,* 2 vols. Frankfurt: Suhrkamp.

———. 1992. *Faktizität und Geltung: Beiträge zur Diskurstheorie des Rechts und des demokratischen Rechtsstaats.* Frankfurt: Suhrkamp.

———. 1997. "Kant's Idea of Perpetual Peace, with the Benefit of Two Hundred Years' Hindsight." In *Perpetual Peace: Essays on Kant's Cosmopolitan Ideals,* ed. James Bohman and Matthias Lutz-Bachmann, 113–53. Cambridge, MA: MIT Press.

———. 1998. *Between Facts and Norms: Contributions to a Discourse Theory of Law and Democracy.* Cambridge, MA: MIT Press.

———. 1999. "Zur Legitimation durch Menschenrechte." In *Das Recht der Republik,* ed. H. Brunkhorst and P. Niesen. Frankfurt: Suhrkamp.

Hacking, Ian. 1990. *The Taming of Chance.* Cambridge: Cambridge University Press.

Hall, Peter, and David Soskice, eds. 2001. *Varieties of Capitalism: The Institutional Foundations of Comparative Advantage.* Oxford: Oxford University Press.

Hall, Robert, and Chad Jones. 1999. "Why Do Some Countries Produce So Much More Output per Worker Than Others?" *Quarterly Journal of Economics* 114:83–116.

Harris, J. W. 1996. *Property and Justice.* Oxford: Oxford University Press.

Hart, H. L. A. 1982. *Essay on Bentham.* Oxford: Oxford University Press.

Haslett, D. W. 1986. "Is Inheritance Justified?" *Philosophy and Public Affairs* 15 (2): 122–55.

Hathaway, Oona. 2002. "Do Human Rights Treaties Make a Difference?" *Yale Law Journal* 111:1935–2042.

Hawthorne, Geoffrey. 1991. *Plausible Worlds: Possibility and Understanding in History and the Social Sciences.* Cambridge: Cambridge University Press.

Hayden, Patrick. 2005. *Cosmopolitan Global Politics.* Burlington: Ashgate.

Hayek, F. A. 1973. *Law, Legislation, and Liberty: A New Statement of the Liberal Principles of Justice and Political Economy,* vol. 1. Chicago: University of Chicago Press.

Hayter, Teresa. 2000. *Open Borders: The Case against Immigration Controls.* London: Pluto Press.

Headrick, Daniel. 1981. *The Tools of Empire. Technology and European Imperialism in the Nineteenth Century.* Oxford: Oxford University Press.

———. 1988. *The Tentacles of Progress. Technology Transfer in the Age of Imperialism, 1850–1940.* Oxford: Oxford University Press.

Hegel, G. W. F. 1990. *Lectures on the History of Philosophy. The Lectures of 1825–26, Volume III: Medieval and Modern Philosophy.* Edited by Robert Brown. Berkeley: University of California Press.

———. 1991. *Elements of the Philosophy of Right,* transl. H. Nisbett. Cambridge: Cambridge University Press.

Held, David. 1995. *Democracy and the Global Order: From the Modern State to Cosmopolitan Governance.* Stanford, CA: Stanford University Press.

———. 2004. *Global Covenant: The Social Democratic Alternative to the Washington Consensus.* Cambridge: Polity Press.

Hellmann, Gunther, Klaus-Dieter Wolf, and Michael Zürn, eds. 2003. *Die Internationalen Beziehungen: Forschungsstand und Perspektiven in Deutschland.* München: Nomos.

Helpman, Elhanan. 2004. *The Mystery of Economic Growth.* Cambridge, MA: Harvard University Press.

Henkin, Louis. 1990. *The Age of Rights.* New York: Columbia University Press.

Herbst, Jeffrey. 2000. *States and Power in Africa.* Princeton, NJ: Princeton University Press.

Herder, Johann Gottfried. 1800. *Outlines of a Philosophy of the History of Man,* trans. T. Churchill. Lincoln's-Inn Fields: Luke Hansard.

Hertel, Thomas, and Roman Keeney. 2006. "What Is at Stake: The Relative Importance of Import Barriers, Export Subsidies, and Domestic Support." In *Poverty and the WTO: Impacts of the Doha Development Agenda,* ed. Thomas Hertel and Alan Winters, 37–63. Washington, DC: World Bank.

Herz, John. 1957. "Rise and Demise of the Territorial State." *World Politics* 9: 473–93.

Hestermeyer, Holger. 2007. *Human Rights and the WTO: The Case of Patents and Access to Medicine.* Oxford: Oxford University Press.

Hettinger, Edwin. 1989. "Justifying Intellectual Property." *Philosophy and Public Affairs* 18:31–52.

Hirschman, Albert. 1991. *The Rhetoric of Reaction: Perversity, Futility, Jeopardy.* Cambridge, MA: Harvard University Press.

Hitler, Adolf. 1941. *Mein Kampf.* München: Verlag Franz Eher Nachfolger.

Hobbes, Thomas. 1991. *Leviathan.* Edited by Richard Tuck. Cambridge: Cambridge University Press.

Hobhouse, L. T. 1994. *Liberalism and Other Writings.* Edited by James Meadowcroft. Cambridge: Cambridge University Press.

Hobsbawm, Eric. 1989. *The Age of Empire: 1875–1914.* New York: Vintage Books.

Hochschild, Adam. 1999. *King Leopold's Ghost: A Story of Greed, Terror, and Heroism in Colonial Africa.* New York: Houghton Mifflin.

Hoeffe, Otfried. 1999. *Demokratie im Zeitalter der Globalisierung*. Munich: Beck.

Hoekman, Bernard. 2002. "The WTO: Functions and Basic Principles." In *Development, Trade, and the WTO: A Handbook,* ed. Bernard Hoekman, Aadiya Mattoo, and Philip English, 41–50. Washington, DC: World Bank.

———. 2004. "Developing Countries and the WTO Doha Round: Market Access, Rules, and Differential Treatment." *Journal of Economic Integration* 19 (2): 205–29.

Hoekman, Bernard, and Michel Kostecki. 2001. *The Political Economy of the World Trading System*. Oxford: Oxford University Press.

Hofrichter, Richard, ed. 2003. *Health and Social Justice: Politics, Ideology, and Inequity in the Distribution of Disease*. San Francisco: Jossey-Bass.

Holland, Alan. 1997. "Substitutability: Or, Why Strong Sustainability Is Weak and Absurdly Strong Sustainability Is Not Absurd." In *Valuing Nature? Economics, Ethics, and Environment,* 119–34. London: Routledge.

———. 1999. "Sustainability: Should We Start from Here?" In Dobson 1999, 46–68.

Honoré, A. M. 1961. "Ownership." In *Making Law Bind: Essays Legal and Philosophical*. Oxford: Clarendon Press.

Hook, Sidney. 1980. "Reflections on Human Rights." In *Philosophy and Public Policy*. Carbondale: Southern Illinois University Press.

Horn, Henrik, and Petros Mavroidis. 2003. "Which WTO Provisions Are Invoked by and against Developing Countries?" CEPR Discussion Paper. London: Center for Economic Policy Research.

Horton, Robin. 1985. "Stateless Societies in the History of West Africa." In *History of West Africa,* ed. J. F. A. Ajayi and Michael Crowder, chap. 3. Burnt Mill: Longmann.

Hospers, John. 1971. *Libertarianism*. Los Angeles: Nash.

Houghton, John. 2004. *Global Warming: The Complete Briefing*. Cambridge: Cambridge University Press.

Howell, Chris. 2003. "Review Article. Varieties of Capitalism: And Then There Was One?" *Comparative Politics* 36 (1): 103–25.

Howse, Robert. 2007. *The WTO System: Law, Politics and Legitimacy*. London: Cameron May.

Hubin, Donald. 1976. "Justice and Future Generations." *Philosophy and Public Affairs* 6:70–83.

Hughes, Justin. 1988. "The Philosophy of Intellectual Property." *Georgetown Law Journal* 77:287–366.

Hume, David. 1975. *Enquiries Concerning Human Understanding and Concerning the Principles of Morals*. Edited by L. A. Selby-Bigge and P. H. Nidditch. Oxford: Clarendon Press.

———. 1978. *A Treatise of Human Nature*. Edited by L. A. Selby-Bigge and P. H. Nidditch. Oxford: Clarendon Press.

Humphreys, Macartan, Jeffrey Sachs, and Joseph Stiglitz, eds. 2007. *Escaping the Resource Curse*. New York: Columbia University Press.

Hunt, Richard. 1974. *The Political Ideas of Marx and Engels: Marxism and Totalitarian Demoracy, 1818–1850*. Pittsburgh: University of Pittsburgh Press.

———. 1984. *The Political Ideas of Marx and Engels: Classical Marxism, 1850–1895*. Pittsburgh: University of Pittsburgh Press.

Hurka, Thomas. 1993. "Ethical Principles." In *Ethics and Climate Change: The Green House Effect,* ed. Harold Coward and Thomas Hurka, 23–38. Calgary: Laurier.

———. 1997. "The Justification of National Partiality." In McKim and McMahan, *Morality of Nationalism,* 139–58.

Ingco, Merlinda, and John Nash, eds. 2004. *Agriculture and the WTO: Creating a Trading System for Development.* Washington, DC: International Bank for Reconstruction and Development/World Bank.

Intergovernmental Panel on Climate Change. 1990. *IPCC—First Assessment Report.* Geneva: Intergovernmental Panel on Climate Change.

———. 1995. *Climate Change 1995: IPCC Second Assessment.* Geneva: Intergovernmental Panel on Climate Change.

———. 2001. *Climate Change 2001: Impacts, Adaptations, and Vulnerability.* Geneva: Intergovernmental Panel on Climate Change

———. 2007a. *Climate Change 2007: The Physical Science Basis. Contribution of Working Group III to the Fourth Assessment Report of the IPCC.* Cambridge: Cambridge University Press.

———. 2007b. *Impacts, Adaptation, and Vulnerability. Contribution of Working Group II to the Fourth Assessment Report of the IPCC.* Cambridge: Cambridge University Press.

———. 2007c. *Mitigation of Climate Change. Contribution of Working Group I to the Fourth Assessment Report of the IPCC.* Cambridge: Cambridge University Press.

International Monetary Fund. 2003. *World Economic Outlook.* Washington, DC: International Monetary Fund.

Irwin, Douglas. 1996. *Against the Tide: An Intellectual History of Free Trade.* Princeton, NJ: Princeton University Press.

———. 2002. *Free Trade under Fire.* Princeton, NJ: Princeton University Press.

Jackson, Robert. 1990. *Quasi-States: Sovereignty, International Relations, and the Third World.* Cambridge: Cambridge University Press.

Jacobs, Michael. 1999. "Sustainable Development as a Contested Concept." In Dobson 1999, 21–45.

Jäckel, Eberhard. 1981. *Hitler's World View: A Blueprint for Power.* Cambridge, MA: Harvard University Press.

Jamieson, Dale. 2001. "Climate Change and Global Environmental Justice." In *Changing the Atmosphere: Expert Knowledge and Global Environmental Governance,* ed. P. Edwards and C. Miller. Cambridge, MA: MIT Press.

———. 2002. "Sustainability and Beyond." In *Morality's Progress: Essays on Humans, Other Animals, and the Rest of Nature,* 321–34. Oxford: Clarendon Press.

Jefferson, Thomas. 1943. "The Invention of Elevators" (Letter, 1813). In *The Complete Jefferson,* ed. Saul Padover, 1015. New York: Dell, Sloane, and Pearce

Jonas, Hans. 1984. *Das Prinzip Verantwortung.* Frankfurt: Suhrkamp.

Jones, Peter. 1994. *Rights.* London: Macmillan.

Joyce, James. 1976. *Finnegans Wake.* New York: Penguin.

———. 1992. *Dubliners*. New York: Penguin.

Judt, Tony. 2006. *Postwar: A History of Europe since 1945*. New York: Penguin.

Julius, A. J. 2003. "Basic Structure and the Value of Equality." *Philosophy and Public Affairs* 31 (4): 321–56.

———. 2006. "Nagel's Atlas." *Philosophy and Public Affairs* 34:176–92.

Kaldor, Mary. 2003. *Global Civil Society: An Answer to War*. Cambridge: Polity Press.

———. 2006. *New and Old Wars*. Cambridge: Polity Press.

Kaiser, Rudolf. 1987. "Chief Seattle's Speech(es): American Origins and European Reception." In *Recovering the Word: Essays on Native American Literature*, ed. B. Swann and A. Krupat, 497–536. Berkeley: University of California Press.

Kamm, Frances. 1996. *Morality, Mortality*. Vol. 2. Oxford: Oxford University Press.

———. 2007. *Intricate Ethics: Rights, Responsibilities, and Permissible Harm*. Oxford: Oxford University Press.

Kant, Immanuel. 1970a. *Kant: Political Writings*. Edited by Hans Reiss. Cambridge: Cambridge University Press.

———. 1970b. *Perpetual Peace: A Philosophical Sketch*. In Kant 1970a.

———. 1970c. *Idea for a Universal History with a Cosmopolitan Purpose*. In Kant 1970a, 41–54.

———. 1981. *Lectures on Ethics*, trans. Louis Infield. Indianapolis: Hackett.

———. 1996. *The Metaphysics of Morals*. In *Immanuel Kant: Practical Philosophy*, ed. Mary Gregor, 353–605. Cambridge: Cambridge University Press.

Kaufmann, D., A. Kraay, and P. Zoido-Lobaton. 2002. "Governance Matters: Updated Indicators for 2001/2002." World Bank Policy Research Department Working Paper 2772. Washington, DC: World Bank.

Kavka, Gregory. 1978. "The Futurity Problem." In *Obligations to Future Generations*, ed. R. I. Sikora and Brian Barry, 186–203. Philadelphia: Temple University Press.

———. 1986. *Hobbesian Moral and Political Theory*. Princeton, NJ: Princeton University Press.

Keene, Edward. 2005. *International Political Thought: A Historical Introduction*. Cambridge: Polity Press.

Kennedy, David. 2004. *The Dark Sides of Virtue: Reassessing International Humanitarianism*. Princeton, NJ: Princeton University Press.

Keohane, Robert. 1984. *After Hegemony: Cooperation and Discord in the World Political Economy*. Princeton, NJ: Princeton University Press.

———. 2006. "Accountability in World Politics." *Scandinavian Political Studies* 29 (2): 75–87.

Keohane, Robert, Stephen Macedo, and Andrew Moravcsik. 2009. "Democracy-Enhancing Multilateralism." *International Organization* 63:1–31.

Keohane, Robert, and Joseph Nye. 2001. "The Club-Model of Multi-Lateral Cooperation and Problems of Democratic Legitimacy." In *Efficiency, Equity, and Legitimacy: The Multilateral Trading System at the Millennium*, ed. Porter, Robert, Pierre Sauvé, Arvind Subramanian, and Americo Beviglia Zampetti, 264–94. Washington, DC: Brookings Institution Press.

———. 2003. "Redefining Accountability for Global Governance." In *Governance in a Global Economy: Political Authority in Transition,* ed. Miles Kahler and David Lake, 386–411. Princeton, NJ: Princeton University Press.

Kersting, Wolfgang. 1984. *Wohlgeordnete Freiheit: Immanuel Kant's Rechts- und Staatsphilosophie.* Berlin: de Gruyter.

Keynes, John Maynard. 2004. *The Economic Consequences of the Peace.* New York: Prometheus Books.

Kiely, Ray. 2010. *Rethinking Imperialism.* New York: Palgrave.

King, Martin Luther Jr. 1963. *Why We Can't Wait.* New York: Harper and Row.

Kingsbury, Benedict. 2008. "Global Administrative Law: Implications for National Courts." In *Seeing the World Whole: Essays in Honor of Sir Kenneth Keith,* ed. Claudia Geiringer and Dean Knight, 101–25. Wellington, NZ: Victoria University Press.

Kingsbury, Benedict, Nico Krisch, and Richard Stewart. 2005. "The Emergence of Global Administrative Law." *Law and Contemporary Problems* 68:15–61.

Kingsbury, Benedict, and Adam Roberts. 1990. "Introduction: Grotian Thought in International Relations." In *Hugo Grotius and International Relations,* ed. Hedley Bull, Benedict Kingsbury, and Adam Roberts, 1–65. Oxford: Clarendon Press.

Kingsbury, Benedict, and Richard Stewart. 2009 "Legitimacy and Accountability in Global Regulatory Governance: The Emerging Global Administrative Law and the Design and Operation of Administrative Tribunals of International Organizations." In *International Administrative Tribunals in a Changing World,* ed. Spyridon Flogaitis. London: Esperia.

Kirzner, Israel. 1978. "Entrepreneurship, Entitlement, and Economic Justice." *Eastern Economic Journal* 4:9–25.

Kleingeld, Pauline. 2004. "Approaching Perpetual Peace: Kant's Defense of a League of States and His Ideal of a World Federation." *European Journal of Philosophy* 12 (3): 304–25.

Kneale, W. C. 1955. "The Idea of Invention." *Proceedings of the British Academy* 41:85–108.

Koh, Harold. 1997. "Why Do Nations Obey International Law?" *Yale Law Journal* 106 (8): 2599–2659.

Kolakowski, Leszek. 2005. *Main Currents of Marxism: The Founders, the Golden Age, the Breakdown.* New York: Norton.

Konwicki, Tadeusz. 1999. *A Minor Apocalypse,* trans. Richard Lourie. Normal, IL: Dalkey Archive Press.

Koonz, Claudia. 2003. *The Nazi Conscience.* Cambridge, MA: Harvard University Press.

Korey, William. 2001. *NGO's and the Universal Declaration of Human Rights: "A Curious Grapevine."* New York: Palgrave Macmillan.

Korsgaard, Christine. 1996. *The Sources of Normativity.* Cambridge: Cambridge University Press.

Krasner, Stephen. 1993. "Westphalia and All That." In *Ideas and Foreign Policy: Beliefs, Institutions, and Political Change,* ed. Judith Goldstein and Robert O. Keohane, 235–65. Ithaca, NY: Cornell University Press.

———. 1999. *Sovereignty—Organized Hypocrisy*. Princeton, NJ: Princeton University Press.

Krebs, Angelika. 1999. *Ethics of Nature: A Map*. Berlin: de Gruyter.

Kremer, Michael, and Rachel Glennerster. 2004. *Strong Medicine*. Princeton, NJ: Princeton University Press.

Kren, George, and Leon Rappoport. 1980. *The Holocaust and the Crisis of Human Behavior*. New York: Holmes and Meyer.

Krishna, Sankaran. 2009. *Globalization and Postcolonialism: Hegemony and Resistance in the Twenty-First Century*. New York: Rowman and Littlefield.

Kropotkin, Petr. 1943. *The State, Its Historic Role*. Albuquerque: A. A. Hennacy.

Krugman, Paul. 1998. "Global Free Trade." In *The Legal and Moral Aspects of International Trade*, ed. A. Qureshi, H. Steinman, and G. Parry, 9–12. London: Routledge.

Krugman, Paul, and Maurice Obstfeld. 2003. *International Economics: Theory and Policy*. Boston: Addison Wesley.

Kuflik, Arthur. 1989. "Moral Foundations of Intellectual Property Rights." In *Owning Scientific and Technical Information: Value and Ethical Issues*, ed. Vivian Weil and John Snapper, chap. 11. New Brunswick, NJ: Rutgers University Press.

Kukathas, Chandran. 2005. "The Case for Open Immigration." In *Contemporary Debates in Applied Ethics*, ed. Andrew Cohen. Oxford: Blackwell.

Kumar, Rahul. 2003. "Who Can Be Wronged?" *Philosophy and Public Affairs* 31 (2): 99–188.

Kurjanska, Malgorzata, and Mathias Risse. 2008. "Fairness in Trade II: Export Subsidies and the Fair Trade Movement." *Politics, Philosophy, and Economics* 7 (1): 29–56.

Kymlicka, Will. 2002. *Contemporary Political Philosophy: An Introduction*. Oxford: Oxford University Press.

Lachlan, James. 2005. "A Neuropsychological Analysis of the Law of Obviousness." In *Death of Patents*, ed. Peter Drahos, 67–109. London: Queen Mary Intellectual Property Research Institute.

Lal, Deepak. 2004. *In Praise of Empires: Globalization and Order*. New York: Palgrave.

Landes, David. 1998. *The Wealth and Poverty of Nations: Why Some Are So Rich and Some So Poor*. New York: Norton.

Larmore, Charles. 2003. "Public Reason." In *The Cambridge Companion to Rawls*, ed. Samuel Freeman. Cambridge: Cambridge University Press.

Lauren, Paul Gordon. 2003. *The Evolution of International Human Rights: Visions Seen*. Philadelphia: University of Pennsylvania Press.

Lawrence, Robert. 1996. *Regionalism, Multilateralism, and Deeper Integration*. Washington, DC: Brookings Institution Press.

———. 2003. *Crimes and Punishments? Retaliation under the WTO*. Washington, DC: Institute for International Economics.

Le Billon, Philippe. 2001. "The Political Ecology of War: Natural Resources and Armed Conflicts." *Political Geography* 20:561–84.

Leary, Virginia. 1996. "The Paradox of Workers' Rights as Human Rights." In *Human Rights, Labor Rights, and International Trade*, ed. Lance Compa and Stephen Diamond, 22–48. Philadelphia: University of Pennsylvania Press.

Lederman, Daniel, and William Maloney, eds. 2006. *Natural Resources: Neither Curse Nor Destiny*. Washington, DC: World Bank.

Leibniz, Gottfried Wilhelm. 1864. "Entretiens de Phlarete et d'Eugene sur la question du temps agitée à Nimwegue touchant le droit d'ambassade des electeurs et princes de le'empire" (1677). In *Die Werke von Leibniz*. Edited by Onno Klopp. 1st Reihe, 3rd Band. Hannover: Klindworth.

Lenman, James. 2002. "On Becoming Extinct." *Pacific Philosophical Quarterly* 83:253–69.

Leopold, Aldo. 1949. *A Sand Country Almanac*. Oxford: Oxford University Press.

Lessig, Lawrence. 2004. *Free Culture: The Nature and Future of Creativity*. New York: Penguin.

Lewellen, Ted. 1992. *Political Anthropology: An Introduction*. London: Bergin and Garvey.

Locke, John. 1988. *Two Treatises of Government*. Edited by Peter Laslett. Cambridge: Cambridge University Press.

Lomborg, Bjørn. 2001. *The Skeptical Environmentalist: Measuring the Real State of the World*. Cambridge: Cambridge University Press.

———, ed. 2007. *Solutions for the World's Biggest Problems*. Cambridge: Cambridge University Press.

Love, James, and Tim Hubbard. 2007. "The Big Idea: Prizes to Stimulate R&D for New Medicines." *Chicago-Kent Law Review* 82 (3): 1519–54.

Lovejoy, Arthur. 1957. *The Great Chain of Being: A Study in the History of an Idea*. Cambridge, MA: Harvard University Press.

Lu, Catherine. 2006. "World Government." In *Stanford Encyclopedia of Philosophy*. http://plato.stanford.edu/archives/win2006/entries/world-government/.

Luban, David. 1980. "The Romance of the Nation-State." *Philosophy & Public Affairs* 9 (4): 392–97.

Macdonald, Margaret. 1984. "Natural Rights." In *Theories of Rights*, ed. Jeremy Waldron, 1–41. Oxford: Oxford University Press.

Mack, Eric. 2009. "What Is Left in Left-Libertarianism?" In de Wijze, Kramer, and Carter 2009, 101–32.

Macklem, Patrick. 2002. "Labor Law beyond Borders." *Journal of International Economic Law* 5 (3): 605–45.

———. 2005. "The Right to Bargain Collectively in International Law: Workers' Right, Human Rights, International Rights?" In *Labor Rights as Human Rights*, ed. Philip Alston, 61–84. Oxford: Oxford University Press.

Macksey, Kenneth, ed. 1995. *The Hitler Options: Alternate Decisions of World War II*. London: Greenhill Books.

Maddison, Angus. 2001. *The World Economy: A Millennial Perspective*. Paris: OECD Development Center.

Maimonides, Moses. 2007. *The Guide for the Perplexed*. Chicago: BN Publishing.

Malanczuk, Peter. 1997. *Akehurst's Modern Introduction to International Law*. 7th ed. London: Routledge.

Malcolm, Noel. 2002. "Hobbes Theory of International Relations." In *Aspects of Hobbes*, 432–57. Oxford: Oxford University Press.

Mann, Michael. 1986/1993. *The Sources of Social Power*. 2 vols. Cambridge: Cambridge University Press.

Marland, G., T.A. Boden, and R. J. Andres. 2006. "Global, Regional, and National CO$_2$ Emissions." In *Trends: A Compendium of Data on Global Change*. Oak Ridge, TN: Carbon Dioxide Information Analysis Center, Oak Ridge National Laboratory, U.S. Department of Energy. http://cdiac.ornl.gov/trends/emis/tre_glob.htm.

Martin, Philip. 2004. "Migration." In *Global Crises, Global Solutions,* ed. Bjørn Lomborg, 443–98. Cambridge: Cambridge University Press.

Martinich, A. P. 1992. *The Two Gods of Leviathan: Thomas Hobbes on Religion and Politics*. Cambridge: Cambridge University Press.

Marx, Karl. 1972. *Capital*. Vol. 3. London: Lawrence and Wishart.

Marshall, Katherine. 2008. *The World Bank: From Reconstruction to Development to Equity*. New York: Routledge.

Maskus, Keith, and Jerome Reichman. 2005a. *International Public Goods and Transfer of Technology under a Globalized Intellectual Property Regime*. Cambridge: Cambridge University Press.

———. 2005b. "The Globalization of Private Knowledge Goods and the Privatization of Global Public Goods." In Maskus and Reichman 2005a.

Mason, Andrew. 1997. "Special Obligations to Compatriots." *Ethics* 107:427–47.

McLellan, David. 1977. *Karl Marx: Selected Writings*. Oxford: Oxford University Press.

McKim, Robert, and Jeff McMahan, eds. 1997. *The Morality of Nationalism*. Oxford: Oxford University Press.

Merry, Sally. 2006. *Human Rights and Gender Violence: Translating International Law into Local Justice*. Chicago: University of Chicago Press.

Michaelowa, Axel. 2007. "Graduation and Deepening." In Aldy and Stavins 2007a, 81–105.

Michalopoulos, Constantine 2002. "WTO Accession." In *Development, Trade, and the WTO: A Handbook,* ed. Bernard Hoekman, Aadiya Mattoo, and Philip English. Washington, DC: World Bank.

Milanovic, Branko. 2005. *Worlds Apart: Measuring International and Global Inequality*. Princeton, NJ: Princeton University Press.

Mill, John Stuart. 1874. "Nature." In *Three Essays on Religion*. London: Longmans, Green, Reader, and Dyer.

———. 1991. *Considerations on Representative Government*. New York: Prometheus Books.

———. 2006. *On Liberty, and the Subjection of Women*. Edited by Alan Ryan. New York: Penguin Books.

Miller, David. 1995. *On Nationality*. Oxford: Clarendon Press.

———. 2001. "Distributing Responsibilities." *Journal of Political Philosophy* 9 (4): 453–71.

———. 2005. "Immigration: The Case for Limits." In *Contemporary Debates in Applied Ethics,* ed. Andrew Cohen. Malden, MA: Blackwell.

———. 2007. *National Responsibility and Global Justice*. Oxford: Oxford University Press.

———. 2008. "Political Philosophy for Earthlings." In *Political Theory: Methods and Approaches,* ed. David Leopold and Marc Stears. Oxford: Oxford University Press.

———. 2009. "Democracy's Domain." *Philosophy and Public Affairs* 37:201–29.

Miller, Richard. 1998. "Cosmopolitan Respect and Patriotic Concern." *Philosophy & Public Affairs* 27:202–24.

———. 2010. *Globalizing Justice: The Ethics of Poverty and Power.* Oxford: Oxford University Press.

Milosz, Czeslaw. 1981. *The Captive Mind.* New York: Vintage Press.

Milton, John. 2000. *Paradise Lost.* Edited by J. Leonard. New York: Penguin

Moellendorf, Darrel. 2002. *Cosmopolitan Justice.* Boulder, CO: Westview Press.

Montefiore, Simon. 2004. "Stalin Flees Moscow in 1941." In Roberts, *What Might Have Been,* 134–53.

Moore, Adam. 1997. "Towards a Lockean Theory of Intellectual Property." In *Intellectual Property: Moral, Legal, and International Dilemmas,* ed. Adam Moore. New York: Rowman and Littlefield.

Moravcsik, Andrew. 2000. "The Origins of International Human Rights Regimes: Democratic Delegation in Postwar Europe." *International Organization* 54 (2): 217–51.

———. 2004. "Is There a 'Democratic Deficit' in World Politics? A Framework for Analysis." *Government and Opposition* 39 (2): 336–63.

———. 2008. "The Myth of Europe's Democratic Deficit." *Intereconomics: Journal of European Economic Policy,* November–December, 331–40.

Morgan, Glyn. 2005. *The Idea of a European Superstate: Public Justification and European Integration.* Princeton, NJ: Princeton University Press.

Morris, Christopher. 1998. *An Essay on the Modern State.* Cambridge: Cambridge University Press.

Morsink, Johannes. 1999. *The Universal Declaration of Human Rights; Origin, Drafting, and Intent.* Philadelphia: University of Pennsylvania Press.

Moyn, Samuel. 2010. *The Last Utopia: Human Rights in History.* Cambridge, MA: Harvard University Press.

Muir, John. 1916. "Anthropocentrism and Predation." Excerpt from *A Thousand Mile Walk to the Gulf.* Rprt. in Gruen and Jamieson 1994.

Mulgan, Tim. 2006. *Future People: A Moderate Consequentialist Account of our Obligations to Future Generations.* Oxford: Clarendon Press.

Müller, Harald. 2007. "Internationale Verhandlungen, Argumente und Verständigungshandeln. Verteidigung, Befunde, Warnung." In Niesen and Herborth, *Anarchie der Kommunikativen Freiheit,* 199–224.

Munzer, Stephen. 1990. *A Theory of Property.* Cambridge: Cambridge University Press.

Murphy, Jeffrie, and Jules Coleman. 1990. *Philosophy of Law: An Introduction to Jurisprudence.* Boulder, CO: Westview Press.

Murphy, Liam. 1998. "Institutions and the Demands of Justice." *Philosophy and Public Affairs* 27 (4): 251–91.

———. 2000. *Moral Demands in Non-Ideal Theory.* Oxford: Oxford University Press.

Mutua, Makau. 2001. "Savages, Victims, and Saviors: The Metaphor of Human Rights." *Harvard International Law Journal* 42:201–45.

———. 2004. "The Complexity of Universalism in Human Rights." In *Human Rights with Modesty,* ed. András Sajó. Leiden: Brill Academic Publishers.

Naess, Arne. 1984. "A Defense of the Deep Ecology Movement." *Environmental Ethics* 6:265–70.

———. 1989. *Ecology, Community, Lifestyle*. Cambridge: Cambridge University Press.

Nagel, Thomas. 1995. "Personal Rights and Public Space." *Philosophy and Public Affairs* 24 (2): 83–107.

———. 1997. "Justice and Nature." *Oxford Journal of Legal Studies* 17 (2): 303–21.

———. 2005. "The Problem of Global Justice." *Philosophy and Public Affairs* 33 (2): 113–47.

Narlikar, Amrita. 2002. "The Politics of Participation: Decision-Making Processes and Developing Countries in the World Trade Organization." *Round Table* 364:171–85.

———. 2005. *The World Trade Organization: A Very Short Introduction*. Oxford: Oxford University Press.

———. 2009. "Law and Legitimacy: The World Trade Organization." In *Routledge Handbook of International Law*, ed. David Armstrong, 294–303. New York: Routledge.

Narveson, Jan. 2001. *The Libertarian Idea*. Ontario: Broadview Press.

Nelson, Eric. 2010. *The Hebrew Republic: Jewish Sources and the Transformation of European Political Thought*. Cambridge, MA: Harvard University Press.

Nett, Roger. 1971. "The Civil Right We Are Not Ready For: The Right of Free Movement of People on the Face of the Earth." *Ethics* 81:212–27.

Neumayer, Eric. 2000. "In Defense of Historical Accountability for Greenhouse Gas Emissions." *Ecological Economics* 33:185–92.

———. 2003. *Weak vs. Strong Sustainability*. 2nd ed. Cheltenham: Elgar.

Nickel, James. 1993. "How Human Rights Generate Duties to Protect and to Provide." *Human Rights Quarterly* 15 (1): 77–86.

———. 2002. "Is Today's International Human Rights System a Global Governance Regime?" *Journal of Ethics* 6:353–71.

———. 2007. *Making Sense of Human Rights*. 2nd ed. Oxford: Blackwell.

Niesen, Peter, and Benjamin Herborth, eds. 2007. *Anarchie der Kommunikativen Freiheit: Jürgen Habermas und die Theorie der Internationalen Politik*. Frankfurt: Suhrkamp.

Nietzsche, Friedrich. 1996. *Human, All Too Human*, trans. R.J. Hollingdale. Cambridge: Cambridge University Press.

Nietzsche, Friedrich. 1998. *On the Genealogy of Morality*, trans. Maudemarie Clark and Alan Swensen. Indianapolis: Hackett.

Nordhaus, William, and Edward Kokkelenberg, eds. 1999. *Nature's Numbers: Expanding the National Economic Accounts to Include the Environment*. Washington, DC: National Academy Press.

North, Douglass. 1990. *Institutions, Institutional Change, and Economic Performance*. Cambridge: Cambridge University Press.

Norton, Bryan. 2005. *Sustainability: A Philosophy of Adaptive Ecosystem Management*. Chicago: University of Chicago Press.

Nozick, Robert. 1974. *Anarchy, State, and Utopia*. New York: Basic Books.

Nussbaum, Martha. 2000. *Women and Human Development: The Capabilities Approach*. Cambridge: Cambridge University Press.

———. 2006. *Frontiers of Justice: Disability, Nationality, Species Membership*. Cambridge, MA: Harvard University Press.

O'Neill, John. 1993. "Future Generations: Present Harms." *Philosophy* 68 (263): 35–51.

O'Neill, Onora. 1986. *Faces of Hunger*. London: Allen and Unwin.

———. 2005. "The Dark Side of Human Rights." *International Affairs* 81: 427–39.

Olivecrona, Karl. 1971. *Law as Fact*. London: Stevens and Sons.

Onuma, Yasuaki, ed. 1993. *A Normative Approach to War: Peace, War, and Justice in Hugo Grotius*. Oxford: Clarendon Press.

Oppenheimer, Franz. 2007. *The State*. New York: Black Rose Books.

Ostrom, Elinor. 1990. *Governing the Commons: The Evolution of Institutions for Collective Action*. Cambridge: Cambridge University Press.

Otsuka, Michael. 2003. *Libertarianism without Inequality*. Oxford: Oxford University Press.

Oxfam. 2002. *Rigged Rules and Double Standards: Trade, Globalization, and the Fight Against Poverty*. Written by Kevin Watkins and Penny Fowler. Oxford: Oxfam.

Pagden, Anthony. 1982. *The Fall of Natural Man: the American Indian and the Origins of Comparative Ethnology*. Cambridge: Cambridge University Press.

———. 2003. "Human Rights, Natural Rights, and Europe's Imperial Legacy." *Political Theory* 31:171–99.

Paine, Lynne Sharp. 1991. "Trade Secrets and the Justification of Intellectual Property: A Comment on Hettinger." *Philosophy and Public Affairs* 20:247–63.

Panagariya, Arvind. 2003. "Think Again: International Trade." *Foreign Policy*, November–December, 20–28.

———. 2004. "Miracles and Debacles: In Defence of Trade Openness." *World Economy* 27 (8): 1149–71.

———. 2005. "Agricultural Liberalization and the Least Developed Countries: Six Fallacies." *World Economy* 28 (9): 1277–99.

Panayotou, Theodore, Jeffrey Sachs, and Alix Zwane. 2002. "Compensation for 'Meaningful Participation' in Climate Change Control: A Modest Proposal and Empirical Analysis." *Journal of Environmental Economics and Management* 43:437–54.

Parfit, Derek. 1984. *Reasons and Persons*. New York: Oxford University Press.

Partridge, Ernest. 1990. "On the Rights of Future Generations." In *Upstream/ Downstream: Issues in Environmental Ethics,* ed. Donald Scherer, 40–66. Philadelphia: Temple University Press.

Passmore, John. 1974. *Man's Responsibility for Nature: Ecological Problems and Western Traditions*. London: Duckworth.

Paul, Ellen F. 1987. *Property Rights and Eminent Domain*. New Brunswick, NJ: Transaction Books.

Pearce, David. 1998. *Economics and Environment: Essays on Ecological Economics and Sustainable Development*. Cheltenham: Elgar.

Pearce, David, Anil Markandya, and Edward Barbier. 1989. *Blueprint for a Green Economy*. London: Earthscan.

Peden, Joseph. 1977. "Property Rights in Celtic Irish Law." *Journal of Libertarian Studies* 1 (2): 81–95.

Penner, J.E. 1997. *The Idea of Property in Law*. Oxford: Oxford University Press.

Pennock, Roland, and John Chapman, eds. 1978. *Anarchism: Nomos XIX*. New York: New York University Press.

Petersmann, Ernst-Ulrich. 2001. "European and International Constitutional Law: Time for Promoting 'Cosmopolitan Democracy' in the WTO." In *The EU and the WTO: Legal and Constitutional Aspects*, ed. Joanna Copestick, Joanne Scott, and Grinne De Brca, 81–110. Oxford: Hart.

Pettit, Philip. 1997. *Republicanism: A Theory of Freedom and Government*. Oxford: Clarendon Press.

Pierson, Paul. 2000. "Increasing Returns, Path Dependence and the Study of Politics." *American Political Science Review* 94:251–68.

Pitts, Jennifer. 2010. "Political Theory of Empire and Imperialism." *Annual Review of Political Science* 13:211–325.

Pogge, Thomas. 1989. *Realizing Rawls*. Ithaca, NY: Cornell University Press.

———. 1994. "Cosmopolitanism and Sovereignty." In *Political Restructuring in Europe: Ethical Perspectives,* ed. Chris Brown, 89–122. London: Routledge.

———. 2002. *World Poverty and Human Rights*. Cambridge: Polity Press.

———. 2005a. "Real World Justice." *Journal of Ethics* 9:29–53.

———. 2005b. "Severe Poverty as a Violation of Negative Duties." *Ethics and International Affairs* 19 (1): 55–83.

———. 2007. "Severe Poverty as a Human Rights Violation." In *Freedom from Poverty as a Human Right: Who Owe What to the Poor?,* ed. Thomas Pogge, 11–53. Oxford: Oxford University Press.

———. 2008a. *World Poverty and Human Rights*. 2nd. ed. Oxford: Polity Press.

———. 2008b. "Access to Medicines." *Public Health Ethics* 1 (2): 73–82.

———. 2009. "Comment on Mathias Risse: 'A Right to Work? A Right to Leisure? Labor Rights as Human Rights.'" *Law and Ethics of Human Rights* 3 (1): 38–47.

Poggi, Gianfranco. 1978. *The Development of the Modern State: A Sociological Introduction*. Stanford, CA: Stanford University Press.

Popper, Karl. 1972. *Objective Knowledge: An Evolutionary Approach*. Oxford: Oxford University Press.

Polanyi, Karl. 1957. *The Great Transformation: The Political and Economic Origins of Our Time*. Boston: Beacon Press.

Porter, Bruce. 1994. *War and the Rise of the State*. New York: Macmillan.

Posner, Eric, and David Weisbach. 2010. *Climate Change Justice*. Princeton, NJ: Princeton University Press.

Pritchett, Lant. 2003. "A Toy Collection, a Socialist Star and a Democratic Dud: Growth Theory, Vietnam, and the Philippines." In Rodrik 2003.

Pritchett, Lant, and David Lindauer. 2002. "What's the Big Idea? Three Generations of Development Advice." *Economia* 3 (1): 1–39.

Pufendorf, Samuel. 1934. *De Jure Naturae et Gentium Libri Octo*, trans. C. H. and W. A. Oldfather. Oxford: Clarendon Press.

Rabkin, Jeremy. 2005. *Law without Nations? Why Constitutional Government Requires Sovereign States*. Princeton, NJ: Princeton University Press.

Raphael. David D. 2001. *Concepts of Justice*. Oxford: Clarendon Press.

Rawls, John. 1993. *Political Liberalism*. New York: Columbia University Press.

———. 1999a. *Collected Papers*. Edited by S. Freeman. Cambridge, MA: Harvard University Press.

———. 1999b. *The Law of Peoples*. Cambridge, MA: Harvard University Press.

———. 1999c. *A Theory of Justice*. Rev. ed. Cambridge, MA: Harvard University Press.

———. 2001. *Justice as Fairness: A Restatement*. Edited by Erin Kelly. Cambridge, MA: Harvard University Press.

Raz, Joseph. 1984. "On the Nature of Rights." *Mind* 93:194–214.

———. 1986. *The Morality of Freedom*. Oxford: Clarendon Press.

———. 2010. "Human Rights without Foundations." In *The Philosophy of International Law*, ed. John Tasioulas and Samantha Besson, 321–39. Oxford: Oxford University Press.

Reader, Soran. 2006a. "Does a Basic Needs Approach Need Capabilities?" *Journal of Political Philosophy* 14 (3): 337–50.

———, ed. 2006b. *The Philosophy of Need*. Cambridge: Cambridge University Press.

———. 2007. *Needs and Moral Necessity*. London: Routledge.

Reed, Esther. 2006. "Property Rights, Genes, and Common Good." *Journal of Religious Ethics* 34 (1): 41–67.

Reeve, Andrew. 1986. *Property*. Atlantic Highlands, NJ: Humanities Press.

———, ed. 1987. *Modern Theories of Exploitation*. London: Sage.

Reinhard, Wolfgang. 1996. *Kleine Geschichte des Kolonialismus*. Stuttgart: Kroener.

Reiss, H. S. 1955. *The Political Thought of the German Romantics*. Oxford: Blackwell.

Renan, Ernest. 1994. *Qu'est-ce qu'une Nation?* Leiden: Academic Press.

Reydams, Luc. 2004. *Universal Jurisdiction: International and Municipal Legal Perspectives*. Oxford: Oxford University Press.

Ricardo, David. 1817. *On the Principles of Political Economy and Taxation*. London: John Murray.

Ridge, Michael. 2003. "Giving the Dead Their Due." *Ethics* 114:38–59.

Rifkin, Jeremy. 2000. *The Age of Access: The New Culture of Hypercapitalism, Where All of Life Is Paid-For Experience*. New York: Penguin.

Risse, Mathias. 2004a. "Arguing for Majority Rule." *Journal of Political Philosophy* 12 (1): 41–64.

———. 2004b. "Does Left-Libertarianism Have Coherent Foundations?" *Politics, Philosophy, and Economics* 3 (3): 337–65.

———. 2005a. "Do We Owe the Poor Assistance or Rectification?" *Ethics and International Affairs* 19 (1): 9–18.

———. 2005b. "How Does the Global Order Harm the Poor?" *Philosophy and Public Affairs* 33 (4): 349–76.

———. 2005c. "What We Owe to the Global Poor." *Journal of Ethics* 9 (1–2): 81–117.

————. 2006. "What to Say about the State." *Social Theory and Practice* 32 (4): 671–98.

————. 2007. "Fairness in Trade I: Obligations from Trading and the Pauper Labor Argument." *Politics, Philosophy, and Economics* 6 (3): 355–77.

————. 2008. "On the Morality of Immigration." *Ethics and International Affairs* 22 (1): 25–33.

————. 2009a. "Common Ownership of the Earth as a Non-Parochial Standpoint: A Contingent Derivation of Human Rights." *European Journal of Philosophy* 17 (2): 277–304.

————. 2009b. "Immigration, Ethics, and the Capabilities Approach." United Nations Development Program on-line Human Development Research Paper Series. http://hdr.undp.org/en/reports/global/hdr2009/papers/.

————. 2009c. "A Right to Work? A Right to Leisure? Labor Rights as Human Rights." *Journal of Law and Ethics of Human Rights* 3 (1): 1–41.

————. 2009d. "The Right to Relocation: Disappearing Island Nations and Common Ownership of the Earth." *Ethics and International Affairs* 23 (3): 281–300.

Risse, Thomas. 2000. "'Let's Argue!' Communicative Action in World Politics." *International Organization* 54 (1): 1–39.

————. 2003. "Transnational Actors in World Politics." In *Handbook of International Relations*, ed. Walter Carlsnaes, Thomas Risse, and Beth Simmons, 255–74. London: Sage.

Risse, Thomas, Stephen Ropp, and Kathryn Sikkink, eds. 1999. *The Power of Human Rights: International Norms and Domestic Change*. Cambridge: Cambridge University Press.

Robb, Graham. 2007. *The Discovery of France: A Historical Geography from the Revolution to the First World War*. New York: Norton.

Roberts, Andrew, ed. 2004. *What Might Have Been: Leading Historians on Twelve "What Ifs" of History*. London: Phoenix.

Robinson, Joan. 1958. *The Accumulation of Capital*. Homewood, IL: Irwin.

Rodriguez, Francisco, and Dani Rodrik. 2000. "Trade Policy and Economic Growth: A Skeptic's Guide to the Cross-National Evidence." In *Macroeconomics Annual 2000*, ed. Ben Bernanke and Kenneth Rogoff. Cambridge, MA: MIT Press.

Rodriguez, Francisco, and Jeffrey Sachs. 1999. "Why Do Resource-Abundant Economies Grow More Slowly?" *Journal of Economic Growth* 4 (3): 277–303.

Rodrik, Dani, ed. 2003. *In Search of Prosperity: Analytical Narratives on Economic Growth*. Princeton, NJ: Princeton University Press.

————. 2007. *One Economics, Many Recipes: Globalization, Institutions, and Economic Growth*. Princeton, NJ: Princeton University Press.

Rodrik, Dani, Arvind Subramanian and Francesco Trebbi. 2004. "The Primacy of Institutions over Geography and Integration in Economic Development." *Journal of Economic Growth* 9 (2): 131–65.

Roemer, John. 1985. "Should Marxists Be Interested in Exploitation?" *Philosophy and Public Affairs* 14 (1): 30–65.

————. 1996. *Theories of Distributive Justice*. Cambridge, MA: Harvard University Press.

———. 1998. *Equality of Opportunity*. Cambridge, MA: Harvard University Press.

Rorty, Richard. 1993. "Sentimentality, Rationality, and Sentimentality." In *On Human Rights*, ed. S. Shute and S. Hurley. New York: Basic Books.

Ross, Michael. 2001. "Does Oil Hinder Democracy?" *World Politics* 53 (3): 325–61.

———. 2003. "The Natural Resource Curse: How Wealth Can Make You Poor." In *Natural Resources and Violent Conflict: Options and Actions*, ed. I. Bannon and P. Collier, 1–37. Washington, DC: World Bank.

Rothbard, Murray. 1974. *Egalitarianism as a Revolt against Nature, and Other Essays*. Auburn, TX: Von Mises Institute.

———. 1996. *For a New Liberty: The Libertarian Manifesto*. San Francisco: Fox and Wilkes.

———. 1998. *The Ethics of Liberty*. New York: New York University Press.

Rousseau, Jean-Jacques. 1968. *The Social Contract*, trans. Maurice Cranston. New York: Penguin

———. 1979. *Emile*. Edited by Allan Bloom. New York: Basic Books.

Routley, Richard, and Val Routley. 1980. "Human Chauvinism and Environmental Ethics." In *Environmental Philosophy*, ed. D. Mannison, M. A. McRobbie, and R. Routley, 96–189. Canberra: Australian National University.

Ruggie, John. 1998. "Territoriality and Millennium's End." In *Constructing the World Polity: Essays on International Institutionalization*. New York: Taylor and Francis.

———. 2005. "American Exceptionalism, Exemptionalism, and Global Governance." In *American Exceptionalism and Human Rights*, ed. Michael Ignatieff, 304–39. Princeton, NJ: Princeton University Press.

———. 2007. "Business and Human Rights: The Evolving International Agenda." *American Journal of International Law* 101 (4): 819–40.

———. 2008. *Promotion and Protection of Human Rights: Human Rights Questions, Including Alternative Approaches for Improving the Effective Enjoyment of Human Rights and Fundamental Freedoms*. 63rd session of the General Assembly, Third Committee, United Nations, October 28.

Rummel, R. J. 1994. *Death by Government*. New Brunswick, NJ: Transaction Publishers.

Russell, Bertrand. 1919. "A Free Man's Worship." In *Mysticism and Logic, and Other Essays*, 46–58. New York: Longmans, Green.

Russell, Conrad. 1985. "The Catholic Wind." In *For Want of a Horse: Choice and Chance in History*, ed. John Merriman, 103–7. Lexington, KY: Stephen Green Press.

Ryan, Alan. 1993. "Introduction." In *Justice*. Oxford: Oxford University Press.

Sachs, Jeffrey. 2001. "Tropical Underdevelopment." National Bureau of Economic Research Working Paper w81119. Cambridge, MA: National Bureau of Economic Research.

———. 2003. "Institutions Don't Rule: Direct Effects of Geography on Per Capita Income." National Bureau of Economic Research Working Paper No. 9490. Cambridge, MA: National Bureau of Economic Research.

Sachs, Jeffrey, and Andrew Warner. 1995. "Natural Resource Abundance and Economic Growth." National Bureau of Economic Research Working Paper No. 5398. Cambridge, MA: National Bureau of Economic Research.

———. 2001. "The Curse of Natural Resources." *European Economic Review* 45:827–38.

Sagoff, Mark. 2008. *The Economy of the Earth: Philosophy, Law, and the Environment*. Cambridge: Cambridge University Press.

Salter, John. 2001. "Hugo Grotius: Property and Consent." *Political Theory* 29: 537–55.

———. 2005. "Grotius and Pufendorf on the Right of Necessity." *History of Political Thought* 26:284–302.

Sample, Ruth. 2003. *Exploitation: What It Is and Why It Is Wrong*. Lanham, MD: Rowman and Littlefield.

Sands, Philippe. 2003. *Principles of International Environmental Law*. Cambridge: Cambridge University Press.

Sangiovanni, Andrea. 2007. "Global Justice, Reciprocity, and the State." *Philosophy and Public Affairs* 35 (1): 3–39.

Sauer, Carl Ortwin. 1963. *Land and Life: A Selection from the Writings of Carl Ortwin Sauer*. Edited by John Leighly. Berkeley: University of California Press.

Scanlon, T. M. 1998. *What We Owe To Each Other*. Cambridge, MA: Harvard University Press.

———. 2003a. "Rights, Goals, and Fairness." In Scanlon 2003c, 26–42.

———. 2003b. "Human Rights as a Neutral Concern." In Scanlon 2003c, 113–24.

———. 2003c. *The Difficulty of Tolerance: Essays in Political Philosophy*. Cambridge: Cambridge University Press.

———. 2003d. "The Diversity of Objections to Inequality." In Scanlon 2003c, 202–19.

Scheffler, Samuel. 2001a. *Boundaries and Allegiances: Problems of Justice in Liberal Thought*. Oxford: Oxford University Press.

———. 2001b. "Conceptions of Cosmopolitanism." In Scheffler 2001a, 111–31.

———. 2003. "What Is Egalitarianism?" *Philosophy and Public Affairs* 31:5–40.

Schelling, Thomas. 1995. "Intergenerational Discounting." *Energy Policy* 23:495–501.

Schmitt, Carl. 1941. *Völkerrechtliche Grossraum-Ordnung*. Wien: Deutscher Rechtsverlag.

———. 2008. *Constitutional Theory*. Durham, NC: Duke University Press.

Schneewind, J. B. 1998. *The Invention of Autonomy: A History of Modern Moral Philosophy*. Cambridge: Cambridge University Press.

Schueklenk, Udo, and Richard Ashcroft. 2002. "Affordable Access to Medication in Developing Countries: Conflicts between Ethical and Economic Imperatives." *Journal of Medicine and Philosophy* 27 (2): 179–95.

Scott, James. 1998. *Seeing Like a State: How Certain Schemes to Improve the Human Condition Have Failed*. New Haven, CT: Yale University Press.

Sell, Susan. 2003. *Private Power, Public Law: The Globalization of Intellectual Property Rights*. Cambridge: Cambridge University Press.

Sen, Amartya. 1980. "Equality of What?" In *Tanner Lectures on Human Values*, ed. S. McMurrin. Cambridge: Cambridge University Press.

———. 1985. *Commodities and Capabilities*. Amsterdam: North Holland.

———. 1993. "Capability and Well-being." In *The Quality of Life,* ed. Amartya Sen and Martha Nussbaum, 30–53. Oxford: Oxford University Press.

———. 1997. *Resources, Values, and Development*. Cambridge, MA: Harvard University Press.

———. 1999. *Development as Freedom*. New York: Random House.

———. 2004. "Elements of a Theory of Human Rights." *Philosophy and Public Affairs* 32 (4): 315–57.

———. 2009. *The Idea of Justice*. Cambridge, MA: Harvard University Press.

Shachar, Ayelet. 2009. *The Birthright Lottery: Citizenship and Global Inequality*. Cambridge, MA: Harvard University Press.

Shaffer, Gregory, Victor Mosoti, and Asif Quereshi. 2003. "Towards a Development-Support Dispute Settlement System in the WTO." *Sustainable Development and Trade Issues*. ICTSD Resource Paper No 5. http://ictsd.net/i/dsu/11342/.

Shaw, George Bernard. 1928. *The Intelligent Woman's Guide to Socialism and Capitalism*. New York: Brentano's.

Sher, George. 1980. "Ancient Wrongs and Modern Rights." *Philosophy and Public Affairs* 10:3–17.

Shiffrin, Seana. 1999. "Wrongful Life, Procreative Responsibility, and the Significance of Harm." *Legal Theory* 5:117–84.

———. 2001. "Lockean Arguments for Private Intellectual Property" In *New Essays in the Legal and Political Theory of Property*, ed. S. Munzer. Cambridge: Cambridge University Press.

———. 2007. "Intellectual Property." In *A Companion to Contemporary Political Philosophy*, ed. Robert Goodin, Philip Pettit, and Thomas Pogge, chap. 36. Oxford: Blackwell.

Shotwell, James. 1934. *The Origins of the International Labor Organization*. New York: Columbia University Press.

Shue, Henry. 1996. "Environmental Change and the Varieties of Justice." In *Earthly Goods: Environmental Change and Social Justice*, ed. Fen Osler Hamilton and Judith Reppy, 9–29. Ithaca, NY: Cornell University Press.

———. 1999. "Global Environment and International Inequality." *International Affairs* 75 (3): 531–45.

———. 2001. "Climate." In *A Companion to Environmental Philosophy*, ed. D. Jamieson, 449–59. Oxford: Blackwell.

Sidgwick, Henry. 2005. *The Elements of Politics*. London: Elibron Classics.

Sieyès, Emmanuel Joseph. 2003. *Political Writings*. Edited by Michael Sonenscher. Indianapolis: Hackett.

Simmons, A. John. 2001a. "Human Rights and World Citizenship: Human Rights in Locke and Kant." Chap. 9 in Simmons, *Justification and Legitimacy.*

———. 2001b. *Justification and Legitimacy: Essays on Rights and Obligations*. Cambridge: Cambridge University Press.

———. 2010. "Ideal and Non-Ideal Theory." *Philosophy and Public Affairs* 38 (1): 5–37.

Simmons, Beth. 2009. *Mobilizing for Human Rights: International Law in Domestic Politics*. New York: Cambridge University Press.

Simms, Andrew. 2005. *Ecological Debt: The Health of the Planet and the Wealth of Nations*. London: Pluto Press.

Singer, Peter. 1972. "Famine, Affluence, and Morality." *Philosophy and Public Affairs* 1 (1): 229–43.

———. 1993. *Practical Ethics*. Cambridge: Cambridge University Press.

———. 2002a. "One Atmosphere." Chap. 2 in Singer 2002b.

———. 2002b. *One World: The Ethics of Globalization*. New Haven, CT: Yale University Press.

Skinner, Quentin. 1989. "The State." In *Political Innovation and Conceptual Change*, ed. T. Ball, R. Hanson, and J. Farr, chap. 5. Cambridge: Cambridge University Press.

Smith, Adam. 1978. *Lectures on Jurisprudence*. Edited by R. L. Meek, D. D. Raphael, and P. G. Stein. Indianapolis: Liberty Classics.

Smith, K. 1991. "Allocating Responsibility for Global Warming: The Natural Debt Index." *Ambio* 20:95–96.

Solow, Robert. 1986. "On the Intergenerational Allocation of Natural Resources." *Scandinavian Journal of Economics* 88:141–49.

———. 1992. "Sustainability: An Economist's Perspective." In *Economics of the Environment: Selected Readings,* ed. Robert Stavins, 505–13. New York: Norton.

Solzhenitsyn, Alexander. 2009. *In the First Circle*, trans. Harry Willetts. New York: Macmillan.

Soros, George. 2002. *George Soros on Globalization*. New York: PublicAffairs.

Spruyt, Hendrik. 1994. *The Sovereign State and Its Competitors*. Princeton, NJ: Princeton University Press.

Squire, J. C., ed. 1931. *If, or History Rewritten*. New York: Viking Press.

Sreenivasan, Gopal. 2000. "What Is the General Will?" *Philosophical Review* 109:545–81.

———. 2010. "Duties and Their Direction." *Ethics* 120:465–95.

Stavins, Robert, ed. 2000. *Economics of the Environment: Selected Readings*. New York: Norton.

Stein, Gertrude. 1995. *The Geographical History of America*. Baltimore, MD: Johns Hopkins University Press.

Steinberg, Richard H. 2002. "In the Shadow of Law or Power? Consensus-based Bargaining and Outcomes in the GATT/WTO." *International Organization,* Spring, 339–74.

Steiner, Henry, Philip Alston, and Ryan Goodman. 2007. *International Human Rights in Context*. Oxford: Oxford University Press.

Steiner, Hillel. 1983. "The Rights of Future Generations." In *Energy and the Future,* ed. Douglas Maclean and Peter Brown, 151–65. Totowa, NJ: Rowman and Littlefield.

———. 1992. "Libertarianism and the Transnational Migration of People." In Barry and Goodin 1992.

———. 1994. *An Essay on Rights*. Oxford: Blackwell.

———. 1999. "Silver Spoons and Golden Genes: Talent Differentials and Distributive Justice." In *The Genetic Revolution and Human Rights: 1998 Oxford Amnesty Lectures*, ed. J. Burley. Oxford: Oxford University Press.

Stemplowska, Zofia. 2008. "What's Ideal about Ideal Theory?" *Social Theory and Practice* 34:319–40.

Sterckx, Sigrid. 2005. "The Ethics of Patenting: Uneasy Justifications." In *Death of Patents*, ed. Peter Drahos, 175–212. London: Queen Mary Intellectual Property Research Institute.

Stiglitz, Joseph, and Andrew Charlton. 2006. *Fair Trade for All: How Trade Can Promote Development*. Oxford: Oxford University Press.

Streeck, Wolfgang, and Kozo Yamamura, eds. 2001. *The Origins of Nonliberal Capitalism: Germany and Japan in Comparison*. Ithaca, NY: Cornell University Press.

Stumpf, Christoph. 2006. *The Grotian Theology of International Law: Hugo Grotius and the Moral Foundations of International Relations*. Berlin: de Gruyter.

Subrahmanyam, Sanjay. 2005. *Explorations in Connected History*. New Delhi: Oxford University Press.

Swift, Adam. 2008. "The Value of Philosophy in Non-Ideal Circumstances." *Social Theory and Practice* 34 (3): 363–87.

Tamir, Yael. 1993. *Liberal Nationalism*. Princeton, NJ: Princeton University Press.

Tan, Kok-Chor. 2004. *Justice without Borders: Cosmopolitanism, Nationalism, and Patriotism*. Cambridge: Cambridge University Press.

Tanaka, Tadashi. 1993. "State and Governing Power." In Onuma 1993, 122–47.

Tasioulas, John. 2010. "Taking Rights out of Human Rights." *Ethics* 120:647–78.

Thelen, Kathleen. 1999. "Historical Institutionalism in Comparative Politics." *Annual Review of Political Science* 2:364–404.

Thompson, Dennis. 1987. *Political Ethics and Public Office*. Cambridge, MA: Harvard University Press.

Thompson, E. P. 1973. "Open Letter to Leszek Kolakowski." *Socialist Register* 10 (ed. John Saville and Ralf Miliband).

Thomson, Garrett. 1987. *Needs*. London: Routledge.

Tierney, Brian. 1997. *The Idea of Natural Rights: Studies on Natural Rights, Natural Law, and Church Law*. Atlanta, GA: Scholars Press.

Tilly, Charles. 1990. *Coercion, Capital, and European States, AD 990–1990*. Cambridge: Blackwell.

Toebes, Brigit. 1999. *The Right to Health as a Human Right in International Law*. Antwerp: Intersentia.

Traxler, Martino. 2002. "Fair Chore Division for Climate Change." *Social Theory and Practice* 28:101–34.

Trebilcock, Michael, and Robert Howse. 2005. *The Regulation of International Trade*. New York: Routledge.

Tribe, Lawrence. 1976. "Ways Not to Think about Plastic Trees." In *When Values Conflict: Essays on Environmental Analysis, Discourse, and Decision*, ed. L. Tribe, C. Schelling, and J. Voss, 61–91. Cambridge: Ballinger Publishing.

Tuck, Richard. 1979. *Natural Rights Theories: Their Origin and Development*. Cambridge: Cambridge University Press.

———. 1999. *The Rights of War and Peace: Political Thought and the International Order from Grotius to Kant*. Oxford: Oxford University Press.

Tugendhat, Ernst. 1993. *Vorlesungen über Ethik*. Frankfurt: Suhrkamp.

Tully, James. 1980. *A Discourse on Property: John Locke and His Adversaries.* Cambridge: Cambridge University Press.

Tushnet, Mark. 1995. "Immigration policy and Liberal Political Theory." In *Justice in Immigration,* ed. Warren Schwartz. Cambridge: Cambridge University Press.

United Nations. 2001. *Report of the High-Level Panel on Financing for Development.* New York: United Nations. http://www.un.org/reports/financing.

———. 2003. *Human Development Report 2003. Millennium Development Goals: A Compact Among Nations to End Human Poverty.* New York: United Nations. http://hdr.undp.org/en/reports/global/hdr2003.

U.S. International Trade Commission. 1997. *The Dynamic Effects of Trade Liberalization: An Empirical Analysis, Investigation 332-375.* Publication No. 3069. Washington, DC: U.S. International Trade Commission.

Vallentyne, Peter, and Hillel Steiner, eds. 2000a. *Left-Libertarianism and Its Critics: The Contemporary Debate.* New York: Palgrave.

———, eds. 2000b. *The Origins of Left-Libertarianism: An Anthology of Historical Writings.* New York: Palgrave.

Vallentyne, Peter, Hillel Steiner, and Michael Otsuka. 2005. "Why Left-Libertarianism is Not Incoherent, Indeterminate, or Irrelevant." *Philosophy and Public Affairs* 33:201–15.

Van de Walle, Nicolas, and Timothy Johnston. 1996. *Improving Aid to Africa.* Baltimore, MD: Johns Hopkins University Press.

Vanderheiden, Steve. 2008. *Atmospheric Justice: A Political Theory of Climate Change.* Oxford: Oxford University Press.

Vattel, Emerich de. 1805. *The Law of Nations, or Principles of the Law of Nature Applied to the Conduct and Affairs of Nations and Sovereigns.* Translated from the French. Northampton, MA: Thomas Pomroy.

Velasco, Andres. 2002. "Dependency Theory." *Foreign Policy,* November–December, 44–45.

Vernon, Richard. 2002. "What Is Crime against Humanity?" *Journal of Political Philosophy* 10:231–49.

———. 2010. *Cosmopolitan Regard: Political Membership and Global Justice.* Cambridge: Cambridge University Press.

Vincent, Andrew. 1987. *Theories of the State.* Oxford: Blackwell.

Vitoria, Francisco de. 1991. *Political Writings.* Edited by A. Pagden and J. Lawrance. Cambridge: Cambridge University Press.

Wacziarg, R., and K. H. Welch. 2008. "Trade Liberalization and Growth: New Evidence." *World Bank Economic Review* 22 (2): 187–231.

Waldron, Jeremy. 1988. *The Right to Private Property.* Oxford: Clarendon Press.

———. 1992. "Superseding Past Injustice." *Ethics* 103:4–28.

———. 1993a. "From Authors to Copiers: Individual Rights and Social Values in Intellectual Property." *Chicago-Kent Law Review* 68:841–87.

———. 1993b. *Liberal Rights: Collected Papers, 1981–1991.* Cambridge: Cambridge University Press.

Wallerstein, Immanuel. 1980. *The Modern World-System I: Capitalist Agriculture and the Origins of the European World-Economy in the Sixteenth Century.* New York: Academic Press.

Waltz, Kenneth. 1959. *Man, the State, and War: A Theoretical Analysis*. New York: Columbia University Press.

Walzer, Michael. 1970. *Obligations*. Cambridge, MA: Harvard University Press.

———. 1983. *Spheres of Justice*. New York: Basic Books.

Weber, Max. 1921. "Politik als Beruf." In *Gesammelte Politische Schriften*. Munich: Duncker and Humblot.

Weil, Simone. 1971. *The Need for Roots*. New York: Harper and Row

———. 1986. "Human Personality." In *Simon Weil: An Anthology*, ed. Sian Miles, 49–79. New York: Grove Press.

Weiss, Edith Brown. 1988. *In Fairness to Future Generations: International Law, Common Patrimony, and Intergenerational Equity*. Dobbs Ferry, NY: Transnational Publishers.

Wellman, Christopher. 2003. "Nationalism and Secession." In *A Companion to Applied Ethics*, ed. R. G. Frey and C. Wellman, 267–78. Oxford: Blackwell.

———. 2008. "Immigration and Freedom of Association." *Ethics* 119:109–41.

Wells, H. G. 1920. *The Outline of History: Being a Plain History of Life and Mankind*. Garden City, NY: Garden City Books

———. 1940. *The Rights of Man, or What Are We Fighting For?* New York: Penguin.

Wenar, Leif. 1998. "Original Acquisition of Private Property." *Mind* 107:799–819.

———. 2005. "The Nature of Rights." *Philosophy and Public Affairs* 33:223–53.

———. 2006. "Why Rawls Is Not a Cosmopolitan Egalitarian." In *Rawls' Law of Peoples: A Realistic Utopia?*, ed. R. Martin and D. Reidy. Oxford: Blackwell.

———. 2008. "Property Rights and the Resource Curse." *Philosophy and Public Affairs* 36 (1): 2–32.

Wendt, Alexander. 2003. "Why a World State Is Inevitable: Teleology and the Logic of Anarchy." *European Journal of International Relations* 9 (4): 491–542.

Wertheimer, Alan. 1996. *Exploitation*. Princeton, NJ: Princeton University Press.

Wesseling, H. L. 2004. The European Colonial Empires, 1815–1919. London: Harlow: Pearson.

White, Lynn. 1967. "The Historical Roots of Our Ecological Crisis." *Science* 55:1203–7.

Whitman, Walt. 1961. *Walt Whitman's Leaves of Grass*. Edited by Malcolm Cowley. New York: Viking Press.

Wiggins, David. 1987. "Claims of Need." In Wiggins, *Needs, Values, Truth*, 1–57. Oxford: Oxford University Press.

———. 2000. "Nature, Respect for Nature, and the Human Scale of Values." *Proceedings of the Aristotelian Society* 100 (1): 1–32.

Wight, Martin. 1966. "Why Is There No International Theory?" In *Diplomatic Investigations: Essays in the Theory of International Politics*, ed. H. Butterfield and M. Wight. London: Allen and Unwin.

Wilkinson, Richard. 1996. *Unhealthy Societies: The Inflictions of Inequality*. London: Routledge.

Williams, Andrew. 1998. "Incentives, Inequality, and Publicity." *Philosophy and Public Affairs* 27 (3): 225–47.

Williams, Bernard. 1981. *Moral Luck*. Cambridge: Cambridge University Press.

———. 1993. *Morality: An Introduction to Ethics*. Cambridge: Cambridge University Press.

———. 1995. "Must a Concern for the Environment Be Centered on Human Beings?" In Williams, *Making Sense of Humanity and other Philosophical Essays*, 233–41. Cambridge: Cambridge University Press.

———. 2005a. "Human Rights and Relativism." In Williams, *In the Beginning Was the Deed*, chap. 6.

———. 2005b. "The Idea of Equality." In Williams, *In the Beginning Was the Deed*, chap. 8.

———. 2005c. "In the Beginning Was the Deed." In Williams, *In the Beginning Was the Deed*, chap. 2.

———. 2005d. *In the Beginning Was the Deed: Realism and Moralism in Political Argument*. Edited by Geoffrey Hawthorn. Princeton, NJ: Princeton University Press.

Williams, Michael. 1996. "Hobbes and International Relations: A Reconsideration." *International Organization* 50 (2): 213–36.

Wilson, Edward O. 1984. *Biophilia*. Cambridge, MA: Harvard University Press.

———. 1993. *The Diversity of Life*. New York: Norton.

Wilson, James. 2009. "Could There Be a Right to Own Intellectual Property?" *Law and Philosophy* 28 (4): 393–427.

Winham, Gilbert. 1998. "Explanations of Developing Country Behaviour in the GATT Uruguay Round Negotiation." *World Competition Law and Economics Review* 21:109–34.

Winichakul, Thongchai. 1994. *Siam Mapped: A History of the Geo-Body of a Nation*. Honolulu: University of Hawaii Press.

Winters, Alan, Neil McCulloch, and Andrew McKay. 2004. "Trade Liberalization and Poverty: The Evidence So Far." *Journal of Economic Literature* 52: 72–115.

Winthrop, Robert. 1869. *The Life and Letters of John Winthrop, Governor of the Massachusetts-Bay Company at their Emigration to New England, 1630*. Boston: Little, Brown.

Wolf, Martin. 2004. *Why Globalization Works*. New Haven, CT: Yale University Press.

Wolf, Susan. 1992. "Morality and Partiality." *Philosophical Perspectives* 6:243–59.

Wolff, Jonathan. 1996. "Anarchism and Skepticism." In *For and Against the State: New Philosophical Readings*, ed. John Sanders and Jan Narveson, 99–119. London: Rowman and Littlefield.

———. 2009. "Global Justice and Norms of Cooperation: The 'Layers of Justice' View." In de Wijze, Kramer, and Carter 2009, 34–53.

Woods, Ngaire. 2006. *The Globalizers: The IMF, the World Bank, and Their Borrowers*. Ithaca, NY: Cornell University Press.

World Bank. 1998. {to come}

———. 2000. *World Development Report 2000/2001*. Washington, DC: World Bank.

———. 2002. *World Development Indicators.* CD-ROM. Washington, DC: World Bank.

———. 2004. *World Development Indicators.* Washington, DC: World Bank

World Commission on Environment and Development. 1987. *Our Common Future.* Oxford: Oxford University Press.

Wright, Quincy. 1949. "Relationship between Different Categories of Human Rights." In *Human Rights: Comments and Interpretations.* UNESCO. New York: Columbia University Press.

Yanagihara, Masaharu. 1993. "Dominium and Imperium." In Onuma 1993, 147–67.

Young, Peyton. 1995. *Equity.* Princeton, NJ: Princeton University Press.

Young, Robert. 2001. *Postcolonialism: An Historical Introduction.* Oxford: Blackwell.

Ypi, Lea, Robert Goodin, and Christian Barry. 2009. "Associative Duties, Global Justice, and the Colonies." *Philosophy and Public Affairs* 37 (2): 103–35.

Index

ability to pay principle, 202–3, 205
Abizadeh, Arash, 289
absorptive capacity, of the atmosphere, 189, 194–98
accountability: analysis of, 335–37; means of discharging obligations for, 339–41; of states, 337–41, 354–56; of WTO, 357
acquisition of property, 110–11
adverse possession, 166
African Charter on Human and Peoples' Rights, 149
agency, 77
Agreement on Trade-Related Aspects of Intellectual Property Rights (TRIPs), 232, 243, 348, 400n18
agreements, private ownership and, 98, 101–3
agricultural subsidies, 261–63, 267
agro-ecological zones methodology, 156
Alliance of Small Island States (AOSIS), 146
anarchism, 313–14, 322–23, 406n4
Anderson, Kym, 263–64
animals, 114, 119
Antarctica, 192
Anthropocene era, 167
antidumping measures, 262
antirealism, about ideas, 239–41
apartheid, 275
arbitrary factors, and justice: 9–10, 38–39, 44, 58, 83–84, 121–22, 164, 288–89, 362n8, 379n8
Archibugi, Daniele, 343
Arendt, Hannah, 90, 117–18
Aristotle, 333
Arrhenius, Svante, 200
assistance, duty of: demands of, 80-81, 264, 370n13, 410n2; for human rights protection, 227–28, 264; immigration policy and, 162; for institution building, 64, 68–69, 80, 201, 213, 264, 265, 333; for persons outside the state, 80; for the poor, 293, 333; Rawls on, 15,

64, 330, 365n20, 410n2; shared past as context for, 301–2; trade and, 265, 272, 275, 350, 352, 353; transnational, 357–59
associative rights, 91, 136, 144, 212, 215
asymmetrical capacity to shape the earth, 178–79
atheism, 124
atmosphere: absorptive capacity of, 189, 194–95; accountability for emissions into, 198–201; goods provided by, 194–98; ownership of, 188–89; regulation of, 189, 193–206
Auerbach, Bruce, 390n11
Augustine, Saint, 27
Australia, 161
Authenticity Thesis, 68
autonomy, 121
Autonomy Principle, 42–44

Baier, Annette, 176, 389n3
Barry, Brian, 80, 389n3
Barry, Christian, 299–300, 302, 354
Barton, John, 352–53, 412n6
basic needs. See needs
basic structure of society, 13, 30, 36
Beck, Roy, 385n1
Becker, Lawrence, 238
Beckerman, Wilfred, 389n3
Beerbohm, Eric, 407n14
Beitz, Charles, 42, 48, 53–55, 57–59, 62, 71, 72, 372n14
Benn, Gottfried, 371n9
Bentham, Jeremy, 367n7
Berlin, Isaiah, 34, 315, 318
Bible, 167, 175, 178, 397n14
biospheric egalitarianism, 120, 381n20
Black, Samuel, 82
Blackstone, William, 108, 109
Blake, Michael, 25, 42–44, 48, 50, 370n14, 385n15
Blake, William, 287, 290
Bloomberg, Michael, 273
borders, 287–90